SPEAKING OF ANIMALS

Speaking of Animals
A DICTIONARY OF ANIMAL METAPHORS

Robert A. Palmatier

GREENWOOD PRESS
Westport, Connecticut • London

Library of Congress Cataloging-in-Publication Data

Palmatier, Robert A. (Robert Allen)
  Speaking of animals : a dictionary of animal metaphors / Robert A.
Palmatier.
    p. cm.
  Includes bibliographical references.
  ISBN 0–313–29490–9 (alk. paper)
  1. English language—Etymology—Dictionaries. 2. English
language—Terms and phrases. 3. Animals—Folklore—Dictionaries.
4. Metaphor—Dictionaries. I. Title.
PE1583.P33   1995
423'.1—dc20   94–29273

British Library Cataloguing in Publication Data is available.

Library of Congress Catalog Card Number: 94–29273
ISBN: 0–313–29490–9

First published in 1995

Greenwood Press, 88 Post Road West, Westport, CT   06881
An imprint of Greenwood Publishing Group, Inc.

Printed in the United States of America

The paper used in this book complies with the
Permanent Paper Standard issued by the National
Information Standards Organization (Z39.48–1984).

P

To

My
Loving
and
Supportive
Family

My mother, Cecile;
My brother, Malcolm, and his family;
My son, David, his wife, Linda, and my grandsons, Justin and Daniel;
My daughter, Denise, and my granddaughter, Kelly.

CONTENTS

PREFACE

There are so many animal phrases and expressions that a book listing them all would become a small dictionary.
Teri Degler, *Straight from the Horse's Mouth*, xiii

Speaking of Animals (SOA) is the first comprehensive American dictionary of animal metaphors to be *organized alphabetically by metaphor* rather than by animal. The only other comprehensive American dictionaries of animal metaphors, *The Animal Things We Say* (ATWS: 1983) and *It's Raining Cats and Dogs* (IRCD: 1989), are either organized alphabetically by animal (ATWS: Part One) or by animal behavior (IRCD and ATWS: Part Two). The rationale for the focus on metaphor in SOA is to enable the reader to locate instantly a metaphor that is either animal-based, e.g., *put on the dog*, or that is suspected to be animal-based, e.g., *bite the hand that feeds you*. Furthermore, there are a number of metaphors, such as *cynic* and *sarcasm*, that one would never suspect of being animal-based and that would be overlooked in a dictionary organized by animal. (All of the preceding metaphors are dog-based.) To compensate for the change in focus, all of the nearly 3,000 metaphors in SOA have been listed under the appropriate animal in the Classification of Metaphors According to Animal, which follows the entries.

Speaking of Animals is also a *referenced* dictionary, based on over thirty published works (*see References* for a list of books and abbreviations) that either restrict themselves to animal metaphors (ATWS, IRCD, SHM) or include animal metaphors along with other metaphors (LCRH, ST), idioms (AID, CI, DEI, ID), clichés (DOC), euphemisms (DEOD), slang terms (NDAS), Americanisms (CH, DA, DAE, IHAT, LTA), word and phrase origins (EWPO, MDWPO), curious words and expressions (HF, HOI, HTB, THT), literary words (BDPF), Indo-European roots

(ROE), "crazy" words and puns (CE, GTP), political words (SPD), and just plain words (SOED, WNNCD, WNWD).

Speaking of Animals not only uses a broad definition of "animal metaphor" but includes words and expressions that *appear* to be animal metaphors but are actually not. These latter terms are marked with an asterisk following "Source," e.g., "Source: CAT (*)." In regard to the broadness of definition, the coverage is not restricted to metaphors that apply only to humans (e.g., *cat burglar*) but includes those that apply also to other animals (e.g., *catfish*) and even to plants (e.g., *catkin*). The dictionary includes similes (e.g., *like the cat that ate the canary*), proverbs (e.g., *curiosity killed the cat*), idioms (e.g., *let the cat out of the bag*), slang (e.g., *cat around*), literary references (e.g., *green-eyed monster*), and popular expressions (e.g., *Cat got your tongue?*). False metaphors, such as *catamaran, catatonic, catsup,* and *catty-corner* are included in order to identify them as such and to attempt to explain the coincidence (as in the first two examples) or the false etymology (as in the last two). Metaphors that are believed to be animal-based but cannot be proved to be are identified with a question mark following the "Source," e.g., "Source: CAT (?)." (*See* Reading the Entries for help in interpreting the contents.)

People have been fascinated with animals since Adam, who, according to Genesis 2:19–20, was given the responsibility of naming all of the animals: "And out of the ground the Lord God formed every beast of the field, and every fowl of the air; and brought them unto Adam to see what he would call them: and whatsoever Adam called every living creature, that was the name thereof." However, Adam may have neglected to name the fish: "And Adam gave names to all cattle, and to the fowl of the air, and to every beast of the field." (It is not known whether Adam eventually ran out of names and began to apply metaphors, such as *mule deer* and *zebra finch*, to the subspecies at the end of the line.) By Noah's time, all of the animals that occupied the land and the air had been named, but, understandably, fish were not included in the pairs of species that were carried in the ark. It is interesting to note that in Modern English, the number of metaphorical names is much higher among fish than among mammals, birds, reptiles, and insects.

Fascination with animals is strong in modern America. The mascots of our political parties are mammals: the *donkey* (Democrats), the *elephant* (Republicans), and even the *bull moose* (Theodore Roosevelt's independent party in 1912). The nicknames for members of Congress are related to birds: *left-wing* (liberals), *right-wing* (conservatives); *doves* (make peace), *hawks* (make war). In the stock market, a *bull* market is a rising market, while a *bear* market is a falling market; a *bear* is a stockbroker who sells when prices are high, while a *bull* is one who buys when they are low. American automobile manufacturers have a fondness for animal names: e.g., *Cougar, Mustang,* and *Thunderbird* (Ford); *Colt, Eagle,* and *Viper* (Chrysler); *Firebird, Skyhawk,* and *Skylark* (General Motors). Animal names are particularly popular for sports teams, both at the amateur and professional levels: e.g., the *Gators* (Univ. of Florida), the *Razorbacks* (Univ. of Arkansas), and the *Wildcats* (Univ. of Arizona); the *Bulls* (Chicago basketball), the *Bears* (Chicago football), and the *Cubs* (Chicago baseball). Fraternal organizations have such names as *Elks*, *Lions*, and *Moose*; and Boy Scouts start out as *Cub* Scouts and end up as *Eagle* Scouts.

For the purpose of this dictionary, an *animal* is defined as "a living *being* other than a human." This is a controversial definition, because *animal* is often defined as "a living *thing* capable of spontaneous movement"—i.e., animals in the SOA sense plus humans. The rationale for separating humans from other animals in the dictionary is language: Humans have it; animals don't. Humans name animals; as far as we know, animals don't name humans. Humans create metaphors; animals don't. Furthermore, our metaphors speak of humans as *behaving like animals* or having *animal instincts*, *animal magnetism*, or *animal passions*. In other words, humans regard themselves as superior to the other, or "lower," animals. *You animal!* is one of the strongest insults in our language.

Speaking of Animals will be of interest to linguists, philologists, lexicographers, and teachers of English as a second or foreign language; to biologists, zoologists, naturalists, and directors of nature centers, wildlife parks, and zoos; to historians, students of American culture, students of popular culture, and members of various animal rights organizations. In regard to animal rights, the dictionary takes a neutral stance between human rights and animal rights: i.e., (1) the right of humans to exploit animals for their own pleasure, comfort, profit, and survival, and (2) the right of animals to live a natural life and die a natural death, without human interference or exploitation. These are the extremes, of course: Most animal rights groups recognize the dependence of humans on animals, and of animals on humans, for the survival of both. What they insist on is humane and ethical treatment, especially by humans.

ACKNOWLEDGMENTS

I wish to recognize several departments and individuals at Western Michigan University for their generous support of this project. In the Department of Foreign Languages and Literatures, I would like to thank my former chairman, Peter Krawutschke, his successor, John Benson, and the administrative assistant, Patricia Duzan; my former faculty colleagues Daniel Hendriksen (especially), Robert Griffin, Benjamin Ebling, Johannes Kissel, and George Osmun; and my former graduate students in Introduction to Linguistics, Sociolinguistics, and Seminar in Linguistics. Further, I wish to express my gratitude to Harold L. Ray, former chairman of the Department of Health, Physical Education, and Recreation, and my collaborator on *Sports Talk: A Dictionary of Sports Metaphors* (Greenwood Press, 1989). In Waldo Library, the professional staff of the Reference section, especially Gordon Eriksen, were invaluable.

I also wish to thank the staff of the Portage Public Library, particularly Frank Hemphill, City Librarian; the staff of the John Rollins Bookstore in Portage, Michigan; and all of the animals in my backyard.

ABBREVIATIONS AND SYMBOLS

ABBREVIATIONS

adj.	adjective
adv.	adverb
Amer.	American
approx.	approximately
Ar.	Arabic
Braz. Port.	Brazilian Portuguese
Brit.	British
ca.	about
cent.	century
dim.	diminutive
Du.	Dutch
Eng.	English
esp.	especially
fig.	figuratively
fr.	from
Fr.	French
gen.	generally
Ger.	German
Gk.	Greek
Gmc.	Germanic

Heb.	Hebrew
I.E.	Indo-European
It.	Italian
Lat.	Latin
lit.	literally
L.Lat.	Late Latin
M.E.	Middle English
M.Fr.	Middle French
M.Lat.	Medieval Latin
Mod. Eng.	Modern English
Mod.Fr.	Modern French
n	noun
N.D.	no date
neg.	negative
O.E.	Old English
O.Fr.	Old French
O.H.G.	Old High German
O.It.	Old Italian
O.N.	Old Norse
O.N.Fr.	Old North French
orig.	originally
pl.	plural
Port.	Portuguese
q.v.	which see
sing.	singular
Skt.	Sanskrit
Sp.	Spanish
U.S.	United States
usu.	usually
v	verb
V.Lat.	Vulgar Latin
WWI	World War One
WWII	World War Two

SYMBOLS

(*)	not an animal metaphor
(?)	possibly an animal metaphor

REFERENCES

KEY TO WORKS CITED

AID   Richard A. Spears, *NTC's American Idioms Dictionary* (Lincolnwood, Ill.: National Textbook Company, 1987).

ATWS   Darryl Lyman, *The Animal Things We Say* (Middle Village, N.Y.: Johnathan David Publishers, 1983).

BDPF   Ivor H. Evans, ed., *Brewer's Dictionary of Phrase and Fable*, rev. Centenary Ed. (New York: Harper & Row, 1981).

CE   Richard Lederer, *Crazy English* (New York: Pocket Books, 1989).

CH   Elizabeth B. Canterbury, *Cliff Hangers* (Springfield, Ill.: Phillip H. Wagner, N.D.).

CI   E. M. Kirkpatrick and C. M. Schwarz, eds., *Chambers Idioms* (Edinburgh: W & R Chambers, 1982).

DA   Mitford M. Matthews, ed., *A Dictionary of Americanisms* (Chicago: University of Chicago Press, 1951).

DAE   William A. Craigie and James R. Hulbert, eds., *A Dictionary of American English on Historical Principles* (Chicago: University Press, 1938).

DEI   Daphne M. Gulland and David G. Hinds-Howell, *Dictionary of English Idioms* (London: Penguin Books, 1986).

DEOD   Hugh Rawson, *A Dictionary of Euphemisms and Other Doubletalk* (New York: Crown Publishers, 1981).

DOC   James Rogers, *The Dictionary of Cliches* (New York: Facts on File, 1985).

EWPO	Robert Hendrickson, *The Facts on File Encyclopedia of Word and Phrase Origins* (New York: Facts on File, 1987).
GTP	Richard Lederer, *Get Thee to a Punnery* (Charleston, S.C.: Wyrick & Co., 1988).
HF	Charles Earle Funk, *Horsefeathers* (New York: Harper & Row, 1958; reprint, New York: Perennial Library, 1986).
HOI	Charles Earle Funk, *A Hog on Ice* (New York: Harper & Row, 1948; reprint, New York: Harper Colophon Books, 1985).
HTB	Charles Earle Funk, *Heavens to Betsy* (New York: Harper & Row, 1955; reprint, New York: Perennial Library, 1986).
ID	Suzanne Brock, *Idiom's Delight* (New York: Times Books, 1988).
IHAT	Stuart Berg Flexner, *I Hear America Talking* (New York: Simon & Schuster, 1976).
IRCD	Christine Ammer, *It's Raining Cats and Dogs* (New York: Dell Publishing, 1989).
LCRH	Robert Claiborne, *Loose Cannons and Red Herrings: A Book of Lost Metaphors* (New York: W. W. Norton, 1988).
LTA	Stuart Berg Flexner, *Listening to America* (New York: Simon & Schuster, 1982).
MDWPO	William Morris and Mary Morris, *Morris Dictionary of Word and Phrase Origins*, 2d ed. (New York: Harper & Row, 1988).
NDAS	Robert L. Chapman, ed., *New Dictionary of American Slang* (New York: Harper & Row, 1986).
ROE	Robert Claiborne, *The Roots of English* (New York: Times Books, 1989).
SHM	Teri Degler, *Straight from the Horse's Mouth* (New York: Henry Holt & Co., 1989).
SOED	C. T. Onions, rev. and ed., *The Shorter Oxford English Dictionary on Historical Principles*, rev. 3d. ed. (Oxford: Clarendon Press, 1944).
SPD	William Safire, *Safire's Political Dictionary*, 3d ed. (New York: Ballantine Books, 1978).
ST	Robert A. Palmatier and Harold L. Ray, *Sports Talk: A Dictionary of Sports Metaphors* (Westport, Conn.: Greenwood Press, 1989).
THT	Charles Earle Funk, *Thereby Hangs a Tale* (New York: Harper & Row, 1950; reprint, New York: Harper Colophon Books, 1985).
WNNCD	Frederick C. Mish, Editor in Chief, *Webster's Ninth New Collegiate Dictionary* (Springfield, Mass.: Merriam-Webster, 1983).
WNWD	David B. Guralnik, Editor in Chief, *Webster's New World Dictionary of the American Language*, 2d college ed. (New York: Simon & Schuster, 1982).

WORKS CONSULTED

Arnett, Ross H., Jr., and Richard L. Jacques. *Simon and Schuster's Guide to Insects.* New York: Simon & Schuster, 1981.

Bliss, Dorothy E. *Shrimps, Lobsters and Crabs.* New York: Columbia University Press, 1990.

Boitani, Luigi, and Stefania Bartoli. *Simon & Schuster's Guide to Mammals.* Edited by Sydney Anderson. New York: Simon & Schuster, 1983.

Bologna, Gianfranco. *Simon & Schuster's Guide to Birds of the World.* Edited by John Bull. New York: Simon & Schuster, 1981.

Boschung, Herbert T., Jr., James D. Williams, Daniel W. Gotshall, David K. Caldwell, and Melba C. Caldwell. *The Audubon Society Field Guide to North American Fishes, Whales, and Dolphins.* New York: Alfred A. Knopf, 1983.

Capula, Massimo. *Simon & Schuster's Guide to Reptiles and Amphibians of the World.* Edited by John L. Behler. New York: Simon & Schuster, 1989.

Pope, John A., Jr., Editor in Chief. *Book of North American Birds.* Pleasantville, N.Y.: The Reader's Digest Association, 1990.

NOTE

WNNCD was used as the primary source for spellings, dates, etymologies, and meanings. WNWD was used as the primary source for identification of Americanisms and the secondary source for spellings, etymologies, and meanings.

READING THE ENTRIES

A typical entry in the dictionary consists of the following elements: an entry *heading*, consisting of the full or constant form of the metaphor; an illustration of the *grammatical use* of the metaphor; a *synonym* for or *definition* of the meaning of the metaphor; the *date* of the first recorded use of the *metaphor* in English (where possible); the name of the animal (or class of animals) that is the *source* of the metaphor; the *date* of the first recorded use of the *animal name*; a discussion of the *connection* between the animal and the metaphor; coded *references* to the works in which the metaphor is recognized as a figure of speech; *informative cross-references* to other entries in the dictionary; and *comparative cross-references* to other entries in the dictionary.

The entry for *barfly* illustrates all of these elements:

BARFLY   *a barfly.* A frequenter of bars. WNNCD: 1910. Source: FLY. WNNCD: O.E. Just as flies are attracted to garbage, carrion, and excrement, in which they lay their eggs, barflies are drawn to barrooms and taverns, where they deposit their money for drinks. The fly's eggs become larvae—called "maggots"—which produce more flies; the barfly's dollars contribute to the purchase of alcohol for the barfly's next visit. ATWS; IRCD. *See also* Fly (n) (1). *Compare* Gadfly.

"BARFLY" is the full form of the metaphor. "*A barfly*" illustrates that the metaphor is a noun. "WNNCD: 1910" indicates that the first recorded use of the metaphor in English was 1910, according to *Webster's Ninth New Collegiate Dictionary* (WNNCD). "Source: FLY" attributes the animal source of the metaphor to the fly. "WNNCD: O.E." indicates that the earliest recorded use of *fly* as the name for an insect was in Old English. The text of the entry points out the similarities between the insect fly and the human "fly." "ATWS" and "IRCD" are coded references to two works in the "Key to Works Cited": *The Animal Things We Say* (ATWS) and *It's Raining Cats and Dogs* (IRCD). "*See also* Fly (n) (1)" is a cross-reference to an entry that provides further information about flies. And "*Compare* Gadfly" is a cross-reference to a contrasting metaphor that also has *fly* as its base.

A

A *the letter A.* The first letter of the English alphabet. Source: OX. A is for *alpha*, the first letter of the Greek alphabet, which derives from the Phoenician symbol ꓘ, a representation of the head of an ox (*aleph*). Note the snout at the bottom, the ears—or possibly the yoke—in the middle, and the horns at the top. The symbol was turned 180 degrees and borrowed for the Greek alphabet and eventually for the Roman and English alphabets. (Turned only 90 degrees, counterclockwise, the symbol became the cursive form of *A* in the Hebrew and Greek alphabets.) The letter *L* also derives from Phoenician, where it was the symbol for *lamed* "oxgoad." ATWS; BDPF; EWPO. *See also* Alphabet. *Compare* C; G; R.

AARDVARK *an aardvark.* A South African termite-eater. WNNCD: 1833. Source: PIG. *Aardvark* is Afrikaans for "earth pig" (*aard* "earth" + *vark* "pig"). The *aardvark* resembles the pig in its thick, almost hairless skin, its short legs, and its blunt snout; but pigs have larger heads, shorter snouts, small, curly tails, and hooves rather than claws; further, aardvarks are omnivorous. EWPO; HF.

ABET *to aid and abet someone.* To assist someone in conducting an activity or carrying out a plan (often a criminal one). WNNCD: 14th cent. Source: DOG. *Abet* is the English form of O.Fr. *abeter* "to hound on"—i.e., to urge on a dog that is baiting a tethered bear in the medieval "sport" of bearbaiting. Abetting a dog is a far cry from *abetting* a criminal, which involves providing such favors as food, shelter, transportation, and money. *Abet* can also have a more positive sense, as in a plan that *abets* the cause of justice. SOED; ST; THT. *Compare* Harass.

ABOVE THE APES   *a little above the apes.* Lacking in intelligence, manners, tact, and sophistication: uncouth, uncivilized, subhuman. Source: APE. WNNCD: O.E. Primates are divided into nonanthropoids (monkeys) and anthropoids (apes). The only primate that is *above the apes* is the human, though some humans are not very far removed, considering their behavior. CE. *See also* Ape (n); Big Ape.

ABUZZ   *to be abuzz with anticipation or excitement.* For a crowd of people to murmur to each other as they await an arrival, an announcement, or the beginning of an event. WNNCD: 1859. Source: BEE. In this metaphor, the crowd of people is likened to a swarm of bees buzzing in unison as they go about their work making honeycombs and honey, and awaiting the arrival of the forager bees with their supply of nectar. *See also* Buzz (v); Buzz Session.

ADAM'S OFF OX   *to not know someone from Adam's off ox.* To have absolutely no knowledge of, or acquaintance with, someone. Source: OX. WNNCD: O.E. The original expression was "to not know someone from Adam." Adam is portrayed as as ox driver, walking to the left of two yoked oxen pulling a cart or a plow. The driver is aware of the "near ox," but he is unable to see the "off ox." So even Adam didn't know his *off ox.* EWPO; HOI; MDWPO; SHM.

AEGIS   *under the aegis of.* Under the sponsorship or protection of. Source: GOAT. *Aegis* is the Latin form of the Greek word *aigis*, meaning "goatskin," from *aig-* "goat." In Greek mythology, the shield of Zeus was covered with goatskin, as was that of Athena. The physical protection that it afforded them has been replaced by financial, moral, or legal support in the modern metaphor. ATWS; THT.

AFTER AWHILE, CROCODILE   *After awhile, crocodile!* See you later, friend! ATWS: 1930s. Source: CROCODILE. WNNCD: 14th cent. The alligator, crocodile, and hummingbird lent their names as terms of address to swing musicians and their followers during the 1930s and 1940s. However, the borrowings were based solely on rhyme (e.g., awh*ile*—crocod*ile*), not on behavior or appearance. CE. *See also* See You later, Alligator; What's the Word, Hummingbird.

AGGREGATE   *See* Congregate.

AIN'T THAT A HOOT   *Ain't that a hoot!* Isn't that a laugh! Source: OWL. A *hoot* (WNNCD: 15th cent.) is the cry of the "hoot owl," or Great Horned Owl, of North America. It is typically uttered in a series of four hoots, intended for friendly communication with members of the owl's own family and as a warning to other male hoot owls and other birds of prey. This expression contrasts sharply with *Not Give a Hoot* and *Not Worth a Hoot* (both of which *see*), in which *hoot* is something insignificant or worthless. *See also* Hoot (n).

ALBANY BEEF *sturgeon.* EWPO: 1791. Source: CATTLE. *Albany beef* is a euphemism for the flesh of the large fish called a *sturgeon.* At the turn of the 18th and 19th cents., poverty-stricken New Yorkers turned to sturgeon, which were readily available in the Hudson River, as a substitute for the much more expensive meat of cattle. Albany, the present capital of New York State, is located up the Hudson River from New York City. DEOD; EWPO. *Compare* Cape Cod Turkey; City Chicken; Hoover Hog; Texas Turkey; Welsh Rabbit.

ALBATROSS AROUND YOUR NECK *an albatross around your neck.* A heavy burden for you to bear, one that is both unwanted and undeserved: a curse; a "cross." DOC: ca. 1800. Source: ALBATROSS. WNNCD: 1564. The metaphor derives from the large seabird in Coleridge's "Rime of the Ancient Mariner" (1798) that was hung around the neck of the unfortunate sailor who shot it. The albatross was regarded as a good-luck symbol because of its ability to fly, or "soar," without flapping its wings. The name of the bird is a corruption of Sp. *alcatraz* "pelican," from Ar. *al ghatas* "sea eagle," but the bird is also known as a *gooney bird* and a *Cape Hope sheep* (q.v.). In England, an *albatross* is a *double eagle* (q.v.) in golf. ATWS; BDPF; DEI; DOC; EWPO; IRCD; LCRH; MDWPO. *Compare* Have a Monkey on Your Back.

ALL AFLUTTER *See* Flutter.

ALLEY CAT *an alley cat.* A sexually promiscuous woman. Source: CAT. WNNCD: O.E. Literally, an alley cat is a homeless, stray, mixed-breed cat that roams the alleys for food and sex. Figuratively, an *alley cat* was orig. a streetwalker or prostitute, but now the term can be applied to any woman of loose morals who seeks sexual gratification wherever she can find it. ATWS; HTB; NDAS. *Compare* Tomcat.

ALLIGATOR (n) *an alligator.* An American crocodilian that differs from the African and Asian crocodile in its smaller size and broader snout. WNNCD: 1568. Source: LIZARD. Spanish explorers in the 16th cent. named this reptile *el lagarto* "the lizard"; the article and noun later fused into *elagarto*, eventually producing *alligator.* In the 1930s the term *alligator* was applied to a swing musician or a male devotee of swing music: a *hepcat* (q.v.). This application was coincident with the popularity of the parting, *See you later, alligator* (q.v.). ATWS; EWPO.

ALLIGATOR (v) *to alligator.* For varnish or paint to crack, as from weathering, in the form of little squares. Source: ALLIGATOR. WNNCD: 1568. The alligator is a North American crocodilian whose back and tail are covered with bony plates. The squares of weathered paint and varnish are analogous to the armor plates of the alligator. ATWS. *See also* Alligator (n).

ALLIGATOR CLIP   *an alligator clip.* A spring-operated metal clamp with long jaws and jagged teeth that is used to make temporary electrical connections. WNNCD: ca. 1941. Source: ALLIGATOR. WNNCD: 1568. The "long jaws" and "jagged teeth" allude to the alligator, which is more populous on the Gulf Coast than the similarly equipped crocodile. ATWS. *See also* Alligator (n).

ALLIGATOR GAR   *an alligator gar.* A large freshwater fish—up to 10 feet long and 300 pounds in weight—of the Ohio and Mississippi rivers and the inland Gulf Coast. Source: ALLIGATOR. WNNCD: 1568. The alligator gar is probably so called because of its large size and the fact that it inhabits some of the same coastal rivers and bayous as the alligator. The *alligator snapper,* a snapping turtle up to five feet long and 150 pounds in weight, is also large for its species and probably gets its name from coexisting with the alligator in the rivers of the Gulf Coast. *See also* Alligator (n).

ALLIGATOR PEAR   *an alligator pear.* The pear-shaped avocado—the fruit of the avocado tree. WNNCD: 1763. Source: ALLIGATOR (?). WNNCD: 1568. An avocado is not shaped like an alligator, but the bumpy green skin is similar. However, the *alligator* in *alligator pear* is probably a mispronunciation of Sp. *aquacate* "avocado," from Aztec *ahucatl* "avocado." ATWS; EWPO; MDWPO. *See also* Alligator (n); Alligator (v).

ALLIGATOR SNAPPER   *See* Alligator Gar.

ALPHABET   *an alphabet.* The ordered set of letters, including both consonants and vowels, of a Greco-Roman writing system. WNNCD: 15th cent. Source: OX. *Alphabet* is a combination of the names of the first two letters of the Greek ordered set: *alpha* and *beta.* These letters were derived from the names of the first two symbols—both consonants—of the Phoenician ordered set: *aleph* "ox" and *beth* "house." Therefore, an *alphabet* is literally an "ox house." BDPF. *See also* A.

ALSO-RAN   *an also-ran.* A distant finisher: a loser. Source: HORSE. In horse racing, an *also-ran* (WNNCD: 1896) is a horse that *finishes out of the money* (q.v.): i.e., it neither *wins* (1st place), *places* (2nd place), nor *shows* (3rd place). EWPO states that the term comes from the heading "Also Ran," under which newspapers once listed the names of horses that finished fourth or lower in a race. Among humans, an *also-ran* is a candidate for a job or an office who is not one of the top finishers: i.e., is not on a "short list" of applicants or does not finish among the top three in an election. *Also-ran* carries the connotation of someone who is not only a loser but is lacking in competitiveness and need not be taken seriously. ATWS; CI; HTB; ST.

AMBLE   *an amble; to amble.* A slow walk; to walk slowly. WNNCD: 14th cent. Source: HORSE. To *amble* over to the store to buy some groceries is simply to take your time—to walk without any hurry. For a horse, however, an amble is a particular gait, one in which the two legs on each side move together in a stride. The result is the single gait of the horse that most resembles the gait of humans. ATWS.

AMERICAN EAGLE   *an American eagle.* A U.S. ten-dollar gold piece (1794–1933) with the image of an eagle on the reverse side. Source: EAGLE. WNNCD: 13th cent. The eagle on the back of the ten-dollar gold coin is the *bald eagle* (q.v.), which has appeared on the Great Seal of the United States since 1782. It is the national emblem. BDPF; IHAT; LTA; SPD. *See also* Double Eagle; Eagle Flies on Friday; Spread Eagle; When the Eagle Flies.

ANDIRONS   Firedogs. WNNCD: 14th cent. Source: COW. *Andiron* is a blend of *andera* (Gaulish for "heifer") and *iron*. A pair of *andirons* is used to support logs, laid crosswise on them, above the hearth of a fireplace. The cow enters the metaphor because a cow's head once decorated the top end of each of the metal posts on the outside. *Firedogs* (WNNCD: 1792) were named for the four short legs that supported the *andirons*. The word is probably a loan translation of Fr. *chenet* "andirons" (lit. "little dog," fr. *chien* "dog"). HF; IRCD: THT; WNWD.

ANGELS ON HORSEBACK   *See* Pigs in the Blanket.

ANGRY AS A BEAR   *See* Cross as a Bear.

ANIMAL   *an animal.* A person who is irrational, immoral, or uncivilized. Source: ANIMAL. WNNCD: 14th cent. Natural objects are divided into animals, plants, and minerals, of which animals and plants are classified as living things. Animals differ from plants in being capable of spontaneous movement. The *animal kingdom* (WNNCD: 1847) is divided into mammals, birds, fish, reptiles, insects, and a few other categories; but popular usage of the term *animal* contrasts mammals with nonmammals, or humans with nonhumans (the "lower animals"). It is these last two senses that apply to persons who *behave like animals* (i.e., like other mammals) or are *lower than the animals* (i.e., are like birds, fish, reptiles, insects, etc.). An example of "animal" behavior can be seen in the film *Animal House*, in which the members of the Alpha Rho Epsilon fraternity behave like the nonhuman primates in their Greek acronym ("APE"): eating, sleeping, drinking, playing, fighting, and lusting. They are *party animals*, with *animal passions*. A civilized group of individuals, such as a company of dancers, singers, or actors, is a *different animal* entirely. ATWS; DEI. *See also* Political Animal.

ANIMAL CRACKER   *an animal cracker.* A small cookie in the shape of an animal. WNNCD: 1897. Source: ANIMAL. WNNCD: 14th cent. The original animal crackers were cookies in the form of certain animals that appeared in the circus or the zoo, such as lions, tigers, elephants, and bears—all of them mammals and all of them wild. Thus, the cookie industry has given us another definition of the word *animal* (q.v.).

ANIMAL INSTINCTS   *See* Animal Magnetism.

ANIMAL MAGNETISM   Physical charm; sex appeal. Source: ANIMAL. WNNCD: 14th cent. The inventor of the clinical use of hypnosis was the German physician F. A. Mesmer (1734–1815), who attributed his ability to hypnotize patients to a mysterious force that he called *animal magnetism. Mesmerism* (WNNCD: 1784), as hypnosis was first called in English, eliminated the patient's inhibitions and revealed his/her *animal instincts*—the drives, such as for food, sex, etc., that are shared by both animals and humans. The term *animal magnetism* has since been popularized to mean the physical—esp. sexual—charm that attracts members of the opposite sex like a magnet.

ANIMAL PASSIONS   *See* Animal.

ANTENNA   *an antenna.* A metal rod, or assembly of rods, for sending or receiving radio or television signals. Source: ARTHROPOD (insects, myriapods, crustaceans). WNNCD: 1877. All arthropods have a pair of "feelers," or *antennae* (WNNCD: 1646), on their heads; and crustaceans have two pairs. These sensory organs are the basis for the name of the telecommunication device known as the *antenna*, although it can not only receive signals but also send them.

ANT LION   *an ant lion.* The larva of a four-winged fly. WNNCD: 1815. Source: ANT (WNNCD: O.E.); LION (WNNCD: 12th cent.). The ant lion is neither an ant nor a lion. The larva gets the name *ant* because it feeds on ants that fall into the pit that it digs in the sand or mud. It may get the name *lion* because of its large size and voracious appetite. HF.

ANTS IN YOUR PANTS   *to have ants in your pants.* To be nervous, fidgety, and impatient. DOC: ca. 1933. Source: ANT. WNNCD: O.E. Persons with ants in their pants behave as if a colony of ants were crawling up their legs, inside their clothing, and they have to twist and turn in order to shake them off. AID; ATWS; CE; DOC; SHM. *Compare* Antsy.

ANTSY   *to be antsy.* To be nervous, fidgety, and impatient. WNNCD: 1951. Source: ANT. WNNCD: O.E. The ant is a "nervous" creature—always on the move, scurrying about, frequently changing directions. An *antsy* person is one who, like the ant, can't seem to stand still. AID; EWPO; SHM. *Compare* Ants in Your Pants.

APE (adj.)   *to be ape.* To be outstanding, such as the work of a great artist or the performance of a great athlete. Source: APE. WNNCD: O.E. The ape alluded to in this metaphor is probably the "great ape," or anthropoid ape, esp. the *gorilla* (q.v.), which is the largest of the apes (males up to 6.5 feet tall, 500 pounds in weight). NDAS. *See also* Ape (n); Big Ape.

APE (n) *an ape.* A large, awkward, unattractive, and uncultured male. Source: APE. WNNCD: O.E. The ape in this metaphor is probably the *gorilla* (q.v.), the largest of the anthropoid apes and the one closest in size to the human. ATWS; IRCD. *See also* Big Ape.

APE (v) *to ape someone.* To imitate someone's behavior—usu. crudely and mockingly. WNNCD: 1632. Source: APE. WNNCD: O.E. The allusion is probably to the ability of the monkey (a nonanthropoid primate) or the chimpanzee (an anthropoid primate) to mimic the behavior of their human caretakers or spectators, as in a zoo. ATWS; DEI; IRCD. *See also* Monkey See, Monkey Do.

AQUILINE *an aquiline nose.* A hooked nose. Source: EAGLE. WNNCD: 13th cent. The eagle's upper beak is much longer than its lower one and curves down over it like a giant hook. The hook is used to tear the flesh of a dead or dying prey into bite-size pieces for the eagle's young. An *aquiline*, or "eagle-like," nose on a human hooks down toward the upper lip in the same manner. ATWS. *See also* Eagle Beak. *Compare* Hawk-nosed.

ARCTIC *the arctic (or Arctic).* The region surrounding the north pole—from approx. 65 degrees north. WNNCD: 14th cent. Source: BEAR. WNNCD: O.E. The far north is named for the bear (Gk. *arktos*), which appears in the northern constellations *Ursa Major* "great bear" and *Ursa Minor* "little bear." The polar bear inhabits these arctic regions, where it endures arctic cold and long arctic winters. The opposite pole, the "anti-arctic," is called the *antarctic* (or Antarctic). EWPO; LCRH; ROE.

ARE YOU A MAN OR A MOUSE *Are you a man or a mouse?* Are you a courageous person or a coward? (The assumption is that you are a coward). EWPO: 1541. Source: MOUSE. WNNCD: O.E. The question is usu. used by a woman to shame a man into doing something that he is reluctant or afraid to do, but it could also be asked of a son by his father. The assumption is that the askee is timid and fearful, like the common house mouse, which is seldom seen or heard. ATWS; IRCD.

AROUSE THE TIGER *to arouse—or bring out—the tiger in someone.* To bring out the suppressed aggressiveness, ferocity, or bloodthirstiness in someone. Source: TIGER. WNNCD: O.E. Humans, as civilized beings, tend to suppress their *animal instincts* (q.v.); but competition can make them as aggressive, ferocious, and bloodthirsty as a tiger, which is the Lord of the Indian Jungle. (Tigers do not now—and perhaps never did—inhabit sub-Saharan Africa.) *See also* Tiger.

ASININE *to be asinine.* For your actions or utterances to reflect your stupidity or bad judgment. WNNCD: 1610. Source: ASS. WNNCD: O.E. To be asinine is to behave like an *ass* (Lat. *asinus*)—i.e., like a *donkey* (ca. 1785). The donkey has long been stereotyped as a stupid animal; but in the survival sense, it is smarter than the horse. ATWS; CE. *See also* Ass; Feel like an Ass; Make an Ass of Yourself.

ASPHALT JUNGLE *See* It's a Jungle Out There.

ASPIC Clear jelly, made of meat stock and used to prepare a meat or vegetable mold. WNNCD: 1789. Source: SNAKE. WNNCD: O.E. In French, an *aspic* is either a meat jelly or an asp viper, a poisonous snake found in France and much of Southwestern Europe. The snake came first, and the jelly was named after it, perhaps because both are cold to the touch. EWPO.

ASS *an ass.* A stupid, stubborn, or contemptible person. LTA: 1400. Source: ASS. WNNCD: O.E. The ass, or donkey, has always had a lower position of respectability than the horse, either because of its smaller size (it is hard to ride) or its greater obstinance (it is hard to control). The homophonous *ass* "buttocks" is from a different source: O.E. *ærs* "ears." ATWS; IRCD. *See also* Asinine; Smart Ass. *Compare* Horse's Ass.

AS THE CROW FLIES "How far is it from here to there?" "Fifteen miles by car; ten miles *as the crow flies*"—i.e., as measured along a straight line drawn on a map. IRCD: 1838. Source: CROW. WNNCD: O.E. The crow has the advantage of traveling in the air, where there are no obstructions or detours. However, the crow is a notoriously non-straight-line flier, unlike wild ducks or geese. It was probably selected for this metaphor because it is so common and audacious. AID; ATWS; BDPF; CI; DEI; DOC; MDWPO.

AS WELL BE HANGED FOR A SHEEP AS A LAMB *You might as well be hanged for a sheep as a lamb.* If you intend to commit a little crime, you might just as well commit a bigger one that carries the same punishment. IRCD: 1678. Source: SHEEP; LAMB. WNNCD: O.E. The punishment for stealing a lamb was once the same as that for stealing a sheep: hanging. The metaphor has been softened in more recent times (EWPO: early-19th cent.) to mean that when opportunity knocks, you might as well take advantage of it, regardless of the consequences. BDPF; CI; DEI.

AT BAY *to hold—or keep—someone or something at bay.* To hold or keep someone or something in check. Source: DOG. Dogs hold (or keep) a quarry *at bay* (DOC: 1530) by barking loudly when the animal is cornered or holed. Their *baying* (fr. Fr. *abai*) keeps the quarry in place and alerts the hunters to its location. People try to hold disease, flood, or famine *in abeyance* (same source) so that it doesn't get any worse; and police officers hold criminals *at bay* until they can be captured and jailed. AID; DEI; DOC; EWPO; HOI; ST. *See also* Bring to Bay.

AT EACH OTHER'S THROATS *See* Dogfight.

AT FAULT *to be at fault.* To be guilty of a misdeed. SOED: 1833. Source: DOG. In a fox hunt, the hounds are said to be *at fault* (SOED: 1592) when they have lost the scent of the fox. At this time they *run riot* (EWPO: 1410), or search about uncontrollably for the proper scent, often picking up the scent of a different animal and chasing off *on the wrong track* (q.v.). People *run riot* (EWPO: 16th cent.) when they act uncontrollably; diseases and other natural disasters *run riot* when they are totally out of control. BDPF; CI; ST.

AT LOGGERHEADS *to be at loggerheads with someone.* To have a serious disagreement with someone. DOC: 1680. Source: TURTLE (?). The loggerhead is a large marine turtle with a head as large as a block of wood (a *logger*). When two loggerheads have a disagreement, they go at it with their powerful jaws. People who are *at loggerheads* with each other are engaged in a violent argument. However, such human confrontations may derive from the 19th cent. game of *loggerheads*, played by sailors tossing a long iron bar with a large bulbous head that was used onboard ship for melting tar (DA: 1871). ST.

AT ONE FELL SWOOP *to happen at—or in—one fell swoop.* For a goal to be achieved by a single, sudden action. EWPO: 1606. Source: KITE. In Shakespeare's *Macbeth* (Act IV, Scene 3), Macduff bewails the murder of his wife and children— by Macbeth—as if by a *hell-kite*: at one *fell* ("deadly") *swoop* ("dive"). The kite, a small hawk with a deeply forked tail, can dive extremely fast, catching its prey either on the ground or in the air. AID; ATWS; CI; DOC. *Compare* Kill two Birds with one Stone.

ATTA BOY *See* Down, Boy.

AT THE DROP OF A HAT Instantly. Source: HORSE. Horse races were once started when the starter swept his hat toward the ground. The horses were *jockeying for position* at the starting post, *raring to go* (WNNCD: 1909), and hoping not to be *left at the post* (q.v.). Once the race began, the horses ran *hell bent for leather* (WNNCD: 1875), sometimes *neck and neck* (WNNCD: 1799), each trying to get the *inside track* (WNNCD: 1857). The winner was usually a *shoo-in* (SPD: 1900), but at the end of the race all of the horses looked like they had been *rode hard and put away wet* (Tennessee Ernie Ford: 1950s). All of these expressions apply equally well to *human* contests and contestants. AID; ATWS; BDPF; CH; CI; LCRH; NDAS; ST.

AT THE END OF YOUR TETHER *See* End of Your Tether.

AUGUR   *to augur well for something.* To show promise for a successful beginning of something. Source: BIRD. An *augur* (WNNCD: 14th cent.—fr. Lat. *avis* "bird" + *garrire* "to tell") was the Roman successor to the *auspex*, or "bird-watcher," who divined, by observing the flocking and feeding habits of birds, whether the time was *auspicious* (WNNCD: 1601) for an event to occur. An *augury* (WNNCD: 14th cent.) was an omen, based not only on observation of birds but on other chance events, that could foretell the proper time to conduct a ceremony or to *inaugurate* (WNNCD: 1606) a public official into office. In modern times, something *augurs well* for success if its future looks good to the business or political analysts. EWPO. *See also* Auspices.

AUGURY   *See* Augur.

AUSPICES   *under the auspices of someone or something.* As a result of the support, guidance, or patronage of a person or organization. Source: BIRD. Modern "benefits" are often sponsored by a wealthy patron. In ancient Rome, major activities were never undertaken without the advice of an *auspex*, or "bird-watcher" (fr. Lat. *avis* "bird" + *specere* "to look at"). The auspex observed how the birds were flocking and what they were eating, and determined whether it was an *auspicious* (WNNCD: 1601) or "favorable" time to act. ATWS; EWPO; LCRH. *See also* Augur.

AUSPICIOUS   *See* Auspices.

AUTOGRAPH HOUND   *See* Hound (n).

AVIATION   The engineering, manufacture, and operation of craft that are heavier than air. WNNCD: 1866. Source: BIRD. All senses of *aviation* derive from Lat. *avis* "bird." Following the word *aviation* came *aviate* "to fly" (WNNCD: 1887), *aviator* "a male pilot" (WNNCD: 1887), and *aviatrix* "a female pilot" (WNNCD: 1910). Female pilots are now usu. called *aviators*, along with male pilots. All aircraft are heavier than air, of course, though some, such as the balloon and the dirigible, can be filled with gas, such as hot air or helium, that causes them to become lighter than air. Birds are also heavier than air, but they are able to achieve flight by flapping their wings—more like a *helicopter* (q.v.) than a fixed-wing plane—until they get up to speed. ATWS.

B

BACKBITE *to backbite.* To speak maliciously of someone behind their back. WNNCD: 12th cent. Source: ANIMAL. Backbiting among animals consists of one individual attacking another—usu. of the same species—from the back. This behavior usu. takes place between siblings or between a young animal and a parent, and the parent soon lets the offspring know that this is not the way to behave. Backbiting among humans involves talking about others behind their backs, or figuratively stabbing them in the back with malicious gossip. CE.

BACK IN HARNESS *See* Die in Harness.

BACK THE WRONG HORSE *to back the wrong horse.* To support a losing cause. Source: HORSE. WNNCD: O.E. In horse racing, to "back the wrong horse" is to bet on a loser. In politics, it is to support a losing candidate; in business it is to invest in a losing concern; and in general, it is to put your trust in the wrong person. ATWS; BDPF; DEI; IRCD; ST.

BACKTRACK *See* Track Down.

BAD EGG *a bad egg.* A no-good, rotten person. EWPO: ca. 1850. Source: CHICKEN. A bad chicken's egg is one that is either old, stale, or rotten or contains a dead baby chick. Its condition can be determined by candling, but it is readily apparent by smelling: It smells like a rotten egg. People who are *rotten eggs* may look wholesome, but their bad deeds "smell to high heaven." CI; DEI; HOI. *See also* Last one in Is a Rotten Egg. *Compare* Good Egg.

BADGER *to badger someone.* To annoy, pester, harass, or torment someone, as a lawyer might do to a witness. WNNCD: 1794. Source: BADGER. WNNCD: 1523. It was not the badger that was guilty of this behavior but the dogs—dachshunds, or "badger hounds"—that were *sicced* (q.v.) on the captive animal in the former "sport" of badger-baiting. The badger was tethered in a barrel and bitten by the dogs whenever it tried to get out. The game usu. ended with the badger's death. ATWS; BDPF; DEI; EWPO; HTB; IRCD; LCRH; MDWPO; SHM; ST.

BADGER GAME *the badger game.* A confidence game in which a woman invites a man to her hotel room, and, while they are engaging in sex, her "husband" suddenly appears, threatening blackmail and sometimes claiming to have photos. SHM: 1920. Source: BADGER. WNNCD: 1523. In this human version of badger-baiting, the victim is the "badger," and the con artists are the "dogs." Instead of being killed, the victim is forced to pay hush-money. ATWS; EWPO; HTB; MDWPO; NDAS. *See also* Badger. *Compare* Cat and Mouse Game.

BAG *to bag something.* To accomplish a goal: get a job, wrap up a deal, make a conquest, etc. Source: ANIMAL. The verb *bag* is a shortening and functional shift of the noun *game bag.* After an animal—esp. a bird or a small mammal—has been killed and retrieved, it is placed in a game bag, or "bagged" (SOED: 1814). Once the game is "in the bag," the pursuit of that particular quarry is over, though other kill may be added to the bag. Metaphorically, a goal is *in the bag* (EWPO: 1925) when it is either accomplished (i.e., reached) or as good as accomplished (i.e., within reach). A "mixed bag" of game is a game bag that contains either animals of different species or animals of the same species that are of different size or quality. A metaphorical *mixed bag* (WNNCD: 1926) is either a goal that is achieved with mixed results—some good, some bad—or a collection of people or things that are of mixed kind or quality. AID; ATWS; BDPF; CI; DEI; DOC; HOI; ID; LCRH; ST.

BAIT (1) *a bait; to bait.* A lure; to lure someone into a trap. Source: ANIMAL. An angler's bait is the worm, minnow, feather, or artificial lure that is attached to, or equipped with, one or more hooks. A hunter's lure is a live or artificial decoy, a deposit of food or grain, or simply a scent—all intended to draw the prey into the range of a gun, net, or trap. When an animal *takes the bait,* it strikes at the hook, approaches the decoy, or enters the trap. People also *bait the hook,* set out *decoys,* and *bait the trap* for other people: i.e., they attempt to trick them into incriminating themselves or falling for a scam. A person who succumbs to the temptation is said to *bite* (q.v.), or *take the bait.* The term *bait and switch* (WNNCD: 1967) is used for a sales tactic in which an item is advertised at a low price (the "bait") to lure customers into the store; then, when the customer arrives, he/she is told that the item is inferior and that he/she should buy a more expensive one (the "switch"). ATWS; ST. *Compare* Bait (2).

BAIT (2) *to bait someone.* To torment, persecute, or harass someone. Source: ANIMAL. *Bait* (fr. O.N. *beita* "to cause to bite") orig. meant to set dogs on tethered animals, such as bears, bulls, and badgers (WNNCD: 13th cent.). This ancient "sport" is now illegal, but baiting continues in the form of lawyers *badgering* (q.v.) witnesses, children teasing other children, and adults attacking each other verbally. ATWS; WNWD. *Compare* Bait (1).

BAIT AND SWITCH *See* Bait (1).

BAIT THE HOOK *See* Bait (1).

BAIT THE TRAP *See* Bait (1).

BALD AS A COOT *to be as bald as a coot.* To be completely bald. EWPO: 15th cent. Source: COOT. WNNCD: 14th cent. The coot is a black, ducklike bird (actually a "rail") whose white upper bill extends onto its forehead, giving it the appearance of being completely bald, although the rest of its head is covered with short feathers. ATWS; BDPF; DEI; DOC; MDWPO. *See also* Old Coot. *Compare* Bald as an Eagle.

BALD AS AN EAGLE *to be as bald as an eagle.* To have lost all of the hair on your head. Source: EAGLE. WNNCD: 13th cent. The analogy is to the bald eagle, which appears on the Great Seal of the United States and many items of currency, and is the official national bird. The bald eagle is not really bald: It simply has white feathers on its head and neck, with brown feathers on the rest of its body. CH. *Compare* Bald as a Coot.

BALLHAWK *See* Hawk (v) (2).

BAND SHELL *See* Shell (n).

BANTAM *See* Bantam Rooster.

BANTAM ROOSTER *a bantam—or bantie—rooster.* A tough little guy. WNNCD: 1915. Source: ROOSTER. WNNCD: O.E. The actor James Cagney was the epitome of a man of small stature whose cocky, combative, and pugnacious nature more than made up for his lack of size. Cagney was sometimes called a *bantam rooster*, because the male of this miniature breed of chickens—imported from Bantam, Java (WNNCD: 1749)—developed into a fierce fighting cock. *Bantam* became synonymous with "miniature" ca. 1900 and was applied to a weight class in boxing (late-19th cent.) and a small British automobile (early-20th cent.). ATWS; BDPF; EWPO; MDWPO. *See also* Bantamweight.

BANTAMWEIGHT   *a bantamweight.* A person of little influence; a boxer in the weight class just above *flyweight* (q.v.) and just below *featherweight* (q.v.). (*A bantam* really is lighter than a *feather.*) WNNCD: 1884. Source: ROOSTER. Compared to a heavyweight, a bantamweight is like a *bantam rooster* (q.v.): small but *feisty* (q.v.). The weight division for "bantams" is from 113 to 119 pounds—118 for professionals. ATWS; LTA.

BARFLY   *a barfly.* A frequenter of bars. WNNCD: 1910. Source: FLY. WNNCD: O.E. Just as flies are attracted to garbage, carrion, and excrement, in which they lay their eggs, barflies are drawn to barrooms and taverns, where they deposit their money for drinks. The fly's eggs become larvae—called "maggots"—which produce more flies; the barfly's dollars contribute to the purchase of alcohol for the barfly's next visit. ATWS; IRCD. *See also* Fly (n) (1). *Compare* Gadfly.

BARK   *to bark at someone; to bark orders at someone; to bark your wares.* To snap at someone in an angry tone; to shout commands like a drill instructor; to advertise your goods or services in a loud voice. Source: DOG. The bark of a dog is short, sharp, loud, somewhat threatening, and almost always annoying. People *bark* at other people when they are unhappy with their performance or are in a bad mood. Drill instructors *bark* at their trainees so that they can be heard and be more likely to be obeyed. *Barkers* (WNNCD: 1699) stand outside sideshows at circuses and carnivals, enticing passersby to come in and see their shows. ATWS; IRCD.

BARK AT THE MOON   *to bark—or bay—at the* moon. To complain loudly but futilely. Source: DOG. A full moon seems to incite barking—baying, howling— by both dogs and wolves (the close cousins of dogs). Why this happens is not certain, though the watchdog is trained to sound an alarm when anything untoward occurs, and a bright light in the sky certainly qualifies. People who *bark at the moon* are protesting against something that they have no control over and cannot change. ATWS; BDPF. *See also* Watchdog.

BARKER   *See* Bark.

BARKING DOGS   *See* Dogs Are Barking.

BARKING DOGS SELDOM BITE   Bullies are not usu. as dangerous as they seem—or sound. Source: DOG. WNNCD: O.E. Barking dogs seldom bite, because it is impossible to bark and bite at the same time. Furthermore, watchdogs come in all shapes and sizes, and even a harmless little dog can bark loudly enough to scare away an intruder, though the dog may sneak away if the intruder gets too close. In that case, the dog's *bark is* (said to be) *worse than its bite;* i.e., the dog is not as dangerous as it pretends to be. People who complain and protest loudly have chosen language as their weapon, so they are not to be feared—at least as long as they keep talking. ATWS; BDPF; CI; DEI; IRCD.

BARK IS WORSE THAN YOUR BITE *See* Barking Dogs seldom Bite.

BARK LIKE A DOG *to bark like a dog.* To utter a bark, a growl, a howl, a snarl, a woof, a yap, a yelp, or a yip. Source: DOG. WNNCD: O.E. Dogs not only *bark* (WNNCD: O.E.), or utter a short, loud cry: they also *growl* (WNNCD: early-18th cent.), or make a low, guttural sound; they *howl* (WNNCD: 14th cent.), or make a loud, sustained sound; they *snarl* (WNNCD: 1589), or make an angry, surly sound; they *woof* (WNNCD: 1804), or make a low, gruff sound; they *yap* (WNNCD: 1668), or make a shrill, snappish sound; they *yelp* (WNNCD: 1553), or make a short, sharp sound; and they *yip* (WNNCD: 1907), or make a sharp, shrill sound. People also *bark* (q.v.); they *growl* (or at least their stomachs do), and the dog's *grrr* is probably fashioned from the first two consonants of this word; they *howl* (as does the wind) when they're in pain; they *snarl* (and gnash their teeth) when they are angry; they *woof* (as do their stereos) when they are talking trash; they *yap* (using their *yap*, or mouth) when they chat or gossip; they *yelp* when they squeal with delight; and they *yip* when they talk incessantly. ATWS; EWPO; LTA.

BARK UP THE WRONG TREE *to bark up the wrong tree.* To look for something in the wrong place; to ask for help from the wrong person. DAE: 1832. Source: DOG. Coon hounds are trained to hunt raccoons at night, when they are most active. The dogs are supposed to tree the coon and then bark at the foot of the tree until the hunters come to shoot it. If the hunters discover that, in the dark, the hounds have gathered under the wrong tree, or the coon has climbed into another one, they may accuse the dogs of "barking up the wrong tree." Figuratively, humans *bark up the wrong tree* when they have been misinformed about the true location of something or the proper source of information about something. AID; ATWS; BDPF; CI; DOC; EWPO; HOI; IRCD; LCRH; LTA; MDWPO; ST.

BARNACLE *a barnacle.* A marine crustacean that secures itself to rocks, docks, boats, and whales. Source: GOOSE. The shellfish called the *barnacle* is named after the European goose, called a *barnacle (goose),* which winters on the continent and summers in the arctic. The metaphor is probably based on the similarity between the long, bare neck of the goose (Celtic *bernik*) and the long, feathery stalk of the crustacean. EWPO.

BARNYARD EPITHET *See* Barnyard Language.

BARNYARD HUMOR *See* Barnyard Language.

BARNYARD LANGUAGE   Language that employs slang terms for various body parts of, sexual activities engaged in by, and manure produced by farm animals. Source: ANIMAL. *Barnyard language* is regarded as earthy and smutty, and for this reason it is frequently used in macho talk, dirty jokes, and vulgar epithets. The attraction of *barnyard humor* (WNNCD: 1927) and *barnyard epithets* (EWPO: 1970) seems to be their shock value to outsiders. Some of the most popular barnyard epithets are *chickenshit* (EWPO: 1930s), *bullshit* (WNNCD: 1942), and *horseshit* (WNNCD: 1946), all of which *see*.

BAT AN EYE   *never batted an eye*. Never blinked (an eye)—even when taken by surprise. WNNCD: 1838. Source: HAWK; FALCON. In the metaphor, *eye* has been substituted for *wing*. A falcon, or female hawk trained for the hunt, "bats," or beats, its wings impatiently when the hood is removed, anticipating a flight for game. But it is still held by the *jess*, or cord attached to its feet, until the right moment arrives. ATWS; EWPO.

BAT HOUSE   *a bat house*. An insane asylum. Source: BAT. WNNCD: 14th cent. Bats are often characterized as being "crazy" because, although they are mammals, they fly like birds, and some species even migrate, like *birds of passage* (q.v.). In addition, they have the strange habit of sleeping in the daytime, hanging upside down in a cave (their "bat house") along with thousands of other bats. ATWS. *See also* Bats; Bats in Your Belfry.

BATMAN   *a batman*. A uniformed servant of a British military officer. WNNCD: 1755. Source: BAT (*). *Batman* is not an animal metaphor. The *bat* in *batman* is not a "flying mouse" but a packsaddle that was once carried by a *bathorse*. The *batman's* job was orig. to load the packsaddle with the officer's baggage. MDWPO.

BATS   *to drive someone bats*. To drive someone crazy. WNNCD: 1939. Source: BAT. WNNCD: 14th cent. *Bats* is a shortening of the expression "to have *bats in your belfry*" (q.v.). The bat, or flying mouse (Ger. *Fledermaus*), has been considered crazy since the beginning of the 20th cent. (If God had wanted mice to fly, He would have given them wings!) ATWS; EWPO; LCRH. *See also* Bat House; Batty. *Compare* Crazy as a Bedbug; Crazy as a Loon.

BATS IN YOUR BELFRY   *to have bats in your belfry*. To be crazy in the head. EWPO: 1907. Source: BAT. WNNCD: 14th cent. The image is that of wild ideas ("bats") flying around in your cranium ("belfry"). If bats are crazy enough to sleep—during the daytime, hanging upside down, along with thousands of others—in the bell tower of a church, then when the bells ring it must be pandemonium. AID; ATWS; BDPF; CE; CI; DEI; DOC; HOI; ID; IRCD; LCRH; MDWPO; SHM. *See also* Bat House; Bats; Batty. *Compare* Butterflies in Your Stomach.

BATTERING RAM   *a battering ram.* A wooden beam or steel pipe used to break down doors or walls. WNNCD: 1611. Source: SHEEP. The ancient *battering ram* was a huge log suspended from chains and swung back and forth to batter down the walls and gates of an enemy fort. The Roman version was called an *aries*, or "ram," either because of the butting nature of the device or the fact that the business end of the beam bore an iron head resembling that of a ram. The modern *battering ram*, used by police and fire fighters for breaking down doors, is a large steel pipe with loops on either side that serve as handles and a circular plate on the front. The handles resemble the horns of a large adult male sheep, or "ram." ATWS; EWPO; IRCD; THT. *See also* Knock Heads; Ram (v); Ramrod.

BATTLE ROYAL   *a battle royal.* A free-for-all involving many combatants. WNNCD: 1672. Source: COCK. *Battle royal* derives from the name of a cockfight in which an even number of cocks are placed in a pit and allowed to fight until half of them are dead. Then, after the pit is cleared and the remaining cocks are rested, the fight is resumed, in the same fashion, until only one survives. This is the basis for the type of elimination tournament used in both professional tennis and collegiate basketball, although those participants play only one opponent at a time. *Battle royal* has also been used to describe medieval jousting tournaments, free-for-all boxing matches, and a fight to the death between two queen bees. DEI; DOC; EWPO; LCRH; MDWPO; ST. *Compare* Sudden Death.

BATTY   *to be—or go—batty.* To be or go crazy. IRCD: early-20th cent. Source BAT. WNNCD: 14th cent. *Batty*, like *bats* (WNNCD: 1939), is probably derived from the expression *bats in your belfry* (WNNCD: 1907), although *batty* has been around since 1590 with the meaning "resembling a bat." The bat has been regarded as a crazy-looking, crazy-behaving animal throughout the 20th cent. *See also* Bat House; Bats; Bats in Your Belfry. *Compare* Loony.

BAWL   *to bawl; to bawl someone out.* To cry (WNNCD: 1570); to reprimand someone vocally (WNNCD: 1905). Source: COW; DOG. A cow "bawls"—or bellows—when its udder is full and milking time has been delayed. A dog "bawls"—or howls—when it is hungry for food or companionship. Babies *bawl* when their stomachs are empty; children *bawl* when they don't get their own way; and adults *bawl* when they are overcome with grief or depression. To *bawl someone out* is to reprimand them loudly for a transgression or misdemeanor. EWPO.

BAYING   *See* At Bay.

BEACH BUNNY   *a beach bunny.* A female groupie whose presence at the surfing beach is more for decoration than for sport. IHAT: 1960s. Source: RABBIT. *Bunny* (WNNCD: 1690) has long been an affectionate name for a young rabbit because of its cute little "cottontail" (Scottish *bun* "rabbit's tail"). Cute little *beach bunnies* hang out at beaches, admiring the surfers and looking for some action of a different sort. *See also* Bunny. *Compare* Snow Bunny.

BEACHED WHALE   *to look like a beached whale.* For a person—or a pet—to be so fat that their individual features are almost indistinguishable, and movement is severely restricted or impossible without assistance. Source: WHALE. WNNCD: O.E. For unknown reasons, some of the smaller whales, such as the pygmy sperm whale and the pilot whale, strand themselves en masse on beaches, where they are helpless and certain to die if not assisted back to the ocean. *See also* Blubber.

BEAK   *See* Bill.

BEAR (1)   *a bear.* A stockbroker who sells heavily while prices are high—in the expectation that they will soon drop: a pessimist. SHM: 1721. Source: BEAR. WNNCD: O.E. This metaphor originated in England in a proverb about a man who sold a bearskin before killing the bear. Because the stockbroker sold his stock before the market "died," he was called a *bearskin jobber,* later shortened to *bear.* (Nowadays, a "bearskin jobber" would be considered a "futures" trader on the "commodities" market.) The *bear* is regarded as a pessimist because he/she sees doom ahead; but the broker can buy back those same stocks at a much lower price when the market goes into hibernation. ATWS; CE; DEI; HOI; IRCD; LCRH; LTA; MDWPO. *See also* Bearish; Bear Market. *Compare* Bullish; Bull Market.

BEAR (2)   *a bear for punishment; a bear for work.* A glutton for punishment; a workaholic. LTA: 1840s. Source: BEAR. WNNCD: O.E. The brown—or "grizzly"—bear of the northwestern United States and western Canada is known for its huge size, and great strength and endurance. A carnivore, it relentlessly pursues its prey and is extremely difficult to stop, even with a high-powered rifle. A human who endures—and even seems to enjoy—rough treatment is said to be a "*bear* for punishment"; and one who is driven to work long hours at hard labor is called a "*bear* for work." ATWS; EWPO. *See also* Bear (3); Bearish; Cross as a Bear; Loaded for Bear.

BEAR (3)   *a bear of a man; a bear of a task.* A huge, strong man; a difficult, frightening task. Source: BEAR. WNNCD: O.E. The largest bears are the brown bear—known in western North America as the grizzly and the Kodiak—and the polar bear of the Arctic. All of these species of bear can weigh up to three-quarters of a ton and are considered very dangerous to humans. A *bear of a man* appears to be as big and strong as a bear; and *a bear of a task,* such as a college examination, seems to be as frightening and difficult to deal with as a bear. ATWS; CE; IRCD; SHM. *See also* Bear (2); Bear (4).

BEAR (4)   *a bear.* A highway patrol officer; a state police officer. Source: BEAR. WNNCD: O.E. *Bear* is CB ("citizens band") jargon for a "cop," esp. one in a police car. A *bear in the air* is an officer in a helicopter or light plane who spots speeders on the highway and relays the information to the *bear* on the ground. Both "bears" are named for *Smokey (the) Bear*, the original nickname for a highway police officer. NDAS.

BEARD THE LION   *to beard the lion in his den.* To confront an adversary on his/her own turf. EWPO: 1808 (Sir Walter Scott's *Marmion*). Source: LION. WNNCD: 12th cent. The male lion does not have a beard, but it does have a mane that encircles its head; and, seen from a distance, full face, the lower part of the mane does look like a beard. At any rate, to *beard* a lion would be to get close enough to it to pull its "beard"—a rather foolhardy thing to do. Scott's metaphor seems to combine the leonine encounters of two different Old Testament heroes: *David*, who caught a lion by his beard and smote him for stealing a lamb (I Samuel 17:34–35), and *Daniel*, who was sealed into a lion's den for praying to God rather than to Darius (Daniel 6:16–23). AID; ATWS; BDPF; CI; DEI; DOC; EWPO; HOI; ID; IRCD. *Compare* Bell the Cat.

BEAR FOR PUNISHMENT   *See* BEAR (2).

BEAR FOR WORK   *See* BEAR (2).

BEAR HUG   *a bear hug.* A tight, total, and usu. affectionate embrace. WNNCD: 1921. Source: BEAR. WNNCD: O.E. In a normal embrace between two humans, each person puts his/her arms around the upper body of the other. With a *bear hug*, however, the single embracer wraps his/her arms around both the body *and* the arms of the surprised embracee, usu. from behind. The *bear hug* is also a "hold" in professional wrestling, used to immobilize the arms of the opponent in preparation for a "takedown." The American black bear (eastern United States) and brown bear (western United States) use the hug for the same reason. ATWS; IRCD.

BEAR IN THE AIR   *See* Bear (4).

BEARISH   *to be bearish.* To be gruff and surly (WNNCD: 1744); to be pessimistic about the direction of the stock market. Source: BEAR. WNNCD: O.E. The wild bear is not docile and submissive like the performing bear in the circus—or fawning and begging like the bear on display in the zoo. Instead, it is rough and gruff and intimidating—like some humans. When humans who play the stock market perceive that prices have reached their peak and are about to decline, they sell their stock and go into hibernation, like the bear, because they are pessimistic about any rise in price in the near future. IRCD. *See also* Bear (1); Bear Market. *Compare* Bullish.

BEAR MARKET   *a bear market.* A high but declining stock market. SHM: 1721. Source: BEAR. WNNCD: O.E. A bear market is a market for *bears*—those who follow the stockbroker's creed of "buy low, sell high" by selling their stock while the prices are high. One would guess that the *bear market* was named after a bear getting ready for hibernation, doubling its weight before a long winter of fasting. But the fact is that it was named for a proverbial *bearskin jobber* who sold a skin before the bear was even captured. IRCD; LCRH. *See also* Bear (1); Bearish. *Compare* Bull Market.

BEAR OF A MAN   *See* Bear (3).

BEAR OF A TASK   *See* Bear (3).

BEARS IN THE WOODS   *Do bears———in the woods?* (Fill in the blank with any bodily function.) Is the Pope Catholic? (Of course he is.) Source: BEAR. WNNCD: O.E. American brown bears are large (up to three-quarters of a ton) powerful carnivores that are the prey of no other animal except the human. They have the run of the fields, streams, and woods of the northwest and can do—and do do—whatever they want to there. *Compare* Six-hundred Pound Gorilla.

BEAST   *a beast.* A brute. Source: ANIMAL. *Beast* has variously meant (1) an animal as opposed to a plant (WNNCD: 13th cent.); (2) a "lower" animal as opposed to humans; (3) a four-legged mammal as opposed to all other animals; (4) a domesticated animal as opposed to the wild animals; and (5) a human (esp. a male) who behaves like an animal. A human *beast* is brutal, coarse, contemptible, cruel, and lacking in intelligence, morality, reason, and self-control—i.e., is *bestial* (WNNCD: 14th cent.) or displays signs of *bestiality* (WNNCD: 14th cent.), although such qualities are sometimes excused as being the *nature of the beast* (i.e., "Boys will be boys"). A man who is forced to do menial work sometimes regards himself as a *beast of burden,* and a person's nemesis is sometimes called his/her *bête noire,* or "black beast" (WNNCD: 1844). A couple composed of a beautiful young woman and a homely man are sometimes called *beauty and the beast,* and a couple engaged in the act of sex are said to "make the *beast with two backs.*" Finally, and strangely, *beastly* cold weather (WNNCD: 1834) is weather that is *fit for neither man nor beast.* ATWS; BDPF; DEI; DOC; LTA; MDWPO. *See also* Send a Dog out.

BEASTLY   *See* Beast.

BEAST OF BURDEN   *See* Beast.

BEAST WITH TWO BACKS   *See* Beast.

BEAT A DEAD HORSE *to beat—or flog—a dead horse.* To attempt to revive a dead issue or pursue a lost cause. EWPO: 1867. Source: HORSE. WNNCD: O.E. It is pointless to beat a dead horse in hopes of getting it to move, just as it is futile to attempt to bring up an issue that was settled long ago or to try to breathe life into a cause that has already been lost. The expression was first used in regard to the British Parliament of 1867, which was so apathetic to a reform bill that trying to get it to act was like *flogging a dead horse.* AID; ATWS; BDPF; CI; DEI; DOC; HOI; HTB; IRCD; NDAS. *See also* Pay for a Dead Horse.

BEAUTY AND THE BEAST *See* Beast.

BEAVER *See* Shoot a Beaver.

BEAVERBOARD Hard, thin, brown fiberboard (called "pegboard" when perforated) that is used for wall panels and clipboards. WNNCD: 1909. (Orig. a trademark: *Beaver Board.*) Source: BEAVER. WNNCD: O.E. The coat of the American beaver is thick and brown, but *beaverboard* is probably named after the beaver's tail, which is hard and flat, like a paddle, and is used to slap the water as a warning signal. *See also* Busy as a Beaver.

BEAVER SHOT *See* Shoot a Beaver.

BEDBUG LETTER *a bedbug letter.* A letter of apology from a respectable hotel to a recent guest who has complained of bedbugs. (The catch is that it's a *form* letter.) MDWPO: 19th cent. Source: BEDBUG. WNNCD: 1808. The bedbug—a "halfwinged," bloodsucking insect—is so called because it inhabits human beds. LTA.

BEE *a bee.* A voluntary gathering of people for work or play. Source: BEE (?). WNNCD: O.E. As a *voluntary* gathering, this term is an Americanism. The word *bee* was already in existence in medieval England for *compulsory* service to the church or crown, but the colonists associated it instead with the busyness of bees. The earliest recorded *bee* in America was the *husking bee* (LTA: 1693), followed by the *spinning bee* (EWPO: 1769), the *quilting bee* (LTA: early 1800s), and the *spelling bee* (WNNCD: 1872). Barn-building *bees* and church-building *bees* were held throughout the period. ATWS; IRCD; MDWPO; SHM; WNWD. *See also* Beehive of Activity; Busy as a Bee.

BEEF (n) *to have a beef with someone.* To have a grudge against someone. Source: CATTLE. Cattle, or "beef," complain loudly when they have not been fed, and cows complain loudly when they have not been milked. These conditions are probably the source of the metaphorical senses of argument, complaint, grudge, and protest. ATWS. *See also* Beef (v). *Compare* Have A Bone to Pick.

BEEF (v)   *to beef about something.* To complain about something. LTA: 1880. Source: CATTLE. *Beef* almost certainly relates to cattle, but the exact association is unknown. The best guess is that the word is an Australian nickname for "cattle" and alludes to the loud bawling or bellowing that steers (and cows) make when they have not been fed (or milked). DEI; LCRH. *See also* Beef (n).

BEEFCAKE   A photographic display of muscular males. WNNCD: 1949. Source: CATTLE. *Beefcake* is the male counterpart to *cheesecake,* the photographic display of shapely females. *Beef* alludes to the sleek, muscular bodies of prime steers, which bring top dollar at the cattle auction. EWPO; MDWPO. *See also* Beef up.

BEEF UP   *to beef something up.* To increase the strength, power, or weight of something. WNNCD: 1941. Source: CATTLE. Body builders *beef up* their bodies—i.e., add muscle and strength—through weightlifting. Campaign managers *beef up* their political campaigns by increasing the media coverage of their candidates. Advertising managers *beef up* their advertising by increasing the size, amount, and diversity of their advertising. Cattle raisers beef up their steers by increasing the amount and quality of their feed prior to marketing. ATWS.

BEEHIVE HAIRDO   *a beehive hairdo.* A women's hair style, popular in the 1950s and 1960s, which featured a conelike pile of hair on top of the head. Source: BEE. WNNCD: O.E. This hairdo, which was popularized by Pricilla Presley, was named after the commercial *beehive* (WNNCD: 14th cent.)—a wooden box for containing a hive of honeybees—but it could just as well have been named after the *hive* (WNNCD: O.E.) itself. In nature, bees crowd together on a tree or the side of a building in the form of a vertical oval or ellipse. So a woman wearing a beehive hairdo looked like she had a hive of bees on her head. *See also* Beehive of Activity.

BEEHIVE OF ACTIVITY   *a beehive of activity.* A busy, noisy, crowded place or scene. Source: BEE. WNNCD: O.E. A *hive* (WNNCD: O.E.) is a colony of honeybees, and a *beehive* (WNNCD: 14th cent.) is a wooden box for containing them. Inside the box, the worker bees, or "house bees," are *abuzz* (q.v.) with activity as they build the wax comb, feed the eggs that the queen bee lays in the hexagonal cells, clean the cells after the eggs hatch, receive nectar from the "foraging bees," manufacture honey, and deposit the honey in the empty cells. Such a busy scene is duplicated on the floor of the stock exchange or a political convention, in the city room of a newspaper, in the ward room of a police station, etc. ATWS; DOC; IRCD. *See also* Busy as a Bee.

BEE IN YOUR BONNET   *to have a bee in your bonnet.* To be obsessed with an idea. EWPO: 1648. Source: BEE. WNNCD: O.E. Obsession with a single idea can make a person appear eccentric, irrational, or even insane. The same is true of a lady of fashion—or a common beekeeper—whose veil over their broadbrimmed hat is invaded by a single bee: a lot of eccentric and irrational behavior can follow, leading persons who are unaware of the situation to wonder if the subject has gone insane. AID; ATWS; CI; DEI; DOC; HF; HOI; ID; IRCD; SHM. *Compare* Bug in Your Ear.

BEELINE *to make a beeline for someplace.* To proceed to a place rapidly and directly. WNNCD: 1830. Source: BEE. WNNCD: O.E. Forager bees proceed to flowering trees, bushes, and plants on the basis of instructions given to them in the hive by their scouts. They learn the approximate direction and distance but have to rely on scent once they approach the general area. However, on their way back to the hive they know exactly where to go and make a direct and rapid flight. People make *beelines* on foot, in cars, on horses, in speedboats, etc., but their route is usually not as straight as that of the airborne bee. AID; ATWS; BDPF; CI; DEI; IRCD; SHM. *Compare* As the Crow Flies.

BEE'S KNEES *You're the bee's knees.* You're the nicest, cutest person in all the world. IHAT: 1923. Source: BEE. WNNCD: O.E. Bees do have knees, but it is unlikely that most people have seen them; so this is probably a fanciful metaphor, conceived for its rhyme. Similar expressions are *You're the cat's meow* (q.v.) and *You're the cat's pajamas* (q.v.). CI; LTA.

BEESWAX *Mind your own beeswax! None of your beeswax!* Mind your own business! None of your business! LTA: 1920. Source: BEE. WNNCD: O.E. *Beeswax* (WNNCD: 1676) is the brownish wax melted down from the honeycombs of bees. (It is also the substance left over in a child's mouth when he/she pops in a chunk of honey-filled honeycomb and chews it until all of the honey has been extracted.) Beeswax is used in many products, from candles to polishes, and for many purposes, from seating toilets to waxing bowstrings. In the expressions cited, *beeswax* is a euphemism for *business*—to soften the force of the retorts. AID; WNWD. *See also* Honeycombed.

BEETLE (n) *a beetle.* The original two-door, air-cooled, rear-engine Volkswagen (or "VW"), which was first manufactured in Germany in the late 1930s and first introduced into the United States in 1949. (It was later called a *bug*.) IRCD: 1950s. Source: BEETLE. WNNCD: O.E. The VW *beetle* resembled the high, curved shell of the bug that it was named after. (The "Fab Four" called themselves *Beatles*, not *Beetles*.) ATWS. *See also* Beetle (v); Beetlebrained; Beetle-browed.

BEETLE (v) *to beetle (over).* To overhang, or project over: e.g., for a cliff to *beetle over* its base toward the sea. WNNCD: 1602. Source: BEETLE. WNNCD: O.E. The two *antennae* (q.v.) of the beetle project from either side of its head and overhang its eyes, mouth, and pincers, giving it a threatening appearance. IRCD. *See also* Beetle (n); Beetle-browed.

BEETLEBRAIN   *See* Beetlebrained.

BEETLEBRAINED   *to be beetlebrained.* To be mentally incompetent. Source: BEETLE. WNNCD: O.E. The beetle is the smallest of all insects and therefore has a very small "brain." However, the beetle has been around for a very long time and has produced more species than any other animal, so it must be doing something right. A *bettlebrained* person, also called a *beetlebrain*, has a brain the size of a beetle's. ATWS. *See also* Beetle (n). *Compare* Beetle-browed.

BEETLE-BROWED   *to be beetle-browed.* To have long, shaggy eyebrows that overhang your eyes and give your face a perpetual scowl or frown. WNNCD: 14th cent. Source: BEETLE. WNNCD: O.E. The beetle does not have eyebrows, but it does have two *antennae* (q.v.) that project from its head—either forward or to the sides, near the eyes. ATWS; BDPF; IRCD; LTA. *See also* Beetle (v).

BEGGAR ON HORSEBACK   *See* If Wishes Were Horses.

BEHAVE LIKE AN ANIMAL   *See* Animal.

BEHEMOTH   *a behemoth.* Something of monstrous size or power. Source: HIPPOPOTAMUS. In the book of Job (40:15–24), the *behemoth* (fr. Heb. for "great animal") was described as an animal of enormous size and strength that had bones of brass or iron, a tail like a cedar tree, and a mouth that could drink up the entire River Jordan. This doesn't sound much like a *hippopotamus* (q.v.), but that's the animal with which the behemoth has most often been identified. A modern *behemoth* is any machine of enormous size or power that moves on the land (such as a tank), on the sea (such as a battleship), or in the air (such as a jumbo jet). ATWS; MDWPO. *Compare* Leviathan.

BELLOW   *to bellow.* To cry out, unrestrainedly, in a loud, deep, powerful voice. Source: BULL. To *bellow* is to make the characteristic cry of a bull (fr. O.E. *byggian* "to roar"). The sound is one of warning and threat. (The more restrained cow is said to *moo*, and cattle are generally said to *low.*) Humans *bellow* when they are angry or in pain. ATWS; WNWD. *See also* Roar like a Bull. *Compare* Croon.

BELL THE CAT   *Who will bell the cat?* Who will sacrifice their life for the common good? IRCD: ca.1377. Source: CAT. WNNCD: O.E. The English version of this metaphor first appeared in *Piers Plowman*, but the question has been asked since ancient Greece. In an Aesop fable, a family of mice met to decide what to do about the cat that was terrorizing their members. The conclusion was reached that the best solution was to hang a bell around the cat's neck so that they could hear it coming. But no one was willing to volunteer for this dangerous mission. Moral: Deeds speak louder than words. ATWS; BDPF; CI; DEI; DOC; EWPO; HOI; ID; SHM. *Compare* Beard the Lion; Sprinkle Salt on Its Tail.

BELLWETHER *a bellwether.* A leader or trendsetter. WNNCD: 15th cent. Source: SHEEP. To the sheep farmer, a *bellwether* is the *wether*, or castrated male sheep, that wears a bell around its neck and leads the flock wherever the farmer leads the bellwether. To the fashion industry it is the setter of trends; to the politician it is the predictor of a trend: "As Maine goes, so goes the nation." ATWS; BDPF; EWPO; LCRH; MDWPO; SPD.

BERSERK *to go berserk.* To become wild, crazy, violent, and dangerous. WNNCD: 1851. Source: BEAR. *Berserk* is a loan translation of the O.N. noun *berserkr* "bear shirt." The reference is to an ancient bear-shirted warrior called Berserkr, a ferocious fighter who was invulnerable in battle in spite of his lack of body armor. This recklessness is reflected in the adjective *berserk*, which implies a disregard for the life and health of oneself and others. ATWS; LCRH; MDWPO; THT.

BESTIAL *See* Beast.

BESTIALITY *See* Beast.

BÊTE NOIRE *See* Beast.

BE THERE WITH BELLS ON *to be there with bells on.* To be delighted to accept an invitation. Source: HORSE. Horses that once pulled buggies and sleighs sometimes wore harnesses that were equipped with bells. The bells were delightful to the ear, but they may orig. have had a more serious function, such as to warn pedestrians of the vehicle's presence or to scare away animal predators that were in the path. MDWPO.

BEWILDERING *See* Wilderness.

BIG APE *You big ape!* You big lug/lout/lummox! That is: You clumsy fool! (Usually said affectionately by a woman to a large male friend.) LTA: 1831. Source: APE. WNNCD: O.E. The largest of the apes is the gorilla, which can reach 6.5 feet in height and 500 pounds in weight. The only primate taller than the gorilla is the human. *See also* Ape (n); Gorilla. *Compare* Big Baboon; Big Ox.

BIG AS AN ELEPHANT *to be as big as an elephant.* To be very fat or very pregnant. Source: ELEPHANT. WNNCD: 14th cent. No human has ever grown to be as big as an adult elephant (up to 13,000 pounds), so this is an exaggerated metaphor. It is usu. used to describe a person whom you have not seen for some time. In the case of a pregnant woman, it is somewhat complimentary; in the case of an obese man or woman, it is probably not. CH. *Compare* Big as an Ox.

BIG AS AN OX *to be as big as an ox.* For a male child to be much bigger than average for his age. Source: OX. WNNCD. O.E. Oxen are pretty big: they can weigh well over a ton. Humans never come close to that weight, so there is a healthy bit of hyperbole in this metaphor. An ox is an adult steer—i.e., a castrated bull—that is used as a draft animal. Oxen are seldom seen in America, where they have been replaced by the horse, mule, and tractor, except in Frontier Day celebrations. *See also* Big Ox; Strong as an Ox. *Compare* Big as an Elephant.

BIG BABOON *You big baboon!* You ugly brute! Source: BABOON. WNNCD: 15th cent. The baboon, a primate found in Africa and Arabia, has always been regarded as an ugly brutish creature, so much so that in the 15th cent. it was identified with the grotesque figure of the gargoyle. But in spite of its apelike body and doglike face, it is thought to be the most intelligent of the nonanthropoid primates. ATWS; IRCD. *Compare* Big Ape; Big Ox.

BIG BRUTE *See* Brute.

BIG BUCKS *to make or pay big bucks.* To make or pay a lot of money. WNNCD: 1976. Source: DEER. The adult male white-tailed deer, or *buck*, can reach a weight of up to 450 pounds, but that is not the focus of this metaphor. Instead, the metaphor is based on the monetary value of the silver dollar that replaced the buckhorn knife, also called a *buck*, as a marker of the dealer in a game of poker in the Wild West. The winner of the game could earn a big pot, or lots of silver dollars. *See also* Buck (n); Fast Buck; Pass the Buck.

BIG ENOUGH TO CHOKE A HORSE *See* Enough to Kill an Elephant.

BIG FISH IN A SMALL POND *to be a big fish in a small pond.* To hold an important position in a relatively unimportant organization. Source: FISH. WNNCD: O.E. The notion is that the big fish in a small pond would be a little fish if it were in a lake or ocean. Small-college scholars and athletes often learn the truth of this metaphor, as do state senators and representatives who are elected to the U.S. Congress, and governors who are elected President of the United States. CE; DEI; NDAS.

BIG OX *a big ox.* A big and strong—but also clumsy and stupid—man. Source: OX. WNNCD: O.E. An ox is a steer that is employed as a beast of burden. (Unemployed steers are the source of most of our beef.) Oxen have long been regarded as less intelligent, less agile, and less beautiful than horses, although they weigh about the same and perform pretty much the same work. ATWS. *See also* Clumsy as an Ox; Dumb as an Ox; Dumb Ox; Strong as an Ox. *Compare* Big Ape; Big Baboon.

BILL *a bill.* The visor of a cap. Source: BIRD. A bird's *bill* (WNNCD: O.E.), or *beak* (WNNCD: 13th cent.), is the horny projection of its jaws. (Both words have also been applied to the jaws of a turtle.) Of the two terms, *bill* sometimes refers separately to the upper bill and the lower bill, while *beak* usu. refers to the two bills together, as a single unit. The visor of a cap resembles the upper bill of a widemouthed bird; and, in profile, the combination of a baseball cap and a batting helmet resembles the upper and lower bills of a bird. (Batting helmets are usu. made to be worn without a cap nowadays.) The term *beak* is also used for the human nose; but *beaker* (WNNCD: 14th cent.), a container for liquid with a projecting lip, is from a different source. ATWS. *See also* Eagle Beak.

BILL AND COO *to bill and coo.* For young lovers to kiss and caress each other amorously while whispering sweet nothings in each other's ears. Source: DOVE; PIGEON. Doves and pigeons *bill* (q.v.)—i.e., rub their beaks, or "bills," together— and *coo* (q.v.)—i.e., make soft murmuring sounds—when showing affection or endearment for each other. ATWS; IRCD.

BIRD *a bird.* A *clay pigeon* (q.v.); a *queer duck* (q.v.); a *young chick* (q.v.); a badminton *shuttlecock* (q.v.); a *birdie* (q.v.); a *goose* (q.v.); a Bronx cheer; a finger; an airplane. Source: BIRD. WNNCD: O.E. All senses and functions of *bird* derive from O.E. *bridd* "a young bird." *Clay pigeons* don't have wings and feathers, but they do fly through the air like birds. A *queer duck* is someone who acts like a "different breed of bird." *Chick*, for "young woman," is the American equivalent of Brit. *bird*. A *shuttlecock* not only has feathers but also flies. A *birdie* is a "little eagle": one stroke under par on a hole in golf. To give someone a *goose* is to give them a poke in the bottom, as a goose does to retreating humans. To give someone a "Bronx cheer" is to give them a razzberry, the equivalent of a Brit. *bird*. To give someone the "finger" is to *flip them the bird.* Any heavier-than-air craft is called a *bird*—from an airplane or helicopter to a space shuttle or rocket. A *wounded bird* is an airplane that has been damaged in flight; and a *birdfarm* (IHAT: 1960s) is an aircraft carrier. HOI; LCRH.

BIRDBRAIN *See* Featherbrain.

BIRDBRAINED *See* Featherbrain.

BIRDCAGE *a birdcage.* An inner office whose walls consist of steel bars or wire mesh. Source: BIRD. WNNCD: O.E. A cage for birds is usu. a cylinder of wire mesh with a flat floor and a top that tapers to a hook for hanging from a metal frame. The bird is able to see out—but not fly out—and the people are able to see in. A *birdcage* for humans is usu. found in a factory or a money-lending institution. It also has two-way visibility, but its purpose is to keep the outsiders out rather than the insider in. A *bird in a gilded cage* is either a canary in a goldplated birdcage or a prisoner in a luxurious "prison," such as a castle. *Compare* Fishbowl.

BIRD DIDN'T FLY   *See* Bird Has Flown.

BIRD DOG   *a bird dog.* A detective or private investigator. Source: DOG. WNNCD: O.E. Police detectives, insurance investigators, and investigative reporters all have the same goal: to search for and retrieve the facts of the case. Search and retrieval are also the goals of the canine "bird dog" (WNNCD: 1888), which is trained to hunt for fowl on land and to retrieve them from the land or water once they have been shot. To *bird-dog* someone, on the other hand, is to watch or follow them closely (WNNCD: 1943), or to pursue another man's wife or girlfriend; and to *bird-dog* a job is to see it through to completion. ATWS; NDAS; SPD; ST.

BIRD-DOG   *See* Bird Dog.

BIRDFARM   *See* Bird.

BIRD HAS FLOWN   *The bird has flown.* The prisoner has escaped. Source: BIRD. WNNCD: O.E. The bird in this metaphor is a *jailbird* (q.v.), a frequent inmate of a jail or prison; and the implication is that the individual has *flown the coop* (q.v.) before. A variant of this expression, *That bird has flown*, means that the matter is closed; and another variant, "The *bird didn't fly*," means that the hoped-for action did not take place. DEI; IRCD.

BIRDIE   *a birdie.* A score of one stroke under par on a golf hole. IRCD: ca. 1921. Source: BIRD. WNNCD: O.E. *Birdie*, or "little bird," may have derived from the earlier *eagle* (q.v.): a score of two strokes under par on a hole. At any rate, both shots "fly" into the hole in fewer than the regulation number of strokes. *Birdie* was also used for the badminton *shuttlecock* (q.v.) in the 19th cent., and both "birdies" can also be called *birds*. To *birdie* a golf hole (WNNCD: 1948) is to complete it in one stroke under par. ATWS; BDPF; EWPO; IRCD.

BIRDIEBACK   *See* Piggyback (adv.).

BIRD IN THE HAND   *A bird in the hand is worth two in the bush.* (A proverb.) Be satisfied with what you have. IRCD: ca. 1470. Source: BIRD. WNNCD: O.E. This proverb reflects the moral of two different Aesop fables from the 6th cent. B.C. The scene is that of a hunter who snares one or more birds but is tempted to release them in hopes of catching even larger birds the next time. The moral is: Be happy with what you already have, because your next try might net you nothing at all. AID; ATWS; BDPF; CI; DEI; DOC; EWPO; ID; ST.

BIRD LEGS   Long, skinny legs. Source: BIRD. WNNCD: O.E. The legs of a stork, crane, or heron are long and thin and seem to lack any flesh or muscle: i.e., they seem to consist of only skin and bones. That is the appearance of the legs of a person with *bird legs*, although human leg bones are almost solid, while birds' legs are hollow.

BIRD OF ILL OMEN   *a bird of ill omen*. A symbol of bad luck. Source: BIRD. WNNCD: O.E. The owl—the "funeral bird"—is a symbol of bad luck in many eastern Mediterranean cultures; and the raven, or crow, is a symbol of bad luck in America. The albatross is sometimes thought to be a bad-luck bird, but that is not the case. An albatross that lands on a ship and refuses to leave is not indicating that there is no land within flying distance: it simply cannot take off from a hard, flat surface. People who are *birds of ill omen* are frequent bearers of bad tidings or prophets of doom. ATWS; BDPF; DEI; IRCD. *Compare* Albatross around Your Neck.

BIRD OF PARADISE   *a bird of paradise*. A tropical African plant. Source: BIRD. WNNCD: O.E. The *bird of paradise* plant, a member of the banana family, has a blue and orange flower, which, together with the petals, resembles the shape and coloring of the bird of the same name. *That* bird of paradise is a brilliantly colored songbird of New Guinea. WNWD.

BIRD OF PASSAGE   *a bird of passage*. An itinerant person (WNNCD: 1732); a borrowing from an exotic language. Source: BIRD. WNNCD: O.E. Literally, a bird of passage is a migrating bird; but the metaphorical sense of "wanderer" appeared earlier than the literal meaning. Some migratory birds travel thousands of miles every fall to avoid cold weather. People who do this are called *snowbirds* (q.v.), or *birds of passage*, though the latter term applies also to people who simply travel a lot, or always seem to be on the go. Exotic words travel from one language to another but maintain their home base, like migratory birds. ATWS; BDPF; DEI; IRCD; ROE.

BIRDS AND THE BEES   *to tell a child about the birds and the bees*. To give a child informal, and sometimes indirect, information about human sexuality and reproduction. CI: 19th cent. Source: BIRD; BEE. WNNCD: O.E. Sex education at home usually consists of the father telling the son, and the mother telling the daughter, about adolescence, human reproduction, and birth control. However, in the Victorian age, the subject of reproduction was presented indirectly, by pointing out that birds and bees—and even fleas—do it: i.e., mate, lay eggs, etc. *Birds* and *bees* were probably selected because they were familiar creatures whose reproduction was never witnessed, unlike that of dogs, for example. AID; ATWS; CI; LCRH; MDWPO; NDAS.

BIRD'S-EYE VIEW   *a bird's-eye view*. An overall view, or overview. WNNCD: 1762. Source: BIRD. WNNCD: O.E. Before the 18th cent., the only bird's-eye view of the world by humans was from the top of a mountain. Earthbound artists and cartographers had to imagine what the world would look like from on high.

The birds knew, but they wouldn't tell. The balloon gave its occupants a view approximating that of the birds, but the airplane reached and exceeded that height. Now, the crew of a spacecraft has an overall view, not only of a part of the earth but of the entire planet—but it is still called a *bird's-eye view.* ATWS; BDPF; CI; DEI; DOC; IRCD. *Compare* Worm's-eye View.

BIRDS OF A FEATHER   *Birds of a feather flock together.* (A proverb.) People of like mind tend to gravitate toward each other. DOC: 1680. Source: BIRD. WNNCD: O.E. Birds of the same species (or "feather") usually associate (or "flock") only with each other, though some birds tolerate birds of other species while feeding. Humans tend to group together on the basis of gender, race, culture, nationality, religion, education, wealth, politics, etc. The proverb is sometimes used sarcastically of a person who associates with others of a different, and usu. negative, quality. AID; ATWS; BDPF; CI; IRCD.

BITCH (n)   *a bitch.* A devious, selfish, heartless, malicious, or domineering woman; a complicated, arduous, difficult, disagreeable, or unpleasant task. Source: DOG. Literally, a bitch is a female dog (O.E. *bicce*). In the 15th cent., *bitch* was applied also to a lewd or immoral woman; and by the 20th cent. it had come to mean a malicious or domineering woman. (A *rich bitch* is simply a very wealthy woman.) The application of *bitch* to a difficult or unpleasant problem or task occurred in 1928. All of these negative senses derive from the polygamous behavior of the female dog and her disagreeable nature when she is in heat. ATWS; EWPO; IHAT; IRCD; LTA; NDAS. *See also* Bitch (v); Son of a Bitch.

BITCH (v)   *to bitch.* To complain. LTA: 1920s. Source: DOG. A female dog, or bitch, is disagreeable when she is in heat: she whines and paces, and generally makes life miserable for her owners. When humans—whether female or male— *bitch,* they find fault with just about everything. Such complainers are said to be *bitchy* (WNNCD: 1937); and a *bitchy remark* is one that is rude, insulting, or nasty. *Bitching,* a related adjective from the 1980s, has an almost opposite meaning: If something is *bitchin',* it's "cool." ATWS; CE; IRCD; NDAS. *See also* Bitch (n).

BITCHING   *See* Bitch (v).

BITCHY   *See* Bitch (v).

BITE   *to bite.* To fall for a trick or go along with a joke. Source: FISH. A fish bites when it strikes at a baited hook or lure. People *bite* when they are suckered into a phony deal or when they play "straight man" to the teller of a joke or riddle: "What did the fish say to the angler?" "Okay, I'll bite. What *did* the fish say to the angler?" People who succumb to this sort of temptation are said to *rise to the bait* or *take the bait.* ATWS; CI; DEI; ST.

BITE THE HAND THAT FEEDS YOU   *to bite the hand that feeds you.* To act ungratefully toward a benefactor. DOC: 1711. Source: DOG. *Man's best friend* (q.v.) and faithful companion, the dog, has a short memory when it comes to being awakened out of a sound sleep or being teased, harassed, or otherwise abused: it reverts to its *animal instincts* and *turns on you.* The result is usu. a bite for the human and punishment for the dog. People who "forget which side their bread is buttered on" sometimes stick up for principles that are not those of their benefactor, in which case they also suffer for their self-defeating behavior. AID; ATWS; BDPF; DEI; MDWPO. *See also* Let Sleeping Dogs Lie. *Compare* Kill the Goose that Laid the Golden Eggs.

BITTEN BY THE BUG   *See* Bug (n) (3).

BITTER AS WORMWOOD   *to be as bitter as wormwood.* To be extremely bitter. (Proverbs 5:4—"But her end is bitter as wormwood.") Source: WORM (*). WNNCD: O.E. Wormwood is a European herb that is the source of a bitter-tasting, dark green oil used in making absinthe; but worms have nothing to do with this production. The word *wormwood* is derived from O.E. *wer* "man" + *mōd* "courage." Perhaps that is what an Old English mother said to her son in the spring when she forced him to partake of the annual vermifuge: "Courage!" Courage was certainly needed to down the first *absinthe* (1612), which consisted of a green liqueur laced with *wormwood.* *Wormwood* also had a reputation as an aphrodisiac—to give a man sexual courage. At any rate, no worm—and no wood—was involved. CE; DEI; EWPO; HF; IRCD; WNWD. *See also* Vermouth. *Compare* Spanish Worm.

BLACK AS A CROW   *to be as black as a crow.* To be completely dark or completely black. Source: CROW. WNNCD: O.E. The American crow is totally black in color: its beak, its eyes, its feathers, its legs, its claws. The crow's color was probably the basis for the term *Jim Crow,* which was first applied to a blackface song-and-dance man in a minstrel show (1835) and later to laws that discriminated against black people: *Jim Crow Laws.* BDPF; MDWPO; NDAS; SPD. *See also* Raven-haired.

BLACK COW   *a black cow.* A root beer float. Source: COW. WNNCD: O.E. A black cow consists of chocolate ice cream scooped into a large glass of root beer. It is actually a chocolate soda made with root beer instead of clear soda water, giving it less carbonation. A *brown cow* (q.v.) is a vanilla soda made with root beer and a scoop of vanilla ice cream. LTA.

BLACK SHEEP   *the black sheep of the family.* The disreputable member of a reputable social group—the one nobody wants to talk about. WNNCD: 1792. Source: SHEEP. WNNCD: O.E. The occasional black sheep is a problem to the farmer because its wool is worthless (though its mutton tastes the same and there is no evidence that it is rejected by the other sheep). Superstition has also associated the *black sheep* with the goat—the *Judas sheep* (q.v.)—and the Devil. AID; ATWS; BDPF; CI; DEI; DOC; EWPO; ID; IRCD; MDWPO.

BLAZE *a blaze.* A light mark on a tree where the bark has been removed to mark a trail. Source: HORSE. The trail marker is named for the white mark on the upper part of a horse's head: a *blaze* (WNNCD: 1639). From the noun has come a verb, to *blaze*, meaning to notch a tree with an ax or hatchet in order to guide those who follow (WNNCD: 1750). To *blaze a trail* has acquired the metaphorical sense of "innovate" or "pioneer": e.g., to *blaze new trails* in manufacturing. EWPO; WNWD.

BLAZE A TRAIL *See* Blaze.

BLEED LIKE A STUCK PIG *to bleed like a stuck pig.* To bleed profusely. Source: PIG. WNNCD: 13th cent. Domestic pigs are usu. slaughtered by bleeding them to death. The pig is hung by its feet from a wooden frame (or "gallows"); its throat is cut (or "stuck") with a *pig sticker* (q.v.); and the blood is collected in a bucket, which may be kicked over by the pig in its death throes. However, the expression may ultimately derive from the ancient sport of wild boar hunting, in which the pig was stuck with a spear carried by a rider on horseback. IRCD. *See also* Kick the Bucket.

BLIND AS A BAT *to be as blind as a bat.* To be totally blind: "stone blind." DOC: 1588. Source: BAT. WNNCD: 14th cent. Bats have long been assumed to be blind, because they are nocturnal animals that locate their prey (usu. flying insects) by means of sonar ("echolocation"). However, all bats are sighted, and some bats have excellent sight, since their food source must be identified by color (and scent). AID; ATWS; BDPF; CI; DEI; IRCD. *See also* Old Bat.

BLIND PIG *a blind pig.* A speakeasy. EWPO: 1840. Source: PIG. WNNCD: 13th cent. Why an establishment where alcoholic beverages are sold illegally is named after the pig, esp. a blind pig, is uncertain. It may be because the officers of the law, sometimes called *pigs*, are blind to its existence—or because the cheap liquor that is sold there can blind the drinkers, or at least make them "blind drunk." IHAT; MDWPO; SHM. *Compare* Blind Tiger.

BLIND TIGER *a blind tiger.* An unlicensed saloon: a "speakeasy." WNNCD: 1857. Source: TIGER. WNNCD: O.E. How the tiger came to be associated with a speakeasy is uncertain, but it may have resulted from the fact that gambling establishments in mid-19th cent. America often provided informal—and therefore illegal—bars for the benefit of their customers. One of the most popular card games of the period was "faro" (from *Pharoah*), which was also known as "tiger." A *blind tiger* was a faro house that had an illegal bar. It is also likely that the cheap whiskey sold at the "tiger" could make you "blind drunk." EWPO; HOI; IHAT; MDWPO; SHM. *See also* Kitty. *Compare* Blind Pig.

BLOODHOUND   *See* Hound (n).

BLOODSUCKER   *a bloodsucker.* A person who bleeds others of their money or property. Source: LEECH. The leech, or *bloodsucker* (WNNCD: 14th cent.), is a freshwater worm that sucks the blood of fish and swimmers. It was used for centuries by physicians for therapeutic bloodletting, and its value is now being recognized again for treating specific illnesses. ATWS; BDPF; DEI. *See also* Leech. *Compare* Sponge (n).

BLOODTHIRSTY   *to be bloodthirsty.* To be ready, willing, and able to wound or kill someone. WNNCD: 1535. Source: ANIMAL. The date of the metaphor eliminates an origin in the human *vampire* (WNNCD: 1734), though the vampire *bat* of Mexico is within range. More likely, the thirst for blood derives from the *bloodsucker* (q.v.) and the *leech* (q.v.), along with the everpresent mosquito, whose nutrition comes entirely from animal and human blood. A person who is *bloodthirsty* is *out for blood*—i.e., is eager to cause someone to shed blood—or is willing to *go for the jugular* (q.v.)—i.e., is willing to cause someone to bleed to death: a *bloodthirsty killer.* WNWD.

BLUBBER   Excessive body fat on humans. (A slang expression.) WNNCD: 15th cent. Source: WHALE. The blubber, or body fat of whales (and other large marine mammals) is extensive, because they are warm-blooded animals that swim in northern seas or at cold depths of southern seas. ATWS. *See also* Beached Whale.

BLUE DOG   *See* Red Dog.

BOA   *a boa.* A long scarf of fabric, fur, or feathers that is worn by women. Source: SNAKE. The snake called a *boa* (WNNCD: 14th cent.—fr. Lat. *boa* "water snake") is a long (up to 18 feet) constrictor of South and Central America and Mexico. It is attractively colored (tan, reddish brown) and is sometimes worn draped around the neck by snake fanciers and exotic dancers. Fur and feather *boas* were most popular during the first half of the 20th cent.; long knit *boas* are still popular, esp. at football games.

BOBTAIL   *a bobtail.* A "semi" tractor traveling without a trailer. Source: HORSE. Literally, a bobtail is a horse whose tail has been cut short or *bobbed* (WNNCD: 1798): a "bobtailed nag." This operation used to be performed esp. for horses that drew buggies or sleighs, so that the tail would not fly into the face of the driver. A related metaphor, *ragtag and bobtail* "the riffraff or rabble" (WNNCD: 1882), derives from a mismatched team of two substandard horses: one with a ragged tail (*ragtag*) and one with a bobbed tail (*bobtail*). The term *bob* is also used for a woman's short haircut. ATWS; DOC; HTB.

BOLD AS A LION   *See* Brave as a Lion.

BOLL WEEVIL   *a boll weevil.* A Southern Democrat who votes Republican once he/she is elected to Congress. Source: WEEVIL. WNNCD: 1895. The boll weevil, a cotton-eating beetle, entered the United States from Mexico in the late 1800s and spread throughout the South, doing tremendous damage to the cotton industry before it was brought under control by chemicals. NDAS. *Compare* Copperhead.

BOMBAST   Inflated, padded, or pretentious language. WNNCD: 1589. Source: SILKWORM. The silkworm is the larva of an Asian moth (Lat. *bombyx*). The caterpillar constructs its cocoon of the silken fibers that it produces. When *bombyx* was first borrowed into English (fr. M.Fr.), as *bombast*, it meant "cotton padding," not silk padding. ATWS. *See also* Silk; Silken; Silky.

BONE OF CONTENTION   *See* Bone to Pick.

BONE TO PICK   *to have a bone to pick with someone.* To have an argument, complaint, dispute, grievance, or problem to settle with someone. DOC: 16th cent. Source: DOG. Dogs are carnivorous, and they like nothing better than to chew the meat off a bone. However, a dog does not like to share its bone with another dog; consequently, if you throw a bone between two dogs, it becomes a *bone of contention* for them, and they spend their time fighting over the bone rather than enjoying the meat on it. For humans, a *bone of contention* is a minor grievance to settle with someone—in a more civilized fashion. A related expression, to *throw someone a bone*, means to give someone a little encouragement or enticement—or simply a hint. ATWS; BDPF; CI; DEI; EWPO; HOI; HTB; ID; LCRH; MDWPO.

BONFIRE   *a bonfire.* A large fire set in the outdoors as part of a celebration or feast, or for the purpose of disposing of excess wood or leaves. WNNCD: 15th cent. Source: ANIMAL. In medieval England, a bonfire was lit. a *bone fire* (fr. O.E. *bān* "bone")—i.e., a burning of the animal bones that had piled up over the course of the past year. The occasion was orig. a pagan festival but later became associated with a saint's day: June 24th. The celebration has been perpetuated in America with a huge bonfire on the night before a big football game—in the fall, and with no Christian overtones. EWPO.

BOO   *to boo.* To express disappointment, disapproval, or contempt by uttering *Boo!* WNNCD: 1816. Source: OX. Crowds have been *booing* their disapproval since early in the 19th cent.; but the noun *boo* goes back to 1575, and the interjection *Boo!*, used to frighten someone, goes back even farther, to 1430. It all started with the lowing of oxen (Lat. *bous*). EWPO; SOED.

BOOBIRD   *a boobird.* A heckling fan at a sports event. Source: BIRD. WNNCD: O.E. *Boobirds* boo the members of their own team every chance they get. The word *boobird* is probably patterned after *bluebird*, though the term may have originated in Toronto, where the Blue Jays had a number of *boobirds* in their early days. The bluebird is a bird of happiness (BDPF: 1910); the *boobird* is a bird of unhappiness. NDAS.

BOOBY HATCH   *a booby hatch.* An insane asylum, or a place resembling one. WNNCD: 1897. Source: BOOBY. The *booby* (fr. Sp. *bobo* "fool") is a small tropical seabird that likes to perch on the hatch (called a *booby hatch*) of a ship, where it displays an awkwardness not seen when it is aloft. ATWS. *Compare* Loony Bin.

BOOKWORM   *a bookworm.* A person who spends much of the time with his/her nose in a book. WNNCD: 1599. Source: WORM. WNNCD: O.E. The literal *bookworm* is an insect larva that devours books by feeding on their paste and binding. Human *bookworms* also "devour" books, but without destroying them. They "feed" on the contents of the pages between the glued and pasted covers. *Bookworms* are to the humanities what "nerds" are to the sciences. ATWS; CI; ID; IRCD; WNWD.

BOSTON CRAB   *a Boston crab.* A hold in professional wrestling in which the extremities of a prone opponent are entwined in the arms and legs of the proponent, who bends the opponent's back upward. Source: CRAB. WNNCD: O.E. The opponent in a *Boston crab* hold looks like the crustacean turned over on its back: in a vulnerable position, with its appendages extended upward. *See also* Crab (n).

BOTTOM FEEDER   *a bottom feeder.* A scum of society. Source: FISH. Among fish, a bottom feeder—or a "bottom fish"—is one such as a sucker, which feeds on the bottom of a lake or stream, cleaning up the "crumbs" left over by the predator fish. It is the garbage collector of the fish world. Human *bottom feeders* are small-time operators who concentrate on the scraps left over by the big-time operators.

BOTTOMLESS PIT   *See* Pitfall.

BRAND   *a brand.* A line of products of a single company; a trademark. Source: ANIMAL. The *brand* as a "trademark" derives from the 16th cent. practice of marking both manufactured products and livestock with a hot iron that bore the symbol of the producer or owner. (It is not certain which came first.) The livestock that were *branded* were those that had little or no hair, such as the cattle, horses, mules, donkeys, and swine—but not the sheep or goats. Nowadays, only cattle are hot-branded; other livestock are *earmarked* (q.v.), painted, or tagged. At one time criminals were also *branded* with a hot iron, as both a mark of identification and a symbol of disgrace. The term *brand name* (WNNCD: 1922) is also based on the noun *brand*. EWPO.

BRAND NAME   *See* Brand.

BRAVE AS A LION   *to be as brave—or as bold—as a lion.* To have enormous courage. Source: LION. WNNCD: 12th cent. The lion has been a symbol of courage since at least the 12th cent., when King Richard I of England was dubbed *Coeur de lion* ("lion heart") for his bravery in the Third Crusade. The lion's reputation is based on the fact that *she* (the lioness) is not afraid to attack animals much larger than herself. ATWS; DEI. *See also* Lionhearted.

BRAVE THE LION'S DEN   *to brave the lion's den.* To dare to go where danger lurks. Source: LION. WNNCD: 12th cent. Lions don't build dens, but they do seek shelter in caves and rock overhangs. If you entered a lion's "den," you would find a "pride" of ten or so assorted males, females, and young—all resentful of your presence. It would be analogous to facing an angry crowd or an irate boss. *See also* Beard the Lion; Lion's Den.

BRAY LIKE A DONKEY   *to bray like a donkey.* To laugh or cry loudly, harshly, or discordantly. Source: DONKEY. WNNCD: ca. 1785. The original expression was "to bray like an ass" (WNNCD: 14th cent.), but *ass* was replaced by the euphemistic *donkey* (from the name *Duncan?*) at about the time that *ass* acquired the additional meaning of "buttocks." The donkey's bray is the source of the imitative *hee haw*. ATWS. *Compare* Make an Ass of Yourself.

BREAK COVER   *to break cover.* To suddenly come out of hiding. Source: ANIMAL. When hunters are around, game birds, such as pheasants and quail, and small mammals, such as rabbits and fox, *lie low* (DOC: 1880)—i.e., take cover in the brush or in a hole in the ground. When the hunter, or his/her dogs, gets too close, the animal usu. breaks cover in a flurry of feathers or fur. People who have committed a crime or have escaped from prison or jail also *take cover* or *hole up* (q.v.) in expectation of being hunted by the police. When the officers get too close, the criminals sometimes *break cover* in order to avoid capture or find a better hiding place. BDPF; CI; ST.

BREAK OUT OF THE PACK   *See* Pull away from the Field.

BREAK OUT OF YOUR SHELL   *to break out of your shell.* To emerge from social or psychological isolation. Source: BIRD. A baby bird is "born" in a shell, grows there, and then pecks its way out when it reaches a certain point of development.

The presence of *break* in the metaphor eliminates snakes and turtles as a source, because their eggs are usu. soft-shelled. (Dinosaurs, however, apparently had hard-shelled eggs.) *Compare* Come out of Your Shell.

BREED (n)   *See* Different Breed of Cat.

BREED (v)   *to breed something.* To lead to or cause something. Source: ANIMAL. To breed animals is to mate them in order to produce the very best offspring, which are then carefully raised for food (e.g., rabbits), for work (e.g., horses), for show (e.g., cats), or for sale (e.g., dogs). Metaphorically, the wrong conditions sometimes produce unfortunate results: e.g., familiarity *breeds* contempt; unemployment *breeds* poverty; and poverty *breeds* crime. ATWS.

BREED LIKE RABBITS   *See* Multiply like Rabbits.

BRIDAL PATH   *See* Get Hitched.

BRIDLE   *to bridle at something.*   To take offense at something. Source: HORSE. WNNCD: O.E. A horse takes offense at being *reined in* by raising its neck and drawing back its head, so that the reins slacken somewhat and reduce the pressure on the bit. People do precisely the same thing—straighten their neck, put their chin on their chest—when they wish to show resentment, scorn, or hostility at something that has been said or done. A *bridle* (WNNCD: O.E.) is a harness for the horse's head that contains a bit and attached reins. (Without the bit and reins, it is called a *halter*, q.v.) The term *unbridled* (14th cent.) means "unrestrained," as when the bridle is removed from a horse, or a person's enthusiasm is allowed to become unbounded. ATWS; BDPF; CE; GTP.

BRIGHT AS A LARK   *to be as bright as a lark.* To be as sharp as a tack: alert, intelligent. Source: LARK. WNNCD: O.E. The European lark, esp. the skylark, has a beautiful, clear song. While the female is minding the nest, the male soars up to several hundred feet in the air, sings his bright song while flying in a circle, then tucks in his wings and dives straight to the ground. *See also* Happy as a Lark; Sing like a Lark.

BRIGHT-EYED AND BUSHY-TAILED   *to be bright-eyed and bushy-tailed.* To be eager, alert, energetic, and vivacious. DOC: 1930s. Source: FOX (WNNCD: O.E.); SQUIRREL (WNNCD: 14th cent.). Both the fox and the squirrel are noted for their alertness and their long bushy tails. (The *squirrel*—lit. "shade-tail"—spreads its tail over its back like an umbrella to protect itself from sun and rain.) DOC gives the source as "squirrel"; however, the date of the citation favors the source as "fox." The fox "stole," the pelt of an entire red fox, including the head, was very popular in the 1930s, draped around the neck of a fashionable woman, with the glass eyes and bushy tail prominently displayed for the viewer. Perhaps it is no wonder that the most common American squirrel is called the "fox squirrel." ATWS; CE; EWPO; NDAS.

BRING HOME THE BACON   *to bring home the bacon.* To serve as the breadwinner of the family. EWPO: 1925. Source: PIG. Americans associate this metaphor with the catching of a greased pig at a country fair, the reward for which was the pig itself, which could then be turned into bacon, ham, pork, etc. To the English, the association is with the Dunmow Flitch, a side of bacon awarded to the most devoted married couple at an annual ceremony held in Dunmow, England, from 1111–1772. The word *bacon* has been synonymous with "prize" since 1725. AID; BDPF; CE; DEI; DOC; HOI; ID; LCRH; MDWPO; SHM; ST. *See also* Like Catching a Greased Pig; Save Your Bacon.

BRING IN A RINGER   *See* Ringer.

BRING TO BAY   *to bring someone or something to bay.* To corner a criminal; to check a potential disaster. Source: DOG. Hunting dogs bring a quarry to bay when they hole it up or corner it. At this point they are *in full cry*—i.e., *baying* (fr. O.Fr. *abai*) at their loudest. The police *bring* a criminal *to bay* when they give him/her no means of escape; and a flood or fire is *brought to bay* when it is held in check and not allowed to spread. ATWS; CI; DEI; DOC; ST. *See also* At Bay.

BRING TO HEEL   *to bring someone to heel.* To get someone under your control. Source: DOG. When a trained dog is told to "Heel!" it is expected to stand or walk at the heels, or side, of the trainer: i.e., it is "brought to heel." When a person is *brought to heel*, he/she is brought in line, made to conform, or forced to yield to authority. WNWD. *Compare* Bring to Bay.

BRISTLE WITH ANGER   *to bristle with anger.* To react indignantly to an insult or affront to your character. Source: PORCUPINE. The porcupine (lit. "spiny pig"), or hedgehog, shows its anger by making its hundreds of stiff, sharp bristles, on its entire body and tail, stand erect. *See also* Porcupinefish; Prickly as a Hedgehog.

BROKEN WING   *See* Wing (n).

BROOD   *a brood; to brood.* The children of one family; to worry about something. Source: BIRD. A mother bird sits on her eggs until they *hatch* (q.v.); then she cares for her half dozen or so baby birds until they are able to fend for themselves. Among humans, a *brood* of children is the (usu.) large number of children in a single family: e.g., "Here come the Joneses and their brood." When humans, either male or female, *brood*, they are not incubating their children but are sitting alone, thinking gloomy thoughts, such as how to pay for their children's education. ATWS.

BROUGHT TO BAY   *See* Bring to Bay.

BROUGHT TO HEEL   *See* Bring to Heel.

BROWN COW   *How now, brown cow?* Hi! What's new? Source: COW. WNNCD: O.E. In 18th cent. Scotland, *brown cow* was a euphemism for "beer," and the way to order another pint of beer was to ask, "How now, brown cow?" (DOC: 1725). The full expression has persisted (probably because of the assonance of its (*-ows-*) as a greeting to friends and a pronunciation exercise of the sort used by Professor Higgins in *My Fair Lady*. A *brown cow* is also a vanilla soda made with root bear instead of fizzy water. *Compare* Black Cow.

BROWSE   *to browse.* To examine an assortment of things randomly and casually. EWPO: 1823. Source: ANIMAL. Animals *graze* when they randomly eat things that are growing on the ground, such as grasses, weeds and flowers; they *browse* when they casually eat shoots, twigs, and leaves (i.e., *browse*) that are growing on bushes, shrubs, and trees. People *browse* when they examine the contents of something, such as a department store, a library, a bookstore, or an individual book. *Browsing* is indoor window-shopping: You're not there to buy anything, just to sample it—much like the animal that stretches its neck to reach a single leaf on a low-hanging limb. ATWS; MDWPO.

BRUSH-HOG   *a brush-hog (or bush-hog).* A machine for cutting brush. Source: HOG. WNNCD: O.E. A brush-hog is a walking or riding mower with a horizontal rotary or reciprocating blade on the front that is capable of cutting down brush, bushes, and saplings. The word *hog* may have been included in the name because the machine resembles a wild boar crashing through the underbrush.

BRUTAL   *See* Brute.

BRUTE   *a brute.* A big, dumb physical man: a *big brute.* Source: ANIMAL. A *brute* is literally a big dumb animal (fr. Lat. *brutus* "stupid, heavy")—i.e., a *beast* (q.v.), such as an ox. Human *brutes* are not only big and dumb like the ox: they can also be ruthless and cruel (i.e., *brutal*—WNNCD: 15th cent.) or unrefined and insensitive (i.e., *brutish*—WNNCD: 1534); and they usu. achieve their goals by using *brute force* or *brute strength* rather than reason. ATWS. *See also* Beast.

BRUTE FORCE   *See* Brute.

BRUTE STRENGTH   *See* Brute.

BRUTISH   *See* Brute.

B.S.   *See* Bullshit (n).

BUCK (n)   *a buck.* A dollar. LTA: 1856. Source: DEER. *Buck,* meaning a U.S. dollar, has two likely and overlapping origins, both pointing to the adult male deer, or "buck." The first is a *buckskin* (q.v.), the hide of an adult male deer, that was used for barter by Native Americans and later as money by European traders. The second is a *buckhorn knife* or *buck* which was used as an indicator of the dealer in Western poker games in the 1870s. When the knife was replaced by a silver dollar, the coin was also called a *buck.* Now, a *buck* is a monetary value, whether in the form of a silver dollar, a dollar bill, or simply a number: $1.00. ATWS; BDPF; DAE; EWPO; IRCD; MDWPO; NDAS; SPD; ST. *See also* Big Bucks; Fast Buck; Pass the Buck.

BUCK (v)   *to buck (for) something.* To resist something; to charge something; to strengthen something. Source: GOAT. *Bucking* is usu. associated with a horse rearing up to dislodge its rider, but that in itself is a metaphor, because the action alludes to the rearing up of a male goat, or *buck* (O.E. *bucca*) before it butts another male goat. To *buck a trend* is to rise up against it; to *buck the odds* is to charge ahead in spite of them; to *buck for a raise* (or promotion) is to fight for a higher salary; and to *buck up* (WNNCD: 1844) is to pull yourself together in spite of adversity. Sawyers *buck* wood; football players *buck* the line; and airplanes *buck* headwinds. ATWS; IRCD; WNWD.

BUCK A TREND   *See* Buck (v).

BUCKEYE   *a buckeye.* A horse-chestnut tree, or the nut or flower thereof. WNNCD: 1763. Source: DEER. Ohio is known as the "Buckeye State" because that is where the similarity was first noticed between the large, glossy, dark-brown seed of the *horse-chestnut tree* (WNNCD: 1597) and the large, glossy, dark-brown eye of the buck deer. The word *buckeye* was then applied to the tree, the flower, the citizens of the State, and the students of the State University. BDPF; EWPO; WNWD.

BUCK FEVER   Nervous excitement of an inexperienced hunter. WNNCD: 1841. Source: DEER. The metaphor derives from the flustered condition of a first-time hunter sighting his/her first buck deer. In more recent times the term has also been applied to the various excuses used by deer hunters to be absent from work or school during deer season. It is comparable to "blue flu" among police officers. IRCD.

BUCK FOR A RAISE   *See* Buck (v).

BUCK NAKED   *to be buck naked.* To be totally naked. WNNCD: 1943. Source: DEER (?). The connection between *buck* "totally" and *buck* "adult male deer" is tenuous. *Buck naked* may mean "naked as a buck," or *buck* may have been confused with *buff* (q.v.), as in "in the *buff*" (q.v.), or *butt*, as in *butt naked*. This metaphor has to be labeled "origin unknown."

BUCK PASSER *See* Pass the Buck.

BUCK PRIVATE *a buck private.* A private of the lowest grade. WNNCD: 1918. Source: DEER. Although a *buck* is an adult male deer (fr. O.E. *bucca*), in recent times the word has also come to mean a young challenger to the status of the adult male. In the Army and Marines, a *buck private* has the lowest grade of the lowest rank—not even meriting a stripe. His/her challenge is to make it to private first class. IRCD. *See also* Young Buck.

BUCKRAM Coarse-woven, stiffened cotton or linen fabric used to interline the hems of garments, the bands of hats, and the spines of hardbound books. WNNCD: 13th cent. Source: GOAT (*); SHEEP (*). *Buckram* looks like it ought to be an animal metaphor, composed of *buck* "adult male goat" and *ram* "adult male sheep"; but it is not. It is an alteration of *Bokhara*, a city in Central Asia where the fabric originated. HF. *See also* Gossamer.

BUCKSAW *a bucksaw.* A one-way, one-person, two-handed saw. WNNCD: 1856. Source: GOAT. The bucksaw is designed for use with a *sawbuck* (q.v.). It consists of a horizontal blade stretched between two vertical handles. The word *buck* in the name suggests the kind of forward charge that is characteristic of a male goat, or *buck*, competing for ewes in the mating season—or at just about any other time of the year. WNWD.

BUCKSKIN *a buckskin.* A horse with a yellowish-gray coat, and a black mane and tail. Source: DEER. The color of a buckskin is that of the skin of an adult male deer, or "buck," which ranges from light tan to dark gray (WNNCD: 14th cent.). The deer, however, has no mane, and its shorter tail is white on the underside. The term *buckskin* is also used for breeches, jackets, and shoes that are made of napped deerskin. WNWD. *See also* Buck (n); White Bucks.

BUCK SLIP *a buck slip.* A routing slip. NDAS: early 1940s. Source: DEER. A buck slip, or *buck sheet*, is a piece of paper containing the names of the persons who are supposed to read or examine the document to which the slip is attached. When each reader has done so, he/she checks off his/her name and passes the document on to another person whose name appears on the slip. The term derives from the metaphor *to pass the buck* (q.v.), where the *buck* was orig. a buckhorn knife. MDWPO; ST. *See also* Buck (n); Buck Stops here.

BUCK STOPS HERE *The buck stops here.* This is the end of the line for responsibility and blame. DOC: late 1940s. Source: DEER. The *buck* in this metaphor alludes to the buckhorn knife that was used as a marker of the dealer in poker games in the Wild West of the 1870s. If the player so designated preferred not to deal, he could *pass the buck* (q.v.) to the player on his left. President Truman (1945–1953) put such a sign on his desk to indicate that he took full responsibility for all of his actions. CI; IRCD; SPD; ST. *See also* Buck (n); Buck Slip.

BUCK THE ODDS   *See* Buck (v).

BUCK TOOTH   *a buck tooth.* A protruding upper-front tooth. WNNCD: 1753. Source: DEER. Deer do not have protruding upper incisors, but the term *buck* (fr. O.E. *bucca* "stag or male deer") has been extended to males of other animals, such as the goat and rabbit, the latter of which *does* have extremely long front teeth. *Buck teeth* on humans are thought to be caused by excessive thumbsucking in infancy.

BUCK UP   *See* Buck (v).

BUCOLIC   Pastoral; rustic, WNNCD: 1613. Source: CATTLE; COW. *Bucolic* suggests a beautiful scene of cattle (Gk. *bous* "head of cattle") grazing in lush grass on sunny, flower-covered hillsides, watched over by a cowherd (Gk. *kolos* "herder"). This romantic setting has come to symbolize rural life as it used to be, "in the good old days": calm, quiet, peaceful, and well-ordered. ATWS; ROE.

BUFF (adj.)   *the color buff.* A yellowish, orangish tan. WNNCD: 1695. Source: BUFFALO. WNNCD: 1511. The source of *buff* must be the American buffalo, or "bison," because the coat of the European bison is brown. The American buffalo has brown hindquarters and a dark brown head, but the forequarters are light brown or tan. BDPF; EWPO; MDWPO. *See also* Buff (n) (1); Buff (n) (2); Buff (v).

BUFF (n) (1)   *a buff.* A devotee, fan, enthusiast, or aficionado: e.g., a sports *buff*, a film *buff*. LTA: 1931. Source: BUFFALO. WNNCD: 1511. The original *buffs* were "fire buffs": volunteer New York City firemen who were issued buffalo robes for fighting fires in the winters of the early 1800s. The robes were buff-colored and came from the pelts of the American buffalo. ATWS; EWPO; MDWPO. *See also* Buff (adj.); Buff (n) (2); Buff (v).

BUFF (n) (2)   *the buff.* The bare skin: e.g., "to strip to the *buff*." DEOD: ca. 1600. Source: BUFFALO. WNNCD: 1511. The American buffalo, or "bison," furnished the early settlers with both buffalo *robes*, made from the hide and hair of the forequarters of the animal, and buff-colored *leather*, tanned, but not dyed, to an orange-yellow color. The word *buff* is a clipped form of the word *buffalo*. ATWS. *See also* Buff (adj.); Buff (n) (1).

BUFF (v)   *to buff something.* To shine or polish something. WNNCD: 1885. Source: BUFFALO. WNNCD: 1511. The verb *buff* is short for *buffalo*, the name of the American bison, whose hide was used in the 19th cent. to polish metal surfaces. The tanned hide was also the source of the adj. *buff* (q.v.), which is a chamois color. ATWS; EWPO. *See also* Buff (n) (1); Buff (n) (2). *Compare* Chamois (adj.).

BUFFALO   *to buffalo someone.* To baffle or bewilder someone. WNNCD: 1903. Source: BUFFALO. WNNCD: 1511. The American buffalo (or, more properly, "bison") is a large, powerful animal—enough so as to frighten and intimidate an Easterner who sees it for the first time. The verb was probably in use for about 30 years before first appearing in print. ATWS; DOC; IHAT; IRCD. *See also* Buffaloed. *Compare* Bully (v).

BUFFALOED   *to be buffaloed.* To be confused, mystified, or overwhelmed. DOC: 1904. Source: BUFFALO. WNNCD: 1511. The American buffalo, one of the largest animals on the continent—six feet tall at the shoulders, over one ton in weight—is the King of the Western Prairie. It goes wherever it pleases, and its only predator is the human. *See also* Buffalo.

BUFFALOFISH   *a buffalofish.* A fish of the sucker family that is found in the Mississippi and Ohio River valleys. WNNCD: 1768. Source: BUFFALO. WNNCD: 1511. The *buffalofish* is a large fish with a humped back, like that of the American buffalo (or "bison"). IHAT. *Compare* Bullhead.

BUFFALO WINGS   Barbequed chicken wings. Source: BUFFALO (*). WNNCD: 1511. Buffaloes don't have wings, so this is not an animal metaphor. The name comes from the city of Buffalo, New York, where the delicacy was first prepared. (*Compare* "Chicago-style pizza.") Even the name of the city does not derive from the animal but from Fr. *beau fleuve* "beautiful river." IRCD. *Compare* City Chicken; Texas Turkey.

BUG (n) (1)   *a bug.* A person with an attraction to, or obsession for, certain actions or objects. IRCD: 1870s. Source: BUG. WNNCD: 1622. The *bedbug*, a "true" bug of the order *Hemiptera* (half-winged insects), seems to be obsessed with hiding in beds and sucking the blood of their human occupants. This obsession carries over to people who are "hooked" on starting fires (a *firebug*, q.v.), dancing wildly (a *jitterbug*, q.v.), trashing the neighborhood (a *litterbug*, q.v.), or taking pictures (a *shutterbug*—WNNCD: 1941). The term *bug* competes with *buff*, q.v. (e.g., a music *buff*), which suggests a person who is a little more sophisticated and a lot less violent. ATWS; CI; EWPO. *See also* Kissing Bug; Lovebug; Travel Bug.

BUG (n) (2)   *a bug.* A flaw, fault, defect, imperfection, or error in a mechanical or electrical system. ATWS: 1889. Source: BUG. WNNCD. 1622. The first metaphorical *bug* was found in Thomas Edison's phonograph. Later, bugs appeared in automobiles and home appliances, and now they affect computer programs. This problem with bugs probably alludes to the M.E. sense of *bugge*, "something terrifying or obnoxious," the meaning before the word was applied to insects. DEOD; EWPO; IRCD; THT. *See also* Bug (n) (3); Bugaboo; Bugbear; Debug.

BUG (n) (3)   *to come down with a/the bug*. To have, get, or catch a cold, virus, or the flu. IRCD: ca. 1900. Source: BUG. WNNCD: 1622. This sense of *bug* probably derives from the microscopic size of the germ that causes the diseases from which all humans suffer. "True" bugs, such as bedbugs and other halfwinged insects, are not microscopic, but they are small, and some of them do transmit diseases such as sleeping sickness (the assassin bug). Computers are also susceptible to the virus carried by *bugs* planted in their software. To be *bitten by the bug* is either to have contracted influenza or to have an irresistible urge to pursue something. ATWS; BDPF; CI; NDAS. *See also* Bug (n) (1); Bug (n) (2).

BUG (n) (4)   *a bug*. A tiny electronic listening device. ATWS: 1940s. Source: BUG. WNNCD: 1622. *Bug* was first applied to surveillance equipment in the 1920s, when it may have developed as a shortening of *burglar* (alarm), as pronounced in a r-less dialect. By the late 1940s it had come to mean a wireless microphone hidden under a desk, above a lamp, inside a telephone, or even in the olive of a martini. Now it is thought of as any tiny intruder that is as obnoxious as the bedbug. EWPO; IRCD; SPD. *See also* Bug (n) (2); Bug (n) (3); Bug (v) (1); Debug.

BUG (v) (1)   *to bug something*. To plant a tiny listening device in a room, car, phone, etc. IRCD: ca. 1945. Source: BUG. WNNCD: 1622. Electronic transmitters are so small that they can be installed inside a house or car phone, under a desk top, above a lamp, etc. Their size was the inspiration for their name: no bigger than an insect. A place that had been so equipped was said to be *bugged*, and the verb *debug* (q.v.) soon appeared on the scene. ATWS; DEI; EWPO; SPD. *See also* Bug (n) (2); Bug (n) (3); Bug (n) (4); Bug (v) (2).

BUG (v) (2)   *to bug someone*. To bother, annoy, or irritate someone. WNNCD: 1949. Source: BUG. WNNCD: 1622. In the broadest sense, a bug is an insect, and many insects, such as the housefly, are a source of great annoyance to humans. Therefore, to *bug* someone is to pester them—accosting them, being shooed away, and immediately returning. The response is often *Stop bugging me!* or *Bug off!* AID; ATWS; EWPO; SPD. *See also* Bug (v) (1).

BUGABOO   *a bugaboo*. A frightening ghost or goblin. WNNCD: 1740. Source: BUG (*). WNNCD: 1622. *Bug* and *bugaboo* come from the same Welsh word: *bwg* "ghost." *Bwg* took on the meaning "a terrifying little creature" (the insect), while *bugaboo* (the *boo* either for alliteration or in imitation of what ghosts say) took on the meaning of a terrifying—and invisible—large creature (the *hobgoblin*). In M.E., *bugge* meant "scarecrow." IRCD; THT. *See also* Bugbear.

BUGBEAR *a bugbear*. An imaginary object of fear or dread. WNNCD: 1581. Source: BUG (WNNCD: 1622); BEAR (WNNCD: O.E.). The original *bugbear* was a ghost or goblin that was created by parents to frighten children into behaving. *Bug*, from Welsh *bwg* "ghost," was combined with *bear* (fr. O.E. *bera*) to call up the vision of a giant—but invisible—hobgoblin. Nowadays, a *bugbear* is more like a bear *cub*: a source of constant irritation. BDPF; THT; WNWD. *See also* Bugaboo.

BUG BOY *a bug boy*. An apprentice jockey—of either sex. Source: BUG. WNNCD: 1622. The *bug boy* gets his/her name from the asterisk, or little "star," that appears next to his/her name in a racing program. The handicap system gives a rookie three *bugs* (three stars) and a ten-pound reduction in the weight to be carried, while an experienced apprentice gets one *bug* and a five-pound reduction. (The normal weight for a full-fledged jockey, who must *add* weight if necessary, is 126 pounds.) ATWS; MDWPO.

BUG-EYED *see* Bug out.

BUGGY (adj.) *to be buggy*. To be crazy. IRCD: 18th cent. Source: BUG. WNNCD: 1622. The bug's relationship to insanity is unclear. The allusion may be to the fact that "true" bugs "drive people crazy" by sucking blood from their sleeping bodies (the bedbug), infecting them with diseases such as sleeping sickness (the assassin bug), destroying their crops (the plant bug), or generally stinking up the place (the stink bug). The original meaning of *buggy* was "infested with bugs" (WNNCD: 1714). (The noun *buggy*, meaning "light carriage," is from an unknown source.) ATWS. *See also* Bughouse (adj.); Crazy as a Bedbug.

BUGGY (n) *See* Buggy (adj.).

BUGGY (v) *to buggy a map*. To plot the location of rocks and trees and other permanent or semipermanent objects on a surveyor's map or blueprint. Source: BUG. WNNCD: 1622. When a surveyor has established the dimensions and elevations of a piece of land and produced a map or blueprint, it is the job of the surveyor's assistant, using the surveyor's notes, to fill in the location of natural objects, such as trees and rocks, and man-made objects, such as houses and barns. Some marks are so small—e.g., for young trees—that they resemble *bugs* sitting on the map.

BUGHOUSE *to be bughouse; a bughouse*. To be insane (WNNCD: 1891); an insane asylum (WNNCD: 1902). Source: BUG. WNNCD: 1622. A *bughouse* is a place for people who are *bughouse*. Both words are ultimately derived from 18th cent. *buggy* (q.v.), which orig. meant "infested with bugs" but soon added the metaphorical meaning "insane." Many insects, such as wasps and ants, build "houses" that are populated with individuals that seem to have lost their individuality. ATWS; BDPF; IHAT; IRCD.

BUG IN YOUR EAR   *to have a bug in your ear.* To have an idea in your brain. LTA: ca. 1900. Source: BUG. WNNCD: 1622. The allusion of this metaphor may be to the earwig, a small insect that travels at night and invades homes—but has never been found in a human ear. More likely, the metaphor compares (1) the childish act of placing a real bug in the ear of a sleeping sibling or parent, resulting in instant arousal, to (2) the audible dropping of a hint to someone in order to bring about some action. A person with a *bug in his/her ear* is thought to be "up to something." ATWS; IRCD. *Compare* Cute as a Bug's Ear.

BUGLE   *a bugle.* A short, valveless "trumpet" that is used in the military for playing taps and reveille. WNNCD: 14th cent. Source: OX. In medieval times, *bugle* referred not only to a hunting or drinking horn but to a young ox (Lat. *buculus*, diminutive of *bos* "ox"). The horn was removed from the ox's head, reamed out, and punctured at the tip. Bugles are now made of brass. ATWS; EWPO; THT; WNWD. *See also* Greenhorn.

BUG OFF   *to bug off (or out).* To beat a hasty retreat. Source: BUG. WNNCD: 1622. A person who is being annoyed (or *bugged*) by someone might say *Bug off!* (or *Bug out!*), meaning "Get off my back!" (or "Get out of here!"). The expression probably derives from the same command given to a fly or other annoying insect—along with a wave of the hand or a slap with the fly swatter. AID; EWPO; IRCD. *See also* Bug (v) (2). *Compare* Buzz off.

BUG OUT   *to bug out.* For your eyes to bulge out. Source: BUG. WNNCD: 1622. Not all bugs, or "insects," have bulging eyes; but the compound eyes of bees, flies, and grasshoppers are huge and protrude well beyond the exoskeleton. A person whose eyes bulge out—e.g., in surprise—is said to be *bug-eyed* (WNNCD: 1922); one whose eyes bulge out all the time may have *exophthalmos*, usu. caused by hyperthyroidism. ATWS; BDPF; IRCD. *Compare* Bug off.

BUILD A BETTER MOUSETRAP   *Build a better mousetrap, and the world will beat a path to your door.* If you can find a simple solution to a complex problem— or if you can improve on an age-old product—you will become rich and famous. EWPO: 1889. Source: MOUSE. WNNCD: O.E. The age-old mousetrap, consisting of a cheese-loaded trigger that releases a spring-loaded bail, was finally improved upon in the 1990s, so presumably the world is beating a path to the inventor's door. IRCD; MDWPO. *See also* Mousetrap.

BUILD A FIRE UNDER *to build a fire under someone.* To shock someone out of their obstinance or lethargy and get them back to work again. Source: MULE. This is an early Americanism, so exaggeration can be expected; but it is possible that farmers sometimes actually resorted to building a fire under a balky mule to get it to move. Mules have the reputation of being the stubbornest animals alive. EWPO. *See also* Mule (1); Mulish; Stubborn as a Mule.

BULIMIA An eating disorder characterized by (1) a constant craving for food, (2) a fear of gaining weight, and (3) a series of binges and purges of the food eaten. WNNCD: 14th cent. Source: OX. To have *bulimia* is to have "the appetite of an ox" (fr. Gk. *boulimia* "great hunger," fr. *bous* "head of cattle, or ox" + *limos* "hunger"), to satisfy that appetite by bingeing, but then to allay the fear of gaining weight by purging.

BULL (1) *a bull.* The adult male of various large animals. Source: BULL. WNNCD: O.E. *Bull* orig. meant "an uncastrated adult male bovine" (WNNCD: O.E. *oxa*). The meaning has been broadened to include the adult males of such large animals as the elephant, the whale, the moose, and the seal. (An adult male of the largest variety of seal is called a *bull elephant seal.*) *See also* Bull (2); Bull (3); Bull (4).

BULL (2) *a bull.* A trader who buys stock heavily while the price is low—either with the expectation that the price will rise, or with the hope that the large purchase will encourage its rise. LTA: 1761. Source: BULL. WNNCD: O.E. A *bull* is a trader who takes advantage of a *bull market* (q.v.): a stock market that is low but shows promise of charging ahead rapidly, like an adult male bovine. ATWS; BDPF; CE; DEI; HOI; IRCD; MDWPO; SHM. *See also* Bullish. *Compare* Bear.

BULL (3) *a bull.* A prison guard; a bailiff. Source: BULL (?). WNNCD: O.E. Since the 19th cent., a male with a brawny physique has been referred to as a *bull*; and because individuals of such large size were often selected as police officers, the meaning was broadened to include prison guards and bailiffs. (Note the bailiff "Bull" on the TV series *Night Court.*) However, one source states that the origin is Spanish Gypsy *bul* "policeman" (IHAT: 1893). ATWS.

BULL (4) *a lot of bull.* A lot of nonsense; a pack of lies. WNNCD: 1914. Source: BULL. WNNCD: O.E. *Bull* is a euphemistic shortening of *bullshit* (q.v.), which first appeared in print in the following year (WNNCD: 1915). Both words meant "boastful talk," "exaggerated nonsense," or "incredible lies" at that time. Since then, the synonyms *jive* and *crap* have been added. It is likely that both *bull* and *bullshit* originated at least 50 years earlier. BDPF; EWPO; IHAT; LTA; MDWPO. *See also* Bullshit (v); Bull Session; No Bull; Shoot the Bull.

BULLDOG (n) *a bulldog.* A tenacious individual who hangs on and won't let go. WNNCD: 1848. Source: BULL. WNNCD: O.E. The *bulldog* is so named, not because it has a very large head (though it does) but because it was specially bred for fighting bulls—in a "sport" called *bullbaiting*—back in 12th cent. England. The English bullfight differed from the Spanish bullfight in that the bull was tethered, and the fighting was done by dogs rather than by people. The *bulldog* was trained to grab the cartilage surrounding one of the bull's nostrils and hang on for dear life. People who have such persistence are said to be *as tenacious as a bulldog.* ATWS; BDPF; IRCD. *See also* Bulldog (v); Bulldog Edition.

BULLDOG (v) *to bulldog a steer.* To wrestle a steer to the ground. WNNCD: 1842. Source: BULLDOG. WNNCD: 1500. In the *bulldogging* contest of a modern rodeo, a cowboy leaps from the back of a horse onto the neck of a steer, grabs a horn in each hand, twists the steer's neck, and wrestles it to the ground. The procedure is named for the bulldog because, in 12th cent. England, this dog was bred to "bait" bulls by grabbing their nostrils in its jaws and hanging on for dear life. ATWS; EWPO; IRCD. *See also* Bulldog (n).

BULLDOG EDITION *a bulldog edition.* The morning edition of a daily newspaper. EWPO: 1890s. Source: BULLDOG. WNNCD: 1500. In merry old England, the bulldog was especially bred and trained to "bait" bulls by grabbing their nostrils and refusing to let go. The editor of the *bulldog edition* of a metropolitan newspaper faces a similar challenge: to hang on all night and put together a paper that will trounce the competition in the morning. If the results don't *feed the bulldog,* then the effort was unsuccessful. NDAS. *See also* Bulldog (n).

BULLDOZE *to bulldoze your way.* To force your way through obstacles (WNNCD: 1876); to level land, trees, buildings, etc. (SHM: 1925). Source: BULL. WNNCD: O.E. The bull is like the *six-hundred pound gorilla* (q.v.): it goes wherever it wants to. The punishment for doing so in the 19th cent. was a *dose* of the *bullwhip* (q.v.): i.e., a *bulldose.* Altered to *bulldoze,* the word soon became a verb meaning "to have your way through coercion, threat, or violence." With the appearance of the mechanical *bulldozer* (q.v.) in 1925, the verb took on the additional meaning of "leveling" everything in sight. EWPO; IRCD; NDAS. *See also* Bull Your Way.

BULLDOZER *a bulldozer.* One who gets his/her way through coercion, threat, or violence (WNNCD: 1876); a tractor with a large blade on the front for leveling land, trees, or buildings (SHM: 1925). Source: BULL. WNNCD: O.E. A bulldozer was orig. a rancher who controlled bulls with a *bullwhip* (q.v.); then it became a name for a person who achieved the same results with people, using words and fists. Today, a *bulldozer* is a large piece of earth-moving equipment that is sometimes called on to topple trees and level small buildings. The name was also once given to the operator of such equipment. ATWS; EWPO; LCRH; MDWPO; TNT. *See also* Bulldoze.

BULLFINCH *a bullfinch.* A small European bird with a small head, and a heavy neck and body. WNNCD: 1570. Source: BULL. WNNCD: O.E. The *bullfinch* has such a rounded body that it seems to have no neck at all. Many small birds are built this way, but this one has the honor of being compared to the male bovine, which has to have a powerful neck to hold up its huge head and horns. IRCD. *See also* Bullnecked.

BULLFROG *a bullfrog.* A large frog with a big head and mouth, a heavy body, and a deep voice. WNNCD: 1698. Source: BULL. WNNCD: O.E. The *bullfrog* is so named because of its large size—like the size of a bull compared with that of a cow—and its deep, loud voice—like the roar of a bull compared with the *moo* of a cow. IHAT; WNWD. *See also* Bullfinch; Bull Snake.

BULLHEAD *a bullhead.* A small freshwater catfish of the eastern United States. Source: BULL. WNNCD: O.E. The bullhead is so called because it has a large head, like a bull. Otherwise, it is just another *catfish* (q.v.)—with a wide mouth; four pairs of *barbels,* or "feelers," on its upper and lower jaws; scaleless skin; and dangerous, spiny fins. The name was first used—in England, in the 15th cent.— for a *sculpin,* a small, partly scaled fish without barbels, and then transferred to the Eastern freshwater catfish in colonial times. WNWD. *See also* Bullheaded.

BULLHEADED *to be bullheaded.* To be stubborn and headstrong. WNNCD: 1818. Source: BULL. WNNCD: O.E. This adj. is probably derived directly from *bull* + *head* rather than from the name of the small freshwater catfish of the eastern United States, the *bullhead* (q.v.). A bull has a large head—made to seem even larger because of the huge horns—and such a large body to go with it that it yields to no other animal and is practically unstoppable in a charge. CH; IRCD. *Compare* Pigheaded.

BULLHORN *a bullhorn.* A fixed loudspeaker on a maritime vessel (WNNCD: 1942); a portable microphone-loudspeaker used by police officers and firefighters. Source: BULL. WNNCD: O.E. Bulls have horns, of course, and the horns of bulls have been fashioned into noisemakers for thousands of years; but the loudspeaker mounted on a ship and the combination loudspeaker and microphone carried by a police officer or firefighter are so called because of their great volume—equal to that of a roaring bull. ATWS; IRCD; NDAS. *See also* Bugle; Bullroar.

BULL IN A CHINA SHOP *like a bull in a china shop.* Without regard for the feelings or property of others. HOI: 1834. Source: BULL. WNNCD: O.E. The metaphor is an amplification of an Aesop fable about an ass in a potter's shop. A bull would be totally out of place in a china shop and would probably cause a considerable amount of damage. Human *bulls* are thoughtless, tactless, and un-diplomatic—to say nothing about being clumsy and destructive. AID; ATWS; BDPE; CI; DEI; DOC; ID; IRCD; SHM.

BULLISH *to be bullish about something.* To be optimistic or enthusiastic about something, such as the stock market or the country (to be "*bullish* on America"). Source: BULL. WNNCD: O.E. To be *bullish* about the stock market is to predict a gradual shift from a falling market (a *bear market* [q.v.]) to a rising market (a *bull market* [q.v.]). This is the time to buy—before stock prices go much higher. IRCD. *See also* Bull (2). *Compare* Bearish.

BULL MARKET *a bull market.* A low but rising stock market. SHM: 1721. Source: BULL. WNNCD: O.E. A *bull market* is not yet charging ahead like a bull, but it shows signs of doing so. According to the stockbroker's creed—"buy low, sell high"—it is the time to buy, because a *bull market* will be followed by a *bear market* (q.v.), and the mood of the market will shift from optimism to pessimism. BDPF; IRCD; LCRH. *See also* Bull (2); Bullish. *Compare* Bear Market.

BULLNECKED *to be bullnecked.* To have a short, thick, powerful neck. Source: BULL. WNNCD: O.E. *Bullnecked* appeared in print sometime later than *bull neck* (WNNCD: 1936) "a neck like that of a bull." The bull is large in every way, from its huge head to its enormous horns, and a powerful neck is needed to hold up the heavy head and horns. A human with such a physique—usu. a wrestler, football player, or body builder—is sometimes called "Bull," like the bailiff on the TV show *Night Court.* IRCD; WNWD.

BULLPEN *a bullpen.* A large detention cell for prisoners waiting to appear in court (WNNCD: 1809); an area outside the left or right foul lines—or beyond the outfield fence—of a baseball park where pitchers warm up before being called into the game (LTA: ca. 1910). Source: BULL. WNNCD: O.E. Literally, a bullpen (or *bull pen*) is an enclosure for holding bulls before they appear at an auction or in a bullfight. Figuratively, a temporary holding tank for prisoners is called a *bullpen* because the prisoners are herded together rather than kept in individual cells. (And they are guarded by *bulls*!) The warm-up area for relief pitchers is called a *bullpen* because it was once located under a billboard advertising Bull Durham chewing tobacco. The relief pitchers for a team are also referred to as "the *bullpen.*" AID; ATWS; IRCD; NDAS. *See also* Have Someone in the Bullpen.

BULLROAR *See* Roar like a Bull.

BULL-ROARER *See* Roar like a Bull.

BULL SESSION *a bull session.* An informal gossip session (orig. for men). WNNCD: 1926. Source: BULL. WNNCD: O.E. Nowadays, both men and women participate in *bull sessions*—together or separately. The session was not named *bull* because it was for males only but because that was where people could *shoot the bull* (q.v.): i.e., engage in idle conversation without threat of recrimination. BDPF; HOI; HTB: IRCD; LTA.

BULL'S-EYE   *a bull's-eye.* A firearm target; the center of a firearm or archery target; a shot therein. IRCD: 17th cent. Source: BULL. WNNCD: O.E. Small white round targets with a solid black center were first used in firearm contests in the 17th cent., followed by large round multicolored targets with a yellow or gold center that were used in archery contests. The former were called "*bull's-eye* targets," presumably for the resemblance of the center to the large dark eye of a bull. The center of the archery target—also called a *bull's eye*—resembles the eye of a bull more than the firearm target does, because it is surrounded by a red ring, like the bloodshot eye of a defeated bull in the bullring. ATWS; EWPO; WNWD. *See also* Bull's-eye Glass; Hit the Bull's-eye; See Red.

BULL'S-EYE GLASS   Thick, circular glass. WNNCD: 1825. Source: BULL. WNNCD: O.E. *Bull's-eye glass* is so called because of its resemblance either to the eye of a bull or to the center of a "bull's-eye target." The term *bull's-eye* was first used for a small skylight in the deck of a ship. Later, it was applied to (1) a large round window on a ship or building (a *bull's-eye window*), (2) the small round window of a lantern (a *bull's-eye lantern*), and (3) the small round lens of a camera (a *bull's-eye lens*). In addition, *bull's-eye glass* is often used for translucent partitions in bars and restaurants: it resembles the bottoms of numerous beer bottles and is sometimes called "bottle glass." ATWS; BDPF; IRCD; WNWD. *See also* Bull's-eye. *Compare* Fish-eye Lens.

BULL'S-EYE LANTERN   *See* Bull's-eye Glass.

BULL'S-EYE LENS   *See* Bull's-eye Glass.

BULL'S-EYE WINDOW   *See* Bull's-eye Glass.

BULLSHIT (n)   Nonsense, lies, doubletalk, jive, "crap." WNNCD: 1915. Source: BULL. WNNCD: O.E. Literally, bullshit is the excrement of bulls: "bull manure." The word occurred in speech long before it first appeared in print, so the development of its metaphorical use is rather speculative. It was supposedly used by soldiers in the Civil War, along with the synonymous short form, *bull*, a euphemism. Besides *bull*, another euphemism, *B.S.* (the initials), appeared shortly before WWI. EWPO; IHAT; IRCD; LTA; SHM. *See also* Bullshit (v). *Compare* Chickenshit; Horseshit.

BULLSHIT (v)   *to bullshit someone.* To lie to, deceive, or mislead someone. WNNCD: 1942. Source: BULL. WNNCD: O.E. The verb *bullshit* is derived from the noun *bullshit* (WNNCD: 1915, q.v.); however, the sense of lying, deceiving, or misleading is reminiscent of the M.E. verb *bull* "to cheat" (fr. O.Fr. *bouler* "to lie boastfully"). Mod. Eng. *bull* is no longer used as a verb with this meaning. SHM.

BULLSHOT   *a bullshot.* A mixed drink made of bouillon and either gin or vodka. WNNCD: 1964. Source: BULL (?). WNNCD: O.E. This cocktail consists of a shot of clear spirits and a shot of *bouillon*, which sounds like *bull* and is usu. processed from beef. The drink is also *as strong as a bull* (q.v.). WNWD.

BULL SNAKE   *a bull snake.* A large nonpoisonous snake of North America. WNNCD: 1784. Source: BULL. WNNCD: O.E. The *bull snake* is so called because of its large size—like that of a bull compared with other bovines—not because of its speed or power or threat to others of its kind. The harmless reptile feeds primarily on rodents and is also called a "gopher snake." WNWD. *See also* Bullfinch; Bullfrog.

BULLWHIP   *a bullwhip.* A long rawhide whip with a braided lash. WNNCD: 1852. Source: BULL. WNNCD: O.E. The *bullwhip* was used by cowboys in the American West for rounding up cattle, including bulls; but the name of the whip probably relates more to its size—up to 25 feet long—than to its application to adult male bovines. The bull is one of the largest animals on the ranch, reaching a weight of over 2,000 pounds. ATWS; IRCD.

BULLY   *a bully.* A person who "picks on" or intimidates others who are smaller or weaker. Source: BULL (*). WNNCD: O.E. *Bully* is not derived from *bull* "an uncastrated adult male bovine," but its meaning has been influenced by the behavior of that animal. The true source is Du. *boel* "lover," which acquired the meaning "sweatheart"—and, later, "pimp"—when it was borrowed into English (WNNCD: 1538). However, the bull presides over its harem of cows, and it *bullies* other males that try to service them. CE; WNWD. *See also* Bully Beef.

BULLY BEEF   Corned beef. WNNCD: 1753. Source: BULL (*). WNNCD: O.E. *Bully beef* is beef, and it could very well be from a bull; but the name comes from the way in which the meat is processed. It is boiled, as the source denotes: Fr. *bouilli* "boiled beef." Besides being boiled, *bully beef* can be also pickled in *brine*, which is made from granules (or "corns") of salt. BDPF. *See also* Bully.

BULL YOUR WAY   *to bull your way through a crowd (etc.).* To force your way through a crowd (etc.). WNNCD: 1884. Source: BULL. WNNCD: O.E. The adult male bovine is a large (over one ton) and powerful animal with long horns and a nasty disposition. It can force its way through a herd of cattle—or a crowd of people—with the greatest of ease. People who shove or shoulder their way through a crowd are behaving like angry bulls. ATWS; IRCD. *See also* Bulldoze.

BULRUSH *a bulrush (or bullrush).* A large rush or sedge found along riverbanks; a cattail (Brit.); a papyrus. WNNCD: 15th cent. Source: BULL. WNNCD: O.E. The name of this aquatic plant suggests that the reeds move in the current or the wind like bulls rushing through a field of grain. However, the *bull* in *bulrush* simply alludes to the large size and strength of the stems of the plant. The baby Moses was floating in an "ark" made of bulrushes when he was found by Pharoah's daughter (Exodus 2:3–10). EWPO; WNWD.

BUM STEER *to give someone a bum steer.* To give someone bad advice. WNNCD: 1894. Source: CATTLE (?). One source, CI, attributes this expression to the American bartering or selling of a worthless steer to someone who then complains about being given a "bum steer." All of the other sources reject the expression as an animal metaphor and state that it simply refers to giving misleading directions: "steering someone wrong." CE; LTA; WNWD.

BUNNY *a bunny.* A female sports groupie. IHAT: 1960s. Source: RABBIT. The word *bunny* is a diminutive of Scottish *bun* "rabbit's tail" and has become an affectionate substitute for *rabbit*, esp. a cute little rabbit (WNNCD: 1690). The meaning was extended in the 1960s to include cute little human females who decorate surfing beaches and ski resorts without actually participating in the sports. ATWS; BDPF; EWPO; IHAT; IRCD; NDAS. *See also* Beach Bunny; Snow Bunny.

BUNNY HOP *the bunny hop.* A "snake" dance popular during WWII. CE: 1940s. Source: RABBIT. WNNCD: 14th cent. Rabbits seldom walk. Instead, they hop, even for a short distance, with the hind legs together, functioning as one. Humans dance the *bunny hop* in much the same way. The dancers form a single file, facing in the same direction, with their hands on the hips of the person in front of them. Everyone swings their right foot out and back, then their left foot out and back, and then hops forward once, backward once, and forward again three times. The pattern is then repeated. The *bunny hop* is similar to another dance, the "bunny hug," which originated ca. 1910. ATWS; IRCD. *Compare* Fox-trot; Monkey; Snake Dance.

BUNS *the buns.* The buttocks. Source: RABBIT. This slang term for the human "bottom" derives from Scottish English *bun* "rabbit, or rabbit's tail." Since rabbits are usu. seen hopping away, the analogy may be to the rabbit's posterior. ATWS. *See also* Bunny. *Compare* Ass.

BURRITO *a burrito.* A rolled tortilla filled with meat, beans, cheese, or other ingredients. WNNCD: 1957. Source: BURRO. WNNCD: 1800. A *burro* (fr. late Lat. for "small horse") is a small, thick bodied donkey that is used as a pack animal. *Burrito* (fr. Sp. *burrito* "little donkey") is a double diminutive: a small version of a small horse. But a burrito resembles neither a horse nor a donkey. WNWD.

BURROW   *to burrow.* To tunnel; to penetrate; to nestle. Source: ANIMAL. Many animals burrow in the ground to build a nest or construct a temporary shelter or permanent home. Humans *burrow* into the ground to build a tunnel; they *burrow* into the rubble to rescue survivors of an earthquake; they *burrow* into a pile of papers on their desk to find the one that is lost; they *burrow* into a crime syndicate to uncover their secrets; and they *burrow* under the covers to get some sleep. ATWS. *See also* Mole.

BURY YOUR HEAD IN THE SAND   *to bury your head in the sand.* To pretend that a crisis or threat does not really exist. IRCD: 1623. Source: OSTRICH. The ostrich, which once inhabited not only Australia and southern Africa but also India and the Middle East, was thought to bury its head in the sand when attacked, in the belief that if it could not see, it could not be seen. (Children cover their eyes for the same reason.) Also: *to hide your head in the sand, to stick your head in the sand.* ATWS; BDPF; DEI.

BUSH-HOG   *See* Brush-hog.

BUSY AS A BEAVER   *to be as busy as a beaver.* To be extremely busy, working hard and fast all the time. EWPO: early 1700s. Source: BEAVER. WNNCD: O.E. The beaver's life is not an easy one. It must cut down many trees, some of them large, along the side of the stream; it must arrange them in the form of a dam; and it must build a large lodge, with underwater entrances, before winter comes. AID; DOC; IRCD. *See also* Eager Beaver; Work like a Beaver. *Compare* Busy as a Bee.

BUSY AS A BEE   *to be as busy as a bee.* To be in constant motion. EWPO: 1387 (Chaucer's *Canterbury Tales*). Source: BEE. WNNCD: O.E. Most bees, including the queen bee, work at a feverish pace. Of the worker bees—all of them infertile females—the forager bees collect nectar and transfer it to the house bees, who convert it into honey to feed themselves, the queen, and the eggs that the queen lays. Only the male drones are idle until the time comes when they mate with the queen bee, in midair; and then they fall dead from the exertion. No human is as busy as a *busy bee.* AID; ATWS; DEI; MDWPO; NDAS. *See also* Beehive of Activity. *Compare* Busy as a Beaver.

BUSY BEE   *See* Busy as a Bee.

BUTCHER   *a butcher.* A meat dealer; a brutal murderer; a sloppy builder or repair person. WNNCD: 14th cent. Source: GOAT. A butcher was orig. a slaughterer of goats (O.Fr. *bouchier*, fr. O.E. *bucca*, an adult male goat, or "buck").

Butchers now deal in all kinds of meat, but they leave the slaughtering to slaughter houses. Criminal *butchers* engage in ruthless killing of other humans; and incompetent workers *butcher* their jobs or make a product worse off than it was when they started. DEI; EWPO; ROE; THT. *See also* Buck (n).

BUTT *See* Butt in.

BUTTERFLIES IN YOUR STOMACH *to have—or get—butterflies in your stomach.* To have or develop a nervous stomach as a result of anxiety or anticipation. Source: BUTTERFLY. WNNCD: O.E. The image in this metaphor is that of butterflies flitting about in your stomach, keeping you in a constant state of nervousness before participating in an important event, such as a speech or a performance. AID; CI; DEI. *See also* Feel the Butterflies. *Compare* Ants in Your Pants; Bats in Your Belfry.

BUTTERFLY FISH *a butterfly fish.* A brilliantly colored fish of the tropical seas; a West African freshwater fish with large, winglike pectoral fins. WNNCD: 1740. Source: BUTTERFLY. WNNCD: O.E. Butterflies are often brilliantly colored—although they are named after the color of butter: yellow—and can have a wingspan of up to 5.5 inches. *See also* Butterfly Shrimp.

BUTTERFLY SHRIMP (Also called *butterflied shrimp.*) Shrimp that have been cut down the back and split wide open before being broiled or deep-fried. WNNCD: 1954. Source: BUTTERFLY. WNNCD: O.E. The butterfly is a four-winged insect with the larger front wings overlapping the smaller rear wings. The pairs of wings are often raised, touching each other, when the butterfly is at rest; when they are lowered, they produce a beautiful display. *See also* Butterfly Fish.

BUTTERFLY STROKE *the butterfly stroke.* (Also called *the butterfly.*) A swimming stroke in which the swimmer, in a prone position, extends both arms, simultaneously, in a circular motion away from the head, while kicking with the legs together. Source: BUTTERFLY. WNNCD: O.E. The allusion is to the butterfly raising and lowering its wings while warming in the sun before its first flight of the day. *See also* Butterfly Fish; Butterfly Shrimp; Butterfly Table; Butterfly Valve. *Compare* Dolphin Kick; Porpoise (v).

BUTTERFLY TABLE *a butterfly table.* A table with hinged leaves on the perimeter ("drop leaves") that can be lowered when not in use. Source: BUTTERFLY. WNNCD: O.E. This is an upside-down metaphor: The (pairs of) wings of the butterfly are *raised*, like those of some WWII aircraft carrier planes, when not in use. The *bird* might have been a better analogue. *See also* Butterfly Shrimp; Butterfly Valve.

BUTTERFLY VALVE   *a butterfly valve*. A "double clack" valve, consisting of two "wings," on a single hinge, which rise to permit outflow (of liquid or air) but fall back in a horizontal position to prevent inflow (as in a carburetor). WNNCD: 1865. Source: BUTTERFLY. WNNCD: O.E. This is a better metaphor than *butterfly table* (q.v.), because the "wings" flap up and back, like those of the butterfly, rather than down and back. *See also* Butterfly Stroke.

BUTT HEADS   *to butt heads*. To clash. Source: SHEEP. Both goats and sheep are "butters"; but adult male goats, or "bucks," strike at each other's bodies with their short, sharp horns, while adult male sheep, or "rams," strike at each other's heads with their long, curved horns. The most spectacular head-butters are the mountain sheep, or "bighorns," which can weigh over 300 pounds, and the white Dall (or Dall's) sheep, which can weigh over 200 pounds. Football players *butt heads*, literally, when they crash into each other across a line of scrimmage; and labor negotiators and politicians *butt heads*, figuratively, when they clash over issues. *See also* Butt in.

BUTT IN   *to butt in*. To intrude. WNNCD: 1900. Source: GOAT. Goats are among the principal "butters" of the animal world, and young goats of both sexes learn to *butt* (WNNCD: 13th cent.), or strike with the head, at a very early age. People *butt in* when they interrupt other people, interfere in other people's business, or meddle in other people's affairs; and a person who does so is known as a *buttinsky* (WNNCD: 1902). *Compare* Butt Heads; Kibitz.

BUY A PIG IN A POKE   *to buy a pig in a poke*. To buy something sight unseen. MDWPO: 1562. Source: PIG. WNNCD: 13th cent. A *poke* is a burlap bag in which suckling pigs were once sold. Unscrupulous sellers sometimes substituted a cat for the pig—getting away with the fraud unless the buyer opened the bag first and *let the cat out of the bag* (q.v.). *Caveat emptor*: "Let the buyer beware." AID; BDPF; CI; DEI; DOC; HOI; ID; MDWPO; ST.

BUZZ (n)   *a buzz*. A buzzing sound (WNNCD: 1627); a signal or call; a drug-induced "high." Source: BEE. *Buzz* is an imitation of the "ZZZZZ" sound made by a swarm of bees. It is used metaphorically for the sound of a murmuring crowd (or for the "rumor" that the crowd produces), for the sound of an electric *buzzer* (q.v.) (or the "summons" that it commands), and for the sound that reportedly occurs inside the head of a consumer of alcohol or drugs (a "high"). BDPF. *See also* Buzz (v); Hum.

BUZZ (v)   *to buzz*. To make a buzzing sound (WNNCD: 14th cent.); to summon someone with a *buzzer* (q.v.); to move about quickly; to fly low over a building or a crowd of people. Source: BEE. A swarm of bees makes a "ZZZZZ" sound that is captured in English as *buzz*. All the while the bees are scurrying about, looking for a new home or attacking a human target. The *buzzing* of people by an airplane probably alludes to the *drone* (q.v.) of the engine of the early biplanes. ATWS. *See also* Buzz (n); Hum.

BUZZARDS ARE CIRCLING *The buzzards are circling.* The money-hungry heirs, creditors, and profiteers are eagerly awaiting the death of a wealthy person. Source: BUZZARD. WNNCD: 13th cent. The buzzard, or "turkey vulture," is a large scavenger bird that circles over a downed animal, waiting for it to die before eating it. *See also* Old Buzzard.

BUZZ BOMB *a buzz bomb.* A German "flying bomb" of the London Blitz of WWII. WNNCD: 1944. Source: BEE. Nazi Germany aimed two kinds of *buzz bombs* at London in the early 1940s: a V1 jet and a V2 rocket. The former made a buzzing sound like that of an angry bee, while the latter approached without warning. Swarming bees buzz loudly as they seek a new home. IHAT. *See also* Buzz (n); Buzz (v).

BUZZER *a buzzer.* An electrical signaling device. Source: BEE. A buzzer makes a buzzing sound: loud, low, and prolonged, like the sound of a swarm of bees. It is used to *buzz*, or notify, someone of a visitor, a phone call, the completion of a drying cycle, etc. It is also used in indoor sports, such as basketball and ice hockey, to signal the end of a period or a game. *See also* Buzz (v).

BUZZ OFF *Buzz off!* Get lost! Source: BEE. *Buzz off!* is a command given to both bothersome bees and annoying people. The bee is expected to fly away, buzzing as it goes; the person is expected to go away and bother someone else. Usually neither pest obeys the order nor takes kindly to it. ATWS; CE. *Compare* Bug off.

BUZZ SESSION *a buzz session.* A discussion session following a lecture, symposium, performance, film, etc. Source: BEE. The buzz session is so called because the members of the small discussion group speak in low tones in order not to disturb the other groups. The mood is friendly, like that of honeybees in the hive, rather than angry, like bees swarming in search of a new home. MDWPO. *See also* Abuzz.

BUZZWORD *a buzzword.* An important-sounding word that is used to impress others. WNNCD: 1967. Source: BEE. *Buzzwords* are used by technicians and politicians as part of the jargons of their professions. When first used, they are poorly understood by the members of the audience, but they are nevertheless adopted and repeated because they sound impressive and lend an air of sophistication. *Buzzwords* are also called "in" words, "vogue" words, "code" words, and "catch phrases." An example of a buzzword is the verb *interface* (WNNCD: 1964), which gave a computational spin to the meaning of the earlier noun, "a common boundary between two bodies, such as oil and water" (WNNCD: 1882). The *buzz* in *buzzword* comes from the fact that the word is on everybody's lips, like the buzzing in a colony of bees. CI: MDWPO; SPD. *Compare* Weasel Word.

BY LEAPS AND BOUNDS   *to grow by leaps and bounds.* To grow rapidly and beneficially. DOC: 1880s. Source: ANIMAL. Some animals not only *grow* by leaps and bounds—they also *go* by leaps and bounds. Among the more spectacular leapers and bounders are the antelope (and the deer), the rabbit (and the hare), the frog (and the toad), and the kangaroo (and the wallaby). When a business— or the productivity of a business—grows *by leaps and bounds,* it is making rapid progress, breaking records every quarter. Industries also grow this way, as do institutions and governments. AID; CI; DEI.

BY THE NAPE OF THE NECK   *to grab someone by the nape of the neck.* To grab someone by the skin on the back of the neck. Source: ANIMAL. Dogs and cats pick up their puppies and kittens in this fashion—closing their jaws on the loose fold of skin on the back of the neck, lifting them up, and carrying them back to where they belong. People sometimes pick up small dogs and cats in this way, which reduces the chance of being bitten or scratched; but the only humans who have enough skin at the back of the neck to grab are children. AID.

C

C   The third letter of the English alphabet. Source: CAMEL. The Lat. *C* was derived from the Gk. *gamma*, which came from the Phoenician *gimel*, which meant "camel." The letter represented both the K sound and the G sound until the 3rd cent. B.C. In Mod. Eng., *C* represents both the K sound and the S sound. ATWS; BDPF; EWPO. *See also* G.

CAB   *a cab.* A taxicab, or "taxi." Source: GOAT. *Cab* is short for *cabriolet* (q.v.), a light, two-wheeled carriage that was used for hire in the early-19th cent. The vehicle tended to bounce around like a goat; hence the name *cabriolet*—fr. Fr. *cabriole* (q.v.), fr. Fr. *capriole* (q.v.), fr. Lat. *caper* (q.v.) "male goat." The more stable *taxicab*, or "metered cab," came along with the advent of the automobile, in 1907. (Joke: "Call me a cab." "O.K.: You're a cab.") BDPF; ROE.

CABRIOLE (1)   *a cabriole.* A ballet leap in which one leg is extended to the side and the other brought up to strike it. WNNCD: 1805. Source: GOAT. Goats, along with sheep and antelopes, are noted for their leaping ability. *Cabriole* is an alteration of *capriole* (q.v.) "a playful leap," which is derived from Lat. *caper* (q.v.) "a male goat." The leap is performed by a male dancer and is extremely difficult to execute. WNWD. *See also* Cabriolet.

CABRIOLE (2)   *a cabriole.* The leg of a piece of furniture that cures outward, then inward, then tapers to a foot grasping a ball. Source: GOAT. Goats lack claws and are unable to grasp anything, so this is a rather fanciful metaphor. *Cabriole*—a modification of Fr. *capriole* (q.v.), fr. Lat. *caper* (q.v.) "a male goat"—may simply allude to the fact that most pieces of furniture, like most goats, have four legs. WNWD. *See also* Cabriolet.

CABRIOLET *a cabriolet.* A small convertible coupe. Source: GOAT. *Cabriolet,* the dim. of *cabriole* (q.v.), orig. referred to a small, lightweight, two-wheeled, one-horse carriage with springs and a folding top (WNNCD: 1764). It is said to have leaped around like a goat because of its unsteady nature. The convertible coupe automobile retains the size and toplessness of the carriage but has four wheels on the ground for stability. ATWS; LTA; MDWPO; ROE. *See also* Cab.

CACKLE *to cackle.* To make the characteristic sound of a chicken. WNNCD: 13th cent. Source: CHICKEN. The chicken has furnished us with many echoic words—all beginning with the letter *C*—that are imitative of its various cries. *Chick* (q.v.) itself—also called *cheep*—is both the chirp of a baby chick and the call used by humans to summon the chickens: "Here chick, chick, chick!" *Cackle* is both the cry that a hen makes after *laying an egg* (q.v.) and the chattering sound made by human gossipers. *Cluck* (WNNCD: 15th. cent.) is both what a hen does to call her chicks and what a human does, by flipping the tongue, to express satisfaction or dissatisfaction. *Chuckle* (WNNCD: 1803) is equivalent to a *coo* among chickens, but to humans it is soft, low-toned laughter. The rooster also gets into the act with *cock* (WNNCD: O.E.), as in *cock-a-doodle-doo,* and *crow* (WNNCD: O.E.), which humans do to brag about themselves. ATWS; EWPO; WNWD. *See also* Dumb Cluck.

CAGED LION *to be as nervous as a caged lion.* To be nervous, anxious, frustrated, and frantic. Source: LION. WNNCD: 12th cent. The King of Beasts does not enjoy being kept in a cage at a circus or zoo. He paces back and forth, paws at the bars, charges at the onlookers, and roars with rage. People behave much the same way when they are denied participation in an event or are delayed in their participation. CH. *Compare* Like a Caged Animal.

CAJOLE *to cajole someone into doing something.* To coax, convince, or persuade someone with flattery, nagging, or false promises. WNNCD: 1645. Source: JAY. *Cajole* is a modified borrowing of Fr. *cajoler* "to chatter like a jay in a cage" (fr. O.N.Fr. *gaiole* "bird cage"). The European jay, like the American blue jay, is a noisy, chattering "bully bird" that always seems to get its own way. ATWS; THT.

CALF *the calf of your leg.* The fleshy, muscular bulge on the upper back portion of your lower leg. IRCD: ca. 1300. Source: CALF (?). WNNCD: O.E. The dates would suggest that the *calf* of the human leg could be named after the unborn *calf* of the domestic cow—that is, while it is still a "bulge" in the mother's abdomen. However, both words are probably derived from an I.E. root meaning "to swell." (Compare O.H.G. *kalf* "calf of the cow" and O.N. *kalfi* "calf of the leg.") ATWS.

CALF EYES *to make calf eyes at someone.* To flirt with someone. Source: CALF. WNNCD: O.E. The eyes of a calf are large, innocent, and pleading (for milk). The eyes of a flirt are also large (eyebrows raised) and pleading (for sexual favors), but are not so innocent. ATWS. *Compare* Cow Eyes; Snake Eyes.

CALF FRIES   To a tourist, these are pieces of fried veal; but to a native (esp. of Texas) they are fried calf testicles—the by-product of the conversion of a bull-calf into a steer. Source: CALF. WNNCD: O.E. A calf is the offspring of a domestic cow, a wild buffalo, an elephant, or a whale. The bovine *calf* is the unfortunate basis for this metaphor. *See also* Lamb's Fries. *Compare* Mountain Oysters; Prairie Oysters; Rocky Mountain Oysters.

CALL OFF YOUR DOGS   *Call off your dogs!* Terminate the search! Source: DOG. WNNCD: O.E. This command is given to the huntsman at a foxhunt when the dogs have lost the scent of the fox or have started following an old trail or the scent of another animal. Metaphorically, it is used by the police to call off a search or investigation that is leading nowhere—and by a civilian who is being *hounded* (q.v.) by reporters, photographers, bill collectors, or the police themselves. AID; ATWS; BDPF; DEI; HTB; ST.

CAMEL   *the color camel.* A light, yellowish brown color. Source: CAMEL. WNNCD: O.E. (by way of Lat. and Gk.—of Semitic origin). The color "camel" is that of the North African or Middle Eastern dromedary (a one-humped camel)—not that of the Asian or Bactrian camel (a two-humped camel), whose coat is a darker brown. Other members of the camel family are the smaller guanaco, llama, and vicuña—all of the South American Andes. ATWS. *Compare* Buff; Canary Yellow.

CAMELOPARD   *a camelopard.* A giraffe. WNNCD: 14th cent. Source: CAMEL (WNNCD: O.E.); LEOPARD (WNNCD: 13th cent.). Before the giraffe was called a *giraffe* (WNNCD: 1594), this Central African animal—whose long neck resembles that of the *camel* (q.v.), and whose brown spots on a lighter background resemble those of the *leopard* (q.v.)—was called a *camelopard.* (Others have called it "an animal designed by a committee.") HF.

CAMEL'S HAIR   The material from which camel's hair brushes (for artists) and camel's hair coats (for patrons) are made. WNNCD: 14th cent. Source: CAMEL. WNNCD: O.E. Nowadays, *camel's hair* brushes are made of the tail hair of squirrels, and *camel's hair* coats are often made of a mixture of camel's hair and wool; but the light yellowish brown color is the same, and so is the soft texture. EWPO. *Compare* Frog Hair.

CAMEL THAT POKED ITS NOSE IN THE TENT   *the camel that poked its nose in the tent.* The thing that came back to haunt you. Source: CAMEL. WNNCD: O.E. Some things refuse to go away—like sins of the past, issues that were once thought to be settled (such as abortion and euthanasia), and camels. The one that poked its nose in the tent probably figured in a proverb or fable—now lost, but certain to return. *Compare* Go through the Eye of a Needle; Straw that Broke the Camel's Back.

CANAPÉ   *a canapé.* An appetizer consisting of a piece of bread or cracker topped with cheese spread, liverwurst, etc. WNNCD: 1890. Source: MOSQUITO. *Canapé*, the appetizer, derives from *canopy* (q.v.), the mosquito netting over a bed. Apparently, someone saw a resemblance between the pastry base and the bed, and between the tasty spread and the netting. MDWPO.

CANARD   *a canard.* A lie; a hoax; a vicious rumor; a false story. WNNCD: ca. 1864. Source: DUCK. *Canard* is French for "duck." The metaphorical meaning in English comes from the French expression *vendre un canard à moitié*: "to half-sell a duck," or "to sell a half-duck." Since it is impossible to sell half of a live duck, the seller is guilty of a half-truth: it *is* a duck, but you only get *half* of it. ATWS; BDPF; EWPO; LCRH; MDWPO; THT. *Compare* Buy a Pig in a Poke.

CANARY (1)   *a canary.* A female singer of contemporary or popular songs. IRCD: late-19th cent. Source: CANARY. (N.D.) The canary is a small yellow songbird that has been kept as a caged pet since the late-15th cent.: "a bird in a gilded cage." It enjoys singing along with piano music just as the human *canary* does. ATWS. *See also* Sing like a Canary.

CANARY (2)   *a canary.* An informer—i.e., a criminal who *squeals* (q.v.) or *rats* (q.v.) on his/her accomplices. LTA: 1940. Source: CANARY. (N.D.) The canary *bird* sings its heart out, in its little cage, for a reward of bird seed. The *human* canary sings his or her heart out, in a big "cage," for a plea bargain and a reduced sentence. ATWS; IRCD. *See also* Canary (1); Sing like a Canary. *Compare* Fink; Rat Fink; Stool Pigeon.

CANARY YELLOW   A light, pale, pastel yellow. WNNCD: 1865. Source: CANARY. (N.D.) The wild canary of the Canary Islands, off the westernmost Atlantic coast of North Africa, has a brownish-gray upper part that has been bred out in captive birds over the past half century. *Canary yellow* is now the color of the caged canary that is still a popular pet and singing companion. *Compare* Buff; Camel; Chamois.

CANCER   The fourth sign of the zodiac; the disease characterized by the uncontrolled growth of a malignancy. WNNCD: M.E. Source: CRAB. The ancient Greeks named a northern constellation *karkinos* "crab" because it resembled the eight-legged crustacean of the same name. The Roman cognate of the Greek word, *cancer*, became the basis of our Mod. Eng. name for (1) the constellation, (2) the astrological sign (capitalized), and (3) the clinical or metaphorical disease. BDPF. *See also* Crabgrass. *Compare* Canker.

CANINE APPETITE   *See* Canine Tooth.

CANINE TOOTH   *a canine tooth, or canine.* An eyetooth. WNNCD: 14th cent. Source: DOG. The noun *canine* (fr. Lat. *canis* "dog") was applied in English to the doglike cuspid before it was applied to the dog itself. The adj. *canine*, as in *a canine appetite* "a voracious appetite," did not appear until three centuries later (WNNCD: 1623). The *canine tooth* is so called because it resembles one of the four long, pointed, conical cuspids—two in the upper jaw (called *eyeteeth*) and two in the lower jaw (called "stomach teeth")—that are found in the mouth of a dog. Lat. *canis* is also the basis for the word *canary* "Island of the Dogs" (WNNCD: 1584) and may have influenced the word *cannibal* "man-eater" (WNNCD: 1553), a corruption of *Caribales* "the natives of the Caribbean Islands." BDPF; EWPO; THT.

CANKER   *a canker sore.* A spreading, ulcerlike sore in the mouth. WNNCD: 13th cent. Source: CRAB. Both *canker* and *cancer* are derived from Lat. *cancer* "crab," the eight-legged crustacean. The difference between them is that a *cancer* is malignant and uncontrolled, while a *canker* is nonmalignant and controllable (in modern times). Both words can be used metaphorically for a source of corruption or destruction. WNWD. *Compare* Cancer.

CANNIBAL   *See* Canine Tooth.

CAN OF WORMS   *a can of worms.* A source of potentially messy problems: a Pandora's box. WNNCD: 1969. Source: WORM. WNNCD: O.E. In cane pole fishing, a *can of worms* is just that: a tin can of angleworms or night crawlers for use as bait. Reaching into the wormy mess to select the next victim is bad enough, but spilling them on the deck of the boat is even worse. In or out of the can, they smell to high heaven on a hot, sultry day. AID; ATWS; LCRH; MDWPO; ST. *See also* Open a Can of Worms.

CANOPY   *a canopy.* An overhead covering—such as a netting over a bed, an awning or marquee, or the leafy top of a forest. Source: MOSQUITO. *Canopy* is from Gk. *kōnōpeion* "a mosquito or gnat." The Romans borrowed *kōnōpeion* as *conopeum* and narrowed the meaning to "mosquito netting." Since then the meaning has broadened considerably. EWPO; THT. *Compare* Canapé.

CAN'T MAKE AN OMELET WITHOUT BREAKING EGGS   *You can't make an omelet without breaking eggs.* Nothing can be accomplished without sacrifice. EWPO: 1859. Source: CHICKEN. In making an *omelet*, it is the chicken's eggs that are sacrificed; in making *coq au vin*, it is the chicken itself that must be given up. More profound endeavors involve the sacrifice of valuable time, energy, property, and even lives. BDPF; DEI.

CAPE COD TURKEY   Baked codfish. EWPO: ca. 1850. Source: TURKEY. WNNCD: 1555. The turkey is the largest American bird—four feet tall, up to 40 pounds—and has been associated with Thanksgiving ever since the Pilgrims. When hard-pressed mid-19th cent. New Englanders substituted cod for turkey at Thanksgiving time, they called it *Cape Cod turkey*. DEOD; IRCD; MDWPO. *See also* Texas Turkey. *Compare* Albany Beef; Hoover Hog; Welsh Rabbit.

CAPE HOPE SHEEP   *a Cape (Hope) sheep*. An albatross. Source: SHEEP. WNNCD: O.E. The albatross received this nickname because it "flocked" in great numbers on the Cape of Good Hope (South Africa). Unlike many other animals with disguised names, the albatross was not eaten by passing sailors, because it was regarded as a bird with mystical powers. *See also* Albatross around Your Neck. *Compare* Cape Cod Turkey; Texas Turkey.

CAPER   *a caper*. A frolic or escapade; a prank or crime. Source: GOAT. WNNCD: O.E. *Caper* comes directly from Lat. *caper* "a male goat." Goats are known for their playful leaps and bounds, and the earliest use of this noun in English described a "frolicsome leap" (WNNCD: 1592). Later, the word acquired the meaning of an unauthorized adventure, then a childish prank, and finally an illegal act or criminal case. ATWS; ROE; THT. *See also* Cab; Cabriole; Cabriolet; Capricious; Capriole; Cut a Caper.

CAPITAL   Wealth; possessions. WNNCD: 1611. Source: CATTLE. The net worth of an individual or institution is a combination of their cash and their assets. At one time, your *capital* (fr. Lat. *capitalis*) consisted only of your assets— specifically, the number of head of cattle that you owned. The association of wealth with the possession of cattle is ancient, preceding even the Greek and Roman civilizations. EWPO. *Compare* Chattel.

CAPRICE   *a caprice*. A sudden, unexpected, and unpredictable action or change of state. WNNCD: 1667. Source: HEDGEHOG. Literally, *caprice* means "hedge-hog head" (fr. It. *capo* "head" + *riccio* "hedgehog")—i.e., a head of hair suddenly standing on end as a result of fright or shock, like the spines of a hedgehog. The European hedgehog, a cousin of the American porcupine, has no spines on its head; but when it is threatened, it instantly raises the footlong quills on its back and tail. *Caprice* can also mean an impulsive action, done on a whim—something that does not fit the hedgehog's instinctive behavior but does fit the *capricious* (q.v.) behavior of the goat (Lat. *caper* "male goat"), which has also influenced the meaning of this word. ATWS; THT. *See also* Hedgehog; Prickly as a Hedgehog.

CAPRICIOUS   *to be capricious*. To be unpredictable or impulsive. WNNCD: 1601. Source: GOAT; HEDGEHOG. *Capricious* and *caprice* (q.v.) are derived from the same It. word, *capriccio*, meaning "hedgehog head," or "hair suddenly standing on end like the spines of a hedgehog." However, the meanings of both words have been influenced by the similar root *capr-*, as in Lat. *caper* "male goat" and *capra* "female goat." The "unpredictable" meaning of *capricious* comes from the frightened hedgehog, the "impulsive" meaning from the playful goat. THT; WNWD. *See also* Caper; Cut a Caper.

CAPRIOLE   *a capriole.* A playful leap by a human (WNNCD: 1594); a backward kick of the hind legs by a horse during a vertical leap. Source: GOAT. The Austrian Lippizaner horses are famous for their execution of the *capriole*, which is usu. performed without a rider. Human leaps are nothing in comparison with these. Goat leaps are somewhere in between: They leap higher than humans but lack the backward kick of the Lippizaners. WNWD. *Compare* Cabriole.

CARD SHARK   *a card shark.* A hustler who suckers others into losing their money in card games. Source: SHARK. WNNCD: 1569. Though the term was orig. *cardsharp(er)* (WNNCD: 1859), the use of *shark* as "swindler" goes back to 1599; so the 1859 usage may have been a softening, or euphemism. The *card shark* preys on other humans the way the marine shark preys on other fish. ID. *See also* Loan Shark; Pool Shark; Shark.

CARROT-AND-STICK   *a carrot-and-stick approach (or policy).* The practice of alternating reward and punishment. WNNCD: 1951. Source: DONKEY. The car- rot-and-stick approach is a practical attempt to get a stubborn donkey to move. A raw carrot, suspended on a string from the end of a pole, is dangled in front of the donkey's nose by the rider. If that doesn't work, or if the animal moves only a short way, the rider then whacks the donkey on the rump with a stick. With people and governments, the policy amounts to rewarding obedience and punishing disobedience. DEI; MDWPO; ST. *See also* Build a Fire under; Like a Carrot to a Donkey.

CASH COW   *a cash cow.* A revenue producer that never seems to run dry. Source: COW. WNNCD: O.E. A *cash cow* is analogous to a milch cow that never seems to dry up. Just as you can always count on the cow to supply milk, you can always depend on a popular product, or a rich relative, to produce money. In colleges and universities, the football program is often a *cash cow* that can be tapped to support other sports. IRCD. *Compare* Fat Cat.

CAST   *See* Cast about.

CAST ABOUT   *to cast about for something.* To conduct a random search for something or someone. Source: DOG. A tracking dog, unlike a coursing dog, follows its prey by scent rather than by sight. If the dog has lost the scent, it will cast about, or sniff around, until it picks it up again. (A pack of hunting dogs— or actors—is called a *cast*). People *cast about* for help in solving their problems, and they also *cast about* in their minds, as when they need a name to go with a face. AID; BDPF. *See also* Sniff out.

CAST PEARLS BEFORE SWINE   *to cast pearls before swine.* To give expensive gifts to persons who do not appreciate their value. Source: PIG. The expression is found in Matthew 7:6: "Give not that which is holy unto the dogs, neither cast ye your pearls before swine, lest they tramp them under their feet, and turn again and rend you." The "pearls" referred to may be of wealth or wisdom, but there is also a possibility that they may be crumbs of the eucharist bread. At any rate, the passage is from the Sermon on the Mount, and the *dog* and *swine* references are probably to the Philistines. AID; ATWS; BDPF; CI; DEI; DOC; HTB; ID; IRCD; SHM.

CAT   *a cool cat.* (Usu. male.) A *hepcat* (WNNCD: ca. 1925); a *hipster* (WNNCD: 1941); a *hippy* (WNNCD: 1953); a *cool dude.* Source: CAT. WNNCD: O.E. The original "cool cat," the *hepcat,* was a devotee of jazz music; the *hipster* became interested in fashionable clothes and drugs; the *hippy* turned away from fashion to embrace peace and communal living; the *cool dude* has reentered society to become a sophisticated, albeit streetwise, leader in the asphalt jungle. The roots *hep-* and *hip-* may derive from West African (Wolof) *hipi* "for a cat to open its eyes." ATWS; BDPF; CE; IRCD; LTA. *Compare* Alley Cat; Cathouse; Catty.

CATAMARAN   *a catamaran.* A twin-hulled boat. LTA: 1884. Source: CAT (*). WNNCD: O.E. *Catamaran* is not an animal metaphor; but because the name is often abbreviated to *cat,* the word is worthy of mention. The original *catamaran* was a log raft, with or without sails (WNNCD: 1673). The word comes from Tamil *kattumaran* "tied trees."

CAT AND MOUSE GAME   See Play Cat and Mouse.

CAT AROUND   *See* Tomcat.

CAT BURGLAR   *a cat burglar.* A "second-story man." WNNCD: 1925. Source: CAT. WNNCD: O.E. Cats are excellent climbers; however, unlike squirrels, they are unable to come down a tree headfirst: they must leap down, from limb to limb. *Cat burglars* are also excellent climbers—of tree, trellises, and drainpipes— but they are able to climb back down, feet first, after they have stolen something from the second or higher story of the house or apartment. *Second-story man* (WNNCD: 1903) was an earlier name for a *cat burglar.* ATWS; IRCD; LTA.

CATCALL   *a catcall.* A loud cry of impatience or disapproval. WNNCD: 1749. Source: CAT. WNNCD: O.E. In America, the standard cry of disapproval at a sporting event or political rally is a *boo,* which sounds more like the *moo* of an unmilked cow than the howl of a sex-starved cat. In England, the standard sound of dissatisfaction at a performance of any kind is a whistle, which sounds more like an angry parrot than a cat or any other mammal. Cats do meow a lot, and they do shriek when they are involved in a fight with another cat, but neither cry sounds much like a "catcall," British or American. EWPO states that the original *catcall* was actually a small noisemaker (like a roll-up party favor?) whose shrieking sound was eventually replaced by an unaided whistle in the 17th cent. (EWPO: 1659). ATWS; BDPF; DEI; IRCD; MDWPO. *See also* Caterwaul. *Compare* Wolf Whistle.

CATCH A CRAB *to catch a crab*. To make a faulty stroke of the oar—either missing the water completely or failing to raise the oar entirely out of the water after a deep stroke. EWPO: 19th cent. Source: CRAB. WNNCD: O.E. This expression probably arose as an excuse offered by an oarsman who slowed down the boat with a faulty stroke: "What happened?" "I caught a crab on my oar." (Crabs—aggressive, eight-legged crustaceans—*do* sometimes cling to oars.) BDPF; DEI; MDWPO. *See also* Crab; Crabby.

CATCH MORE FLIES *You can catch more flies with honey than with vinegar*. You can make more friends—sales, money, etc.—by being nice than by being mean. Source: FLY. WNNCD: O.E. Flies are attracted by anything sweet, such as honey, but are repelled by anything bitter, such as vinegar. Comrades and customers are partial to sweet talk, although it is ineffective if perceived as insincere. DOC. *See also* Draw People like Flies.

CATCHPOLE *a catchpole*. A bill collector. WNNCD: ca. 11th cent. Source: CHICKEN. In Mod. Eng., *catchpole* is a nickname for a bill collector, but in O.E. it referred to a tax collector, and in M.E. it meant an officer of the court who arrested people for nonpayment of debts. Literally, a *catchpole* is a "chicken chaser" (fr. O.N.Fr. *cache* "to catch" + *poul* "cock"). HF; WNWD.

CATCH SOMEONE OFF STRIDE *See* Take Something in Stride.

CATERPILLAR *a caterpillar*. The wormlike larva of a moth or butterfly. WNNCD: 15th cent. Source: CAT. WNNCD: O.E. A *caterpillar* bears no resemblance to an active and agile cat except for the fur, esp. on its tail. Some caterpillars, such as the "wooly bear," have a coat of brown and black hair whose density is said to predict the intensity of the coming winter; and the larva of a clothes moth actually constructs its own coat out of the wool in which it resides. Literally, *caterpillar* means "hairy cat" (fr. Lat *catta* "cat" + *pilosus* "hair"), but the *-pillar* part of the word has sometimes been confused with the root *pill-* "plunder," as in *pillage*, because many caterpillars destroy trees by stripping off their leaves. *Caterpillar* is also the nickname for the cars on a roller coaster, and is the trademark for a metal-treaded tractor whose movement resembles that of the many-legged larva. ATWS; EWPO; IRCD; ROE; THT; WNWD. *See also* Cattail.

CATERWAUL   *to caterwaul.* To argue or quarrel noisily. WNNCD: 14th cent. Source: CAT. WNNCD: O.E. The *cater* in *caterwaul* is the *tomcat* (q.v.), and the *waul* is the wail that the tomcat makes when it senses a cat in heat. When a group of male cats gather beneath the window of such a female, they perform a concert that is probably the most horrible collection of sounds ever heard. Quarreling people don't even come close to this cacophony. ATWS; HF; IRCD. *See also* Like a Cat in Heat.

CATFIGHT   *a catfight.* A physical or verbal battle between two or more women. Source: CAT. WNNCD: O.E. A feline catfight is a vicious battle between two cats—of either gender—who *make the fur fly* (q.v.). The association of the cat with the female of the human species can be seen also in *cathouse* (q.v.) and *catty* (q.v.). Catfights between either cats or humans are usually noisy and violent. DOC; NDAS. *See also* Fight like Cats and Dogs.

CATFISH   *a catfish.* A large-headed fish with four pairs of barbels, or feelers— above, below, and beside the mouth. WNNCD: 1612. Source: CAT. WNNCD: O.E. The whiskerlike barbels of this fish are the basis for its analogy to a cat, whose whiskers are much more numerous. Some people believe that the barbels are poisonous, but it is the pectoral fins of certain catfish that contain venom. IHAT. *Compare* Bullhead.

CAT GOT YOUR TONGUE   *Cat got your tongue?* Why are you so silent? DOC: 19th cent. Source: CAT. WNNCD: O.E. This question is usually asked of a shy or reticent child by a parent or other adult. The notion of a cat rendering a child speechless comes from an ancient belief that a cat can suck the breath from a sleeping child. With a young child, parents sometimes play the "cat" by placing the back of their hand on the child's face and then, while withdrawing their hand, stick the thumb between the first and second fingers, giving the appearance that they have removed the child's tongue (or nose). Nobody is fooled by this little game. AID; ATWS; DEI.

CATGUT   The material used for the strings of violins and tennis rackets. WNNCD: 1599. Source: CAT. WNNCD: O.E. Nowadays, *catgut* is likely to be made of a synthetic material, such as nylon; but in the past, the strings of musical and athletic instruments were always made of the gut, or small intestines, of animals. However, the cat was never one of these animals: the strings were made of the guts of sheep, lambs, cows, horses, and mules. The presence of *cat* in the name may be due to the fact that the strings were strong and durable and seemed to *have nine lives* (q.v.). BDPF; EWPO; IRCD.

CATHOUSE   *a cathouse.* A blue-collar house of prostitution. WNNCD: 1931. Source: CAT. WNNCD: O.E. *Cathouse* is a 20th cent. American slang term for a cheap bordello, but the association of the cat with prostitution goes back to

15th cent. England (DEOD: 1401). Cats, both male and female, are known for their sexual promiscuity, and a "loose woman" has been called an *alley cat* (q.v.) for some time. Domestic cats are not kept in separate houses, like dogs, but roam the neighborhood looking for sexual satisfaction. However, an abandoned house might very well serve as a home for stray cats, thus serving as a literal *cathouse.* ATWS; BDPF; EWPO; IRCD; NDAS. *See also* Cat around. *Compare* Chicken Ranch.

CAT IS OUT OF THE BAG *See* Let the Cat out of the Bag.

CATKIN *See* Pussy Willow.

CATLIKE *See* Move like a Cat.

CATNAP *a catnap.* A short, light sleep, esp. in the daytime. WNNCD: 1823. Source: CAT. WNNCD: O.E. Cats are light sleepers. They can doze off at any time, but the slightest sound will arouse them. *Catnap* is an extension of M.E. *nap* (same meaning), which is derived from the O.E. verb *hnappian* "to doze." For people, a *catnap* is the same thing as a nap, though perhaps briefer and shallower. ATWS; IRCD; LTA.

CAT ON A HOT TIN ROOF *to be as nervous—or as busy—as a cat on a hot tin roof.* To be uncomfortable, restless, or frantic. EWPO: ca. 1900. Source: CAT. WNNCD: O.E. The phrase was the title of a Tennessee Williams play in 1955 but originated half a cent. earlier. Tin roofs were common on farm buildings and sheds in 1900, and they got very hot during the summer. A cat on such a roof would be beside itself with anxiety, hopping up and down, trying to get off as quickly as possible. Nervous people in an analogous situation become *antsy* (q.v.) and impatient; busy people get busier and more frantic. Both the cat and the people wish they were somewhere else. ATWS; DOC; MDWPO. *Compare* Fish out of Water.

CAT-O'-NINE-TAILS *See* Room to Swing a Cat in.

CAT SCAN *a CAT scan.* A computerized imaging of soft internal tissues. WNNCD: 1975. Source: CAT (*). WNNCD: O.E. CAT is an acronym for Computerized Axial Tomography, so *CAT scan* is not an animal metaphor. However, approx. fifteen years after the name was coined, it was changed to *CT scan* (ca. 1990), for reasons unknown. The reason may have been that upon hearing the old name, children who were about to undergo the process imagined that there was a cat inside the machine that was about to look them over. At any rate, the term *CAT scan* is now obsolete, after a very short life.

CAT'S CRADLE   A children's game played with a loop of string that is formed into the shape of a cradle on the fingers of one player's hands and then passed to the other player to create a different form. WNNCD: 1768. Source: CAT (*). WNNCD: O.E. *Cat's cradle* is not an animal metaphor. The term is a folk etymological modification of 14th cent. *cratch-cradle*, the original name of the game. A *cratch*, from O.Fr. *creche* "manger," was a medieval crib for storing fodder. The open framework of the crib and the resemblance of the crib to a cradle were the inspiration for the name of the game. BDPF; EWPO; IRCD.

CAT'S-EYE   *a cat's eye.* An iridescent gemstone (WNNCD: 1599); a child's marble containing overlapping circles. Source: CAT. WNNCD: O.E. The domestic cat has unusual eyes: they glow in the dark, and the pupils consist of vertical slits rather than perfect circles. The *cat's-eye* gem is named for the rainbowlike effect of the reflection given off by the eye of the cat, while the *cat's-eye* marble is named after the shape of its pupils. (Some reptiles also have oval pupils.) ATWS; BDPF; IRCD; WNWD. *See also* Eyes like a Cat.

CAT'S MEOW   *the cat's meow.* Something special. IHAT: 1922. Source: CAT. WNNCD: O.E. "You're the cat's meow!"—as said by a man to a woman—means something like "You're a doll!" A person who *thinks* of him-/herself as the *cat's meow* has an inflated ego. The meow is one of the most defining features of a cat, and *meow* (WNNCD: 1873) is found in many of the languages of the world. An older, more British term for the cat's cry is *mew* (WNNCD: 1596). When uttered alone, esp. by one woman about another, *Meow!* means "Catty!" (q.v.). A variation of "You're the *cat's meow*" is "You're the *cat's whiskers.*" DOC; IRCD; MDWPO. *See also* Cat's Pajamas.

CAT'S PAJAMAS   *the cat's pajamas.* Something special. IHAT: 1920. Source: CAT. WNNCD: O.E. Someone who is the *cat's pajamas* is remarkably attractive or talented. A person who *thinks* of him-/herself as the *cat's pajamas* is kidding him-/herself. This expression is earlier than *cat's meow* (q.v.) and *cat's whiskers*. Cats don't wear pajamas, of course, so one that did would be something special indeed. BDPF; CI; DEI; DOC; LTA; MDWPO.

CAT'S PAW   *a cat's paw.* A dupe or pawn. Source: CAT. WNNCD: O.E. In the Aesop fable, a monkey duped a cat into letting the monkey use the cat's paw to draw hot chestnuts from the fire. The monkey got the chestnuts, and the cat got a singed paw. Since then, people who allow themselves to serve as a tool or pawn for someone else—and consequently *get burned*—have been called *cat's paws*; and doing someone else's dirty work for them has been called *pulling chestnuts out of the fire.* The term *cat's paw* is also used to describe (1) a soft breeze that barely ruffles the surface of the water (like a cat stepping lightly across it), and (2) a sailor's knot for hitching a rope to a hook suspended from a block and tackle. ATWS; BDPF; DEI; DOC; EWPO; HTB; LCRH; MDWPO; SHM.

CATSUP   Ketchup: tomato puree. WNNCD: 1690. Source: CAT (*). WNNCD: O.E. *Catsup* is not an animal metaphor: i.e., it does not refer to a *cat's supper*. Instead, it is a fancy spelling of *ketchup* on the menus of expensive restaurants. Why *cat-* replaced *ketch-* is anybody's guess, because the word has always been pronounced *ketch-up*. *Ketchup* is from Malay *kechap* "spiced fish sauce." EWPO.

CAT'S WHISKERS   *See* Cat's Meow.

CATTAIL   *a cattail*. A tall marsh reed with a soft brown furry covering near the top. WNNCD: 1548. Source: CAT. WNNCD: O.E. A *cattail* looks like a *hot dog* (q.v.) impaled lengthwise on a stick (a "corn dog"); but to the person who first named it, it must have looked like the upright tail of a very large cat wandering through the marsh. The leaves of the *cattail* plant are used for weaving chair seats and mats. IRCD. *See also* Caterpillar. *Compare* Pussy Willow.

CAT THAT ATE THE CANARY   *to look like the cat that ate—or swallowed— the canary*. To look guilty, smug, or self-satisfied. IRCD: 1871. Source: CAT; CANARY. When a canary owner returns home and finds Tabby *grinning like a Cheshire cat* (q.v.), it's a good bet that the cat has killed and eaten the canary. People who are guilty, or have just gotten away with something, usu. wear a *sheepish grin* (q.v.), while persons who are concealing a pleasant secret or are very pleased with themselves, like a cat, usu. grin from ear to ear. Cats—and people— also eat goldfish, though people don't usu. smile afterwards. AID; ATWS; DEI; LTA.

CATTLE (1)   *to be treated like (a herd of) cattle*. To be crowded into a small enclosure or herded around from place to place. Source: CATTLE. WNNCD: 13th cent. People do not enjoy being packed into an elevator, subway, room, etc., because they are being denied their "space" and their freedom. Cattle also complain about being herded into a pen in a stockyard, though that is probably due to their sense of impending doom. *Compare* Packed like Sardines.

CATTLE (2)   *to behave like (a herd of) cattle*. For people to forego their independence and move with the crowd. Source: CATTLE. WNNCD: 13th cent. All bovine animals, whether domesticated or wild, congregate in herds. However, unlike members of the deer family, which also "herd," cattle lack strong leadership. Therefore, they go wherever the rest of the herd goes. People who behave this way are sometimes contemptuously called *cattle*. *Compare* Herd Mentality; March like Lemmings.

CATTLE CALL   *a cattle call*. A mass audition of actors, dancers, musicians, etc. WNNCD: 1952. Source: CATTLE. WNNCD: 13th cent. Cattle, esp. cows, are called in from their daytime grazing in the fields by yelling "Co Boss! Co Boss!"—

perhaps from "Come Boss!" (fr. Lat. *bos*, Gk. *bous* "cow"). Performers are invited to mass auditions through advertisements and the posting of notices. NDAS.

CATTLE PROD   *a cattle prod.* An electrified stick that jolts the recipient into moving faster or in a different direction. Source: CATTLE. WNNCD: O.E. Cattle prods are used in the stockyards for moving cattle and other shorthaired livestock from pen to pen, up and down ramps, etc. The same electrified prod is sometimes used by police for controlling crowds during a riot. WNWD. *Compare* Goad.

CATTY   *to be catty; a catty remark.* For a woman to engage in malicious gossip about another woman; a spiteful remark. WNNCD: 1903. Source: CAT. WNNCD: O.E. Cats are sly, secretive, and sometimes malicious, but they don't deserve to be the basis for this metaphor. Gossipers probably do more damage than cats ever did. The proper caution to a person who has uttered a catty remark is to say *Meow!*, which means "You're being catty." ATWS; DEI; IRCD; LTA. *See also* Cat's Meow.

CATTY-CORNER   *See* Kitty-corner.

CATWALK   *a catwalk.* A narrow ledge, as around a building or on the side of a bridge. WNNCD: 1885. Source: CAT. WNNCD: O.E. A cat is a surefooted animal and can negotiate even the narrowest of ledges. A *catwalk* is a walkway that is just wide enough for a cat to walk on and therefore difficult and dangerous for people to use. A narrow hanging walkway is also called a *catwalk.* ATWS.

CAUGHT IN A TRAP   *See* Trap.

CAUGHT IN THE WEB   *See* Web of Deceit.

CAUGHT LIKE A RAT IN A TRAP   *to be caught like a rat in a trap.* To be suckered into a bad deal. Source: RAT. WNNCD: O.E. The standard *rattrap* (q.v.) is a larger version—about three times the size—of the old-fashioned mousetrap. It also is baited with cheddar cheese (called *rat trap cheese*), and the bail is also sprung when the rodent takes a nibble. ATWS.

CAUGHT NAPPING   *to be caught napping.* To be caught off guard or unprepared. Source: ANIMAL. A hunted animal is caught napping when it is discovered sleeping in its hiding place. Result: death. A person who is *caught napping* is either asleep on the job, unprepared for a sudden development, or unaware of a development that has already taken place. Result: dismissal. ST.

CAVALCADE   *a cavalcade.* A procession of vehicles, floats, ships, acts, etc. WNNCD: 1644. Source: HORSE. A cavalcade was orig. a parade of riders on horseback (fr. O.It. *cavalcate*, fr. Lat. *caballus* "horse"). Now, a parade may begin with horseback riders, but it may continue with open automobiles, decorated floats, clowns, motorcycles, bands, etc. A *cavalcade* on the water may consist of motorboats, sailboats, yachts, and tall ships; and a more metaphorical *cavalcade* may consist of a collection or succession of "stars" or star vehicles at a premiere, film festival, or benefit—or on a radio show, telethon, or awards ceremony. ATWS.

CAVIAR TO THE GENERAL *to be caviar to the general.* To be too sophisticated to be appreciated by the masses. DEI: ca. 1602 (Shakespeare's *Hamlet*, Act II, Scene 2: "The play, I remember, pleased not the million; 'twas caviary to the general"). Source: FISH. Caviar is an acquired taste: if you haven't already acquired the taste, you're probably not going to like it. The salty delicacy is processed from the roe, or eggs, of large fish, such as the sturgeon. Children sometimes refer to tapioca pudding as *fish eggs*. EWPO; MDWPO; NDAS.

CHAMELEON *a chameleon.* A "quick-change artist": a person who constantly changes his/her appearance, attitude, character, mood, or loyalty. Source: CHAMELEON. WNNCD: 14th cent. The chameleon, or "ground lion," is a lizard capable of changing the color of its skin to match that of its surroundings. *Chameleon* is a double metaphor: fr. Gk. *chamai* "ground" + *leōn* "lion." ATWS; BDPF; HF.

CHAMOIS *a chamois.* A soft, absorbent "cloth" used for washing, drying, and cleaning hard surfaces. Source: ANTELOPE. The *chamois* (WNNCD: 1560), a goatlike antelope of the mountainous parts of Europe, was the original source of the polishing cloth called a *chamois.* Nowadays, the skin of the *chamois* has pretty much been replaced by sheepskin or suedelike cotton cloth; but the tannish yellow color, also called *chamois,* has been preserved. To *chamois* a car is to wash it, dry it, and/or polish it, using a *chamois* cloth. ATWS.

CHANGE HORSES IN MIDSTREAM *to change horses in midstream.* To change leaders during a crisis; to change strategy during a campaign. Source: HORSE. WNNCD: O.E. In an address to the Republican National Convention in June 1864, President Abraham Lincoln congratulated his party for deciding not to "swap horses while crossing the river"—i.e., for not nominating someone else as the party's candidate while the Civil War was still going on. The analogy was to a rider switching horses halfway across a river—a dangerous maneuver—rather than waiting until he/she gets to the other side. The "swapping" metaphor has since been altered to *change horses in midstream* or *change horses in the middle of the stream.* AID; ATWS; BDPF; CI; DEI; EWPO; HOI; IRCD; SPD.

CHANGE OF PACE *See* Keep Pace with.

CHARLEY HORSE   *a charley horse.* A cramp in the thigh. WNNCD: 1888. Source: HORSE. *Charley horse* originated among the Chicago White Stockings baseball players in the late 1880s who likened their cramped thighs to the legs of the broken-down horse, named Charley, that pulled the roller to pack down the infield of their ballpark. (The manager at the time was Charlie Comiskey, but his first name has never been linked to the name of the affliction.) Now, anyone, including horses, can get a *charley horse*, usu. as a result of strain from overwork. AID; ATWS; EWPO; HTB; IRCD; LTA; ST.

CHASE YOUR TAIL   *to be chasing your tail.* To be getting nowhere, accomplishing nothing. Source: DOG. A dog sometimes *runs around in circles* trying to chase its own tail. The effort is usually unsuccessful and leads to further frustration for the distracted animal. Dogs—and cats—also circle around several times before lying down, perhaps *harking back* (q.v.) to the habits of their wild ancestors. Draft animals—such as the ox, horse, and mule—also go around in circles when they push the end of a wooden pole around a mill; and rabbits evade dogs by running around in circles and coming back to where they started from. People who are *going—or running—around in circles, chasing their own tails,* are wasting their time, making absolutely no progress. AID. *Compare* Run Circles around.

CHAT   *See* Chatter.

CHATTEL   Personal property—i.e., property other than real estate. WNNCD: 14th cent. Source: CATTLE. In the fiefdoms of the Middle Ages, all *real* property—land and buildings—was owned by the crown. The only thing owned by the farmer was his cattle and other livestock. Both *cattle* and *chattel* derive from M.Lat. *capitalis* "head (as in 'head of cattle') or personal property." EWPO; THT. *See also* Capital; Fee; Pecuniary.

CHATTER   *to chatter.* To talk rapidly and indistinctly (EWPO: ca. 1225); for your upper and lower teeth to strike each other repeatedly and involuntarily; for the brakes of your car to vibrate noisily when applied. Source: BIRD. Birds are the original chatterers, but squirrels and humans also utter sounds that are repetitive and meaningless. *Chat* (WNNCD: 1530) is recorded later than *chatter*, and it has a slightly different meaning ("to make small talk"); but *chat* is a close approximation to the call of certain birds, such as the magpie. When your teeth *chatter* from the cold, they sound like the incessant *chak-chak-chak* of a magpie, or the angry jawing of a squirrel. Machines *chatter* when they are not properly balanced or have defective parts. A *chatterbox* (WNNCD: 1774) is a person, not a machine, who talks incessantly. ATWS; WNWD. *See also* Chatter like a Magpie.

CHATTERBOX   *See* Chatter.

CHATTER LIKE A MAGPIE   *to chatter like a magpie.* For a child (esp.) to talk incessantly. Source: MAGPIE. WNNCD: 1605. The magpie, a rather large bird of Europe, Asia, and North America, is known for its noisy *chatter* (q.v.). In fact, the word *chatter* may derive from the call of the magpie: *chak-chak-chak.* DEI. *See also* Magpie.

CHAUVINIST PIG   *See* Male Chauvinist Pig.

CHEVAL GLASS   *a cheval glass.* A full-length mirror in a (usu.) wooden frame, on which it can be tilted vertically. WNNCD: 1828. Source: HORSE. *Cheval* is the French word for "horse." It is also used in both French and English to mean a wooden framework on which something can be supported: e.g., Eng. *sawhorse* (q.v.) and *clotheshorse* (q.v.). In the case of the *cheval horse*, what is supported is the mirror, or "glass." BDPF. *Compare* Easel.

CHEVRON   *a chevron.* An insignia worn on the upper sleeve of a military or police uniform to indicate the rank of the wearer. Source: GOAT. *Chevron* derives ultimately from the Lat. root *capr-* "goat." The connection lies in the goat's V-shaped horns, which first gave rise to Fr. *chevron* "rafter" and eventually to the modern insignia, which, however, is an inverted V. ROE; WNWD. *See also* Caper.

CHEW SOMEONE OUT   *to chew someone out.* To reprimand someone; to bawl someone out. WNNCD: 1943. Source: ANIMAL. When a drill sergeant *chews out* a buck private, the private feels like a wild animal that has fallen prey to a predator and is having its insides eaten while it is still alive. This grizzly scene has pretty much faded from the common usage of the metaphor, which can be substituted for such weaker terms as *scold* and *call on the carpet.* AID; DOC; ID. *See also* Bawl.

CHEW YOUR CUD   *See* Ruminate.

CHICK   *a (young) chick.* An attractive young woman. IRCD: 1930s. Source: CHICKEN. WNNCD: O.E. A barnyard chick is a cute and cuddly little yellow ball of down: a newly hatched or days-old baby chicken. (*Chick* is short for *chicken*, and both are imitative of the sound that chickens make.) *Chick* was used in the 19th cent. for "a foolish young *girl*." In the late 1930s, *chick*, meaning something like "a dumb blonde," came to compete with *chick* meaning "an attractive and sophisticated young *woman*": a *hip chick* or a *slick chick* (IRCD: ca. 1940). An expression that was popular in the 1950s was "The chicks are back!" ATWS; CE; IHAT; LTA; NDAS. *Compare* Bird.

CHICKEN (adj.)   *to be chicken.* To be timid, fearful, cowardly, or "yellow." WNNCD: 1941. Source: CHICKEN. WNNCD: O.E. A female chicken, or *hen* (q.v.), is protective of her baby chicks but is otherwise not aggressive like her male counterpart, the *rooster* (q.v.) or *cock* (q.v.): she would rather run away than fight. Humans who are *chicken* are reluctant to try anything that looks dangerous or illegal and seldom succumb to "dares." DEI; IRCD; LTA. *See also* Chicken (n); Chickenhearted; Chicken-livered; Chicken Outfit; Chicken Switch.

CHICKEN (n) *a chicken; the game of chicken.* A coward; the game of "dare." LTA: 1930s. Source: CHICKEN. WNNCD: O.E. Female chickens, or *hens*, unlike male chickens, or *roosters*, are not known for their aggressiveness. Humans are sometimes called *chickens* if they refuse to participate in something dangerous or back out once they have become involved. In the game of *chicken*, one person dares the other to stay the course while they are driving straight at each other on motorized vehicles. The one who swerves off at the last moment is a *chicken*. ATWS; CE; DOC; LTA. *See also* Chicken (adj.); Chicken out; Play Chicken.

CHICKEN COLONEL *a chicken colonel.* A full colonel in the U.S. Army, Air Force, or Marines. WNNCD: 1947. Source: CHICKEN. WNNCD: O.E. The insignia for a full colonel is an eagle, which is the basis for the metaphor. The term *chicken* also serves to contrast the full colonel with a lieutenant colonel, whose insignia is a silver oak leaf. The misrepresentation of an eagle as a domestic fowl can also be seen in the nickname for the WWII discharge medal: a "ruptured duck." IRCD. *See also* Chicken Outfit.

CHICKEN FEED An insignificant amount of money. WNNCD: 1836. Source: CHICKEN. WNNCD: O.E. Grain that is too small in size or poor in quality for human use is thrown on the ground for the chickens to eat. Salaries, bonuses, and profits that are meager or paltry are analogized to this "throwaway" food. People who *work for chicken feed* receive very little money for their efforts. AID; ATWS; BDPF; CI; DEI; EWPO; IRCD; LTA. *Compare* Work for Peanuts.

CHICKENHEARTED *to be chickenhearted.* To be cowardly. WNNCD: 1681. Source: CHICKEN. WNNCD: O.E. To be *chickenhearted* is to have the heart— i.e., the courage—of a chicken, which, unlike the rooster or gamecock, usu. runs away from a fight. This is the earliest of the "chicken = coward" metaphors and is even earlier than the contrasting "lion = courage" metaphor: *lionhearted* (q.v.). ATWS; BDPF; DEI; ID; LTA. *See also* Chicken (adj.); Chicken (n); Chicken-livered; Chicken out.

CHICKEN IN EVERY POT *a chicken in every pot.* Prosperity for everyone. LTA: 1928. Source: CHICKEN. WNNCD: O.E. This phrase was a slogan of the 1928 presidential campaign of Herbert Hoover, whose campaign literature urged voters to support the party that had "put a chicken in every pot" during the preceding seven years of the Republican administration. DOC; EWPO; IRCD; SPD. *See also* Rubber-chicken Circuit.

CHICKEN INSPECTOR   *a chicken inspector.* A self-appointed inspector of *chicks* (q.v.). Source: CHICKEN. WNNCD: O.E. In the early 1940s, high school boys used to flash a card with this title on it to convince innocent high school girls to allow them to conduct a "body search." The stupid trick never worked, of course, but it serves to illustrate the equation of *chicken* (or *chick* [q.v.]) with "young woman" at that time.

CHICKEN-LIVERED   *to be chicken-livered.* To be cowardly. WNNCD: 1872. Source: CHICKEN. WNNCD: O.E. *Chicken-livered* is the equivalent of the earlier *chickenhearted* (WNNCD: 1681 [q.v.]). The difference lies in where one believes courage resides: in the heart or in the liver. The female chicken, or *hen*, has the reputation of being much less aggressive than the male rooster, or *cock.* ATWS; BDPF; EWPO; IRCD. *See also* Chicken (adj.); Chicken (n); Chicken out. *Compare* Lionhearted.

CHICKEN LOBSTER   *a chicken lobster.* A lobster that weighs less than a pound. Source: CHICKEN. WNNCD: O.E. In this metaphor, *chicken* is used in the sense of "small" or "trivial"; i.e., the lobster is too small to have any commercial value. Chickens are small, of course, and when they stop producing eggs they are expendable; but the reference is probably to baby chicks, which are even smaller. IRCD. *See also* Chicken Pox; Chickenshit; Chickweed.

CHICKEN OUT   *to chicken out.* To drop out of an activity from fear or cowardice. WNNCD: 1943. Source: CHICKEN. WNNCD: O.E. Cocks, or roosters, seldom walk away from a fight, but hens, or chickens, avoid fighting and are regarded as *cowards* (q.v.). A person who wriggles out of an obligation or a dare— i.e., one who *chickens out*—is also considered a coward (or a *chicken*). This applies esp. to a participant in a game of *chicken* (q.v.) who veers off at the last moment to avoid a head-on collision. AID; ATWS; DEI; DOC; IRCD; LTA. *See also* Chicken (adj.); Chicken (n); Play Chicken.

CHICKEN OUTFIT   *A chicken outfit.* An organization that is characterized by pettiness and unnecessary discipline. WNWD: WWII military slang. Source: CHICKEN. WNNCD: O.E. In this metaphor, *chicken* is probably short for *chickenshit* (q.v.)—i.e., "as petty and worthless as manure." A *chicken outfit* was a platoon, company, battalion, division, or army that a WWII serviceperson found demeaning and wanted to get out of. Now, the term can be applied to any organization, such as a business or a college, that the member finds petty or worthless. *See also* Chicken Colonel. *Compare* Mickey Mouse.

CHICKEN POX   A contagious disease, usu. affecting children, that is characterized by numerous small eruptions on the skin. WNNCD: 1727. Source: CHICKEN. WNNCD: O.E. Children call the disease "chicken *pops,*" either by mispronunciation or because the eruptions "pop up" all over the body and then burst when scratched. The word *chicken* in the name of this herpeslike disease may simply characterize it as "trivial," at least compared with small pox; however, although the child acquires lifelong immunity to the disease, the same individual may develop the more serious "shingles" as an adult. There may also have been an influence from the pebbled appearance of the skin of a plucked chicken, which looks as if it has numerous "pimples." IRCD. *See also* Chicken Lobster; Chickenshit; Chickweed. *Compare* Goose Bumps; Gooseflesh; Goose Pimples.

CHICKEN RANCH   *a chicken ranch.* A country brothel. EWPO: early 1900s. Source: CHICKEN. WNNCD: O.E. A literal chicken ranch is a farm that is dedicated to the raising of chickens and eggs, sometimes in buildings as long as a football field. A metaphorical *chicken ranch* is a rural bordello where the farmers sometimes pay for the service with chickens. The original Chicken Ranch was made famous in the Broadway and Hollywood musical, *The Best Little Whorehouse in Texas.*

CHICKENS COME HOME TO ROOST   *The chickens always come home to roost.* Your ill words and deeds always come back to haunt you. EWPO: 1810 (Robert Southey, "The Curse of Kehama"). Source: CHICKEN. WNNCD: O.E. The original expression, a modification of Southey's line, was: "Curses, like chickens, always come home to roost." Since that time, ill deeds have joined ill words, and the modern expression is almost equivalent to "a bad penny always returns." Chickens roam the barnyard during the daytime but always come back to the henhouse at night to roost. ATWS; BDPF; CI; DEI; DOC; IRCD; MDWPO. *See also* Go to Bed with the Chickens.

CHICKEN SCRATCHES   Illegible handwriting. EWPO: 1956. Source: CHICKEN. WNNCD: O.E. A page of illegible handwriting looks like a plot of barnyard dirt that a flock of chickens has tracked up all day while scratching for food. Chicken scratches are sometimes referred to as *chicken tracks*, although the latter term is also used for the isolated—and unwanted—marks made on paper by the printer. ID. *Compare* Pedigree.

CHICKENSHIT   Petty rules and regulations. EWPO: 1930s. Source: CHICKEN. WNNCD: O.E. Chickens are the source of manure that messes up the barnyard and is worthless as fertilizer. The triviality of this by-product of chickens was transferred to petty and disagreeable military regulations in the 1930s and shortened to *chicken* during WWII. IRCD; LTA. *See also* Chicken Colonel; Chicken Outfit.

CHICKEN SWITCH   *a chicken switch.* A button or lever used by a pilot to eject from a plane—or by a laboratory subject to terminate an experiment. Source: CHICKEN. WNNCD: O.E. The *chicken* in *chicken switch* refers to the female domestic fowl, or *hen*, that is thought to be cowardly and lacking in "guts." The lab experiment is a good measure of courage, but the pilot whose plane is in trouble has no choice but to "bail out." *See also* Chicken (adj.); Chicken out.

CHICKEN TRACKS *See* Chicken Scratches.

CHICKWEED A small-leaved, tiny-flowered plant in the pink family. WNNCD: 14th cent. Source: CHICKEN. WNNCD: O.E. The *chick* in *chickweed* is an indicator of small size, like that of the baby chicks of a mother hen. It also indicates triviality and worthlessness: *Chickweed* has no value except its beauty. IRCD. *See also* Chicken Lobster; Chickenshit.

CHILI DOG *See* Hot Dog.

CHIMERA *a chimera*. A fanciful illusion; a wild scheme. Source: GOAT. In Greek mythology, a *chimera* (fr. Gk. *chimaira* "she-goat") was a fire-breathing monster with the head of a lion, the body of a goat, and the tail of a serpent. Today, a *chimera* is a monster of a different kind: a fabrication of the mind; an impossible dream. BDPF; MDWPO.

CHIPMUNK CHEEKS Protruding cheeks, such as those of a child with a mouthful of food or candy—or a baseball player with a chaw of tobacco (in one cheek at a time). Source: CHIPMUNK. WNNCD: 1832. The small North American ground squirrel uses its cheek pouches to temporarily store nuts and seeds before taking them to its underground home.

CHIVALRY IS NOT DEAD There are still some men who know how to treat a woman. Source: HORSE. Chivalry was a concept of 13th and 14th cent. romances in Western Europe—esp. in France, England, and Germany, and esp. regarding the Arthurian legend and the quest for the Holy Grail—when knighthood was in flower. A knight, or *chevalier* (lit. "horseman," fr. Fr. *cheval* "horse"), was expected to live by the code of *chivalry* (or "knighthood," fr. Fr. *chevalerie* "men on horseback"), which entailed gallantry, generosity, courtesy, and high-minded treatment of women. (Proper knights kissed only their horses, as did cowboys in later Western movies.) Chivalry was dead by the end of the 14th cent., but knighthood is still in flower when men open doors for women. BDPF; THT.

CHOMP AT THE BIT *to chomp—or champ—at the bit*. To be anxious or impatient; to be *raring to go* (q.v.). Source: HORSE. The metal *bit* is the only part of the bridle that goes in the horse's mouth—crossways, above the tongue and between the teeth, with a rein attached at either end. Horses don't like bits, and they try to get rid of them by moving them around with their tongue and biting them with their teeth. Uninformed observers of horses chomping at their bits have taken this action to be a sign of impatience to get moving, but it is actually a sign of discomfort and irritation. *Chomp* (WNNCD: 1847) is a modified form of 14th cent. *champ*. AID; ATWS; WNWD. *See also* Take the Bit.

CHOWHOUND   *See* Hound (n).

CHUBBY   *to be chubby*. To be plump or well-rounded. WNNCD: 1722. Source: FISH (*chub*: 15th cent.). A chub is a freshwater fish of the carp family that has a thick, fat, bullet-shaped head. It inhabits rivers of Northern Europe, where it is easily caught because of its slow movement. *Chubby* is an ameliorative adj. when applied to children (a "*chubby* little rascal") but a pejorative adj. when applied to adults (X is "a little *chubby*"). ATWS; EWPO; SHM.

CITY CHICKEN   Imitation chicken legs. Source: CHICKEN. WNNCD: O.E. City chicken is ground up pork and veal formed on a stick in the shape of a drumstick. (In some areas, it is a shish kebab consisting of alternating pieces of veal and pork skewered on a stick.) The *city* part of the name suggests a more elegant dish than the leg of a real chicken. *Compare* Buffalo Wings; Cape Cod Turkey; Hoover Hog; Mock Turtle Soup; Pigs in the Blanket; Texas Turkey; Welsh Rabbit.

CLAM   *a clam*. A dollar. Source: CLAM. WNNCD: 1520. The clam is a marine bivalve mollusk or freshwater mussel that is easy to catch and delicious to eat. Its hard shell, which was once used as money by Native Americans, is shaped some-what like the American silver dollar. Both facts probably contributed to the met-aphorical use of *clam* for "one dollar." ATWS. *Compare* Sawbuck.

CLAMBAKE   *a clambake*. A large gathering of friends and relatives for fun and games. WNNCD: 1835. Source: CLAM. WNNCD: 1520. The clambake was orig. a social gathering at the seashore at which clams were baked or steamed on heated rocks under seaweed. The presence of clams is no longer necessary. The most famous *clambake* was the former Bing Crosby Golf Tournament at Pebble Beach, California. ATWS; ID; NDAS. *See also* Happy as a Clam.

CLAMMY   *to be clammy*. To be cold, damp, soft, and sticky: e.g., "*clammy* hands." WNNCD: 14th cent. Source: CLAM (*). WNNCD: 1520. The word *clam*, for the marine bivalve mollusk, does not appear until more than a century after *clammy*, so the latter is not an animal metaphor. *Clammy* is probably fr. M.E. *clammen* "to smear," which is related to O.E. *claeg* "clay." IRCD. *See also* Cold Fish.

CLAMSHELL   *a clamshell*. A bucket, as for excavation or dredging, which hangs from the cables of a crane and has two hinged jaws at the bottom that can be forced together. WNNCD: 1877. Source: CLAM. WNNCD: 1520. The shell of a hard-shell clam consists of two "valves" (or half-shells) that are held tightly together except when feeding. The scallop, also a bivalve, propels itself through the water by opening and shutting its valves. The pair of doors on the bottom of a cargo plane is also called a *clamshell*. *See also* Shut up like a Clam.

CLAM UP *to clam up*. To refuse to talk. WNNCD: 1916. Source: CLAM. WNNCD: 1520. When the hard-shell clam, a bivalve mollusk, is threatened, it retracts its "neck" (or "siphon") and its "foot" into its shell and closes the two halves tightly. In this metaphor the jaws of the human are likened to the half-shells of a clam. When you feel threatened, shut your mouth. AID; ATWS; EWPO; IRCD; NDAS. *See also* Shut up like a Clam.

CLAW (n) *a claw*. The forked end of a hammer head or wrecking bar; the three- (or four-) pronged "hand" of a machine used to pick up logs, brush, or cheap prizes. Source: BIRD. The claws of a bird, unlike those of a mammal or reptile, are designed to hold onto a limb (with both feet) or to grasp a prey and pick it up (with a single foot). Most birds have one or two claws (or "toes") in back and two or three claws in front—but never more than a total of four claws on each foot. The fork at the back of the head of a *clawhammer* resembles the front claws of a bird with two front toes. The *mechanical claw* found in penny arcades consists of three evenly spaced prongs, hanging from a tiny *crane* (q.v.), that *hovers* (q.v.) over a pile of prizes on the floor of the glass box and then suddenly falls on one other than the "diamond" ring or the "gold" watch. The logger's "claw" is designed to grasp and lift, but it consists of two opposing claws on each side, as on the foot of a macaw. ST. *See also* Claw (v).

CLAW (v) *to claw your way out; to claw your way to the top*. To achieve freedom or success the hard way. Source: ANIMAL. While the senses of the noun *claw* (q.v.) derive primarily from the bird, the senses of the verb *claw* derive primarily from the mammal. A big cat that is caught in a *pitfall* (q.v.) tries to extricate itself by clawing its way up the dirt walls to the top of the hole; and a rat that is trapped in the hot or cold air system of your house tries to *claw* its way up the galvanized steel ducts to the register. Figuratively, people who find themselves in a predicament try to *claw their way out* by any means possible; and people who *claw their way to the top* manage to achieve success by working their fingers to the bone.

CLAWHAMMER *See* Claw (n).

CLAW YOUR WAY OUT *See* Claw (v).

CLAW YOUR WAY TO THE TOP *See* Claw (v).

CLAY PIGEON *a clay pigeon*. A "flying saucer" made of baked clay that is hurled into the air from a "trap" and used as a target for shotgun shooters in the sport of "skeet" (earlier called "trapshooting"). WNNCD: 1888. Source: PIGEON.

WNNCD: 14th cent. A *clay pigeon* resembles a real pigeon—the gray rock pigeon that was introduced into North America from Europe—only in its flight, which is away from the shooter at considerable speed. ATWS; IRCD; ST. *See also* Pigeon; Pigeon Has Flown. *Compare* Sitting Duck.

CLEAN AS A HOUND'S TOOTH   *to be as clean as a hound's tooth.* To be free of guilt or wrongdoing. Source: DOG. A hound's teeth, esp. its *canine teeth* (q.v.), are sparkling clean if the dog is given enough bones to chew on. Looked at from the front, the two rows of white teeth resemble the weave of *houndstooth check* (WNNCD: 1937): the pattern of angular rows of broken or jagged checks in a color contrasting with the background. DOC; IRCD.

CLEAR AWAY THE COBWEBS   *to clear away the cobwebs.* To clear your head—after waking up from a fitful sleep or suffering a hangover—by splashing cold water on your face or downing your first cup of coffee. Source: SPIDER. Spiders spin their webs in dark, deserted places. When you enter these places, your progress is impeded—and your vision obscured—by the cobwebs, which you must brush aside to proceed. BDPF; MDWPO. *See also* Cobwebs in Your Head; Spider's Web.

CLEVER AS A FOX   *See* Sly as a Fox.

CLIMB LIKE A MONKEY   *to climb like a monkey.* For a child—a *little monkey* (q.v.)—to climb and swing on a *jungle gym* (q.v.) with the greatest of ease. Source: MONKEY. WNNCD: ca. 1530. Monkeys—the nonanthropoid or "tailed" primates—are arboreal, spending most of their time in trees: climbing with great speed and agility and swinging from limb to limb, or "brachiating." Tarzan, a human primate, is probably the most famous brachiator, however. *See also* Monkey Bars.

CLING LIKE A LEECH   *to cling (to someone) like a leech.* To attach yourself to someone in a condition of total dependency. Source: LEECH. WNNCD: O.E. The *leech* (q.v.), or *bloodsucker* (q.v.), clings to a fish by means of its suckers and lives off the blood until the fish dies. Human waders are also attacked by leeches, and they find them very difficult to remove. DEI. *See also* Stick to Someone like a Leech.

CLIP SOMEONE'S WINGS   *to clip someone's wings.* To curtail someone's power; to "ground" a child. Source: CHICKEN. All chickens are domesticated, and they all get their wings—or at least one of their wings—clipped to prevent them from *flying the coop* (q.v.). People who abuse their privileges or exceed their power *have their wings clipped* by less drastic means: children are "grounded," and politicians are censured or recalled. AID; ATWS; BDPF; CI; DEI.

CLOSE ON SOMEONE'S HEELS   *See* In Hot Pursuit.

CLOTHESHORSE   *a clotheshorse.* A man's clothes rack (WNNCD: 1775); a female "fashion plate." Source: HORSE. WNNCD: O.E. Originally, a clotheshorse was a small wooden framework—consisting of a pedestal, a post, and a hanger—on which a man's clothes could be hung for donning on the following morning. The post was sometimes topped by a horse's head, but the *clotheshorse* was so called because it was a small wooden framework, like the woodsman's *sawhorse* (q.v.). Later, the name was also applied to a stylish woman who wore a different outfit every day and looked like the pictures in a fashion magazine. CH. *See also* Cheval Glass. *Compare* Easel.

CLOUD-CUCKOO-LAND   An impractical or unrealistic scheme or design. WNNCD: 1899. Source: CUCKOO. WNNCD: 13th cent. In Aristophanes' play, *The Birds* (ca. 400 B.C.), the birds erected a city in the air, Cloud-cuckoo-land, where everything was perfect. It has become the model for a foolish undertaking. Cuckoo birds are associated with craziness because of their monotonous call (*kuk-kuk*) and their habit of laying their eggs in the nests of other birds. CI; DOC. *See also* Cuckoo (adj.); Cuckoo (n); Cuckoo's Nest.

CLUMSY AS AN OX   *to be as clumsy as an ox.* To be extremely clumsy. Source: OX. WNNCD: O.E. The ox—a steer that is used as a draft animal—has probably gained its reputation for clumsiness from its comparison with the horse. Horses run and race, and prance and gallop. Oxen plod. Horses respond to jerks on the reins. Oxen respond to goads. Even bulls—noncastrated male bovines—are regarded as clumsy. CE. *See also* Bull in a China Shop.

CLUTCH (n) (1)   *a clutch.* A grasp; power or control; a critical situation. Source: ANIMAL. An animal's *clutch* (WNNCD: 13th cent.) is the seizure of something in its claws. A human *clutch* is the seizure of something in your hands (e.g., a *clutch bag*) or the possession of power or control over someone else (e.g., to *have someone in your clutches*). An automobile *clutch* is a mechanical device for disengaging or engaging the engine; and a sports *clutch* is a critical situation in which a *clutch hitter*—i.e., one who is *good in the clutch*—is expected to *come through in the clutch*—i.e., get a *clutch hit.* ATWS. *See also* Clutch (v).

CLUTCH (n) (2)   *a clutch.* A small group of children. Source: CHICKEN. A literal *clutch* (WNNCD: 1721) is a *brood* (q.v.) of baby chicks, numbering up to approx. a dozen. A metaphorical *clutch* consists of the children of a single family or a group of children under the supervision of an adult: e.g., a *clutch* of four-year-olds. The word is not related to the verb *clutch* (q.v.), "to grab a handful of something."

CLUTCH (v)   *to clutch.* To "choke." Source: ANIMAL. A *clutch* is a critical situation in a sports event. If a participant fails to come through with a pass or hit a basket or make a goal that should have been made, he/she is said to have *clutched*, or "choked." That is, the athlete behaves as though a predator has seized him/her by the throat and deprived him/her of the oxygen necessary to perform the act. The symbol for such a failure, often made by the athlete him-/herself, is the grasping of the throat with the thumb and fingers of one hand. The noun *clutch* derives from the verb *clutch* (WNNCD: O.E.). *See also* Clutch (n) (1).

CLUTCH BAG   *See* Clutch (n) (1).

CLUTCH HIT   *See* Clutch (n) (1).

CLUTCH HITTER   *See* Clutch (n) (1).

COBWEBS IN YOUR HEAD   *to have cobwebs in your head.* For your mind to be filled with confusion, doubts, disorder, or too many bad memories. Source: SPIDER. A *cobweb* (WNNCD: 14th cent.) is a web that the spider (M.E. *coppe*) spins in dark, deserted places to trap insects. A confused mind is one that is cluttered with too many random thoughts to make any sense. ATWS. *See also* Clear away the Cobwebs.

COCCYX   *the coccyx.* The tailbone of a human (or anthropoid ape). WNNCD: 1615. Source: CUCKOO. WNNCD: 13th cent. The bill of the cuckoo bird (Gk. *kakkyx*) is not straight but curves downward. The lower part of the spinal column of a human curves outward, terminating in the tailbone. Why the Greeks picked the cuckoo as the model for this condition is uncertain, since many birds—e.g., the wrens and warblers—have curved beaks.

COCK (n)   *a cock.* A spout, tap, valve, or faucet for controlling the flow of liquid or gas; a hammer in the lock of a firearm that causes the release of the firing pin or discharge of the percussion cap. Source: COCK. WNNCD: O.E. Both the faucet and the hammer are compared to the shape of the head and comb of a cock, or rooster. A *petcock* (WNNCD: 1864—perhaps fr. *petite* + *cock*) is a small *cock*, or shut-off valve. ATWS; HF; IRCD; WNWD. *See also* Cock (v).

COCK (v)   *to cock something.* To draw back the hammer of a firearm; to skew the position of your hat, your head, a part of your head, or your arm. Source: COCK. WNNCD: O.E. When the hammer of a firearm is drawn back, it looks like the profile of the head and comb of a cock, or rooster. This change in attitude, like turning the valve of a *cock* (q.v.), is reflected in the metaphors *cock your arm*, *cock your ears*, *cock your eye*, *cock your hat*, and *cock your head*—all of which *see*. ATWS; IRCD.

COCKADE *a cockade.* An ornament, such as a rosette or *panache* (q.v.), worn on a cap or hat. WNNCD: 1709. Source: COCK. WNNCD: O.E. The *cockade* orig. indicated a person's rank, office, or honor; but now, in the form of a single feather in a hatband, it serves merely as a decoration. The term is based on Fr. *cocarde* "vain," which is derived from Fr. *coq* "cock" (fr. O.E. *cocc*). The metaphor alludes to the *crest* (q.v.) or *coxcomb* (q.v.) of a cock or rooster. IRCD. *Compare* Feather in Your Cap.

COCK-AND-BULL STORY *a cock-and-bull story.* A tall or farfetched tale: a *canard* (q.v.). WNNCD: 1795. Source: COCK; BULL. WNNCD: O.E. The *cock-and-bull story* probably derives from a classical (e.g., Aesop), medieval (e.g., Chaucer), or early modern (e.g., La Fontaine) animal fable about a cock and a bull, but such a tale has never been found. In its absence, attempts have been made to link the phrase with a tavern by the same name—or with two taverns, each with one of the names—in which tall tales were told by the inebriated customers. This search has been more successful, but the incredible nature of the stories most likely suggests an old animal fable in which a cock and a bull debate their sexual prowess and dominance over their competition. AID; ATWS; BDPF; CI; DEI; DOC; EWPO; HOI; IRCD; LTA; MDWPO; NDAS; SHM. *Compare* Shaggy-dog Story.

COCKBOAT *a cockboat, or cock.* A small boat, kept aboard a ship for rowing the captain ashore. WNNCD: 15th cent. Source: COCK. WNNCD: O.E. The *cockboat* is so called either because it is so small, compared to the size of the ship, or because it is reserved for the captain, the master of the ship. The helmsman of a cockboat is its *coxswain* (q.v.), "cock's swain." EWPO; HF.

COCKEYED *to be cockeyed.* To be cross-eyed, crooked (like a picture), or crazy (like an idea). WNNCD: 1821. Source: COCK. WNNCD: O.E. A cock, or rooster, is not cross-eyed—i.e., with eyes turned inward—but it does *cock its head* (q.v.) when looking with one eye at something too close for it to see with both eyes. This tilting of the head is the basis for the application of *cockeyed* to a crooked picture or a crazy idea. (The opposite of *cockeyed* is *walleyed*.) ATWS; BDPF; IRCD; ST. *See also* Cock (v).

COCKFIGHT *a cockfight.* A skirmish between two lightweight combatants who are unlikely to do much harm to each other. Source: COCK. WNNCD: O.E. The combatants in a *real* cockfight are expected to maim or even kill each other. Gamecocks are small, but they are armed with metal spurs on the back part of their lower legs. Though the action is not as loud and vicious as that of a *dogfight* (q.v.), it is sufficient to attract gamblers and spectators in large numbers. Cockfighting was practiced in ancient Greece and Rome and now is probably the most universal of all games involving animals. BDPF; ST. *See also* Bantam Rooster; Bantamweight.

COCKHORSE *to ride a cockhorse.* For a child to ride either (1) a *rocking horse* (WNNCD: 1540), (2) a *hobbyhorse* (WNNCD: 1557), or (3) an adult's foot. Source: COCK; HORSE. WNNCD: O.E. In the rocking horse and hobbyhorse metaphors, *cock* refers to a male horse. In the "foot" metaphor, *cock* refers to the crossed (or "cocked") leg of the adult on whose foot the child is "riding." BDPF; HF; WNWD. *See also* Cock (v).

COCKLE *a cockle finish.* A puckered finish on expensive stationery. WNNCD: 15th cent. Source: COCKLE. WNNCD: 14th cent. The uneven nature of the finish on expensive paper is analogous to the surface of the shells of a bivalve mollusk, such as a cockle or *scallop* (q.v.), which has raised, bumpy ribs. WNWD.

COCK OF THE WALK *to think you're the cock of the walk.* To imagine yourself to be the most important person in an organization: to be conceited or overbearing. DAE: 1835. Source: COCK. WNNCD: O.E. On the farm, the cock, or rooster, not only *rules the roost* (q.v.), or chicken coop, but dominates the *walk*, or chicken yard. No other cock is allowed to enter the walk, where the chickens feed and breed. ATWS; BDPF; CI; DEI; DOC; EWPO; HOI; SHM; ST. *See also* Cocksure; Cocky.

COCKPIT *a cockpit.* The place where the pilot/driver of an airplane, speedboat, or racing car sits. ATWS: WWI. Source: COCK. WNNCD: O.E. The pilot of a WWI fighter plane sat in an open cockpit, as do the drivers of Indy-type racers and the pilots/drivers of most speedboats, but the term *cockpit* applies also to the *enclosed* cabin of a modern airplane, racing boat, or racing car. Literally, a cockpit is the *pit* in which *gamecocks* fight at a *cockfight* (q.v.)—now illegal in most parts of the United States. It's where the action is. In its earliest use as a metaphor (Prologue to Shakespeare's *Henry V*, 1599), *cockpit* referred to a battlefield; and Belgium has since been referred to as "the *cockpit* of Europe" because so many battles have been fought there. The earliest application of *cockpit* to a vehicle was for the cabin of a ship (SHM: ca. 1700). BDPF; EWPO; IRCD; LCRH; MDWPO; ST. *See also* Pit Stop.

COCKROACH *a cockroach.* A wood louse: a large nocturnal insect that infests homes, esp. where food or water is present, and is extremely difficult to eradicate. WNNCD: 1623. Source: COCK; CATERPILLAR. *Cockroach* is a folk etymology of Sp. *cucaracha,* lit. "caterpillar roach." A *cockroach* is neither a cock nor a caterpillar, so this is a double metaphor. The cockroach was first attested to in English by Captain John Smith of the Virginia Colony. IHAT; WNWD.

COCKSURE *to be cocksure.* To be boldly self-confident. WNNCD: 1603. Source: COCK. WNNCD: O.E. To be *cocksure* is to be as sure and determined as a cock—the rooster that crows every morning at the break of day. However, the meaning of the word has been influenced by the meanings of such analogues of *cock* as (1) the *petcock* that secures the liquid in a barrel, and (2) the cocked hammer that prevents a firearm from discharging. *Cocksure* also implies conceit and arrogance. ATWS; BDPF; EWPO; HF; IRCD; ST. *See also* Cock (n); Cocky.

COCKTAIL   *a cocktail*. A before-dinner mixed drink; an early-in-the-dinner cup of fruit. WNNCD: 1806. Source: COCK. WNNCD: O.E. It is not certain how the tail of a cock has come to be associated with an aperitif or an appetizer. While it is true that gamecocks in training were once fed a mixture of ale and liquor, called *cockale*, and that the winner of a cockfight—i.e., the one with the most tailfeathers left—was once toasted with a drink, the most likely source seems to be either (1) the *cocktailings*, or leftovers, from various bottles of wine or liquor, or (2) the folk etymologizing of Fr. *coquetel* "mixed-wine drink" or Aztec *xochitl* "cactus juice." The fruit cup may derive from Fr. *coquetier* "egg cup." BDPF; EWPO; HF; IRCD; LTA; SHM. *Compare* Cold Duck; Rooster Tail.

COCKY   *to be cocky*. To be conceited, arrogant, and overbearing. WNNCD: 1768. Source: COCK; WNNCD: O.E. On the farm, the cock, or rooster, *rules the roost* (q.v.) with a brash self-confidence—announcing the break of day, having the run of the females, chasing away the other males, eating whatever and wherever he wants, and generally playing the role of *cock of the walk* (q.v.) to the hilt. He is the embodiment of *machismo*. ATWS; ID; IRCD; LCRH; ST. *See also* Cocksure.

COCK YOUR ARM   *to cock your arm (or wrist)*. To bend your arm and draw it back, possibly with a bent wrist, in preparation for throwing a baseball or football. Source: COCK. WNNCD: O.E. *Cocking* the arm or wrist derives from the action of *cocking* a firearm—i.e., altering its position so that it resembles the angular profile of the head and comb of a cock, or rooster. *See also* Cock (v); Cock Your Ears; Cock Your Eye; Cock Your Hat; Cock Your Head.

COCK YOUR EARS   *to cock your ears*. To prick up your ears. Source: COCK. WNNCD: O.E. Dogs and cats prick up their ears when they hear a far-off sound. Horses and mules not only prick up their ears but can rotate them 180 degrees for better coverage. Humans can neither prick up nor rotate their ears; instead, they turn their head so that their better ear "faces" the sound. ATWS; BDPF. *See also* Cock (v); Cock Your Arm; Cock Your Hat; Cock Your Head.

COCK YOUR EYE   *See* Cock Your Head.

COCK YOUR HAT   *to cock your hat*. To wear your hat on the side of your head. Source: COCK. WNNCD: O.E. *Cocking your hat* is a means of calling attention to yourself or revealing a *cocky* (q.v.) attitude. The analogy is the same as that for *cocking* your arm, ears, or head: you are altering the position of something so that it resembles the profile of the head and—in this case "crestfallen"—comb of a cock. ATWS; BDPF. *See also* Cock (v); Cock Your Arm; Cock Your Ears; Cock Your Head.

COCK YOUR HEAD   *to cock your head (and/or eye)*. To tilt your head sideways, while at the same time closing one eye. Source: COCK. WNNCD: O.E. This is the instinctive behavior of a bird—such as a cock, or cock robin—when looking at something too close for it to see with both eyes. The robin also cocks its head to improve its hearing of a worm moving in the ground. For the human, it is an act of questioning, doubting, or puzzling. BDPF; DEI. *See also* Cock (v); Cockeyed; Cock Your Arm; Cock Your Ears; Cock Your Hat.

COCK YOUR WRIST   *See* Cock Your Arm.

COCOON (n)   *a cocoon*. A protective covering used to *mothball* (q.v.) military equipment; a physical or psychological retreat from society. Source: INSECT. An insect larva protects itself with an envelope of silken filament—a *cocoon* (q.v.)— during its pupal stage. Humans protect military equipment in a similar way, and they sometimes retreat from society—either physically (to their place of abode) or psychologically (to a state of depression). ATWS; WNWD. *See also* Cocoon (v); Cocooning; Cocoon Stage.

COCOON (v)   *to cocoon something*. To protect something—such as inactive military equipment—in a envelope of waterproof cloth or plastic. WNNCD: 1881. Source: INSECT. The larva of an insect spins an envelope of silken filament to protect itself during its pupal stage. Humans protect their unused military equipment in a similar way—covering it with a tarpaulin or spraying it with plastic. *See also* Cocoon (n); Cocooning; Cocoon Stage. *Compare* Mothball (v).

COCOONING   Withdrawing from society to a physical retreat. Source: INSECT. Insects cover themselves in a coat of silken filament to protect themselves during their pupal stage. Humans—esp. couples—sometimes protect themselves from society by holing up in their house, apartment, etc., for an extended period of relaxation or lovemaking. *See also* Cocoon (n); Cocoon Stage.

COCOON STAGE   *in the cocoon stage*. In its infancy: e.g., an idea that is "in its cocoon stage." Source: INSECT. The stages of an insect metamorphosis are egg, larva, pupa, and adult. The pupa is the "cocoon stage," in which the larva covers itself in a protective envelope of silk, from which the adult will eventually emerge. An idea is in the *cocoon stage* when it is still rather fuzzy and undeveloped. *See also* Cocoon (n); Cocoon (v).

CODA   *See* Queue.

CODFISH ARISTOCRACY   *the codfish aristocracy.* (A derogatory term.) The nouveau riche of mid-19th cent. Boston whose wealth came from the codfishing industry. HTB: ca. 1850. Source: COD. WNNCD: 14th cent. The codfish, or *cod*, is a major food fish of the North Atlantic. The commonplace nature of the fish may have contributed to the ridicule of those profiting from it—like junk dealers in the 20th cent. EWPO.

CODPIECE   *a codpiece.* A flap of cloth attached to the front of men's breeches to conceal the opening. WNNCD: 15th cent. Source: COD (*). WNNCD: 14th cent. The term suggests a codfish hung from the belt in this area, but this is not an animal metaphor: the source is M.E. *cod* "scrotum." The modern term is *fly* (q.v.).

COLD AS A MACKEREL   *to be as cold as a mackerel.* To be dead—or feel dead to the touch. Source: MACKEREL. WNNCD: 14th cent. The Atlantic mackerel is a cold-blooded animal, and when it is pulled from the water it feels cold to the human touch. Any common fish would have served for this metaphor. *See also* Cold-blooded; Cold Fish; Dead as a Mackerel.

COLD-BLOODED   *to be cold-blooded.* To be without mercy. WNNCD: 1595. Source: FISH (*). Technically, this is not an animal metaphor, since the adjective was applied to cold-blooded murderers—who murder *in cold blood*—before it was applied to fish (or reptiles). Technically, also, fish are not cold-blooded, because their body temperature adjusts to the temperature of the surrounding water; and in very warm water their temperature can be as high as that of a human. At any rate, *cold-blooded* is a metaphor for lack of kindness and consideration in humans. It is also applied to persons who are unusually sensitive to the cold. BDPF. *See also* Cold as a Mackerel; Cold Fish.

COLD DUCK   A blend of two sparkling wines: burgundy and champagne. WNNCD: 1969. Source: DUCK. WNNCD: O.E. *Cold duck* is a loan translation of Ger. *kalte Ente*, "cold duck," which MDWPO reports is a modification of Ger. *kalte Ende*, "cold end." The speculation is that waiters made it a practice to pour the leftover wine from champagne and burgundy bottles into a single bottle, creating a new mixture that they called *kalte Ende* but later changed to *kalte Ente*, "cold duck."

COLD FISH   *a cold fish.* A person who is without warmth or feelings. WNNCD: 1924. Source: FISH. WNNCD: O.E. A cold fish is a *dead fish* (q.v.); however, since fish are *cold-blooded* (q.v.), they often warm up in the bottom of the boat or creel after being caught. Nevertheless, a person who is a *cold fish* might as well be dead, because he/she finds no comfort in, or friendship for, other humans. You can identify such a person by the handshake: if it feels like you're holding a dead fish in your hand, you have just shaken hands with a *cold fish*. AID; BDPF; DEI; NDAS. *See also* Cold as a Mackerel.

COLD SHOULDER   *to give someone the cold shoulder.* To show indifference to or snub someone. WNNCD: 1816. Source: SHEEP. Nowadays, women give the *cold shoulder* to the unwanted advances of men; but in the early 19th cent. hostesses actually gave a cold shoulder of mutton to unwanted guests, at least according to Sir Walter Scott, who first recorded this practice. EWPO; WNWD.

COLD TURKEY   *to quit cold turkey.* To terminate the use of an addictive substance—e.g., alcohol, drugs, tobacco—abruptly, without gradual withdrawal. IRCD: ca. 1920. Source: TURKEY. WNNCD: 1555. The reference to *turkey* is unclear. It may be to the blunt language associated with *talking turkey* (q.v.), or it may be that the *goose bumps* (q.v.) on a shivering addict resemble the skin of a plucked turkey. ATWS; DOC; LCRH; LTA; NDAS. *Compare* Cold Duck.

COLTISH   *to be coltish.* To be frisky, frolicsome, or playful; to be uninhibited or undisciplined. WNNCD: 14th cent. Source: HORSE. Colts, or young male horses, are able to stand soon after birth, and they spend the rest of their youthful lives learning how to run and play and get in all sorts of trouble. An elderly person (esp. a male) is said to be *coltish* when he sheds his inhibitions and begins to behave *like a young colt* or becomes *as frisky as a young colt. Coltish* behavior in younger persons is seen as a sign of lack of discipline or control. ATWS; BDPF; GTP; IRCD.

COLUMBINE   *a columbine.* A plant of the buttercup family whose red, white, or blue flower has irregular, spurred petals. WNNCD: 14th cent. Source: DOVE. *Columbine* means "like a dove" (fr. Lat. *columba* "dove"). Medieval Europeans thought that the cluster of petals on the flower looked like a flock of (white) doves. ATWS; EWPO. *Compare* Palomino.

COME A CROPPER   *to come a cropper.* To suffer a misfortune, failure, or defeat. WNNCD: 1858. Source: HORSE. Originally, this expression meant to "fall off a horse"—i.e., to fall over the horse's neck, or *cropper*. Figuratively, *to come a cropper* means to suffer a serious loss of fortune, position, or reputation. A related expression, to *fall neck and crop*, meaning "to suffer a complete failure," orig. referred to the horse, not the rider. In such a fall the horse fell down completely—from its neck to its *crop* (or "rump"), where the whip, or *crop*, falls. AID; CI; DOC; EWPO; MDWPO; SOED; ST.

COME BACK TO THE FIELD   *See* Pull away from the Field.

COME DOWN WITH THE BUG   *See* Bug (n) (3).

COME HOME TO ROOST   *See* Chickens Come Home to Roost.

COME IN LIKE A LAMB   *If March comes in like a lamb, it will go out like a lion.* If the weather at the beginning of the month of March is clement, the weather at the end of the month will be inclement—and vice versa. Source: LAMB (WNNCD: O.E.); LION (WNNCD: 12th cent.). This is an old farmer's tale, based on the meek and gentle nature of the lamb, and the bold and ferocious nature of the lion. BDPF. *See also* Bold as a Lion; Gentle as a Lamb; Meek as a Lamb.

COME IN LIKE A LION   *See* Come in like a Lamb.

COME OFF IT   *See* Get on Your High Horse.

COME OFF YOUR PERCH   *See* Perch.

COME OUT OF THE WOODWORK   *to come out of the woodwork.* To come out of nowhere. Source: COCKROACH. WNNCD: 1623. You win the lottery and all sorts of shirttail relatives and "friends" start *coming out of the woodwork* to get their share. Cockroaches lit. come of the the woodwork at night to get their share of leftover food and drink, esp. in the kitchen area of the home. *See also* Cockroach.

COME OUT OF YOUR SHELL   *to come out of your shell.* To lose your inhibitions or end a period of withdrawal from society. Source: SNAIL; TORTOISE. The land snail retreats into its shell when threatened; when the threat passes, it can emerge either partially or completely. The tortoise, or land turtle, can retract its head, legs, and tail into its shell in times of danger, but it is permanently attached to its shell and cannot emerge completely. To *draw someone out of their shell* is to successfully encourage someone to loosen up or reenter society. BDPF; DEI. *Compare* Break out of Your Shell.

COME STRAIGHT FROM THE HORSE'S MOUTH   *See* Straight from the Horse's Mouth.

COME THROUGH IN THE CLUTCH   *See* Clutch (n) (1).

COME TO THE END OF YOUR TETHER   *See* End of Your Tether.

CONGREGATE   *to congregate.* To gather together; to assemble as a group. WNNCD: 15th cent. Source: ANIMAL. Most *hoofed* animals congregate as a *herd* (q.v.); most *feathered* animals—and sheep—congregate as a *flock* (q.v.). The root of the verb *congregate* is Lat. *greg-* (or *grex*) "herd or flock," and the Lat. verb *congregare* means "to come together as a herd or flock." People congregate when they form a group or a crowd; and a *congregation* (WNNCD: 14th cent.) is the membership of a church—i.e., the minister's (or "shepherd's") *flock*. People who enjoy the company of other people with similar interests are said to be *gregarious* (WNNCD: 1668)—i.e., they tend to flock together, like *birds of a feather*. An *aggregate* (WNNCD: 15th cent.) is the sum total of the parts that make up a mass; and in the construction business, *aggregate* is the loose sand and gravel that is mixed with cement and water to form concrete. To *segregate* (WNNCD: 1542) is to set some of the group apart from the rest; and to be *egregious* (WNNCD: 1578) is to stand out from the rest of the crowd by being conspicuously bad—e.g., an *egregious error*. LCRH; MDWPO; THT. *See also* Herd (n); Herd (v); Rise above the Herd.

CONGREGATION   *See* Congregate.

CONSTABLE   *a constable*. A police officer below the rank of sergeant (Brit.); a peace officer below the rank of sheriff (Amer.). Source: HORSE. *Constable* derives from late Lat. *comes stabuli* "master of the stable." In medieval France, *constable* came to be applied to the head of the royal cavalry, and later to the head of the entire army. In medieval England, *constable* was applied to an officer of the royal household, and later to a warden of a castle or fortified town. Now, the connotation of "horse keeper" has been lost completely. ATWS; THT.

COO   *to coo*. For a baby (usu. between three and six months of age) to make soft, murmuring sounds of pleasure—as opposed to the earlier cries of hunger (etc.) and the later sounds of babbling. WNNCD: 1670. Source: DOVE; PIGEON. Doves and pigeons *coo* (an imitative word), as do young lovers (to each other) and parents (to their young infants). ATWS. *See also* Bill and Coo.

COOK SOMEONE'S GOOSE   *to cook someone's goose*. To get revenge on someone. DOC: 1851. Source: GOOSE. WNNCD: O.E. Most sources believe that this expression is based on the fable of the goose that laid the golden eggs. The greedy and impatient farmer killed the goose, expecting to find a cache of golden eggs inside; but there were none. All he could salvage was the goose itself, which he had for dinner. He had *cooked his own goose!* AID; ATWS; BDPF; CI; DEI; EWPO; HOI; LCRH; LTA; SHM. *See also* Gone Goose; Goose Is Cooked; Kill the Goose that Laid the Golden Eggs.

COOL YOUR HEELS   *to cool your heels*. To wait, or be forced to wait. Source: HORSE. A horse doesn't have "heels," but it does have fetlocks, which are comparable to human heels. (A horse doesn't have fingers or toes, either, but the hooves are comparable to combined fingernails/toenails.) After a long hot trip, a horse's metal shoes become overheated, in turn causing the hooves to become overheated. The remedy is to let the horse rest, esp. in the shade, or to let it stand in shallow water for a period of time. People "get hot" *because* they are made to wait, whether out of neglect or by design. A VIP sometimes lets a not very important person wait just to emphasize his/her superiority. MDWPO.

COON'S AGE   *not in a coon's age.* Not for a very long time. ("I haven't seen you in a coon's age.") WNNCD: 1844. Source: RACCOON. WNNCD: 1608. The raccoon (or *coon*: 1742) is a masked, ring-tailed mammal of North America. It was once thought to live for a very long time, but its life span is actually only a dozen years or so. This is still a long time not to see a friend. AID; ATWS; BDPF; DOC; EWPO; IRCD. *Compare* Since Hector Was a Pup.

COOP   *a coop.* A place of confinement. Source: CHICKEN. A coop was orig. a wicket pen in which chickens (or geese) were confined at night to roost (WNNCD: 14th cent.). The modern coop is either a pole barn with sides of *chicken wire* (q.v.) or a long, enclosed building, as on a *chicken ranch* (q.v.). As a place of confinement for humans, *coop* usu. refers to a prison, a jail, or a holding cell in a police station. ATWS. *See also* Cooped up; Fly the Coop.

COOPED UP   *to be cooped up.* To be confined in a small or crowded space. WNNCD: 1563. Source: CHICKEN. Chickens are cooped up at night, in a *coop* (q.v.), to roost and lay eggs. Humans who are *cooped up* feel as if they're locked in a chicken coop with hundreds of their own kind. This feeling of claustrophobia occurs in crowded elevators, crowded cars (esp. coupes?), and snowbound homes, where the condition is known as *cabin fever*. *See also* Fly the Coop; Nobody here but Us Chickens.

COPPERHEAD   *a copperhead.* A Northerner, or a Southerner living in the North, who sympathized with the Confederacy during the Civil War. SPD: 1860s. Source: SNAKE. The *copperhead* snake (WNNCD: 1775) is a poisonous viper, with a copper-colored head, that inhabits the eastern and central United States, although it is primarily identified with the South. It is related to the *rattlesnake* (q.v.) but lacks the rattles, so it strikes without warning. The human *copperhead*—the term is still in use—is a traitor to his/her group: a *maverick* (q.v.). ATWS; LCRH. *Compare* Gypsy Moth.

COPYCAT   *a copycat.* A mimic or impressionist. WNNCD: 1896. Source: CAT. WNNCD: O.E. Unlike monkeys and parrots, cats are not good mimics of other animals and show little interest in copying the gestures or sounds of humans. Therefore, the cat appears in this metaphor more for the alliteration than for the sense. However, humans are very good *copycats*, as seen in music, painting, fashion, architecture, etc. A *copycat killer* is one who kills in imitation of an earlier murderer, and a *copycat crime* is one that is inspired by and mimics a crime committed earlier. In the 1970s there was a TV show called *The Copycats* that consisted of sketches by famous impressionists. AID; ATWS; DEI; IRCD; LTA; NDAS. *Compare* Monkey See, Monkey Do.

COPYCAT CRIME *See* Copycat.

COPYCAT KILLER *See* Copycat.

COQUET *See* Coquetry.

COQUETRY Flirtation. WNNCD: 1656. Source: COCK. WNNCD: O.E. Literally, *coquetry* is "strutting like a little rooster"—fr. Fr. *coquet* (WNNCD: 1691) "a male flirt," the dim. of Fr. *coq* "cock." Oddly enough, the earliest of the "flirtacious" words to come into English from French was *coquette* (WNNCD: 1611) "a female flirt"; so a *coquette* is "a female flirt who struts around like a male flirt." The cock, of course, is known for its amorous advances and swaggering behavior. ATWS; WNWD.

COQUETTE *See* Coquetry.

CORMORANT *a cormorant.* A greedy or gluttonous person. Source: RAVEN. *Cormorant* is a double metaphor. First, the cormorant is named for the raven (Lat. *corvus marinus* "raven of the sea") and is also called a "crow duck" and a "water turkey." The similarity to the raven is the black coloring; the similarity to the duck is the webbed feet; and the similarity to the turkey is the large size. Second, the feeding habits of the cormorant contribute to the human metaphor. Cormorants are diving birds, and they feed primarily on fish. They are such good fishers that in the Far East they are employed for that purpose; and in the Galapagos they walk directly into the water, without flying in. People who can't get enough of anything, including food, are like the cormorant.

CORN DOG *See* Hot Dog.

CORNET *See* Horn.

CORRAL *to corral something.* To contain a brush fire; to round up votes for a candidate; to rope in a job. Source: ANIMAL. A *corral* (WNNCD: 1582) is an enclosure for holding livestock, such as cows and horses. To *corral* livestock is to drive them into such an enclosure (WNNCD: 1847). When people *corral* fires, voters, or jobs, they round them up and *rope them in* (q.v.), as if they were wild horses or domestic cattle. WNWD.

CORRODE *See* Erode.

COUNT NOSES *to count noses.* To count the number of persons present. Source: HORSE. WNNCD: O.E. For some strange reason, horses are counted by the nose, while cattle are counted by the entire head (e.g., "six *head* of cattle"). Since each animal has only one head and one nose, the system works; but it would work just as well to count tails—or to count eyes or ears and divide by two. BDPF.

COUNT SHEEP   *to count sheep.* To attempt to induce sleep through mental gymnastics. Source: SHEEP. WNNCD: O.E. Some insomniacs try to induce sleep by counting imaginary sheep jumping over an imaginary fence: one, two, three, zzzzz. (The sheep was probably selected for this metaphor because it is soft, cuddly, and nonthreatening.) Others work multiplication problems or try to remember the names of all their friends: one, two, three, zzzzz.

COUNT YOUR CHICKENS   *See* Don't Count Your Chickens before They Hatch.

COVER YOUR TRACKS   *to cover (up) your tracks.* To conceal evidence of your movements or activities. DAE: 1865. Source: FOX. The fox covers its tracks in a fox hunt by doubling back (or *backtracking* [q.v.]) on its own tracks, by running in the tracks of another animal, or by running in or across a stream. Humans cover their tracks, literally, by dragging a leafy branch behind them, or, figuratively, by establishing a personal, paper, or electronic alibi. DEI; ST. *See also* Throw Someone off the Track.

COVEY   *a covey.* A small group or cluster. Source: BIRD. A *covey* of birds (WNNCD: 14th cent.—fr. O.Fr. *cover* "to sit on or brood") is a family or small flock of birds. A *covey of critics* is either a congregation of critics or a small number of individual critics. Terms of assembly are often alliterative when applied to humans: e.g., *a bevy of beauties.*

COW (n)   Milk or cream; a large, untidy, or unattractive woman. Source: COW. WNNCD: O.E. To order some *cow* is to ask for a glass of milk or some cream for your coffee—a case of metonymy, or "whole for the part." To call a woman a *cow,* however, is just plain bad taste, regardless of how unappealing she is. The bovine cow is fat, flabby, and filthy, and it is regarded as loose, stupid, and easily *cowed* (q.v.). The term *cow* is also applied to adult females among nonbovine animals whose adult males are called *bulls:* elephants, moose, and whales. ATWS; IRCD; NDAS; WNWD.

COW (v)   *to cow someone.* To intimidate someone. WNNCD: 1605. Source: COW (*). WNNCD: O.E. To *cow* someone is to make that person *cower* with fear, but neither verb is derived from the name of the bovine. Cow (v) comes from O.N. *kuga* "to subdue," and *cower* comes from O.N. *kura* "to be afraid." However, the timidity of the cow has influenced the meaning of both words. WNWD. *Compare* Coward.

COWARD   *See* Tail between Your Legs.

COWCATCHER   *a cowcatcher.* A plow-shaped apparatus on the front of a locomotive (WNNCD: 1838); a "secondary" commercial just before a radio or TV program. Source: COW. WNNCD: O.E. *Cowcatchers* were orig. designed to clear cows off the tracks, killing them in the process; but now they are more likely to encounter cars and trucks. The media *cowcatcher* is analogous to the plowlike apparatus in that it occurs before the primary object: the sponsoring commercial. ATWS.

COW COLLEGE   *a cow college.* An agricultural land-grant college or university (WNNCD: 1913); a provincial college or university that lacks sophistication and culture. Source: COW. WNNCD: O.E. Land-grant colleges were established in 1862 with a grant of land from the Federal Government and a mission to teach agricultural subjects, such as the raising of cattle. Many of them still exist, and retain the word *State* in their title—e.g., Michigan State University, formerly Michigan State Agricultural College. *Cow college,* at first a nickname for such institutions, has broadened its meaning to include younger, less traditional colleges that may be located in rural areas but offer no instruction in agriculture whatsoever. IRCD; WNWD. *See also* Cow Town.

COWER   *See* Cow (v).

COW-EYED   *See* Cow Eyes.

COW EYES   Large, dark, beautiful, innocent eyes. Source: COW. WNNCD: O.E. In the *Iliad,* Homer described Hera, the wife-sister of Zeus, as "the *cow-eyed Hera*"—a flattering description. To *make cow eyes* at someone is to entice someone with a wide-eyed, innocent expression. Cows are regarded as stupid and ugly, but most people agree that they have beautiful eyes. WNWD. *Compare* Buckeye; Bull's-eye; Sheep's Eyes.

COWLICK   *a cowlick.* A patch of hair, usu. at the back of the head, that grows in all directions, or in a direction different from that of the other hair. WNNCD: 1598. Source: COW. WNNCD: O.E. A cow licks its hair by turning its head and neck to one side, sticking out its long tongue, and reaching an itch about one-third of the way back on its body. The result is a swirl of hair pointing in all directions. The cow's *cowlick* is temporary; the human's is permanent. ATWS; BDPF; IRCD; MDWPO.

COWSLIP   *a cowslip.* A wildflower of the buttercup family that is called "primrose" in England and "marsh marigold" in the United States. WNNCD: O.E. Source: COW. WNNCD: O.E. The *cowslip* is so called not because its yellow or purple flower resembles the lip of a cow but because the plant is usu. found growing in cow dung (O.E. *cu* "cow" + *slyppe* "dung"). The name *marigold* (*Mary*

+ *gold*) reflects the yellowish variety of the wildflower. EWPO; HF; IRCD; MDWPO.

COW TOWN   *a cow town*. A small rural town. Source: COW. WNNCD: O.E. The original cow town was a town from which cattle were shipped, or a city where cattle were marketed (WNNCD: 1885). *Cow town* now suggests the provincial setting of a peaceful little town where cattle may once have roamed but no longer necessarily do so. IRCD. *See also* Cow College.

COXCOMB   *a coxcomb*. A conceited fool. Source: COCK. WNNCD: O.E. Literally, a *coxcomb* is the red *comb*, or "crest," of a *cock*, or "rooster." The metaphor was first applied to the drooping, red-striped cap of a court jester, or "fool" (WNNCD: 1573). Then it was applied to anyone who acted like a fool; and later it was applied to a silly, vain, or conceited person. ATWS; BDPF; HF; IRCD. *See also* Cockade; Crest; Crestfallen.

COXSWAIN   *a coxswain*. The helmsman of a small boat; the "conductor" of a racing shell. Source: COCK. WNNCD: O.E. A coxswain was orig. the *swain*, or "servant," who steered the *cock*, or *cockboat* (q.v.), that took the captain to and from the ship and shore. Now, a *coxswain* is the steersman of any boat—or the person in the back seat of a shell who faces forward and calls out the rhythm to the scullers. EWPO; HF; WNWD.

COYOTE   *You coyote!* You dirty rotten scoundrel! Source: COYOTE. WNNCD: 1759. The coyote, a smaller cousin of the American wolf, inhabits the western states, where it preys on stray sheep and calves, and has earned the hatred of livestock ranchers. Human *coyotes* may also rustle livestock, but they are more likely to be caught cheating at cards. ATWS.

CRAB (n)   *a crab*. ("Don't be such a crab!") A cranky, disagreeable, irritable, or ill-tempered person. WNNCD: 1580. Source: CRAB. WNNCD: O.E. The crab is a crustacean that can hang on stubbornly, with its eight legs and two pincers, when anything tries to dislodge it. It also has a crooked, sideways walk and a disagreeable nature. ATWS; BDPF; IRCD; LTA. *See also* Catch a Crab; Crab Apple; Crabby.

CRAB (v)   *to crab about something*. To carp, complain, or *grouse* (q.v.) about something. IRCD: ca. 1810. Source: CRAB. WNNCD: O.E. The crab, an eight-legged crustacean with two menacing pincers extending from the front of its round shell, is rather odd in both appearance and behavior. Its sideways method of locomotion has inspired a word for an airplane flying at an angle in a crosswind: to *crab*. ATWS; NDAS. *See also* Crab (n); Crab Apple; Crabby.

CRAB APPLE   *a crab apple.* The small, sour, multicolored fruit of the wild crab apple tree. WNNCD: 1712. Source: CRAB. WNNCD: O.E. The metaphor is based on the odd appearance and disagreeable nature of the crab, a crustacean with four pairs of legs and a pair of claws radiating from its round shell. The crab walks sideways, hides in the shells of other shellfish, and clings stubbornly to something when caught. *See also* Crab (n); Crab (v); Crabby.

CRABBED   *to be crabbed* (two syllables): *e.g., crabbed handwriting.* To be so small or intricate as to be difficult to decipher. WNNCD: 14th cent. Source: CRAB. WNNCD: O.E. The crab has a reputation for being difficult to figure out. It nests in the shells of other, larger crustaceans; it looks menacing with its eight legs and two pincers; and it walks sideways and leaves an unusual track. ATWS; IRCD. *See also* Crab (n); Crab (v); Crab Apple. *Compare* Chicken Scratches; Pedigree.

CRABBY   *to be crabby.* To be bad-tempered, cranky, disagreeable, or sour. WNNCD: 1776. Source: CRAB. WNNCD: O.E. The crab, a crustacean, is often described as being "cross-current and contradiction," partly because of its sideways or angular locomotion and partly because it is stubborn and even malicious. Armed with menacing claws, it invades the shells of other crustaceans, leaving only when it feels like it. ATWS; EWPO; IRCD. *See also* Crab (n); Crab (v); Crab Apple.

CRAB GRASS   A pesky grass that sends forth many stems, spreads rapidly, and is hard to eradicate; it is regarded as a "weed" by most homeowners. WNNCD: 1743. Source: CRAB. WNNCD: O.E. This grass is named for the crab because of the many appendages radiating from a central source. The crab, which has ten appendages, has the same undesirable reputation among other marine animals as the grass does on land. WNWD. *See also* Crab (n); Crabbed; Crabby.

CRAB LOUSE   *a crab louse.* A sucking louse that inhabits the pubic areas of the human body and creates considerable discomfort. WNNCD: 1547. Source: CRAB. WNNCD: O.E. The metaphor is based on the fact that the tiny louse bears a strong resemblance—in number of legs and overall shape—to the crustacean known as a *crab.* A person who is infested with *crab lice* is said to have (the) *crabs.* IRCD; WNWD. *See also* Crab (n).

CRABS   *See* Crab Louse.

CRANBERRY   *a cranberry.* The small, hard, red fruit of the cranberry bush. WNNCD: 1647. Source: CRANE. WNNCD: O.E. *Cranberry* is an altered borrowing of Low Ger. *kraanbere* (fr. *kraan* "crane" + *bere* "berry"). The *cranberry* is named after the crane because its flower resembles a crane's head and neck. The crane is a tall wading bird with long thin legs and a long neck. It frequents wetlands such as *cranberry* bogs. EWPO; HF. *See also* Crane. *Compare* Crowberry; Gooseberry.

CRANE *a crane.* An elevated girder—either vertical or horizontal—equipped for lifting heavy objects at a construction site. Source: CRANE. WNNCD: O.E. The crane is a large wading bird with long thin legs and a very long neck. The metaphor is based on the resemblance of the motorized vertical crane not only to the long neck of the bird but to the head and beak as well. ATWS; EWPO; IRCD; LCRH. *See also* Crane Your Neck.

CRANESBILL *a cranesbill.* A geranium plant or flower. WNNCD: 1548. Source: CRANE. WNNCD: O.E. The *cranesbill*, or *crane's-bill*, is named for the long bill of the European crane, which resembles the long beak of the seed pods of the geranium plant. (The word *geranium* meant "little crane" in Classical Greek.) WNWD. *See also* Crane; Crane Your Neck.

CRANE YOUR NECK *to crane your neck.* To stretch and twist your neck in order to get a better view. IRCD: 18th cent. Source: CRANE. WNNCD: O.E. The crane, the largest of the wading birds, stands almost five feet tall and has an excellent view of everything that goes on in the marshes. Humans wish they had a crane's long neck when they are stuck in a crowd. ATWS; LCRH. *See also* Crane.

CRAWFISH *to crawfish.* To retreat from a position. WNNCD: 1842. Source: FISH. WNNCD: O.E. Although a crawfish—or *crawdad* or *crayfish* (q.v.)—is not a "true" fish, it is popularly classified as a *shellfish*. The metaphor is based on the fact that all lobsterlike crustaceans, including the crawfish, have the capability of moving rapidly backward by forcing their large, flexible tail downward, again and again, until they have retreated from danger. Politicians who back away from a stated position or a campaign promise are said to *crawfish* on those issues. LCRH. *Compare* Backtrack.

CRAWL INTO YOUR SHELL *to crawl into—or retreat into—your shell.* To become reclusive and uncommunicative: to withdraw from society. Source: SNAIL. The land snail is able to withdraw entirely from its shell—or it may withdraw partially and drag the shell along behind. However, if the snail senses danger or bad weather, it backs completely into its shell until the unpleasantness passes. (The hermit crab crawls backwards into an empty snail shell and adopts it as its home.) ATWS; BDPF. *See also* Withdraw into Your Shell. *Compare* Come out of Your Shell.

CRAWL UNDER A ROCK *to feel like crawling under a rock.* To feel embarrassed, chagrined, or mortified. Source: ANIMAL. Some small animals—such as bugs, lizards, and worms—crawl under a rock when they are preyed upon. For example, the Berber's skink, a foot-long lizard of North Africa, hides under a stone when it is pursued or alarmed. People have no such alternative, but they often hide their face in their hands when they are humiliated or shocked. A person who *looks like something that just crawled out from under a rock* is sometimes told to "Crawl back under your rock!" The expression *to leave no stone unturned*—i.e., to conduct a careful search—may derive from hunting for fishing worms under rocks. *Compare* Bury Your Head in the Sand.

CRAYFISH   *a crayfish.* A small, lobsterlike, freshwater, crustacean; a large, lobsterlike, marine crustacean. WNNCD: 14th cent. Source: FISH. WNNCD: O.E. *Crayfish* is a folk etymological interpretation of M.Fr. *crevice* "crab," which was probably a modified borrowing of O.H.G. *Krebiz*, with the same meaning. An alternative form, *crawfish* (q.v.), appeared in England in 1624; and a Gulf coast regional form, *crawdad*, appeared in American English in the 19th cent. A freshwater *crayfish* has large claws, like a lobster, while the saltwater *crayfish*—a *rock lobster* (ca. 1884) or *spiny lobster* (WNNCD: 1819)—has miniscule claws. Neither crustacean is a crab, however, and neither is a true "fish." EWPO; WNWD.

CRAZY AS A BEDBUG   *to be as crazy as a bedbug.* To be mentally unstable, totally irrational, or insane. LTA: 1832. Source: BEDBUG. WNNCD: 1808. Bedbugs aren't "crazy," but they cause humans to become so—attacking them in their beds and sucking their blood. ATWS; IHAT. *See also* Don't Let the Bedbugs Bite. *Compare* Crazy as a Coot; Crazy as a Loon.

CRAZY AS A COOT   *to be as crazy as a coot.* To be completely insane. IRCD: 16th cent. Source: COOT. WNNCD: 14th cent. The eccentric behavior of the coot, a ducklike bird, occurs during the breeding season, when the male flaps its wings, sits on its tail, and slashes out with its claws. Only the female coot makes any sense of these actions. CE; DOC; EWPO. *See also* Old Coot. *Compare* Crazy as a Bedbug; Crazy as a Loon.

CRAZY AS A LOON   *to be as crazy as a loon.* To be comically deranged. IHAT: 1832. Source: LOON. WNNCD: 1634. The loon (fr. Du. *loen*) is a ducklike bird with a daggerlike bill. Its craziness stems from its awkwardness on land (its legs are set far back for diving), its need to run on top of the water to become airborne, and its maniacal nighttime cry. AID; ATWS; ID; SHM. *Compare* Crazy as a Bedbug; Crazy as a Coot.

CRAZY LIKE A FOX   *to be crazy like a fox.* To appear crazy but really be clever, cunning, and sly. DOC: 1944 (the title of a book by S. J. Perelman). Source: FOX. WNNCD: O.E. The "crazy" things that a fox does to outwit the hounds, like running in streams and on top of stone walls, are not crazy at all but quite intelligent—and often quite successful. IRCD. *See also* Cunning as a Fox; Sly as a Fox. *Compare* Know a Hawk from a Handsaw.

CREATURE COMFORTS   The basic needs of life: food, drink, warmth, security, etc. WNNCD: 1659. Source: ANIMAL. Creature comforts are those things that are necessary to sustain the life of all "creatures"—both animals (i.e., lower animals) and humans. The phrase is used almost apologetically, as if it were embarrassing for humans to be identified with wild animals, such as *predators* (q.v.), and farm animals, such as *beasts of burden* (q.v.). A *creature of habit* is a person whose life is totally predictable, like the daily, seasonal, and lifetime routine of a lower animal, which is based on genes and conditioning rather than rational decision-making. DEI.

CREATURE OF HABIT   *See* Creature Comforts.

CREEP   *a creep*. A disgusting, obnoxious, or frightening person. Source: INSECT. A *creep* is someone who is *creepy* (q.v.) or gives you the *creeps* (q.v.): i.e., someone who reminds you of a crawling insect. The thought of an insect crawling over your skin is the basis for the term *creep show*, "a scary movie or play," one that causes you to shiver with fear. LCRH.

CREEPS   *for something to give you the creeps*. For something to give you a feeling of apprehension or horror. Source: INSECT. Having an insect crawling over your skin can cause your flesh to "creep." It is an unpleasant and distressing sensation, usu. followed by shuddering, scratching, and shedding of clothing. A human who causes the same reaction is called a *creep* (q.v.), and a frightening film or play is called a *creep show*. LCRH. *See also* Creepy.

CREEP SHOW   *See* Creeps.

CREEPY   *to be creepy*. To be frightening or revolting. WNNCD: 1831. Source: INSECT. The sensation of one or more insects crawling unnoticed over your skin is enough to cause your flesh to crawl in response. The same reaction can be caused by a scary story, film, or play—or even an obnoxious acquaintance—all of which can be called *creepy*. *See also* Creep; Creeps.

CREST (n)   *a crest*. The highest part of a hill, wave, drama, musical composition, etc. Source: COCK. The fleshy red matter on top of the head of a *cock* (q.v.) is called its *crest* (WNNCD: 14th cent.) or its *coxcomb* (q.v.). The name of this topmost part of the cock has become a metaphor for the highest point of just about anything—from physical phenomena (e.g., ridges and peaks) to psychological phenomena (e.g., climaxes and culminations). *Crest* has also been applied to a decoration on the top of a human head: the *cockade* (q.v.), plume, or rosette on a hat or cap. The verb *crest* is derived from the noun *crest*. ATWS.

CREST (v)   *See* Crest (n).

CRESTFALLEN   *to be crestfallen.* To be dejected, defeated, or humiliated. Source: COCK. The metaphor is based on the drooping crest, or *comb*, of a cock, esp. that of a gamecock that has gotten the worst of it in a cockfight. It was first applied, metaphorically, to the drooping cap, or *coxcomb* (q.v.), of a court jester but now applies to anyone who hangs his/her head in shame. ATWS; ID; ST. *See also* Crest (n).

CRICKET (1)   *the game of cricket.* The British counterpart to American baseball. WNNCD: 1598. Source: CRICKET. 14th cent. *Cricket* is much older than baseball, has two goals (each with a goal stake, or "wicket"), uses more players, and seems to go on forever. However, both games use a ball and involve a pitcher (or "bowler") throwing the ball at a batter (or "batsman"). The name of the game derives from the name of the insect (M.E. *criket*, fr. M.Fr. *criquet*), which is of imitative origin. The resemblance is between the sound of the bat hitting the ball and the "chirp" produced by a male cricket rubbing its wings together. ST. *See also* Cricket (2); Not Cricket.

CRICKET (2)   *a cricket.* A child's toy. Source: CRICKET. WNNCD: 14th cent. A child's *cricket* is a small metal dome, often painted to look like a beetle, with a flexible steel band attached underneath. When the band is pressed with the thumb, a sharp click (or "crick") can be heard, delighting the child and terrifying the parents. The sound made by the toy is similar to, but louder than, the sound produced by the male insect rubbing its wings together. *See also* Cricket (1).

CRIMSON   *the color crimson.* A deep purplish red or scarlet color. WNNCD: 15th cent. Source: INSECT; WORM. The ultimate source of *crimson* is Skt. *krmi* "worm," which added the meaning "insect" when it spread to Arabic and Latin. The insect in question is the *kermes*, or "scale insect," which inhabits Mediterranean oaks. When killed, dried, and crushed, it produces a dark red dye. EWPO. *Compare* Vermilion.

CROAK   *to croak.* To die. Source: FROG. The "death rattle" of a dying human somewhat resembles the deep, throaty, gurgling sound of a frog's *croak* (WNNCD: 15th cent.)—at least enough to have produced this metaphor. The verb is also used to describe the hoarse voice of a living person. ATWS; BDPF. *See also* Frog in Your Throat.

CROAK LIKE A FROG   *See* Frog in Your Throat.

CROCODILE   *a crocodile.* A reptile of tropical and subtropical Africa, southeast Asia, and northern Australia: the largest of the crocodilians. WNNCD: 14th cent. Source: WORM. The ancient Greeks perceived the crocodile (fr. Gk. *krokodilos* "lizard") as a "shingle or pebble worm" (fr. Gk. *kroke* "shingle or pebble" + *drilos* "worm")—the former because of its armored plates and gravel haunts, and the latter because of its long, sinuous body and tail. (The Nile crocodile can attain a length of 20 feet.) ATWS; EWPO; LTA. *See also* Crocodile Tears. *Compare* Alligator.

CROCODILE TEARS *to shed crocodile tears.* To feign sorrow. WNNCD: 1563. Source: CROCODILE. WNNCD: 14th cent. The sorrow is false because, contrary to what world traveler Sir John Mandeville wrote in 1400, the crocodile cannot shed tears while eating its victims, nor does it moan or cry to lure them to its lair. The crocodile is the largest of the legged reptiles—up to 20 feet in length—and inhabits the continents of Africa, Asia, and Australia. AID; ATWS; BDPF; CI; DEI; DOC; EWPO; HOI; ID; IRCD; LCRH; MDWPO; SHM.

CROOKED AS A DOG'S HIND LEG *See* Dogleg.

CROON *to croon.* To sing a popular song—esp. a ballad—in a soft, gentle voice. Source: BULL. It's a long road from the bellowing of Scottish bulls (Scottish *croon* "to bellow") to the relaxed singing of America's most famous *crooner*, Bing Crosby; but that's the road this word has taken. Crosby's *crooning* was more like the lowing of cattle than the bellowing of bulls. Elvis Presley also *crooned* a few romantic ballads. EWPO. *Compare* Bellow.

CROONER *See* Croon.

CROSS AS A BEAR *to be as cross as a bear.* To be in a bad mood: peevish, angry, ill-tempered, *disgruntled* (q.v.). LTA: 1840s. Source: BEAR. WNNCD: O.E. The phrase is short for "to be as cross—or angry—as a bear with a sore head," which is a modification of "like a bear with a sore head" (WNNCD: 1824). The word *sorehead* (WNNCD: 1848), a person with the above qualities, comes from the same source. How did the bear get a sore head? Possibly by being shot in the head by a hunter, or being bitten on the head by a prey; or perhaps by being bitten by dogs while chained to a stake, in the ancient sport of "bear-baiting." But the most likely source is by sticking its head in a hollow tree to get honey—an act that was engineered by Reynard the Fox in a medieval animal fable. ATWS; DEI; EWPO; HTB; IRCD.

CROW *to crow about something.* To brag about your own victory or gloat about your opponent's defeat. Source: COCK. It is ironic that the name of the cry of the admired cock (or rooster) and the name of the much-despised crow (or raven) come from the same O.E. verb, *crawan* "to crow." (The crow actually *caws* rather than *crows*.) The rooster is the barnyard's alarm clock, exultantly crowing the break of day; and the gamecock is said to crow over his fallen opponent after a victory in the cockpit. Humans *crow* about anything that they are proud of. ATWS; BDPF; EWPO; IRCD.

CROWBAR   *a crowbar.* A long black iron or steel bar with a point at one end and a wedge at the other—used as a prying tool. WNNCD: 1748. Source: CROW. WNNCD: O.E. The *crowbar* was probably so named because it was all black and had a beaklike point at one end—like the crow. However, the modern *wrecking bar* (WNNCD: 1943), a much smaller and lighter prying bar, looks much more like a crow, because one end is curved and has a notch, like a claw. ATWS; EWPO; HF; IRCD; MDWPO; WNWD. *See also* Crowfoot.

CROWBERRY   *a crowberry.* An evergreen alpine shrub, or its fruit. WNNCD: 1597. Source: CROW. WNNCD: O.E. The fruit of the *crowberry* is black. That is about the only resemblance that the shrub has to a crow, unless the crow regarded the tasteless berry as a delicacy back in the 16th cent. Modern crows eat almost anything, from berries to bunnies. *Compare* Cranberry; Gooseberry.

CROWFOOT   *a crowfoot.* A plant of the buttercup family, for which this is a common name. WNNCD: 15th cent. Source: CROW. WNNCD: O.E. The metaphor is based on the cleft lobes of the leaves of the buttercup plant, which vaguely resemble a crow's foot. The word *crowfoot* is also a nautical term for a light pulley equipped with small lines to raise and lower a canopy or awning. WNWD. *Compare* Crow's-feet.

CROW'S-FEET   Tiny lines radiating from the outer corners of the eyes. EWPO: 1372. Source: CROW. WNNCD: O.E. Wrinkles! One of the first signs of aging—or perhaps of too many years of squinting. The lines look somewhat like the footprint of a crow, as first observed by Chaucer in *Troilus and Criseyde.* ATWS; DEI; ID; IRCD. *Compare* Crowfoot.

CROW'S NEST   *a crow's nest.* A lookout station located high on the mast of a sailing ship. WNNCD: 1818. Source: CROW. WNNCD: O.E. Crows like to nest as high in a tree as possible—from 50 to 70 feet, approx. the height of the mast of a "tall ship." The term has been adopted for any elevated, partly enclosed platform, as on a telephone pole. ATWS; EWPO; IRCD. *Compare* In the Catbird Seat.

CRY OVER SPILLED MILK   *Don't cry over spilled—or spilt—milk.* There's no use grieving over something that is abundant and can be easily replaced. Source: COW. Unlike horses, cows can kick in both directions—forward and backward. The forward kick is aimed at the milker, but it sometimes hits the pail. Not to worry! There are two more teats to go, and another milking will take place in twelve hours. DOC; EWPO. *See also* Bawl.

CRY WOLF   *to cry wolf.* To sound one too many false alarms or tell one too many lies: Sooner or later, nobody will believe you anymore. Source: WOLF. WNNCD: O.E. Wolves are natural predators of most other animals—larger or smaller than themselves, wild or domestic. In the Aesop fable, a bored and lonely shepherd boy falsely cried "Wolf!" in order to get some attention. When neighboring shepherds came running, they found nothing and left. After awhile he falsely cried "Wolf!" again, and the scene was repeated. When a wolf actually did appear, he cried "Wolf!" a third time, but no one came to help him, and the sheep were killed. AID; ATWS; BDPF; CI; DEI; DOC; HTB; IRCD; LCRH.

CUB REPORTER *a cub reporter.* A young, inexperienced reporter for a newspaper. Source: ANIMAL. An animal *cub* (WNNCD: 1530) is a young bear, coyote, fox, wolf, lion, or tiger. The implication is that the apprentice reporter is as helpless as the young of a wild ursine, canine, or feline. *Cub Scout* (WNNCD: ca. 1935—a proper noun), is the name for a "junior" Boy Scout from the age of eight to ten. A *Chicago Cub* (also a proper noun) is a member of the Chicago National League baseball club, whose symbol is a bear cub. ATWS.

CUCKOLD *a cuckold.* A man whose wife is unfaithful to him. WNNCD: 13th cent. Source: CUCKOO. WNNCD: 13th cent. The female cuckoo bird is unfaithful to her mate in two ways: first, she is polyandrous; and second, she lays the eggs of his offspring in the nests of other birds, which hatch and raise them as their own. Polyandry is not unusual among birds, but parasitism of this sort is. (Cowbirds also do it.) *Cuckold* was borrowed from O.Fr. *cucuault.* ATWS: BDPF; EWPO; IRCD; LCRH; WNWD. *See also* Cuckoo (n); Cuckoo's Nest.

CUCKOO (adj.) *to be cuckoo.* To be foolish, demented, or insane. IHAT: 1918. Source: CUCKOO. WNNCD: 13th cent. The cuckoo bird is said to be foolish or crazy because (1) the male has a "crazy" call (*kuk-kuk*), (2) its mate "fools around," (3) she lays her eggs in the nests of other birds, and (4) the male lets her get away with it. No wonder that *cuckold* (q.v.) derives from *cuckoo* (O.Fr. *coucou* or *cucu*). IRCD. *See also* Cloud-cuckoo-land; Cuckoo (n); Cuckoo's Nest.

CUCKOO (n) *a cuckoo.* A foolish, demented, or insane person. EWPO: 16th cent. Source: CUCKOO. WNNCD: 13th cent. The cuckoo is regarded as a silly, laughable bird because of its monotonous call (*kuk-kuk*) and its habit of depositing its eggs in the nests of other birds. But it has furnished us with many metaphors: *Cloud-cuckoo-land; Coccyx; Cuckold; Cuckoo Clock; Cuckoo's Nest;* and *Cuckoo Spit* (all of which *see*). ATWS; EWPO.

CUCKOO CLOCK *a cuckoo clock.* A clock from which a small wooden cuckoo bird appears to sound the hours with its monotonous cry *kuk-kuk.* WNNCD: 1789. Source: CUCKOO. WNNCD: 13th cent. The fact that the *cuckoo clock* appeared only half a century after the bird received its imitative name illustrates the popularity of the cuckoo as a kind of resident clown. It is, however, a furtive bird in the wild, seldom seen. ATWS; WNWD. *See also* Cuckoo (n).

CUCKOO'S NEST   *a cuckoo's nest.* An insane asylum, as in the 1975 film *One Flew Over the Cuckoo's Nest.* Source: CUCKOO. WNNCD: 13th cent. The cuckoo bird prefers to lay its eggs in the nests of other birds, so the reference here is probably to those other nests, in which the parasite eggs are raised along with the host eggs, producing an interesting family, especially at feeding time. *See also* Cuckold; Cuckoo (n).

CUCKOO SPIT   A frothy secretion on plants. WNNCD: 1592. Source: CUCKOO. WNNCD: 13th cent. Why the frothy secretion on plants is named for the cuckoo bird is unknown: Cuckoos don't spit, and they don't deposit frothy secretions by any other means. The froth is produced by the nymphs of the spittlebug, which suck juice from the plants and excrete it as foam. The foam serves as a protection for the nymphs as they undergo their various moltings on their way to becoming adults. Perhaps the "spit" is blamed on the cuckoo because this bird deposits its eggs wherever it pleases. WNWD. *See also* Cuckoo's Nest.

CUD   *See* Ruminate.

CUDDLY AS A BEAR   *to be as cuddly as a bear.* To be as warm and comfy and snuggly as a *teddy bear* (q.v.). Source: BEAR. WNNCD: O.E. Teddy bears are stuffed toys in the likeness of bear cubs, which are cute, cuddly, innocent, and eager for affection. They will soon grow into large, vicious adult bears that would like nothing better than to cuddle you to death.

CUNNING AS A FOX   *See* Sly as a Fox.

CUR   *a cur.* A cowardly or despicable person. Source: DOG. Originally, a cur was a growling dog (fr. M.E. *curdogge*—fr. *curren* "to growl" + *dogge* "dog"); but by the 13th cent., a cur was an inferior or worthless dog, or a dog of mixed breed: a *mongrel.* Figuratively, a *cur* is a contemptible or cowardly person—i.e., one who is as brave as a barking dog. ATWS; EWPO; IRCD; WNWD. *See also* Barking Dogs seldom Bite; Bark Is Worse than Your Bite.

CURIOSITY KILLED THE CAT   Excessive nosiness can be dangerous. Source: CAT. WNNCD: O.E. There is probably some long-lost fable about a cat that poked its nose in other animals' business one too many times and died in the final attempt. The cat was probably selected for the proverb because cats can afford to be curious: they *have nine lives* (q.v.). People don't, so they have to be careful. AID; ATWS; CE; CI; DEI.

CURRY FAVOR   *to curry favor from someone.* To flatter someone for personal gain. DOC: 1510. Source: HORSE. *To curry favor* was orig. *to curry Fauvel.* Fauvel was the cunning, duplicitous, chestnut-colored horse-hero of the 14th cent. French satirical poem, *Roman de Fauvel.* From this allegorical romance came the

English expression *to curry Fauvel*—i.e., to groom a horse in hopes of enlisting some of its power. In the 15th cent., the expression was altered to *to curry favel*; and, in the early 16th cent., in the form of *to curry favor*, it was generalized to mean "to fawn on someone insincerely and duplicitously." ATWS; BDPF; EWPO; HOI; LCRH; MDWPO.

CURSES, LIKE CHICKENS, ALWAYS COME HOME TO ROOST *See* Chickens Come Home to Roost.

CURTAIL *See* Tail (v).

CUT A CAPER *to cut a caper; to cut capers.* To frolic about in a playful manner (HTB: 1600); to play tricks or pranks. Source: GOAT. To "cut a caper" was first described by the verb *caper* (WNNCD: 1588), which appeared earlier than the noun *caper* (q.v.). That verb has pretty much been replaced by the phrase in question; and the earlier meaning, "to frolic" (as in Shakespeare's *Twelfth Night*— Act I, Scene 3), has been augmented by the sense of committing a malicious, or even criminal, act. The source of all "capers" is Lat. *caper* "male goat"—the goat being famous for its leaps and antics. HTB; WNWD.

CUTE AS A BUG'S EAR *to be as cute as—or cuter than—a bug's ear.* For a child to be incredibly cute. Source: BUG. WNNCD: 1622. The child's cuteness is incredible because bugs don't have ears—they have *antennae* (q.v.), or "feelers." In this case, cuteness is being equated with smallness: small ears + small nose + small eyes + small head = "cute." HTB. *Compare* Bug in Your Ear.

CYNIC *a cynic.* A faultfinding critic; a pessimist. WNNCD: 1547. Source: DOG. *Cynic* derives, by way of Latin, from Gk. *kynikos* "doglike." The term was first applied to the followers, including Diogenes, of an ancient Greek school of philosophers who lived a doglike existence on the streets of Athens. They not only rejected all forms of comfort for themselves but criticized others, sometimes rudely and insolently, for their wealth and luxury. Another "dog" metaphor from Classical Greek, *cynosure* "a center of attention or interest" (fr. Gk. *kynosoura*, lit. "dog's tail," fr. the Gk. root *kyn-* "dog") refers to the constellation Ursa Minor, whose tail of stars ends in Polaris, the Pole Star or North Star, around which all other constellations were once thought to revolve. ATWS; BDPF; EWPO; LCRH; MDWPO; ROE; THT; WNWD. *See also* Dog's Life. *Compare* Gadfly.

CYNOSURE *See* Cynic.

D

DANDELION *a dandelion*. A yellow-flowered herb. WNNCD: 14th cent. Source: LION. WNNCD: 12th cent. The dandelion consists of numerous serrated green leaves, growing close to the ground, out of the center of which rises a single daisy-like flower on a long stem. The leaves are sometimes prepared as "greens," and the flowers are sometimes fermented as wine; but the plant is usually regarded as an obnoxious weed. The name, which derives fr. M.Fr. *dent de lion* "lion's tooth," is based on a resemblance between the serrated leaves of the plant and the sharp teeth of the lion. EWPO; HF; ID.

DARK HORSE *a dark horse*. A contestant or candidate about whom little is known but who makes a surprisingly good showing in a race. WNNCD: 1831. Source: HORSE. WNNCD: O.E. The original dark horse was an established race-horse whose coat was dyed darker and who was entered in a race under a different name. Because the horse was unknown by that name, the odds were long, and the horse paid off well when it won. A *dark horse* in politics is an unexpected nominee who nevertheless threatens to pull off a win; and a *dark horse* in business is a company that comes out of nowhere to make a name for itself. ATWS; BDPF; CI; DEI; DOC; EWPO; HTB; IRCD; MDWPO; SPD; ST. *See also* Ringer.

DARNING EGG *a darning egg*. An ovoid object that is inserted in a sock to facilitate darning. Source: CHICKEN. The original darning egg was probably a small dried gourd, since the modern plastic version usu. has a handle. However, the *nest egg* (q.v.) may also have been used, since it was made of porcelain or glass and provided a smooth, hard surface to stitch against.

DEAD AS A DODO   *to be as dead as a dodo.* To be long gone and forgotten. Source: DODO. WNNCD: 1628. Spats, bustles, and five-cent cigars are all *dead as a dodo*; and an idea, plan, or proposal is *as dead as a dodo* when it is rejected and never considered again. The dodo, a large flightless bird of two islands in the Indian Ocean, became extinct about 1700, when the last member of the species was eaten by a pig (or a colonist). AID; ATWS; BDPF; CI; DEI; HTB. *See also* Dodo; Dumb Dodo. *Compare* Dead as a Herring; Dead as a Mackerel.

DEAD AS A HERRING   *to be as dead as a herring.* To be positively dead. IRCD: 16th cent. Source: HERRING. WNNCD: O.E. Dead fish smell bad enough; but when they are salted and smoked, as a *red herring* (q.v.) is, they smell even worse. The strong odor of the red herring has been used to advantage by foxhunters for training foxhounds—and by opponents of foxhunting for diverting foxhounds from the true path of the fox. A metaphorical *red herring* has been used to advantage by authors for diverting readers of mystery novels from the true villain, and by politicians for diverting voters from the true issues. ATWS; HTB. *See also* Draw a Red Herring. *Compare* Dead as a Mackerel.

DEAD AS A MACKEREL   *to be as dead as a mackerel.* To be stone-cold dead. Source: MACKEREL. WNNCD: 14th cent. The fact that the mackerel is such a common food fish probably accounts for this metaphor (but *see also* Dead as a Herring). The mackerel is caught live but is quite dead by the time it reaches port. ATWS; DOC. *See also* Cold as a Mackerel. *Compare* Dead as a Dodo.

DEAD DUCK   *a dead duck.* An easy mark; a hopeless victim; a lost cause. IRCD: ca. 1867. Source: DUCK. WNNCD: O.E. There are various degrees of deadness in ducks. A *sitting duck* (q.v.), i.e., one that is sitting on the water or on the ground, is an easy—and illegal—mark; a *lame duck* (q.v.) is one that has been shot and wounded; a *dead duck* is one that has been shot and killed; and *duck soup* (q.v.) is what will become of all three. People often find themselves in one or more of these conditions. AID; ATWS; CI; ST.

DEAD FISH   Visiting relatives: "Visiting relatives are like dead fish. After three days they begin to smell." Source: FISH. WNNCD: O.E. Actually, *dead fish* begin to smell a lot sooner than that—esp. if they have not been cleaned and refrigerated. A contrast between dead fish and visiting relatives is that the former are lured into your boat, while the latter usu. descend on you without invitation. *See also* Cold Fish; Fishy. *Compare* Dead Duck.

DEAD HORSE   *See* Pay for a Dead Horse.

DEAD RINGER   *See* Ringer.

DEAD SET ON   *to be dead set on doing something.* For someone to be insistent on doing something—usu. against the advice of others. DA: 1848. Source: DOG. A bird dog, such as a "setter" or "pointer," is "dead set" on a bird in its cover when it remains absolutely still, with one foreleg raised and its nose pointing directly at the hidden quarry. Children are *dead set on* doing things that their parents disapprove of, and adults are *dead set on* doing things that they probably shouldn't do or can't afford to do. ST.

DEAF AS AN ADDER   *to be as deaf as an adder.* To be totally oblivious to the entreaties of others. Source: SNAKE. A person who is *as deaf as an adder* is not physically deaf but simply refuses to listen. The earliest report of the adder's "deafness" is Psalm 58:4–5, referring to the wicked: "They are like the deaf adder that stoppeth her ear; which will not harken to the voice of the charmer." The adder was thought to resist the powers of the snake charmer by sticking its tail in one "ear" and holding the other "ear" to the ground. BDPF; EWPO; HTB.

DEATH TRAP   *See* Trap.

DEBUG   *to debug a room (etc.); to debug a computer program.* WNNCD: 1950. Source: BUG. WNNCD: 1622. A room that is *bugged* with hidden eavesdropping devices can be *debugged* by "sweeping" it with electronic detection equipment, locating the *bugs*, and removing them. Locating a *bug* in a computer program is not quite so simple: It means checking and rechecking all of the commands to find the flaw in the logic. (Debugging the back yard can be done with a bug zapper.) *See also* Bug (n) (2); Bug (v) (1).

DECOY   *a decoy.* A lure for attracting game or for trapping criminals. Source: BIRD. *Decoy* is an altered borrowing of Du. *de kooi* "the cage." The original decoy was a net that was thrown over a pond to capture waterfowl (WNNCD: 1641). Later, a live bird, such as a pigeon, was tied to a stool, on land, to lure other birds there (EWPO: 1830). Nowadays, a decoy is either (1) an artificial bird or other animal that is so realistic that it draws others of the same species to that place, or (2) an undercover police officer who poses as a drug dealer or prostitute to "entrap" criminals. ATWS; ST; WNWD. *See also* Stool Pigeon.

DELPHINIUM   A genus name for a large group of plants, also called "larkspur," of the buttercup family. WNNCD: 1664. Source: DOLPHIN. WNNCD: 14th cent. The delphinium, or "little dolphin" (fr. Gk. *delphinion,* dim. of *delphin* "dolphin"), is so called because its nectar gland has a bottle-nose shape resembling that of many dolphins. ATWS.

DEN   *a den.* A hideout; a secluded room; a small pack of Cub Scouts. Source: ANIMAL. An animal den is the lair of a wild, predatory animal, such as a bear, lion, or wolf. It is the secluded place, such as a cave, shelter, or hole, in which the animal sleeps and bears its young. A human *den* is (1) a secluded place where thieves hide out from the law, (2) a room in the house that is reserved for work or quiet play, or (3) a group of Cub Scouts that is smaller than a pack. A *den of thieves* (EWPO: 1719) is not only a physical hideout but can be any center of illicit, immoral, or illegal activities. A household *den* is the room that used to be called the "library." And a *den mother* (WNNCD: 1946) is either the adult leader of a Cub Scout *den* or, more figuratively, the informal leader of any small group of people. ATWS; DEI. *See also* Lion's Den. *Compare* Mother Hen.

DEN MOTHER   *See* Den.

DEN OF THIEVES   *See* Den.

DESCRIPTION OF AN ELEPHANT   *See* See the Elephant.

DESERT RAT   *a desert rat.* A hermit who lives in and off of the desert; a person who uses the desert for recreation. Source: RAT. WNNCD: O.E. Various rats go by the name "desert rat," including the desert wood rat, or *pack rat* (q.v.), which inhabits the deserts of the southwestern United States. But the most famous desert rats are the ones in the Saraha Desert who gave their name to the British tank troops of the North African campaign in WWII: "Desert Rats." NDAS. *Compare* Dock Rat; River Rat; Rug Rat; Shop Rat.

DEWLAP   *a dewlap.* A loose fold of skin hanging under the chin of an elderly person. Source: COW. Various animals have *dewlaps* (WNNCD: 14th cent.), but the most prominent one is on the mature cow. It hangs so low on the cow's neck that it "laps the dew" on the vegetation that the cow is grazing in. The *dewlap* on a human is a sign of advancing age and is a prime candidate for plastic surgery. HF; WNWD. *See also* Lap. *Compare* Turkey Wattles.

DIDN'T TURN A HAIR   *He/she didn't turn a hair.* He/she didn't *bat an eye* (q.v.). Source: HORSE. To *turn a hair* is to show signs of distress. A horse "turns a hair" when it sweats so much that its normally smooth coat becomes rough and disarrayed. People *turn a hair* when they become disturbed with someone's behavior or remarks, or become distressed over someone's illness or death. EWPO.

DIE IN HARNESS   *to die in harness.* To die with your boots on: still active, still working. Source: HORSE. A horse that dies in harness is at work, since horses are harnessed only when needed to pull a load. The first metaphorical use of the expression appeared in Shakespeare's *Macbeth* (ca. 1606), just before the battle with Macduff at Dunsinane Castle, when Macbeth said: "At least we'll die with harness on our back." (There may be a pun on *harness* here, since not only were Macbeth and his men in full armor but they were carrying leafy boughs from Birnam Wood.) A related expression, *to be or get back in harness,* refers to a return to work after a long vacation or illness: "It's great to be *back in harness again!*" ATWS; BDPF; CH; DEI; DOC; MDWPO. *See also* Get Hitched.

DIE LIKE A DOG *to die like a dog.* To die a miserable, shameful death. IRCD: 1529. Source: DOG. WNNCD: O.E. The dog has long been regarded as the lowest of domestic animals. Kicking or beating a stray dog was generally accepted in the Renaissance period in England, because such dogs had no feelings and served no useful purpose. When a dog was killed, it died whimpering, like a coward, without honor or dignity. People who *die like dogs* either die such a shameful and miserable death or die a senseless death, for no good reason. A related expression, *to gun them down like dogs,* reflects all of these conditions. BDPF; DEI; EWPO.

DIFFERENT ANIMAL *See* Animal.

DIFFERENT BREED OF CAT *a different breed of cat.* Someone or something that is completely different from the rest. Source: CAT. WNNCD: O.E. Out-of-towners sometimes say that New Yorkers are a "different breed of cat," meaning, presumably, that they are completely different from all other Americans. There are many breeds of cats, but cats themselves seem to pay more attention to gender and friendliness than to breed. *Compare* Horse of a Different Color.

DINOSAUR *a dinosaur.* A surviving member of a dying breed: an anachronism. Source: DINOSAUR. WNNCD: 1841 or 1842. No one knows exactly why the once dominant dinosaur became extinct approx. 65 million years ago, but the extinction may have been caused by meteorites striking the earth and kicking up dust that blocked the sun and killed the dinosaur's food supply. (Other guesses are excessive heat or cold.) An example of a human *dinosaur* is a lexicographer who handwrites his/her material instead of keyboarding it. ATWS. *See also* Last Dinosaur.

DIRTY DOG *a dirty dog.* A mean, despicable person. DOC: 1928. Source: DOG. WNNCD: O.E. In spite of the fact that the dog is *man's best friend* (q.v.)—helping us hunt, herding our livestock, and guarding our property—people have long regarded the dog as the lowest of domesticated animals; and a *dirty* dog is the lowest of all dogs. Humans who are *dirty dogs* are evil, sly, devious, and morally reprehensible—the lowest of all humans. BDPF; DEI; EWPO; IRCD. *See also* Yellow Dog. *Compare* Dirty Rat.

DIRTY RAT *You dirty rat!* You filthy vermin! IRCD: ca. 1931. Source: RAT. WNNCD: O.E. This epithet is closely identified with James Cagney and the gangster roles he played in films in the early 1930s. (To do an impersonation of Cagney, all you have to do is double your fists, sway from side to side, and say "You dirty rat!") But the actor claimed he never said it. Rats are associated with filth and disease (carried by their fleas and ticks), but one of the principal disease carriers, the brown rat, is the ancestor of the antiseptic white rat that is used in laboratory experiments and often kept as a pet.

DISGRUNTLED *to be disgruntled.* To be annoyed or discontented. WNNCD: 1682. Source: HOG. Hogs grunt when they are contented; humans grunt when they are discontented. The *dis-* in *disgruntled* is more like that in *dispense* than that in *disobey*: i.e., *disgruntled* workers have not stopped working—they are attempting to show their dissatisfaction while on the job. LCRH. *See also* Grunt (n); Grunt (v).

DOCK RAT *a dock rat.* A homeless person who finds food and shelter on the docks. Source: RAT. WNNCD: O.E. The original dock rat was probably the Norway rat, or brown rat, which is partial to water and whose hind feet are webbed. It is the rat that boards ships and carries plague and typhus to other countries. The homeless person is regarded as much a pest on the docks as is the brown rat. NDAS. *Compare* River Rat; Rug Rat; Shop Rat.

DODO *a dodo.* A stupid person: "You dodo!" Source: DODO. WNNCD: 1628. The *dodo* (fr. Port. *dondo* "silly, stupid") is an extinct bird of the Reunion and Maritius islands in the Indian Ocean. The bird was regarded as stupid by the European colonists who discovered—and ate—it in the 16th cent. because it was fat, flightless, and easily caught. It was extinct by ca. 1700. ATWS; EWPO; LTA. *See also* Dead as a Dodo; Dumb Dodo.

DOG (n) *a dog.* An unattractive woman (MDWPO: 1950); an ineffective racehorse; an unsuccessful literary or theatrical production. Source: DOG. WNNCD: O.E. The negative connotation of *dog* probably derives from the lowly status of the dog among domestic animals. In spite of the important work that dogs do for humans—hunting, herding, and guarding—they have long been regarded as dirty, lazy, good-for-nothing animals. Therefore, anything undesirable, such as a homely woman, or ineffective, such as an over-the-hill race horse, or unsuccessful, such as a flop play, can be called a *dog.* ATWS; NDAS.

DOG (v) *to dog someone's footsteps.* To follow someone closely and persistently. WNNCD: 1519. Source: DOG. WNNCD: O.E. A hunting dog is trained to follow the sight or scent of a quarry until it is found or killed. A bloodhound tracks an escaped criminal in the same way, and so does a human bloodhound, or detective, although the track is more often a paper trail. Reporters and photographers sometimes *dog the heels* of celebrities; people sometimes *dog* other people until they get what they want; and projects are sometimes *dogged* (one syllable)—i.e., "plagued" or "hampered"—by bad weather or equipment problems. ATWS; IRCD; ST. *See also* Hound (v).

DOG AND PONY SHOW   *a dog and pony show.* An elaborate sales pitch or public relations presentation. WNNCD: 1970. Source: DOG; HORSE. WNNCD: O.E. In show biz parlance, a dog and pony show is a *one-ring circus*, with nothing more than a trick dog and a *one-trick pony.* In PR parlance, a dog and pony show is a traveling sales pitch, with charts and diagrams and multimedia effects. The term is contemptuous when used about someone else's "circus," but is excusatory when used by presenters about their own presentation. LCRH; MDWPO; NDAS; ST.

DOG-CHEAP   *See* Dog-tired.

DOG COLLAR   *a dog collar.* A priest's collar; a woman's choker. Source: DOG. WNNCD: O.E. Dogs wear a leather collar around their necks as a mark of identification and as a "belt" to which a leash or chain can be attended. On humans, a narrow band of white cloth at the top of the vestments identifies the wearer as a priest or minister; and a snug-fitting band of cloth around the neck identifies the wearer as a woman of style. (The choker is sometimes leather and may be decorated with sparkling stones.) When a dog *slips its collar*, it is free to go where it pleases; when a person does so, he/she has escaped from jail. BDPF; NDAS.

DOG DAYS   *the dog days of summer.* The hot, sultry days of July and August; any period of inactivity or business slowdown. WNNCD: 1538. Source: DOG. WNNCD: O.E. *Dog days* is a translation of Lat. *caniculares dies*, which had the same meaning. The Romans believed that the rising of the Dog Star (Sirius) just before sunrise in early July increased the heat of the sun during the rest of that month. Strengthening the metaphor was the fact that dogs sometimes went mad during that period of time. In modern times, the Dog Star now rises in August, and the metaphor has been broadened to include any period during which business is slow, and people—and dogs—are inactive. ATWS; BDPF; DEI; EWPO; HOI; IRCD; LCRH; MDWPO; SHM.

DOG-EAR   *See* Dog-eared.

DOG-EARED   *a dog-eared page; a dog-eared book.* A page, the corner of which has been turned down to mark the place for the reader; a book that is shabby and worn. WNNCD: 1784. Source: DOG. WNNCD: O.E. To *dog-ear* a page (WNNCD: 1725) is to fold over the corner so that it looks like one of the bent-over ears of certain hounds and collies. (Collies' ears are sometimes surgically altered to make them droop.) A dog-eared book is one that has been read by so many people that all of the pages have been dog-eared, and the covers and spine are in shambles. ATWS; BDPF; DEI; IRCD.

DOG EAT DOG   *to be dog eat dog.* To be ruthless and savage. Source: DOG. WNNCD: O.E. When dogs kill a prey, they sometimes fight over it *tooth and nail* (q.v.), valuing the prize more than their own life or that of their fellows. Competition in the world of business is like a *dogfight* (q.v.): It's *dog eat dog* out there; It's a *dog-eat-dog world* (WNNCD: 1834); It's *every man for himself*; It's the *survival of the fittest*. Dogs don't usu. eat other dogs, and people don't usu. eat other people; but neither genus hesitates to eliminate others of the same species. ATWS; CE; CI; DOC; IRCD; LTA; SHM; WNWD.

DOG-EAT-DOG WORLD   *See* Dog Eat Dog.

DOGFACE   *a dogface, or dog soldier*. An infantry soldier; a noncommissioned officer in the infantry. WNNCD: 1941. Source: DOG. WNNCD: O.E. The infantry is the *nitty-gritty* (q.v.) outfit of the armed services, the one that does the dirty work. The analogy is to the hunting dog, which tracks its prey on foot and sometimes encounters strong resistance. The earlier version of this WWII term was *doughboy* (WNNCD: 1867), which was used during WWI. The application of the term *dogface* to a noncommissioned officer, such as a sergeant, probably comes from the infantry privates themselves. ATWS; WNWD.

DOGFIGHT   *to develop into a dogfight*. For a dispute between two people to turn into a serious altercation. DAE: 1865. Source: DOG. WNNCD: O.E. Literally, a *dogfight* (WNNCD: 1656) is a fight between two dogs, whether spontaneous or prearranged. The dogs *fight tooth and nail* (q.v.), go *at each other's throats*, and try to kill each other. Human *dogfights* are highly animated but seldom physical. A WWI *dogfight* was a battle in the air between two (or more) airplanes, which fired at each other but didn't actually touch. ATWS; CI; DEI; IRCD; ST. *Compare* Fight like Cats and Dogs.

DOGGED   *to be dogged* (two syllables). To be marked by persistence, obstinance, or stubborn determination. WNNCD: 1653. Source: DOG. WNNCD: O.E. Hunting dogs pursue their quarry relentlessly—i.e., with *dogged determination*—but the *bulldog* (q.v.) is probably the most *dogged* of all dogs. As the name implies, bulldogs were orig. bred and trained to bait bulls by clamping their jaws on the bull's nostrils and hanging on *doggedly* until the bull gave up. People display *doggedness* by refusing, like the bulldog, to give up, even under the most trying circumstances. ATWS; ID; IRCD; MDWPO.

DOGGEDLY   *See* Dogged.

DOGGEDNESS   *See* Dogged.

DOGGEREL   *See* Dog Latin.

DOGGIE BAG   *a doggie—or doggy—bag*. A paper bag used for taking home leftovers from a meal at a restaurant. WNNCD: 1963. Source: DOG. WNNCD:

O.E. *Doggie bag* is an Americanism that originated with a request to a waiter or waitress for a bag in which to carry home the leftover meat (esp.) to give to the family dog. The intention may have been sincere in the beginning, but soon the *doggie bag* included leftover pasta, side orders, and dessert, which most dogs would not be interested in. The *doggie bag* is now an excuse for buying a large steak, because it can feed you on the following day also. WNWD.

DOGGONE   *Doggone it!* (A euphemism). God damn it! WNNCD: 1828. Source: DOG. WNNCD: O.E. Over the years, people have gone to great lengths to soften forbidden expressions. (Other euphemisms for *God damn it!* are *Gosh darn it!* and *Dag nab it!*) The innocent dog figures into this one because *God* spelled backwards is *Dog. Doggone* is also used attributively, as in *That doggone cat!* ATWS; BDPF; CE; HF.

DOGHOUSE   *See* In the Doghouse.

DOG IN THE MANGER   *a dog in the manger.* A mean-spirited person who denies access by others to something that he/she has no need or use for. WNNCD: 1573. Source: DOG. WNNCD: O.E. The allusion is to an Aesop fable in which a snarling dog moves into a manger and refuses to allow an ox to eat the hay that the dog itself has no appetite for. A modern *dog in the manger* is a person who maintains an "attractive nuisance" but denies use of it to others. In government, when "the dogs are in the manger," there is strong opposition to a proposal. ATWS; BDPF; CH; CI; DEI; DOC; HOI; IRCD; LCRH; SHM.

DOG IT   *to dog it.* To do as little as possible to get a job done. LTA: 1920. Source: DOG. WNNCD: O.E. Lazy people give less than 100% effort on a job—working halfheartedly and failing to do their best. Why the dog is the basis for this metaphor is uncertain. Hunting dogs do sometimes stop to water a bush or investigate a hole in the ground or chase a nongame animal, but they usu. *work like a dog* (q.v.) and wind up *dog-tired* (q.v.) at the end of the day. This is another example of the undeserved disparagement of *man's best friend* (q.v.). ATWS.

DOG LATIN   False Latin. EWPO: mid-18th cent. Source: DOG. WNNCD: O.E. Dog Latin, a mixture of Latin and English, is like a mongrel dog: a mixed breed. The term was first used by school children who, unable to produce correct Latin, introduced English words in the place of Latin ones. It was also the original name for what is now called *pig latin* (WNNCD: 1931—q.v.). The same association of *dog* with "spurious" occurs in the word *doggerel* (WNNCD: 1630), which was first used by Chaucer in the form *rym dogerel.* Also called *dog rhyme,* the term has come to mean "bad verse," written by a hack or intended only for comic effect. ATWS; BDPF; CI; HF; IRCD.

DOGLEG *a dogleg.* A bend in the road; an angled fairway on the golf course. WNNCD: ca. 1909. Source: DOG. WNNCD: O.E. A dog's front leg is straight, from the "elbow" to the paw; but its hind leg is crooked, with a backward bend halfway down. An angled road or fairway has a bend either to the left or the right, analogous to the hind leg of a dog (as viewed from the dog's left or right side, respectively—reading upward). In golf, the bend is called a *dogleg left* or *dogleg right* (WNNCD: 1889), and the fairway is said to *dogleg* (WNNCD: 1947) in one of these directions. The expression *crooked as a dog's hind leg* is a direct metaphor for dishonesty, but *straight as a dog's hind leg* carries with it a bit of sarcasm. ATWS; LTA.

DO GOOBERS EAT GOPHERS, OR DO GOPHERS EAT GOOBERS *Do goobers eat gophers, or do gophers eat goobers?* (A riddle.) The answer is: Gophers eat goobers—i.e., "peanuts." Source: GOPHER. (N.D.) The gopher, or thirteen-lined ground squirrel, is omnivorous, eating just about everything, including peanuts and other gophers. It is the nemesis of groundskeepers at golf courses, parks, and peanut farms.

DOG PADDLE *the dog paddle.* A basic swimming stroke, executed with the arms paddling, the legs kicking, and the head sticking out of the water. WNNCD: 1904. Source: DOG. WNNCD: O.E. All dogs are able to swim—though some, such as retrievers, enjoy it more than others—and they all swim in the same way: front legs paddling, back legs kicking, and head always above the surface of the water. Nonswimming humans instinctively use the *dogpaddle* when they are thrown in the water, and some of them actually survive. ATWS; IRCD. *Compare* Butterfly; Dolphin Kick; Frog Kick.

DOG RHYME *See* Dog Latin.

DOG'S AGE *a dog's age.* A long time. Source: DOG. WNNCD: O.E. The life expectancy of a dog is between ten and fifteen years. In human years, that may not seem like a long time; but in *dog years*—i.e., actual years multiplied by seven—it is: 70 to 105 years. A seven-year-old child might say that he/she was actually 49 years old—"in dog years." BDPF. *Compare* Coon's Age.

DOGS ARE BARKING *My dogs are barking.* My feet are killing me. IRCD: 1930s. Source: DOG. WNNCD: O.E. Feet have been called *dogs* since the early 20th cent. (IHAT: ca. 1910). The analogy may be to the *watchdog* (q.v.), which warns its owner that trouble is brewing. The solution to the problem of *barking dogs* is to remove your shoes and rub your feet. NDAS. *Also* My Dogs Are Tired.

DOGS ARE IN THE MANGER *See* Dog in the Manger.

DOGS ARE TIRED *See* Dogs are Barking.

DOG'S LETTER *the dog's letter.* The letter *R.* HF: 1636. Source: DOG. WNNCD: O.E. Ben Jonson called "R" the *dog's letter* because the sound associated with the letter resembled the snarling of a dog; but the Romans had come to the same conclusion much earlier. The reference is probably a postvocalic "R," as in *brr* and *grr,* the representations of the sounds of shuddering and growling, respectively. One hundred fifty years after Jonson made his statement, the postvocalic "R" was dropped from the King's English—and from certain dialects of American English—where shuddering people and growling dogs now presumably say *buh* and *guh.* EWPO.

DOG'S LIFE   *See* Lead a Dog's Life.

DOGS OF WAR   *the dogs of war.* The horrors of war; those who profit from war. Source: DOG. WNNCD: O.E. In Shakespeare's *Julius Caesar* (1599), Mark Antony prophecies that dead Caesar's spirit will "Cry 'Havoc!' and *let slip the dogs of war*" on Brutus and his co-conspirators (Act III, Scene 1). The metaphorical *dogs of war* that Antony catalogues in this soliloquy are famine and fire, maiming and killing, and atrocities against women and children. One basis for the metaphor is the slipping off of the collars of greyhounds to signal the start of a dog race. Another is the releasing of the *dogs,* or "catches," on crossbows to free the strings that propel the bolts. Modern *dogs of war* are arms dealers and mercenaries who profit from the hostilities. BDPF; DEI; DOC; IRCD; ST.

DOG SOMEONE'S HEELS   *See* Dog (v).

DOG TAGS   Military identification tags. EWPO: ca. 1918. Source: DOG. WNNCD: O.E. Canine *dog tags* (WNNCD: 1918) and military *dog tags* were named at about the same time, but the latter were named for the former. A dog wears a single metal tag, containing its license number, on its collar; a person in the armed forces wears two tags, each with their name and ID number, on a chain around their neck: one for the body and one for the records. The military tags were orig. bare aluminum, but they made so much noise clanging against each other that they were later framed in rubber. Plans are being made to embed a computer chip in the tags to provide more information. ATWS; BDPF.

DOG-TIRED   *to be dog-tired.* To be completely exhausted. WNNCD: ca. 1552. Source: DOG. WNNCD: O.E. To be *dog-tired* is to be as tired as a working dog— i.e., a hunting dog or a herding dog—at the end of a long, hard day. The dog is too tired to even eat, and just wants to curl up and go to sleep. People usually become *dog-tired* as a result of overworking or overexercising. Another use of the word *dog* as an intensifier occurs in the term *dog-cheap,* meaning "extremely cheap" or "dirt-cheap." ATWS; BDPF; DEI; IRCD. *See also* Dogs Are Barking; Work like a Dog.

DOGTOWN *See* Try It on the Dog.

DOG WATCH *the dog watch.* A suppertime watch aboard ship (WNNCD: 1700); a night shift at a factory. Source: DOG (*). WNNCD: O.E. The shipboard watch from 4 P.M. to 8 P.M. was split up into two two-hour watches—from 4 P.M. to 6 P.M. and 6 P.M. to 8 P.M.—so that everyone could have time to eat supper. The shortened—or *docked*—watch came to be called the "dog" watch by folk etymology. In more recent times the term has been applied to the last—or "third"—shift at a factory (from 11 P.M. to 7 A.M.), which occurs almost entirely in the dead of night, when watchdogs are usu. the only ones up and about. BDPF; EWPO; HF; IRCD; MDWPO.

DOG YEARS *See* Dog's Age.

DOLPHIN KICK *a dolphin kick.* A kicking of both legs, underwater, tight together, at the same time, as in the *butterfly stroke* (q.v.). Source: DOLPHIN. WNNCD: 14th cent. All mammals of the whale class—whales, dolphins, porpoises—have horizontal tail fins, rather than the vertical tail fins of fish. So dolphins propel themselves through the water by raising and lowering their tails, instead of by moving them from side to side. ATWS. *Compare* Porpoise (v).

DONKEY ENGINE *a donkey engine.* A small locomotive used to switch railroad cars or pull ships through a lock; a small auxiliary engine used to pump liquids or to hoist loads at a construction site. WNNCD: 1858. Source: DONKEY. WNNCD: ca. 1785. The donkey has always played second fiddle to the horse— consider *horsepower* rather than "donkeypower"—so the small or unglamorous sources of energy are often named after the donkey. ATWS; BDPF. *See also* Donkeywork.

DONKEY'S YEARS A very long time. WNNCD: 1916. Source: DONKEY. WNNCD: ca. 1785. The donkey's lifespan was once approx. the same as that of a human (50 years or so), but now it is much shorter. DOC suggests that the metaphor may be a play on "donkey's ears," which are also quite long. *Compare* Coon's Age; Dog's Age; Dog Years.

DONKEYWORK Hard, boring, monotonous, "no-brain" work. WNNCD: 1920. Source: DONKEY. WNNCD: ca. 1785. Water buffalo and oxen did the heavy pulling in older times, while the camel and the donkey (or *ass*) did the heavy carrying. All of these jobs were routine and unglamorous. When the horse came along, with its speed and ability to carry knights in shining armor, the donkey, although also an equine, lost even more status by comparison. By the 20th cent., *donkeywork* was work that required little intelligence. DEI. *See also* Donkey Engine.

DON'T COUNT YOUR CHICKENS BEFORE THEY HATCH *Don't count your chickens before they hatch!* Don't count on something happening until it actually does. MDWPO: ca. 1575. Source: CHICKEN. WNNCD: O.E. This warning is the moral of an Aesop fable about a farmmaid who, while carrying a basket of eggs to market, daydreamed of how she could make a fortune by selling the eggs, buying a goose, selling the goose, buying a cow, etc.—until she suddenly dropped the basket and broke all of the eggs. (In another version of the tale, the woman was carrying a pail of milk.) AID; ATWS; BDPF; CI; DEI; DOC; EWPO; ID; IRCD. *See also* Don't Put All Your Eggs in one Basket. *Compare* Bird in the Hand.

DON'T GIVE A LICK *See* Lick and a Promise.

DON'T KNOW SIC 'EM *See* Sic.

DON'T LET THE BEDBUGS BITE *Sleep tight! Don't let the bedbugs bite!* A popular way of saying good night to children who are on their way to bed. Source: BEDBUG. WNNCD: 1808. The children may not even know what a bedbug is, but the parents probably know all too well that they are bloodsucking bugs that infest filthy beds. *See also* Bedbug Letter; Crazy as a Bedbug.

DON'T LOOK A GIFT HORSE IN THE MOUTH *See* Look a Gift Horse in the Mouth.

DON'T PUT ALL YOUR EGGS IN ONE BASKET *Don't put all your eggs in one basket!* Don't risk everything on a single venture. EWPO: 1894. Source: CHICKEN. This metaphor may derive from the same Aesop fable as *Don't Count Your Chickens before They Hatch* (q.v.). In that fable a farmmaid collects the eggs in the morning, puts them in a single basket, and drops the basket, causing all the eggs to break. (If she had put them in two baskets, half of the eggs might have survived.) A positive version of the warning—"Put all your eggs in one basket, and WATCH THAT BASKET"—has been attributed to both Andrew Carnegie and Mark Twain (*Pudd'nhead Wilson*, 1894). ATWS; BDPF; CE; CI; DOC. *See also* Nest Egg.

DOODLEBUG *a doodlebug.* A divining rod; a dune buggy. Source: BUG. WNNCD: 1622. A divining rod is a small forked branch, about a yard long, that is used to locate underground supplies of water, oil, gas, and minerals. The diviner holds the branch by the two forks, with the straight part forward. When the end of the branch suddenly dips down, that's where the treasure is. This sense of *doodlebug*—from *dawdle* "to move aimlessly" + *bug* "insect"—derives from the behavior of the larva of the *ant lion* (q.v.)—also called a *doodlebug*—which obtains its food by burrowing into the sand and waiting for ants to fall in after it. *Doodlebug*, the vehicle, combines the "aimless" sense of *dawdle* and the "off-the-road" character of *bugs*. It can refer to any small or stripped-down car, truck, or airplane. HF; WNWD.

DORMOUSE   *a dormouse*. A small nocturnal rodent, with a bushy tail, that hibernates in northern climes. WNNCD: 15th cent. Source: MOUSE. WNNCD: O.E. A *dormouse* (fr. Fr. *dormir* "to sleep") is not a mouse. The metaphor is based on the mouselike appearance of the dormouse's head and body only; if it had been based on the appearance of its tail, the animal could just as well have been called a "dorsquirrel"—i.e., a hibernating squirrel. (Squirrels and mice don't hibernate.) *Compare* Titmouse.

DOUBLE BACK   *See* Track down.

DOUBLE EAGLE (1)   *a double eagle*. A U.S. twenty-dollar gold piece (1796–1929) with the image of an eagle on the reverse side. Source: EAGLE. WNNCD: 13th cent. The *double eagle* was so called because it had double the value of an *American Eagle* (q.v.), a ten-dollar gold piece that was minted two years earlier. (There was also a "half eagle," worth five dollars.) The eagle on all of these coins is the one on the Great Seal of the United States: a bald eagle. LTA. *See also* Eagle Flies on Friday; When the Eagle Flies.

DOUBLE EAGLE (2)   *a double eagle*. A score of three strokes below par on a golf hole. Source: EAGLE. WNNCD: 13th cent. A *double eagle* is so called because it is twice as many strokes below a *birdie* (q.v.) as an *eagle* (q.v.). It yields a score of two on a par five hole and one on a par four hole. The latter is the rarest shot in golf. Also a verb: to *double eagle* a hole. *See also* Albatross.

DOVE   *a dove*. A pacifist: one who prefers talking to fighting. IRCD: 1962. Source: DOVE. WNNCD: 13th cent. The dove has been a symbol of peace since biblical and classical times. In international affairs, a *dove* is a legislator who favors negotiation and compromise as an alternative to violence and war. ATWS; BDPF; IHAT; MDWPO; SPD. *See also* Dove of Peace; Dovish; Gentle as a Dove; Hold out the Olive Branch. *Compare* Hawk (n) (1).

DOVE OF PEACE   *a dove of peace*. The dove as a symbol of peace. Source: DOVE. WNNCD: 13th cent. The dove, esp. the white dove, has been a symbol of peace since biblical and classical times. Today, a profile of a dove with an olive branch in its mouth is instantly recognizable, and it is not uncommon for a flock of white doves to be released at an outdoor international gathering. DEI. *See also* Dove; Hold out the Olive Branch.

DOVETAIL (n)   *a dovetail*. A joint in cabinetmaking in which a series of wedge-shaped mortises fits perfectly into a series of V-shaped tenons. WNNCD: 1565. Source: DOVE. WNNCD: 13th cent. A *dovetail*, or *dovetail joint*, is the result of joining two pieces of wood, usu. at right angles, without the use of nails, screws, staples, or pegs (though glue is sometimes applied). The joint resembles the perfectly interlocked tail feathers of a dove. (The joint was orig. called a "swallowtail joint."). ATWS; HF; IRCD. *See also* Dovetail (v).

DOVETAIL (v) *to dovetail.* To fit together perfectly, like clasped hands. WNNCD: 1656. Source: DOVE. WNNCD: 13th cent. The tail feathers of a dove cross and interwine with each other perfectly. The same is true not only of clasped hands—and ideas—but of furniture, in which a mortise and a tenon fit together perfectly to form a joint. ATWS. *See also* Dovetail (n).

DOVISH *to be dovish.* To support alternatives to violence and war. Source: DOVE. WNNCD: 13th cent. The dove has been a symbol of peace since biblical and classical times. A legislator who is *dovish* on international affairs is not necessarily a *dove* (q.v.), but is one who views war as a last resort, following negotiation and appeasement. *See also* Dove of Peace; Hold out the Olive Branch. *Compare* Hawkish.

DOWN Something soft and fluffy. Source: BIRD. *Down* refers either to (1) the fine, soft feathers of a baby bird or (2) the short, fluffy breast feathers of an adult bird (WNNCD: 14th cent.). Birds sometimes line their nests with down to keep the eggs from breaking and to make brooding more comfortable for the adults. In the 20th cent. the term *down* has been applied to anything—animal, vegetable, or synthetic—that is as fine and soft and fluffy—i.e., as *downy*—as the down of birds. (Joke: How do you get down off an elephant? You don't: you get down off a duck.) ATWS; WNWD.

DOWN, BOY *Down, boy!* Restrain yourself! Source: DOG. *Down, boy!* is a command from a doghandler to a dog that is jumping up on a visitor. Figuratively, it is a command from a wife to her husband who is eyeing an attractive female; or it can be a silent command from a man to himself, under the same circumstances. A related expression, *Atta Boy!* (fr. *That a boy!*, fr. *That's a boy!*) is a shout of approval from a doghandler whose dog has obeyed his/her commands. Figuratively, it is an expression of approval from a parent (usu. the father) to a son who has acted commendably.

DOWN THE STRETCH *See* In the Homestretch.

DOWN-TO-EARTH *to be down-to-earth.* To be practical and realistic. WNNCD: 1932. Source: BIRD (?). A down-to-earth person is one who has his/her feet on the ground, not his/her head in the clouds. Birds spend much of their time in the air, where they are free to fly wherever they fancy. Both birds and people can be *brought down to earth* by shooting them—or their dreams—full of holes. Domestic fowl are prevented from *flying the coop* (q.v.) by *clipping their wings* (q.v.); and children are *grounded* by their parents when they run afoul of the rules of the household.

DRACONIAN *See* Dragon Lady.

DRAGONFLY *a dragonfly*. A four-winged flying insect with a long narrow body that inhabits marshes, swamps, and lakes. (It is also called a "devil's darning needle" and a *mosquito hawk*, q.v.) WNNCD: 1626. Source: DRAGON. WNNCD: 13th cent. The dragonfly is so called either because of its unusual shape and size (for a fly) or because its larva, or "nymph," can actually eat crayfish. The term *dragon* is still in use for certain large lizards. HF; THT. *See also* Dragon Lady.

DRAGONHEAD *See* Dragon Lady.

DRAGON LADY *a dragon lady*. A tough, tyrannical female boss or businesswoman. (Probably from the comic strip of the same name.) Source: DRAGON. WNNCD: 13th cent. The mythical *dragon* (fr. Gk. *drakōn* "serpent") was a monstrous winged saurian with huge teeth and claws that breathed fire and smoke—such as the one that St. George slew in the 3rd cent. and Beowulf killed in the 6th cent., although those dragons were not necessarily female. Dragons are now "extinct," but their name lives on in words like *dragonfly* (q.v.); *dragon's blood* (14th cent.) "dark red palm resin used for coloring and engraving"; *dragon's teeth* (1853) "rows of concrete wedges set in the ground to stop tanks"; *dragonhead* (1784) "a North American mint whose flower petals look like dragon's teeth"; and, of course, the *Komodo dragon* of Indonesia, over ten feet long and weighing over 300 pounds, which has the size and claws but lacks the wings and fire of a mythical dragon. The adj. *draconian* (WNNCD: 1876), meaning "harsh or cruel," also derives from Gk. *drakōn*, but only because it was also the name of a Greek legislator who was tough and strict.

DRAGON'S BLOOD *See* Dragon Lady.

DRAGON'S TEETH *See* Dragon Lady.

DRAW A RED HERRING *to draw a red herring across someone's path*. To create a diversion or distraction; to draw attention away from the real issue. DOC: 19th cent. Source: HERRING. WNNCD: O.E. In the 17th cent., criminals sometimes dragged a *red herring* (q.v.) across their path to distract the pursuing hounds. Opponents of fox hunting also dragged a red herring across the path of the fleeing fox to divert the attention of the foxhounds. Mystery writers introduce *red herrings* as false clues to draw the attention of the reader away from the real culprit, and politicians use *red herrings* to draw the attention of the voters from the real issue. This expression is the source of *red herring* as a deliberate diversion or distraction. BDPF; DEI; EWPO; HOI; SHM. *See also* Dead as a Herring.

DRAW IN YOUR HORNS   *to draw in—or pull in—your horns.* To retreat from a political, forensic, financial, or sexual stance or commitment. EWPO: early 14th cent. Source: SNAIL. The land snail has four hornlike tentacles at the end of its "foot," the middle two of which have eyes at the ends of the stalks. If the partially exposed snail senses—i.e., sees or feels—danger with its tentacles, it backs into the shell that it has been dragging along at the rear. The "horns" are the last part of its body to enter the shell. ATWS; BDPF; CI; DEI; HOI; IRCD. *See also* Pull in Your Eyes.

DRAW PEOPLE LIKE FLIES   *to draw people like flies.* To attract customers or spectators in large numbers. Source: FLY. WNNCD: O.E. Flies are attracted to their natural breeding ground (garbage, carrion, and excrement) and to their natural source of food (flowers, people, and live animals). People are attracted to places and events that satisfy their own basic needs, such as restaurants, theaters, sporting events, and stores. They are not attracted to flies. *See also* Catch More Flies.

DRAW SOMEONE OUT OF THEIR SHELL   *See* Come out of Your Shell.

DRAW THE COLLAR   *to draw—or take—the collar.* For a baseball batter to strike out; for a baseball team to go without any hits or runs in an inning or game. Source: HORSE. The batter or team is said to have been *horse-collared* by the opposing pitcher. The connection between *collar* and "failure" is that the horse collar is ovalshaped, like the numeral zero, and the players have "nothing" to show for their efforts. A horse collar is worn around the neck of a draft horse; it is the part of the harness to which the traces are attached. ATWS; ST. *See also* Duck Egg; Goose Egg; Lay an Egg; Love.

DRINK FROM THE SAME TROUGH   *to drink from the same trough.* To be of the same kind. Source: ANIMAL. On the farm, horses drink from the horse tank (or trough), cows drink from the cow tank (or trough), and hogs eat and drink from the hog trough; i.e., each species of animal has its own source of liquid refreshment. People drink from cups, glasses, and fountains, not from troughs; but the metaphor likens people of the same nature and inclinations to domesticated animals of the same species: i.e., they are "cut from the same cloth." *Compare* Birds of a Feather.

DRINK LIKE A FISH   *to drink like a fish.* To drink too much and too often. IRCD: 1646. Source: FISH. WNNCD: O.E. To *drink like a fish* is to drink as much alcohol as a fish drinks water. However, though saltwater fish take water into their mouths and expel it through their gills, they never ingest it—and freshwater fish ingest very little. So there are no aquaholic fish, but there are plenty of alcoholic humans. ATWS; BDPF; CI; DEI; EWPO; ID; IRCD; SHM; ST. *See also* Loaded to the Gills.

DRIVE SOMEONE BANANAS *See* Go Bananas.

DRIVE SOMEONE BATS *See* Bats.

DRONE (n) (1) *a drone.* A monotonous sound, as of a machine or a long-winded speaker. Source: BEE. The noun *drone* is derived from the O.E. verb *drān* "to make the humming sound of a swarm of bees," which is also the source of the name of the male bee in a beehive: a *drone.* This is rather odd, because drones make up only two percent of the population of the hive and therefore contribute little to the sound level. WNWD. *See also* Drone (n) (2); Drone (v).

DRONE (n) (2) *a drone.* A parasite; a harmless drudge; a pilotless craft. Source: BEE. All of these senses of *drone* derive from the role of the male bee, or *drone,* in a beehive. The male gathers no nectar, makes no honey, and builds no combs. Its sole purpose is to mate with the queen bee—in midair—and then die. In the meantime, the drone lives off the honey produced by the worker bees, like a parasite, and keeps to itself in the corner of the hive, like a drudge. When its moment of glory arrives, however, it flies forth with only one purpose in mind; and when that is accomplished, it becomes expendable—like a remote-controlled ship or plane or missile. ATWS; IRCD; WNWD.

DRONE (v) *to drone (on).* For an engine to make a deep, continuous humming sound; for a person to speak lengthily, boringly, and monotonously on a subject. WNNCD: 1500. Source: BEE. The modern verb *drone* derives from the O.E. verb *drān* "to make the humming sound of a swarm of bees," but somehow it bypassed M.E. entirely. Furthermore, although it is also the source of the noun *drone* "a male bee," the drone does not participate in the work of the hives and contributes little to the buzz of activity. Nevertheless, worker bees *drone,* as do motors and long-winded speakers. ATWS; DEI; WNWD. *See also* Buzz (n); Drone (n) (1); Drone (n) (2); Make Things Hum.

DROP LIKE FLIES *to drop like flies.* For people to collapse, in large numbers, from heat stroke, exhaustion, food poisoning, etc. *Also:* "to fall or *die like flies.*" Source: FLY. WNNCD: O.E. Flies are among the most abundant and widespread insects: they are found wherever humans and animals—and their waste—are. They also have a short life span, meaning that flies *drop like flies* all the time.

DROVES *to move in droves.* To move as a crowd. Source: CATTLE. A *drove* is a group of cattle (or sheep) that is being driven as one body by a *drover* (WNNCD: 14th cent.). People move *in droves*—actually, one drove—when they arrive at or leave a place en masse. The term is also used for flocks of birds—and for swarms of ants and bees—that are migrating from one place to another.

DROWNED RAT   *to look like—or be as wet as—a drowned rat.* To be completely soaked with water, esp. your face and hair. Source: RAT. WNNCD: O.E. To most people, a live rat is an ugly sight, but a dead one is even more disgusting. Finding a drowned rat would be rather unusual, because most rats can swim; and some, such as the water rat, even have partially webbed hind feet. Of the disease-carrying rats, the black rat dislikes swimming, while the brown rat—the one that leaves sinking ships—is an excellent swimmer. It would probably take a typhoon, hurricane, or major flood to drown one of them. ATWS; BDPF; ID; IRCD.

DRUNK AS A SKUNK   *to be as drunk as a skunk.* To be "stinking" drunk. Source: SKUNK. WNNCD: 1634. The skunk, an American *polecat* (q.v.), does not drink, but it does stink. It can shoot a vile-smelling liquid up to 20 feet from glands beneath its tail. Drunks may stink like skunks, but it is probably the rhyme that attracted the skunk to this metaphor. ATWS; CE; DOC. *See also* Skunk (n); Skunk (v).

DUCK (n)   A lightweight cotton fabric resembling sail cloth. WNNCD: 1640. Source: DUCK (*). WNNCD: O.E. *Duck cloth*, or *duck*, is a popular fabric for casual apparel such as pants and skirts, shirts and blouses, and raincoats and jackets. Although it is often worn while sailing, it takes its name from Du. *doek* "cloth," not from English *duck*, the aquatic bird, and is not an animal metaphor. IRCD.

DUCK (v)   *to duck.* To lower your head and shoulders; to stoop down or bend over; to move quickly out of sight. SOED: 1598. Source: DUCK. WNNCD: O.E. Both the noun *duck* "an aquatic bird" and the verb *duck* "to stoop down" derive from a Gmc. root meaning "to dive." Thus, the duck is a "diver," and the act of diving carries the duck's head, neck, and upper body out of sight in the water. Humans usu. *duck down* in response to the cry "Duck!"; and they usu. *duck into* a doorway when they don't want to be seen. IRCD; MDWPO; ST.

DUCKBILLED PLATYPUS   *a duckbilled platypus.* An aquatic mammal of Australia—also called a *duckbill* (WNNCD: 1840) and a *platypus* (WNNCD: 1832). Source: DUCK. WNNCD: O.E. According to the *duck test* (q.v.), the *platypus* (Gk. for "flatfoot") is a duck: it has a bill like a duck; it has webbed feet like a duck; and it lays eggs like a duck. However, it has four legs and a tail like a beaver, and it is a mammal. So much for the duck test. WNWD.

DUCK HOOK   *a duck hook.* A short tee shot in golf that travels hard and fast into the left rough (for a right-handed swinger). Source: DUCK. WNNCD: O.E. The reason for the association with *duck* is uncertain. The legendary golfer Sam Snead is reputed to have said that the *duck hook* is so called because the ball suddenly "ducks down" into the grass. Another possibility is that "Duck!" is the last thing heard before the ball hits the spectators. *See also* Duck (v); Wounded Duck.

DUCKS AND DRAKES   The British original of the American game of "skipping stones." WNNCD: 1583. Source: DUCK. WNNCD: O.E. Skipping stones is a pastime of visitors to the shore of a body of water. The object is to get as many "skips," or bounces, as possible out of a flat stone thrown low and parallel to the surface of the water. In England, the term is also used for squandering money: "To play ducks and drakes with your money" is to throw it away, like skipping stones that eventually disappear. Why the pastime is called *ducks and drakes* is uncertain, although it may be due to the resemblance of the bouncing stones to female and male ducks landing awkwardly on the water. ATWS; BDPF; DEI; HOI; IRCD; LCRH.

DUCK'S EGG   *See* Goose Egg.

DUCK SOUP   *to be as easy as duck soup.* To be extremely easy: child's play; a cinch; a piece of cake. WNNCD: 1912. Source: DUCK. WNNCD: O.E. Recipe for duck soup: "Take one duck . . . ." Getting the duck is the hard part; making soup out of it is easy. Actually, getting the duck can also be easy if the duck is shot illegally—i.e., while sitting on the ground or water—or if you have a dog along to retrieve it for you. AID; ATWS; CE; CH; DOC; HTB; IRCD; LTA; ST. *See also* Dead Duck; Lame Duck; Sitting Duck.

DUCKTAIL   *a ducktail.* A hair style in which the long hair on both sides of the head is combed to form a vertical ridge at the back. WNNCD: 1947. Source: DUCK. WNNCD: O.E. The *ducktail* haircut is named after the tail of a duck, which is the only part of the duck that is visible when it tips over to dive. The feathers meet at the back and are tapered to a point. The hair style was popular with teenagers following WWII. ATWS; IRCD.

DUCK TEST   *the duck test.* The test of whether something is really what it is purported to be. Source: DUCK. WNNCD: O.E. The *duck test* was applied by the Democratic Congress in 1989 to determine whether President Bush's financial proposal was really a tax: "If it looks like a duck (or tax), waddles like a duck (or tax), and quacks like a duck (or tax), then it's probably a duck (or tax)." *See also* Duckbilled Platypus.

DUCK WALK   *to do the duck walk.* To walk bent over, with your hands around your ankles and your toes pointed outward; to walk "hunkered down," with your hands on top of your head or grasping a rifle or guitar. Source: DUCK. WNNCD: O.E. Ducks have short legs and walk with their large webbed feet pointed outward. Imitations of this walk are used in children's races (using the bent-over position) or in military calisthenics (using the squatting position). Rock star

Chuck Berry is famous for playing his guitar while moving across the stage hunkered down in a modified *duck walk*. IRCD. *See also* Duck Test; Shoot the Duck; Waddle like a Duck.

DUCKY   *to be (just) ducky.* To be just fine. (Sometimes a sarcasm). WNNCD: 1819. Source: DUCK. WNNCD: O.E. Since about 1830, *ducky* has been broadened in America to mean not only "fine" or "satisfactory" but "wonderful" or "marvelous." As sarcasm, an exclamation like "Well, isn't that just *ducky!*" means something like "Isn't that a fine *kettle of fish* (q.v.)!" *Ducky* suggests a peaceful scene of a family of ducks floating on the calm water, but it probably derives from the expression *a fine day for ducks* (q.v.), meaning "a miserable (rainy) day for humans." ATWS; IRCD; LTA.

DUMB AS AN OX   *to be as dumb as an ox.* To be stupid. Source: OX. WNNCD: O.E. The ox—a steer that is used as a draft animal—has probably gained its reputation for stupidity from its comparison with the horse. Horses are harnessed; oxen are yoked. Horses are reined; oxen are goaded. Horses are ridden; oxen are not. Horses are raced; oxen are not, etc. In other words, oxen are thought capable of menial work only. CH. *See also* Dumb Ox; Lummox. *Compare* Clumsy as an Ox.

DUMB BUNNY   *You dumb bunny!* You stupid idiot! LTA: 1922. Source: RABBIT. *Bunny* has been an affectionate name for "rabbit" since 1690. *Dumb bunny* is an affectionate scolding for a naughty child, a bumbling sibling, or a spouse. Rabbits are "dumb" only in the sense of "making no sound"; otherwise, they are very good at locating vegetables in the garden at night and in surviving many predators, including humans. *Compare* Dumb Dodo; Dumb Ox.

DUMB CLUCK   *a dumb cluck.* A naive or stupid person. Source: CHICKEN. The *cluck* in this metaphor is a metonymous name for the chicken, which, although never given much credit for intelligence, is smart enough to know how many chicks she has and how to round them up by calling "Cluck! Cluck!" Human *dumb clucks* lack either sophistication or brains—or both. ATWS; CE. *See also* Cackle. *Compare* Dumb Bunny; Dumb Dodo; Dumb Ox.

DUMB DODO   *You dumb dodo!* You stupid idiot! LTA: 1930. Source: DODO. WNNCD: 1628. The extinct dodo bird, formerly of two islands east of Madagascar, is, in a sense, being blamed for its own extinction (ca. 1700). It was too easy for the European colonists to catch it, and it was too tasty for them to resist it. It was too "dumb" to survive. *See also* Dodo; Dead as a Dodo. *Compare* Dumb Ox.

DUMB OX   *a dumb ox.* A stupid person (usu. male). Source: OX. WNNCD: O.E. The most famous *dumb ox* was Thomas Aquinas, who was tagged with this nickname by his teacher, Albertus Magnus (ca. 1250), because he was so "stupid."

Oxen are thought to be dumb because they do only menial work. Unlike horses, they do not run, race, prance, or gallop; and they do not respond to reins the way horses do. EWPO; IRCD. *See also* Dumb as an Ox; Lummox. *Compare* Dumb Bunny; Dumb Dodo.

DUMMOX   *See* Lummox.

DUST BUNNY   *a dust bunny*. A dust ball under a bed. Source: RABBIT. The balls of dust that accumulate under a bed over a period of time are gray and furry and resemble little *hares*. (Rabbits are born naked, blind, and immobile; hares are born furred, sighted, and mobile.) Calling them "little rabbits" is not a big mistake, but giving each of them a name means that it's time to vacuum. *Compare* Dust Pussy.

DUST PUSSY   *a dust pussy*. A ball of dust that accumulates in an out-of-the-way place, such as under a bed. Source: CAT. A *dust pussy* is so named because it resembles a furry little kitten, or "pussy," all curled up in a ball asleep. *Pussy* (WNNCD: 1878) is short for the earlier *pussycat* (WNNCD: 1805). *Compare* Dust Bunny; Wood Pussy.

DYED-IN-THE-WOOL   *a dyed-in-the-wool conservative*. A staunch political conservative. WNNCD: 1579. Source: SHEEP. Wool that is dyed before it is processed (i.e., dyed *in the wool*) is more highly valued than wool that is dyed after it is woven or fashioned into a garment. Its color is fast and firm, like the views of a conservative. DOC.

DYING QUAIL   *a dying quail*. A fly ball, in baseball, that suddenly drops just beyond the infielders: a "Texas leaguer"; a "cheap pop fly." Source: QUAIL. WNNCD: 14th cent. The quail, like the partridge and grouse, is a game bird. When it is shot in the air by a hunter, it drops immediately to the ground. *See also* Quail (v). *Compare* Wounded Duck.

E

EAGER BEAVER *an eager beaver.* An overly zealous person who works harder or longer than necessary—and then volunteers for more—in order to impress his/her superior, and as a result alienates his/her associates. WNNCD: 1943. Source: BEAVER. WNNCD: O.E. The beaver, a semiaquatic mammal, and the bee, a flying insect, are recognized as the most industrious of all animals. ATWS; BDPF; CI; DOC; EWPO; HOI; HTB; IRCD. *See also* Busy as a Beaver; Work like a Beaver. *Compare* Busy as a Bee.

EAGLE *an eagle.* A score of two strokes below par on a golf hole. Source: EAGLE. WNNCD: 13th cent. The golf *eagle* is probably so called because it is a more "majestic" score than a *birdie* (q.v.) (one stroke below par). It yields a net score of three on a par five hole, two on a par four hole, and one—a "hole in one"—on a par three hole. To "make an eagle" is to *eagle* the hole. The *American eagle* coin (q.v.) was also called an *eagle* for short. ATWS. *See also* Double Eagle.

EAGLE BEAK A pejorative name for a person with an aquiline nose; the nose itself. Source: EAGLE. WNNCD: 13th cent. A person with an *eagle beak* has a long nose that hooks downward toward the upper lip. The analogy is to the upper beak of a bald or golden eagle, which hooks down over the shorter lower beak and has the function of tearing apart the carcass of a dead or dying animal. *See also* Aquiline. *Compare* Hawk-nosed.

EAGLE EYE *to have an eagle eye.* To have a keen sense of sight or insight. WNNCD: 1802. Source: EAGLE. WNNCD: 13th cent. The bald eagle or golden eagle can spot a mouse a quarter of a mile away from its perch high in a tree or while soaring high in the air. Human vision is not that good, but attention to detail and nuance brings it closer. Also: *to watch someone with an eagle eye.* ATWS; BDPF; DEI; DOC. *See also* Eagle-eyed; Eye of an Eagle; Legal Eagle.

EAGLE-EYED *to be eagle-eyed.* To have a keen sense of sight or insight. Source: EAGLE. WNNCD: 13th cent. An eagle-eyed person has a good eye for detail and an instinct for the feelings of others. The American eagle is noted for its extraordinary eyesight, although it has little sympathy for the animals—large (e.g., deer) and small (e.g., mice)—that it preys on. IRCD; SHM. *See also* Eagle Eye; Eye of an Eagle; Legal Eagle.

EAGLE FLIES ON FRIDAY *The eagle flies on Friday.* Friday is payday. IRCD: 1898. Source: EAGLE. WNNCD: 13th cent. This expression, attributed to Black slang, is thought to refer to the former payment of workers in ten-dollar gold pieces, nicknamed "eagles," although the eagle has appeared on the back of many coins, including the current quarter, and on many bills, including the current one-dollar bill. NDAS. *See also* Spread Eagle; When the Eagle Flies.

EAGLE HAS LANDED *The eagle has landed.* The expected has occurred. Source: EAGLE. WNNCD: 13th cent. This utterance in 1969 proclaimed to the world that the lunar landing module, the Eagle, had landed safely on the moon. Previously, it had circled the moon looking for an appropriate landing place, just as an eagle seeks out its prey from on high. *See also* Eagle Eye; Soar like an Eagle.

EARLY BIRD *See* Early Bird Catches the Worm.

EARLY BIRD CATCHES THE WORM *The early bird catches—or gets—the worm.* First come, first served. DOC: 1636. Source: BIRD; WORM. WNNCD: O.E. The robin is a familiar figure, early in the morning after a rain, pulling a worm from its hole or picking one up from the sidewalk before it returns to its hole. For humans, an *early bird* (WNNCD: ca. 1890) is a person who gets up early, arrives early, or acts promptly on a tip. Both "early birds" are more likely to succeed than those who get up late, arrive late, or procrastinate. Humans have a choice, but diurnal birds instinctively stir when the sun rises. AID; ATWS; BDPF; CE; CI; DEI; DOC; ID; IRCD.

EARMARK (n) *to have all the earmarks of something.* To have all the distinguishing features of something—such as a riot, a recession, or a tax. Source: CATTLE. Literally, an earmark is a notch in the ear of a domesticated animal, esp. a bovine animal, for the purpose of identification—a form of "branding" (WNNCD: 15th cent.). Figuratively, an *earmark* is an indication of the impending development of something sinister. ATWS; EWPO; LCRH; MDWPO. *See also* Earmark (v). *Compare* Dog-ear (n).

EARMARK (v)   *to earmark something.* To set aside, or designate, something for a specific purpose or use. Source: CATTLE. Farmers earmark cattle and other domesticated animals, such as pigs and sheep, for the purpose of identifying them in case they are lost or stolen (WNNCD: 1591). Organizations *earmark* funds for a particular use by setting them aside so that they will not be used for other purposes. Funds so designated are said to be *earmarked* for that use only. ATWS; BDPF; EWPO; LCRH; MDWPO. *See also* Earmark (n). *Compare* Dog-ear (v).

EARN YOUR WINGS   *See* Sprout Wings.

EASEL   *an easel.* A three—or four—legged wooden framework for supporting a painter's canvas. WNNCD: 1634. Source: ASS. WNNCD: O.E. The *ass* (Du. *ezel*), or donkey, is the proverbial beast of burden. The load that it carries was once supported by a wooden framework consisting of connected *sawhorses* (q.v.). The donkey bore this burden with ease, as an artist's *easel* does the canvas. (In French, an *easel* is "a little horse": *chevalet*.) ATWS; EWPO; LCRH; THT. *See also* Ass.

EASY AS DUCK SOUP   *See* Duck Soup.

EAT A HORSE   *See* Eat like a Horse.

EAT CROW   *to eat crow.* To swallow your pride, admit defeat, and accept the consequences. SPD: 1851. Source: CROW. WNNCD: O.E. Losing is distasteful, and so is crow. Unlike the chicken, duck, pheasant, or turkey, the crow is a scavenger, and eating it would be repulsive to many people. Furthermore, although the crow is a fairly large bird, its meat is said to be tough and sparse. The only thing worse might be to eat vulture. AID; ATWS; BDPF; CE; DOC; EWPO; HOI; ID; IRCD; LCRH; SHM.

EAT HIGH OFF THE HOG   *to eat high off—or on—the hog.* To live well; to eat expensive food. Source: HOG. WNNCD: O.E. The expensive cuts of pork are those that are found on the upper hind legs and hips (the "hams"), the upper front legs and shoulders (the "picnics"), and the upper and lower sides (the "loins" and "bacon"). The less expensive cuts are those found on the perimeter: the feet, knuckles, hocks, belly, and jowls. To eat the latter is to *eat low on the hog.* AID; BDPF; EWPO. *See also* Live High on the Hog.

EAT HUMBLE PIE   *to eat humble pie.* To submit to humiliation; to apologize under pressure. WNNCD: 1830. Source: DEER. To "eat *humble* pie" is a 19th cent. version of the medieval English expression "to eat *umble* pie"—i.e., to eat the internal organs, or "umbles," of a deer. When a huntsman presented the carcass of a deer to the lord of the manor, the lord and his family got the venison, while the huntsman and his comrades got the heart, liver, kidneys, etc., which were usu. prepared as a pie. The unequal division of meat was thought to be humiliating to the huntsman, leading to the association of *umble* with *humble*. In the 20th cent., *to eat humble pie* is approx. the equivalent of the milder *to eat your hat* or *to eat crow* (q.v.). AID; ATWS; BDPF; CE; CH; CI; DEI; DOC; EWPO; HOI.

EAT LIKE A BIRD   *to eat like a bird.* To eat very little; to pick at your food. Source: BIRD. WNNCD: O.E. Many of the commonest birds, such as the sparrow, are quite small, and consequently they do not consume a great amount of food in one day. Furthermore, much of the eating time is spent pecking at the ground, picking up a morsel, dropping it, picking it up again, etc. Such birds appear to eat very little, but a sparrow can easily eat 100% of its bodyweight every day, while a human eats only about 1.5% of their bodyweight in a single day. Therefore, humans who *eat like a bird* eat the amount that a small bird does, but not the relative percentage of their bodyweight that either a bird or a normal person does. AID; ATWS; IRCD.

EAT LIKE A HORSE   *to eat like a horse.* To eat in excess or without restraint. Source: HORSE. WNNCD: O.E. The horse is a strange subject for this metaphor. Horses are herbivorous, and they eat hay and grain slowly and steadily. Furthermore, a horse eats approx. the same percentage of its bodyweight daily—approx. 1.5%—as a human, although the average horse weighs about ten times as much as a human. Therefore, a human who eats ten times as much as he/she normally does—say two pounds—would have to eat approx. twenty pounds a day in order to "eat like a horse." Another metaphor involving eating and horses—"to be so hungry you could *eat a horse*"—means that you could eat approx. 1,000 pounds at one sitting. AID; ATWS; CI; DEI; ID.

EAT LIKE A PIG   *to eat like a pig.* To gulp down your food, making loud noises and creating a mess. Source: PIG. WNNCD: 13th cent. Children are often accused of *eating like pigs*, as are some adults. Pigs—and hogs—are usu. fed "slop"—liquid garbage—out of a trough. While eating, they grunt a lot and spill the slop onto the floor or ground; and they never seem to get enough, although they don't eat much more in one day than humans their own size. DEI; ID. *See also* Make a Pig of Yourself; Pig out. *Compare* Eat like a Horse.

EAT OUT OF YOUR HAND   *to have someone eating out of your hand.* To have someone in your power or control. DOC: 1921. Source: ANIMAL. Domesticated animals are dependent on humans for their food—whether by being fed in the barn or being let out to graze. Wild animals that are enticed to eat food out of your hand are sometimes regarded as "tame," but mostly they are just hungry—and they can still *bite the hand that feeds them* (q.v.). Animals in the wild can become dependent on humans for food, just as humans can become submissive to other humans who dominate them. AID.

EAT YOUR FIRST OYSTER   *like eating your first oyster.* A little scary, like eating your first peach. (T. S. Eliot's "The Love Song of J. Alfred Prufrock": "Do I dare to eat a peach?") Source: OYSTER. WNNCD: 14th cent. Raw oysters are often served *on the half shell* (q.v.) and ingested by lifting the shell to your mouth, letting the loose body of the oyster slide in, and swallowing it. *See also* Mountain Oyster; Prairie Oyster.

EGGHEAD   *an egghead.* A highbrow or intellectual (usu. male). WNNCD: 1952. Source: CHICKEN. WNNCD: O.E. This metaphor derives from the 1952 presidential campaign of Adlai Stevenson, who was a highbrow—both literally (he was almost bald) and figuratively (he was a cultivated person)—and an intellectual (he was a university professor). Technically, an *egghead* should be completely bald, so that his smooth round head resembles a chicken's egg, at least from above or behind; but Stevenson's appearance was close enough to earn him this moniker. (LTA and MDWPO cite earlier occurrences of the metaphor.) ATWS; CE; DEI; SPD.

EGG ON   *to egg someone on.* To incite someone to unwise action. WNNCD: 13th cent. Source: CHICKEN (*). WNNCD: O.E. *Egg on* calls forth the image of someone throwing hen's eggs at someone else in order to get that person to do something that is not in his/her best interests. However, *egg on* is not an animal metaphor. It derives from O.N. *eggja* "edge," a cognate of O.E. *ecg* "edge." Therefore, to *egg* someone on is to push them closer to the *edge* of danger or criminality. AID; CI; DEI; EWPO.

EGG ON YOUR FACE   *to have egg on your face.* To have embarrassed or incriminated yourself. Source: WEASEL. When the farmer catches the weasel crawling out of the henhouse, it usu. has egg on its face, attesting to its guilt: the weasel has spent the night killing chickens and sucking eggs. ATWS. *See also* Walk on Eggs; Weasel out.

EGGPLANT   *an eggplant.* The smooth, ovoid, blackish-purple fruit of the herb of the same name. WNNCD: 1767. Source: CHICKEN. The edible eggplant is so called because of its egglike smoothness and shape, although it is closer in size to a turkey egg than a chicken egg. The analogy is not based on the color: chicken eggs are usu. white or brown. The color *eggplant* is a metaphor in its own right. EWPO.

EGREGIOUS   *See* Congregate.

ELEPHANT DOG   *an elephant dog.* A tiny but noisy watchdog. Source: ELEPHANT. WNNCD: 14th cent. This is a joke. A toy poodle, though noisy, is too small to frighten away even a kitten; but the owner defends its usefulness by saying, "Well, you haven't seen any elephants around here lately, have you?"

ELEPHANT EAR *an elephant ear.* A large, thin, flat, glazed pastry. Source: ELEPHANT. WNNCD: 14th cent. Elephant ears are a favorite offering at fairs and carnivals. At one foot in diameter, these honey-glazed "cookies" are almost a meal in themselves. The pastry is closer in size to the ear of the Asian elephant, but it is shaped more like the giant "fan" of the African elephant. *See also* Elephant Mitt. *Compare* Elephant's Ear.

ELEPHANTIASIS A medical condition that involves enlargement of the limbs and thickening of the surrounding skin. WNNCD: 1581. Source: ELEPHANT. WNNCD: 14th cent. This disease was so named by the ancient Greeks (Gk. *elephantiasis,* fr. Gk. *elephant*) because the resulting enlargement and thickening resembled the appendages of a pachyderm. The Romans, who borrowed the term, linked the disease with leprosy, but it is now known to be caused by obstruction of the lymph system by parasitic worms. The condition of the Elephant Man, Joseph Merrick, was first described as *elephantiasis,* then as neurofibromatosis, and finally as Proteus syndrome. ATWS. *See also* Elephantine.

ELEPHANTINE *to be elephantine.* To be of massive size or possess enormous strength. WNNCD: 1630. Source: ELEPHANT. WNNCD: 14th cent. The African elephant is the world's largest land animal, weighing up to 13,000 pounds, with a length of close to 25 feet and a height of approx. 13 feet. The Indian elephant is slightly smaller: just under 12,000 pounds, just over 21 feet long, approx. 10.5 feet high. Such size implies great strength, and Indian elephants are trained to do heavy work that is impossible for humans. The metaphor is applied to objects of considerable size and power, such as engines and dynamos, and even to long and ponderous sentences, as in some of William Faulkner's stories. ATWS; CE. *See also* Elephantiasis.

ELEPHANT IN THE ROOM *See* See the Elephant.

ELEPHANT MITT *an elephant mitt.* A catcher's mitt used with a knuckleball pitcher. Source: ELEPHANT. WNNCD: 14th cent. The *elephant mitt* is so called because it is larger than a regular catcher's mitt and is shaped like the ear of an elephant. The mitt was designed to catch the unpredictable pitches of a knuckleballer, which are slow but extremely erratic. *Compare* Elephant Ear; Elephant's Ear.

ELEPHANT SEAL *an elephant seal.* The largest member of the seal-walrus family. WNNCD: 1841. Source: ELEPHANT. WNNCD: 14th cent. The *elephant seal* is so called because of its size. Just as the elephant is the largest member of its class (land animals), the *elephant seal* is the largest member of its own class (aquatic *pinnipeds,* or "fin-footed mammals"). The Asian elephant and the elephant seal are approx. the same length (20 feet), but the pachyderm weighs almost twice as much as the seal (6 tons to 3.5 tons).

ELEPHANT'S EAR   *an elephant's ear.* An ornamental taro plant with enormous heart-shaped leaves; a variety of begonia plant with large showy leaves; a false morel, or "beefsteak," mushroom. Source: ELEPHANT. WNNCD: 14th cent. The ear in question is that of an African elephant, whose "fans" are twice the size of those in the Indian elephant. The false morel, a fungus, does not have leaves, but it is shaped like a leaf—or an elephant's ear. WNWD. *Compare* Elephant Ear.

EMPTY NEST   *See* Empty-nest Syndrome.

EMPTY NESTER   *See* Empty-nest Syndrome.

EMPTY-NEST SYNDROME   *the empty-nest syndrome.* The feelings of emptiness and loneliness felt by the parents of children who have grown up and left home. Source: BIRD. In this metaphor, the *nest* (q.v.) is the home in which the children were raised, the *empty nest* is the home after the children have departed, and the *empty nesters* (WNNCD: 1971) are the parents who thought they would be happy to see the children *leave the nest* but now wish they would return. The implication is that birds feel the same way when their brood hatches, fledges, and flies; but that is questionable, since many birds lay more than one clutch of eggs annually, and their nest is full again before long. NDAS.

END OF YOUR TETHER   *to be at—or come to—the end of your tether.* To have exhausted all of your options or resources. DOC: 1809. Source: ANIMAL. A domestic animal is tethered—i.e., attached by a rope to a stake—in order to restrict its area of grazing and/or to prevent it from running away or chasing after other animals. Human tethers are invisible, for the most part. They consist of limits on one's finances, patience, energy, and options. A person who has come to the *end of his/her tether* has run out of alternatives for survival and is "at his/her wit's end." AID; ATWS; BDPF; CI; EWPO; HOI; ID.

ENOUGH TO KILL AN ELEPHANT   *to have taken enough alcohol, drugs, pills, or poison to kill an elephant.* To have overdosed on alcohol, drugs, pills, or poison. Source: ELEPHANT. WNNCD: 14th cent. The elephant is the world's largest land animal, weighing up to 13,000 pounds. The assumption is that it would take approx. one hundred times the amount needed to kill a human to kill an elephant. (But it would probably take a hundred humans to administer the dose.) A related expression, *big enough to choke a horse,* refers to a roll of bills, not a drug or poison. NDAS.

ENTRAPMENT   *See* Trap.

ERASE   *to erase something.* To rub or scratch something out; to delete or nullify something. WNNCD: 1605. Source: RAT. WNNCD: O.E. The I.E. root *red-* "to gnaw or scratch" provides us not only with the English (and French) word *rat* "the gnawer and scratcher" but the Latin verbal roots *rad-* "to scratch" (from which *erase* derives) and *rod-* "to gnaw." The analogy is to the behavior of the rat, which can scratch its way through the ground or gnaw its way through wood. Other descendants of Latin *rad-* are *rascal* "an unprincipled adult or mischievous child" (WNNCD: 15th cent.); *rash* "a series of eruptions or events" (WNNCD: 1709); and *raze* "to level a building or a beard" (WNNCD: 1547). *See also* Erode.

ERODE *to erode*. To eat away at something; to be eaten away by something. WNNCD: 1612. Source: RAT. WNNCD: O.E. The I.E. root *red-* "to gnaw or scratch" provides us not only with the word *rat* "the gnawer and scratcher" but the Latin verbal roots *rod-* "to gnaw" (from which *erode* derives) and *rad-* "to scratch." The analogy is to the behavior of the rat, which can gnaw through wood or scratch its way through the ground underneath. Other descendants of Latin *rod-* are *corrode* "for metal to be eaten away by chemical action" (WNNCD: 15th cent.) and *rodent* "a ratlike mammal" (WNNCD: 1541). EWPO; ROE. *See also* Erase.

EVERY DOG HAS HIS DAY Every person can expect to get at least one opportunity for success, wealth, power, etc. EWPO: early-19th cent. Source: DOG. WNNCD: O.E. The dog is regarded as the lowest of all domesticated animals, because it does not earn its keep by killing pests (as the cat does), helping haul loads (as horses, mules, and oxen do), providing food for the table (as cows, pigs, and chickens do), or providing fiber for clothing (as sheep and goats do). Yet even the lowest domestic animal can find its moment of glory by chasing away thieves, pulling a child from the water, warning a family about a fire, etc. And even the most insignificant of humans can expect "fifteen minutes of fame" (Andy Warhol). AID; ATWS; BDPF; CI; DEI; HTB; ID.

EYE LIKE A HAWK *to have an eye like a hawk*. To have a sharp eye for details. Source: HAWK. WNNCD: O.E. The hawk perches high in a tree or soars high in the air looking for its prey on the ground. Its keen vision allows it to spot a small mammal under cover of brush or a fish underwater. A person with remarkable eyesight is sometimes called "Hawkeye," as in *The Last of the Mohicans* and *M*A*S*H*. *See also* Hawk-eyed; Watch Someone like a Hawk. *Compare* Eye of an Eagle.

EYE OF AN EAGLE *to have the eye(s) of an eagle*. To have a keen eye for detail. Source: EAGLE. WNNCD: 13th cent. The eagle is noted for its amazing eyesight. It can see a tiny mouse from high up in the air or when perched in a tall tree. A human who can spot details in a painting, or errors in a manuscript, is said to have the same kind of vision. *See also* Eagle Eye; Eagle-eyed; Legal Eagle.

EYES LIKE A CAT *to have eyes like a cat*. To have sharp vision, esp. in the dark. Source: CAT. WNNCD: O.E. Cats are nocturnal animals, and their eyes have an additional layer that reflects more light to the retina and greatly improves their night vision. (It also causes their eyes to shine in artificial light, such as that of a flash camera.) People who see well in the dark are said to have *eyes like a cat*, or to be *cat-eyed*. ATWS. *See also* Cat's-eye.

F

FADE IN THE STRETCH *See* In the Homestretch.

FAIR GAME *See* Open Season.

FALL INTO A TRAP *See* Trap.

FALL NECK AND CROP *See* Come a Cropper.

FALL OF A SPARROW *the fall of a sparrow.* A seemingly insignificant event. Source: SPARROW. WNNCD: O.E. Matthew 10:29 states that God is aware of everything, even the death of a single sparrow. The English sparrow is a very small bird, a very common bird, and its song is undistinguished. But it was introduced into America to catch insects, and it does that very well.

FALL OFF A HORSE *What should you do if you fall off a horse? Get right back on.* What should you do if you suffer a setback? Try, try again. Source: HORSE. WNNCD: O.E. A riding horse seems to know when it is being ridden by an inexperienced rider. Such a rider is more likely to get thrown than an experienced one, and the fallen rider is also likely to become *horse shy* unless he/she retrieves the horse and gets back in the saddle immediately. People who suffer a rejection are reminded of this maxim and are urged to get back into action as soon as possible. ST. *See also* Gun-shy.

FALL OFF THE PACE *See* Keep Pace with.

FALL PREY TO *See* Prey on.

FARRAGO   *a farrago.* A hodgepodge. WNNCD: 1632. Source: CATTLE. Farrago is lit. "cattle fodder," a mixture of barley and other grains (fr. Lat. *farrago* "mixed fodder"). In its metaphorical sense, a *farrago* is a confused mixture of things: e.g., a *farrago* of fears, doubts, or nonsense. Cattle feed has not changed much in the past 2,000 years, but *farrago* has. EWPO. *Compare* Chicken Feed; Feel Your Oats; Know Your Oats; Off Your Feed.

FAST BUCK   *to make a fast buck.* To make a quick, and possibly dishonest, dollar. Source: DEER. WNNCD: O.E. The adult male deer, or "buck," is a very fast animal, but this metaphor is based on the deer's antlers, which were once used to make the handle of a buckhorn knife. The knife was used as an indicator of the dealer in late-19th cent. Western poker games—until it was replaced by the silver dollar, or "buck." Hence the monetary value and the shady source of income. WNWD. *See also* Big Bucks; Buck (n); Buck Stops here.

FAT AS A PIG   *to be as fat as a pig.* To be uncustomarily overweight or obese. Source: PIG. WNNCD: 13th cent. The purpose of raising a pig is to fatten it up for sale or slaughter. It used to be believed that the fatter the pig the better, but now a "sleek" pig is preferred to a very fat one. Humans who are said to be *as fat as a pig* are usu. either not present at the time or are children. CH. *See also* Eat like a Pig; Make a Pig of Yourself.

FAT CAT   *a fat cat.* A wealthy benefactor, esp. to political campaigns. WNNCD: 1928. Source: CAT. WNNCD: O.E. To most people a fat cat is the pampered cartoon feline Garfield, who spends most of his time eating and sleeping and getting his way with just about everything and everybody. But to a politician, a *fat cat* is a wealthy supporter of the candidates of a particular political party who makes generous contributions in return for certain favors. In more recent times, the metaphor has been extended to include a wealthy person who simply enjoys the life of the rich and famous. ATWS; CE; DOC; IRCD; NDAS; SPD.

FAWN   *the color fawn.* A light grayish brown. Source: DEER. Fawn is supposedly the color of a young deer (WNNCD: 14th cent.); but the young of most deer around the world have coats that are speckled with white, so this is an imperfect metaphor. Oddly enough, the verb *fawn*, as in *fawn on* (q.v.), does not derive from the name of these cute little animals. ATWS.

FAWN ON   *to fawn on someone.* To show unrestrained, insincere affection for someone. Source: DOG. Dogs show *sincere* affection for their caretakers by licking their boots and jumping up on them—wagging their tails all the while. (WNNCD: 15th cent.) People show *insincere* affection for someone by groveling, flattering, and figuratively *licking their boots*—all for the purpose of gaining favor. The *fawn* in *fawn on* does not derive from the name for a young deer but from the O.E. verb *fagnian* "to rejoice." ATWS; CE; DEI. *Compare* Curry Favor.

FEATHER (n) *a feather.* A fringe of hair on the back of the lower legs of certain dogs and horses. Source: BIRD. All senses and functions of *feather* derive from O.E. *fether,* which is a cognate of Gk. *pteron* "wing." Birds are the only animals that have natural feathers, but tufts of hair on certain mammals, including humans (on the back of the neck), are given the same name. *Feather* has also been applied to: (1) a flaw in the eye or in a precious gem; (2) a condition of health or appearance: *in fine feather* (q.v.); and (3) a genus or species: *birds of a feather* (q.v.). Something that is *as light as a feather* is extremely light, as the usual answer to the question "Which is heavier, a pound of feathers or a pound of lead?" confirms. AID; ATWS. *See also* Feather (v).

FEATHER (v) *to feather an oar or a propeller blade.* To position the blade of an oar or a propeller so that it is parallel to the direction of movement. Source: BIRD. An oar is *feathered* when it is returned horizontally to its rowing position. During this time, the water remaining on the blade flies off in a feathery spray. The propeller blades of an airplane are *feathered* when the engine has failed or the pilot is trying to save fuel. The only thing *feathery* about this procedure is that the blades now act like little wings. ATWS; BDPF; ID. *See also* Feather (n). *Compare* Catch a Crab.

FEATHERBED *to featherbed.* For a union to negotiate a contract that limits production or requires more workers than necessary to do the job. WNNCD: 1947. Source: BIRD. A *feather bed* (WNNCD: O.E.) is a mattress cover filled with duck or goose feathers and *down* (q.v.). It is the softest and most comfortable of mattresses. *Featherbedding* (WNNCD: 1921) is the practice of reducing the work load while at the same time retaining the work force. It results in jobs that outsiders regard as soft and cushy, like a feather bed. ATWS; EWPO; LCRH; WNWD. *See also* Feather Your Nest.

FEATHERBRAIN *a featherbrain.* A stupid, foolish, or scatterbrained person. WNNCD: 1839. Source: BIRD. A *featherbrained* person (LTA: 1820) has a brain that is as *light as a feather* (q.v.) and is therefore incapable of behaving like a normal human being. A later variant of this metaphor is *birdbrain* (WNNCD: 1943). A *birdbrained* person (IRCD: 1920s) has a brain the size of a bird's—still too small to control human behavior. Birds of different species have different size brains—the hummingbird's is quite tiny—but each is of adequate size to suit the needs of that particular species. ATWS; CE; LCRH. *Compare* Featherweight.

FEATHERBRAINED *See* Featherbrain.

FEATHER IN YOUR CAP *a feather in your cap.* A mark of achievement, distinction, or honor. Source: BIRD. The American use of this metaphor probably derives from the practice among Native American Indians of adding an eagle feather to their headband as a mark of distinction in hunting or battle. European settlers adopted this practice by placing a feather of the bird that they had killed in the headband of their cap or hat. (Men's hats are sometimes still sold with a feather in the hatband in America.) Yankee Doodle stuck a feather in his cap to increase his status among the townspeople. Nowadays, a *feather in your cap* is simply a figurative honor; e.g., a positive accomplishment of any kind, such as a big sale or a promotion, can be *a feather in your cap*. AID; ATWS; BDPF; CI; DEI; DOC; EWPO; HOI; LCRH; SHM. *Compare* Cockade.

FEATHERWEIGHT   *a featherweight.* A boxer in the weight class between *bantamweight* (q.v.) and *lightweight*: 119 pounds to 126 pounds (professional); 120 pounds to 125 pounds (amateur). WNNCD: 1812. Source: BIRD. Compared to a heavyweight boxer, a *featherweight* is *as light as a feather* (q.v.); and compared to a heavyweight of business or industry, a *featherweight* is a person of little influence or importance. ATWS; LTA.

FEATHERY   *See* Feather (v).

FEATHER YOUR NEST   *to feather your (own) nest.* To improve your condition in life, esp. at someone's else's expense. DOC: 1553. Source: BIRD. *Feathering your nest* can be as innocent as providing for your own comfort in the present or building up a *nest egg* (q.v.) for the future. However, the metaphor has acquired overtones of corruption, as when public officials abuse their power and siphon off money for their own use. When birds have finished building their nest of twigs, some of them pluck downy feathers from their breast and line the nest with them. This is done not only for the sake of the fragile eggs but also for the comfort of the adult birds themselves. AID; ATWS; BDPF; CI; DEI; DOC; EWPO; HOI; ID; IRCD.

FEE   *a fee.* A charge for use or services. Source: CATTLE. *Fee* derives from O.E. *feoh* "cattle or property" but was influenced by O.Fr. *fief* "a feudal estate held in return for service." Both words have a Gmc. origin. The long association of cattle with wealth can be seen in Lat. *pecus* "cattle" and *pecunia* "money." ATWS; BDPF; EWPO; WNWD. *See also* Capital; Chattel; Pecuniary.

FEEDING FRENZY   *a feeding frenzy.* A wild and disorderly scramble for something. Source: FISH. Meateating fish, such as the shark and the piranha, go crazy when a chunk of fresh meat is thrown into the water. They fight over the meat, attack each other, and generally behave like humans at a blue-light special or a rock concert. Other animals, such as chickens and hogs, also engage in *feeding frenzies.*

FEED THE BULLDOG   *See* Bulldog Edition.

FEED THE FISHES *to feed the fishes.* To drown in the ocean, esp. as a result of foul play. Source: FISH. WNNCD: O.E. Big fish eat little fish, and some of the big fish, such as the sharks, have a taste for human flesh. A dead body would not last long among a pack of sharks. (The metaphor is also applied to seasick persons vomiting over the rail of a ship.) A milder expression for sinking to a watery grave is *to sleep with the fishes*, as following death and burial at sea. BDPF; DEI.

FEED THE KITTY *See* Sweeten the Kitty.

FEEL LIKE AN ASS *to feel like an ass.* To feel like a fool. Source: ASS. WNNCD: O.E. The ass, or donkey, has long been regarded as a stupid animal because, unlike its cousin the horse, its role has been primarily that of a beast of burden. To *feel like an ass* is to feel chagrined because of a foolish action or utterance. *See also* Ass; Make an Ass of Yourself.

FEEL THE BUTTERFLIES *to feel the butterflies.* To have a nervous stomach, caused by anxiety or anticipation. Source: BUTTERFLY. WNNCD: O.E. The feeling is that of having a thousand butterflies flying around in your empty stomach, keeping you in a constant state of nervous tension. Stage fright is one of the major causes. The situation is not as serious as having *bats in your belfry* (q.v.).

FEEL YOUR OATS *to feel your oats.* To be full of pep and energy; to feel frisky and playful. EWPO: 1843. Source: HORSE. A horse "feels its oats" when it reacts to a meal of high-energy grain by behaving like a frisky colt (or filly)—racing around the corral, rearing up on its hind legs, nipping at its stablemates, and refusing to come when called. (Horses—and humans—who are *full of beans* react in the same way.) People *feel their oats* by acting like kids again, although the reaction is not usually to a bowl of oatmeal but to some particularly good news, or simply to a good night's sleep. A related expression, *to know your oats*, i.e., to be a good judge of talent, probably derives from the metaphor *a good judge of horseflesh* (q.v.). (Horses are sometimes called "oat-eaters.") BDPF; LCRH; MDWPO; ST.

FEISTY *to be feisty.* To be full of spirit. Source: DOG. In Colonial America, a *feist* was a small, belligerent dog (WNNCD: 1770). From this noun derived the adj. *feisty* (WNNCD: 1896), which orig. meant "nervous and fidgety" but came to mean "lively and frisky." Now it can also mean "quarrelsome and belligerent." *Feisty* pretty well describes many of the characters played by the late James Cagney. EWPO; WNWD.

FELINE *See* Move like a Cat.

FENCED IN *to be fenced in.* To be or feel restrained in your freedom of action. Source: ANIMAL. The primary purpose of a fence or hedgerow is to restrain the freedom of movement of livestock. A person who is *fenced in* feels *cooped up* (q.v.) or restricted in his/her ability to accomplish something. Similar expressions, such as *to be all tied up* and *to be fit to be tied*, probably derive from sailing rather than from restraining animals. AID.

FERAL   *See* Fierce.

FEROCIOUS   *See* Fierce.

FERRET OUT   *to ferret something out.* To uncover something—e.g., the truth—after a painstaking search. SOED: 1577. Source: FERRET. WNNCD: 14th cent. The ferret is a small weasel-like animal that has been used for centuries to hunt rats and rabbits by entering their burrows and driving them out. Its nickname is the "little thief" (V.Lat. *furrittus*, dim. of Lat. *fur* "thief"). ATWS; DEI; EWPO.

FIERCE   *to be fierce.* To be hostile, violent, savage, intense, or unrestrained. WNNCD: 14th cent. Source: ANIMAL. To be *fierce* is lit. to be "wild" (fr. Lat. *ferus* "wild or savage," which is from an I.E. root meaning "wild animal"). A *fierce* battle is a savage one; a *fierce* temper is a violent one; and a *fierce* pain is an intense one. A *feral* animal (WNNCD: 1604) is one that is either wild or has returned to the wild (fr. Lat. *feralis* "wild"); and a *feral* child is one that has lived with, or been raised by, wild animals, like Romulus and Remus. To be *ferocious* (WNNCD: 1646) is lit. to be "wild-eyed" (fr. Lat. *ferus* + *oc-* "eye"). A *ferocious* animal is a fierce-looking one; a *ferocious* attack is a savage one; and *ferocious* heat is intense heat. ROE.

FIGHT LIKE A TIGER   *to fight like a tiger.* To fight ferociously, savagely, and relentlessly. Source: TIGER. WNNCD: O.E. The Indian tiger is a ferocious hunter—ambushing animals much larger (such as the water buffalo) and faster (such as the deer) than itself and pursuing them until it makes a kill. Human *tigers* often make up for their lack of size or status by displaying unusual aggressiveness. (*Tiger* is a favorite name for undersized prizefighters.) DEI. *See also* Arouse the Tiger. *Compare* Fight like Cats and Dogs.

FIGHT LIKE CATS AND DOGS   *to fight like cats and dogs.* To fight a mortal battle. Source: CAT; DOG. WNNCD: O.E. Cats and dogs are natural—and mortal—enemies, and when they fight, they *fight tooth and nail* (WNNCD: 1550); i.e., the dog's teeth and the cat's claws (or "nails") inflict considerable damage. (The cat usu. wins.) People who *fight like cats and dogs* "pull no punches," with "no holds barred" (to mix a couple of "ring" metaphors). A similar expression, *to fight like cats in a bag*, suggests a cruel game for the amusement of sadistic humans. DOC; ID. *See also* Catfight; Make the Fur Fly; Rain Cats and Dogs.

FIGHT LIKE CATS IN A BAG   *See* Fight like Cats and Dogs.

FIGHT TOOTH AND NAIL   *See* Fight like Cats and Dogs.

FILLY   *a filly.* A vivacious young girl or woman. IRCD: 18th cent. Source: HORSE. An equine filly is a female horse under the age of four years (WNNCD: 15th cent.). A human *filly* is a teenage girl or young woman who is as lively and spirited as a young horse. The term *filly* is still in use as a metaphor, but it has pretty much been replaced in England by *bird* (q.v.) and in America by *chick* (q.v.). ATWS; WNWD.

FIN   *a fin.* One of a pair of vertical projections at the rear of an automobile; one of a pair of horizontal projections on the side of a submarine; one of numerous horizontal ribs on a radiator or air-cooled engine. Source: FISH. All senses of *fin* derive from the spiny membranes found on the body of a "true" fish: dorsal fins, pectoral fins, pelvic fins, anal fins, and the caudal fin, or "tail." (The fins on whales and porpoises are named after those of the fish.) The fish uses its caudal fin to produce forward movement; it uses the pectoral fins to change directions; and it uses the other fins to stabilize its upright position in the water. The *fins* on the submarine—and some airplanes—are there for stability; the *fins* on a radiator or small engine are designed to produce cooling; and the *fins* on an automobile— esp. those of the 1940s to 1960s—are strictly decorative. (*Fin* as a five-dollar bill is from Yiddish *finf* "five.") ATWS; EWPO. *Compare* Flipper.

FINE DAY FOR DUCKS   *a fine day for ducks.* A rainy day. IRCD: early-19th cent. Source: DUCK. WNNCD: O.E. Because ducks are aquatic birds, and rain-drops roll off them *like water off a duck's back* (q.v.), they think rainy days are just *ducky* (q.v.). Humans, who lack the duck's oily feathers, think otherwise. Also: *nice day for ducks; nice weather for ducks; nice weather if you're a duck.* ATWS.

FINISH OUT OF THE MONEY   *See* Also-ran.

FINK   *a fink.* A contemptuous person (WNNCD: 1903); an informant or squealer. Source: BIRD. Persons are held in contempt by their colleagues when they betray them by informing the authorities of their dirty deeds. Such informers are called *stool pigeons* (q.v.), *canaries* (q.v.), or *finks. Fink* is the Ger. word for "finch," and a canary is also a finch. All finches are songbirds, so the notion of "singing" on one's colleagues follows logically. A *rat fink* (q.v.) is the worst kind of fink: one who *rats* (q.v.) on his/her fellows out of revenge rather than fear of prosecution. EWPO; LCRH; MDWPO. *See also* Sing like a Bird.

FIREBUG   *a firebug.* An arsonist. WNNCD: 1872. Source: BUG. WNNCD: 1622. There really is an insect—a stink bug—called a *fire bug* (a "calico bug" or "harlequin bug"), but it is so called because of its flaming reddish orange markings rather than an obsession for starting fires. Earlier terms for *firebug* were *arsonist*

(WNNCD: 1680) and *pyromaniac* (WNNCD: 1842). A *political firebug* is someone who likes to start political fires. BDPF; DEI; EWPO; IRCD. *See also* Bug (n) (1).

FIREDOGS   *See* Andirons.

FIREFLY   *a firefly*. A small flying beetle that produces a bright intermittent light during courtship. WNNCD: 1658. Source: FLY. WNNCD: O.E. Among the many classes of insects, flies belong to the order *Diptera* ("two-wings"), while beetles belong to the order *Coleoptera* ("sheath-wings"). That is, a beetle, such as the firefly, has four wings, the outer pair of which form a sheath over the body, and is not a fly at all. The larval stage of a *firefly*, which also emits light, is called a "glow worm." CE.

FIRE HORSE   *See* Old Fire Horse.

FISH (v) (1)   *to fish for something*. To search for something by indirect means. IRCD: 17th cent. Source: FISH. WNNCD: O.E. Fishing is not as simple and direct as reaching into the water and pulling out a fish. It is usu. done by such indirect means as dropping a line with a baited hook into water that may or may not contain fish, which you couldn't see even if they were there. Metaphorically, people *fish* for coins in their pocket—or keys in their purse—by groping and feeling; and they *fish for information and compliments* by feigning ignorance and inferiority, respectively. AID; ATWS; BDPF; DEI; ST. *See also* Fish (v) (2).

FISH (v) (2)   *to fish someone out of the water; to fish something out of a container*. To rescue someone from the water; to extract something from a container. SOED: 1632. Source: FISH. WNNCD: O.E. The process of *fishing* a drowning person out of the water is much like that of landing a fish: remove them from the water to the boat or dock. The process of *fishing* your keys out of your purse—or a coin out of your pocket—is more difficult. You must fish *for* the article before you can fish it *out*. You can't *see* what you're doing and must rely on groping and feeling. It's like fishing for fish in a barrel of oil. ATWS; ST. *See also* Fish (v) (1).

FISHBOWL   *to live or work in a fishbowl*. To live or work under conditions that provide little or no privacy. Source: FISH. WNNCD: O.E. Literally, a fishbowl is a glass bowl in which goldfish or other miniature fish are kept as pets (WNNCD: 1906). Figuratively, a *fishbowl* is either (1) a glassed-in office, often in the center of a larger room, where your every action is visible to those outside, or (2) the high-visibility life of a celebrity, whose every move is reported in newspapers and magazines and on television. IRCD.

FISH EGGS   *See* Caviar to the General.

FISHEYE *to give someone the fisheye.* To glare at someone with a hard, condemning look. Source: FISH. WNNCD: O.E. Most fish have large, dark, bulging eyes that are incapable of closing or blinking. The fixed stare of a fish on a dinner plate seems to say, "You're not going to eat me, are you?" If *fisheye looks* could kill, there would be daggers in the air. ATWS. *See also* Fish-eye Lens.

FISH-EYE LENS *a fish-eye lens.* A highly convex, wide-angle camera lens that covers an angle of 180 degrees and produces a circular image. WNNCD: 1942. Source: FISH. WNNCD: O.E. The *fish-eye lens* bulges out like the eye of a fish, and the round picture that it produces looks like a reflection in the eye of a dead fish. *Fish-eye* photographs are interesting but highly distorted. ATWS; WNWD. *See also* Fisheye.

FISH FOR COMPLIMENTS *See* Fish (v) (1).

FISH FOR INFORMATION *See* Fish (v) (1).

FISHING EXPEDITION *a fishing expedition.* A search for incriminating evidence of any kind. WNNCD: 1925. Source: FISH. WNNCD: O.E. When you go fishing, you never know what, if anything, you will catch. When detectives or lawyers interview suspects, they have no idea what, if anything, they will uncover. The same applies to Congressional committees and investigative reporters, although these "anglers" may have partisan or pecuniary reasons, respectively, for hoping that they will uncover something incriminating or embarrassing. ATWS; DEI; DEOD; IRCD; SPD; ST. *See also* Fish (v) (1).

FISH IN TROUBLED WATERS *to fish in troubled waters.* To capitalize on someone else's misfortune. EWPO: 19th cent. Source: FISH. WNNCD: O.E. Fish don't bite any better in bad weather than in good; but the wind and the rain may drive most of the anglers away, and the ones who remain can catch their limit. In times of political and economic unrest, most people suffer, but those who take advantage of the troubled situation can make a killing. ATWS; BDPF; CI; DEI; DOC; HOI; IRCD; ST.

FISH OR CUT BAIT *to fish or cut bait.* To make up your mind to take action or get out of the way and support those who do. IRCD: 1876. Source: FISH. WNNCD: O.E. On a commercial fishing boat, when a school of fish is sighted, there is a frenzy of activity on board. Some of the crew are fishing, and some are cutting up trash fish for bait. There are no other jobs, and there is no place for idlers. You must decide which job to take. Similar modern expressions are "Make yourself useful" and "Do something positive." AID; ATWS; DAE; DOC; EWPO; HTB; LCRH; MDWPO; ST.

FISH OUT *See* Fish (v) (2).

FISH OUT OF WATER   *to be (like) a fish out of water.* To be totally out of your element. EWPO: ca. 1380. Source: FISH. WNNCD: O.E. The fish's element is the water. When it is caught, it flops helplessly on the ground, because it lacks legs and cannot extract oxygen from the air. The human's element is the land. Humans are out of their element when they find themselves in unfamiliar surroundings, such as a strange culture or a job for which they are not trained. Consequently, they feel awkward and helpless, like the fish. AID; ATWS; BDPF; CI; DEI; DOC; HTB; ID; IRCD; ST.

FISH STORY   *a fish story.* A tall tale. WNNCD: 1819. Source: FISH. WNNCD: O.E. Anglers are famous for their exaggerated stories of incredibly large fish that *took the bait* (q.v.), *ran with the line* (q.v.), then managed to *get off the hook* (q.v.). Gullible listeners are likely to swallow the story *hook, line, and sinker* (q.v.), because there is no corpus delicti to prove otherwise. ATWS; DAE; IRCD; ST. *See also* One that Got away. *Compare* Shaggy-dog Story.

FISHTAIL   *to fishtail.* For the rear end of a self-propelled vehicle or its trailer to move from side to side. WNNCD: 1927. Source: FISH. WNNCD: O.E. Fish propel themselves by moving their vertical tail from side to side. (Whales and porpoises do so by moving their horizontal tail up and down.) The side-to-side movement of the fish's tail was first associated with the swinging of an airplane's tail in this fashion to reduce speed. Later, the term was applied to (1) a rear-wheel drive land vehicle whose rear end swerves out of control on ice, mud, or gravel, and (2) a trailer that fails to track properly and swerves from side to side. ATWS; NDAS; ST. *Compare* Porpoise (v).

FISHWIFE   *a fishwife.* A vulgar, foul-mouthed, abusive woman. Source: FISH. WNNCD: O.E. In the 15th cent., a *fishwife* was simply a woman who sold fish; but the coarse, scolding nature of the female fishseller led to a blanket indictment of all vulgar and abusive women as *fishwives.* The term is also slang for the wife of a homosexual man. DEI; IRCD; NDAS. *See also* Shrew; Tarred with the Same Brush.

FISHY   *to smell, taste, look, or sound fishy.* To seem suspicious, doubtful, or questionable. IRCD: 1844. Source: FISH. WNNCD: O.E. *Fishy* was first applied to the smell or taste of food that had been cooked in pots previously used for cooking fish (WNNCD: 1547). Later, it was applied to anything that didn't look or sound exactly right, such as a *fish story* (q.v.). ATWS; DOC; ST.

FIT FOR NEITHER MAN NOR BEAST   *See* Beast.

FLAT AS A FLOUNDER   *to knock someone as flat as a flounder.* To knock someone down or out. Source: FISH. The *flounder* (WNNCD: 14th cent.), along with the halibut, turbot, and sole, is a flatfish. It has a highly compressed body and, as an adult, both swims and rests in a horizontal position. It also has both eyes on the same side of its head, a condition that may or may not apply to a knocked-out prizefighter. BDPF. *See also* Flounder.

FLEABAG *a fleabag.* A cheap or run-down hotel or motel. IRCD: 1920s. Source: FLEA. WNNCD: O.E. A *fleabag* was orig. a mattress infested with fleas, the tiny (1 mm.), wingless, leaping insects that feed on the blood of humans and other hairy mammals. Then the term was expanded to cover an establishment in which such mattresses might be found. A run-down horse is also called a *fleabag.* ATWS; LTA. *See also* Flea-bitten; My Dog Has Fleas; Thick as Fleas.

FLEA-BITTEN *to be flea-bitten.* For a horse or dog to have a light-colored coat flecked with reddish spots. WNNCD: 1570. Source: FLEA. WNNCD: O.E. The flea, a tiny, wingless, bloodsucking insect, is red, and so are the marks it leaves on a light-skinned person. The human condition has been transferred to the color of certain short-haired domestic animals. ATWS; EWPO; HF. *See also* Fleabag; My Dog Has Fleas; Thick as Fleas.

FLEA-FLICKER *a flea-flicker.* A play in football in which the quarterback receives the ball from the center, hands it off to a running back, and retreats a few yards. The back then turns and laterals the ball to the quarterback, who throws a forward pass. Source: FLEA. WNNCD: O.E. The metaphor is based on the leaping ability of the flea (the football), which can move from cat to dog to human, and back, with the greatest of ease. *See also* My Dog Has Fleas.

FLEA IN YOUR EAR *to be sent away with a flea in your ear.* To be given a stinging oral rebuff, rebuke, reproof, or warning. IRCD: 1580. Source: FLEA. WNNCD: O.E. The analogy is to the agony of a dog, or other hairy mammal, that is being attacked by a flea. When the flea enters its ear, the dog becomes hysterical—scratching, whining, and rolling on the ground. ATWS; CI; DEI; HOI; IRCD; LCRH. *Compare* Bug in Your Ear.

FLEA MARKET *a flea market.* A market for secondhand goods and antiques. WNNCD: 1922. Source: FLEA. WNNCD: O.E. The implication is that the clothes or upholstered furniture sold at a flea market are infested with fleas, the tiny bloodsucking insects that nest in woven material but leap to and from animals and humans. The origin of the name is probably the Parisian *Marche aux Puces* ("flea market"), although it may be the 17th cent. Dutch *Vlie Market* in Manhattan. CI; EWPO; IRCD; LTA; MDWPO.

FLEDGLING *See* Full-fledged.

FLEECE *to fleece someone.* To cheat or defraud someone. WNNCD: 1537. Source: SHEEP. To *fleece* someone is to strip them of their goods or cash through fraud, extortion, or other illegal or unfair means. The analogy is to the shearing of sheep, during which the wool, or "fleece," is removed from the entire body, leaving the sheep without protection from the elements. ATWS; ID. *Compare* Pluck a Pigeon.

FLEECY   *to be fleecy.* To be soft and fluffy. WNNCD: 1590. Source: GOAT; SHEEP. Cotton balls are white and fleecy, and so are puffy clouds; but fleecy things need not be white or in their natural state. When the wool of goats or sheep is dyed and spun and woven, it can produce a cloth that is soft and fluffy. The most popular goats for this purpose are the cashmere and the angora (for mohair). ATWS.

FLIES   *See* Fly (n) (1).

FLIPPER   *a flipper.* One of a pair of rubber "fins" worn on the feet by skin divers and scuba divers to increase their swimming speed and improve their mobility. Source: SEAL. Along with dolphins, porpoises, and whales, seals and walruses have front flippers; but only the large-eared seal, or *sea lion* (q.v.), has functional *rear* flippers like those worn by swimmers. *See also* Like a Trained Seal.

FLIP THE BIRD   *See* Give Someone the Bird.

FLOAT LIKE A BUTTERFLY   *to float like a butterfly, sting like a bee.* For a boxer to be light on his feet but heavy on his punches. (Muhammad Ali: ca. 1970.) Source: BUTTERFLY; BEE. WNNCD: O.E. The butterfly is light on its wings and hard to catch. The bee is a persistent and vicious attacker. *See also* Sting (v). *Compare* Light as a Feather.

FLOCK   *a flock; to flock.* A supervised or unsupervised group of people; for people to assemble or move as a group. Source: ANIMAL. The noun *flock* is currently used to describe groups of *animals*, such as birds and sheep, and groups of *people*, such as congregations and tourists. The unsupervised senses of *flock*, as for tourists, derive from flocks of birds; the supervised senses of *flock*, as for congregations, derive from flocks of sheep. The sense of the verb *flock* (WNNCD: 14th cent.), as in "to *flock* to the beach," derives from the unsupervised sense of the noun *flock* (WNNCD: O.E.). When people *flock*, they swarm like a flock of birds. ATWS; LCRH. *See also* Pastor.

FLOG A DEAD HORSE   *See* Beat a Dead Horse.

FLOUNDER   *to flounder.* To struggle; to fail. WNNCD: 1592. Source: FISH (*). *Flounder* is not exactly an animal metaphor. When someone's career is *floundering*, it does resemble a fish, such as a flounder, flopping around in the bottom of the boat, struggling to survive. However, *flounder* is an alteration of *founder*

(WNNCD: 14th cent.), which orig. referred to a boat that was sinking or "going to the bottom." The confusion may have come from the flounder's habit of swimming horizontally, rather than vertically, and lying on the sandy bottom with its eye-side up, giving the appearance that it is either injured or dead, respectively. *See also* Flat as a Flounder. *Compare* Go Belly up.

FLUSH OUT   *to flush someone out.* To drive someone, such as an escaped criminal, from his/her place of concealment. Source: BIRD. All senses of *flush* (WNNCD: 13th cent.) derive from the sound of a gamebird breaking from its cover and flying away rapidly. The bird beats its wings frantically in order to take off—sometimes vertically—without a running start. The sound symbolic nature of the word has been preserved in the *flushing* of a toilet, but it has been lost in the *flushing* of a criminal from his/her hiding place. ST.

FLUTTER   *to flutter.* To vibrate irregularly. Source: BIRD. All senses and functions of *flutter* derive from the O.E. verb *floterian* "to float or flutter." The original flutterer was the bird, which flaps its wings rapidly while flying, courting, or defending. The word was also applied to sails, flags, and flames, which flap in the breeze with irregular motions. In modern times, the *flutter* of engines, television pictures, and hearts is a sign of trouble; but when female hearts are *all aflutter*, they are beating rapidly from the pangs of love. ATWS.

FLY (n) (1)   *a fly.* A two- (or four-) winged insect; a garment closing; a high batted ball; the space high above a stage; the endpaper of a book. Source: BIRD. The common housefly is named for the verb *fly* that describes the flight of a bird. The *fly* of a pair of pants is the flap that covers—or "flies over"—the zipper. A *fly ball* (WNNCD: 1867) is a baseball hit high in the air to the outfield, where it may be caught *on the fly* (DAE: 1868), i.e., while running; a *pop fly* (WNNCD: 1887) is one hit high in the infield. The *flies* of a theater are the open spaces high above the stage where equipment and scenery are hung. A *flyleaf* (WNNCD: 1832) is one of the two unnumbered sheets of blank paper, at the beginning and end of a book, over which the hard cover is bound. Riddle: *What has four wheels and flies?* Solution: A garbage truck. DOC; IRCD; ST; WNWD. *See also* Fly (v); Tie Flies. *Compare* Fly (n) (2).

FLY (n) (2)   *a fly.* A fishhook adorned with feathers to resemble a large flying insect. Source: FLY. WNNCD: O.E. The fishhook so adorned is used in the sport of *fly fishing* (q.v.). Feathers are tied to the hook to make the fish—e.g., a trout—think that they are the wings of a flying insect—e.g., a caddis fly. *See also* Tie Flies. *Compare* Fly (n) (1).

FLY (v)   *to fly.* To move through space or time. Source: BIRD. Birds fly with the aid of their feathered wings, and they are the basis for this metaphor. (Bats and insects also have wings, but they lack feathers.) Humans *fly* with the aid of manufactured wings, either fixed or rotating; and they even *fly* without wings, as in balloons and rockets. If the conditions are *top flight* (WNNCD: 1934), they can be *flying high* in a *high-flying* career; but if they lose their heads, they may *fly off the handle* or *fly into a rage*. People who are *flighty* are capricious and volatile, and their ideas seldom *fly* because they can't *get off the ground*. Bullets, *fly*, flags *fly*, feathers *fly*, and fur *flies*. Time also *flies*. ATWS; BDPF; IRCD. *See also* Fly (n) (1); Fly (n) (2).

FLY BALL   *See* Fly (n) (1).

FLY BLIND   *See* Wing (v).

FLY-BY-NIGHT   *a fly-by-night; a fly-by-night operation.* A person who avoids creditors by sudden flight (WNNCD: 1822); a fraudulent company that leaves town after swindling its customers (WNNCD: 1914). Source: BIRD (?). If *fly-by-night* is an animal metaphor, it probably refers to migratory birds that feed on a farmer's crops in the daytime and then fly away during the night. (The bat is also a candidate.) However, it is possible that the term derives from the early-19th cent. belief that witches fly by night after doing their dirty work in the daytime. AID; CH; CI; DOC; EWPO; HTB.

FLY BY THE SEAT OF YOUR PANTS   *See* Wing (v).

FLY FISHING   Fishing with fishhooks adorned with feathers to resemble large flying insects. WNNCD: 1653. Source: FLY. WNNCD: O.E. Fly fishing, or *fly casting* (WNNCD: ca. 1889), is usu. done while standing in a trout stream. The *fly* is attached to a long line that runs through the eyelets of a long flexible rod. The trout thinks that the hook looks like one of its favorite insects, the caddis fly. *See also* Fly (n) (2); Tie Flies.

FLYING FOX   *a flying fox.* A fruit bat. WNNCD: 1759. Source: FOX. WNNCD: O.E. Foxes don't fly, so the metaphor is probably based on the physical resemblance of the two mammals. Many fruit bats have caninelike muzzles, large eyes, and long ears like those of the fox; and the bat is sometimes reddish, silver, or gray—typical fox colors. The bushy tail is absent, of course, on the tailless bats.

FLY IN THE FACE OF   *to fly in the face—or the teeth—of something.* To defy convention, danger, logic, etc. DOC: 1553. Source: BIRD. One defense that birds use against predators is to fly directly at them, time after time. Crows do this to squirrels, attempting to knock them off their perch so that they will fall to the ground and become injured. Chickens do it to cats, dogs, foxes, and weasels when they invade the barnyard or henhouse. Birds even attack people this way when they wander too near a nesting place. People *fly in the face of* custom or reason when they simply ignore it and behave like a bird. AID; ATWS; BDPF; DEI.

FLY IN THE OINTMENT *a fly in the ointment.* A small problem that can ruin an otherwise perfect plan or project. Source: FLY. WNNCD: O.E. The sense of this metaphor was expressed in Ecclesiastes 10:1—"Dead flies cause the ointment of the apothecary to send forth a stinking savour: so doth a little folly him that is in reputation for wisdom and honour." The ointment was presumably a perfumed cosmetic that had attracted the flies and suffocated them. They stank like the misdeeds of an otherwise honorable person. AID; ATWS; BDPF; DEI; DOC; EWPO; HOI; IRCD; LCRH; SHM.

FLY IN THE TEETH OF *See* Fly in the Face of.

FLYLEAF *See* Fly (n) (1).

FLY ON THE WALL *I'd love to be a (little) fly on the wall.* I'd love to hear what they're saying behind those closed doors. Source: FLY. WNNCD: O.E. A fly on the wall of a closed meeting room would go completely unnoticed but could hear every private word that was spoken there. Fortunately, or unfortunately, the fly can't communicate to other flies what it has heard. Gossipy people can—and do. ATWS. *Compare* Wish I Could Be a Little Mouse.

FLYSPECK *a flyspeck.* A tiny speck of dirt on a paper, mirror, lens, etc; something small or insignificant. Source: FLY. WNNCD: O.E. Literally, a *flyspeck* is a speck of fly excrement (WNNCD: 1847). The meaning was first broadened to include (1) the spoor of any "bug," such as a spider, then (2) any foreign speck of dirt or ash, and finally (3) anything small and insignificant (the planet Earth is a *flyspeck* in the cosmos). ATWS.

FLY THE COOP *to fly the coop.* To escape from confinement. DOC: mid-19th cent. Source: CHICKEN. If a poultry raiser fails to *clip the wings* (q.v.) of his/her chickens, or to secure the gate or door of their *coop* (q.v.), they are likely to fly away, at least for a short distance and a short time, and lay their eggs in the fields or become prey to animals such as the cat, dog, fox, or weasel. Humans who *fly the coop* are either criminals who escape from jail or prison, or grown children who finally decide to *leave the nest* (q.v.). AID; ATWS; BDPF; HOI; LCRH. *Compare* Slip the Collar.

FLYWEIGHT *a flyweight.* A boxer fighting in the lightest division of amateur and professional boxing—maximum weight 112 pounds. WNNCD: 1911. Source: FLY. WNNCD: O.E. The fly is not the lightest in weight of all flying animals—the gnat and the mosquito weigh even less—but at a fraction of an ounce it is certainly lighter than a chicken (*compare* Bantamweight) or even the feather of a chicken (*compare* Featherweight). The name is also used for the division: the *flyweight division*. ATWS; LTA.

FOAM AT THE MOUTH   *to foam at the mouth.* To be uncontrollably angry. DOC: 1440. Source: DOG. A dog foams at the mouth when it becomes uncontrollably angry or when it is suffering from distemper or rabies. The foam is a frothy mass of aerated saliva that collects in the mouth and drips from the lips. People don't actually produce foam when they are angry, but they can show all of the other symptoms of a rabid dog. Horses also foam at the mouth—but from hard riding, not anger. DEI; WNWD. *Compare* Work Yourself into a Lather.

FOLLOW SOMEONE AROUND LIKE A PUPPY DOG   *to follow someone around like a puppy dog.* To attach yourself to someone as if they were your mother. Source: DOG. WNNCD: O.E. When a puppy is a few months old, it often adopts one of its caretakers, male or female, as its surrogate mother, *following them anywhere.* If it loses track of its "mother," it gets a sad, tearful, helpless look: a *lost-puppy look.* Other baby animals also behave in this way, and so do toddlers, although they are usu. looking for "Daddy."

FOLLOW YOU ANYWHERE   *See* Follow Someone around like a Puppy Dog.

FOOD FOR WORMS   *to be food for worms.* To be dead and buried (or not buried). Source: WORM. WNNCD: O.E. The "worm" referred to in this metaphor is probably the maggot, or larva of a fly. Maggots are not "true" (i.e., annelid) worms, so in this case *worm* itself is a metaphor. Maggots feed on dead or dying animals, as in Job 24:20—"The worm shall feed sweetly on him." ATWS; BDPF; IRCD. *See also* Worm-eaten; Worm (3). *Compare* Feed the Fishes.

FOOT-IN-MOUTH DISEASE   *to have foot-in-mouth disease.* To have a habit of saying the wrong thing at the wrong time. SPD: 1950s. Source: CATTLE. This human affliction, also known as "putting your foot in your mouth," is named for the contagious disease of cattle called "foot-*and*-mouth disease" (also known as "hoof-and-mouth disease"), which produces ulcers on the foot, mouth, and udder of cows. AID; ATWS; DOC.

FOR THE BIRDS   *to be (strictly) for the birds.* To be worthless, ridiculous, or nonsensical. DOC: 1951 (J. D. Salinger's *Catcher in the Rye*). Source: BIRD. WNNCD: O.E. On the farm, grain that is too small or too old for human consumption is thrown to the chickens. In the city, birds find undigested grain in the manure of carriage and police horses, and it has been suggested that *for the birds* is a euphemism for *horseshit* (q.v.). At any rate, if it is fit only for birds, it is unfit for humans. AID; ATWS; CI; ID; IRCD; LCRH. *Compare* Chickenfeed.

FOUL YOUR OWN NEST *to foul your own nest.* To disgrace your own family; to destroy your own environment. DOC: 1440. Source: BIRD. The metaphor derives from the proverb, "It is an ill bird that fouls its own nest." Birds spend a lot of time building their nests and lining them with down; so they are unlikely to defecate in them, although the baby birds do. Humans *foul their own nest* by speaking ill of their family members or bringing disgrace on them or themselves. People also *foul their own nest* by polluting their environment with acid rain, oil spills, etc. DEI. *See also* Feather Your Nest.

FOX *a fox.* An attractive young woman. IHAT: 1963. Source: FOX. WNNCD: O.E. The red or silver fox—the color depending on the latitude—is regarded as a beautiful creature. It is one of the few animals whose entire pelt, including muzzle and feet, has been worn by *foxy ladies* (q.v.). The metaphor has been attributed to Muhammad Ali, when he was Cassius Clay. DEOD; IHAT; SHM. *See also* Sly Old Fox.

FOX AND GEESE A children's game played on a spoked wheel marked out in the snow. Also: *foxes and geese.* Source: FOX; GOOSE. WNNCD: O.E. A designated player (the "fox") starts in the center (the hub of the wheel) and tries to tag the other players (the "geese"), who start on the rim, using only the stomped paths. The game is over when all of the "geese" have been tagged. The game is modeled on the natural attraction of the fox to fowl of all kinds. *See also* Fox in the Henhouse.

FOXFIRE Phosphorescent light from a luminous fungus growing on decayed wood. WNNCD: 15th cent. Source: FOX. WNNCD: O.E. *Foxfire* is said to have an eerie glow resembling the brilliant coloring of a red, silver, or gray fox. The gray fox, for example, features the colors gray, reddish brown, white, and black. The red fox is reddish colored in the subarctic zones and mostly silver in the arctic zones. IRCD.

FOX GUARDING THE HENHOUSE *The fox is guarding the henhouse.* A conflict of interests exists. Source: FOX; HEN. WNNCD: O.E. This expression is often used when a coach is also appointed athletic director, a field manager is also asked to serve as general manager, or an agency is asked to conduct an investigation of itself. It is difficult, and perhaps impossible, to be objective under these circumstances, just as it is for the lucky fox. *See also* Put the Fox in Charge of the Henhouse.

FOXHOLE *a foxhole.* A shallow pit dug by a soldier for protection from enemy fire. WNNCD: 1919. Source: FOX. WNNCD: O.E. The fox digs much deeper pits, or "dens," than the soldier—usu. with multiple entrances and sometimes with multiple chambers. The military foxhole—first called a *slit trench*—was developed during WWI and has been enlarged, improved, and relied on ever since. BDPF; IRCD; ST.

FOX SQUIRREL   *a fox squirrel.* A large, bushy-tailed squirrel of the eastern United States. Source: FOX. WNNCD: O.E. The tail of the fox squirrel is not as large as that of the red, silver, or gray fox; but it is just as prominent, equaling approx. the total length of the animal's body. The tails of both mammals were once sought after as decorations for the tips of car radio antennas, and both animals are described as *bright-eyed and bushy-tailed* (q.v.).

FOX-TROT   *a fox-trot (or fox trot).* A dance step, or the accompanying music, in 4/4 time. EWPO: 1915. Source: FOX. WNNCD: O.E. The fox figures only indirectly in this metaphor. *Fox-trot* was first recorded in 1872 as the gait of a horse in a fox hunt. The term was adapted to a dance step performed by the actor Harry Fox in a Broadway musical in 1913, and soon after to the dance music itself. The "close" dancing used with the fox-trot competed with the *jitterbug* (q.v.) in the 1940s, and was almost eliminated by the "separated" dancing of the 1950s and early 1960s and the disco dancing of the late 1960s and the 1970s. ATWS; BDPF; IRCD; ST; WNWD.

FOXY LADY   *a foxy lady.* A physically attractive young woman. DEOD: 1976. Source: FOX. WNNCD: O.E. *Foxy* is derived from *fox* (q.v.), which is attributed to Muhammad Ali (IHAT: 1963). The metaphor is based either on the beautiful appearance of the animal in the wild or the fact that classy ladies often wore fox stoles in the 1960s. A *stone fox* is a totally sexy woman, with *stone* functioning as it does in *stone blind* "totally blind." ATWS; IRCD; SHM.

FRAIDY-CAT   *See* Scaredy-cat.

FREE AS A BIRD   *to be as free as a bird.* To be able to come and go whenever and wherever you please. DOC: 1533. Source: BIRD. WNNCD: O.E. Because they are able to fly, birds can ignore the terrain that restricts the movement of land creatures and the waterlines that limit the travel of sea creatures. However, birds are not quite as free as they seem to be, because sooner or later they have to *come down to earth* to eat, rest, or nest. Humans kid themselves when they imagine that retirement will allow them to be *as free as a bird.* It will simply bring new responsibilities. AID; ATWS; DEI. *Compare* As the Crow Flies.

FRET   *to fret.* To worry. Source: ANIMAL. To *fret* is literally "to devour" (fr. O.E. *fretan*), as one wild animal devours another. Figuratively, to *fret* is to be devoured by anxiety, as if anxiety were a wild animal gnawing away at your innards. The expression *What's eating you?* probably derives from this experience. EWPO.

FRISKY AS A YOUNG COLT *See* Coltish.

FROG (1) *a frog.* The "nut" of a violin bow, which contains a screw for tightening the horsehairs. Source: FROG. WNNCD: O.E. The *frog* of a violin bow bears no physical resemblance whatsoever to the amphibian, so perhaps the metaphor is based on the legendary jumping ability of frogs (as in Calaveras County): the bow *jumps* over the strings. IRCD. *See also* Frog (2); Frog (3); Frog (4); Frog (5).

FROG (2) *a frog.* A braided loop for securing a button—as opposed to a buttonhole. Source: FROG. WNNCD: O.E. The metaphor may be based on the resemblance of a button in a loop to a frog sitting on a lily pad—or to a fly nestled in a frog's curled tongue. The term is also used for a leather or metal loop attached to a belt to hold a tool, such as a hammer. *See also* Frog (1); Frog (3); Frog (4); Frog (5).

FROG (3) *a frog.* A device placed at the bottom of a vase or bowl for securing the stems of cut flowers (in holes or on spikes). Source: FROG. WNNCD: O.E. The florist's *frog* sits at the bottom of the container, in water, and is usu. colored green—all of which features resemble the behavior and appearance of the amphibian. IRCD. *See also* Frog (1); Frog (2); Frog (4); Frog (5).

FROG (4) *a frog.* The triangular pad extending from the "heel" to the center of the hoof of a horse or other solid-hoofed animal. Source: FROG. WNNCD: O.E. The *frog* of a horse's hoof resembles a large amphibian, as seen from below, in its shape (triangular), its softness (compared to the rest of the hoof), and its size. *See also* Frog (1); Frog (2); Frog (3); Frog (5).

FROG (5) *a frog.* A crossing or switching plate on a railroad track to permit one track to cross another or merge with another. IHAT: 1847. Source: FROG. WNNCD: O.E. The metaphor may be based on the amphibian's legendary jumping ability—in this case, for a train to "jump" from one track to another. *See also* Frog (1); Frog (2); Frog (3); Frog (4).

FROG HAIR *the frog hair.* The fringe of slightly longer grass around the very short grass of a golfing green. Source: FROG. WNNCD: O.E. Frogs are smooth-skinned amphibians—often green (like summer grass) or brown (like dormant winter grass). Of course, frogs don't have hair, but a golf green does look a little like a frog sitting on a lily pad: green on green. *See also* Frog (2).

FROG IN YOUR THROAT *to have a frog in your throat.* To have laryngitis, hoarseness of the throat, or partial loss of voice. IRCD: 19th cent. Source: FROG. WNNCD: O.E. When you have a *frog in your throat,* you *croak like a frog.* IRCD states that frogs were used in the Middle Ages to inhale infection from a patient's body—a sort of reverse mouth-to-mouth. ATWS; BDPF; DEI; ID. *See also* Croak.

FROG KICK   *a frog kick.* The kicking motion used in the breaststroke: legs bent, knees pointed outward, legs straightened and brought together sharply. The kick alternates with the arm stroke. WNNCD: 1940. Source: FROG. WNNCD: O.E. This is exactly how the frog swims, and frog legs look very much like human legs. The *frog kick* is also used in the *dog paddle* (q.v.). IRCD. *Compare* Dolphin Kick; Porpoise (v).

FROGMAN   *a frogman.* A scuba diver (esp. military) equipped with face mask, wet suit, flippers, and breathing apparatus. WNNCD: 1945. Source: FROG. WNNCD: O.E. When so equipped, esp. in black rubber, the frogman (or frog person) looks very much like an amphibian. Frogmen are invaluable for underwater operations during wartime and for rescue and salvage operations during peacetime. IRCD.

FROG SPIT   A slimy mass of algae that forms on the still water of marshes and ponds. WNNCD: 1825. Source: FROG. WNNCD: O.E. Frogs don't spit. This metaphor may be based on the fact that frogs, as amphibians, frequent marshes and ponds on which a thick coat of algae has accumulated. When the green frog sticks its head through the green algae, it looks like it belongs to him/her. *Compare* Cuckoo Spit.

FROG STICKER   *a frog sticker.* A dagger or bayonet. NDAS: early 1800s. Source: FROG. WNNCD: O.E. The *frog sticker* was probably never used to kill frogs. Its purpose was to kill people. It was named for the frog because it was a *small* weapon, used only at close quarters. *Compare* Pig Sticker; Toad Sticker.

FULL AS A TICK   *to be as full as a tick.* To have consumed a considerable amount of food or drink. Source: TICK. WNNCD: 14th cent. The tick is a tiny bloodsucking insect, related to the smaller mite, that bloats itself with the blood of mammals and conveys diseases from animals to humans. *See also* Tight as a Tick. *Compare* Don't Let the Bedbugs Bite.

FULL-FLEDGED   *to be full-fledged.* To be mature or fully developed. WNNCD: 1883. Source: BIRD. A full-fledged bird is one that has acquired its full plumage and is an accomplished flier. Among humans, a *full-fledged* doctor, lawyer, or plumber is one who has completed his/her education and apprenticeship and is now practicing his/her profession or occupation. A *fledgling* bird (WNNCD: 1830), on the other hand, is one that has just acquired its feathers and is attempting its first flight. For humans, a *fledgling* author, business, or nation is one that has just appeared on the scene and is still young and inexperienced. (A *fledgling* disturbance can soon turn into a *full-fledged* riot.) ATWS; EWPO. *See also* In Fine Feather.

FULL OF BEANS   *See* Feel Your Oats.

FUNGUS   *a fungus*. A parasitic plant—a mold, mildew, mushroom, or yeast— that lacks chlorophyll and lives on dead or decaying matter. WNNCD: 1527. Source: SPONGE. The sponge is an animal, not a plant, but it does attach itself to other objects, and its tan-colored, interlaced elastic fibers do make it look more like flora than fauna. ATWS.

FUR WILL FLY   *See* Make the Fur Fly.

G

G   *The letter G.* The seventh letter of the English alphabet. Source: CAMEL. The modern letter G developed in the 3rd cent. B.C., when the Romans altered the letter C to spell the g sound. The source of C (and G) is the Greek *gamma*, from the Phoenician *gimel* "camel," which was shaped like the dip in the camel's neck. ATWS; BDPF; EWPO. *See also* C.

GABRIEL'S HOUNDS   *See* Hounds of Hell.

GADFLY   *a gadfly.* A persistent critic of social institutions and their leaders. Source: FLY. WNNCD: O.E. A gadfly is lit. a "goad-fly"—i.e., a fly that annoys wild or domestic animals by persistently biting them, sucking their blood, and sometimes killing them. Social activists, such as Ralph Nader, use biting criticism to goad bureaucrats into doing a better job for their customers or constituents. The original *gadfly* was Socrates. ATWS; CE; IRCD; LCRH; MDWPO.

GALLOP   *to gallop.* To advance rapidly and uncontrollably. Source: HORSE. Old French had two dialectal forms for "gallop": Parisian French *galoper* and Norman French *waloper*. From the former comes the English word *gallop* (WNNCD: 15th cent.), which orig. referred to the headlong rush of a horse, during which all four feet left the ground at the same time. Now, pneumonia *gallops*, inflation *gallops*, the crime rate *gallops*, etc. From the latter form comes the English word *wallop* (WNNCD: 14th cent.), which orig. meant the same as *gallop* (for the horse) but later acquired the meaning "to beat, thrash, trounce, or lambaste." From this verb developed the noun *wallop* (WNNCD: ca. 1823) "a powerful blow, force, or impact," as in *to pack a wallop.* ATWS; WNWD.

GAMBIT   *See* Gams.

GAMBOL   *See* Gams.

GAME   *to be game.* To be resolute, tough, or courageous. WNNCD: ca. 1787. Source: COCK. The adj. (or adv.) *game* is derived from the noun *gamecock* "a fighting cock." The gamecock displays *gameness* by never giving up in its battle in the *cockpit* (q.v.); i.e., it has a lot of *grit* (q.v.). Humans who are *game* are usu. athletes who "play through" their injuries—or heroes who rescue people from floods and fires in spite of the danger. ATWS; BDPF.

GAMS   Women's legs. EWPO: ca. 1900. Source: HORSE. In the 16th cent., a *gam*, spelled *gambe* or *gamba*, was the hind leg of a horse. In the 17th cent., a *gam* was the wooden leg of a stringed musical instrument: e.g., It. *viole da gamba* "leg viol, or cello." In the 18th cent., a *gam*, also spelled *gamb*, was a human leg of a member of either sex (WNNCD: 1781). Today, a woman who is said to have "a good set of *gams*" has a shapely pair of legs. The word *gambol* (WNNCD: 1508) "to leap about in play" derives fr. M.Fr. *gambole* "the spring of a horse." An opening *gambit* in chess (WNNCD: 1656) is a sacrificial move to "trip up" your opponent.

GANDY DANCER   *a gandy dancer.* A railroad worker on a section gang. WNNCD: 1923. Source: GOOSE (?). *Gandy dancer* may not be an animal metaphor. While it is true that section hands look a little like hungry geese (or *ganders*) pecking at the ground when they hammer in spikes—and like waddling geese when they try to walk on the rails—the word *gandy* probably derives from the name of the Chicago toolmaker that produced much of the track laying/straightening equipment: The Gandy Manufacturing Company. EWPO; IHAT; MDWPO. *See also* Take a Gander.

GAS HOG   *a gas hog.* An old car that gets low mileage and lots of "fill-ups." Source: HOG. WNNCD: O.E. A *gas hog* has an insatiable thirst for gas, just as a domestic hog has an insatiable thirst—or hunger—for swill or hogslop. They never seem to get enough "fuel." *See also* Hog (n) (1); Hog (v).

GENTLE AS A DOVE   *to be as gentle as a dove.* To be tender, passive, and peace-loving. Source: DOVE. WNNCD: 13th cent. Doves—and pigeons, their larger and more urban cousins—are neither birds of prey, like hawks and owls, nor birds who feed on the prey of other animals, like buzzards and vultures. They eat seed, grains, and an occasional insect, and mind their own business. DEI. *See also* Dove of Peace. *Compare* Gentle as a Lamb .

GENTLE AS A LAMB   *to be as gentle as a lamb.* To be calm and peaceful, meek and mild, thoughtful and considerate. Source: LAMB. WNNCD: O.E. The lamb has long been regarded as a gentle animal—nonaggressive, nonpredatory, non-violent. Perhaps this was one reason for its popularity as a sacrificial animal. Nowadays, a person who is *as gentle as a lamb* would not hurt a flea (or fly, or lamb). IRCD. *See also* Innocent as a Lamb; Meek as a Lamb. *Compare* Gentle as a Dove.

GERANIUM   *a geranium.* A plant of the geranium family; a flower of this plant. WNNCD: 1548. Source: CRANE. *Geranium* lit. means "little crane" (fr. Gk. *geranion*, dim. of *geranos* "crane"). The metaphor is based on the resemblance of the long seed pods of the geranium plant to the long neck and beak of the European wading bird known as a *crane* (q.v.). ATWS; EWPO; WNWD. *See also* Cranesbill.

GERRYMANDER   *to gerrymander.* To divide up voting districts in order to favor one political party—as was done by Governor Elbridge Gerry of Massachusetts. WNNCD: 1812. Source: SALAMANDER. WNNCD: 14th cent. *Gerrymander* is a blend of *Gerry* and *salamander* (q.v.). The metaphor was based on the salamanderlike shape of the resulting map. EWPO; THT.

GET A BITE   *to get a bite.* To get an offer; to get a response to an offer. Source: FISH. An angler gets a bite when a fish strikes at his/her baited hook or lure. A businessperson *gets a bite* when a customer responds to his/her offer or makes a counteroffer. A similar expression, *to get a nibble*, implies a strike at the bait rather than the hook; in business, this is a show of interest but not yet of money. SOED; ST. *See also* Get a Rise out of.

GET ALL YOUR DUCKS IN A ROW   *to get all your ducks in a row.* To get all your affairs in order; to get things properly organized. Source: DUCK. WNNCD: O.E. When a family of ducks travels on the land or water, they move in single file, led by one of the parents (usu. the mother). This scene is probably the ultimate source of the metaphor. However, other possible sources include: (1) the game of *duck pins* (also named for the aquatic bird), in which the half-size pins must be set by hand before the next (half-size) ball is thrown, and (2) the game of shooting mechanical "ducks" in a shooting gallery: If you hit *all of the ducks in a row*, you get a prize. AID; BDPF; MDWPO; ST.

GET A NIBBLE   *See* Get a Bite.

GET A RISE OUT OF SOMEONE   *to get a rise out of someone.* To provoke a reaction, esp. an angry reaction, from someone. Source: FISH. A flycaster gets a rise out of a fish when the fish comes to the surface to strike at the moving lure. A practical joker *gets a rise out of someone* when the latter falls victim to the "joke"; a salesperson *gets a rise out of* a customer when the latter *takes the bait* (q.v.); and a debater *gets a rise out of* his/her opponent when the latter takes offense at a "low blow." ATWS; EWPO. *See also* Get a Bite; Hooked.

GET BURNED   *See* Cat's Paw.

GET HITCHED   *to get hitched.* To get married. Source: HORSE. When a horse gets hitched, it gets harnessed to a load, usu. along with another horse. The two horses, which are said to be "in double harness," must work together, in unison, or they will cancel out each other's efforts. When two people *get hitched*, they get married, and from that time they *travel in double harness*, which demands the same kind of cooperation. A related expression, "to go down the *bridal path*," also derives—by punning—from equine terminology. A *bridle path* (WNNCD: 1811) is a trail for horseback riding. A *bridegroom*, however, is not the bride's horse servant but the bride's *man* (fr. O.E. *guma* "man"). CE; CH; NDAS.

GET HOOKED   *See* Hooked.

GET IN YOUR HAIR   *to get in your hair.* For someone or something to annoy or irritate you persistently. EWPO: 1851. Source: LOUSE. The reference is to the eggs, or "nits," of the tiny head louse, which become attached to the hairs of your head and can be transferred to others by the common use of combs, pillows, etc. Bats have also been accused, probably falsely, of getting caught in women's long hair. ATWS; EWPO; LTA. *See also* Louse. *Compare* Get under Your Skin.

GET IT IN THE NECK   *to get it in the neck.* To be defeated, reprimanded, punished, or fired. HTB: 1887. Source: CHICKEN. The chicken "gets it in the neck" when its head is chopped off with an axe—the quickest and easiest way to kill a chicken. The sudden and unexpected action equates to human defeat, rebuke, punishment, and termination. This metaphor is sometimes shortened to *to get the axe* and is the basis for the later expressions *to stick your neck out* (q.v.) and *to put your neck on the line* (q.v.). AID; BDPF; HOI; LTA. *Compare* Sudden Death.

GET IT STRAIGHT FROM THE HORSE'S MOUTH   *See* Straight from the Horse's Mouth.

GET OFF YOUR HIGH HORSE   *See* Get on Your High Horse.

GET ON THE HORN   *See* Horn.

GET ON THE STICK   *See* Hobby.

GET ON YOUR HIGH HORSE   *to get on your high horse.* To become arrogant or haughty. WNNCD: 14th cent. Source: HORSE. WNNCD: O.E. In medieval pageants and tournaments, the royals and nobles rode horses that were bigger than those of their inferiors, giving them an air of superiority and haughtiness. Figuratively, to *get on or ride a high horse* is to suddenly put on airs or affect an attitude of superiority and arrogance. A contrasting expression, *to get off your high horse*, means to *come down to earth* and stop acting so *high and mighty*. The expression *Come off it!* may have been derived from the command "Get off your high horse!" ATWS; BDPF; CH; CI; DEI; DOC; EWPO; HOI; ID; IRCD; LCRH; ST. *See also* Down-to-earth.

GET ON YOUR HORSE   *to get on your horse.* To get ready, get busy, get moving. Source: HORSE. WNNCD: O.E. *Get on your horse* has a meaning similar to *get on the stick*, although the latter expression derives from children riding a *hobbyhorse* (q.v.), while the former comes from cowboys, pony express riders, and mounted posses getting ready to mount up and go to work.

GET OUT OF HAND   *See* Keep a Tight Rein.

GET SOMEONE'S GOAT   *to get someone's goat.* To anger, annoy, irritate, or exasperate someone. SOED: 1912. Source: GOAT (?). WNNCD: O.E. The origin of this metaphor is uncertain, but it may have something to do with the "kidnapping" (lit.) of a pet goat from the stall of a racehorse that is expected to race on the following day. The racehorse becomes upset over the absence of its stablemate, has a fitful night, and runs poorly in the race, which is won by a horse that the kidnappers have bet on. No other reasonable explanation has been offered for this metaphor. ATWS; BDPF; CE; CI; DEI; DOC; EWPO; HOI; HTB; IRCD; LCRH; MDWPO; SHM; ST. *See also* Kidnap.

GET THE AX   *See* Get It in the Neck.

GET THE MONKEY OFF YOUR BACK   *to get the monkey off your back.* To finally shake a persistent problem, such as an alcohol or drug addiction. IRCD: 1940s. Source: MONKEY. WNNCD: ca. 1530. In this metaphor, an addiction is likened to a wild monkey jumping on your back and refusing to let go. It is always with you, like a curse. Getting rid of it "takes the weight off your shoulders." *See also* Have a Monkey on Your Back.

GET UNDER YOUR SKIN   *to get under your skin.* For something to either annoy or captivate you. Source: INSECT. A number of ticks and mites (which are actually arachnids, not insects) burrow into human skin and set up housekeeping (or, rather, bloodsucking) there. Their presence can be extremely irritating, much like that of a person whom you can't stand. Cole Porter mixed the metaphor by having the love bug (actually a fly) infect you with love that you can't resist: "I've got you under my skin." ATWS; BDPF. *See also* Jigger.

GET UP WITH THE BIRDS   *See* Go to Bed with the Chickens.

GET UP WITH THE CHICKENS   *See* Go to Bed with the Chickens.

GET WIND OF SOMETHING *to get wind of something.* To hear rumors about something that is supposed to be a secret. Source: ANIMAL. Most mammals have a keen sense of smell, and they are able to recognize the scent of another animal some distance away if the wind is blowing in the right direction. This is why hunters stake out a position downwind from the place where they expect their prey to appear—and why animals move downwind from where they expect the hunters to be. Figuratively, to *get wind of something* is to sense that something secret is going on or is about to happen, although the sense employed is usu. hearing rather than smell. ATWS.

GET YOUR BACK UP *to get your back up.* To take offense; to become angry or annoyed. EWPO: 18th cent. Source: CAT. When a cat becomes aroused to anger or is spoiling for a fight, it arches its back, and the hairs on its back stand straight up. This action is the basis for the metaphor *get your back up* and perhaps for *make your hair stand on end.* People don't actually arch their backs when they become angry, but the hair on the back of their necks does stand on end when they have a *hair-raising experience* (WNNCD: 1900). This last-mentioned phrase is the source of the adjective *hairy,* in the sense of "scary or tricky." ATWS; BDPF; CI; DOC; HTB; LCRH; MDWPO. *Compare* Get Your Hackles Up.

GET YOUR HACKLES UP *to get your hackles up.* To become fighting mad. Source: COCK. Hackles are the long feathers surrounding the neck of a rooster or gamecock. When the cock becomes angry, it raises its hackles as a sign of its readiness to fight. When humans *get their hackles up,* the hair on the back of their neck stands on end; and for dogs and cats, it is the hair on their back and neck. ATWS. *See also* Raise Someone's Hackles. *Compare* Get Your Back up.

GHOTI George Bernard Shaw's fanciful spelling of *fish* (1912). Source: FISH. To illustrate the chaotic nature of English spelling, Shaw took the final two letters of *laugh* (*gh*), the first vowel of *women* (*o*), and the middle two letters of *nation* (*ti*) and put them together, with the same phonetic values, to form the word *ghoti* "fish." MDWPO. *Compare* ICHTHUS.

GIFT HORSE *See* Look a Gift Horse in the Mouth.

GIVE SOMEONE A BUM STEER *See* Bum Steer.

GIVE SOMEONE FREE REIN *to give someone free rein.* To give someone complete freedom to think and act as they please. WNNCD: 1952. Source: HORSE. A rider or driver gives a horse free rein by relaxing the reins and allowing it to go at whatever speed it wishes. People are *given free rein* when they are allowed to make their own decisions and to act on them as they see fit. A synonymous expression, *to give someone their head,* focuses on the freedom of the head of the horse from the restricting control of the reins by the driver. ATWS; BDPF; CI; ST. *Compare* Give Someone Some Line; Take the Bit.

GIVE SOMEONE SOME LINE   *to give someone some line.* To give someone some slack. Source: FISH. After a fish has *taken the bait* (q.v.), it may swim away from the boat or dock. In that case, the best thing to do is to give it some line, or let it run with the hook or lure until it tires out. In the case of people—esp. adolescents—it is sometimes wise to relax control on a non-lethal issue until they get bored and can be *reeled (back) in* (q.v.). *Running with the line* applies to allowing a practical joker or teller of tall tales to have their way, knowing that the end is near. ST. *Compare* Give Someone Free Rein.

GIVE SOMEONE THE BIRD   *to give someone the bird.* To hiss at someone (HOI: 1859); to give someone the "razzberry" (WNNCD: ca. 1919); to give someone the "finger." Source: BIRD. WNNCD: O.E. The *bird* that was given to actors in the 19th cent. was a gooselike hiss from the audience. The early-20th cent. *bird* was a Bronx cheer, or "razzberry," from the Yankee fans. The latest *bird* is the raised middle finger of one hand—given in situations where vocal communication is impossible, as from the driver of one car to another. All of these "birds" convey disapproval or contempt, and the last mentioned, also called *flipping the bird*, can lead to your arrest in some communities. ATWS; BDPF; CI; DEI; HOI; IRCD; LCRH; LTA; NDAS.

GIVE SOMEONE THEIR HEAD   *See* Give Someone Free Rein.

GOAD   *to goad someone into doing something.* To pressure someone into action or acceptance. Source: CATTLE. Cattle are goaded into moving more rapidly or in a particular direction by the use of a long stick (an "ox-goad") or an electrified stick (a *cattle prod* [q.v.]). People are usu. *goaded* by words, but prods are sometimes used to control crowds in a riot.

GO APE   *to go ape.* To go (temporarily) wild or crazy. WNNCD: 1959. Source: APE. WNNCD: O.E. The allusion is to the monkey (a nonanthropoid primate) or the chimpanzee (an anthropoid ape), both of which become wildly excited at the prospect of food or the threat of danger. IRCD. *See also* Ape (adj.); Go Ape over. *Compare* Go Bananas.

GO APE OVER   *to go ape over something or someone.* To become wildly excited about something or someone, such as a rock star. IRCD: 1960s. Source: APE. WNNCD: O.E. The monkeys and the chimpanzees (nonanthropoid and anthropoid primates, respectively) become wildly excited about the prospect of being fed, esp. by visitors at a zoo. AID; ATWS. *See also* Ape (adj.); Go Ape. *Compare* Go Bananas.

GO AROUND IN CIRCLES   *See* Chase Your Tail.

GOAT   *See* Get Someone's Goat; Hero to Goat; Old Goat; Scapegoat.

GOATEE   *a goatee.* A small, pointed chin beard. WNNCD: 1844. Source: GOAT. WNNCD: O.E. The *goatee* (lit. "little goat") is fashioned after the beard that hangs below the chin of an adult male goat, or billygoat, and it was orig. called a "billygoat beard." It was first worn by Uncle Sam in 1868 but declined in popularity shortly thereafter. The female goat, or *nanny* (q.v.), also has a goatee. ATWS; EWPO; IRCD. *Compare* Muttonchops.

GOATSUCKER   *a goatsucker.* A nighthawk or whippoorwill. WNNCD: 1611. Source: GOAT. WNNCD: O.E. *Goatsucker* is an English translation of Lat. *caprimulgus* "goat milk." It was believed in ancient times that the widemouthed nightjar, the European cousin of the American nighthawk, sucked the milk from goats at night. Actually, goatsuckers feed primarily on insects, which they scoop up in their big mouths while flying at high speeds and low altitudes. ATWS; WNWD.

GO BANANAS   *to go bananas.* To go crazy. WNNCD: 1968. Source: MONKEY. "Go bananas" is what a monkey in the zoo does when it catches sight of a zoo keeper or visitor with a bunch of its favorite fruit. It goes even crazier when the holder of the bananas tempts or teases the animal before giving the fruit up. People *go bananas* when they watch something hilarious, such as monkeys, or get incredibly lucky. Also: *drive someone bananas.* AID; CI; DOC. *Compare* Go Ape; Go Ape over.

GOBBLEDYGOOK   The unintelligible jargon of government officialese. WNNCD: 1944. Source: TURKEY. EWPO states that this word was invented by U.S. Rep. Maury Maverick, who complained, in writing, about Washington bureaucratic language, comparing it to the pompous *gobbling* of tom turkeys at courtship time. (*Gook* is not recorded separately until 1949.) ATWS; SPD. *See also* Gobble up; Talk Turkey.

GOBBLE UP   *to gobble something up.* To devour something, such as food or written matter, rapidly and greedily. WNNCD: 1601. Source: TURKEY (?). Male turkeys, or "gobblers," make a guttural sound (a "gobble") when they are asserting themselves or trying to attract females. They also swallow what they eat hurriedly, although they do not "gobble" at the same time. To *gobble (up)* is a combination of the sound made by the turkey and the unrelated word *gob* "lump," as in "to eat *gobs* of food." ATWS.

GO BELLY UP   *to go belly up.* To go bankrupt. WNNCD: 1939. Source: FISH. When a fish dies, it rises to the surface of the water, either because its air sac has ruptured or gases have begun to build up in its belly. When a business goes bankrupt and "dies," it is said to go belly up like the fish. (Hognose snakes also go belly up when threatened.) The same can be said of an individual or a scheme. MDWPO; ST. *Compare* Turn Turtle.

GO DOWN TO THE WIRE   *to go down to the wire.* To be determined at the very last minute, or by the very last vote. Source: HORSE. A *wire* is the finish line at a racecourse. It is an actual steel wire strung high above the horses' heads to aid the officials in deciding which horse comes *under the wire* first. In case two or more horses seem to have finished at the same time, the race is declared a *photo finish* (WNNCD: 1936), and the results are delayed until the photographs can be examined. A horse that leads the race from start to finish is said to *lead from wire to wire,* and a horse that loses to another horse at the finish line is said to *take the winner to the wire.* All of these racing expressions can be applied to people, esp. political candidates engaged in a close race; but *under the wire* is usu. reserved for activities with a deadline, such as filing for office. AID; DAE; NDAS; ST.

GO FLY A KITE   *See* Kite (n).

GO FOR THE JUGULAR   *to go for the jugular.* To attack an opponent in his/her most vulnerable spot. Source: ANIMAL. The *jugular vein* (WNNCD: 1597) is a prominent blood vessel that appears on either side of the neck and carries blood from the brain to the heart. It is a favorite point of attack for smaller animals, such as the hyena, on larger animals, such as the gnu, which then slowly bleeds to death. A person who has an *instinct for the jugular* is able to sense where an opponent's weakness lies and to attack it with deadly consequences. *Jugular* itself (WNNCD: 1615) is a metaphor, deriving from I.E. *yugo* "yoke" (q.v.), the wooden framework that joins oxen together in a team. DEI; SPD; WNWD.

GO FULL TILT   *to go full tilt.* To go at top speed. WNNCD: 1600. Source: HORSE. In medieval jousting tournaments, a horse and rider were going at full tilt when the rider's lance was lowered to the horizontal and the horse was galloping at full speed toward the opponent. Unhorsed people *go (at) full tilt* when they marshall all of their energy and work as hard and as fast as they can. ST.

GO GET 'EM, TIGER   *Go get 'em, Tiger!* (Sarcastic words of encouragement to someone who doesn't have a ghost of a chance of succeeding.) Source: TIGER. WNNCD: O.E. The tiger is a fierce, savage, bloodthirsty animal—quite the opposite of an incompetent human who thinks he can take on the world. The allusion may be to the holder of a "tiger" hand in poker: no face cards, no pairs, no potential flush or straight. Winning with such a hand is possible only by bluffing. ID. *See also* Arouse the Tiger; Have a Tiger by the Tail; Ride a Tiger.

GO HOG-WILD   *to go hog-wild.* For a person or a machine to go completely out of control. WNNCD: 1904. Source: HOG. WNNCD: O.E. Young people do this at rock concerts; adults do it at blue light specials; and cars do it when the accelerator gets stuck. Domestic hogs also do this when they are being fed, ringed, or rounded up for slaughter; and wild boars do it when they're being hunted down by horses and dogs. ATWS; BDPF; EWPO; HTB; IRCD.

GO INTO HIBERNATION   *to go into hibernation.* To go into seclusion. Source: ANIMAL. The mammals that go into hibernation—also known as the "seven sleepers"—are, in alphabetical order: the badger, the bat, the bear, the dormouse, the groundhog (or woodchuck), the ground squirrel (or chipmunk or gopher), and the hedgehog (or porcupine). People *go into hibernation* every winter when they stay inside to keep warm and come outside only to take out the garbage or shovel the walk. People also *go into hibernation* at any time of the year when they *hole up* (q.v.) in order to avoid prosecution or to seek peace and quiet. *See also* Cocoon (v).

GONE COON   *a gone coon.* A person who is in deep trouble: a *sitting duck* (q.v.). EWPO: ca. 1780. Source: RACCOON. WNNCD: 1608. The raccoon (or *coon*: 1742) is a nocturnal arboreal animal of the eastern United States. It is hunted at night with "coon dogs," and when it is treed it is in great danger of being shot and killed. ATWS; MDWPO. *See also* Out on a Limb. *Compare* Dead Duck; Gone Goose.

GONE GOOSE   *to be a gone goose.* To be done for, dead, or about to be dead. HTB: 1830. Source: GOOSE. WNNCD: O.E. *Gone* has meant "dead" since 1538 (WNNCD). Adding *goose* was probably inspired by the Revolutionary War metaphor *gone coon* (q.v.), which referred to an enemy soldier who was cornered (or treed) and about to be shot. A *gone goose* is someone who is about to be metaphorically killed, plucked, and served up for dinner. ATWS; EWPO; LTA. *See also* Cook Someone's Goose; Goose Is Cooked. *Compare* Dead Duck.

GOOD CATCH   *a good catch.* An outstanding candidate for a mate. Source: FISH. A good catch of fish is either a large number of fish caught or a number of large fish caught. It can also be a single large fish caught: a "prize catch." Among humans, a *good catch* is a potentially good choice for a husband or a wife, based on wealth, occupation, appearance, etc.; and a *prize catch* is the best of all possible choices. But you have to *land* him/her (q.v.) first. ST.

GOOD EGG   *a good egg.* A good person; a nice guy. EWPO: ca. 1900. Source: CHICKEN. A *good* egg is one which, when held in front of a bright light (orig. a candle) shows an intact yolk, a runny "white," no blood clots, no cracks in the shell, and no signs of the development of a baby chick (!). Good, or "fresh," eggs, therefore, are without flaws, like people who are wholesome, kind, and considerate. HOI. *Compare* Bad Egg.

GOOD IN THE CLUTCH   *See* Clutch (n) (1).

GOOD JUDGE OF HORSEFLESH   *a good judge of horseflesh.* A man with good taste in women. Source: HORSE. WNNCD: O.E. A buyer, trader, breeder, or racer of horses who is a good judge of horseflesh is able to size up the potential value of a horse just by looking at it or watching it perform. A bachelor is a *good judge of horseflesh* if he consistently escorts beautiful women or manages to convince the most beautiful one to be his bride. Granted, the woman is being equated with horseflesh; but at the wedding, it is the man who becomes the *groom*. *See also* Get Hitched; Horse Trade.

GO ON A FISHING EXPEDITION   *See* Fishing Expedition.

GO ON A RAMPAGE   *See* Rampant.

GOOSE (n)   *a goose.* A tailor's smoothing iron; a poke in the bottom. Source: GOOSE. WNNCD: O.E. The tailor's smoothing—or pressing—iron is an old-fashioned, stovetop-heated implement with a long handle that curves over the body of the tool from back to front to allow access into pockets, under collars, etc. It is called a *goose* because it resembles the heavy body of a goose with its long neck turned backward over its body. A poke between the buttocks is called a *goose* because geese sometimes chase people away by biting them on the bottom as they retreat. BDPF; THT. *See also* Goose (v); Gooseneck; Silly Goose.

GOOSE (v)   *to goose someone or something.* To poke someone between the buttocks (WNNCD: 1879); to accelerate the progress of something (EWPO: 1920s). Source: GOOSE. WNNCD: O.E. The adult goose, male or female, is a formidable protector of its young. When humans get too close, it hisses at them, attacks them, and bites their behinds as they run away. Humans have adopted this behavior to startle other humans, whose sudden inspiration of air resembles the expirational hiss of a goose. *Goose* is also used for accelerating the speed of a vehicle ("*Goose* it!") or for increasing the productivity of a business (by *goosing* the sales or ratings). IRCD; LTA.

GOOSEBERRY   *a gooseberry.* A tart berry that resembles the smaller currant. WNNCD: 1532. Source: GOOSE (?). WNNCD: O.E. This is a suspicious metaphor. There is no mention in the sources of geese being partial to gooseberries, and neither the berry nor the shrub bears any resemblance to a goose. WNWD suggests that *gooseberry* may be a folk etymology for an earlier *groseberry*, or "large berry." HF. *See also* Goshawk.

GOOSE BUMPS   *See* Goose Pimples.

GOOSE EGG   *a goose egg.* Nothing: a score of zero. WNNCD: 1866. Source: GOOSE. WNNCD: O.E. The "big fat zero" chalked up on the scoreboard at 19th cent. baseball games reminded Americans of a *goose egg*, while the same zero reminded English cricket fans of a *duck's egg* and French tennis fans of a *chicken's egg*. DAE; DEI; HOI; IRCD; LTA; ST. *See also* Lay an Egg.

GOOSEFLESH   *See* Goose Pimples.

GOOSE HANGS HIGH   *The goose hangs high.* All's right with the world. LTA: 1866. Source: GOOSE. WNNCD: O.E. The meaning of the metaphor is clear— all is well and wonderful—but it is not clear how the goose figures in. LCRH reports that the expression was orig. "The goose *honks* high," i.e., the geese are flying high because the weather is so fair. ATWS states that a goose was once hung outside an inn as a symbol of good fare inside, thereby suggesting the metaphor. HOI; MDWPO. *See also* Gossamer; Halcyon Days.

GOOSE IS COOKED   *Your goose is cooked.* You're done for, finished, washed up. IRCD: 1851. Source: GOOSE. WNNCD: O.E. You Fool! You killed—and cooked—the goose that laid the golden eggs. Now, because of your impatience and greed, you have lost your steady income and have only a cooked goose to show for it. (This is probably what the farmer's wife said to him in the Aesop fable.) HOI. *See also* Cook Someone's Goose; Gone Goose; Kill the Goose that Laid the Golden Eggs.

GOOSENECK   *See* Gooseneck Lamp.

GOOSENECK LAMP   *a gooseneck lamp.* A household lamp at the end of a flexible metal arm that can be bent into just about any shape. Source: GOOSE. WNNCD: O.E. The word *gooseneck*, for anything curved like the neck for a goose (WNNCD: 1688), was current long before electricity was harnessed. The modern electric *gooseneck lamp*, which comes in both floor and table models, allows the user to aim the light exactly where he/she wants to. ATWS; IRCD. *See also* Goose (n); Loose as a Goose; Loosey-goosey; Take a Gander.

GOOSE PIMPLES   Bumps that appear on the skin as a result of cold, fright, empathy, or patriotism. WNNCD: 1889. Source: GOOSE. WNNCD: O.E. The analogy is to the skin of a plucked goose, whose feathers have been harvested for quill pens, pillows, etc. The tiny muscles that once lifted the feathers contract, forming hundreds of little bumps on the skin. In humans, the follicles of hair on the arms and legs stand on end when a person shivers with cold or fear or reacts emotionally to the playing of the national anthem or the viewing of a touching scene in a movie. Other terms for this phenomenon are *gooseflesh* (WNNCD:

1810) and *goose bumps* (WNNCD: 1933). AID; ATWS; BDPF; DEI; EWPO; ID; IRCD; LTA. *See also* Get Your Back up.

GOOSE STEP   *the goose step.* The slow, straight-legged, lockkneed, highkicking parade step used by military personnel, palace guards, and drum majors. IRCD: 1900. Source: GOOSE. WNNCD: O.E. *Goose-stepping* soldiers look like a flock of geese marching in unison, although geese don't have to lock their knees, since they have none. The *goose step* is usu. associated with Hitler's and Mussolini's troops passing in review in the 1930s and 1940s, but the term had been in use for several decades before that time and was probably based on an 1806 exercise in calisthenics in which a stationary individual swung one leg at a time, back and forth, in order to demonstrate his/her balance. ATWS; BDPF; DEI; EWPO; LTA.

GOOSE THAT LAID THE GOLDEN EGGS   *See* Kill the Goose that Laid the Golden Eggs.

GO OUT ON A LIMB   *See* Up a Tree.

GOPHER   *a gopher (or gofer).* An errand boy or girl whose job it is to *go for* this and *go for* that. SPD: 1966. Source: GOPHER (?). (N.D.) The gopher, or "thirteen-lined ground squirrel," is usu. seen in parks or on golf courses "going for" the nearest of the many holes that it has dug. In fact, the name of the rodent may derive from Fr. *gaufre* "honeycomb." The "errand boy/girl" metaphor may have originated in the theater (EWPO: 1940s). IHAT; MDWPO. *See also* Gopher Ball; Gopher Pitch.

GOPHER BALL   *a gopher ball.* A baseball that is hit for a home run. WNNCD: ca. 1949. Source: GOPHER. (N.D.) The last sight one has of a *gopher* (q.v.) is when it dives into its hole. The last sight one has of a *gopher ball* is when it dives into the outfield stands. MDWPO. *See also* Gopher Pitch.

GOPHER PITCH   *a gopher pitch.* A pitch that results in a baseball being hit for a home run. Source: GOPHER. (N.D.) The *gopher* (q.v.) is usu. seen scurrying for its hole (it has many). If you throw a stone at one, that's exactly what it will do. If a pitcher throws a bad pitch at a batter, the ball is likely to scurry for the stands. *See also* Gopher Ball.

GORILLA   *a gorilla.* A hired thug; a "goon." LTA: 1926. Source: GORILLA. WNNCD: 1853. The gorilla, the largest of the anthropoid apes, is better known for its size—up to 6.5 feet tall and 500 pounds in weight—than its intelligence, although it has been proved capable of learning American Sign Language. Song parody: "Gorilla my dreams, I love you." ATWS; EWPO; MDWPO. *See also* Six-hundred Pound Gorilla.

GOSHAWK   *a goshawk*. A short-winged, long-tailed hawk of northern Europe, Asia, and America. WNNCD: O.E. Source: GOOSE. WNNCD: O.E. The goshawk, or "goose hawk" (fr. O.E. *gōs* "goose" + *hafoc* "hawk"), is so called not because it preys on geese, which are much too large (up to 42 inches long) for the hawk to handle, but because it is a fairly *large* hawk (up to 23 inches long), at least compared to a *sparrow hawk* (up to 15 inches long). *See also* Gooseberry.

GOSSAMER   A gauzelike fabric: delicate, light, and airy. Source: GOOSE. WNNCD: O.E. *Gossamer* is a blend of *goose* and *summer—goosesummer—*also known in England as St. Martin's Summer and in America as Indian Summer: the *halcyon days* (q.v.) of November when cobwebs float lazily through the warm air and summer seems to have returned. How does *goose* figure into all this? It seems that in England a goose is served on November 11 in honor of St. Martin, who died on this day in 397 after killing and eating a goose. EWPO; MDWPO; THT.

GO STAG   *to go stag*. For a male to attend a dance or party without a female date. Source: DEER. In Europe, a *stag* (WNNCD: 1843) is the adult male of the red deer, which is approx. fifty percent larger than the adult male, or *buck*, of the American white-tailed deer. During the mating season, in late winter, the stag rounds up a large harem and never lacks for a female until the season is over. During the rest of the year, it *goes stag*. AID; ATWS; IRCD. *See also* Stag Line; Stag Movie; Stag Party.

GO SUCK AN EGG   *See* Teach Your Grandmother to Suck Eggs.

GO THROUGH THE EYE OF A NEEDLE   *to go through the eye of a needle*. To do something impossible. Source: CAMEL. "It is easier for a camel to go through the eye of a needle, than for a rich man to enter into the kingdom of God" (Matthew 19:24). The camel, or "dromedary," of North Africa and the Middle East is a large animal—almost seven feet tall at the shoulder, with a long dipping neck—that would even have trouble going through the "needle's eye" gate of an ancient walled city. EWPO; MDWPO. *See also* Camel that Poked His Nose in the Tent.

GO THROUGH THE PACES   *See* Put Someone Through Their Paces.

GO TO BED WITH THE CHICKENS   *to go to bed with the chickens*. To go to bed early. Source: CHICKEN. WNNCD: O.E. Chickens get up at daybreak, when the cock crows; they roam the barnyard all day, feeding and pecking; then they go to the henhouse at sundown to roost and brood. People who *get up with the chickens (or the birds)* arise early, at dawn or earlier; and those who *go to bed with the chickens* retire early, at sundown or shortly thereafter. AID; ATWS. *See also* Chickens Come Home to Roost.

GO TO POT   *to go to pot.* To be ruined. EWPO: ca. 1600. Source: ANIMAL. In the Elizabethan era, the best cuts of hunted game and slaughtered animals went to the lord and ladies, while the poorer cuts and leftovers went into a stew pot for the servants and farmhands. The conversion of a healthy animal into a pot of stew became the basis for a metaphor for ruin in general, and now marriages, businesses, health, and even lives can *go to pot.* AID; DEI. *Compare* Go to the Dogs.

GO TO THE DOGS   *to go to the dogs.* To fall into disrepair or disrepute. IRCD: 1619. Source: DOG. WNNCD: O.E. When food becomes unfit for human consumption, it is time to *throw it to the dogs* (BDPF: Shakespeare's *Macbeth*, 1606). When a piece of real estate *goes to the dogs*, it becomes run down and dilapidated; and when humans *go to the dogs*, they show disregard for their appearance or reputation. Once again, the dog is being treated as the lowest of all domestic animals. AID; ATWS; BDPF; CI; DEI; DOC; EWPO; HTB; LCRH. *See also* Dog (n). *Compare* Go to Pot.

GO WHOLE HOG   *to go (the) whole hog.* To go all the way. WNNCD: 1829. Source: HOG. WNNCD: O.E. This expression may derive from an anecdocte about a novice thief who took only a ham when he could have stolen the whole hog (LCRH), but most sources link it to the Irish nickname for a British shilling: a "hog." It seems that bartenders in Irish pubs urged their parsimonious customers to spend the "whole hog," or shilling, rather than order only one drink at a time. Nowadays, the expression is likely to come from a new-car salesperson who tells you that if you want to *go whole hog* you should buy the more expensive model. AID; ATWS; BDPF; CI; DEI; DOC; EWPO; HOI; IRCD; MDWPO; SHM.

GRACEFUL AS A SWAN   *to be as graceful as a swan.* To move with beauty, lightness, grace, and dignity. Source: SWAN. WNNCD: O.E. The metaphor is probably based on the aquatic/aerial behavior of the pure-white mute swan, which has a neck a yard long and a wing span of over seven feet. Both the mute swan and the somewhat smaller black swan were introduced into the United States from elsewhere—the former from Europe and the latter from Australia. Also: *to have the grace of a swan.*

GRASSHOPPER (1)   *a grasshopper.* A green alcoholic mixed drink consisting of crème de menthe, crème de cacao, and crème de cow. Source: GRASSHOPPER. WNNCD: 14th cent. The most common grasshopper in the United States is green or greenish yellow. It feeds on grasses, and it hops—or flies—from one feast to another. IRCD. *See also* Grasshopper (2); Grasshopper Pie.

GRASSHOPPER (2)   *a grasshopper.* An oil pump in a California oil field. Source: GRASSHOPPER. WNNCD: 14th cent. The American grasshopper is small (approx. one inch long) and green (or greenish yellow), but its profile (large head higher than its body) does bear a resemblance to the large black oil pump, whose "head" moves up and down to "feed." *See also* Grasshopper (1). *Compare* Donkey Engine.

GRASSHOPPER PIE *a grasshopper pie.* A bottom-crusted pie filled with mint ice cream or mint chiffon. Source: GRASSHOPPER. WNNCD: 14th cent. As with the mixed drink called a *grasshopper*, the pie draws its name from the color of the ingredients: green, like the American insect. IRCD. *See also* Grasshopper (1).

GRAZE *See* Browse.

GREASE MONKEY *a grease monkey.* A mechanic. WNNCD: 1928. Source: MONKEY. WNNCD: ca. 1530. *Grease monkey* was orig. applied to airplane mechanics, but its meaning has been extended to include other mechanics, esp. automobile mechanics. The analogy may be due to the agility that mechanics must have to work in tight spots under the hood of a car—or under the car itself—and also to the fact that their hands are always dirty. IRCD. *See also* Monkey Wrench.

GREAT HORNED OWL *See* Horn.

GREEN AROUND THE GILLS *to look a little green around the gills.* To look sick, esp. seasick. Source: FISH. Humans don't have gills; but if they did, they would be located on the neck, just below the lower jaw, where they would be visible to others. A person who looks a little *green around the gills* has an ashen, or off-color, appearance, usu. as a result of nausea or diarrhea. AID; ATWS. *See also* Loaded to the Gills; Stuffed to the Gills.

GREEN DOG *See* Red Dog.

GREEN-EYED MONSTER *the green-eyed monster.* Jealousy. WNNCD: 1604 (Shakespeare's *Othello*, Act III, Scene 3—Iago to Othello: "O, beware, my lord, of jealousy:/ It is the green-ey'd monster, which doth mock/ The meat it feeds on."). Source: CAT. The *green-eyed monster* is the cat, which toys with its captive, the mouse, before killing it—just as Othello toys with the mind of his wife, Desdemona, before smothering her. Both Othello and the cat are jealous of their possessions, and they tolerate no (real or imagined) infidelity. Some but not all, cats do have green eyes. BDPF; CI; DOC; EWPO; LCRH. *See also* Play Cat and Mouse.

GREENHORN *a greenhorn.* A rookie; a newcomer; a novice; a neophyte. WNNCD: 1682. Source: OX. Among bovines, a "greenhorn" is a young ox, with immature (or "green") horns, that is still untrained as a draft animal. Among humans, the term *greenhorn* was first applied to army recruits but is now used for any new or inexperienced member of a workplace or organization. ATWS; EWPO; HF; LCRH. *See also* Bugle.

GREGARIOUS   *See* Congregate.

GREYHOUND   *a greyhound.* A swift, slender, graceful runner, as in the sprint races of the sport of track. Source: GREYHOUND. WNNCD: O.E. The dog by this name is a swift, slender, graceful runner that was once used to chase game but is now used to chase a mechanical rabbit in dog races. Its likeness appears on the bus by the same name.

GRIN LIKE A CHESHIRE CAT   *to grin like a Cheshire cat.* To smile broadly, mischievously, or inscrutably. WNNCD: 1866 (Lewis Carroll's *Alice's Adventures in Wonderland*, 1865). Source: CAT: WNNCD: O.E. The inscrutable grin of the Cheshire cat in *Alice* was the last part of it to vanish as the cat gradually faded from view. The connection with Cheshire, a county in Northwest England, is uncertain. There are three theories: (1) The cat's grin was like that on the face of Warden Thomas *Caterlin* when he killed or tortured poachers in the Cheshire forest. (2) The grin resembled the expression of the lion on a coat of arms that appeared on many Cheshire inns. (3) The grin seemed to be present on Cheshire cheese that was once molded in the form of a cat's face: When the cheese was eaten, the grin was the last part to disappear. None of the theories seems more likely than Carroll's lively imagination. BDPF; CI; DEI; EWPO; HOI; IRCD; SHM.

GRIT   *to have (a lot of) grit.* To have a lot of courage and determination. Source: COCK. Cocks are not the only birds that swallow "grit"—sand, gravel, pebbles, and other granules—to aid in the breaking down of food in their gizzards; but the courage of the gamecock in the pits is attributed to the special diet of grit and grain that they are fed during their training. LCRH. *See also* Game.

GROOM   *to groom someone for an important position; to be well-groomed.* To prepare someone for assuming an important office; to be neat and attractive (WNNCD: 1886). Source: HORSE. To "groom" orig. meant to clean and brush the coat of a horse (WNNCD: 1809). Later, the verb was applied to caring for one's own appearance, esp. the hair; and even later, *groom* was used to describe the careful mowing and trimming of a lawn. Finally, the word *groom* was applied to the education and training of a potential candidate for political office, with attention to the hair being only a minor part of the preparation. ATWS. *Compare* Curry Favor.

GROUNDHOG   *a groundhog.* A woodchuck. WNNCD: 1784. Source: HOG. WNNCD: O.E. *Groundhog* is the name by which a *woodchuck* (WNNCD: 1674) is called in the Northeastern United States—esp. in Pennsylvania, where Punxsutawney Phil pokes his nose out of his hole every February 2 to forecast whether there will be six more weeks of winter. (There *will* be if he sees his shadow.)

However, Phil is not a hog but a large rodent that looks like a beaver without the paddletail. The *hog* part of the name comes from its hoglike habit of digging up the ground, although for the groundhog this is to create a burrow in which it can hibernate during the winter—except for Groundhog Day, of course. The groundhog is also called a *whistle pig*. EWPO; HF.

GROUND LION *See* Chameleon.

GROUSE *to grouse about something*. To complain or grumble about something. WNNCD: 1887. Source: GROUSE. WNNCD: 1531. The origin of the verb *grouse* is unknown, but the noun *grouse* describes a smallish, plump game bird, the male of which, in some species, is brilliantly colored and produces soft, low "thumping" sounds in its bulging throat sacks during courtship. LTA.

GROW BY LEAPS AND BOUNDS *See* By Leaps and Bounds.

GROWL *See* Bark like a Dog.

GROWL LIKE A BEAR *to growl like a bear*. To act surly or mean. Source: BEAR. WNNCD: O.E. Bears are not very vocal animals, but they do growl like a large dog when they are angry. The sound is deep, guttural, and threatening. Humans who vocalize this way are usu. *cross as a bear* (q.v.)—out of sorts, in a bad mood—although some are always this way. *See also* Growl.

GRUB Food. Source: INSECT. Spouse #1: "What are we having for dinner?" Spouse #2: "I'll see what I can dig up." A *grub* is the wormlike larva of an insect (WNNCD: 15th cent., fr. M.E. *grubbe*, fr. *grubben* "to dig"). Grubs feed on underground roots and are themselves fed on by moles. The association of *grub* with "food" goes back at least to WWII, when it competed with *chow*. ATWS. *See also* Grubby; See What I Can Dig Up.

GRUBBY *to be grubby*. To be dirty, grimy, slovenly, sloppy, or base. Source: INSECT. *Grubby* orig. meant "infested with fly maggots," i.e., "covered with grubs" (WNNCD: 1725). A grub is the wormlike larva of an insect, of which maggots are one example. The meaning of *grubby* has been extended from a dead animal covered with maggots to (1) human hands and faces covered with dirt, (2) the slovenly appearance of clothes and hair, and (3) contemptible motives in business and politics. (*Grubbies* are old, worn, comfortable clothes.) ATWS. *See also* Grub.

GRUNT (n) *a grunt*. A snort (WNNCD: 1553); an Army or Marine footsoldier (WNNCD: 1960s). Source: HOG. The human *grunt* is a short, deep nasal sound uttered in times of physical strain, social annoyance, or just plain disgust. It very much resembles the sound made by a hog. Army and Marine *grunts* probably make more of these sounds than most people do, considering that the term originated during the Vietnam War; but they may also be so called because they spend most of their combat time wallowing in the mud and dirt, like their porcine counterparts. *See also* Grunt (v).

GRUNT (v) *to grunt.* To snort. WNNCD: O.E. Source: HOG. Pigs squeal, but hogs grunt. Their grunt is a short, deep, nasal sound uttered as a sign of contentment. Humans *grunt* in the same fashion when they are annoyed or discontented (i.e., *disgruntled* [q.v.]), or when they are suffering physical strain. Tennis star Monica Seles used to grunt whenever she hit a ground stroke, causing some of her opponents to object to the distraction. ATWS. *See also* Grunt (n).

GUESS WHICH WAY THE CAT WILL JUMP *See* Which Way the Cat Will Jump.

GUINEA PIG *a guinea pig.* An animal or human subject of laboratory research and testing. Source: PIG. WNNCD: 13th cent. The Brazilian *guinea pig* (WNNCD: 1664)—a small, large-headed and almost tailless rodent, or "cavy"—was imported into Europe in the 17th cent., domesticated as a pet, and later used for experimentation in the laboratory because of its gentle nature and its reasonably high reproductivity. However, it is not a pig, and it does not come from Guinea, a country on the West coast of Africa, now called Equatorial Guinea. The "pig" label may have come from its large head, stout body, and short tail. The "Guinea" label may be a reminder of the Portuguese slave trade of the 17th cent. in which ships carrying slaves from African Guinea to Brazil returned to Portugal with exotic treasures, including the Guinea pig. AID; ATWS; BDPF; CE; CI; DEI; EWPO; ID; IRCD.

GULL (n) *a gull.* A person who is easily tricked or cheated: a dupe. WNNCD: 1594. Source: GULL. WNNCD: 15th cent. It is possible that the metaphor is based on the use of *gull* in the 14th cent. for an unfledged, and therefore impressionable, bird. However, it seems just as likely that the metaphor derives from M.E. *golle* "throat," since the gull is omnivorous and will "swallow anything." CE; IRCD. *See also* Gull (v); Gullible.

GULL (v) *to gull someone.* To deceive or dupe someone. WNNCD: 1550. Source: GULL. WNNCD: 15th cent. The origin of this metaphor is uncertain. It may derive from the impressionability of young birds in general (called *gulls* in the 14th cent.) or from the fact that both young and adult *gulls* will "swallow anything" (fr. M.E. *golle* "throat or gullet"). The appearance of the verb almost fifty years before the noun (1594) deepens the mystery. CE; EWPO; IRCD; LCRH. *See also* Gull (n); Gullible.

GULLIBLE *to be gullible.* To be easily tricked, cheated, deceived, or duped. WNNCD: 1818. Source: GULL. WNNCD: 15th cent. The connection between *gull* and *gullible* may be that a *gullible* person is as innocent as a young "bird" (M.E. *gull*), which permits the adult bird to ram just about anything down its "throat" (M.E. *golle*). IRCD. *See also* Gull (n); Gull (v).

GULL-WING   *a gull-wing door or car*. An automobile door that opens *up* rather than forward or backward—as on the 1954 Mercedes-Benz 300SL and the 1981– 82 DeLorean; the automobile itself. Source: GULL. WNNCD: 15th cent. The wings of the herring gull are long and angular, much more so than those of most other birds. The "wings" of a *gull-wing* car are also angular and curved, like those of the gull. *See also* Gull (n).

GUN-SHY   *to be gun-shy*. To be unduly cautious, distrustful, or afraid. Source: DOG. A dog that is *gun-shy* (WNNCD: 1884) is afraid of the sound of a gunshot, and consequently is useless for hunting. A person who is *gun-shy* is afraid of taking a chance, probably on the basis of negative past experiences, and is there-fore unable to function normally in certain situations. The meaning of the word has been extended, by analogy, to the fear of being photographed: *camera-shy*. SOED; ST.

GUN THEM DOWN LIKE DOGS   *See* Die like a Dog.

GUTTERSNIPE   *a guttersnipe*. A street urchin; a tramp. WNNCD: 1869. Source: SNIPE. WNNCD: 14th cent. The snipe is a small, long-billed bird that frequents marshes, bogs, and swamps. A *guttersnipe* was orig. a homeless child who collected rags from the street gutters. Later, the term was applied to a homeless person of any age who wanders the streets and finds cast-off food and clothing in the trash. ATWS; DEI; HF; IRCD. *See also* Urchin.

GYPSY MOTH   *a gypsy moth*. A northern congressman who, during a conser-vative administration, crosses party lines to vote with the liberals of the other party. Source: MOTH. WNNCD: O.E. The caterpillar of the *gypsy moth* (WNNCD: 1819), which was introduced into the United States in 1869, has done consid-erable damage here by defoliating and eventually killing many old trees— presumably as the liberal congressman has helped to destroy much conservative legislation. NDAS. *Compare* Boll Weevil; Copperhead.

H

HACK *See* Hackneyed.

HACKNEY *See* Hackneyed.

HACKNEYED *to be hackneyed.* To be stale or trite. WNNCD: 1749. Source: HORSE. *Hackneyed* derives from the M.E. noun *hakeney* "a horse used for riding or driving" (WNNCD: 14th cent.). In the 16th cent., *hackney* was applied to a horse no longer suitable for riding or racing that was hired out for pulling a light carriage. In the early-18th cent., *hackney* came to be applied to the carriage itself and was shortened to *hack* (WNNCD: ca. 1721), which survives as the word for a modern taxicab or its driver. In the mid-18th cent., the adj. *hackneyed* appeared with the meaning "lacking in freshness"—like the worn-out *jade* (q.v.) but refer-ring to writing that was stale or trite. In the late-18th cent., the term *hack writer* was first used to refer to someone who hired out to write *hackneyed prose* (LTA: 1796), and in the early-19th cent. a writer of this sort was referred to as a *hack* for the first time (SPD: 1807). ATWS; BDPF; LCRH; MDWPO.

HACK WRITER *See* Hackneyed.

HAGGARD *to be haggard.* To appear wild-looking, emaciated, or gaunt. SOED: 1697. Source: FALCON. A *haggard* (WNNCD: 1567) was an adult female hawk caught wild and not yet tamed—or untamable—for falconry. The female hawk was the one used for hunting in the Renaissance period, perhaps because it was larger than the male; but it was usu. raised specifically for that purpose. (The male was called a *tiercel*, later *tercel*.) ST.

HAIR OF THE DOG *the hair of the dog that bit you.* A drink on the "morning after" to remedy a hangover from the night before. HTB: 1546. Source: DOG. WNNCD: O.E. The Romans practiced an early form of homeopathic medicine on a dogbite victim by applying some of the burnt hair of the dog to the wound. (It didn't work, esp. if the dog was rabid.) In the 16th cent., *hair of the dog* became a metaphor for "curing" a hangover by imbibing "more of the same"—i.e., using the Latin principle of "like cures like." (That didn't work either.) Modern medicine has employed the principle in the development of vaccines that contain live or dead microorganisms of the offending virus. (That works.) AID; ATWS; BDPF; CI; DEI; DOC; EWPO; HOI; IRCD; LCRH; SHM.

HAIR-RAISING EXPERIENCE *See* Get Your Back up.

HAIRY *See* Get Your Back up.

HALCYON DAYS Happy days, golden days: a time of peace, tranquility, and prosperity. Source: KINGFISHER. The *kingfisher* (WNNCD: 15th cent.) is a small, brilliantly colored Eurasian bird that was believed by the ancient Greeks to have the power to calm the waters of the sea when it built its nest there during the winter solstice. Actually, it nests at the end of a tunnel that it digs in the bank of a river. ATWS; DEI; EWPO; LCRH; THT. *See also* Kingfish. *Compare* Dog Days.

HALTER *a halter.* A minimal blouse for women that covers the chest only and is secured above by straps around the neck and below by straps behind the back. Source: HORSE. The women's halter resembles the horse's halter only in the sense that both consist of straps and little else. The horse's halter is essentially a *bridle* (q.v.) that a horse wears when it is not working. (A rope can be attached to the halter for leading.) Halters are also used for mules, donkeys, and cows. ATWS.

HAM (1) *a ham.* An overactor. MDWPO: 1880s. Source: HOG. To the butcher, a ham is the (usu. smoked) thigh of a hog, which is separated from the skin by a sizable layer of fat. Because this ham fat was used by performers in minstrel shows to remove the lampblack from their faces, such performers became known in the mid-1800s as "hamfatters." Later, the expression was shortened to *ham* and applied to actors generally who overplayed their parts, exaggerated their perform-ances, or tried to *ham it up* (q.v.). AID; EWPO; HF; HTB; LCRH.

HAM (2) *a ham.* An operator of a federally licensed amateur radio station. Source: HOG (?). WNNCD: O.E. This is probably not an animal metaphor. The *ham* in *ham radio* and *ham radio operator* is said to derive not from the name for the thigh of a hog but from the first syllable of the word *amateur*. No one is sure where the *h* came from, although it may have come from the *ham-handed* (q.v.) way in which the *hams* operated their telegraph keys. GTP; LCRH; MDWPO.

HAM ACTOR *See* Ham (1).

HAM-HANDED *to be ham-handed (or ham-fisted)*. To lack dexterity or grace. WNNCD: 1918. Source: HOG. At the first level of metaphor, a person who is *ham-handed* has hands the size of hams; at the second level, the *ham-handed* person is clumsy, like a *bull in a china shop* (q.v.); and at the third level, the *ham-handed* person is heavy-handed and tactless. DEI; CI; LCRH; WNNCD.

HAM IT UP *to ham it up*. To overact. WNNCD: 1933. Source: HOG. A *ham actor* is one who, like the performers in 19th cent. minstrel shows, overplays his part to the point of silliness. To *ham it up* is to perform a role with exaggerated gestures and speech—to "show off." The *ham* in the expression derives from the hamfat that the minstrels used to remove their blackface makeup. AID; BDPF; GTP. *See also* Ham (1).

HAM RADIO *See* Ham (2).

HAM RADIO OPERATOR *See* Ham (2).

HANDLE WITH KID GLOVES *to handle (or treat) someone (or something) with kid gloves*. To treat someone or something with the greatest consideration and respect. Source: GOAT. *Kid gloves* are fine leather gloves made from the skin of young goats (or "kids"), which is thin enough to permit the wearer to feel through them, and soft enough to prevent damage to the object that is felt. Handling a touchy person, a priceless object, or a delicate situation requires the same kind of careful treatment. ATWS; CI; DEI; DOC; ID. *See also* Kid-glove Treatment.

HANGDOG LOOK *a hangdog look or expression*. A look of shame, guilt, desperation, or defeat. WNNCD: 1677. Source: DOG. WNNCD: O.E. *Hangdog look* alludes to the facial expression of a hanged dog. In late medieval and renaissance England, dogs could be charged, convicted, and hanged for certain crimes. The appearance of a hanged dog didn't discourage other dogs from committing crimes against the state, but it made quite an impression on the citizenry, because this metaphor has been around for over 300 years. People have a *hangdog* demeanor when they are abject, cowed, dejected, or desperate. A related expression, "to stay *until the last dog is hung*" (MDWPO: 1902), refers to the lynching of criminals, or *dirty dogs* (q.v.), in the American West. ATWS; BDPF; DEI; EWPO; HF; IRCD. *See also* Die like a Dog.

HAPPY AS A CLAM *to be as happy as a clam*. To be deleriously happy. DOC: 1838. Source: CLAM. WNNCD: 1520. This metaphor refers to the Atlantic soft-shell clam, with a thin, elongated shell, that buries itself in the sand and can be dug up easily at low tide. The original form of the metaphor was "to be as happy as a clam *at high tide*," when clamdigging is impractical. AID; ATWS; BDPF; EWPO; IRCD; SHM. *Compare* Happy as a Lark.

HAPPY AS A LARK *to be as happy as a lark.* To be deleriously happy. Source: LARK. WNNCD: O.E. The European skylark has a bright and cheerful song, which it sings, early in the morning during the breeding season, high in the air (up to 800 feet) as it circles the nesting area. Then it folds its wings and dives at a high rate of speed toward the ground. AID; ATWS; CI; DEI; GTP; ID. *See also* Bright as a Lark; Sing like a Lark. *Compare* Happy as a Clam.

HARASS *to harass someone.* To annoy, worry, trouble, or torment someone. Source: DOG. In medieval France, *Hare!* was an interjection used to *sic* (q.v.) a dog on an animal or person. From *hare* developed M.Fr. *harer* "to set a dog on"; and from *harer* came Mod.Fr. *harasser* "to wear out." In the 17th cent., the English borrowed *harass* to mean "to worry the enemy with repeated raids"; and in modern America *harass* means "to abuse someone with unwanted attention." The pronunciation of *harass* has changed, for some Americans, from the original stress on the final syllable, as in French, to stress on the initial syllable. EWPO. *Compare* Abet.

HARD-BITTEN *See* Take the Bit.

HARD-BOILED *to be hard-boiled.* To be tough and demanding. WNNCD: 1886. Source: CHICKEN. The *hard-boiled* boss behaves as if his/her head has been cooked in hot water until all pity and sentiment have been boiled away. Most drill sergeants are like this, as well as some construction bosses and office managers. (In cookbooks, the term is usu. *hard-cooked*.) BDPF; WNWD.

HARD ON SOMEONE'S HEELS *See* In Hot Pursuit.

HARD SELL *See* Hard-shell/Soft-shell.

HARD-SHELL CONSERVATIVE *See* Hard-shell/Soft-shell.

HARD-SHELL/SOFT-SHELL Rigid/flexible. Source: ANIMAL. The attributives *hard-shell* and *soft-shell* first referred to the rigidity or flexibility of the shells of turtles, clams, and crabs. In all cases, *soft-shell* appeared before *hardshell*: the soft-shelled turtle (WNNCD: 1771); the soft-shell clam, or *quahog* (WNNCD: 1796); the hard-shell clam (WNNCD: 1799); the soft-shell crab, i.e., one that has recently shed its shell (WNNCD: 1805); and the hard-shell crab (WNNCD: 1902). The first metaphorical use of these modifiers, however, emphasized rigidity: e.g., a *hard-shell conservative*, one who is stiff and uncompromising (WNNCD: 1838). More recently, the attributive modifiers have been used to distinguish flexibility in taco shells: a *hard-shell taco* and a *soft-shell taco*. It is also likely that the merchandising term *hard sell* "the use of high-pressure sales tactics" (WNNCD: 1952) and *soft sell* "the use of gentle persuasion" (WNNCD: 1954) were influenced by the terms *hard-shell* and *soft-shell*. BDPF; WNWD. *See also* Shell (n).

HARD-SHELL TACO   *See* Hard-shell/Soft-shell.

HARD TO SWALLOW   *See* Stick in Your Craw.

HARE AND HOUNDS   A paper chase. WNNCD: 14th cent. Source: HARE; HOUND. WNNCD: O.E. In medieval England, *hare and hounds* was a cross-country game in which a runner, acting as the "hare," set off in advance, leaving a trail of paper for the other runners, the "hounds," to follow in order to catch him/her. (In a real hunt, the only trail that the hare leaves for the hounds is the scent.) Currently, a *paper chase* is the pursuit of a law degree, and a *paper trail* is the record of a transaction that investigators must follow to nab a white-collar criminal. ATWS; BDPF; DEI; IRCD. *See also* Run with the Hare and Run with the Hounds. *Compare* Fox and Geese.

HAREBRAINED   *a harebrained scheme*. A foolish or foolhardy plan or idea. WNNCD: 1534. Source: HARE. WNNCD: O.E. A *harebrained scheme* is one that has been thought up by someone who has a brain the size of a hare's. Hares do have small brains, compared with humans, but they are neither foolish nor foolhardy. Their habit of *backtracking* (q.v.) may seem foolish to humans, but to dogs it is a brilliant maneuver. ATWS; BDPF; DEI; IRCD. *See also* Mad as a March Hare. *Compare* Beetlebrained; Birdbrained.

HARELIP   *a harelip*. A cleft upper lip. WNNCD: 1567. Source: HARE. WNNCD: O.E. The congenital deformity called a *harelip* is named after the split upper lip of the hare, for which it is a normal feature. Since many other animals have a split upper lip (e.g., the big cats), it must be assumed that the familiarity with the hare prompted the metaphor. ATWS; BDPF; IRCD. *Compare* Beetle-browed; Pigeon-toed.

HARK BACK   *to hark back to something*. To return to, or recall, an earlier subject or event. WNNCD: 1834. Source: DOG. When foxhounds have lost the scent of the fox, the huntsman calls them back to the fresher track by yelling "Hark!" Speakers *hark back*, or return, to a topic mentioned earlier; and an occurrence in the present can *hark back to*, or remind you of, an event in the past. ATWS; BDPF; ST.

HARNESS   *to harness energy*. To control and utilize natural energy for the benefit of humans. Source: HORSE. A harness is the network of leather straps in which a horse (or mule) is outfitted for pulling a load (WNNCD: 14th cent.). To harness a horse is to equip it with this gear (WNNCD: 14th cent.). To *harness* the energy of the sun, moon, wind, waves, storms, etc., is to convert their energy into forms that can be controlled and utilized by humans. The resulting energy is often measured in *horsepower* (q.v.) or in *watts* (1/746th of a horsepower).

HARRIDAN *a harridan.* A disreputable woman. WNNCD: 1700. Source: HORSE. *Harridan* is probably a modification of Fr. *haridelle* "a worn-out horse: an old nag." There are many metaphors comparing unfriendly women with vicious or violent animals. EWPO; WNWD. *See also* Jade: Shrew; Vixen.

HARRIER *a harrier.* A cross-country runner. Source: HARE. WNNCD: O.E. A *harrier* was orig. one of the pack of dogs used for hunting hares. Later the term was applied to a member of the "hound" team in a game of *hare and hounds* (q.v.). In modern times it refers to a member of a school cross-country team, which is hunting for nothing more than a win. MDWPO. *Compare* Rabbit.

HATCH *to hatch a plan or plot.* To come up with a plan or plot in secret. Source: BIRD. A mother bird sits on her eggs in a secluded nest until they hatch, or *break out of their shells* (q.v.). Her job is to produce a *brood* (q.v.) of half a dozen or so baby birds in order to maintain the survival of the species. Humans *hatch* plots and plans, not eggs; and their goal seems to be the survival of a philosophy or ideology. ATWS. *See also* Brood.

HAVE A BEAR BY THE TAIL *to have a bear by the tail.* To be in double jeopardy. EWPO: early-19th cent. Source: BEAR. WNNCD: O.E. The tails of American bears are so short—maximum of five inches—that they are barely noticeable. Grabbing one by its tail would be a foolhardy thing to do, putting you in a lose-lose situation: If you hang on, you will be dragged to death; if you let go, you will be mauled to death. LCRH; MDWPO. *Compare* Have a Tiger by the Tail.

HAVE A BURR UNDER YOUR SADDLE *See* Saddled with.

HAVE A COW *to have a cow.* To have an anxiety attack. Source: COW. WNNCD: O.E. On the TV show "The Simpsons," Bart Simpson says "Don't have a cow, man!" meaning "Don't get all upset about it." Bart is likening an anxiety attack to giving birth to a cow—a frightening thought. Normally, cows are the ones that give birth to cows—i.e., bull calves and heiffer calves. *Compare* Have Kittens.

HAVE A MONKEY ON YOUR BACK *to have a monkey on your back.* To have a problem that is hard to shake, such as an addiction to drugs or alcohol. IRCD: ca. 1942. Source: MONKEY. WNNCD: ca. 1530. The analogy may be to the organ grinder's monkey, which often perched on his shoulder; or it may be to a drug-induced nightmare of a wild monkey jumping on your back and refusing to let go. SHM. *Compare* Albatross around Your Neck; Have a Bear by the Tail; Have a Tiger by the Tail.

HAVE ANTS IN YOUR PANTS   *See* Ants in Your Pants.

HAVE A RING THROUGH YOUR NOSE   *See* Lead Someone around by the Nose.

HAVE AS MANY LIVES AS A CAT   *See* Have Nine Lives.

HAVE A TIGER BY THE TAIL   *to have a tiger by the tail.* To be in an unexpectedly precarious or dangerous position—one in which the only options are bad ones. Source: TIGER. WNNCD: O.E. If you lit. have a tiger by the tail, you have two options: to hold on or let go. Either way, you will be devoured by the tiger. (In the game of poker, if you are dealt a worthless hand known as a *tiger*—no face cards, no pairs, no potential straight or flush—your only option is to bluff, which is also dangerous.) ATWS; DEI; DOC; SHM. *See also* Ride a Tiger. *Compare* Have a Bear by the Tail.

HAVE BUTTERFLIES IN YOUR STOMACH   *See* Butterflies in Your Stomach.

HAVE EYES LIKE A CAT   *See* Eyes like a Cat.

HAVE KITTENS   *to have kittens.* To be nervous or upset. LTA: 1900. Source: CAT. When a mother cat is ready to have her kittens, she anxiously seeks out the proper place for their delivery. The delivery itself is a risky time, because then the cat and her helpless kittens are extremely vulnerable to predators. Following the delivery, the mother is exhausted but must attend to the nursing of her half dozen or so babies. People who are *having kittens* are not only nervous but are often angry or enraged. ATWS; CI. *Compare* Have a Cow.

HAVE MORE MONEY THAN FLEAS   *to have more money than fleas.* To have more money than you can count. Source: FLEA. WNNCD: O.E. It would be impossible to count the fleas on a dog's back, because they are so tiny (1 mm. in length), so numerous, and so active (noted for their leaping ability). *Flea-bitten* (q.v.) people who have more money than fleas are rich. *See also* Thick as Fleas.

HAVE NINE LIVES   *to have nine lives.* To be able to survive any disaster or setback. EWPO: 1546. Source: CAT. The notion that a cat has nine lives is part of medieval folklore, probably based on the fact that cats are curious and durable animals: they are suspicious of everything, get in a lot of trouble, and always manage to *land on their feet* (q.v.) when they fall. A person who *has as many lives as a cat* always seems to come out of a setback smelling like a rose—at least until the tenth time. In Shakespeare's *Romeo and Juliet* (ca. 1597), Mercutio answers

Tybalt's question, "What wouldst thou have with me?" by saying, "Good King of Cats, nothing but one of your nine lives." ATWS; BDPF; IRCD; MDWPO.

HAVE SOMEONE IN THE BULLPEN *to have someone in the bullpen.* To have someone in reserve. LTA: 1910. Source: BULL. WNNCD: O.E. The bullpen in this metaphor is the warm-up area for relief pitchers in a baseball stadium, which in outdoor parks is usu. located outside the left or right foul lines. At one time, the bullpen was often guarded by a bull on a billboard advertising Bull Durham chewing tobacco. MDWPO: ST. *See also* Bull (1); Bullpen.

HAVE SOMEONE IN YOUR CLUTCHES *See* Clutch (n) (1).

HAVE YOUR CAGE RATTLED *to have your cage rattled.* To be intimidated by someone or something; to be shocked into reality. Source: MONKEY. The tables are being turned in this metaphor, in which the human is compared to a caged monkey whose bars are being rattled by the keeper or visitor in order to stir up some action or simply harass the animals. Monkeys also rattle their own cages to intimidate other monkeys. *See also* Rattle Someone's Cage.

HAVE YOUR WINGS CLIPPED *See* Clip Someone's Wings.

HAWK (V) (1) *a hawk.* A militant: one who advocates military buildup and military response. IRCD: 1962. Source: HAWK. WNNCD: O.E. The human *hawk*—orig. a *warhawk* (BDPF: 1811)—is a legislator or executive officer who believes that a strong offense is the best defense, as in the Cuban Missile Crisis. More recently, the term has also come to mean a businessperson who advocates vigorous, aggressive action. The feathered hawk is an aggressive bird of prey. ATWS; IHAT. *See also* Hawkish. *Compare* Dove.

HAWK (n) (2) *a hawk.* A mortarboard: a square piece of board or metal, with a short wooden handle attached underneath, on which masons and plasterers carry their mortar in one hand while working with the other. WNNCD: 1854. Source: HAWK. WNNCD: O.E. It is uncertain why the portable mortarboard is named after the hawk, but it may be because falconers hold their hawks in this fashion, perched on one hand. *See also* Know a Hawk from a Handsaw.

HAWK (v) (1) *to hawk your wares.* To offer goods for sale—e.g., newspapers in the street, refreshments at a stadium—by calling out their name. WNNCD: 1713. Source: HAWK (*). WNNCD: O.E. This is not an animal metaphor. *Hawk* is a back-formation from *hawker* (WNNCD: 1512), "a peddler," which is an alteration of Ger. *Höker* (fr. *hoken* "to peddle"). The bird is in no way involved in this derivation.

HAWK (v) (2)   *to hawk the ball.* To steal the ball from an opponent (or a teammate). Source: HAWK. WNNCD: O.E. To hawk the ball is to seize it before the nearest player can get his/her hands on it. In football this is an interception or a fumble recovery; in basketball it is a pick, a steal, or the recovery of a turnover; in baseball it is a diving stop or catch, sometimes at the expense of a teammate. (The perpetrator of such an act is called a *ballhawk.*) All of these actions resemble the aggressive behavior of the hawk, which seizes its prey in the water, on the ground, or in the air.

HAWK-EYED   *to be hawk-eyed.* To have keen vision. Source: HAWK. WNNCD: O.E. During the time of the American frontier, a hunter was *hawk-eyed* if he had miraculous aim with a muzzle-loading firearm, as in Cooper's *Last of the Mohicans.* Today, someone who is *hawk-eyed* has a sharp eye for details: e.g., copy editors, surgeons (as on M*A*S*H), and art critics. ATWS; IRCD. *See also* Eye like a Hawk; Watch Someone like a Hawk. *Compare* Eagle-eyed; Eye of an Eagle.

HAWKISH   *to be hawkish.* To be militant: to support military buildup and response. Source: HAWK. WNNCD: O.E. The hawk is a symbol of aggressive behavior. Unlike the vulture, which waits for its meal to die, the hawk attacks its live prey on the ground, in the water, or in the air. Humans exhibit *hawkish* behavior when they advocate war, or, more recently, when they aggressively pursue commercial goals. IRCD. *See also* Hawk (n) (1). *Compare* Dovish.

HAWK-NOSED   *to be hawk-nosed.* To have a long nose that hooks downward toward the upper lip. IRCD: 16th cent. Source: HAWK. WNNCD: O.E. The analogy is to the upper beak of a hawk (or eagle or owl), which hooks down over the shorter lower beak and has the function of tearing apart the carcass of an animal. *Hawk-nosed* males, esp. athletes, are sometimes given the name "Hawk" for this reason. *Compare* Aquiline; Eagle Beak.

HEAD-IN-THE-SAND   *a head-in-the-sand attitude or approach.* A belief that if you ignore a problem long enough, it will go away. Source: OSTRICH. The two-toed flightless ostrich, the largest living bird, was once thought to stick its head in the sand when it was threatened or attacked, believing that if it could not see, it could not be seen. Its territory has now shrunk from three continents to Australia and southern Africa. *See also* Bury Your Head in the Sand; Ostrichlike.

HEDGEHOG   *a hedgehog.* A European cousin of the American porcupine. WNNCD: 15th cent. Source: HOG. WNNCD: O.E. The hedgehog and the *porcupine* (q.v.) (fr. Lat. *porcus*: "pig" + *spina* "spine") are both named for swine, but they are actually large rodents—up to 55 and 40 pounds, respectively—and look nothing like hogs or pigs. Like the hog, however, they are both "rooters," and the roots of hedges figure in the name of the hedgehog. HF. *See also* Hedgehog Gene.

HEDGEHOG GENE *a hedgehog gene.* The gene that is responsible for transforming embryos into vertebrate animals. Source: HEDGEHOG. WNNCD: 15th cent. The *hedgehog gene* controls the development of body parts such as wings, paws, and flippers—as well as brains, spines, and spinal cords. It is named for the hedgehog because it can cause a fly to sprout bristles when the growth gene from a hedgehog is implanted in it. The discovery of the hedgehog gene was reported by the New York *Times* in January 1994. *See also* Hedgehog.

HEE HAW *See* Bray like a Donkey.

HELICOPTER *See* Whirlybird.

HELL BENT FOR LEATHER *See* At the Drop of a Hat.

HELLCAT *a hellcat.* A witch (WNNCD: 1605); a *shrew* (q.v.). Source: CAT. WNNCD: O.E. Nowadays, a *hellcat* is a sharp-tongued, ill-tempered woman: a "woman from hell." However, in the 17th cent. a *hellcat* really was believed to come from hell, or at least possessed evil powers associated with the Devil, who sometimes appeared in the form of a black cat. IRCD.

HEN PARTY *a hen party.* A social gathering for women only. WNNCD: 1885. Source: HEN. WNNCD: O.E. A hen party is the female version of a *stag party* (q.v.), which is for men only. In the barnyard, the hens are usu. found on the ground, tending to their chicks, while the rooster perches on a fence post, enjoying his harem. They have separate roles. DEI; IRCD.

HENPECK *to henpeck someone.* For a nagging wife to dominate her husband. WNNCD: 1688. Source: HEN. WNNCD: O.E. According to the *pecking order* (q.v.) of chickens, the most dominant hen is allowed to peck any other hen without being pecked back, and it is possible that she may even assert the same dominance over young roosters. Socrates was said to have undergone such treatment by his wife, Xanthippe. ATWS; IRCD. *See also* Henpecked Husband.

HENPECKED *See* Henpecked Husband.

HENPECKED HUSBAND *a henpecked husband.* A husband who is dominated by his nagging wife. Source: HEN. WNNCD: O.E. The most famous henpecked husband was Socrates, who was said by Richard Steele (IRCD: 1712) to be the "undoubted head of the sect of the hen-pecked." The aggressor was his wife, Xanthippe. Hens peck other hens—and sometimes young roosters—to establish their dominance in the *pecking order* (q.v.). BDPF; CI; DEI; EWPO. *See also* Henpeck.

HEPCAT *See* Cat.

HERD (n)   *the herd.* The masses. Source: ANIMAL. Literally, a *herd* (WNNCD: 12th cent.) is a group of ungulate, or "hoofed," animals that either live and move together in the wild (as do bison, caribou, deer, elk, and moose) or are *herded* together by human caretakers (as are cattle, goats, sheep, and swine). Figuratively, a *herd* is either a congregation of people who have assembled for a common purpose; or the entire mass of people who are under the control of a common leader. In either case, a *herd mentality* sometimes develops, in which people either follow the example of their neighbors or follow the dictates of their leader— mindlessly, without independent thought. To *rise above the herd* is to assert your independence and think for yourself, esp. in the areas of ethics, morality, justice, and common sense. The bull, buck, ram, and boar manage to control their own destiny because of their size and strength. ATWS. *See also* Herd (v). *Compare* Egregious.

HERD (v)   *to herd people around or together.* To assemble people in a group or move them in a group from one place to another. Source. ANIMAL. People who herd cows, goats, sheep, and swine go by the names *cowherd, goatherd, shepherd* (for *sheepherder*), and *swineherd*, respectively. Their job is to see that the animals stay together while grazing and move together from pasture to pen, and vice versa. People who *herd* other people are, e.g., teachers who keep their pupils together while on a field trip, ushers who let people into or out of an auditorium or stadium, and police officers who transfer prisoners from one lockup to another. ATWS. *See also* Gregarious; Herd (n).

HERD MENTALITY   *See* Herd (n).

HERD OF ELEPHANTS   *to move like a herd of elephants.* For a large crowd of people to move ponderously and noisily toward a goal. Source: ELEPHANT. WNNCD: 14th cent. African elephants travel in herds of up to one hundred individuals, led by an elderly female, esp. in times of drought. The dusty scene is one of mass confusion and irresistible force. A comparable scene on the human level is an angry mob marching toward a government building or the stage of a rock concert. *Compare* Herd of Turtles.

HERD OF TURTLES   *to move like a herd of turtles.* For a crowd of people or cars to move at a *snail's pace* (q.v.). Source: TURTLE. WNNCD: 1657. This is a playful metaphor. Turtles do not herd together like cattle; and "true" turtles, i.e., sea turtles, move quite rapidly in the water. However, it is true that land turtles, i.e., tortoises, have a very slow gait, and some do migrate to a common area at nesting time, as in the Galapagos Islands. *Compare* Herd of Elephants.

HERO TO GOAT   *to go from hero to goat.* To go from success to failure. Source: GOAT. WNNCD: O.E. The *goat* in this metaphor is the biblical *scapegoat* (q.v.), on whom disgrace is heaped and exile is expected. Earlier, that same person may have been honored and glorified, like the other goat that was sacrificed to God. Human scapegoats, however, may return from the wilderness and live to enjoy herodom once more. ID.

HERPES   Either of two viral diseases that are characterized by blistering of the skin or the mucous membrane. WNNCD: 14th cent. Source: SNAKE. *Herpes* is Greek for "serpent," or "the creeping one." It is an appropriate name for cold sores (*herpes simplex*) and a venereal virus (*herpes genitalis*, also known as "the creeping crud"). Both varieties appear, spread, cause pain and suffering, then disappear, like the poisonous snake. *Compare* Canker.

HERRINGBONE   *See* Herringbone Pattern.

HERRINGBONE PATTERN   *a herringbone pattern*. A pattern consisting of a column of nested Vs alternating with a column of inverted Vs. WNNCD: 1598. Source: HERRING. WNNCD: O.E. This pattern of weaving, stitching, bricklaying, etc. is named for the skeleton of the fish called a *herring*—or, rather, for the skeletons of several herring laid head to tail. The small bones that project diagonally from the spine point backwards, away from the head. A twilled fabric woven with this pattern is called a *herringbone twill*, and a suit made of this twill is called a *herringbone suit*. The pattern also appears in the snow after skiers have *herringboned* up a slope with ski tips widely spread. BDPF; IRCD; MDWPO.

HERRINGBONE SUIT   *See* Herringbone Pattern.

HERRINGBONE TWILL   *See* Herringbone Pattern.

HIDE   *See* Hide nor Hair.

HIDEBOUND   *to be hidebound*. To be narrow-minded, rigidly opinionated, or ultraconservative. Source: CATTLE. Hidebound cattle are those which, because of disease or starvation, are so emaciated that their hide *sticks to their ribs* and cannot be removed after slaughtering (WNNCD: 1559). *Hidebound* people are those whose minds are so inelastic that they can not accept new ideas. ATWS; EWPO; HF; LCRH; SPD.

HIDE NOR HAIR   *I haven't seen hide nor hair of him in ten years.* He hasn't been around here in ten years. DOC: 1857. Source: ANIMAL. The *hide* of an animal is its skin, and the *hair* is its fur. When the fur of the animal has been removed from the hide, i.e., when it has been "dressed" or "tanned," it is called *leather;* and when the fur is left on the hide, i.e., when it is left "undressed," it is called a *skin* (e.g., a bearskin rug or a coonskin cap). If you have seen *neither hide nor hair* of someone, you have seen no part of them whatsoever. When a parent threatens to *tan a child's hide* (DOC: 1842), the threat usu. leads to nothing more than a spanking, which results in reddish skin; but when an animal hide is tanned, the color is changed to tan as a result of the use of tannin. A person or animal that *hides* in order to avoid punishment or death is lit. trying to *save their own hide*. AID; ATWS; EWPO; HOI; HTB; MDWPO.

HIDE YOUR HEAD IN THE SAND   *See* Bury Your Head in the Sand.

HIGH AS A KITE   *See* Kite (n).

HIGH AS AN ELEPHANT'S EYE   *to be as high as an elephant's eye*. To be over ten feet tall. Source: ELEPHANT. WNNCD: 14th cent. In the musical *Oklahoma!* it was the corn that was as high as an elephant's eye (from the song "O, What a Beautiful Morning"). The African elephant, which stands up to 13 feet tall at the shoulder, was probably familiar to early Oklahomans from visits there by the Barnum and Bailey Circus.

HIGHTAIL IT   *to hightail it out of here*. To get out of here as quickly as possible. WNNCD: 1925. Source: ANIMAL. When a deer or horse or rabbit is "spooked," it races away with its tail raised to the fullest height. In the case of the white-tailed deer, the raising of the "flag"—brown above, white below—is a signal to the other deer to take off. In the case of the horse, the raised tail can also be a sign of pleasure and pride, as when the horse is galloping around the lot or participating in dressage. For people, the expression probably derives from the cowboys of the Old West, who *hightailed it home*, along with their horses, when the work was done. The cottontail rabbit also raises its tail—brownish gray above, fluffy white below—when it becomes alarmed. AID; EWPO; IHAT; MDWPO; NDAS; ST.

HIP CHICK   *See* Chick.

HIPPOPOTAMUS   *a hippopotamus*. An amphibious mammal of sub-Saharan Africa. WNNCD: 14th cent. Source: HORSE. The hippopotamus is a large (up to 2.5 tons) pachyderm that spends most of its daylight hours in the water. Because of its size and aquatic nature, the ancient Greeks called it a "river horse" (Gr. *hippos* "horse" + *potamos* "river"), although it looks very little like a horse: huge head, fat body, short legs, no tail to speak of. The hippopotamus is actually more like a *sea cow* (q.v.), because it gives birth to its "calf" underwater and also nurses it there. ATWS; EWPO; IHAT. *See also* Behemoth.

HIT THE BULL'S-EYE   *to hit the bull's-eye*. To hit the center of the target; to "hit the nail on the head." Source: BULL. WNNCD: O.E. A *bull's-eye* (q.v.) is the center of a firearm target, an archery target, a dartboard, etc. Hitting it yields the highest score in a competition, and doing so metaphorically wins you the highest respect of your peers. CI; DEI; ST; WNWD.

HOBBLED   *to be hobbled by something.* To be impeded, hampered, or handicapped by something. Source: HORSE. A horse is hobbled by having two of its legs, usu. on the same side, tied together. The purpose of temporarily handicapping the horse in this way is to prevent it from straying, esp. when there is no tree around to tie it to. In the short period of 1910–1914, women were *hobbled* when they wore a *hobble skirt* (WNNCD: 1911), one that was so tight around the ankles that they couldn't walk. Prisoners who are considered dangerous or prone to escape are *hobbled* by having their ankles connected with a chain that is barely long enough for them to take a short step. BDPF; WNWD. *Compare* Pester.

HOBBLE SKIRT   *See* Hobbled.

HOBBY   *a hobby.* A personal pastime or avocation. WNNCD: 1816. Source: HORSE. Originally, a hobby was a small horse, or pony, that could be ridden by children (EWPO: 1375). In the 16th cent., *hobby* was combined with *horse* to describe the character played in the Morris Dance by a man wearing a wicker framework draped in the shape of a horse: a *hobbyhorse* (WNNCD: 1557). Later in that century, the hobbyhorse was adapted as a children's toy consisting of a stick, with the image of a horse's head on one end, that the child could "ride." (The expression *get on the stick* may come from this source.) In the 17th cent., the term *hobbyhorse* was applied to a child's *rocking horse*, or *cockhorse*, which was later suspended by springs from a framework. In the 18th cent., the expression *to ride a hobbyhorse* arose, meaning "to dwell on a pet theory as persistently as a child rides its hobbyhorse." Later in that century, *hobbyhorse* acquired the meaning "avocation or pastime"; and in the early-19th cent., the term was shortened to *hobby*, which has now come full circle. ATWS; BDPF; DEI; HF; IRCD; MDWPO; SHM; SOED; ST; THT. *See also* Get on Your Horse.

HOBBYHORSE   *See* Hobby.

HOBSON'S CHOICE   A choice with no options. WNNCD: 1649. Source: HORSE. Thomas Hobson, an English liveryman of the early 1600s, did not permit his customers to rent a particular horse but required them to "choose" the horse nearest to the door. That is, they had no choice at all. Hobson's system of rotating his stock was good for the horses, but the customers probably weren't very pleased. Patrons at budget barber shops sometimes feel the same way. BDPF; EWPO; SHM.

HOG (n) (1)   *a hog.* A dirty, greedy glutton. Source: HOG. WNNCD: O.E. Hogs are relatively clean animals when they are kept inside; but when they are kept outside, in a pigpen, they love to *wallow* (q.v.) in the mud. Hogs are also selfish, refusing to share the feeding trough with their peers; and they have insatiable appetites for just about any kind of food, including garbage. Being called a *hog* is worse than being called a *pig*. ATWS; BDPF. *See also* Pig (2).

HOG (n) (2) *a hog.* A large heavy motorcycle, esp. a Harley-Davidson. Source: HOG. WNNCD: O.E. *Hog* is an affectionate name for a Harley or other monster bike. The analogy is probably to the large size and rounded shape of a domestic boar, although the wild boar may have influenced the metaphor also. IRCD. *See also* Gas Hog; Road Hog.

HOG (v) *to hog something.* To attempt to monopolize something, such as food, attention, conversation, the limelight, or the road. IRCD: 1887. Source: HOG. WNNCD: O.E. The hog is a greedy, gluttonous, bullyish, selfish animal by nature: it wants the food, mud, space, etc., all to itself. Human *hogs* want more than their fair share of anything—but by nurture rather than by nature. ATWS; BDPF; DEI; DOC. *See also* Hog (n) (1).

HOGBACK *a hogback.* A sharp ridge with steep sides: a "razorback." WNNCD: 1834. Source: HOG. WNNCD: O.E. Hogs have a long, straight back; but in domestic hogs the spine is well protected by fat (or "fatback"). The reference is probably to the wild, long-legged, thin-bodied razorback hog of the southeastern United States (WNNCD: 1849), after which the University of Arkansas Razorbacks are named. WNWD.

HOG HEAVEN *to be in hog heaven.* To be surrounded by an abundance of normally forbidden "fruits." Source: HOG. WNNCD: O.E. If hogs dream, or at least daydream, they probably imagine a world quite different from the one they inhabit: fields of clover instead of ponds of mud; solid food instead of liquid garbage; endless tables instead of crowded troughs; warm beds instead of cold floors; etc. That's *hog heaven.* *See also* Like a Pig in Clover; Rolling in Clover.

HOG LATIN *See* Pig Latin.

HOGNOSE SNAKE *a hognose snake.* A false, or nonpoisonous, "puff adder." WNNCD: 1736. Source: HOG. WNNCD: O.E. The false puff adder is named after the hog because it has an unusual, upturned snout that it uses to borrow underground in search of food and more comfortable temperatures. It resembles the highly venomous puff adder because, when threatened, it hoods its neck, puffs up its body, hisses, and then *rolls over and plays dead* (q.v.). *See also* Go Belly up.

HOGSHEAD *a hogshead.* A large wooden barrel capable of holding between 63 gallons (the U.S. measure) and 140 gallons of liquid. WNNCD: 14th cent. Source: HOG. WNNCD: O.E. Why such a cask was named after a hog's head (M.E. *hoggeshede*) is uncertain. It may have been because the container was double the size of the normal barrel (31 gallons), just as the head of a mammoth boar is at least twice the size of that of a large pig. ATWS; GTP; HF; IRCD.

HOG THE LIMELIGHT *See* Hog (v).

HOG THE ROAD   *See* Hog (v); Road Hog.

HOG-TIE   *to hog-tie someone; to be hog-tied.* To render someone helpless; to be rendered helpless. Source: HOG. WNNCD: O.E. When a hog is being taken to slaughter, its four feet are tied together, causing it to lie on its side helpless (WNNCD: 1894). The same operation is performed on a calf in the calf-roping event of a rodeo, and it is sometimes used by robbers to immobilize their victims. (The hands and feet are tied together *behind* the victim's back.) The expression may be the source of another metaphor: to be *(all) tied up* at the moment. ATWS; GTP; IRCD.

HOGWASH   Nonsense; garbage. EWPO: ca. 1700. Source: HOG. WNNCD: O.E. Literally, *hogwash* is not the water left from washing a hog but the water left over from washing dishes or clothes, combined with scraps of garbage to form the slop, or "swill," that is fed to hogs. It is as unfit for human consumption as cheap liquor, meaningless talk, bad journalism, or misleading propaganda. ATWS; HF; IHAT; IRCD.

HOLD AT BAY   *See* At Bay.

HOLD OUT THE OLIVE BRANCH   *to hold out the olive branch.* To make a gesture of peace and goodwill. Source: DOVE. WNNCD: 13th cent. The dove and the olive branch have been symbols of peace since biblical times. In Genesis 8: 8–12, as the flood receded, Noah sent out a dove, three times, to discover whether there were any signs of life. The first time, it returned to the ark "empty-handed." The second time, the dove returned with an olive leaf in its beak, symbolizing peace with God. The third time it did not return at all. ATWS. *See also* Dove; Dove of Peace; Gentle as a Dove.

HOLD YOUR HORSES   *Hold your horses!* Not so fast! Take it easy! Slow down! HTB: 1844. Source: HORSE. WNNCD: O.E. In harness racing, the horses do not wait in a starting gate for the race to begin. At one time, the sulky riders had to maneuver their horses to the starting line on the run. After a few false starts, the starter would tell those who "jumped the gun" to *hold your horses*—i.e., get your horses under control so that they don't cross the starting line before the signal is given. (Nowadays, harness races are started behind a pace car with folding "wings.") People who are told to *hold their horses* are too impatient or impetuous for their own good. AID; ATWS; BDPF; CI; DEI; EWPO; HOI; IRCD; LCRH; ST.

HOLE UP   *to hole up.* To seek refuge or peace of mind in a safe or quiet place. WNNCD: 1875. Source: ANIMAL. Some mammals, such as the rabbit and the fox, hole up daily, as part of their normal routine; some mammals hole up seasonally, as with the "seven sleepers," who *go into hibernation* (q.v.) every winter; and some mammals take refuge in a hole, brushpile, or other cover when they are pursued. People hole up when they are pursued by the law, by bill collectors, by paparazzi, by fans, by relatives—or when they just want some peace and quiet.

HOLY CATS   *Holy cats!* Wow! Source: CAT. WNNCD: O.E. *Holy cats!* is probably a euphemism for Holy Christ! Cats may have been treated like royalty in ancient Egypt, but in medieval Europe they were thought to be instruments of the Devil, esp. if they were black. Their selection for this euphemism was probably due to their familiarity and the initial C. ATWS. *See also* Hellcat. *Compare* Holy Cow; Holy Mackerel; Holy Moley.

HOLY COW   *Holy cow!* Amazing! Unbelievable! Source: COW. WNNCD: O.E. *Holy cow!* is probably a euphemism for Holy Christ! No one knows how old it is, but it was popularized, simultaneously, by two baseball announcers in the 1950s: Harry Caray with the St. Louis Cardinals and Phil Rizzuto with the New York Yankees. Both of them used the expression to describe a home run, or a great play, by a member of their own team. *Compare* Holy Cats; Holy Mackerel; Holy Moley.

HOLY MACKEREL   *Holy Mackerel!* Wow! ATWS: 1899. Source: MACKEREL. WNNCD: 14th cent. The Atlantic mackerel is a common food fish on the East Coast and has therefore been a popular entree on holy days—although perhaps not as popular as the halibut, or "holy flatfish." *Mackerel* is probably a euphemism for *Moses: Holy Moses! Compare* Holy Cats; Holy Cow; Holy Moley.

HOLY MOLEY   *Holy moley!* Holy smokes! Source: MOLE (?). WNNCD: 14th cent. *Holy moley!* may be a euphemism for *Holy Moses!* The mole is a familiar burrowing animal that can easily turn a lawn into a giant molehill. Moles have had many oaths aimed at them, but they are only seeking out grubs and insects to maintain their survival. CE. *See also* Mole. *Compare* Holy Cats; Holy Cow; Holy Mackerel.

HOME, JAMES   *Home, James! And don't spare the horses!* Take me home. EWPO: 1600s. Source: HORSE. *James* was a name of convenience for the driver of the carriage of a wealthy or noble family in the 17th cent. When the family emerged from the opera or a soiree, they instructed the driver to take them home by saying, "Home, James!" "Don't spare the horses!" was a command to get there as soon as possible, regardless of how lathered the horses might get. In modern times, *Home, James!*—with no mention of horses—is usu. an instruction from a wife, who has just been picked up at work, to her husband, regardless of what his real name is. *Compare* Whoa, Nellie.

HONEY   *a honey of a black eye (etc.).* A perfectly formed black eye. Source: BEE. Honey is the sweet, sticky liquid produced by honeybees from the nectar of flowers. It was one of the primary sources of sucrose before the discovery of sugarcane and sugar beets. Therefore, it came to be regarded as the superlative example of sweetness—as in the term of endearment for a sweetheart, *Honey* (EWPO: 1880s), and, eventually, for other objects and actions: e.g., a *honey* of a car; a *honey* of a race. ATWS. *See also* Sweet as Honey.

HONEYCOMB *See* Honeycombed.

HONEYCOMBED *to be honeycombed.* To be full of holes. WNNCD: 1774. Source: BEE. In the beehive, the honeybees construct a hexagonal-celled comb of *beeswax* (q.v.) in which to raise their young—and, later, to store their honey. Humans have utilized the principle of the *honeycomb* (WNNCD: O.E.) in the manufacture of building and packaging materials that are cellular in makeup and therefore lighter in weight, although just as strong as necessary. *Honeycombed* objects are also found in nature, such as porous rock and wood and the underground tunnels of burrowing animals. ATWS.

HONEYMOON *a honeymoon.* A vacation for newlyweds. WNNCD: 1546. Source: BEE. A honeymoon orig. lasted one month (a "moon") and was expected to be as "sweet" as the marriage would ever get. Now, a *honeymoon* is also a short period of harmony granted to a new leader: Once *the honeymoon is over*, the cooperation ceases unless the leader has won over most of the followers by that time. ATWS; DEI.

HONEYMOON IS OVER *See* Honeymoon.

HONK (n) *See* Honk (v).

HONK (v) *to honk.* To sound the horn of a car or other vehicle. Source: GOOSE. When geese fly in their characteristic V-formation, they make a lot of noise, continually "honking" signals to each other regarding their place in line and perhaps their speed, direction, and destination. Strangely enough, the imitative word *honk* was not applied to the goose's vocalization until the 19th cent.: 1835 for the act of *honking*, and 1854 for the *honk* itself (WNNCD). The transfer of the word to the sound, or sounding, of a bulbtype horn, as on a bicycle, came later in that century. ATWS. *See also* Honker.

HONKER *a honker.* Your nose. Source: GOOSE. The sound of blowing your nose is associated with the honking sound made by geese in flight. For the geese, the *honk* is an important means of communication; for the human, it is an unavoidable embarrassment. *Honker* is also sometimes used, negatively, to suggest a large or bulbous nose. *See also* Honk (v). *Compare* Bill; Snout.

HOODWINK *to hoodwink someone.* To dupe, deceive, or trick someone. Source: FALCON. The falcon, a female hawk trained for the hunt, was *hoodwinked*

(WNNCD: 1562), or blindfolded, with a leather hood over its head and eyes while being transported to the field. When the hood was removed, the bird *batted its wings* until being tossed into the air. HF; ID; ST. *See also* Bat an Eye.

HOOFER *See* Hoof It.

HOOF IT *to hoof it.* To walk. WNNCD: 1641. Source: ANIMAL. The verb *hoof* derives from the noun *hoof* (fr. O.E. *hōf*), which refers to the horny matter that connects the toes of most farm animals and many wild animals, such as the deer, elephant, giraffe, and rhinocerous. *Hooves* (or *hoofs*) correspond to the claws of other mammals, such as bears, cats, and dogs, and to the nails of humans and other primates. Ungulate (or "hoofed") mammals, such as the horse, walk completely on their hooves, but humans who "*hoof it* over to the store" get there on their entire feet. A *hoofer* (WNNCD: 1918) is a professional dancer who lives by his/her feet. ATWS. *See also* On the Hoof. *Compare* Amble; Shank's Mares.

HOOKED *to be—or get—hooked on something.* To become addicted to something, such as books, music, or drugs. Source: FISH. A fish gets hooked when it *takes the bait*, or gets caught on the angler's baited hook or lure. Humans *get hooked* when they can't get enough of a harmless pleasure or a dangerous drug. Earlier, *to be hooked* meant to be seduced into matrimony by a member of the opposite sex (esp. a female). BDPF; ST. *See also* Hook, Line, and Sinker.

HOOK, LINE, AND SINKER *to swallow something hook, line, and sinker.* To fall for a practical joke, a swindle, or a preposterous tale. WNNCD: 1838. Source: FISH. This expression is comparable to *lock, stock, and barrel* (for firearms)—i.e., "everything, a total loss." Sometimes a fish will swallow the baited hook and some of the leader line, but it is unlikely that a normal-size fish would ingest the sinker as well. Consequently, the basis for this metaphor is probably a *fish story* (q.v.) about the *one that got away* (q.v.): It was so big that it swallowed everything, including the sinker that was three feet up the line from the hook. A gullible person who believes such a story is said to *swallow it hook, line, and sinker.* ATWS; EWPO; HOI; ID.

HOOT (n) *a hoot.* (*You're a real hoot, aren't you!*) A joker. (You think you're funny, don't you!) Source: OWL. The reference is to the "hoot owl," or Great Horned Owl, which stands two feet high from its "ears" to its tail and is the King of the Forest, preying on everything from hares to hawks. Its typical cry is a series of four hoots. The *hoots* that a joker gets are a mixture of laughs and boos from the audience. *See also* Ain't that a Hoot; Give a Hoot; Hoot (v); Not Worth a Hoot.

HOOT (v) *to hoot your disapproval; to hoot down a speaker.* To shout out your disapproval; to shout down a speaker. WNNCD: 13th cent. Source: OWL. The most famous *hooter* is the "hoot owl," or Great Horned Owl, which inhabits most of the North American continent. The *hooting* that humans do is not necessarily in imitation of the hoot owl, but that's where the word comes from. Baseball fans used to make this sound when "Hoot" Evers came to the plate. WNWD. *See also* Hoot (n).

HOOVER HOG *a Hoover hog.* An armadillo. EWPO: 1930s. Source: HOG. WNNCD: O.E. In the Great Depression, during the first part of which Herbert Hoover was President, hungry residents of the Gulf Coast, esp. in Florida and Texas, began to take a closer look at the little armored animal that had previously been regarded only as a pest. Calling it a hog, or a *Texas turkey* (q.v.), made it sound more appetizing. *Compare* Cape Cod Turkey; Welsh Rabbit.

HOREHOUND A hard candy made from an extract of the mint plant of the same name. HF: 15th cent. Source: DOG (*). WNNCD: O.E. *Horehound* is a folk attempt to make sense of M.E. *horhoune* (fr. O.E. *hār* "hoary" + *hūne* "herb"). It does not allude to an old gray dog, and it is not an animal metaphor.

HORN *a horn.* A wind instrument. Source: ANIMAL. Wind instruments were orig. fashioned from the hollowed out horns of rams and bulls, but now they are made of metal: e.g, the *cornet* (WNNCD: 14th cent.), or "little horn" (fr. Lat. *cornu* "horn"). Because of the sound effect of the horn, the word *horn* has been applied to a fixed loudspeaker, as on a ship, and to the telephone: "*Get on the horn* and start calling people!" The appearance of the horn of an animal has caused the word *horn* to be applied to the pommel of a Western saddle (WNNCD: 1856), to the "ears" of the Great Horned Owl (WNNCD: 1812), to the "spikes" of a *horned toad* (WNNCD: 1806), and to the *antennae* (q.v.) of a yellow jacket or *hornet* (WNNCD: O.E.). *Hornet* lit. means "little horn" in English and is cognate with M.Fr. *cornet*. ATWS; ROE. *See also* Horns of a Dilemma.

HORNED QUESTION *See* Horns of a Dilemma.

HORNED TOAD *See* Horn.

HORNET *See* Horn.

HORNET'S NEST *a hornet's nest.* A peck of trouble: a Pandora's box. WNNCD: 1590. Source: HORNET. WNNCD: O.E. The hornet, a "yellowjacket" or large wasp, builds a nest of paper hanging from the limb of a tree. Anyone who disturbs the nest is in for a violent attack of multiple stings, including the same hornet. ATWS. *See also* Mad as a Hornet; Sting to the Quick; Stir up a Hornet's Nest.

HORN IN ON *See* Lock Horns.

HORNS OF A DILEMMA   *to be (caught) on the horns of a dilemma.* To be forced to make a choice between two unacceptable alternatives. Source: ANIMAL. In the metaphor, a *dilemma* (fr. Gk. *di-* "two" + *lemma* "proposition") is likened to an animal with two sharp horns, either of which could be lethal. To be caught on the horns of such an animal would mean to be in a precarious position: a lose-lose situation. An example of a dilemma, in the form of a *horned question*, is the query, "Have you stopped beating your wife?" If you answer "yes," you imply that you once were in the habit of beating her; and if you answer "no," you confirm that you are still doing do. You're damned if you do and damned if you don't. AID; ATWS; DOC; EWPO; HOI; LCRH. *See also* Horn. *Compare* Hobson's Choice.

HORNY   *to be horny.* To be sexually aroused. LTA: 1889. Source: ANIMAL. Before 1889, only hoofed animals were "horny," i.e., possessed horns. Since 1889, the term *horny* has been applied, first, to a sexually aroused male human (because of the resemblance of the erect penis to an animal's horn), and, later, to a sexually excited human of either sex. CE; EWPO. *See also* Horn.

HORSE   Heroin. NDAS: 20th cent. Source: HORSE. WNNCD: O.E. It is uncertain why *horse* has become a slang term for *heroin* (WNNCD: 1898). One clue might be that horses are fast, and heroin travels fast in the bloodstream to the brain. Another clue could be that horses are big, and heroin is sometimes called "the big H." (*Heroin* was orig. a trademark.)

HORSE-AND-BUGGY   *See* Horse-and-buggy Days.

HORSE-AND-BUGGY DAYS   *the horse-and-buggy days.* The old-fashioned days before the advent of the automobile. WNNCD: 1926. Source: HORSE. WNNCD: O.E. In the "good old days," transportation was achieved by riding either *on* a horse or *behind* a horse pulling a *buggy* (a light, four-wheeled carriage). Nowadays, people who are "behind the times" are said to have a *horse-and-buggy* attitude toward modern life or to take a *horse-and-buggy* approach to modern problems.

HORSE AROUND   *See* Horseplay.

HORSE CHESTNUT   *a horse chestnut tree.* A buckeye. WNNCD: 1597. Source: HORSE. WNNCD: O.E. You might guess that the horse chestnut tree was so called because its shiny brown nuts resembled the droppings, or "road apples," from horses. But you would be wrong. *Horse* is used here in the sense of "big," as in *horseradish* (q.v.); i.e., the seed of the tree is unusually large. Horses do have *chestnuts*, but they are the small black callouses on the inner side of the front legs, just above the knee. The horse's *chestnuts* were probably named for the seeds of the chestnut tree, rather than vice versa. EWPO; HF.

HORSE-COLLAR   *See* Draw the Collar.

HORSEFEATHERS *Horsefeathers!* Nonsense! WNNCD: 1928. Source: HORSE. WNNCD: O.E. Horses don't have feathers, although the long, light, fluffy hair at the back of the lower leg of a horse—esp. a Clydesdale—is sometimes called *feathering.* An interpretation of the metaphor could be that something is about as sensible as the notion that horses can fly (like Pegasus); but almost everyone agrees that *Horsefeathers!* is a euphemism for *Horseshit!* (q.v.), an adjustment required in the comic strip in which it first appeared in the 1920s. (It was also the title of a Marx Brothers film in 1936.) ATWS; EOD; EWPO; HF; IHAT; IRCD. *Compare* When Pigs Fly; Whether Pigs Have Wings.

HORSEHIDE *a horsehide.* A baseball. Source: HORSE. WNNCD: O.E. Nowadays, when you "toss the old *horsehide* around," you're tossing a *cowhide* baseball around, because the ball hasn't been made of horsehide since 1985. The same applies to the professional football, or *pigskin* (q.v.), and the professional basketball, or *round ball,* both of which are also made of cowhide. (College and high school footballs and basketballs are made of a synthetic compound.)

HORSE LATITUDES *the horse latitudes.* The regions of the oceans located 30° north and 30° south of the equator. WNNCD: 1777. Source: HORSE. WNNCD: O.E. The *horse latitudes* would seem to be so called because they form a belt, or cinch, around the middle of the earth; but the fact is that they were named after the region in the Atlantic only, where the pressure is high and the winds are light or calm. In the 18th cent., a ship headed from Europe to the New World that slipped south of the trade winds into the windless *horse latitudes* could be becalmed for days. With food and water running short, the captain might order the horses, which consumed an inordinate amount of each, to be jettisoned into the ocean. ATWS; BDPF; EWPO; IRCD.

HORSELAUGH *a horselaugh.* A loud, coarse, vulgar laugh: a guffaw. WNNCD: 1713. Source: HORSE. WNNCD: O.E. Horses don't laugh, but they do sometimes curl back their lips when they neigh, giving the impression of a sardonic smile. People who laugh boisterously, spontaneously, and unceremoniously convey the impression that they are uncultured or uncivilized, like the horse. ATWS; BDPF; CI; DEI; EWPO; IRCD.

HORSELESS CARRIAGE *See* Iron Horse.

HORSE MARINES *the horse marines.* A fictitious seagoing cavalry. IRCD: mid-19th cent. Source: HORSE. WNNCD: O.E. Horses, and horse soldiers, have been carried on ships since the Age of Exploration began; but the soldiers presumably did not ride their steeds aboard ship, and they certainly did not conduct cavalry charges there. By the middle of the 19th cent., *horse marines* had become an absurd contradiction—Whoever heard of sailors on horseback?—and was the basis for the expression "Tell it to the horse marines," now shortened to *Tell it to* *the marines,* i.e., tell your story to someone as unlikely as the story itself. BDPF; MDWPO.

HORSE OF A DIFFERENT COLOR   *That's a horse of a different—or another—color.* That's a different matter entirely. DOC: 1798. Source: HORSE. WNNCD: O.E. The horse in question is probably a *ringer* (q.v.): a fast horse substituted for a slower one in order to take advantage of the longer odds. A knowledgeable horseperson might utter the expression if he/she noticed the substitution in time. The metaphor was parodied in the movie *The Wizard of Oz* (1939), one of the first color films, in which the horse pulling the Wizard's carriage kept changing colors. AID; ATWS; BDPF; CI; DEI; EWPO; HOI; ID; IRCD; MDWPO; SHM; ST.

HORSE OF ANOTHER COLOR   *See* Horse of a Different Color.

HORSE OPERA   *a horse opera.* A motion picture, radio program, or TV show with a Western theme. WNNCD: 1927. Source: HORSE. WNNCD: O.E. Originally, the *horse opera* was a play with a Western flavor that was performed in the local opera house (IRCD: mid-19th cent.). With the advent of film, the *horse opera* became synonymous with nostalgic stories about the Old West: cowboys and Indians, lawmen in white hats and villains in black hats, saloons, stagecoaches, and, of course, horses. The theme was maintained in radio and television, and the *horse opera* has become a genre in the entertainment industry. ATWS.

HORSEPLAY   Rough and boisterous play, esp. by children. WNNCD: 1589. Source: HORSE. WNNCD: O.E. Young horses are frisky and frolicsome when they are allowed to run free in a large pen or corral. They love to *kick up their heels* (q.v.), bite their playmates, and race around the yard at breakneck speed. Human children also like to engage in *horseplay*—i.e., to *horse around*—when they are left unsupervised, but their play usu. involves wrestling and rolling around on the floor or ground, and it is usu. more destructive than the play of young horses. ATWS; CI; DEI; IRCD.

HORSEPOWER   The power rating of an engine or motor. IRCD: ca. 1800. Source: HORSE. WNNCD: O.E. Horsepower as a unit of measurement of the power of an engine was invented by James Watt, the Scottish developer of the steam engine. After an elaborate calculation of the work that a horse could do in one day, Watt settled on one *horsepower* as a unit "equal to the raising of 33,000 pounds one foot high in one minute." That equates to 550 foot-pounds of work per second in England and 746 watts of power in the United States. (A *watt* is 1/746th of a horsepower.) ATWS; EWPO; WNWD.

HORSE RACE   *a horse race.* A close and exciting contest. Source: HORSE. WNNCD: O.E. A horse race is not very suspenseful if one of the horses *pulls away from the field* (q.v.) and creates a *one-horse race.* The same is true of political campaigns: If a candidate lacks serious competition, the race isn't very exciting. However, if a *dark horse* (q.v.) enters the picture and gives the candidate a *run for his money* (q.v.), then the race is said to be a *horse race*: tight and competitive. CI; DAE; ST.

HORSERADISH A large, white, pungent radish of the mustard family. WNNCD: 1597. Source: HORSE. WNNCD: O.E. The *horseradish* is not named after the horse because it is powerful and fiery but because it is large. It is simply a large white root of the *horseradish* plant, usu. ground up as a relish. The same sense of *horse* appears in the word *horse chestnut* (q.v.). BDPF; EWPO.

HORSE'S ASS *You're a horse's ass!* You're stupid and disgusting. WNNCD: 1970. Source: HORSE. WNNCD: O.E. One would have expected this invective to have appeared in 1770 or 1870 rather than in 1970, because in the "good old days" the rear end of a horse was what the rider of a buggy had to look at all trip long. The reason for the late appearance may have been that by 1970 the word *ass* (q.v.), as in "You're an ass," had lost its association with the donkey and needed reinforcement.

HORSE SENSE Practical wisdom; common sense. WNNCD: 1832. Source: HORSE. WNNCD: O.E. It is unclear why the horse was selected to represent common sense. Horses panic easily, they are afraid of their own shadow, and they make themselves sick by drinking too much water after a hard day's work. The reason may have been that horses are such *creatures of habit* that they can pull a buggy home after the driver has fallen asleep, or that a cutting horse is so highly trained that it can herd cattle even after the rider has fallen off. A more likely explanation for the metaphor is that the term alludes to a *human* who is a *good judge of horseflesh* (q.v.)—a *horse trader* (q.v.). ATWS; CI; DEI; DOC; EWPO; IRCD.

HORSES FOR COURSES *There are horses for courses.* Some people are better suited for certain jobs—or certain job conditions—than others. EWPO: 1898. Source: HORSE. WNNCD: O.E. Some racehorses run better at certain tracks—or under certain track conditions—than others. A "mudder," for example, runs well on a wet track; and a British horse is at an advantage in England, where the horses race clockwise. Some people adjust well to night work, outdoor work, or teamwork, while others prefer day work, indoor work, or independent work. There are "different strokes for different folks." CI; DEI; ST.

HORSESHIT Nonsense, bunk, "crap." WNNCD: 1946. Source: HORSE. WNNCD: O.E. *Horseshit* developed during WWII as a competitor to *bullshit* (q.v.), which had been around since before WWI. Perhaps *horseshit* appeared because *bullshit* had been replaced in polite company by the euphemisms *bull* (q.v.) and *B.S.* (q.v.), and a stronger term was needed. ("Horse manure" sounds a little "wimpy.")

HORSESHOE BAT   *See* Horseshoes.

HORSESHOE BEND   *See* Horseshoes.

HORSESHOE CRAB   *See* Horseshoes.

HORSESHOES   An American game, similar to British *quoits* (WNNCD: 15th cent.), in which U-shaped iron objects are tossed at iron stakes approx. 40 feet away. (In quoits, the missiles are circular.) Source: HORSE. WNNCD: O.E. As the name implies, the original objects thrown in *horseshoes* were "real" horseshoes (WNNCD: 14th cent.)—the U-shaped iron "shoes" that are nailed to the bottom of a horse's hooves to protect them from harm. Horseshoes are also regarded as good-luck symbols and are sometimes nailed above doorways—open side up— so that the *luck won't run out.* A *horseshoe bend* is a U-shaped curve in a river; a *horseshoe crab* (WNNCD: 1797) has a U-shaped body; and a *horseshoe bat* has a U-shaped disc around its nostrils. MDWPO.

HORSE THIEF   *a horse thief.* A scoundrel. Source: HORSE. WNNCD: O.E. In the frontier days, a man's most valuable possession was his horse. It was his primary means of transportation, tilling, and herding, and it was often his only companion. To steal a man's horse was to steal his livelihood, and only a dirty rotten scoundrel would do such a thing. Hanging was automatic. CH.

HORSE TRADE   *a horse trade.* A shrewd bargain. WNNCD: 1846. Source: HORSE. WNNCD: O.E. *Horse trading* has no doubt been going on for as long as there have been horses, and a good horse trader is a tough, smart, hardhearted bargainer. Figurative *horse traders* are businesspersons or politicians who drive a hard bargain and usu. get what they want, even if it means making costly concessions. ATWS; DEI; IRCD; SPD.

HORSE TRADER   *See* Horse Trade.

HORSE TRADING   *See* Horse Trade.

HORSEY SET   *the horsey (or horsy) set.* People who are identified with the ownership or breeding of race horses or the ownership or riding of showhorses, fox hunting horses, or polo ponies. Source: HORSE. WNNCD: O.E. Horses are the most expensive domestic animals to own, maintain, breed, show, or race. The *horsey set* are the closest thing to aristocracy in America. GTP; WNWD.

HOT AND BOTHERED   *See* Work Yourself into a Lather.

HOT DIGGITY DOG   *See* Hot Dog!

HOTDOG *to hotdog.* To show off. WNNCD: 1962. Source: DOG. WNNCD: O.E. *Hotdog* originated in the sports of surfing and skiing, where a *hotdogger* is someone who performs daredevil stunts in order to impress the other skiers. The term may hark back to the frankfurter on a bun sold at baseball parks, where some players like to show off for the hog dog eaters; it may derive from the nickname for a wienershaped surfboard popular in the 1950s; or it may come from the exclamation *Hot dog!* (q.v.). *Hotdoggers* are also called *hot dogs.* ATWS; CE; EWPO; IHAT; ST. *See also* Hot Dog.

HOG DOG *a hot dog.* A hot sausage on a bun. WNNCD: 1900. Source: DOG. WNNCD: O.E. The hog dog was invented at Coney Island, Brooklyn, N.Y., in 1871, and was called a "frankfurter" or "Coney Island" at that time. In approx. 1896, it was sold in the Polo Grounds, home of the New York Giants baseball team, where it was called a "red hot" or a "dachshund sausage." In 1900, a New York cartoonist drew a picture of a dachshund—sometimes called a "wiener dog"—lying in a bun and called it a *hot dog.* The name stuck. Other names for the hog dog are *dog, chili dog* (with chili sauce), *corn dog* (coated with corn meal, skewered on a stick, and deep fried), and *frank.* ATWS; EWPO; HTB; IRCD; ST. *See also* Hotdog; Hot Dog! *Compare* Hush Puppy.

HOT DOG! *Hot Dog!* Wow! Great! WNNCD: 1906. Source: DOG. WNNCD: O.E. This expression of approval or pleasure may have come from the baseball park, where the *hot dog* (q.v.) is the favorite entree, and the favorite sound is "Hot dogs! Get your hot dogs!" The timing is right, because *hot dog* replaced "red hot" in approx. 1900. *Hot dog!* is the basis for the expanded expression *Hot diggity dog!* (IHAT: 1920s); and the sense of approval associated with *Hot dog!* may have contributed to the development of the verb *hotdog* (q.v.). ATWS; IHAT; IRCD.

HOGDOGGER *See* Hotdog.

HOT ON THE TRAIL *See* In Hot Pursuit.

HOT TO TROT *See* Trot (v).

HOUND (n) *a hound.* A relentless pursuer; an avid collector. Source: DOG. *Hound* (fr. O.E. *hund* "dog") has become the basis for a number of compounds relating to searching and collecting. A *bloodhound*, also known as a *sleuthhound* (WNNCD: 1856), is a detective: one who tracks down criminals as relentlessly as the droopy-eared dog of the same name. An *autograph hound* is someone who pursues celebrities in order to obtain their signatures. A *chowhound* (WNNCD: 1942) is a person, orig. in the military, who loves to eat, and gulps down his/her food like a hungry dog. A *rock hound* is either a professional geologist (WNNCD: 1915) or an amateur collector of rocks and minerals. (A child *rock hound* is affectionately called a *pebble pup*.) ATWS; BDPF; IRCD; MDWPO; ST. *See also* Hound (v).

HOUND (v)   *to hound someone*. To pester or harass someone; to pursue someone relentlessly. WNNCD: 1528. Source: DOG. From the noun *hound* (q.v.) comes the verb *to hound*: "to pursue someone as relentlessly as a hound pursues its prey." When the pursuit lacks authorization, however, *hound* has come to mean "to harass someone by stalking or persecuting them." ATWS; BDPF; EWPO; IRCD; SHM; ST. *See also* Dog; Hound (n).

HOUND DOG   *a hound dog*. A good-for-nothing person (esp. male). Source: DOG. WNNCD: O.E. In O.E., *hund* was the generic word for "dog," and *docga* was the name for a male dog; since then, the two words have virtually traded places, with *dog* (M.E. *dogge*) becoming the generic term and *hound* coming to mean a hunting dog. Combining the two words emphasizes the low regard in which a canine, or a good-for-nothing human, is held, as in the 1956 song by Jerry Leiber and Mike Stoller, "You Ain't Nothin' but a Hound Dog." IRCD.

HOUNDS OF HELL   *the hounds of hell*. The leaders of the opposition. DOC: 1867. Source: DOG. In Greek mythology, the "hound of hell" was Cerberus, the guard dog of Hades, who had three heads, which accounts for the plural use of *hounds* in the metaphor. In medieval times, the "hounds of heaven" were known as *Gabriel's hounds*: a flock of migratory geese whose honking resembled the barking of a pack of dogs *in full cry* (q.v.). The wandering geese, guarded by the Archangel Gabriel, were thought to be the souls of unbaptized children waiting for Judgment Day. EWPO.

HOUNDSTOOTH CHECK   *See* Clean as a Hound's Tooth.

HOUSEBROKEN   *See* Rub Someone's Nose in It.

HOVER   *to hover*. To remain suspended in air over a particular spot. WNNCD: 15th cent. Source: BIRD. Not all birds are able to hover. The ones that are good at it are the soaring birds, such as the hawks and gulls; but the best of all is the hummingbird, which not only hovers at the mouth of a flower but is able to fly backwards to retreat from it. People have invented machines that *hover* in air, such as the balloon, the helicopter, and the trademarked Hovercraft, which can travel over either land or water on a cushion of air. Clouds also *hover*, as do debts, guilt, and nosy parents. ATWS.

HOW DO YOU GET DOWN OFF AN ELEPHANT   *See* Down.

HOWL   *See* Bark like a Dog.

HUM *to hum.* To sing with the lips closed. WNNCD: 15th cent. Source: BEE. Unlike *buzz* (q.v.), which refers to the *z*-like sound of bees in flight, *hum* alludes to the *m*-like sound produced by the bees' wings in a hive. Just as *bu-* has been added to *z* to produce the word *buzz*, *hu-* has been added to *m* to produce *hum*. *See also* Humdrum; Make Things Hum.

HUMDRUM *a humdrum existence.* A dull and monotonous life. WNNCD: 1553. Source: BEE. *Humdrum*, a modified reduplication of *hum*, means about the same thing as *hohum* (WNNCD: 1969): "routine; lacking in excitement or incentive." The allusion in both words is to life among the honeybees, where the agenda does not change from day to day or generation to generation. HF. *See also* Hum; Make Things Hum.

HUNGRY AS A BEAR *to be as hungry as a bear.* To have a voracious appetite. Source: BEAR. WNNCD: O.E. Bears are classified as carnivores, but they eat everything, from berries to buffalo, and they all love honey. (One O.E. name for the bear was "bee-wolf," i.e., *Beowulf.*) Eastern American black bears are primarily vegetarians, while Western brown bears, the grizzly and the Kodiak, have a taste for fish; and Alaskan polar bears feed on seals. Bears are hungriest in the early spring, following a long winter of hibernation, and in the late fall, just before hibernation, when they can double their weight in preparation. If you were *as hungry as a bear*, you could probably *eat a horse* (q.v.). AID.

HUNGRY MOUTHS TO FEED *to have a lot of hungry mouths to feed.* To have a large family with a lot of young children. Source: BIRD. Baby birds don't nurse, of course, and they also don't fly; so the parents must spend most of their time rounding up the appropriate food and bringing it back to the nest. There they must (1) pass it to the young bird, from beak to beak (e.g., a grasshopper), or (2) pick the prey apart into small pieces, passing one to each chick (e.g., a fish or rabbit), or (3) regurgitate a partially digested meal directly into the baby's mouth (e.g., "pigeon's milk"). Human parents with a large number of young children to feed must feel a lot like the birds: all of their time and energy seem to be expended for the sake of their young.

HUNT-AND-PECK *the hunt-and-peck method of typing.* The method used by someone who is unfamiliar with the keyboard and the ten-finger style of typing. WNNCD: 1939. Source: BIRD. A *hunt-'n-pecker* resembles a hen hunting for a grain of corn on the ground and then pecking at it once she finds one. There are also overtones of the woodpecker, which hunts for the location of an insect in a tree and then pecks at the bark until it reaches it. Novice typists look puzzlingly at the jumble of letters out of alphabetical order and then strike the key with the same finger they strike all of the other keys with. Some actually become quite good at it.

HUNT-'N-PECKER   *See* Hunt-and-peck.

HUSH PUPPY   *a hush puppy.* A deep fried ball of cornmeal. WNNCD: ca. 1918. Source: DOG. The *hush puppy* originated in the South during the Civil War (WNNCD: early 1860s). How it got its name is uncertain, but the speculation is that it arose from the practice of quieting the dogs who hung around the campfire by throwing them balls of deep-fried cornmeal, along with the admonition, "Hush, puppy!" At any rate, *hush puppies* are now popular throughout the country, where they are standard fare with fish and "chips" (french fries); but the recipe has been relaxed to permit wheat and potato flour, and some people refer to them as "donut holes." ATWS; EWPO; HF; IRCD.

HUSKING BEE   *See* Bee.

HYENA   *a hyena.* A large doglike animal of Central and Southern Africa. WNNCD: 14th cent. Source: HOG. *Hyena* lit. means "female hog, or sow" (fr. Gk. *hys* "hog" + *aina* "feminine"). The hyena is named after the hog because of its bristly mane; but the reason could just as well have been the fact that it has an unattractive muzzle (or "snout") and a short neck, and that it burrows and eats anything, living or dead. WNWD.

I

ICHTHUS   The symbol for Jesus Christ. Source: FISH. The Greek word *ichthus* "fish" was the model for an early Christian acronym constructed from the initial letters of the Greek words for "Jesus Christ, God's Son, Savior." The schematic outline of a fish, resembling the lowercase Greek letter *alpha*, now stands for ICHTHUS, Christ, and the Christian Church. EWPO; IRCD. *Compare* Ghoti.

IF IT HAD BEEN A SNAKE   *If it had been a snake, it would have bitten me.* It was right under my nose. Source: SNAKE. WNNCD: O.E. Most snakes bite, but usu. only when cornered or molested. When you lose something and then find it within your reach, you are as close to it as you should ever get to a wild snake, esp. a poisonous one. *Compare* Nourish a Serpent.

IF WISHES WERE HORSES   *If wishes were horses, beggars would (or could) ride.* (A proverb.) Wishing doesn't make it so. MDWPO: 1670. Source: HORSE. WNNCD: O.E. In the 17th cent., the horse was the primary means of transportation; but horses were expensive, and the poorest people could not afford them. So the beggars "rode their wishes," ignoring the fact that they would never come true. Today, the proverb is uttered when someone substitutes wishes for reality, as the beggars did. A related proverb, "Set a *beggar on horseback* and he'll outride the devil," alludes to the arrogance that accompanies newfound wealth. ATWS; DEI; EWPO.

IMPECUNIOUS   *See* Pecuniary.

IMPERIALIST DOG   *See* Running Dog.

IN ABEYANCE   *See* At Bay.

IN A LATHER   *See* Work Yourself into a Lather.

IN A PIG'S EYE   *In a pig's eye!* No way! Never! Not on your life! DOC: 1872. Source: PIG. WNNCD: 13th cent. Just about every part of the pig has been appropriated for a metaphor, from the squeal to the tail. *Pig's eye* may be a reference to a parlor game similar to *pin the tail on the donkey* (q.v.). In both cases the participant is blindfolded, spun around three times, and told to locate an animal part on a picture hanging on the wall (the donkey) or drawn on the floor (the pig's eye). The results are usu. hilarious. ATWS; IHAT; IRCD; NDAS. *See also* Make a Silk Purse out of a Sow's Ear.

IN AT THE DEATH   *to be in at the death.* To be present at the climax of something. DOC: 1800. Source: DOG. In fox hunting, when the dogs have *run the fox to earth* (q.v), the fox is either killed by the dogs, killed by the huntsman, or captured to run another day. For humans, being *in at the death*, or *in at the kill*, means being a witness to the end of something, such as the demise of an institution or the end of an era. It is a time for both celebration and sorrow. CI; DEI; ST.

IN AT THE KILL   *See* In at the Death.

INAUGURATE   *See* Augur.

IN COLD BLOOD   *See* Cold-blooded.

INDEPENDENT AS A HOG ON ICE   *to be as independent as a hog on ice.* To be cocky, confident, and self-assured. DAE: 1894. Source: HOG. WNNCD: O.E. This is an ironical expression, since a hog on a frozen pond is about as dependent as an animal can be. It can't stand up or move in any direction: it is completely helpless. Some have suggested that the "hog" is a Scottish curling stone that fails to reach its mark and represents a hazard to other curlers, but other sources (e.g., MDWPO) deny this. The explanation may simply be that the domestic hog that is stranded on the ice is regarded as independent because it steadfastly refuses to allow the farmer to help it get off. ATWS; BDPF; DOC; HOI; ST.

IN FINE FEATHER   *to be in fine feather.* To be in good condition—physically, financially, etc. Source: BIRD. A bird is in fine, or "full," feather when it is not molting. Most birds molt twice a year, in the summer and the winter, and during the summer molt they sometimes shed so many feathers that they are unable to fly. People who are *in fine feather* are in good physical, mental, and emotional health and are comfortable enough financially to dress fashionably, with all the trimmings. ATWS; BDPF; DEI.

IN FULL CRY   *See* Bring to Bay.

IN FULL FEATHER   *See* In Fine Feather.

IN HOT PURSUIT   *to be in hot pursuit.* For the police to be close to apprehending someone. Source: DOG. In fox hunting, the hounds are *in full cry* when they are *hot on the trail* of the fox—i.e., when they are *hard (or close) on its heels* or lit. *on its tail.* When the police are *in hot pursuit* of a criminal, they are usu. in a squad car chasing after the suspect's car. The word *hot* refers both to the *baying* (q.v.) of the dogs and the sound of the siren of the police car. DOC; SOED; ST. *See also* At Bay; Bring to Bay.

IN HOT WATER   *to be in hot water.* To be in deep trouble that can only get worse and from which there is no escape. WNNCD: 14th cent. Source: LOBSTER. The live Maine lobster goes straight from the holding tank to the pot of boiling water—unlike most other animals that are already dead before they are cooked and whose troubles are over. DOC. *See also* Look like a Boiled Lobster; Red as a Lobster.

INNOCENT AS A LAMB   *to be as innocent as a lamb.* To be totally without guilt or guile. Source: LAMB. WNNCD: O.E. All young animals are innocent, of course, but the lamb is usu. white, and the color white has long been associated with innocence and purity, as at baptisms and weddings. Regardless of color, black or white, the lamb is a nonthreatening and submissive creature. AID; DOC. *See also* Gentle as a Lamb; Meek as a Lamb.

IN SEASON   *See* Open Season.

INSECT   *an insect.* A trivial, unimportant, or contemptible person. Source: INSECT. WNNCD: 1601. Technically, an insect is a member of the class *Insecta* of the phylum *Arthropoda*. "True" insects have tripartite bodies (head, chest, abdomen), three pairs of legs, and one or two pairs of wings. However, the word *insect* is often applied to noninsects such as spiders and centipedes, and it can also apply to a human who gives you the *creeps* (q.v.). WNWD.

INSIDE TRACK   *See* At the Drop of a Hat.

INSTINCT FOR THE JUGULAR   *See* Go for the Jugular.

IN THE BAG   *See* Bag.

IN THE BUFF   *to be in the buff.* To be in your bare skin: naked. Source: BUFFALO. The shoulder portion of a buffalo hide, which is lighter colored than the rest of the hide, was the part used to make a buffalo robe. This color could be the source of the word *buff* (short for *buffalo*), or the source could be the orangish yellow color of the hide after it has been tanned. At any rate, the metaphor can apply to both light and dark-skinned persons. ATWS; EWPO. *See also* Buff (adj.).

IN THE CATBIRD SEAT *to be (sitting) in the catbird seat.* To be "sitting pretty"—in a position of superiority, advantage, or prominence. WNNCD: 1942. Source: CATBIRD. WNNCD: 1709. The catbird is an American songbird whose song reminds some people of the meowing of a cat and whose perch, like that of a cat, is always the highest one around. The expression was popularized in the 1940s by Dodgers announcer Red Barber and humorist James Thurber. ATWS; DOC; EWPO; IHAT; IRCD; LCRH; MDWPO; NDAS; ST.

IN THE DOGHOUSE *to be in the doghouse.* For a husband to be in a state of disfavor with his wife. DOC: 1904. Source: DOG. WNNCD: O.E. A *doghouse* (WNNCD: 1611) is an outdoor shelter for a dog—dark, damp, dirty, and un-heated. A chastized husband imagines himself living under these conditions with the family dog. The expression derives from the play *Peter Pan* (1904), by James M. Barrie, in which Mr. Darling lives in a doghouse as punishment for mistreating his children's dog, Nana. The term *doghouse* has recently also been applied to an oil crew's shed. AID; ATWS; BDPF; CI; DEI; EWPO; HOI; HTB; IRCD.

IN THE HOMESTRETCH *to be in the homestretch.* To be near the end of a long project. DA: 1866. Source: HORSE. A racehorse is *in the homestretch* (WNNCD: 1841) when it has rounded the final turn and is heading down the final straightaway toward the *wire*. During this time, when it is running straight ahead, the horse is able to stretch out its legs and run at top speed. People are often energized to work harder when they are *coming down the stretch* and can see that the end is near. A horse that *fades in the stretch* has used up most of its energy in the backstretch and has little left when it gets to the homestretch. A person who *fades in the stretch*, such as a candidate at the end of a long political campaign, has run out of energy or money or has lost his/her appeal with the voters. ST.

IN THE RUNNING *See* Off and Running.

IN THE SWIM *to be in the swim.* To be *au courant*: up to date, stylish, among the right people. SOED: 1869. Source: FISH. Literally, a *swim* is either a school of fish or a place where fish normally congregate. When an angler drops a line in a swim, it is like *shooting fish in a barrel* (q.v.): almost too easy. Figuratively, a *swim* is a trend or fashion that it is to your advantage to participate in. When you do, you will be said to be *in the swim of things*. AID; BDPF; CI; DEI.

IN TWO SHAKES OF A LAMB'S TAIL In no time at all. MDWPO: 1840. Source: LAMB. WNNCD: O.E. During their first year of life, lambs still have their tails; but when they are yearlings, their tails are docked and they become sheep.

The expression may refer to the tailless yearling, which can no longer shake its tail: i.e., at *no time* at all. AID; ATWS; BDPF; CI; EWPO; HOI; IRCD; LCRH; ST.

IRON HORSE   *an iron horse.* A steam locomotive. WNNCD: 1840. Source: HORSE. WNNCD: O.E. Before the railroad train appeared in the 1820s, the horse was the primary provider of power for transportation. When the steam locomotive came charging down the tracks, it was dubbed an *iron horse*—still a horse, but now made of iron. The same sort of thing occurred with the automobile: When it came charging down the road in the late-19th cent., it was dubbed a *horseless carriage* (WNNCD: 1895)—still a carriage, but without the horse. ATWS; BDPF; CI; IHAT; IRCD.

ISINGLASS   Mica. Source: FISH. How isinglass came to be another name for mica is somewhat of a mystery. The word is an altered borrowing of Du. *huizenblas* "sturgeon's bladder." The air bladders of sturgeons (and other fish) were used to prepare a semitransparent gelatin—hence the folk etymological change of *blas* to *glass*—which resembled a thin sheet of transparent mica, made from mineral silicates. *Isinglass* of the mineral variety was once used for small windows, or "peepholes," in ovens. ATWS; EWPO; WNWD.

IT'S A JUNGLE OUT THERE   It's every man (*sic*) for himself in this *dog-eat-dog* world (q.v.). Source: ANIMAL. Technically, a *jungle* (WNNCD: 1776) is a tangled mass of tropical vegetation, but the animals that are generally associated with it, such as the lion and the tiger (the "lords" of the African and Indian "jungles," respectively), are more often found in the plains or hills than in the impenetrable tropical forests. The mammals that are the principal inhabitants of the world's jungles are the monkeys; chimpanzees, orangutans, and gorillas. Human *jungles* are large cities and metropolitan areas—the *asphalt jungle* (WNNCD: ca. 1920)—where the battle with crowds and traffic, and the competition in business and industry make life a constant struggle for survival. It's "kill or be killed," and "only the fittest survive." This is the *law of the jungle* (EWPO: late-19th cent.): There are no laws. The same is not true of *hobo jungles* (LTRA: 1910), where behavior is more civilly regulated. CI; DEI. *See also* Jungle Gym.

IVORY TOWER   *to live in an ivory tower.* To be oblivious to the world around you. WNNCD: 1911. Source: ELEPHANT. An ivory tower is literally an "elephant tower," since *ivory* derives from the ancient Egyptian word for "elephant." Elephants don't live in towers made of ivory, and neither do people, although scholars and intellectuals are often accused of behaving as if they did. The university is a prime example of a place where the world inside can receive more attention than the world outside. CI; EWPO. See also Tickle the Ivories.

J

JACKAL *a jackal*. One who does someone else's dirty work. Source: JACKAL. WNNCD: 1603. The jackal, an Old World wild dog, was once believed to be the advance scout for the lion—locating the lion's prey (large game) and driving it (with the help of other jackals) in the lion's direction. It is now known that the jackal simply waits for the lion to finish its meal and then scavenges the rest. ATWS; BDPF; IRCD. *Compare* Cat's Paw; Toady.

JACKANAPES *a jackanapes*. A person (esp. male) who pretends to be better (richer, more cultivated) than he really is. WNNCD: 1522. Source: APE (*). WNNCD: O.E. A jackanapes "apes" his betters, but this is an eponymous expression rather than an animal metaphor. It is based on the nickname, *Jack Napis*, of a 15th cent. Duke of Suffolk who behaved in this way. HF. *See also* Ape (v); Play the Ape.

JACKASS *a jackass*. A stupid or stubborn person: a fool. LTA: 1832. Source: ASS. WNNCD: O.E. A *jackass* is a male donkey (WNNCD: 1727). (The female donkey is called a "jenny.") The *ass* (q.v.) has long been regarded as a stupid and stubborn animal, at least in comparison with the horse; but it is stubborn only because it knows its own limitations. ATWS; BDPF; CE; LCRH; MDWPO. *See also* Asinine. *Compare* Jackrabbit.

JACKRABBIT *a jackrabbit*. A large, long-eared hare of western North America. WNNCD: 1863. Source: ASS. The *jackrabbit* is named after the *jackass* (it was orig. called a *jackass rabbit*) because both animals have extremely long ears. *Jack* has also been applied to fish (no ears!) of larger than average size, e.g., mackerel, salmon, and smelt. ATWS; EWPO; IHAT. *See also* Jackass. *Compare* Mule Rabbit.

JACKRABBIT START *a jackrabbit start.* The sudden acceleration of a motor vehicle from a standing stop. Source: RABBIT. WNNCD: 14th cent. Exhibitionists make *jackrabbit starts* when the light turns green, and drag racers do the same thing when the green starting light goes on. The analogy is to a *jackrabbit* (q.v.) leaping suddenly from cover and bounding quickly away when disturbed by a dog or a hunter. ATWS; ST. *See also* Run like a Scared Rabbit.

JADE *See* Jaded.

JADED *to be jaded.* To be blasé, bored, spoiled, or calloused; to be worn-out, stale, trite, or *hackneyed* (q.v.). Source: HORSE. *Jaded* is derived from the noun *jade* "an old, tired, worn-out, broken-down horse" (WNNCD: 14th cent.). A *jaded* person is like a worthless nag: hardened, calloused, lacking in spirit, and oblivious to pleasure or pain; and a *jaded* art form is old, dull, overused, and hackneyed. The term *jade* is sometimes also applied to a disreputable older woman, esp. a prostitute. ATWS; BDPF; LCRH; MDWPO.

JAILBIRD *a jailbird.* An inmate or prisoner, esp. a repeater. WNNCD: 1618. Source: BIRD. WNNCD: O.E. A jailbird is so called because a prisoner behind bars is like a bird in a cage. And just as the pet bird is sometimes let out to fly around the house and is then caged up again, a habitual criminal is released when his/her term is up but often returns to be locked up once more. A variant of *jailbird* is *yardbird* (WNNCD: ca. 1941): a soldier who is not confined to jail but is disciplined by being restricted to a particular part of the base (the "yard") and assigned menial tasks. DEI; IHAT; IRCD. *Compare* Railbird.

JAY *See* Jaywalker.

JAYWALK *to jaywalk.* To cross the street in a careless, unsafe, or illegal manner, esp. at a location other than the designated crosswalk. WNNCD: 1919. Source: JAY. WNNCD: 14th cent. This is an Americanism, and the *jay* is the American blue jay, a noisy "bully bird" that walks—and flies—anywhere it wants to. (*Jaywalk* is a back-formation from *jaywalker* [q.v.].) ATWS; LCRH.

JAYWALKER *a jaywalker.* A person who crosses the street against the light or at a location other than the designated crosswalk. IHAT: 1917. Source: JAY. WNNCD: 14th cent. A *jaywalker* is one who either walks like a *jaybird* (i.e., anywhere it wants to) or walks like a *jay* (a country bumpkin who is unfamiliar with city laws). BDPF; DEI; EWPO; IRCD; MDWPO.

JELLYFISH *a (spineless) jellyfish.* A person who is lacking in backbone or conviction. LTA: 1911. Source: FISH. WNNCD: O.E. *Jellyfish* is a double metaphor, because this marine animal is an invertebrate, lacking a fixed form, and technically cannot be described as a "fish." *Spineless jellyfish*, therefore, is a redundancy as well as a metaphor. People who can't make up their minds, can't make tough decisions, or lack the courage of their convictions are like the formless jellyfish: they are as firm as jelly. ATWS; CE.

JERK SOMEONE AROUND   *to jerk someone around.* To manipulate someone; to give someone the runaround. Source: DOG. When a dog is being walked *on a short leash* (q.v.), it is not free to go where it wants to; if it tries to do so, the walker jerks the dog back to the proper path. People *jerk other people around* because they are either manipulative, egotistical, or lacking in sensitivity. A related expression, *to jerk someone's chain,* "to needle someone," probably derives from the choke chain used to train dogs: it tightens around the dog's neck when it *strains at the leash* (q.v.). LCRH.

JERK SOMEONE'S CHAIN   *See* Jerk Someone Around.

JIGGER   *a jigger.* A shot glass, or the amount of whiskey contained therein (usu. 1.5 ounces). Source: INSECT. The *jigger* derives its name from the tiny blood-sucking insect, either a flea or a mite, which burrows into the skin of humans and other animals and causes painful welts. (*Jigger* is fr. Wolof *jiga* "insect"; an altered form, *chigger,* is an Americanism.) The analogy is to the size of the shot glass compared with a drinking glass. EWPO; WNWD. *See also* Get under Your Skin.

JIMMINY CRICKETS   *Jimminy crickets!* (A euphemism.) Jesus Christ! Source: CRICKET. WNNCD: 14th cent. The field cricket is a small black insect whose chirping is enjoyed by people throughout the world but whose behavior is detested by those whose houses it invades. (It can eat holes in a nylon curtain in no time flat.) In the singular, *Jimminy Cricket* was the name of an animated figure in Walt Disney's *Pinocchio. See also* Cricket (1); Cricket (2).

JINX   *a jinx.* A bringer of bad luck; a spell of bad luck. WNNCD: 1911. Source: BIRD. The jinx is a wryneck woodpecker that has been used in black magic since the Middle Ages as a charm to cast spells. Eventually, the bird came to be regarded as both a caster of spells and a spell itself. Nowadays, a *jinx* is a person who is the common denominator in a "stretch of bad luck," also called a *jinx.* To *jinx* someone or something is to bring bad luck to them. EWPO. *Compare* Albatross around Your Neck.

JITTERBUG   *the jitterbug.* A vigorous, acrobatic "couples" dance that was performed to "swing" music in the late 1930s and the 1940s. WNNCD: 1938. Source: BUG. WNNCD: 1622. There is no insect by this name. *Jitterbug* is a combination of *jitter* "to move in a nervous or jerky fashion" (WNNCD: 1931) and *bug* "an enthusiast." One who danced in this manner was called a *jitterbug,* which may have been the model for the later *litterbug* (q.v.). To dance the dance was to *jitterbug* (WNNCD: 1939), and this verb was later applied also to "faking out," or "juking," an opponent in such sports as football, basketball, and soccer. IRCD: NDAS; WNWD. *See also* Bug (n) (3).

JOCKEY FOR POSITION   *See* At the Drop of a Hat.

JUDAS SHEEP   *a Judas sheep.* A goat. Source: SHEEP. WNNCD: O.E. In the New Testament, the horned goat was identified with the Devil, as was Judas, the betrayer of Jesus. (The *sheep* was identified with Jesus: *agnus dei* "lamb of God.") Calling the goat a *Judas sheep* was like saying that it was a *black sheep* (q.v.) or a "devil sheep." MDWPO. *See also* Separate the Sheep from the Goats.

JUGULAR   *See* Go for the Jugular.

JUMBO   *jumbo; jumbo-size.* Huge, mammoth, gigantic. WNNCD: 1883. Source: ELEPHANT. WNNCD: 14th cent. *Jumbo* is used to describe a container (e.g., a *jumbo-size* box of detergent or bag of potato chips) or its contents (e.g., *jumbo* or *jumbo-size* shrimp—a popular oxymoron). The metaphor derives from the name of the largest elephant ever captured: the Jumbo of P. T. Barnum's Greatest Show on Earth. Barnum purchased Jumbo in 1881 from the London zoo and exhibited him until he was hit by a train and killed in 1885. Although he weighed over 13,000 pounds, Jumbo was gentle and very popular with the children who rode on his back. BDPF; EWPO. *See also* Elephantine.

JUMP THROUGH HOOPS   *to jump through hoops.* To be forced to perform meaningless tasks; to go out of your way to please someone. Source: ANIMAL. In the circus, dogs and big cats (lions, tigers, leopards, etc.) are often made to jump through hoops as part of the act; and in the case of the cats, the hoops are sometimes set on fire. People *jump through hoops* when they do their best to cater to someone's wishes, or when they are made to do menial tasks as a test of their resolve, as in boot camp. AID; CI; ST. *Compare* Put Someone through Their Paces.

JUNGLE GYM   *a jungle gym.* A playground apparatus consisting of a framework of wooden or metal bars on which children can climb and swing. WNNCD: 1923. Source: MONKEY. *Jungle gym* was orig. a trademark (*Junglegym*) for the playground version of the *monkey bars* (q.v.) found in zoos. The name "Jungle Jim" has also been assumed by various hunters and trainers of wild animals, not necessarily monkeys. *See also* Climb like a Monkey.

K

KANGAROO COURT *a kangaroo court.* An impromptu trial, conducted without any legal authority, in which the verdict—"guilty"—is predetermined. WNNCD: 1853. Source: KANGAROO. WNNCD: 1773. The Australian kangaroo is guilty only by association here, either because the mock courts of the Old West "leapt" to their perverted conclusions or because the convictions were usu. of "claim-jumpers." ATWS; BDPF; DEI; EWPO; HF; HOI; IRCD; LCRH; THT. *See also* Kangaroo Ticket.

KANGAROO RAT *a kangaroo rat.* A desert rat of the southwestern United States. WNNCD: 1867. Source: KANGAROO. WNNCD: 1773. The *kangaroo rat* is a rodent, not a marsupial, but it resembles the Australian kangaroo in the sense that it moves by hopping on its hind legs. The tail is also long—longer than the body—and the rat has chipmunklike "pouches." *Compare* Rat Kangaroo.

KANGAROO TICKET *a kangaroo ticket.* A campaign ticket on which the presidential candidate has less attraction for the voters than the vice presidential candidate. SPD: 1932. Source: KANGAROO. WNNCD: 1773. The female kangaroo carries its offspring in its pouch for almost a year. To some people the baby is more attractive than the mother. *See also* Kangaroo Court; Kangaroo Rat.

KEEP AT BAY *See* At Bay.

KEEP A TIGHT REIN *to keep a tight rein on someone.* To maintain tight control over someone. Source: HORSE. The first thing that a rider or driver learns about controlling a horse (or horses) is to hold the reins tight. The horse understands that tight reins mean that the rider/driver is in control, and it also understands that loose reins mean a lack of control. Without control over the horse it is likely to *get out of hand*—i.e., the control passes out of the hands of the rider/driver to the horse. Humans maintain control over other humans by demanding strict obedience and observing constant vigilance. When a situation *gets out of hand*, the person in charge has lost control over it, and it takes on a life of its own. BDPF; MDWPO; ST. *Compare* On a Short Leash.

KEEPER *a keeper.* A fine specimen of man or woman. Source: FISH. A fish is a "keeper" when it is of legal size. A man or a woman is a *keeper* when he or she is handsome or beautiful, respectively, or is otherwise desirable to a member of the opposite sex. When a fish is below legal size, the angler throws it back; when a person is less than desirable, the analyst simply ignores him or her. ST.

KEEP PACE WITH *to keep pace with someone or something.* To keep up with the competition, the times, the trends, the demands, etc. Source: HORSE. A horse keeps pace with another horse in a race by maintaining the same speed as the other horse and running *neck and neck* (q.v.) with it. A horse that *falls off the pace* of the other horse loses ground to it and falls behind in the race. Businesses that are behind the times lose ground to their competition and are doomed to failure. A *change of pace* is a change of gait for a four-gaited horse, but for baseball pitchers it is a slower version of a fastball (also called a *change-up*); and for people in general it is a departure from the normal routine, like having tea instead of coffee. CI; ST.

KEEP THE WOLF FROM THE DOOR *to keep the wolf from the door.* To barely avoid poverty or starvation. ("It's not much of a job, but it keeps the wolf from the door.") HOI: mid-15th cent. Source: WOLF. WNNCD: O.E. One way to keep the wolf from your door is to toss out some raw meat. When the meat runs out, however, you're a goner. Actually, wolves are more likely to chase sleighs than to besiege houses. AID; ATWS; CI; DEI; IRCD; LCRH; SHM. *See also* Throw Someone to the Wolves.

KEEP TRACK OF *See* Track down.

KETTLE OF FISH *a nice, fine, or pretty kettle of fish.* A nice, fine, or pretty mess you've gotten yourself into. WNNCD: 1742. Source: FISH. WNNCD: O.E. Literally, a kettle of fish is a large cast iron pot, sitting over a roaring fire, filled with pieces of salmon, whitefish, trout, etc., cooking in water laced with beer, wine, or soda pop. The result is a *mess*, in the original sense of "enough food for one meal." Somehow the alternative sense of *mess*, as "a sorry state of affairs," came to be associated with the kettle, perhaps because of the "messiness" involved in eating the contents. *Kettle of fish* has also acquired the meaning "another matter entirely," as in "That's a *different kettle of fish.*" AID; ATWS; CE; CI; DEI; DOC; EWPO; HOI; ID; IRCD; LCRH; MDWPO; SHM; ST.

KIBITZ *to kibitz.* For an onlooker at a card game to offer unwanted advice. WNNCD: 1927. Source: BIRD. This metaphor is based on a bird known in English as a lapwing or pewit, which utters a shrill cry of *pee-weet, pee-weet* when threatened. The cry was interpreted in German as *kiebitz* and in Yiddish as *kibits* and came to be associated with the constant comments of onlookers at card games. A *kibitzer* (WNNCD: 1925) is someone who gives this unwanted advice or criticism. EWPO.

KIBITZER *See* Kibitz.

KICK AGAINST THE PRICKS *to kick against the pricks.* To struggle against fate. Source: OX. The *pricks* are the goads that an ox-driver gives to the oxen— esp. to the "near ox" in the yoke—when he/she wants them to move faster or in a different direction. The oxen sometimes resist the authority by kicking. In Acts 9:5, Christ says to Saul, in a voice from heaven, "I am Jesus, whom thou persecutest: it is hard for thee to kick against the pricks." In this passage, Jesus is the ox-driver, and Saul, who has been persecuting the followers of Jesus, is the "near ox." Jesus gives directions to (or "pricks") Saul, but Saul reacts by resisting (or "kicking") rather than obeying. This behavior is hard for Jesus to accept. BDPF. *Compare* Kick over the Traces.

KICK LIKE A MULE *to have a kick like a mule.* For an alcoholic drink to have a sudden and strong effect on the body. Source: MULE. WNNCD: 13th cent. The mule's kick is like that of the horse, and it is probably just as strong. However, *mule* is also a slang term for "moonshine," and the original expression may have been "have a kick like *mule.*" *See also* Mule (1); Mule (2).

KICK OVER THE TRACES *to kick over the traces.* To throw off all restraint; to achieve independence. Source: HORSE. Traces are the lines on either side of a draft horse's harness that connect to the vehicle being pulled. When a horse kicks over its traces, it either dislodges them by kicking or gets one or both hind legs outside of the lines, allowing it to kick more freely. People *kick over the traces,* metaphorically, when they defy authority and assert their independence. A related expression, *to kick up your heels,* alludes to what a horse does when its harness is removed and it is allowed to roam free in the pasture: it runs, kicks, and acts like a frisky colt. People *kick up their heels* by living it up and having fun, like a bunch of kids. AID; ATWS; BDPF; DEI; DOC; HOI. *Compare* Kick against the Pricks.

KICK THE BUCKET *to kick the bucket.* To die. Source: HOG (?). WNNCD: O.E. This expression probably originated in the suicidal death of humans by hanging. The victim stands on an overturned bucket, throws a rope over a rafter, adjusts the noose, and then kicks away the bucket, causing a slow and painful death. However, there is a possibility that the source is the slaughter of a hog by hanging it by its hind feet from a wooden frame, puncturing its jugular vein, and allowing it to bleed to death. In the process, the animal may kick over the bucket that is there to catch the blood, thus inspiring the metaphor. EWPO. *See also* Bleed like a Stuck Pig.

KICK UP YOUR HEELS   *See* Kick over the Traces.

KID (n)   *a kid.* A child or young person; a son or daughter, regardless of age. EWPO: 1599. Source: GOAT. *Kid* orig. meant only a young goat, less than one year old (WNNCD: 13th cent.). In the late-16th cent. the word was applied, metaphorically, to a young child, probably because of the playful nature of both offspring. In the 19th cent. the meaning of the metaphor was broadened to include human offspring of any age: "How many kids do you have?" The word *kid* is a cognate of Ger. *Kind* "child," as in *kindergarten.* ATWS; BDPF; IRCD; MDWPO. *See also* Kid (v); Kidnap.

KID (v)   *to kid someone; to kid around with someone.* To fool someone; to fool around with someone. WNNCD: ca. 1811. Source: GOAT. Kids, i.e., young goats, enjoy playing with and butting their peers in imitation of their fathers. Human *kids*, i.e., children, are also playful and enjoy teasing and pulling pranks on their siblings and parents. The metaphor started with young children but now applies equally to the behavior of older children and adults: "You're *kidding!*" "Stop *kidding* around!" ATWS; BDPF; EWPO. *See also* Goat; Kid (n).

KIDDING   *See* Kid (v).

KID-GLOVE TREATMENT   Special treatment. Source: GOAT. VIPs, priceless objects, and delicate situations require special care in order to avoid causing offense, doing damage, or exacerbating conditions. Kid gloves—gloves made of the skin of kids, or young goats—are made of leather so thin and soft that the wearer can feel the difference between the obverse and reverse sides of a coin. They are the finest and most expensive of all gloves. DOC. *See also* Handle with Kid Gloves.

KIDNAP   *to kidnap someone or something.* To abduct a person, a person's pet, or a prize animal. WNNCD: 1682. Source: GOAT. This is not exactly an animal metaphor. *Kidnap* is probably a back-formation from *kidnapper:* the *nabber* (or "thief") of a *kid* (or "child"). However, *kid* "child" is a metaphorical extension of *kid* "young goat," so there is an indirect connection to goat. BDPF; WNWD. *See also* Get Someone's Goat.

KILLDEER   *a killdeer.* A North American bird (a "plover") whose cry sounds like *kill deer, kill deer.* WNNCD: 1731. Source: DEER. WNNCD: O.E. *Killdeers* don't kill deer, but they are staunch protectors of their young. When a *killdeer's* nest on the ground is threatened, it *flies in the face* (q.v.) of the predator or pulls the *wounded bird trick* (q.v.)—i.e., it walks away from the nest while pretending that it has a broken wing, thus calling attention to itself as a target and diverting the attacker from the eggs. The *killdeer* cry, however, is uttered in flight, at more peaceful times.

KILL THE FATTED CALF   *to kill the fatted calf.* To prepare an elaborate feast or party in honor of someone's visit or accomplishments. Source: CALF. WNNCD: O.E. The fatted (or "fattened") calf appeared in a New Testament parable (Luke 15:11–32, esp. 23), where it was killed for a feast to honor the return of the Prodigal Son. Lesser occasions would have called for a sheep or goat. AID; ATWS; BDPF; DEI; DOC; EWPO; HTB; IRCD; LCRH. *See also* Worship the Golden Calf.

KILL THE GOOSE THAT LAID THE GOLDEN EGGS   *to kill the goose that laid the golden eggs.* To behave greedily and self-defeatingly. LTA: 1890s. Source: GOOSE. WNNCD: O.E. An Aesop fable tells of a farmer who owned a goose that laid eggs of gold. The farmer became impatient waiting for the eggs to be laid, so he killed the goose to get at all of the golden eggs inside. Not only were there none, but the farmer had deprived himself of all of the eggs that would have been laid in the future. A modern parallel would be to *milk a cash cow dry,* thereby losing all possibility of future revenue. AID; ATWS; BDPF; CI; DEI; DOC; EWPO; IRCD; LCRH; MDWPO. *See also* Cash Cow. *Compare* Bite the Hand that Feeds You.

KILL TWO BIRDS WITH ONE STONE   *to kill two birds with one stone.* To accomplish two goals with a single attempt. DOC: 1656. Source: BIRD. WNNCD: O.E. Nowadays, *killing two birds with one stone* can be as mundane as picking up your laundry while you are dropping off your dry cleaning. However, in the ancient world it was an unusual event for a hunter to kill even one bird, say nothing about two, with a rock from a sling. (*Throwing* rocks was even less effective.) In the modern world, the people who are most concerned with *killing two birds with one stone* are efficiency experts. AID; ATWS; BDPF; CI; DEI; IRCD; ST.

KINGFISH   *a kingfish.* A master of the deal. Source: FISH. WNNCD: O.E. *King-fish* is a cover name for various large marine fish—such as the ocean perch, the sea bass, the mackerel, the tuna, and the swordfish—which are presumably the "kings" of the ocean. A human *kingfish* is more likely to be a king of political deals (like Huey Long) or of business deals (like the pal of Amos and Andy). HF; SPD; *See also* Halcyon Days.

KING OF BEASTS   *See* Lord of the Jungle.

KITE (n)   *a kite.* A child's toy; a bad check; a light sail. Source: KITE. WNNCD: O.E. All senses of the noun *kite* derive from O.E. *cyta* "a high-flying hawk with narrow wings and a forked tail." A child's *kite* is a light framework covered with paper or plastic that is capable of flying high on a long string if you can just get it off the ground. A financial *kite* is an altered check or one that is knowingly drawn against insufficient funds; and a nautical *kite* is a light sail, or spinnaker, that is rigged in front of the main sail when sailing downwind. An unwanted person is sometimes told to *go fly a kite*, and a very drunk person is sometimes described as being *as high as a kite*. ATWS; DEI; ID. *See also* Kite (v).

KITE (v) *to kite a check; to kite prices.* To cash a bad check; to raise prices unfairly. Source: KITE. WNNCD: O.E. All senses of the verb *kite* derive from the noun *kite* (q.v.). To *kite a check* is either to alter a check by increasing the amount to be paid or to write a personal check that you know is not covered by sufficient funds in your account. To *kite prices* is to raise the prices of goods for selected customers. These inflations of amounts are analogous to the soaring flight of the high-flying hawk, or kite.

KITTEN *See* Playful as a Kitten.

KITTENISH *See* Playful as a Kitten.

KITTY *a kitty.* The combined bets in a poker game: a "pot" (WNNCD: 1887); the individual contributions to a solicitation of funds: a "pool." Source: TIGER. The nickname for the 19th cent. game of *faro* was *tiger* (perhaps derived from the tiger sign on Chinese gambling houses), and this name was extended to the pot, or "little tiger": the *kitty*. (IRCD traces *kitty* to Du. *kitte*, a "jug.") The extension to collections at the office occurred in the 20th cent. EWPO. *See also* Blind Tiger; Sweeten the Kitty. *Compare* Piggy Bank.

KITTY-CORNER *to be kitty-corner to something.* To be diagonally opposite to something. Source: CAT (*). *Kitty-corner* is not an animal metaphor. It is a folk interpretation of *catercorner* (WNNCD: 1843), which is also not an animal metaphor. *Cater* (i.e. *catre*) is an O.Fr. spelling of Mod.Fr. *quatre* "four." In M.E., a *cater* was a "four-spot," or a playing card with a spot at each corner. At a four-cornered intersection, the diagonally opposite corners are *catercorner*, or *catty-corner*, to each other. *Kitty-corner* is a dim. form of *catty-corner*. MDWPO.

KIWI *See* Kiwi Fruit.

KIWI FRUIT The fruit of the Chinese Gooseberry. WNNCD: 1966. Source: BIRD. Chinese gooseberries are not the favorite fruit of the kiwi—a flightless, almost wingless, bird of New Zealand. They are called *kiwi fruit* because they are identified with the country whose residents are named for the long-billed, short-legged bird. Most kiwi fruit that is imported to America comes from New Zealand. EWPO.

KNEE-HIGH TO A GRASSHOPPER   *to be knee-high to a grasshopper.* To be very young. DOC: 1851. Source: GRASSHOPPER. WNNCD: 14th cent. The American grasshopper is only about an inch long, and it "stands" only about 3/8th of an inch high. It does have knees, but they are only slightly farther from the ground, so there is a bit of minimization in this metaphor. AID; CI; EWPO; ID; IRCD. *See also* Grasshopper (2). *Compare* Coon's Age.

KNOCK HEADS   *to knock heads.* To engage in a violent confrontation. Source: SHEEP. Among domestic sheep, only the males have horns. However, among wild sheep, such as the American bighorn, or "mountain sheep" (often mistakenly called a mountain *goat*), and the subarctic Dall sheep, or "white sheep" (often called a Dall's sheep), both sexes have horns, but only the males engage in hierarchical headbutting. The clashes are long, loud, exhausting, and dazzling. *See also* Ram (v).

KNOCK ME OVER WITH A FEATHER   *You could have knocked me over with a feather.* I was surprised, astonished, and stunned by the action (or announcement). Source: BIRD. A person who can lit. be knocked over with a feather has been rendered totally helpless, like a beat-up boxer who can be dropped by the touch, rather than the blow, of a glove. Figuratively, a person who has seen a surprising sight or received some shocking bit of news is psychologically helpless, but just as vulnerable. AID; ATWS; BDPF; CI; DEI.

KNOCK SOMEONE OFF THEIR PERCH   *See* Perch.

KNOCK THE TAR OUT OF SOMEONE   *to knock the tar out of someone.* To beat someone senseless. HOI: 20th cent. Source: SHEEP. Tar was once used to treat the sores on sheep and to "brand" them with the farmer's special mark. However, once the tar hardened, it ruined the wool and had to be knocked off with a stick before the next shearing. Thus, to *knock the tar out of someone* is to beat someone as if with a stick. HOI. *See also* Tarred with the Same Brush.

KNOW A HAWK FROM A HANDSAW   *to know a hawk from a handsaw.* To be of sound mind and judgment. Source: HAWK. WNNCD: O.E. In Shakespeare's *Hamlet* (Act II, Scene 2), Hamlet says: "I am but mad north-northwest. When the wind is southerly, I know a hawk from a handsaw." The *hawk* and the *handsaw* are either: (1) a bird and a carpenter's tool; (2) two birds: a hawk and a hernshaw (a young heron); or (3) two worker's tools: a mason's mortarboard and a saw. BDPF; CI; EWPO; LCRH; MDWPO. *See also* Hawk (n) (2).

KNOW YOUR OATS   *See* Feel Your Oats.

KOALA BEAR   *a koala bear.* An arboreal animal of eastern Australia. WNNCD: 1808. Source: BEAR. WNNCD: O.E. A koala bear is not a bear at all but a marsupial, or "pouched" mammal, related to the American possum. The offspring of both species are nursed in the mother's pouch while young; then they are carried on the mother's back for about a year afterwards. The koala is called a *bear* because it is entirely covered with soft fur and is as cuddly as a *teddy bear* (q.v.). Adults average only about 20 pounds in weight. CE. *Compare* Panda Bear.

KOMODO DRAGON *See* Dragon Lady.

L

L *See* A.

LADY-OR-TIGER *a lady-or-tiger situation*. A situation that is fraught with peril: the wrong choice can lead to disaster. Source: TIGER. WNNCD: O.E. In a 19th cent. short story by American author Frank Stockton, entitled "The Lady or the Tiger?", a condemned suitor of a king's daughter was forced to choose between door number one and door number two. Behind one door was his lady love; behind the other was a tiger. The story closes without revealing which choice the suitor made: it was left up to the reader's imagination. MDWPO. *Compare* Horns of a Dilemma.

LAMB *a lamb*. A person who is easily deceived or cheated, esp. in the stock market. Source: LAMB. WNNCD: O. E. The lamb has long been regarded as meek and mild, gentle and peaceful, innocent and trusting. The last-mentioned quality has made it a prime choice for sacrifice; the human "lamb" is a prime target for swindlers. ATWS; IRCD. *See also* Sacrificial Lamb. *Compare* Pigeon.

LAME DUCK *a lame duck*. An officeholder who has failed to be reelected and is serving out the balance of his/her term. DAE: 1863. Source: DUCK. WNNCD: O.E. Before the 20th Amendment to the Constitution (the "Lame Duck Amendment") was passed in the 1930s, an unreelected national official could serve approx. four additional months—November to March—before giving way to his/her successor. During this time, legislation could be passed in a *lame duck session* of Congress that might damage the new administration. The amendment solved this problem by ending the terms of office in January. The same metaphor is used in England to refer to a person who has been wiped out in the stock market.

Literally, a lame duck is a duck that has been wounded but is not yet dead. ATWS; CI; DOC; EWPO; HOI; HTB; IRCD; LCRH; LTA; MDWPO; ST.

LAND   *to land a job (etc.).* To (finally) get a job (etc.). Source: FISH. An angler "lands" a fish by removing it from the water to the land. A jobseeker *lands* a job— or a bidder *lands* a big contract—when the job or contract is removed from the listings and given to the applicant. Fishing and jobseeking require a lot of patience and many attempts before the prize is won. ST.

LAND ON YOUR FEET   *to land on your feet.* To always recover from a personal setback. Source: CAT. Regardless of the position a cat is in when it falls, or is dropped, it always manages to land upright: on its four feet. That may be because—or why—the cat *has nine lives* (q.v.). People who always seem to bounce back after a bout of ill health or a financial, social, legal, marital, or political setback are said to be able to *land on their feet* like the cat. The expression is also applied to gymnasts who always manage to land on their *two* feet after the most difficult routine. ATWS; DEI; ST.

LAP   *to lap the shores.* For soft waves to make a gentle splashing sound as they strike the shore. Source: ANIMAL. Dogs and cats take in liquids not by drinking them, as cows and horses do, but by lapping them up with their tongues. The sound made by this activity is the basis for the extension of *lap* to the sound made by waves touching the shore. To *lap something up* is a metaphor for people eating or drinking noisily or greedily and, more abstractly, for people "eating up" or "drinking in" the words of a book or speaker or the sights or sounds of an attraction. WNWD.

LAP DOG   *See* Put on the Dog.

LAP SOMETHING UP   *See* Lap.

LARK   *a lark.* A spree; an adventure; a good time. WNNCD: ca. 1811. Source: LARK (?). WNNCD: O.E. The origin of this metaphor is uncertain. It may derive from the courting ritual of the skylark, which climbs to 800 feet in the air, sings a beautiful song, and then dives at high speed, with its wings folded, to the ground. Or it may derive from the Brit. Eng. *lake* "sport," from M.E. *laik* "play" and OE. *lac* "contest." BDPF; DEI; EWPO; LCRH. *See also* Happy as a Lark.

LARKSPUR   *a larkspur.* A flower of the buttercup family: a *delphinium* (q.v.). WNNCD: 1578. Source: LARK. WNNCD: O.E. The delphinium is called a *larkspur* because the leaves surrounding the flower are spur-shaped, like the long hind claw of the lark. IRCD.

LAST DINOSAUR   *the last dinosaur.* The last member of a dying breed—human or institutional. Source: DINOSAUR. WNNCD: 1841. No one knows exactly when the last real dinosaur died, but it was probably about 65 million years ago, and its death was probably caused by meteorites striking the earth and kicking up dust that blocked the sun and killed the dinosaur's vegetation and smaller prey. Examples of metaphorical *last dinosaurs* are the last neighborhood grocery store, the last full-service gasoline station, the last man to open a door for a woman, and the last woman to make coffee for her male boss. ATWS. *See also* Dinosaur.

LAST ONE IN IS A ROTTEN EGG   *Last one in is a rotten egg!* The last one in the water stinks. Source: CHICKEN. This expression is a challenge uttered by one of a group of children as he/she runs down the beach toward the water. It is also used when getting on the schoolbus, in a car, on a carnival ride, etc. To a child, nothing is as bad as being last—or smelling the sulfurous smell of a rotten egg. *See also* Bad Egg.

LAST STRAW   *the last straw.* The final indignity. WNNCD: 1848. Source: CAMEL. Any beast of burden, such as the camel, has a limit to the amount of burden that it can bear. Dickens, in *Dombey and Son* (1846–1848), applied this situation to the human condition, where the burden is abuse and indignity. Also: "the *final* straw." AID; CI; EWPO; ID; IRCD. *See also* Straw that Broke the Camel's Back.

LAUGH LIKE A HYENA   *to laugh like a hyena.* To laugh loudly and uncontrollably. Source: HYENA. WNNCD: 14th cent. The "laughing hyena" is the largest of the African hyenas (over six feet long from nose to tip of tail) and also the noisiest, esp. during mating season. Its appearance—like a leopard with a dog's head—and its role as a scavenger may have contributed to the derision associated with it. *See also* Hyena.

LAW OF THE JUNGLE   *See* It's a Jungle out there.

LAY AN EGG   *to lay an egg.* To fail miserably. EWPO: 1870s. Source: DUCK; GOOSE. In 19th cent. baseball, the expression was "to lay a *goose egg*" (q.v.)—i.e., to score no runs in an inning or a game—which was based on the earlier cricket expression "to lay a *duck's egg*" (q.v.). From baseball, the metaphor has passed into the theater (meaning "to bomb") and the stock market (meaning "to plunge"). In general usage, *to lay an egg* is to fail to live up to expectations. AID; ATWS; DOC; HOI; LCRH; MDWPO; ST. *See also* Love.

LEAD A DOG'S LIFE   *to lead a dog's life.* To lead a life of degradation and misery. WNNCD: 16th cent. Source: DOG. WNNCD: O.E. The life of the dog is not like that of other domestic animals, because the dog provides no food for the table, wool for the loom, or power for the wagon. Even a working dog works only sporadically—herding the sheep, bringing in the cows, aiding the hunter, or guarding the property. The rest of the time the dog just lies around, sometimes chained, in the most miserable of conditions, occasionally being thrown a bone. People *lead a dog's life* when they are treated like dogs. AID; ATWS; BDPF; CI; DEI; DOC; EWPO; ID; IRCD.

LEAD A HORSE TO WATER *You can lead a horse to water, but you can't make it drink.* You can't force someone to do what they don't want to do. BDPF: 1546. Source: HORSE. WNNCD: O.E. Horses are large animals, and they need a lot of water, esp. before they go to work in the morning. Leading a horse from the stable to the horse tank (or trough), only to discover that it is not thirsty, is very frustrating, because you have to stay there until the thirst returns. At the end of the day, when the work is over, the horse has just the opposite problem: it refuses to stop drinking and can drink itself sick. The stubborn mule shows much more sense in the same situation: it refuses to drink at all when it is hot and tired and will take water only after it has cooled down. People are more like the horse. ATWS; CI; DOC; IRCD.

LEAD BY A NOSE *See* Win by a Nose.

LEADER OF THE PACK *the leader of the pack.* The ringleader or principal instigator of a group. Source: WOLF. Wolves hunt and travel in a pack of up to 15 members, led by one or two dominant leaders. The leaders identify the prey, lead the attack, and complete the kill. Human *leaders of the pack* usu. head a gang or a band. Frank Sinatra was called the "Leader of the (Rat) Pack" in the early 1960s, but real *rat packs* (q.v.) don't have leaders. *See also* Pack of Wolves; Wolf Pack.

LEAD FROM WIRE TO WIRE *See* Go down to the Wire.

LEAD SOMEONE AROUND BY THE NOSE *to lead someone around by the nose.* To manipulate, dominate, or control someone. DOC: 1581. Source: ANIMAL. In biblical times, the standard means of leading an ass, ox, camel, or water buffalo was by a rope attached to a brass ring passing through the cartilage between its nostrils (Isaiah 37:29); and in the Roman circus, wild animals such as the bear, boar, and lion were controlled in the same manner. In America, oxen were once led in this fashion, but the ring in the boar's nose was to prevent it from rooting in the ground. Men who are *led around by the nose* or *have a ring through their nose* are either *henpecked* (q.v.), i.e., are under the control of a domineering wife, or are easily deceived. In Shakespeare's *Othello* (Act I, Scene 3), Iago characterizes Othello as being "led by the nose/ As asses are"—in reference to Othello's willingness to believe that his wife Desdemona is being unfaithful to him. AID; ATWS; BDPF; CI; DEI; EWPO; HTB.

LEAP AT THE CHANCE   *See* Pounce.

LEAPFROG (n)   A children's game. WNNCD: 1599. Source: FROG. WNNCD: O.E. *Leapfrog* is a game for two players, one of whom bends forward at the waist while the other approaches quickly from the rear, places his/her hands on the bent-over child's back, and vaults over. They then switch roles. Frogs are well-known for their leaping and jumping ability, and a male frog will leap onto the back of a female to help force out her eggs for fertilization. *See also* Leapfrog (v).

LEAPFROG (v)   *to leapfrog over someone or something.* To move ahead of someone; to hurdle over something. WNNCD: 1872. Source: FROG. WNNCD: O.E. When a person is promoted over someone of higher rank, that person is said to *leapfrog* over that individual; and when a planner avoids a difficulty, he/she is said to *leapfrog* over that problem. Soldiers and police officers who advance in successive waves when approaching a hidden danger are also said to *leapfrog* (over) each other. All of these actions are based on the leaping/jumping ability of the frog. ATWS; HF; ID; IRCD; ST. *See also* Leapfrog (n).

LEAPING LIZARDS   *Leapin' Lizards!* An exclamation used by Little Orphan Annie in her comic strip, musical, and films. Source: LIZARD. WNNCD: 14th cent. Some lizards—i.e., small, long-bodied, four-legged reptiles with long, tapering tails—do leap, and some run on their hind legs over the surface of the water, but they usu. do so to escape rather than to frighten children. It is uncertain which one Annie had in mind.

LEAVE NO STONE UNTURNED   *See* Crawl under a Rock.

LED AROUND BY THE NOSE   *See* Lead Someone around by the Nose.

LEECH   *a leech.* A person who lives off the resources of others, giving nothing in return: a *parasite* (q.v.). Source: LEECH. WNNCD: O.E. The leech, or *bloodsucker* (q.v.), is a freshwater worm that attaches itself to a fish and sucks out its blood. The word *leech* is either derived from O.E. *læce* "physician" or is identified with it because physicians for many years used leeches to bleed their patients. ATWS; BDPF; EWPO; IRCD; THT; WNWD. *See also* Cling like a Leech.

LEFT AT THE POST   *See* Off and Running.

LEFT HOLDING THE BAG   *to be left holding the bag.* To be left to take the blame; to be made a fool of. Source: SNIPE. In the childish prank known as a *snipe hunt* (q.v.), a new member of a group is taken to a swamp at night and told to hold a bag (or sack) open while the rest of the members drive some snipe in that direction. They never do, and the poor soul is *left holding the bag* for the rest of the night. *See also* Snipe; Sniper.

LEFT-WING See Wing (n).

LEGAL EAGLE *a legal eagle.* A lawyer. Source: EAGLE. WNNCD: 13th cent. This metaphor owes its existence more to the rhyme than to any resemblance between lawyers and eagles. However, lawyers must have an *eagle eye* (q.v.) for details, and they must pick apart a testimony the way an eagle dismembers a quarry and feeds the pieces to its young (the jury?).

LEONINE *to be leonine.* To be lionlike. WNNCD: 14th cent. Source: LION. WNNCD: 12th cent. *Leonine* has an assortment of meanings. It can refer to a full head of long, wild hair (based on the huge mane of the male lion); it can refer to a one-sided agreement (based on the notion of *lion's share* [q.v.]); and it can refer to internal rhyme at the middle and end of a line of poetry: *leonine verse* (connection unknown). BDPF. *See also* Leonine Contract.

LEONINE CONTRACT *a leonine contract.* A one-sided agreement. Source: LION. WNNCD: 12th cent. A *leonine contract,* or partnership, is one in which one of the two partners is both liable for the losses and ineligible for the profits. The metaphor is based on the Aesop fable of "The Lion and His Fellow Hunters," in which the lion is assisted in the kill by other animals but refuses to allow them to share in the spoils. EWPO; MDWPO; SHM. *See also* Lion's Share.

LEONINE VERSE *See* Leonine.

LEOPARD *a leopard.* One of the "big cats" of sub-Saharan Africa and Southern Asia. WNNCD: 13th cent. Source: LION. WNNCD: 12th cent. The spotted leopard was so named by the ancient Greeks for its resemblance to a lion (Gk. *leōn*), in its length, tawny color, and power, and to a black panther (Gk. *pardos*), in its menacing appearance and black coloring. The prior existence of the black panther suggests that the leopard could really be basically black with light-colored rings (or "rosettes"), rather than basically tan with black spots. BDPF. *See also* Leopard never Changes Its Spots. *Compare* Camelopard.

LEOPARD FROG *a leopard frog.* A common North American frog with numerous brown blotches on a light green background. WNNCD: 1839. Source: LEOPARD. WNNCD: 13th cent. The *leopard frog* is named after the leopard because of its spots. The spots don't actually look that much like "rosettes," but the leopard is famous for its spotted coat, and it was discovered first. *See also* Leopard; Leopard never Changes Its Spots. *Compare* Leopard Seal.

LEOPARD NEVER CHANGES ITS SPOTS *a leopard never changes its spots.* One's character never changes: "Once a crook, always a crook." BDPF: 1597 (Shakespeare's *Richard II*). Source: LEOPARD. WNNCD: 13th cent. The ancient Greeks believed that the leopard was a combination of a lion (*leōn*) and a black panther (*pardos*) because its tawny coat was covered with black spots. But it is possible that the panther is a leopard with just one big black spot—no lions involved. DEI; EWPO; ID. *See also* Leopard; Leopard Seal. *Compare* Camelopard.

LEOPARD SEAL *a leopard seal.* An Antarctic seal with dark spots on its light gray coat. Source: LEOPARD. WNNCD: 13th cent. The leopard seal is a large aquatic mammal, up to 13 feet in length and 800 pounds in weight. Its only physical resemblance to the tropical leopard is the spots, for which the leopard seems to be the universal model, just as the tiger and the zebra are for stripes. *See also* Leopard Frog.

LET SLEEPING DOGS LIE Leave well enough alone. EWPO: 19th cent. Source: DOG. WNNCD: O.E. Waking a sleeping dog can be dangerous: the dog may instinctively bite the hand that wakes it. The warning first appeared in Chaucer's *Troilus and Criseyde* (1374), "It is nought good a slepyng hound to wake," but was changed to its present form in the 1800s. Other sayings that translate the metaphor are: "Don't ask for trouble"; "Don't rock the boat"; and "If it ain't broke, don't fix it." ATWS; BDPF; CI; DEI; DOC; HTB; ID; IRCD.

LET SLIP THE DOGS OF WAR *See* Dogs of War.

LET SOMEONE OFF THE HOOK *See* Off the Hook.

LET THE CAT OUT OF THE BAG *to let the cat out of the bag.* To unintentionally reveal a secret. LTA: 1760. Source: CAT. WNNCD: O.E. Originally, the secret that was unintentionally revealed was that the pig that someone thought they were buying in a poke (a sack) was really a cat that had been substituted by an unscrupulous seller. When the buyer opened the sack to check on the validity of the purchase, they accidentally *let the cat out of the bag*; and once *the cat was out of the bag*, the deception was out in the open. AID; ATWS; BDPF; CI; DEI; DOC; ID; IRCD; LCRH; SHM; ST. *See also* Buy a Pig in a Poke.

LEVIATHAN *a leviathan.* Something large and formidable. Source: CROCODILE. In the book of Job (41:1–34), the *leviathan* (fr. Heb. for "sea monster") was described as a formidable animal of great size and strength that had scales and teeth, breathed fire and smoke, and made the sea boil. This doesn't sound much like a crocodile, but that's the animal with which it has most often been identified. A modern *leviathan* is either an oceangoing ship or a vast bureaucracy, esp. in a totalitarian state. ATWS. *Compare* Behemoth.

LICK AND A PROMISE *to give something a lick and a promise.* To do a superficial or perfunctory job. Source: CAT. A cat gives itself a *complete* bath by licking the fur that it can reach with its tongue, then licking its front feet and cleaning its face and ears with them. A *superficial* bath is one in which the cat licks only its paws and chest—and supposedly "promises" to do the rest later. People who give something a "once over lightly" are giving it a lick but not necessarily a promise. People who *don't give a lick* don't even do the work at all. BDPF; MDWPO. *See also* Lick into Shape.

LICK INTO SHAPE   *to lick someone into shape.* To get someone ready for competition. Source: BEAR. Because bear cubs are born during hibernation, humans seldom see what the cubs look like at birth. Medieval writers created the myth (HOI: ca. 1400) that cubs are born as a shapeless lump of flesh that must be licked into the form of a baby bear by the mother. The writers were probably referring to the amniotic sac in which most mammals are born and which the mother licks away to allow them to move and breathe. Human coaches and drill sergeants *lick their charges into shape* by training them hard until they are ready to perform. ATWS; BDPF; EWPO; LCRH; SHM.

LICK SOMEONE'S BOOTS   See Fawn on.

LICK YOUR CHOPS   *to lick your chops.* To show eagerness or anticipation. Source: DOG. A dog licks its "chops," i.e., its lips and jaws, when it is about to be fed. The action may be intended to clean the mouth before eating or to lick off the drool that accompanies the expectation of food. People also *lick their chops* when something *makes their mouth water* (EWPO: 1555), such as the sight of food or even the description of it on the menu. A related expression, *to stand there with your tongue hanging out,* applies both to dogs who are drooling in the anticipation of food and to people who are excited over the sight of a beautiful member of the opposite sex. These *Pavlovian responses* (WNNCD: 1926) recall Pavlov's dog, which was conditioned to associate the ringing of a bell with the introduction of food; eventually, the dog let its tongue hang out, salivated, and licked its chops whenever the bell rang, even if no food was present. DOC; MDWPO.

LICK YOUR WOUNDS   *to lick your wounds.* To attempt to recover from a psychological blow. Source: ANIMAL. Mammals attempt to cure their *physical* wounds by licking them, i.e., keeping them clean and coating them with saliva. Humans sometimes do the same thing to treat superficial cuts on their hands, but their method of curing *psychological* wounds, such as loss of face, loss of a job, or rejection by a lover, is to apply lots of denial and self pity. DEI.

LIE LIKE A DOG   *to lie like a dog.* To lie outrageously or vindictively. Source: DOG. WNNCD: O.E. It is not clear how the dog figures in this metaphor. Sometimes a dog's *bark is worse than its bite* (q.v.); but whenever it is caught red-handed, it shows its guilt more than any other domestic animal. The reference may be to another metaphor, *dirty dog* (q.v.) "a low and despicable person"—as low and despicable as a dog that *bites the hand that feeds it* (q.v.).

LIE LOW   *See* Break Cover.

LIGHT AS A FEATHER   *See* Feather (n).

LIKE A BAT OUT OF HELL   *to go like a bat out of hell.* To leave suddenly and rapidly. HTB: ca. 1900. Source: BAT. WNNCD: 14th cent. The bat, which spends its days hanging upside down in a dark cave (etc.) and its nights flying nonstop in the dark sky, seems to loathe the light. It would react quickly if it flew too close to the fires of Hell. AID; ATWS; DOC; EWPO; ID; IRCD. *See also* Bats in Your Belfry; Blind as a Bat.

LIKE A BEAR WITH A SORE HEAD   *See* Cross as a Bear.

LIKE A BULL IN A CHINA SHOP   *See* Bull in a China Shop.

LIKE A BULL OUT OF A CHUTE   *to take off like a bull out of a chute.* To leave suddenly and explosively. Source: BULL. WNNCD: O.E. The reference is either to the bullriding event in a rodeo or the entrance of the bull into the ring of a bullfight. In the rodeo, the rider mounts the bull in a small pen bordering the arena; when the gate is opened, the bull bursts out of the enclosure kicking and twisting, trying to throw the rider off its back. In the bullfight, the bull approaches the ring from a long chute, down which it has been driven from the bull pen; when it enters the ring, it usu. charges the first human that gets in its way.

LIKE A CAGED ANIMAL   *See* Like an Animal.

LIKE A CARROT TO A DONKEY   Like candy to a child: a strong incentive. Source: DONKEY. WNNCD: ca. 1785. Donkeys, like their hybrid offspring, mules, are notoriously stubborn, refusing to move when they don't want to. Sometimes an inducement or enticement works: a carrot dangling from a stick just in front of the donkey's nose, so that the animal has to move ahead to get it. DEI. *See also* Carrot-and-stick.

LIKE A CAT IN HEAT   *to act like a cat in heat.* For a woman to seek sexual gratification openly and incessantly. Source: CAT. WNNCD: O.E. In catdom, it is the male cat, or *tomcat* (q.v.), that actually seeks out the female cat in estrus, not the other way around. The expression *to sound like a cat in heat* is also a misnomer: the *caterwauling* (q.v.) sound is made by a chorus of male suitors, not by the females. AID; CI.

LIKE A CHICKEN WITH ITS HEAD CUT OFF   *to run around like a chicken with its head cut off.* To run around in circles: aimlessly, frantically, chaotically. Source: CHICKEN. WNNCD: O.E. A chicken is often able to run around the barnyard for a few minutes after having its head cut off on the chopping block.

This behavior may be the basis for the metaphor *to lose your head*, i.e., to lose your sense of reason or control: to behave irrationally. AID; ATWS. *See also* Get It in the Neck; Stick Your Neck out.

LIKE A CORNERED ANIMAL   *See* Like an Animal.

LIKE A DUCK TO WATER   *to take to something like a duck to water*. To adjust to a new activity with little or no difficulty. Source: DUCK. WNNCD: O.E. Ducks are aquatic birds, so it would be expected that they would adapt well to water. Baby ducks are hatched on land, but they are able to swim and dive within hours of breaking out of their shells. The metaphor applies to humans who adapt to new situations, such as riding a bike or running a business, with the greatest of ease. AID; ATWS; DEI; IRCD.

LIKE A FEMALE LION PROTECTING HER CUBS   *to be like a female lion— or lioness—protecting her cubs*. To be willing to do anything to protect your family, property, honor, etc. Source: LION. WNNCD: 12th cent. The female lion, or *lioness*, is much smaller than the male, but it is she, not the male, who is the primary killer in the family. An intruder to the lion's den can expect a blow to the back that will break the intruder's spinal column. *Compare* Mother Hen.

LIKE A FISH OUT OF WATER   *See* Fish out of Water.

LIKE A FLOCK OF SHEEP   *to behave like a flock of sheep*. To be passive, submissive, and easily led. Source: SHEEP. WNNCD: O.E. Domestic sheep are among the most timid, powerless, and dependent of animals. They will go wherever their leader, the *bellwether* (q.v.), goes, even if it means following him into danger. People who are mindlessly obedient to their leaders are *like a flock of sheep* or a *herd of cattle* (q.v.). ATWS; DEI.

LIKE A HUNTED ANIMAL   *See* Like an Animal.

LIKE A LAMB TO SLAUGHTER   *to go like a lamb to slaughter*. For a person to face pain or punishment without argument or complaint. Source: LAMB. WNNCD: O.E. This expression is an alteration of a passage from Isaiah 53:7— "he is brought as a lamb to the slaughter, and as a sheep before her shearers is dumb, so he openeth not his mouth." The metaphor is based on the ancient practice of sacrificing a lamb to appease a deity. CI; DEI. *See also* Like a Sheep Being Led to Slaughter; Sacrificial Lamb.

LIKE A MOTH TO FLAME   *to be drawn to something like a moth to (a) flame*. To be irresistably attracted to something. Source: MOTH. WNNCD: O.E. Unlike the diurnal butterfly, which must warm itself in the sun before it can fly, the nocturnal moth is able to fly at night, although it is irresistably drawn to the light of a candle or a bulb. DEI. *Compare* Red Flag to a Bull.

LIKE AN ANGRY HORNET   *See* Mad as a Hornet.

LIKE AN ANIMAL   *to behave like an animal.* To display the natural instincts of a wild animal. Source: ANIMAL. *Animal instincts* (q.v.) are the primal drives and urges that are exhibited by wild animals but inhibited by humans. In an emergency, however, humans sometimes resort to animal behavior. For example, a fugitive may behave *like a hunted animal*; a victim may *feel like a cornered animal*; and a prisoner may act *like a caged animal*, pacing back and forth, rattling the bars, and howling with rage.

LIKE AN OCTOPUS   *to be all over someone like an octopus.* For a man to "paw" a woman as if he had eight arms. Source: OCTOPUS. WNNCD: 1758. The octopus (Gk. *oktōpous*) is an eight-footed cephalopod mollusk, related to the squid and the cuttlefish, which have ten feet (or "arms"). A more aggressive masher might be called a "squid." ATWS. *See also* Octopus.

LIKE A PIG IN CLOVER   *to be like a pig in clover.* To be deleriously—and incongruously—happy. Source: PIG. WNNCD: 13th cent. Pigs are usu. associated with mud, not colorful weeds. A pig in a field of clover would be about as wide-eyed and out of place as a hillbilly in Hollywood—wanting to take in everything but not knowing where to start. BDPF; DEI. *See also* Rolling in Clover. *Compare* Like a Fish out of Water.

LIKE A SHEEP BEING LED TO SLAUGHTER   *to be like a sheep being led to slaughter.* To be headed for inevitable destruction. Source: SHEEP. WNNCD: O.E. This expression was used for both King George VI of England and the country of Czechoslovakia, just before the beginning of WWII. King George ascended to the throne in 1936; Czechoslovakia was occupied by Germany in 1938. Domestic sheep are among the most passive of animals and were often used for religious sacrifices in ancient times. *Compare* Like a Lamb to Slaughter.

LIKE A TRAINED SEAL   *to act like a trained—or performing—seal.* To take orders or follow directions, however silly or demeaning, without thought or question. Source: SEAL. WNNCD: O.E. The California sea lion, a large seal of the Pacific coast, is the one usu. trained to perform in circus acts, because it is quite intelligent and has functional hind flippers. *See also* Flipper.

LIKE A YOUNG COLT   *See* Coltish.

LIKE CATCHING A GREASED PIG   *to be like catching a greased pig.* To be practically impossible. Source: PIG. WNNCD: 13th cent. To catch a pig in the barnyard is difficult enough, because pigs move fast, maneuver well, and have practically no hair to grab onto; but to catch one that is covered with grease at a country fair is practically impossible, because the pig keeps slipping out of your grasp. If you succeed, however, you can bring home the bacon (q.v.). BDPF; EWPO; HOI; ST.

LIKE RATS LEAVING A SINKING SHIP *to be like rats leaving a sinking ship.* To be deserting a failing cause or enterprise. Source: RAT. WNNCD: O.E. In the 16th cent. it was believed that rats could sense the impending doom of a ship or a building. Their early departure was a useful sign to humans; but in the metaphor, people who leave a failing campaign or business are regarded as deserters, traitors, or cowards. ATWS; DOC; IRCD; ST. *See also* Dirty Rat. *Compare* Coward.

LIKE SHOOTING FISH IN A BARREL *to be like shooting fish in a barrel.* To be much too easy. LTA: 1939. Source: FISH. WNNCD: O.E. What are fish doing in a barrel, and why are people shooting them? The barrel is legitimate: Sometimes freshly caught fish are kept alive in a barrel of water (or a horse tank) until they are *fished out* (q.v.) for eating. However, the shooting is illegitimate, because it is too simple: There is no sport involved. Actually, if the fish are not swimming on the surface, it would be almost impossible to shoot them; and, anyway, you might shoot a hole in the barrel by mistake. Also: *as easy as shooting fish in a barrel.* ST.

LIKE WATER OFF A DUCK'S BACK *to roll off someone like water off a duck's back.* For criticism or accusations to have absolutely no effect on their target. Source: DUCK. WNNCD: O.E. President Reagan was called the "Teflon president" because the charges of his critics always seemed to roll off his back without sticking. A duck has oil in its feathers that prevents them from getting soaked and rendering the duck unable to fly. AID; ATWS; CI; DEI; IRCD.

LIMPET *a limpet.* A person who clings tightly to someone or something; an explosive designed to cling tightly to the hull of a ship. Source: LIMPET. WNNCD: O.E. The limpet is a gastropod mollusk whose single shell is saucerlike in shape and which clings tightly to a rock or timber when threatened. ATWS.

LION *a lion of industry (etc.).* A person of great importance in a particular field. Source: LION. WNNCD: 12th cent. In the fields (or savannas) of Africa, the lion is the dominant animal: the King of Beasts. He will take on animals much larger than himself, and he has no predators except humans. (Actually, it is the female lion who does most of the killing, although she is not referred to as the "Queen of Beasts.") ATWS. *See also* Social Lion.

LIONHEARTED *to be lionhearted.* To be brave or courageous. WNNCD: 1708. Source: LION. WNNCD: 12th cent. One who is *lionhearted* has the "heart of a lion," as did King Richard I of England (ruled 1189–1199), who was dubbed

Coeur de Lion for his valor in the Third Crusade. (The label was not translated into English from Richard's native French until over half a century later.) The lion is said to have courage because it attacks animals much larger than itself, such as the cape buffalo. However, it is the *lioness* who makes most of the kills. The Cowardly Lion of *The Wizard of Oz* wanted a heart to give him courage, but he might have been better off with a mate. ATWS; IRCD. *See also* Like a Female Lion Protecting Her Cubs. *Compare* Chickenhearted.

LIONIZE   *to lionize someone.* To treat someone royally. WNNCD: 1809. Source: LION. WNNCD: 12th cent. The lion is the King of Beasts, at least in Africa. (The tiger is probably king in India—the only place where the two coexist.) As such, the lion is treated with utmost respect by all other animals, including those much larger and faster. When a person is *lionized*, he/she is treated like royalty—wined and dined and fussed over. The metaphor is based on the earlier expression *to see the lions* (q.v.). ATWS; BDPF; DEI; EWPO; IRCD. *See also* Social Lion.

LION'S DEN   *the lion's den.* A place where great danger lurks. Source: LION. WNNCD: 12th cent. In rocky terrain, lions often take shelter, during the daytime, in caves or rock overhangs. The biblical Daniel was sealed up in a lion's den by King Darius but escaped harm by divine intervention (Daniel 6:16–23). The modern *lion's den* is an arena of competition, such as the pit of the stock exchange or the floor of the U.S. House or Senate. DEI. *See also* Beard the Lion; Brave the Lion's Den. *Compare* Snake Pit.

LION SHALL LIE DOWN WITH THE LAMB   *and the lion shall lie down with the lamb.* Peace will break out. Source: LION; LAMB. This expression appears to be biblical, but it is not. Lions do prey on lambs, but in the famous "little child shall lead them" passage from Isaiah (11:6), "the *wolf* . . . shall dwell with the lamb." The (young) *lion* is paired with the (fatling) calf. The reference is to the coming of the Messiah, when all animals will become tame, and predators will befriend their prey.

LION'S MOUTH   *the lion's mouth.* A dangerous place or situation. Source: LION. WNNCD: 12th cent. Both the Old and the New Testaments equate the *lion's mouth* with danger: "Save me from the lion's mouth" (Psalm 22:21); "and I was delivered out of the mouth of the lion" (II Timothy 4:17). The lion was the most feared of all mammals in biblical times. To slay a lion, as David did, was a great accomplishment; and to escape from a whole den of lions, as Daniel did, was even more miraculous. ATWS. *See also* Put Your Head in the Lion's Mouth.

LION'S SHARE   *the lion's share.* The largest part. WNNCD: 1790. Source: LION. WNNCD: 12th cent. In the Aesop fable, a lion is assisted by two other animals in killing a deer. When it comes to dividing up the spoils, the lion reminds the others that he is the King of Beasts, and he claims the entire carcass. Nowadays, instead of the total share, the *lion's share* is the largest or *best* part of an allotment (as in bonus monies); and the metaphor can also mean the largest and *worst* part (e.g., of the dirty work). ATWS; BDPF; CI; DEI; DOC; EWPO; HOI; ID; IRCD; LCRH; SHM.

LION-TAILED MACAQUE *a lion-tailed macaque.* A monkey of southwestern India. Source: LION. WNNCD: 12th cent. The *lion-tailed macaque* is so named because its fairly short, nonprehensile tail is fluffy at the end; but it could just as well have been called a "lion-*maned* macaque," because it has a fluffy mane of lighter colored hair surrounding its head except at the top. *Compare* Lion Tamarin.

LION TAMARIN *a (golden) lion tamarin.* A marmoset of the mountains southwest of Rio de Janeiro, Brazil. Source: LION. WNNCD: 12th cent. The *golden lion tamarin* is a primate, not a cat. It is named after the lion because it is lion-colored and has a thick *mane* (q.v.) that surrounds its face, like that of the male lion. Another animal that is named for the lion because of its mane is the *sea lion* (q.v.). *Compare* Lion-tailed Macaque.

LITTER *a litter.* A large number of young children in one family. Source: ANIMAL. An animal litter is all of the offspring of a single birth, as to a dog, cat, or pig. A human *litter* is all of the young children of a family, delivered in separate or multiple births. The "pick" of an animal litter is the single individual that is selected as a household pet. The *pick of the litter* in a human family is the child that turns out best in the long run: most attractive, most talented, most successful, etc. *Compare* Runt of the Litter.

LITTERBUG *a litterbug.* A person who throws trash on the ground rather than in the proper container. WNNCD: 1947. Source: BUG. WNNCD: 1622. Many bugs are regarded as obnoxious creatures—biting or stinging people, sucking their blood, infecting them with diseases, etc. Human *bugs*, such as the *firebug* (q.v.) and *litterbug*, are also regarded as obnoxious. *Litterbug* was probably patterned after the earlier *jitterbug* (q.v.), which, although harmless, was regarded as obnoxious by many parents in the 1930s. ATWS; DEI; EWPO; HF; IRCD.

LITTLE BIRD TOLD ME *A little bird told me.* I'd rather not reveal my source. DOC: 1583. Source: BIRD. WNNCD: O.E. A person who answers "A little bird told me" to the question "Where did your hear that?" is either uncertain about the accuracy of the information or is trying to protect him-/herself or his/her informant. A *little bird* was probably selected for the metaphor because such creatures are extremely numerous and totally anonymous. The literary source of the metaphor may be the book of Ecclesiastes (10:20), in which a warning is given not to curse the king or the rich, "for a bird of the air shall carry the voice, and that which hath wings shall tell the matter." AID; ATWS; BDPF; CI; DEI; EWPO; IRCD; SHM. *Compare* Straight from the Horse's Mouth.

LITTLE MONKEY   *a little monkey*. A mischievous child: a "cutup." Source: MONKEY. WNNCD: ca. 1530. As viewed in the zoo, a monkey is an active little animal that delights in tormenting other monkeys—attacking them, stealing from them, and mimicking them (and the onlookers). Children who perform such stunts are affectionately called *little monkeys*, and the term is sometimes applied inappropriately to adults as well. (The *littlest* monkey is the pygmy marmoset, which weighs less than three ounces.)

LIVE HIGH ON THE HOG   *to live high on the hog*. To live well and prosperously. Source: HOG. WNNCD: O.E. This expression is an extension of the metaphor *to eat high on the hog* (q.v.). A person who *lives* high on the hog not only *eats* expensive cuts of meat but is able to afford a luxurious house, car, and all sorts of other material goods. There is also an implication that those who do so are members of the nouveau riche, not accustomed to such affluence. ATWS; BDPF; EWPO; IRCD; LCRH.

LIVE LIKE FIGHTING COCKS   *to live like fighting cocks*. To have an abundance of the best food and drink. Source: COCK. WNNCD: O.E. The fighting cock, or *gamecock*, is bred and trained for *cockfights* (q.v.). This pampered bird is fed the best grain and grit, which it washes down with *cockale* (or *cock's ale*, a mixture of liquor and ale)—all in preparation for a few minutes in the *cockpit* (q.v.). CI. *Compare* Live High on the Hog.

LOADED FOR BEAR   *to be loaded for bear*. To be prepared for anything. HTB: mid-1800s. Source: BEAR. WNNCD: O.E. The black bear of the eastern United States (up to a quarter of a ton) and the brown bear, or *grizzly*, of the western United States (over three quarters of a ton) were the most feared animals of the American frontier. Consequently, pioneers and settlers were never without a firearm that was powerful enough to ward off their attack. Today, the expression *loaded for bear* can be used for an adult preparing to give a presentation at a board meeting or a child heading off for summer camp. Both are probably overequipped for the task. AID; ATWS; EWPO; IRCD; ST.

LOADED TO THE GILLS   *to be loaded to the gills*. To be unquestionably drunk. Source: FISH. The gills of a fish are the organs on either side of the "neck" that extract oxygen from the water. If humans had gills, they would presumably be located in the same place—and serve the same purpose. A person who is *loaded to the gills* is full of alcohol up to the neck, where the gills would be. Also: *stewed to the gills* (DOC: 1949). ATWS; EWPO; LCRH; LTA; MDWPO; SHM; ST. *See also* Drink like a Fish; Green around the Gills; Stuffed to the Gills.

LOAN SHARK   *a loan shark*. A money lender who charges exorbitant rates of interest: a usurer. WNNCD: 1905. Source: SHARK. WNNCD: 1569. A *loan shark* bleeds his/her clients dry. A marine shark will attack any fish or mammal, including humans, and tear them to pieces, thereby attracting other sharks to the smell of blood. IRCD. *See also* Card Shark; Pool Shark.

LOBSTER (1)   *a lobster.* A North Atlantic crustacean with eight walking legs, a large pair of claws, and a long abdomen, or "tail." Source: SPIDER. WNNCD: 14th cent. The word *lobster* (WNNCD: O.E.) lit. means "female spinner" (fr. O.E. *loppe* "spider or spinner" + *ster* "female agent"). Spiders and lobsters have eight walking legs—the basis for the metaphor—but spiders are arachnids and lobsters are crustaceans. Both are arthropods. *Compare* Crayfish; Lobster (2).

LOBSTER (2)   *a lobster.* An Atlantic crustacean with ten legs and a long abdomen, or "tail." Source: LOBSTER. WNNCD: O.E. The difference between Lobster (2), e.g., a *spiny lobster*, and Lobster (1), e.g., a Maine lobster, is that the former has miniscule claws, while the latter has large claws. In other words, Lobster (2) is not a "true" lobster at all but an overgrown *crayfish* (q.v.), also called a *rock lobster* (q.v.) or *langostino*. Lobster lovers don't really care. DEOD; EWPO; HF. *Compare* Lobster (1).

LOBSTER SHIFT   *the lobster shift.* The early morning shift on a newspaper, commencing after the night shift has finished its work. WNNCD: ca. 1933. Source: LOBSTER. WNNCD: O.E. The metaphor apparently originated with the early morning shift of a New York newspaper that began at about the same time as the lobster boats were putting out to sea (approx. 4 A.M.). EWPO; MDWPO. *Compare* Bulldog Edition.

LOCK HORNS   *to lock horns with someone.* To have an angry confrontation with someone. Source: ANIMAL. Horned animals use their horns as weapons, and sometimes the horns of two combatants become so entangled that the animals remain locked together until they die of starvation. This is esp. true of mountain sheep, which retain the same set of horns throughout their lifetime, but also applies to deer, elk, caribou, and moose, whose antlers will eventually fall off if the battle is in early spring. Battles often begin when one male "horns in on" the territory or harem of another male. People *horn in on* other people when they intrude on them or force themselves on them without an invitation (WNNCD 1912). As a result, the host and the unwanted guest may *lock horns* with each other, each willing to die for his/her rights. AID; ATWS; CI; EWPO.

LOCK THE BARN DOOR AFTER THE HORSE IS STOLEN   *to lock the barn door after the horse is stolen.* To take preventive action after the damage has already been done. HTB: 1390. Source: HORSE. WNNCD: O.E. (The original expression was "to lock the stable door after the horse has bolted.") Locking the barn door *after* the horse is stolen is like *putting the cart before the horse* (q.v.): i.e., reversing the natural order of things. Of course, locking the barn door *before* the horse is

stolen doesn't do much good either. A similar expression is "too little, too late."
ATWS; BDPF; CI; DEI; EWPO; ID.

LONE WOLF   *a lone wolf.* A loner: one who prefers to live, act, or work alone.
WNNCD: 1909. Source: WOLF. WNNCD: O.E. In the wild, a "lone wolf" is usu.
a young male that has been banished from the tight-knit pack for having unsuc-
cessfully challenged its leader. Human *lone wolves* simply want to be alone: they
get more work done that way, and they enjoy their independence. ATWS; CI;
DEI; ID; IRCD. *See also* Pack of Wolves; Wolf Pack.

LONG HORSE   *See* Vaulting Horse.

LONG IN THE TOOTH   *to be (a little) long in the tooth.* To be old or aging.
MDWPO: 1852. Source: HORSE. As a horse ages, its permanent teeth become
longer, due partly to their natural growth and partly, esp. in a very old horse, to
receding gums. Long teeth are probably the best clue to a horse's age. People's
gums also recede with age, although not as noticeably as the horse's. To say that
someone is *getting a little long in the tooth* is to suggest, politely, that that person
is about ready to be *put out to pasture* (q.v.). ATWS; CI; DEI; DOC; EWPO; ST.
See also Look a Gift Horse in the Mouth.

LOOK A GIFT HORSE IN THE MOUTH   *Never look a gift horse in the mouth.*
Don't examine a gift too closely, as if estimating its value. (Remember: It's the
thought that counts.) Source: HORSE. WNNCD: O.E. Saint Jerome (ca. 44 A.D.)
said something similar—"Don't find fault with gifts"—but the earliest proponents
of this philosophy were the ancient Trojans (ca. 1200 B.C.), who accepted at face
value a huge *wooden horse* (q.v.) that was left outside the gates of Troy by the
retreating Greeks. The Trojans wheeled the horse inside the gates, not realizing
that it was filled with Greek soldiers—and you know the rest of the story. Looking
at the mouth of a horse is the standard method of determining its age—by the
number, length, and condition of the teeth. (An old horse has fewer, longer, and
poorer teeth.) AID; ATWS; BDPF; CI; DEI; DOC; EWPO; HOI; ID; IRCD; LCRH;
MDWPO; SHM; ST. *See also* Long in the Tooth; Straight from the Horse's Mouth;
Trojan Horse.

LOOK LIKE A BOILED LOBSTER   *to look like a boiled lobster.* To look as red
as a beet, esp. as a result of a severe sunburn. Source: LOBSTER. WNNCD: O.E.
When the live Maine lobster is moved from the holding tank to the pot of boiling
water, its dark green shell gradually turns red, like the skin of a person who has
been out in the sun too long. *See also* In Hot Water; Red as a Lobster.

LOOK LIKE ROADKILL   *to look—or feel—like roadkill.* To look—or feel—as
bad as the flattened carcasses of small animals killed on the highway. Source:
ANIMAL. An animal such as a raccoon, possum, squirrel, or turtle that is struck

and killed by a car or truck is often run over—and over—by other vehicles until it becomes an unrecognizable slab of leather. A person who *looks* like roadkill looks nothing like his/her usual self (at least early in the morning or after partying the night before); and a person who *feels* like roadkill feels banged up and beaten to a pulp. *See also* Roadkill.

LOOK LIKE SOMETHING THAT JUST CRAWLED OUT FROM UNDER A ROCK *See* Crawl under a Rock.

LOOK LIKE SOMETHING THE CAT DRAGGED IN *to look like something the cat dragged in.* To look awful: unkempt, dishevelled, bedraggled, etc. IRCD: ca. 1920. Source: CAT. WNNCD: O.E. What the cat drags in is a mouse or chipmunk that it proudly deposits on the front steps of its adopted home. The animal is dirty, bloody, and either dead or dying. People who look like that are in pretty bad shape, or at least in worse shape than usual. A related expression, *Look what— or who—the cat dragged in!*—meaning "Look who finally showed up"—lacks the implication of messiness but retains the sense of unwillingness of the cat's victim. ATWS; CE; CI; LTA; ST.

LOOK LIKE THE CAT THAT ATE THE CANARY *See* Cat that Ate the Canary.

LOOK WHAT THE CAT DRAGGED IN *See* Look like Something the Cat Dragged in.

LOOK WHAT THE STORK BROUGHT *Look what the stork brought!* Look at our new baby! Source: STORK. WNNCD: O.E. The stork is a very large Old World bird that constructs permanent nests on rooftops or chimneytops and is credited in Germanic folklore with delivering human babies to their families. *See also* Stork Brought Me; Stork Is Coming. *Compare* Look What the Cat Dragged in.

LOONY *to be loony.* To be crazy, eccentric, or weird. WNNCD: 1872. Source: LOON (*). WNNCD: 1634. Because of the pronunciation and spelling of this word—and the existence of the expression *crazy as a loon*—*loony* is often associated with the bird called a *loon.* In addition, a person who is insane is sometimes called a *loony,* and an insane asylum is sometimes called a *loony bin* (WNNCD: 1890). However, the source of *loony* is not the bird but Lat. *luna* "moon": a *lunatic* was once believed to be a person who went crazy during a full moon. ATWS; IRCD; MDWPO. *Compare* Cuckoo's Nest.

LOONY BIN *See* Loony.

244   LOOSE AS A GOOSE

LOOSE AS A GOOSE *to be as loose as a goose.* To be totally relaxed, both physically and mentally. IRCD: mid-20th cent. Source: GOOSE. WNNCD: O.E. Nothing much is loose about a goose except its neck, which is very flexible and agile. Other than that, the metaphor owes more to the rhyme of the bird's name with *loose* than to any physical feature or idiosyncratic behavior of the goose. Also: *loosey-goosey.* CE; GTP; *See also* Gooseneck; Take a Gander.

LOOSEY-GOOSEY *See* Loose as a Goose.

LORD OF THE JUNGLE *the lord of the jungle.* (Often sarcastic: How is the Lord of the Jungle?) To be, or pretend to be, the most powerful person in an organization: a gang leader; a crime boss; a drug kingpin. Source: LION. The male lion is often called the *King of Beasts* and the *Lord of the Jungle*, even though lions prefer open spaces to jungle cover. This is because the lion has no predators except humans. ATWS.

LOSE TRACK OF *See* Track down.

LOSE YOUR HEAD *See* Like a Chicken with Its Head Cut off.

LOST-PUPPY LOOK *See* Follow Someone around like a Puppy Dog.

LOST SHEEP *a lost sheep.* A person who has strayed from the teachings of his/her religion. Source: SHEEP. WNNCD: O.E. The metaphor of the lost sheep is found in both the Old Testament (Psalm 119:176—"I have gone astray like a lost sheep"; Jeremiah 50:6—"My people hath been lost sheep") and the New Testament (Matthew 15:24—"I am not sent but unto the lost sheep of the house of Israel"; and Matthew 18:12—the Parable of the Lost Sheep). ATWS. *Compare* Black Sheep.

LOUNGE LIZARD *a lounge lizard.* A self-styled ladies' man who hangs around cocktail lounges trying to pick up wealthy older women. WNNCD: 1918. Source: LIZARD. WNNCD: 14th cent. Both men and (younger) women regard lounge lizards as one of the lowest forms of life, because they prey on vulnerable creatures (the older women), employ camouflage (the open shirts and gold chains), and are covered with slime (the slicked-back hair). Real lizards are not slimy, but they do prey on hapless insects; and some of them, such as the chameleon, employ camouflage. ATWS; BDPF; IHAT; IRCD; MDWPO; NDAS.

LOUSE *a louse.* A contemptible or detestable person. IRCD: ca. 1915. Source: LOUSE. WNNCD: O.E. The louse is a tiny (3 mm) blood-sucking insect that is parasitic on humans and other mammals. Varieties include body lice ("cooties"), head lice, and pubic lice ("crabs"). All varieties are annoying and irritating, and body lice can transmit diseases such as typhus. ATWS. *See also* Get in Your Hair; Lousy; Lousy with.

LOUSE UP   *to louse something up.* To make a mess of something: to foul something up. WNNCD: 1934. Source: LOUSE. WNNCD: O.E. The parasitic louse makes its host, a human or other mammal, miserable. It sucks the host's blood, lays eggs in its hair, and can infect it with disease. It can ruin a person's happy life. ATWS; IRCD. *See also* Louse; Lousy.

LOUSY   *to be—or feel—lousy.* For something to be incredibly bad (e.g., *lousy* weather, *lousy* food); for someone to feel miserable. IRCD: ca. 1550. Source: LOUSE. WNNCD: O.E. *Lousy* orig. meant "infested with lice" (IRCD: ca. 1377). Later it came to mean "repulsive or contemptible." Now it just means "bad." The louse probably deserves this contempt, since it not only sucks the blood of humans but can also infect them with disease. ATWS; NDAS. *See also* Louse; Louse up; Lousy with.

LOUSY WITH   *to be lousy with something.* To be amply supplied with something: e.g., "*lousy with* money." IRCD: ca. 1918. Source: LOUSE. WNNCD: O.E. The expression can refer to an abundance of anything: "*lousy with* cops," "*lousy with* reporters," etc. A child's hair can be infested with as many head lice as a dog has fleas: thousands. ATWS. *See also* Get in Your Hair; Louse; Lousy. *Compare* More Money than a Dog Has Fleas.

LOVE   A score of "zero" in tennis. EWPO: 1742. Source: CHICKEN. *Love* is the English version of Fr. *l'oeuf* "egg." The French first equated the egg with "nothing" because of its resemblance to the numeral zero, but they have since replaced *l'oeuf* with *zero* in tennis matches, as have all but the English-speaking countries, where "40-*love*" and "six games to *love*" can still be heard. *See also* Duck's Egg; Goose Egg; Lay an Egg.

LOVEBIRDS   *a pair of lovebirds.* An amorous and devoted couple—young or old, married or unmarried. IHAT: 1930s. Source: PARROT. The lovebird is a small, gray-green parrot of tropical Africa, Asia, and South America that shows great affection for its lifetime mate. However, the term is sometimes also applied, mistakenly, to a pair of *turtledoves* (q.v.), or mourning doves, which are less colorful birds. EWPO. *Compare* Lovebug.

LOVEBUG   *the lovebug.* Cupid. Source: BUG. WNNCD: 1622. If you don't watch out, Cupid will shoot you with one of his arrows and you will be hopelessly in love. The insect called a *lovebug* (WNNCD: 1966) doesn't bite people and make them fall in love, but it does amaze them with its ability to mate in the air. Clouds of copulating lovebugs can be seen along southern coastal highways, where they sometimes cover windshields and stop traffic. *See also* Bug (n) (3). *Compare* Love-birds.

LOVE ME, LOVE MY DOG   If you really love me, you love everything about me, including my faults. Source: DOG. WNNCD: O.E. This sentiment was first expressed, in Latin, by Saint Bernard—not the 11th cent. namesake of the dog, Saint Bernard of Menthon, but the 12th cent. founder of the Cistercian Order, Saint Bernard of Clairvaux. As usual, the dog is being treated here as the most insignificant of all human possessions. BDPF; DEI; EWPO; HTB. *See also* Dog (n).

LOVE NEST   *See* Nest (n).

LOVESICK PUPPY   *See* Puppy Love.

LOVEY-DOVEY   *to be (all) lovey-dovey.* For two young lovers to show their affection for each other by *billing and cooing* (q.v.) and otherwise professing their true and enduring love. EWPO: 1819. Source: DOVE. WNNCD: 13th cent. *Lovey-dovey* is an example of rhyming slang. It is based on the belief that doves are not only affectionate toward their mates but are forever true to them. DEI; IRCD. *Compare* Lovebirds.

LOWER THAN A SNAKE'S BELLY   *to be—or feel—lower than—or as low as—a snake's belly.* To be totally contemptible; to feel totally humiliated. Source: SNAKE. WNNCD: O.E. A snake's belly is about as low as you can get, given that snakes don't have legs and have to crawl on the ground. *Lower than a snake's belly* is an epithet for contemptible people, but for chagrined people it is how they feel when they make a major faux pas: "about this high" (measured with the thumb and forefinger). CH. *See also* Crawl into a Hole.

LOWER THAN THE ANIMALS   *See* Animal.

LOW ON THE FOOD CHAIN   *to be low on the food chain.* To be lacking in ambition and intelligence. Source: ANIMAL. The *food chain* (WNNCD: 1926) is a hierarchy of predation among animals. At the top end of the chain are animals that are predators of other animals but prey to none. In Africa, this is the lion, and in India it is the tiger; but worldwide, it is the human. In the middle of the chain are animals that are the prey of those above but predators of those below. Birds, fish, reptiles, and smaller mammals fall pretty much into this category. At the bottom end of the food chain are animals that are predators of no other animals but prey to all of those above. Insects are the primary occupiers of this rung on the ladder. Persons who are described as being *low on the food chain* are among the lowest of the lower animals: They are the little fish that are eaten by the big fish. *See also* Pecking Order.

LUCKY DOG   *You lucky dog!* You lucky guy! Source: DOG. WNNCD: O.E. A dog *leads a dog's life* (q.v.), and it is grateful for small favors, such as a chance to eat, play, or go for a walk. A person who is a *lucky dog* is someone who is favored with luck that he/she doesn't deserve, such as winning the lottery. DEI; IRCD.

LUMMOX   *a lummox.* A clumsy person. WNNCD: 1825. Source: OX. WNNCD: O.E. *Lummox,* an Americanism, is probably a blend of *lumbering* ("plodding") and *ox* ("a working steer"), although it may be an alteration of *dumb ox* (q.v.): a *dummox.* Therefore, a *lummox* may not only be clumsy but also stupid. EWPO. *See also* Clumsy as an Ox; Dumb as an Ox.

LUPUS   Any of various diseases characterized by lesions of the skin. WNNCD: 15th cent. Source: WOLF. It is not clear why these diseases are named for the wolf (Lat. *lupus*). Wolves are not noted for contracting such diseases or for suffering from skin lesions. The connection may lie either in the ferocity of both the disease and the wolf or in the resemblance of the patient to someone who has been attacked by a wolf. ATWS.

LURE   *to lure someone.* To attract someone by the offering of a pleasurable reward. Source: FALCON. When the falconer wishes to recall, or *lure,* the falcon from the pursuit of game, he/she twirls a small animal, such as a mouse or shrew, around his/her head at the end of a cord. A *lure* is also an artificial bait for attracting fish. ST.

M

MACKEREL SKY *a mackerel sky.* A formation of cumulus clouds in the western sky, just after sunset, which has the appearance of a quilted comforter in various hues of red and blue. WNNCD: 1669. Source: MACKEREL. WNNCD: 14th cent. The sides of a mackerel have iridescent scales that give off a rainbow of colors. ATWS; IRCD. *See also* Mother of Pearl.

MAD AS A HORNET *to be as mad as a hornet.* To be violently and uncontrollably angry. IHAT: 1833. Source: HORNET. WNNCD: O.E. The hornet—a large wasp, such as a yellow jacket—becomes enraged if its fragile paper nest, hanging from a limb, is disturbed. Unlike the bee, the hornet can, and does, deliver multiple stings. AID; ATWS; ID; IRCD. *See also* Hornet's Nest; Sting to the Quick; Stir up a Hornet's Nest. *Compare* Mad as a March Hare; Mad as a Wet Hen.

MAD AS A MARCH HARE *to be as mad as a March hare.* To be comically, harmlessly crazy. Source: HARE. WNNCD: O.E. The expression is from Lewis Carroll's *Alice's Adventures in Wonderland,* 1865, in which the March Hare and the Mad Hatter perform all sorts of antics at a tea party with Alice and the Dormouse. Hares were once thought to go crazy during the breeding season, of which March is in the middle. (An alternative interpretation of *March* is "marsh." EWPO.) AID; ATWS; BDPF; IRCD; LCRH; MDWPO; SHM. *Compare* Mad as a Hornet; Mad as a Wet Hen.

MAD AS A WET HEN *to be as mad as—or madder than—a wet hen.* To be upset or angry. IHAT: 1821. Source: HEN. WNNCD: O.E. The hen is a terrestrial bird, not an aquatic one, but it does not seem to mind being out in the rain during the daytime. However, it dislikes having a bucket of water thrown at it—to scare it away or stop its pecking—and it becomes extremely unhappy when locked out of a coop on a rainy night. AID; ATWS; DOC; EWPO; HTB; IRCD. *Compare* Mad as a Hornet; Mad as a March Hare.

MAD DOG *a mad dog.* A crazed killer. Source: DOG. WNNCD: O.E. Literally, a mad dog is a dog suffering from distemper or rabies—one that foams at the mouth, snarls and growls, and refuses to let anyone near it. Figuratively, a *mad dog* is a person (usu. a male) who is dangerously out of control—wrecking everything in sight, attacking both friend and foe, and refusing to surrender or listen to reason. Noel Coward compared "Mad Dogs and Englishmen" in a poem so titled, because they were both crazy enough to "go out in the midday sun," at least in the equatorial colonies. IRCD.

MAGPIE *a (little) magpie.* A person (esp. a child) who talks, or "chatters," incessantly. Source: MAGPIE. WNNCD: 1605. The magpie is a rather large (18-inch long) bird of Eurasia and western North America that is known for its noisy chatter (*chak-chak*) and its tasty contribution to a meat dish that was the original basis for the word *pie.* ATWS. *See also* Chatter like a Magpie; Pie.

MAKE A BEELINE *See* Beeline.

MAKE A MONKEY OUT OF SOMEONE *to make a monkey out of someone.* To make a fool out of someone. LTA: 1899. Source: MONKEY. WNNCD: ca. 1530. To *make a monkey out of someone* is to make that person look foolish, stupid, ridiculous, or ludicrous. This is the impression that people have of monkeys, which have been put on display since the 17th cent., whether in carnivals, circuses, or zoos or on the shoulders of organ grinders. ATWS; CE; CI; DEI; IRCD; MDWPO. *Compare* Make an Ass of Yourself.

MAKE A MOUNTAIN OUT OF A MOLEHILL *to make a mountain out of a molehill.* To make a big issue out of a little one. HTB: 1570. Source: MOLE. WNNCD: 14th cent. A molehill is the raised portion of a lawn above the underground tunnel created by a mole. The problem is that the mole burrows under the *entire* lawn, making it eventually look like a mountain of dirt—or at least that's how it seems to the homeowner. AID; ATWS; CE; DEI; DOC; EWPO; ID; IRCD.

MAKE AN ASS OF YOURSELF *to make an ass of yourself.* To do something stupid or unforgivable: to make a laughing stock of yourself. Source: ASS. WNNCD: O.E. The *ass,* or donkey, has long been considered a stupid and somewhat laughable creature, probably because, although stubborn, it submits passively to its role as a beast of burden. ATWS; DEI. *See also* Ass; Feel like an Ass. *Compare* Make a Monkey out of Someone.

MAKE A PIG OF YOURSELF   *to make a pig of yourself.* To eat too much, too fast, too greedily. Source: PIG. WNNCD: 13th cent. Pigs have voracious appetites—from the time they are *piglets* struggling for a place at their mother's belly, to the time they are *shoats* (up to one year of age) competing for a place at the hog trough, to the time they are *hogs* fighting for a place to root in the yard. CI. *See also* Eat like a Pig; Pig out.

MAKE A SILK PURSE OUT OF A SOW'S EAR   *You can't make a silk purse out of a sow's ear.* You can't do the impossible. DOC: 1579. Source: PIG. WNNCD: 13th cent. Professor Higgins did the impossible in Shaw's *Pygmalion* when he turned a flower girl into a proper lady; but, generally speaking, even the most skilled craftsperson can't make something out of nothing, or something superior out of something inferior. AID; ATWS; BDPF; CI; DEI; EWPO; ID; IRCD.

MAKE A STINK   *to make a stink about something.* To make a strong protest, or public outcry, about something. Source: SKUNK (?). WNNCD: 1634. When a skunk is threatened, it shoots a vile-smelling liquid up to 20 feet from beneath its tail. This is the skunk's protest. Humans make a figurative *stink* when confronted with a threat to their livelihood. AID. *See also* Skunk (n).

MAKE COW EYES   *See* Cow Eyes.

MAKE GREAT STRIDES   *See* Take Something in Stride.

MAKE HEADS OR TAILS   (Usu. neg.) *can't make heads or tails of something.* Can't figure something out or make sense of it. Source: ANIMAL (?). Most animals have a head and a tail, at least in some stage of their development. Animals don't seem to have any trouble distinguishing the head from the tail of other animals, but humans sometimes have this problem, esp. with animals such as porcupines and worms. People also have difficulty deciphering writing that is either ancient or foreign and arguments that are either illogical or contradictory. However, the metaphor may be based on the two sides of a worn coin or the indistinguishable beginning and end of a poorly written story. ATWS; DOC; ST.

MAKE HORNS   *to make horns; to make the horn.* To make a fist, with the first and fourth fingers extended: a gesture of insult or contempt. BDPF: 1652. Source: ANIMAL. The "horns" imply that the person at whom the gesture is directed is a *cuckold* (q.v.), a man who *wears the horns.* Why horns are associated with cuckoldry is uncertain, but EWPO suggests that the source may be the *buck*, which, when another buck steals away its harem, is left only with its horns. At University of Texas (Austin) football games, fans make the two-fingered fist and yell "Hook 'em, Horns!"—urging the Longhorns to defeat their opponents. To a baseball player, the "horn" sign simply means "two outs." *Compare* Flip the Bird.

MAKE SOMEONE'S HACKLES RISE *See* Raise Someone's Hackles.

MAKE THE FEATHERS FLY *to make the feathers fly.* To engage in a violent confrontation. Source: BIRD. Birds that make the feathers fly are usu. males fighting other males to establish their status in the flock or to protect their flock from outsiders. Gamecocks are specially raised and trained to make their opponent's feathers fly off in a cockfight. Physical violence is not necessary for humans to *make their opponent's feathers fly:* spoken or written words usu. suffice. AID; ATWS; BDPF; CH; CI; DEI. *Compare* Make the Fur Fly.

MAKE THE FUR FLY *to make the fur fly.* To engage in a violent argument. DOC: 1663. Source: ANIMAL. When furbearing animals, whether in the wild or in the backyard, engage in a fight, clumps of their fur are often removed by teeth or claws. When *people* engage in a violent argument, the fur that flies is angry words, including insults, threats, and expletives. When a violent argument is expected to take place, it is predicted that *the fur will fly.* AID; ATWS; BDPF; CI; DEI; EWPO; LCRH. *See also* Catfight; Fight like Cats and Dogs; Fight Tooth and Nail. *Compare* Make the Feathers Fly.

MAKE THINGS HUM *to make things hum.* To create a condition of busy and well-ordered activity; to restore a machine to proper working order. Source: BEE. WNNCD: O.E. The beehive is a model of "busyness," accompanied by the *buzz* (q.v.), *drone* (q.v.), and *hum* (q.v.) of the bees' wings: no *hum* = no work. People at work don't actually *hum,* but machines do when they are properly tuned. EWPO. *Compare* Purr like a Kitten.

MAKE YOUR GORGE RISE *to make your gorge rise.* For something to make you sick, disgusted, or revolted. Source: FALCON. The falcon, or female hawk trained for the hunt, is sometimes allowed to eat some of the game that it has caught, storing the food in its gorge, or "crop." If it overeats, it may make itself sick, causing it to regurgitate some of the meat. To the falconers, this is disgusting and revolting. EWPO.

MAKE YOUR HAIR STAND ON END *See* Get Your Back up.

MAKE YOUR MOUTH WATER *See* Lick Your Chops.

MALE CHAUVINIST PIG *a male chauvinist pig.* A man who regards himself as superior to the members of the female sex. IHAT: 1970. Source: PIG. WNNCD: 13th cent. The domestic pig has long been an object of contempt for its slovenly appearance and coarse behavior. The term *chauvinist* was applied by the Women's Liberation movement of the 1970s to men who harass, abuse, or denigrate women or treat them as sex objects. DEI; GTP. *See also* PIG (3).

MAMMOTH   *to be mammoth.* To be enormous, gigantic, immense. WNNCD: 1802. Source: ELEPHANT. The adj. *mammoth* derives from the Russian noun *mamont* "earth," the place where a skeleton of the prehistoric elephant was first discovered. The *wooly mammoth* (WNNCD: 1706) was much larger and hairier than the modern elephant, and its huge tusks curled upwards and inwards until they almost touched. In spite of, or because of, its huge size, the mammoth did not survive the glacial period and became extinct about 10,000 years ago. ATWS; EWPO. *Compare* Jumbo.

MAN BITES DOG   News. DOC: late-19th cent. Source: DOG. WNNCD: O.E. When a dog bites a man, that's not news; but when a man bites a dog, that is. This instruction to *cub reporters* (q.v.) has been attributed to the city editor of the New York *Sun*. Apparently the "cubs" were having trouble distinguishing between what was newsworthy and what was routine or ordinary. EWPO; MDWPO.

MANE   *a mane.* A head of long, full, heavy hair. Source: LION. The human mane is named after the mane of the adult male lion, which surrounds the lion's face like a straggly halo. Other animals that are named after the lion because of their mane are the *lion tamarin* (q.v.) and the *sea lion* (q.v.). The mane of a horse (or donkey or zebra) appears at the top of the head and neck of both males and females. On horses it can grow quite long and is often bobbed or braided for both practical and aesthetic reasons. ATWS.

MANGY   *to be mangy.* To be filthy, worn, seedy, shabby, or sordid; to be low, mean, contemptible, or despicable. Source: DOG. A mangy dog is one that has developed skin lesions—and lost most of its hair—as a result of having parasitic mites that cause mange. The affliction causes the dog to scratch a lot, lose weight, and become irritable and distracted. A mangy dog is not a pretty sight, and neither is a *mangy* carpet, couch, or coat that looks as if it has been attacked by mange. Other animals, and humans, can get mange, but the problem is usu. associated with the dog. IRCD; WNWD.

MAN ON A WHITE HORSE   *See* Man on Horseback.

MAN ON HORSEBACK   *a man on horseback.* A man whose success in the military convinces people to allow him to take charge of the country. WNNCD: 1860. Source: HORSE. WNNCD: O.E. The first American "man on horseback" was Gen. George Washington (1789); others were Gen. Ulysses S. Grant (1869) and Gen. Dwight D. Eisenhower (1953), although Eisenhower had never served in the cavalry. The metaphor is probably based on the familiar statues of famous leaders mounted on horseback. A related expression, *a man on a white horse*, alludes to the "good guys" of medieval jousting tournaments and early Western movies and novels—the ones who defeated the "bad guys" and were rewarded for their actions. EWPO; MDWPO; SPD.

MAN'S BEST FRIEND   *a man's best friend.* The one thing a man can count on the most: his dog, his gun, his horse, his car, etc. Source: DOG. The original expression was "The dog is man's best friend"—i.e., the dog has helped the human race rise to preeminence in the world more than any other animal. Although that contention is arguable, the dog has certainly made an important contribution to human development. It has guarded human lives and property; it has assisted humans in hunting and retrieving game; and it has been a faithful companion to humans during times of loneliness and despair. The term *three-dog night* alludes to this last condition: On an extremely cold night, a hunter or sledder can huddle or sleep with three of his/her dogs in order to survive. *See also* Send a Dog out.

MARCH LIKE LEMMINGS   *to march like lemmings to the sea.* For people to move unthinkingly and unceasingly toward eventual destruction—of themselves, their environment, their culture, their society, and their civilization. Source: LEMMING. WNNCD: 1607. The Norway lemming, a small, furry rodent, is very social and very prolific. Every three years or so its numbers outstrip its food supply, and the entire colony migrates to greener pastures, sometimes toppling over cliffs into the sea in the process. They are not, however, suicidal. DEI; MDWPO.

MARE'S NEST   *a mare's nest.* An imaginary discovery; a deliberate hoax; a confused or complicated situation. WNNCD: 1619. Source: HORSE. Mares don't build nests, so the reported discovery of one would be both remarkable and fraudulent. However, if female horses *did* build nests, they would be as large and complex as the hoax itself—or the doubletalk that accompanies it. ATWS; CI; DEI; DOC; IRCD; LCRH; MDWPO; SHM. *Compare* Can of Worms; Snake Pit; Weasel Word.

MARE WITH THREE LEGS   *See* Two-legged Mare.

MARSHAL (n)   *a marshal (or marshall).* A high-ranking general in the French army; a U.S. peace officer; the ceremonial leader of a parade; a chief fire investigator. Source: HORSE. *Marshal* was borrowed fr. O.Fr. *mareschal*, which in turn was borrowed fr. O.H.G. *marahscalc* "a horse servant." The horse servant rose to become the leader of the king' cavalry and eventually commander of the royal army. Marshals no longer ride horses—except, perhaps, in a parade—but they remain high-ranking officials in the military and paramilitary. From the noun *marshal* comes the verb *marshal* (WNNCD: 15th cent.) "to organize," as in to *marshal troops* or to *marshal arguments.* ATWS; EWPO; MDWPO; ROE.

MARSHAL (v)   *See* Marshal (n).

MAVERICK   *a maverick.* A social or political nonconformist. BDPF: 1880s. Source: CATTLE. *Maverick* started out as a *human* metaphor. When Texas rancher Samuel Maverick failed to brand his calves, his neighbors appropriated them and called them *mavericks* (WNNCD: 1867). Later, the term was applied to a person who refuses to conform to the policies of his/her group or party. ATWS; DEI; EWPO; IHAT; MDWPO.

MAWKISH   *to be mawkish.* To be sickly sentimental. WNNCD: 1697. Source: MAGGOT. The M.E. word for maggot, *mathek* "the grub of a fly," was borrowed from O.N. in the 13th cent. It then took two separate forms, *magotte* and *mawke*, both meaning "maggot"; the latter form became the adj. *mawkish* in the 17th cent. Maggots are usu. associated with dead bodies. EWPO.

MEALY-MOUTHED   *to be mealy-mouthed.* To be sweet-talking but insincere. WNNCD: 1572. Source: BEE. *Mealy-mouthed* is a loan translation of Gk. *melimuthos* "honey mouth" or "honey speech," a compliment in Classical times. A person whose speech is *as sweet as honey* (q.v.) but whose motive is flattery is now regarded as a *sweet-talker. Mealy-mouthed* persons are devious, dishonest, and deceitful. CI; EWPO; LTA. *Compare* Mellifluous.

MECHANICAL CLAW   *See* Claw (n).

MEEK AS A LAMB   *to be as meek as a lamb.* To be kind, gentle, thoughtful, and considerate. Source: LAMB. WNNCD: O.E. Meekness is a virtue to Christians, as stated in the third beatitude of the Sermon on the Mount (Matthew 5:5): "Blessed are the meek: for they shall inherit the earth." Jesus, who spoke the words, is often referred to as *Agnus Dei* "Lamb of God": "Behold the Lamb of God, which taketh away the sin of the world" (John 1:29). DEI. *See also* Gentle as a Lamb; Innocent as a Lamb.

MELLIFLUOUS   *a mellifluous voice.* A voice as *sweet as honey* (q.v.). WNNCD: 15th cent. Source: BEE. Beautiful sounds *flow* (fr. Lat. *flu-*) like *honey* (fr. Lat. *mel-*) from the mouth of someone with a *mellifluous* voice. This is true also of someone who is *mealy-mouthed* (q.v.) (fr. Gk. *meli* "honey" + *muthos* "mouth"), but that *sweet-talker* (q.v.) has the added quality of insincerity.

MEMORY OF AN ELEPHANT   *to have the memory of an elephant.* To have a fantastic memory. Also: *to have a memory like an elephant.* Source: ELEPHANT. WNNCD: 14th cent. It is said that elephants never forget, although what it is that they never forget is seldom mentioned. What they really never forget is where they are supposed to go to die: the elephant burial ground. Salmon also have to remember where to go to die—and not to forget to fertilize the eggs first. ATWS; DEI; IRCD.

MICKEY MOUSE   *a mickey mouse course, rule, job, song, etc.* A silly, petty, or childish course, rule, job, song, etc. WNNCD: 1936. Source: MOUSE. WNNCD: O.E. A *mickey mouse* course is a "no-brainer." A *mickey mouse* rule is a nuisance rule. A *mickey mouse* job is an insignificant one. *Mickey mouse* music is corny, like the background music of a Mickey Mouse cartoon, which Walt Disney created in 1923. As trivial as these applications may seem, *Mickey Mouse* was a password for the Allies' invasion of Normandy in 1944. ATWS; CE; EWPO; LTA; MDWPO; NDAS. *See also* Mickey-mouse.

MICKEY-MOUSE *to mickey-mouse the action in a film.* To parody the action in a cartoon with background music that rises when the animated figure climbs the stairs, falls when the figure tumbles back down, etc. Source: MOUSE. WNNCD: O.E. The practice is an outgrowth of the music that accompanied the early Mickey Mouse cartoons, created by Walt Disney in 1923. ATWS. *See also* Mickey Mouse.

MIGHTY MITE *a mighty mite.* A person of small stature but great strength. Source: MITE. WNNCD: O.E. A mite is a tiny arachnid that is parasitic on animals and plants and is a carrier of certain diseases. *Mighty mite*—an oxymoron like *jumbo shrimp* (q.v.)—is a nickname given, often sarcastically, to a child, or an adult of short stature, who has performed a feat of physical or mental strength, such as tackling a ball-carrier in football or defeating an opponent in a debate. The reference may be to the microscopic mite's ability to have such a devastating effect on humans.

MILK *to milk a snake; to milk a situation.* To extract venom from a poisonous snake; to exploit a situation for profit. Source: COW. A cow is milked by grasping a teat tightly at the top, between the thumb and forefinger, and then closing the fingers from the top down. A snake is *milked* by holding it behind its head and forcing the upper jaw, just back of the fangs, down on the edge of a glass beaker. A situation is *milked* by extracting from it every possible ounce of gain. The metaphor applies to both *milking a cash cow* (q.v.) and telling and retelling a funny joke or a story of your own exploits. DEI.

MILK A CASH COW *to milk a cash cow.* To tap a dependable source of revenue. Source: COW. WNNCD: O.E. The cow is a dependable source of milk. You can milk it in the morning and evening, and come back the next day and do the same thing. (In fact, you must.) A *cash cow* (q.v.) can be milked for money and will then produce new revenue for the next withdrawal. It's like *the goose that laid the golden eggs* (q.v.).

MIND LIKE A STEEL TRAP *See* Trap.

MIND YOUR OWN BEESWAX *See* Beeswax.

MIXED BAG *See* Bag.

MOCK DUCK   A roll of thin, pounded round steak stuffed with cheese, garlic, parsley, and breadcrumbs and cooked in tomato sauce. Source: DUCK. WNNCD: O.E. *Mock duck* can be substituted for real duck (or chicken) and is often served with spaghetti. It is one more of the products of hard times. *Compare* Cape Cod Turkey; City Chicken; Hoover Hog; Mock Turtle Soup; Pigs in the Blanket; Texas Turkey; Welsh Rabbit.

MOCK TURTLENECK   *a mock turtleneck.* A knit shirt/sweater with a false *turtleneck* (q.v.)—i.e., a collar that looks like a double layer of material but consists of only a single layer. Source: TURTLE. WNNCD: 1657. The collar of a *mock turtleneck* shirt or sweater looks pretty much like that of a real one, although perhaps a little shorter. It also looks like the neck of a turtle whose head is extended about halfway out of its shell. *See also* Mock Turtle Soup.

MOCK TURTLE SOUP   Imitation turtle soup, containing meat, such as veal, and wine, but no turtle. WNNCD: 1783. Source: TURTLE. WNNCD: 1657. The green turtle, a large (up to five feet long) sea turtle, is the source of the primary ingredients of real green turtle soup: *calipash*, just below the upper shell, and *calipee*, just above the lower shell. (The former is dull green, the latter light yellow.) *See also* Mock Turtleneck.

MOLE (1)   *a mole.* A machine for digging tunnels. Source: MOLE. WNNCD: 14th cent. The mole is a burrowing animal that digs tunnels just below the surface of the earth, seeking out grubs and insects by feel and smell. It has a pointed snout and powerful front legs, with large claws. The mechanical *mole* also tunnels, but deep below the surface, and in modern times is guided by lasers, as for the French/English Channel Tunnel, or "Chunnel." *See also* Make a Mountain out of a Molehill; Mole (2).

MOLE (2)   *a mole.* An undercover agent who infiltrates an organization and pretends to be one of its loyal members. IRCD: 1970s. Source: MOLE. WNNCD: 14th cent. The spy burrows his/her way into the organization in the same manner that the real mole burrows its way just below the surface of the ground. They are both seeking something—grubs or information—and they both work in the dark. ATWS; DEI; EWPO. *See also* Make a Mountain out of a Molehill; Mole (1).

MOLESKIN   A heavy cotton fabric with a thick, velvety nap. Source: MOLE. WNNCD: 14th cent. *Moleskin* orig. referred to the pelt of a mole (WNNCD: 1668), which was used as recently as the 1980s to make garments and to line shoes and gloves. The imitation product is used esp. as a pad attached to the back of a shoe or foot to prevent rubbing. The color (gray) and the texture (soft) of the ersatz product are very similar to those of the original. (The *mole* on a person's face is from a different source.) *See also* Mole (1); Mole (2).

MOMENT OF TRUTH   *the moment of truth.* The critical test of one's character. WNNCD: 1691. Source: BULL. The *moment of truth* in a bullfight is when the matador faces the defeated bull and thrusts home the final sword for the kill. (In a sense, it is also a *moment of truth* for the bull.) For ordinary humans, a *moment of truth* is a critical moment in one's life when a difficult decision or action could affect everything that happens thereafter. CI; DOC; ST.

MONKEY   *the monkey.* An American dance of the disco period in which the separated partners faced each other, waggled their heads from side to side, and mimicked the action of climbing a grape vine with their hands. IRCD: mid 1960s. Source: MONKEY. WNNCD: ca. 1530. Monkeys are nonanthropoid primates with long (usu. prehensile) tails that spend most of their time climbing and swinging (or "brachiating") in the trees. A TV show of the 1960s that parodied the Beatles was called "The Monkees."

MONKEY AROUND   *to monkey around.* To fool around. WNNCD: 1859. Source: MONKEY. WNNCD: ca. 1530. Monkeys are perceived as curious, mischievous, and spirited little creatures. In the zoo, they jump up and down, climb on the *monkey bars* (q.v.), *rattle their cages* (q.v.), throw bananas, and gen. make a mess of things. Children who *monkey around* act like the monkeys in the zoo: jumping on the furniture, climbing the drapes, banging on the walls, throwing knickknacks at each other, and gen. making a mess of things. ATWS. *See also* Monkey with.

MONKEY BARS   The playground apparatus consisting of a framework of wooden or metal bars on which children can climb and swing: a *jungle gym* (q.v.). WNNCD: 1955. Source: MONKEY. WNNCD: ca. 1530. Monkey bars were orig. constructed in zoos to provide exercise for the monkeys. In the early 1920s they were adapted for use by children—i.e., the *little monkeys* (q.v.)—on school and city playgrounds. *See also* Climb like a Monkey.

MONKEY BUSINESS   Improper conduct, running from lighthearted mischief to unethical, immoral, or illegal activity. WNNCD: 1883. Source: MONKEY. WNNCD: ca. 1530. Monkeys are mischievous creatures—tricking each other, stealing from each other, attacking each other—but they are not governed by ethics, morals, or criminal laws. Humans are supposed to know better, but they sometimes stretch the controls as far as they will go. ATWS; CI; DEI; DOC; EWPO; ID; IRCD. *See also* Monkeyshines.

MONKEY SEE, MONKEY DO   Like father, like son; like mother, like daughter. IRCD: ca. 1920. Source: MONKEY. WNNCD: ca. 1530. Children, or *little monkeys* (q.v.), often imitate the behavior of their parents—their action, their postures, their speech patterns, and, esp., their bad habits. Monkeys in a zoo are accomplished mimics of the people who come to observe them: i.e., they *ape* (q.v.) or *parrot* (q.v.) their behavior. They are great *copycats* (q.v.). *See also* See no Evil.

MONKEYSHINES   Harmless or playful pranks. WNNCD: 1828. Source: MON-KEY. WNNCD: ca. 1530. *Monkeyshines* differ from *monkey business* (q.v.) in the motives and consequences. *Monkey business* is often deliberate and sometimes causes great harm. *Monkeyshines* are usu. childish tricks intended to amuse one's friends or embarrass someone else. Monkeys are famous for their mischievous behavior in zoos. ATWS; EWPO; IRCD.

MONKEY SUIT   *a monkey suit.* A formal dress suit or full dress uniform. IRCD: late-19th cent. Source: MONKEY. WNNCD: ca. 1530. In the 18th cent., organ grinders began to dress their monkeys in bright-colored suits and bellboy caps. The term *monkey suit* was first applied to a full dress military uniform in the mid-19th cent. and to a formal dress civilian suit, or tuxedo, in the late-19th cent.—presumably because the wearers felt that both apparels made them look as foolish as the organ grinder's monkey. ATWS; BDPF; EWPO; MDWPO. *See also* Work for Peanuts.

MONKEY'S UNCLE   *Well I'll be a monkey's uncle!* Well I'll be damned! IRCD: ca. 1926. Source: MONKEY. WNNCD: ca. 1530. How this expression relates to the monkey—or what the uncle of a monkey might be—is unknown. Perhaps the speaker, who has just seen or heard something surprising, is comparing him/herself to his/her excitable relative, the monkey, which manifests surprise by jumping, chattering, and creating confusion. The initial rhyme of *monk-* and *unc-* doesn't hurt either. *Compare* Son of a Bitch.

MONKEY WITH   *to monkey (around) with something.* To fool around, or tamper, with something. ("Who's been *monkeying* with my word processor?") IRCD: ca. 1880. Source: MONKEY. WNNCD: ca. 1530. Monkeys toy with an object that they are not familiar with—examining it from every angle, touching it with their hands and mouth, and provoking it to do its thing. Human *monkeying* runs from innocent attempts to find out how something works to deliberate attempts to sabotage it. ATWS; BDPF; CE; DEI; SHM. *See also* Monkey around.

MONKEY WRENCH   *a monkey wrench.* A wrench with a fixed upper jaw and a movable lower jaw. WNNCD: 1858. Source: MONKEY (?). WNNCD: ca. 1530. There *is* some resemblance between a monkey wrench and the profile of a monkey—the upper part being the head, the lower part the lower jaw, and the handle the monkey's neck. But the date suggests that the wrench was named after the mechanic who invented it, in Springfield, Mass., in 1856: a man named *Monk.* ATWS; EWPO; HF; IRCD. *See also* Grease Monkey; Throw a Wrench in the Works.

MOON DOG   *See* Sun Dog.

MOOSE   *a moose.* A big man; a nickname for a big man. Source: MOOSE. WNNCD: 1603. The North American moose is the largest member of the deer family, standing over six feet tall at the shoulders and weighing up to two-thirds of a ton. It inhabits Canada, Alaska, and the northern part of the contiguous states. ATWS. *Compare* Tiger.

MORE FUN THAN A BARREL OF MONKEYS   *to be more fun than a barrel of monkeys.* To be great fun: comical and hilarious. IRCD: ca. 1920. Source: MONKEY. WNNCD: ca. 1530. Monkeys in the zoo are great fun to watch, because they engage in all sorts of antics, as if they were putting on a show for the visitors. Monkeys don't come in barrels, but if they did, they would be even more hilarious. ATWS; HOI. *Compare* Like Shooting Fish in a Barrel.

MORE MONEY THAN A DOG HAS FLEAS   *See* My Dog Has Fleas.

MORE THAN ONE WAY TO SKIN A CAT   *There's more than one way to skin a cat.* There's more than one way to accomplish just about anything. DOC: 1830s. Source: CAT (?). WNNCD: O.E. There are two ways to skin a cat: by pulling the skin off from head to tail or from tail to head, although it is hard to imagine why anyone would want to do that. A more pleasant source of the expression might be the children's game of *skin the cat,* in which a child jumps up and grabs a small limb or bar, passes his/her legs and body between the separated hands, and winds up facing in the original direction. However, the date of the game (HOI: ca. 1845) is later than the estimated earliest use of the metaphor. ATWS; EWPO; DEI; ID; ST.

MOSQUITO BOAT   *a mosquito boat.* A small patrol boat, called a *PT* ("patrol torpedo") boat in WWII. WNNCD: 1906. Source: MOSQUITO. WNNCD: 1583. The *mosquito boat* was named after the insect because of its small size and its ability to outmaneuver or outrun its pursuers. (It was orig. used for rumrunning.) EWPO; IRCD.

MOSQUITO HAWK   *a mosquito hawk.* A dragonfly (a four-winged flying insect). WNNCD: 1737. Source: MOSQUITO (WNNCD: 1583); HAWK (WNNCD: O.E.). A *dragonfly* (q.v.) is neither a mosquito (which flies but has only two wings) nor a hawk (which also flies but is a bird). This double metaphor can be heard in coastal North Carolina and Virginia.

MOSSBACK   *a mossback.* A reactionary politician who resists progress and change. SPD: 19th cent. Source: TURTLE (?). Sea turtles can live to a very old age, eventually accumulating a growth of moss on their backs; but they never forget where they were born, because that is where they must return to lay their eggs. Dry land turtles, or "tortoises," make the same migrations, but they don't grow moss.

MOTHBALL   *to mothball a ship.* To temporarily deactivate a military vessel, protecting it from rust in anticipation of possible future use. WNNCD: 1943. Source: MOTH. WNNCD: O.E. Mothballs of camphor or naphthalene are used in the household to protect garments made of wool, fur, or feathers from the larvae of the clothes moth. Working parts of the ship are sprayed with a plastic coating to protect them from rust. BDPF. *See also* Mothball Fleet; Put in Mothballs.

MOTHBALL FLEET   *a mothball fleet.* A fleet of naval ships that have been put in protective storage for use at a future time. IRCD: ca. 1946. Source: MOTH. WNNCD: O.E. Working parts of ships are sprayed with a plastic coating to protect them from rust, giving them the appearance of the cocoon of the pupal stage of the moth. *See also* Mothball; Put in Mothballs.

MOTH-EATEN   *to be moth-eaten.* To be antiquated, outmoded, decayed, or decrepit. IRCD: 1900. Source: MOTH. WNNCD: O.E. The larva of the *clothes moth* (WNNCD: 1753) eats holes in clothing that is made of such animal by-products as fur, feathers, and wool. The result is a *moth-eaten* garment (WNNCD: 14th cent.) that looks much older and more used than it really is. ATWS; DEI; EWPO. *Compare* Flea-bitten.

MOTHER CAREY'S CHICKENS   Stormy petrels; falling snow. WNNCD: 1767. Source: CHICKEN. WNNCD: O.E. Stormy—or *storm*—petrels are black and white seabirds that are found in the North and South Atlantic. They are so called because they were once thought to foretell storms or trouble for sailors, who nicknamed them "chickens of the *Dear Mother*" (Lat. *mater cara*). Sailors who associated petrels with snow were probably sailing in the South Atlantic, near Antarctica, where the all-white *snow petrel* flies. Chickens, of course, are not able to fly long distances, even if their wings are not clipped. BDPF; EWPO; HTB; LCRH; WNWD.

MOTHER HEN   *a mother hen.* A mother who is overly protective of her children; an employee, male or female, who treats his/her fellow employees like children. WNNCD: 1954. Source: HEN. WNNCD: O.E. In the barnyard, the mother hen protects her chicks at all cost, *taking them under her wing* (q.v.) when danger approaches. In the workplace, a *mother hen* is a worker with a maternal instinct who smothers his/her colleagues with unwanted attention. ATWS; IRCD.

MOTHER Of PEARL   A hard, shiny, iridescent surface. Source: OYSTER. The mother of *a* pearl is an oyster, and *mater perlawn* (M.Lat. for "oyster") was one of the oyster's original names. Later, *mother of pearl* was applied to the iridescent inner lining of the oyster's shell. Now it can apply to the inner lining of an abalone shell, as well as to an iridescent surface of manufactured products, such as plastic. WNWD. *See also* Pearl; Pearly White.

MOUNTAIN LION *a mountain lion.* A puma or cougar. WNNCD: 1859. Source: LION. WNNCD: 12th cent. The mountain lion—also known as a *catamount* or *panther*—is not really a lion at all but a large North American cat. It looks somewhat like the female African lion—the one without a mane—but it is smaller and has a longer, thicker tail. It is also not the *King of Beasts* (q.v.) in the New World. IHAT. *Compare* Sea Lion.

MOUNTAIN OYSTERS Pig—or lamb—testicles, fried and served as a delicacy, esp. to unsuspecting tourists, in the Rocky Mountain area. Source: OYSTER. WNNCD 14th cent. Oysters, a variety of marine bivalve mollusks, aren't found anywhere near the Rocky Mountain range, so the pioneers from the East Coast substituted the next best thing—pig or lamb testicles, which are routinely removed by farmers to control and bulk up their male animals. NDAS. Also: *Rocky Mountain Oysters. Compare* Prairie Oysters.

MOUSE (1) *a mouse under your eye.* A black eye. Source: MOUSE. WNNCD: O.E. A black eye is a discolored swelling underneath your eye—caused by a blow—that is about the size and color of a little mouse (no tail). The house mouse may have been selected for this metaphor not only because of its size (ca. 3 inches) and color (gray-brown) but because it is one of the most common animals in the world. ATWS; BDPF; IRCD. *See also* Mouse (2). *Compare* Muscle.

MOUSE (2) *a computer mouse.* A small device, attached by a cable to a microcomputer, which, when moved about the table, can cause the cursor to move, in the same direction, on the screen. Source: MOUSE. WNNCD: O.E. The computer *mouse* is a little bit bigger than the common house mouse, but the cord does look like a tail, and the device scurries around on the table the way a real mouse would. IRCD.

MOUSETRAP *a mousetrap.* A scheme or strategem to lure someone to self-destruction. Source: MOUSE. WNNCD: O.E. A conventional mousetrap is baited with cheese to lure the mouse. When the mouse bites into the cheese, a spring-loaded bail is released, striking the mouse and pinning it to the wooden frame, where it dies a slow death. Human *mousetraps* are usu. psychological rather than mechanical. *See also* Build a Better Mousetrap.

MOUSE TYPE Fine print. Source: MOUSE. WNNCD: O.E. *Mouse type* is trade jargon for (1) a disclaimer that accompanies a legal contract, or (2) a list of precautions that accompany an over-the-counter drug or a dangerous household product. Such disclaimers or precautions are usu. put in *fine print* (WNNCD:

1951) so small that they are almost unreadable without a magnifying glass; they look like the tracks or scratchings of a tiny mouse. *Compare* Chicken Scratches.

MOUSY   *to be mousy.* For a person to be shy and retiring; for a person's hair (esp. a woman's) to be plain and unattractive. WNNCD: 1853. Source: MOUSE. WNNCD: O.E. The house mouse is timid, quiet, and seldom seen. When it *is* seen, it reveals a grayish brown coat of the sort worn by all of the other mice in the house—or in the world, for that matter. ATWS.

MOVE LIKE A CAT   *to move like a cat.* To move agilely, gracefully, and quietly. Source: CAT. WNNCD: O.E. The cat is known for its stealthful movement while stalking a prey, and its quick and nimble movement when catching it. A human who *moves like a cat*, or is *as quick as a cat* (DOC: 1855), is either a *cat burglar* (q.v.) or an athlete—such as a shortstop in baseball, a running back in football, or a point guard in basketball. All have *catlike* (WNNCD: 1600) or *feline* moves. ATWS.

MUD PUPPY   *a mud puppy.* A large American salamander. WNNCD: 1882. Source: DOG. The *mud puppy* is an amphibian that is like a perennial puppy: it never matures. It is born in the water, grows up in the water (to a length of up to 17 inches), and spends the rest of its life in the water. The external gills of the larval stage remain in adulthood as reddish brown "feathers," just behind the head. HF; IRCD. *See also* Puppy Dog.

MUGWUMP   *a mugwump.* A person who can't make up his/her mind. Source: BIRD (*). The *mugwump* is an imaginary bird that sits on a fence with its *mug* (or "face") on one side and its *wump* (or "rump") on the other. A human *mugwump* is either a political independent or a person who simply can't make a decision. *Mugwump*, fr. Algonquian *mugquomp* "chief," was first applied, in 1884, to a Republican who couldn't bring himself to support the party ticket. WNNCD. *Compare* Boll Weevil; Copperhead.

MUKLUKS   *a pair of mukluks.* A pair of calf-high boots made of sealskin and having a soft leather sole. WNNCD: 1868. Source: SEAL. The seal is the primary source of leather for *mukluks* (fr. Inuit *muklok* "large seal"), although caribou fur is also used by the Inuit, and light canvas is sometimes substituted by manufacturers. *See also* Flipper; Like a Trained Seal.

MULE (1)   *a mule.* A stubborn or obstinate person. Source: MULE. WNNCD: 13th cent. A mule is a hybrid—the sterile offspring of a male donkey, an *ass* or *jackass*, and a female horse, a *mare*. (The offspring of a male horse, a *stallion*, and a female donkey, a *jenny*, is called a *hinny*.) Mules inherit their size from their mothers, and their stubbornness from their fathers. ATWS; BDPF. *See also* Mulish; Stubborn as a Mule.

MULE (2) Moonshine: cheap, clear liquor from an illegal still. (Also called *white mule.*) Source: MULE. WNNCD: 13th cent. Moonshine may have been called *mule* because (1) it lacks color (or, in the case of the mule, the pretty coloring of a horse), (2) it is illegal (or "unnatural," like the mule's parentage), or (3) it packs a kick like that of a mule. ATWS; LTA. *See also* Kick like a Mule; Mule (1). *Compare* Sheep Dip; Snake Medicine.

MULE (3) *a pair of mules.* A pair of backless slippers. WNNCD: 1582. Source: MULE (*). WNNCD: 13th cent. This is not an animal metaphor. *Mule slippers* derive from those worn by Roman magistrates (Lat. *mulleus*). However, folk etymology has associated the slippers with the animal because mule shoes, like the larger horseshoes, are open in the back. MDWPO. *See also* Mule (1).

MULE DEER *a mule deer.* A large, heavy, long-eared deer of western North America. WNNCD: 1805. Source: MULE. WNNCD: 13th cent. The mule deer is larger and heavier than the familiar white-tailed deer of eastern North America, and it has much longer ears—just as the mule is larger and heavier than its father, the donkey, and has longer ears. The term *mule* has come to mean both "large" and "long-eared." *See also* Mule Ear; Mule Rabbit.

MULE EAR *a mule ear.* A pasty (pronounced *past-y*): a portable meat pie, consisting of beef stew encased in a soft dough pouch, which was once carried by miners in the Upper Peninsula of Michigan but is now sold there to tourists (who invariably pronounce it *paste-y*). Source: MULE. WNNCD: 13th cent. The mule's ears, which it inherits from its father, the jackass, are larger than those of the horse, and they *do* resemble the pasty in size and shape. *Compare* Elephant Ear.

MULE RABBIT *a mule rabbit.* A jackrabbit (q.v.). IHAT: 1857. Source: MULE. WNNCD: 13th cent. Just as the term *jack* (from *jackass*) is used in combination with the name of another animal to signify "large," "male," and "large-eared," *mule* is used here to mean a large, male, long-eared rabbit (actually, a hare). The terms *mule rabbit* and *jackrabbit* are essentially interchangeable. *See also* Mule Deer; Mule Ear.

MULISH *to be mulish.* To be obstinate, unreasonable, inflexible, or stubborn. WNNCD: 1751. Source: MULE. WNNCD: 13th cent. The mule has a reputation for being the stubbornest animal in the world, although it is no more stubborn than its father, the jackass, and its stubbornness is more often than not caused by its understandable unwillingness to carry a load heavier than it can bear—or to drink or eat too soon after strenuous work. IRCD. *See also* Mule (1); Stubborn as a Mule.

MULTIPLY LIKE RABBITS *to multiply like rabbits.* To increase in numbers at an astounding rate. Source: RABBIT. WNNCD: 14th cent. The rabbit is one of the most prolific breeders in the class of mammals. With a gestation period of approx. one month, the female rabbit can produce up to four litters a year, with up to 12 offspring in each, for a total of 48 new offspring in one year, if all survive. Strict vegetarians, rabbits can do considerable harm to gardens and cabbage patches. DEI.

MUSCLE *a muscle.* A bundle of body tissues that contract and swell when their nerves are stimulated. WNNCD: 14th cent. Source: MOUSE. A *muscle* is lit. a "little mouse" (fr. Lat *musculus*, dim. of *mus* "mouse"). The analogy is based on the similarity of the shape and motion of the muscle and the mouse: the flexing muscle looks like a mouse scurrying around under a blanket or rug. ATWS; LCRH; THT. *See also* Mussel. *Compare* Calf.

MUSKET *a musket.* A muzzle-loading firearm. WNNCD: ca. 1587. Source: FLY. *Musket* derives from O.It. *moschetto* "a crossbow arrow, or bolt," which flies to its target on little wings. *Moschetto*, in turn, is a dim. of O.It. *mosca* "fly," which is from Lat. *musca* "fly." Both the crossbow bolt and the musket ball sting like a fly if they hit their target. ROE.

MUSSEL *a mussel.* A marine or freshwater bivalve mollusk with a dark-colored, elongated shell. WNNCD: O.E. Source: MOUSE. A *mussel* is literally a "Little mouse" (fr. Lat. *musculus*, the dim. of *mus* "mouse"). The analogy is based on the size, shape, and color of the mussel and the mouse: small, elongated, and dark. *Mussel* and *muscle* (q.v.) thus derive from the same source, although the former emphasizes color, while the latter focuses on shape and movement. EWPO; THT.

MUTT *a mutt.* A foolish or insignificant person (WNNCD: 1901); a nondescript or mongrel dog (LTA: 1904). Source: SHEEP. *Mutt* is short for *muttonhead* (q.v.) "a dull-witted person"—i.e., one who has the intelligence of a *sheep* (Fr. *mouton*). *Mutt* has also come to mean a short person, though the *Mutt* of the *Mutt and Jeff* cartoon was the tall one. The application of *mutt* to a dog echoes the "insignificant" portion of the definition: a *mutt* is worthless, in the sense that it is not pure bred. *Compare* Cur.

MUTTON CHOPS Full sideburns that extend from the temples to the lower jaws, or "chops." WNNCD: 1865. Source: SHEEP. *Mutton chops* are named after the wool that grows on the sides of the head of a sheep (Fr. *mouton*), but not on the face or forehead. Whiskers of this sort were popular in the 19th cent. and can occasionally be seen today. BDPF; LTA. *Compare* Beetlebrowed; Eagle Beak; Goatee; Sheep's Eyes.

MUTTONHEAD *a muttonhead.* A stupid or dull-witted person. LTA: 1804. Source: SHEEP. Literally, a *muttonhead* is a "sheep's head" (fr. Fr. *mouton* "sheep"). Sheep are not known for their intelligence or initiative. Like the *turkey* (q.v.), they don't know enough to come in out of the rain, they fall down and can't get up, they herd so tightly that they can smother each other, and they show no independence whatsoever. People with these qualities were first called *muttonheads*, then *mutts* (q.v.). *Compare* Sheepshead.

MUZZLE (n) *a muzzle.* A leather harness fitted on the mouth of an animal; the mouth of an animal or firearm. Source: DOG. *Muzzle* derives fr. M.Fr. *musel*, the dim. of *mus* "mouth or snout of an animal"; so a *muzzle* is "a little mouth." The muzzle was first used in the 15th cent. to cover the mouth of a vicious dog in order to prevent it from biting, but it could also be used on other animals, such as horses. In its figurative use, a *muzzle* is a restraint that is placed on people to prevent them from discussing, or expressing their opinion on, a subject—a form of censorship. The *muzzle* of a firearm is the "little mouth" at the end of the barrel where the bullet exits. ATWS; WNWD. *See also* Muzzle (v).

MUZZLE (v) *to muzzle someone; to put a muzzle on someone.* To "gag" someone: to restrain someone's freedom of expression. Source: DOG. A "gag rule" allows a judge to prevent participants in a court action from discussing the case outside the courtroom. Thus, the judge is *muzzling*, or *putting a muzzle on* (q.v.), the participants to prevent them from opening their mouths and communicating information that could damage the case. Dogs have been muzzled, or fitted with muzzles, since the 15th cent. to prevent them from barking or biting. SPD; WNWD. *See also* Muzzle (n).

MY DOG HAS FLEAS A jingle memorized for tuning a ukulele. Source: DOG; FLEA. WNNCD: O.E. Dogs have fleas, and people have *ukuleles* (q.v.), or "jumping fleas." The four strings of a ukulele are tuned—from top to bottom— to the notes E, C, D, G. The four-word jingle matches the four-note sequence. Another expression that links dogs and fleas is "to have *more money than a dog has fleas*" (q.v.), meaning that someone is very wealthy.

MYRMIDONS OF THE LAW *the myrmidons of the law.* Law enforcement personnel, esp. those who carry out orders without question or scruples. WNNCD: 15th cent. Source: ANT. The original *myrmidons* (fr. Gk. *myrmēx* "ant") were warriors, created from ants by Zeus, who fought with Achilles in the Trojan War and received renown for their loyalty and brutality. The modern *myrmidons* are so called because of their obedience, strength, and uniformity of appearance. EWPO.

N

N   The fourteenth letter of the English alphabet. Source: FISH. The Phoenician sign for "N" was called *nun*, meaning "fish." (In the Gk. alphabet, which was based on the Phoenician consonant symbols, *nun* became *nu* but lost its association with a fish.) The Phoenician sign, in turn, was based on an Egyptian hieroglyph, resembling a cursive *n*, that meant "fish," or "the sea." ATWS; BDPF; EWPO. *Compare* Ghoti; ICHTHUS.

NAKED AS A JAYBIRD   *to be as naked as a jaybird*. To be completely naked. Source: JAY. WNNCD: 14th cent. *Jaybird* (WNNCD: 1661) is a nickname for the American blue jay. The adult bird of both sexes is covered with beautiful blue, black, and white feathers; but the hatchlings are featherless—i.e., "naked." AID; ATWS; DOC; ID. *Compare* In the Buff.

NASTY   *See* Nest (n).

NATURE OF THE BEAST   *See* Beast.

NECK AND NECK   *See* At the Drop of a Hat.

NEITHER FISH NOR FOWL   *to be neither fish nor fowl*. To be neither one thing nor another: to be unclassifiable. SHM: 1500s. Source: FISH; FOWL. WNNCD: O.E. The original expression, "to be neither fish nor fowl nor good *red herring* (q.v.)," referred to the three classes of medieval society: the clergy, who ate fresh fish; the nobles, who ate flesh; and the beggars or paupers, who ate smoked herring. Someone or something that could not be *pigeonholed* (q.v.) in one of the first two categories was regarded as being *neither fish nor fowl*. AID; ATWS; BDPF; CI; DEI; HOI; ID; MDWPO. *Compare* Hide nor Hair.

NEITHER HIDE NOR HAIR *See* Hide nor Hair.

NEST (n) *a nest*. A home. Source: BIRD. All functions and senses of *nest* derive from the O.E. noun *nest*, which denoted a structure where a bird could lay its eggs and raise its young. Since the 11th cent., the noun has broadened in meaning to include the domicile of various other animals, such as the ant, the bee, the hornet, the wasp, and the human ("a sweet little *nest*"). Humans sometimes furnish a second *nest*, a *love nest* (EWPO: 1900), that serves as a hideaway for married couples or a trysting place for adulterous lovers. The adj. *nasty* "filthy, disgusting, repugnant" (WNNCD: 14th cent.) may have derived from the noun *nest* (orig. as *nesty*), considering the fact that birds have a tendency to *foul their own nest* (q.v.), esp. if there is more than one brood per year or if the same nest is used for two or more years in succession. ATWS; CE; EWPO. *See also* Empty-nest Syndrome; Nest (v).

NEST (v) *to nest*. To set up housekeeping or start a family. Source: BIRD. The verb *nest* derives from the O.E. noun *nest*. Most birds build a nest in the spring in which to lay their eggs and raise their young. Humans get the *nesting instinct* when they desire to settle down and start a family—also, often, in the spring. The children *nestle* (fr. "little nest") all snug in their beds, and they may *nestle* a kitten in their arms. If the parents are linguists or computer programmers, they may create *nested embeddings*, in which one constituent fits inside another like this year's bird's nest into last year's. ATWS. *See also* Nest (n).

NESTED EMBEDDINGS *See* Nest (v).

NEST EGG *a nest egg*. A cache of money set aside for a rainy day. EWPO: 17th cent. Source: CHICKEN. A literal "nest egg" is a real or artificial egg that is placed in a hen's nest to encourage it to lay more eggs in that particular place. Artificial eggs are made of porcelain or glass and are themselves worth collecting. A financial *nest egg* is "seed" money put aside to encourage more savings in the future. ATWS; CI; DEI; ID; LCRH; MDWPO. *See also* Darning Egg.

NESTING INSTINCT *See* Nest (v).

NESTLE *See* Nest (v).

NEVER LOOK A GIFT HORSE IN THE MOUTH *See* Look a Gift Horse in the Mouth.

NICE DAY FOR DUCKS *See* Fine Day for Ducks.

NICE WEATHER FOR DUCKS   *See* Fine Day for Ducks.

NICE WEATHER IF YOU'RE A DUCK   *See* Fine Day for Ducks.

NIGHTHAWK   *a nighthawk.* A nocturnal person: one who works or plays late into the night. Source: HAWK. WNNCD: O.E. This is a double metaphor, since the nighthawk is not a hawk at all but a *goatsucker* (q.v.), related to the whip-poorwill. Furthermore, hawks do not fly at night. The *nighthawk* uses the cover of darkness to capture moths and other nocturnal insects in its huge mouth. ATWS. *Compare* Night Owl.

NIGHTINGALE   *a nightingale.* A female singer with a beautiful soprano voice. Source: NIGHTINGALE. WNNCD: O.E. The *nightingale* (fr. O.E. *nihtegale* "night singer") is a nocturnal bird admired for its lovely song—unless you're trying to get some sleep. However, the singer is the male, not the female. *See also* Sing like a Bird; Sing like a Canary (1); Sing like a Nightingale.

NIGHTMARE   *a nightmare.* A frightening dream or experience. Source: HORSE (*). The horse is not the basis for this metaphor. Instead of O.E. *mere* "female horse," the source is O.E. *mare* "incubus." The incubus was thought to sit on the chest of sleeping persons in an attempt to suffocate them. When they awoke in a cold sweat they would attribute the disruption of their sleep to a *nightmare*, or "night hag." BDPF; EWPO; HF; MDWPO. *See also* Mare's Nest.

NIGHT OWL   *a night owl.* A night person—one who works nights or just likes to stay up until the wee hours of the morning. WNNCD: 1846. Source: OWL. WNNCD: O.E. Most owls are nocturnal, so *night owl* is somewhat redundant. Owls are able to hunt at night because they have keen, binocular vision and remarkable hearing from all directions, including behind them. They can locate prey in total darkness by the sound. ATWS; CI; DEI; IRCD. *See also* Owl Show. *Compare* Nighthawk.

NINE LIVES   *See* Have Nine Lives.

NIP AT THE HEELS   *to nip at the heels of something.* For someone to be close to success or failure. Source: DOG. A herding dog nips, or bites, at the heels of the livestock that it is tending, in order to get them to move on or in a particular direction. When people *nip at the heels* of success, they are almost there; but when failure is *nipping at their heels*, they are almost doomed. Jack Frost *nips*, but at people's ears and noses; and on a frosty morning people say that it's *nippy* outside. *See also* Hard on the Heels.

NIPPY   *See* Nip at the Heels.

NITPICK   *to nitpick.* To find fault, often unjustifiably, over trivial matters. WNNCD: 1966. Source: NIT. WNNCD: O.E. A nit is the egg of a head louse or body louse. The louse itself is tiny (3 mm), and the egg is even tinier: it can only be "picked"—from the hair—with a nit-comb, not by the fingers or with a regular comb. A *nitpicker* is one who attempts to harvest faults ("nits") that are too small to be noticed. ATWS; CI; ID; LCRH. *See also* Nitpicker; Nit-picking. *Compare* Strain out Gnats and Swallow Camels.

NITPICKER   *a nitpicker.* One who finds fault over trivial matters. WNNCD: 1966. Source: NIT. WNNCD: O.E. This agentive noun suggests monkeys picking fleas from each other's fur; but nits, or louse eggs, are too tiny to be "picked" at all. The *nitpicker* is looking for faults that are too small to be noticed or may not even exist at all. EWPO. *See also* Nitpick; Nit-picking.

NIT-PICKING   *to be nit-picking.* To be finding fault over trivial things. WNNCD: 1956. Source: NIT. WNNCD: O.E. *Nit-picking* is the source of the back-formations *nitpick* (q.v.) and *nitpicker* (q.v.), which have lost the hyphen. All of these words relate to the removal of louse eggs ("nits") from the hair. This would seem to be beneficial, but nits are microscopic and impossible to remove by hand; so *nit-picking* is strictly metaphorical. DEI.

NITTY-GRITTY   *to get down to the nitty-gritty.* To get down to brass tacks; to tell it like it is. WNNCD: 1963. Source: NIT. WNNCD: O.E. Most sources agree that *nitty-gritty* is Black ryming slang based on the *nit* "the tiny egg of the louse" and *grit* "dirt." *To get down to the nitty-gritty* is therefore to reduce an argument to its bare essentials, however harsh or unpleasant. ATWS; CI; IHAT; LTA; NDAS; SPD. *See also* Nitpick; Nitpicker; Nit-picking.

NITWIT   *a nitwit.* A mentally deficient or disturbed person. WNNCD: 1922. Source: NIT (?). WNNCD: O.E. A *nitwit* is someone who has a brain the size of a nit—i.e., very small. Since a nit is the egg of a head louse or body louse, however, it is not certain that it has a brain at all. (EWPO and WNNCD state that *nitwit* is from Ger. dialectal *nit* "not" + Eng. *wit* "sense": "no sense.") ATWS. *Compare* Beetlebrain; Birdbrain.

NO ATHEISTS IN FOXHOLES   *There are no atheists in foxholes.* Imminent death has a way of making believers of us all. Source: FOX. WNNCD. O.E. This expression is attributed to a U.S. Army chaplain on Bataan in WWII. The reference is to the shallow pits, or *foxholes* (q.v.), dug hastily by soldiers to protect themselves from enemy fire. The analogy is to the dens dug by foxes back home. Just as there are no atheists in military foxholes, there are no foxes in them either. BDPF.

NOBODY HERE BUT US CHICKENS Farmer: "Who's in this henhouse?" Thief: "There's nobody here but us chickens." IRCD: late-19th cent. Source: CHICKEN. WNNCD: O.E. Chickens don't talk, so this joke makes the farmer look like a fool if he/she accepts the answer and goes back to bed. The response is also used as a reply to a neighbor who sticks his/her head in the door and asks the same sort of question.

NO BULL *See* Bull (4).

NO CHICKEN *See* No Spring Chicken.

NO FLIES ON ME *There are no flies on me.* There's nothing wrong with me: I'm cunning, shrewd, alive, and kicking. DOC: 1888. Source: FLY. WNNCD: O.E. Flies congregate on dead, dying, wounded, or stationary animals, on which they feed and breed. If there are *no flies on you*, you are probably not only alive and well but also active and alert, not staying in one place long enough to attract them. ATWS; BDPF; CI; DEI; IRCD; LTA; NDAS.

NOM DE PLUME *See* Plume.

NONE OF YOUR BEESWAX *See* Beeswax.

NOSE FOR NEWS *See* Sniff out.

NOSE SOMEONE OUT *See* Win by a Nose.

NO SPRING CHICKEN *You're no spring chicken yourself.* You're not so young either. WNNCD: 1879. Source: CHICKEN. WNNCD: O.E. A shorter form of the expression, *no chicken*, used to be used exclusively for women (LTA: 1730s); but the expanded form, which makes little natural sense, can now be used of either sex. Spring is the birthtime for many animals, including birds, but the domesticated chicken produce eggs year-round. AID; BDPF; CE; CI; DEI; DOC; EWPO; IRCD.

NOT CRICKET *That's not cricket!* That's not fair! SOED: 1902. Source: CRICKET. WNNCD: 14th cent. That's unsportsmanlike—not according to the rules or conventions of the game of cricket, whose name derives from that of the chirping insect. CI; DOC; ST. *See also* Cricket (1); Cricket (2); Jimminy Crickets.

NOT FIT FOR MAN NOR BEAST *See* Beast.

NOT GIVE A HOOT *I don't give a hoot; I wouldn't give two hoots.* I don't care in the least; I couldn't care less. Source: OWL. A *hoot* is the cry of the "hoot owl," or Great Horned Owl of North America. *To not give a hoot* is, lit., to have nothing to say about something—i.e., to show no interest in it whatsoever—just as the hoot owl shows its lack of interest in another hoot owl by not "giving a hoot." *See also* Ain't That a Hoot; Hoot (n); Not Worth a Hoot.

NOT THE ONLY FISH IN THE OCEAN *See* Plenty More Fish in the Ocean.

NOT WORTH A HOOT *to not be worth a hoot.* To be worthless. Source: OWL. WNNCD: O.E. A *hoot* is the cry of the "hoot owl," or Great Horned Owl. The hoot owl hoots to communicate with its mate and to announce its presence to other owls and other birds of prey. It does not, however, hoot to alert its prey to its attack; so the hoot is a peaceful or innocuous cry. (The endangered Northern Spotted Owl *did* turn out to be *worth a hoot* ca. 1990 when it delayed lumbering in its habitat in the northwestern United States.) ATWS; ID. *See also* Ain't that a Hoot; Give a Hoot; Hoot (n).

NOT YET DRY BEHIND THE EARS *See* Still Wet behind the Ears.

NOURISH A SNAKE IN YOUR BOSOM *to nourish—or cherish—a snake in your bosom.* To do a favor for someone, only to be rewarded with ingratitude and treachery. Source: SNAKE. WNNCD: O.E. The expression derives from an Aesop fable about a farmer who put a frozen viper inside his shirt to revive it. When the snake revived, it rewarded the farmer by biting him. Moral: Let frozen vipers lie. ATWS; BDPF; EWPO. *See also* Bite the Hand That Feeds You; Let Sleeping Dogs Lie.

O

OCTOPUS *an octopus.* An organization with eight (or more) branches radiating from, or controlled by, a central plant or headquarters. Source: OCTOPUS. WNNCD: 1758. The octopus is an eight-footed (fr. Gk. *okto* "eight" + *pous* "foot") cephalopod mollusk, related to the squid and cuttlefish, which have ten feet (or "arms"). An organization with more branches than an *octopus* could be—but is not—called a "squid." *See also* Like an Octopus.

ODD DUCK *See* Queer Duck.

OFF AND RUNNING *to be off and running.* For a contest to have begun. DOC: 1967. Source: HORSE. *Off and running* is a modification of what the track announcer says when the horses break out of the starting gate: "And . . . they're off!" If a horse fails to leave the gate, or is slow to do so, it is said to have been *left at the post* (from the post that orig. marked the starting point of a race). As the race proceeds, those horses that are out of contention are said to be *out of the running,* and those that still have a chance to win are said to be *in the running.* A horse that wins the race by a wide margin is said to *win going away,* but even a losing horse can give the fans a *run for their money* if it performs well *in the homestretch* (q.v.). All of these expressions can be applied, as metaphors, to candidates for a political office. BDPF; CI; DEI; LCRH; ST.

OFF THE HOOK *to be—or get—off the hook.* To be relieved of a problem or obligation: to get a reprieve. Source: FISH. If an angler fails to *set the hook* (q.v.) once the fish has *taken the bait* (q.v.), the fish may get free of the hook and even swim away with the bait. A person who is in trouble can be *let off the hook* by the person who put him/her there, just as an angler may release a fish that is too small to keep; but if that same person gets out of trouble on his/her own, he/she is said to *wiggle—or wriggle—off the hook*. AID; ATWS; BDPF; CI; ST.

OFF YOUR FEED *to be off your feed*. To be physically or emotionally ill. Source: HORSE. When a horse is "off its feed," it loses its appetite—a good sign that it is physically ill. When people are *off their feed*, they are more likely to be depressed or distracted, although a good case of "stomach flu" can produce the same effect. ATWS. *Compare* Feel Your Oats.

OLD BAT *an old bat*. A disagreeable, unpleasant, or repulsive old woman. Source: BAT. WNNCD: 14th cent. Throughout the 20th cent., bats have been regarded as repulsive creatures— *fly-by-nights* (q.v.)—that get in your hair, suck your blood, and give you rabies. However, *old bat* may derive from a British slang term for a prostitute who works at night—in the dark—like the bat (EWPO: 1612). ATWS; ID; NDAS. *See also* Bats. *Compare* Old Biddy.

OLD BIDDY *an old biddy*. An elderly woman who is gossipy, meddlesome, and eccentric. Source: HEN (?). WNNCD: O.E. In the barnyard, a *biddy* (WNNCD: 1601) is a hen, esp. an old hen, that is noisy, demanding, and unfriendly, as most hens are. *Biddy* as part of an epithet, however, may derive from a child's pronunciation of a common name for a nanny: *Bridget*. IRCD; WNWD. *Compare* Old Bat.

OLD BIRD *See* Rare Bird.

OLD BUZZARD *an old buzzard*. An unpleasant, unlovable old man. Source: BUZZARD. WNNCD: 13th cent. The buzzard, or turkey vulture, is a large bird that feeds primarily on dead animals and refuse. This habit, plus the fact that the bird's head is "naked" (without feathers), makes it appear unpleasant and unlovable. ATWS; IRCD. *See also* Buzzards Are Circling. *Compare* Old Coot; Old Goat.

OLD CAT Stick ball. Source: CAT (?). WNNCD: O.E. *Stick ball* (WNNCD: 1903) is a street version of baseball. It is played with a broomstick and a child's rubber ball, and the bases are whatever happens to be present at that particular location and time: a fire hydrant, a light pole, a manhole cover, etc. The game is named for the number of bases to be used on any given occasion: "three *old cat*" (three bases), "two *old cat*" (two bases), or "one *old cat*" (one base). The connection between the game and the cat is unknown. LTA.

OLD COOT *an old coot*. An eccentric old man. DOC: 1859. Source: COOT. WNNCD: 14th cent. The coot's "eccentricity" lies in the behavior of the male during the breeding season, although that behavior is normal for male coots and is regarded as eccentric only by human standards. ATWS; EWPO; IRCD. *See also* Crazy as a Coot. *Compare* Old Buzzard; Old Goat.

OLD CROW   *an old crow.* An elderly person who makes a lot of threats but is unable to back them up with action. Source: CROW. WNNCD: O.E. The crow is a noisy bird—so much so that its name has been verbalized for the morning cry of the rooster (or cock): *to crow* (q.v.). But the crow is also a *chicken* (q.v.) when it comes to standing its ground over a *roadkill* (q.v.): it scares easily. CE. *Compare* Old Bat; Old Buzzard; Old Coot.

OLD FIRE HORSE   *an old fire horse.* A veteran or retired fire, police, or military officer. Source: HORSE. WNNCD: O.E. Before the advent of trucks, fire wagons were pulled by a team of horses. The horses became so used to the routine that when the fire bell rang they couldn't wait to leave the firehouse. Even when they were retired and *put out to pasture* (q.v.), they still responded to the sound of a bell like Pavlov's dog. (Old habits are hard to break.) Veteran or retired emergency workers are the same way. They respond to an alarm as if they were still on active duty; and, in the case of military veterans, this can be dangerous to the person who alarms them. *Compare* Old War Horse.

OLD FOX   *See* Sly Old Fox.

OLD GOAT   *an old goat.* A disagreeable, unpleasant, or stubborn old man; a lewd, lascivious, lecherous, or "dirty" old man. Source: GOAT. WNNCD: O.E. The goat has long been associated with the Devil because of its horns, its stubbornness, its lustfulness, and its dirty behavior: it will eat anything, including tin cans. An *old goat* is an established "sinner" who has no redeeming qualities, although he may think he is God's gift to women. ATWS; CH; SHM. *Compare* Old Buzzard; Old Coot; Old Crow.

OLD HEN   *an old hen.* A fussy or meddlesome woman, esp. an elderly one. Source: HEN. WNNCD: O.E. In the barnyard, a *hen* is a female chicken; but in the wild, the word has broadened its meaning to include the adult female of various other birds (e.g.: the *peahen,* as opposed to the *peacock;* the *hen pheasant,* as opposed to the *cock pheasant*); and it has even been extended to sea creatures (such as the female lobster). ATWS; CE; IRCD. *Compare* Old Biddy.

OLD STOMPING GROUND   *your old stomping (or stamping) ground(s).* The neighborhood where you used to live; the places where you used to hang out. WNNCD: 1786. Source: ANIMAL. Literally, a stomping ground is a place where hoofed animals go during the mating season. The females stand around and watch while the males butt heads, lock horns, and bite and kick each other until only one male remains. That male then services every female that will have him. All of this activity results in the grass being trampled down by the animals' hooves. An *old stomping ground* for humans is not necessarily a place where sexual conquests once occurred but the former territory for such activities as going to school, playing on the playground, attending the movies, and generally hanging out with the kids in the neighborhood. ATWS; EWPO; HTB; LCRH.

OLD WAR HORSE   *an old war horse.* A veteran soldier (IRCD: 18th cent.); a veteran politician (IRCD: 19th cent.); a hackneyed work of art (IRCD: 20th cent.). Source: HORSE. WNNCD: O.E. Originally, a *war horse* (WNNCD: 1653) was a military charger, and an *old* war horse was one that had been *put out to pasture* (q.v.) after many campaigns. Figuratively, an *old war horse* is either (1) a veteran or retired soldier or politician who has participated in many military or political campaigns and loves to reminisce about them, or (2) a work of art that has been performed so many times that it has lost its appeal and become stale and trite. BDPF; DEI; SPD. *Compare* Old Fire Horse.

ON A COLD TRAIL   *to be on a cold trail.* To be searching for someone who disappeared long ago and has left no clues as to his/her whereabouts. Source: DOG. Hunting dogs track animals by their scent; when the scent is old and faint, the dogs have little chance of tracking down their quarry successfully. Detectives have the same problem with fugitives who have made a clean getaway. ST.

ON A SHORT LEASH   *to have, keep, or put someone on a short leash.* To have, keep, or put someone under tight control. Source: DOG. A dog is walked on a short leash if it is large, vicious, or playful or has a tendency to wander, visit other dogs or cats, or gen. disobey commands. Parents keep children *on a short leash* by controlling their movement and supervising their activities; and wives keep husbands *on a short leash* by restricting their freedom and accompanying them wherever they go. DOC. *See also* Strain at the Leash.

ONCE BITTEN, TWICE SHY   (A proverb.) One learns from experience, esp. a bad experience. Source: DOG. If a child is bitten by a dog, that child learns the hard way that it is best to *let sleeping dogs lie* (q.v.) and will be more careful the next time. Adults who fall for scams or cons have learned their lesson and will think twice before giving up their hardearned money in the future. BDPF.

ONE-HEARSE TOWN   *See* One-horse Town.

ONE-HORSE RACE   *See* Horse Race.

ONE-HORSE TOWN   *a one-horse town.* A small, unimportant, rural town or village. IRCD: 1884 (Mark Twain's *Huckleberry Finn*). Source: HORSE. WNNCD: O.E. In the "good old days," the number of horses in a small town was close to the number of men who lived there; so a one-horse town must have been a very small one indeed. In those days, the horse was used for riding, pulling wagons and buggies, hauling farm equipment, and turning gins and mills; so a *one-horse town* must also have been very sleepy and impoverished. By analogy, a town with only one funeral parlor is jokingly called a *one-hearse town*. ATWS; BDPF; HOI; LCRH. *Compare* Cow Town.

ONE-RING CIRCUS   *See* Dog and Pony Show.

ONE SWALLOW DOES NOT MAKE A SUMMER   Don't get too optimistic over a little bit of good news. EWPO: 1539. Source: SWALLOW. WNNCD: O.E. The original expression was "One swallow does not make a *spring*" (Aristotle, 4th cent. B.C.); the season was changed in the English version because swallows are the harbingers of *summer* in Britain. (In California, they return to San Juan Capistrano on March 19.) BDPF; CI; DEI; MDWPO. *Compare* Count Your Chickens.

ONE THAT GOT AWAY   *You should have seen the one that got away*. If you think *this* one is big—or beautiful—you should have seen the one that I *almost* caught. IRCD: 1892. Source: FISH. This expression is part of the *fish story* (q.v.), in which an incredibly large fish swallows the angler's bait *hook, line, and sinker* (q.v.) and then swims away with the entire tackle. It is all part of the exaggeration that is associated with fishing.

ONE-TRICK PONY   *See* Dog and Pony Show.

ON SOMEONE'S TAIL   *See* In Hot Pursuit.

ON THE FLY   *See* Fly (n) (1).

ON THE HALF SHELL   *served on the half shell*. Served "open-face(d)," like a sandwich without the top slice of bread—or like chipped beef on toast or *Welsh Rabbit* (q.v.). Source: OYSTER. Raw oysters are commonly served on the interior side of one of their two shells: a *half shell*. The meat on a sandwich served *on the half shell* looks like an oyster lying in one of its shells. *See also* Eat Your First Oyster.

ON THE HOOF   *to be worth X number of dollars on the hoof*. To be worth X number of dollars as is. Source: CATTLE. Cattle are bought from the farmer "on the hoof"—i.e., "live"—and then sold at a higher price when slaughtered and butchered. Used cars that are sold *on the hoof* have not been altered from the condition in which they arrived on the lot. The analogy is between the four hooves of the cow or steer and the four wheels or tires of the car.

ON THE NOSE   *See* Win by a Nose.

ON THE PROWL   *See* Prowl.

ON THE RIGHT/WRONG TRACK *to be on the right or wrong track.* To be headed in the right or wrong direction. Source: DOG. Hunting dogs first track an animal by following its scent; once the animal is sighted, they follow it by sight. When they are *on the right track,* they are following the scent of the intended quarry; when they are *on the wrong track,* they are *at fault* (q.v.) and often pick up the scent of a different animal. People are *on the right or wrong track* when they are headed in the right or wrong direction, following the right or wrong clues, or looking in the right or wrong places. Railroading has adopted these usages for its trains. AID; CI; ST.

ON THE TRACK OF *See* Track down.

ON YOUR OWN HOOK *to do something on your own hook.* To accomplish something all by yourself. Source: FISH. A child often gets assistance from an adult in rigging a fishing line, baiting the hook, casting the lure, hooking the fish, and reeling it in. When the child is old enough, he/she is able to perform these tasks *on his/her own hook*—i.e., independently. Both children and adults get credit for initiating a project and carrying it out all by themselves, without the help of others. MDWPO.

OPEN A CAN OF WORMS *to open a can of worms.* To unnecessarily introduce a set of complicated, and perhaps insoluble, problems: to open a "Pandora's box." Source: WORM. WNNCD: O.E. Pandora probably never went fishing with a cane pole and a can of angleworms—and presumably never spilled them in the boat. But she did, according to Greek mythology, open a forbidden box and let loose a swarm of evils upon the world. AID; ATWS; CE; IRCD. *See also* Can of Worms.

OPEN SEASON *to be open season on certain individuals, groups, or institutions.* To be a time when certain individuals, groups, or institutions are out of favor and subject to criticism, attack, and/or ridicule. Source: ANIMAL. At various times, members of certain professions (such as doctors, lawyers, and politicians) and certain large organizations (such as businesses, churches, and unions) come under fire for questionable practices. During these times it is *open season* on them: i.e., they are *fair game,* or legitimate targets for attack. Animals are fair game for pursuit when they are *in season*: i.e., when the legal time for hunting, fishing, or trapping is in force (WNNCD: 1890); otherwise, they are *out of season.* In some states of the United States it is always *open season* on pests, such as crows, dogfish, and rats. AID; ATWS; BDPF; CI; DEI; LCRH; ST.

OSTRACISM Social banishment (similar to "banning" or "shunning"). Source: OYSTER. WNNCD: 14th cent. *Ostracism* (fr. Gk. *ostrakismos*) was an ancient Greek method of forcing an unwanted citizen into temporary exile by voting him out with a piece of tile resembling an oyster shell (Gk. *ostrakon*). Modern *ostracism* involves informal exclusion from the privileges of the society to which the person still belongs. WNWD. *See also* Ostracize; Solitary as an Oyster.

OSTRACIZE   *to ostracize someone.* To banish someone socially, by general consent. Source: OYSTER. WNNCD: 14th cent. The ancient Greeks voted on the banishment of an unwanted citizen by writing his name on a piece of tile that resembled, and was named after, the oyster shell (Gk. *ostrakon*). *Ostracize* (fr. Gk. *ostrakizein*) no longer means to "exile" but to reject someone socially—to render someone a "nonperson." (It is probably a back-formation from *ostracism* [q.v.].) EWPO; SHM; WNWD.

OSTRICHLIKE   *to assume an ostrichlike position.* To refuse to face reality. Source: OSTRICH. WNNCD: 13th cent. The ostrich, the largest living bird (10 feet tall, over 300 pounds), has three adequate means of defense: to peck with its bill; to kick with its feet; and to run away at high speed. However, because it is flightless, it was once fabled to stick its head in the sand, assuming that if it could not see, it could not be seen. DEI. *See also* Bury Your Head in the Sand; Head-in-the-sand.

OTHER FISH TO FRY   *to have other fish to fry.* To have other, better, or more important things to do. HTB: 1660. Source: FISH. WNNCD: O.E. It is hard to say how this expression would be used in fish frying—perhaps "Don't bother me. I'm not done frying the fish yet." At any rate, as a metaphor the meaning is clear: "I can't help you. I have more urgent things to do." Also: *to have bigger fish to fry.* AID; ATWS; BDPF; CH; CI; DEI; ID; IRCD; ST. *See also* Plenty More Fish in the Ocean.

OUT FOR BLOOD   *See* Bloodthirsty.

OUTFOX   *to outfox someone.* To outsmart someone. WNNCD: 1924. Source: FOX. WNNCD: O.E. The cleverness of the fox has made it a popular subject for animal fables and foxhunts, although in both cases it usu. loses. The fox is a master at covering up its tracks—by retracing its own steps, running in the tracks of another animal, traveling in a stream, or walking on top of a stone wall. Knowledge of these practices gives humans the ability to *outfox* the fox. ATWS; IRCD; ST.

OUT OF SEASON   *See* Open Season.

OUT OF THE RUNNING   *See* Off and Running.

OUT ON A LIMB   *See* Up a Tree.

OVAL   *to be oval.* To be elliptical or oblong. WNNCD: 1577. Source: CHICKEN. Literally, something that is oval is "egg-shaped" (fr. Lat. *ovalis* "of an egg," fr. Lat.

ovum "egg"). A chicken's egg is not a perfect sphere but an elongated spheroid that is large at one end and small at the other. An *oval* racetrack, or *oval*, on the other hand, is a symmetrical ellipsis, with straight sides and similarly rounded ends.

OWLISH *to be owlish.* To look silly, solemn, and wise—all at the same time. WNNCD: 1611. Source: OWL. WNNCD: O.E. The owl looks wise because it has a rather flat, round, humanlike face and large, unblinking eyes. It looks solemn because it can perch for hours without moving a feather, waiting for its prey. And it looks silly because it has "ears," can turn its head 270 degrees, and is remarkably tame for a bird of prey. In other words, it looks something like a *scarecrow* (q.v.). IRCD. *See also* Wise as an Owl; Wise Old Owl.

OWL SHOW *an owl show.* A late-night movie or theatrical performance. Source: OWL. WNNCD: O.E. The owl is noted for its nocturnal habits, sharing that distinction with other flying animals such as the bat (a mammal), the moth (an insect), and the nighthawk (another bird). *Owl shows* are intended for *night owls* (q.v.)—people who have their days and nights reversed. NDAS. *Compare* Dog and Pony Show.

OXBOW *an oxbow.* A U-shaped bend in a river. IHAT: 1780s. Source: OX. WNNCD: O.E. Oxen were not harnessed, like horses and mules, but were yoked, in pairs, under a double-curved beam of wood. The ox's head was held in place under the yoke in a U-shaped wooden collar called an *oxbow.* The word is now pretty much forgotten, or else the "No U-Turn" signs might read "No Oxbow." BDPF; WNWD. *See also* Subjugate; Syzygy; Yoke.

OYSTER WHITE *to be oyster white.* To be an off-white, slightly creamy white color. Source: OYSTER. WNNCD: 14th cent. Oysters are not white on the outside. The inside of their shell is white, but this color is iridescent and is usually called *mother-of-pearl* (q.v.). So *oyster white* is probably named for the pulverized shell, used as a base for paint, or for the color of the body of the oyster itself. WNWD. *See also* Pearl; Pearly White.

P

PACEMAKER   *See* Set the Pace.

PACESETTER   *See* Set the Pace.

PACK A WALLOP   *See* Gallop.

PACKED LIKE SARDINES   *to be packed (in) like sardines.* To be crowded together tightly, as in an automobile, an airplane, a subway car, an elevator, or a small room. Source: SARDINE. WNNCD: 15th cent. It is customary to pack sardines—small or immature fish, such as the European Pilchard—tightly together in small, flat cans, laying them head to tail to get more in. AID; CI; DEI; DOC. *Compare* Herringbone Pattern.

PACK OF WOLVES   *a pack of wolves.* A vicious, bloodthirsty group of human predators. Source: WOLF. WNNCD: O.E. Wolves normally hunt in packs of up to 15 individuals, preying on wild animals as large as elk and bison and on domestic animals as large as calves and sheep. When their natural prey are unavailable, they sometimes pursue humans, as do the reporters and photographers of our media. *See also* Leader of the Pack; Wolf Pack. *Compare* Paparazzi.

PACK RAT   *a pack rat.* A person who collects useless items and never throws any of them away. Source: RAT. WNNCD: O.E. The wood rat of the southwestern United States is also known as a *pack rat* (WNNCD: ca. 1885) because it collects all sorts of things in its nest. Human *pack rats* collect and hoard worthless items—such as wrapping paper, plastic bags, aluminum foil, and string—in their own "nest" and refuse to give them up, even at spring cleaning time. ATWS.

PADLOCK *a padlock.* A removable metal lock, opened by a key or a combination, with a pivoting, U-shaped rod that can be used to secure doors, bicycles, etc. WNNCD: 15th cent. Source: FROG (?); TOAD (?). The origin of the *pad* in *padlock* is unknown. It may be the O.E. word for "frog or toad," based on the resemblance of the body of the lock to the body of an amphibian. It may even be a lily pad, on which frogs like to sit. HF; WNWD.

PALOMINO *a palomino.* A Western horse with a golden coat and a flaxen mane and tail. WNNCD: 1914. Source: DOVE. *Palomino* lit. means "like a dove" or "dovelike" (fr. Span. *paloma* "dove"). When applied to the Spanish horse in America, it means that the coloring is like that of a dove. MDWPO. *Compare* Columbine.

PANACHE *See* Pinnacle.

PANDA BEAR *a panda (bear).* A large, black-and-white mammal of Central China: A Giant Panda. Source: BEAR. WNNCD: O.E. A *panda bear*, or *panda*, is not a bear at all, but it resembles a bear because of its large size (up to 260 pounds), its long body, and its thick fur. (Its head is much larger than that of a "true" bear.) In fact, the Giant Panda is closely related to the Himalayan—or "lesser"—panda, which has red fur and a ringed tail, is about the same size as an American raccoon, and is a member of the raccoon family. The fact that stuffed toys in the form of Giant Pandas have become popular in the United States has contributed to their identification as "bears." CE. *Compare* Koala Bear; Teddy Bear.

PAPARAZZI Free-lance photographers who relentlessly pursue celebrities with the intention of taking unposed photographs of them. WNNCD: 1968. Source: INSECT. In Italian, *paparazzi* lit. means "buzzing insects," but the meaning of the word was broadened—by Federico Fellini in the film *La Dolce Vita*—to cover "swarming photographers." The insects referred to are either bees or flies, both of which buzz as they swarm over humans and other animals. EWPO. *See also* Buzz (v).

PAPER CHASE *See* Hare and Hounds.

PAPER TIGER *a paper tiger.* Someone or something that is menacing only in appearance, not in reality. SPD: 1946. Source: TIGER. WNNCD: O.E. Mao Tsetung first applied this term to the Nationalist forces during the Communist revolution in China following WWII. Later (WNNCD: 1949), he applied it to the United States, meaning that both the United States and the *paper tiger* were weak and ineffective. Mao's use of the term may have alluded to the figures of animals in Chinese new year's celebrations, which look frightening—and growl a little—but are only made of paper. ATWS; DEI; DOC; IRCD; LCRH; MDWPO. *See also* Toothless Tiger.

PAPER TRAIL   *See* Hare and Hounds.

PARASITE   *a parasite.* One who depends on another for subsistence or support—and provides nothing in return. Source: ANIMAL (*). This metaphor has come full circle. The original *parasite* (WNNCD: 1539) was a human who ate at the tables of the rich and famous (WNNCD: Gk. *para* "for" + *sitos* "food"), contributing nothing but flattery. Later, the term was applied to an animal, such as a *leech* (q.v.), which attaches itself to another for sustenance. More recently, the word has been applied once again to "freeloading" humans, although not necessarily those who come to dinner. *See also* Sponge. *Compare* Predator; Scavenger.

PARROT (n)   *a parrot.* One who echoes the words of others, often without understanding them. Source: PARROT. WNNCD: 1525. A parrot is sometimes called a "tape recorder with feathers" because it can so successfully mimic the sounds of its environment (doorbells and phones ringing, dogs barking and cats meowing, police and fire trucks sirening), including human speech—sometimes to the embarrassment of the speakers. ATWS; IRCD. *See also* Parrot (v). *Compare* Monkey See, Monkey Do; Sedulous Ape.

PARROT (v)   *to parrot something.* To repeat something in the exact way that it was just spoken by someone else. WNNCD: 1596. Source: PARROT. WNNCD: 1525. The parrot is the best of the "talking birds." It can mimic, exactly, both animal sounds and sounds produced by inanimate objects, such as chiming clocks and percolating pots. IRCD. *See also* Parrot (n). *Compare* Ape (v).

PARROT-FASHION   *to learn something parrot-fashion.* To learn something by rote, without attention to its meaning. Source: PARROT. WNNCD: 1525. The parrot is able to mimic the speech of humans with great accuracy, but it has no idea what it is "saying" or even that what it is uttering is "speech"—as opposed to the barking of dogs or the slamming of doors. CI; DEI. *See also* Parrot (n); Parrot (v).

PARROT FISH   *a parrot fish.* A multicolored fish whose teeth are fused together in both the upper and lower jaws, one of which usu. closes over the other. WNNCD: 1712. Source: PARROT. WNNCD: 1525. Parrots have no teeth, of course, but the edges of their bills are very sharp, and the upper bill curves down over the lower one. As one might expect, *parrot fish* are herbivores, like parrots.

PARTY ANIMAL   *See* Animal.

PASS THE BUCK   *to pass the buck.* To shift responsibility or blame onto someone else. DOC: 1872 (Mark Twain's *Innocents at Home*). Source: DEER. In poker games in the Old West, the token that was used to identify the dealer was a buckhorn knife, the handle of which was fashioned from the antler of a male deer. If the designated player preferred not to deal, he would *pass the buck* to the player to his left, thereby shifting the responsibility to him. One who did so was called a *buck passer*. ATWS; BDPF; CI; EWPO; HOI; IRCD; LCRH; ST. *See also* Buck (n); Buck Slip; Buck Stops here.

PASTOR   *a pastor.* A minister. WNNCD: 14th cent. Source: ANIMAL. Literally, a *pastor* (fr. Lat. *pastor* "herdsman") is a herder—as of sheep, goats, or other livestock—who watches over the animals while they graze (Lat. *pascere* "to feed"). Metaphorically, a pastor is the *shepherd* (q.v.) of a *flock* (q.v.), i.e., a religious congregation. The sense of *shepherd* as a caretaker of people goes back to the Old Testament, e.g., Psalm 23: "the Lord is my shepherd." The adj. *pastoral* (WNNCD: 15th cent.), which is also derived fr. Lat. *pastor*, orig. described things related to the care of animals; but in the poetry of the English Renaissance (16th cent.), *pastoral* came to mean writing that idealized the life of sheep and shepherds as something peaceful and idyllic. *Pastoral* is also used to describe the role and responsibility of a *pastor*: e.g., *pastoral duties* and *pastoral care.*

PASTORAL   *See* Pastor.

PAVILION   *a pavilion.* A detached or separate structure for special purposes, such as exhibition or entertainment. Source: BUTTERFLY. Originally, a *pavilion* was a large, multicolored Roman tent erected for shelter, meals, and receptions (WNNCD: 13th cent.). The word *pavilion* derives fr. Lat. *papilion* "butterfly" by way of O.Fr. The Roman tents looked like giant butterflies with flapping wings. THT. *Compare* Canapé; Canopy.

PAVLOVIAN RESPONSE   *See* Lick Your Chops.

PAW   *a paw; to paw.* A hand; to maul. Source: ANIMAL. An animal *paw* (WNNCD: 14th cent.) is the clawed foot of a fourlegged mammal. A human *paw* is the hand—usu. a large or heavy one—of a person. A *southpaw* (WNNCD: 1892) is a person who is lefthanded. The term derives from baseball, where oldtime parks were situated so that the pitcher threw toward the west, putting the throwing arm of a lefthander on the south side of the mound. To *paw* someone (WNNCD: 1604) is for a man to handle a woman roughly and sexually, esp. without her consent: "Get your big *paws* off me!" ATWS; ST.

PAY FOR A DEAD HORSE   *to pay for a dead horse.* To continue to pay for something that is now useless or unprofitable. HOI: early-17th cent. Source: HORSE. WNNCD: O.E. You put a down payment on a horse and take possession of it; the horse dies, but you must continue to pay for it anyway. The same applies to a car that is bought on time but becomes inoperable, wrecked, or stolen before it is fully paid for. *Dead horse* also applies to prepayment for work to be done later: if the recipient spends the money before the work begins, he/she is working for nothing. HF; HTB; IRCD. *See also* Beat a Dead Horse.

PEARL *the color pearl*. A bluish gray color. Source: OYSTER. Natural pearls are not *pearly white* (q.v.), like most imitation pearls: they are bluish gray. Gemologists know this, but they rely more on the feel of the pearl than on the color, rubbing it against their teeth to detect a gritty surface on the natural pearl. ATWS. *See also* Mother-of-pearl; Oyster White.

PEARL DIVER *a pearl diver*. A dishwasher in a restaurant. Source: OYSTER. Japanese pearl divers (usu. women) dive for Great Pearl Oysters, which may or may not contain pearls. (That is determined after they are taken to the surface.) A dishwasher in a restaurant plunges his/her hands into the soapy dishwater *fishing for* (q.v.) silverware or pieces of crockery, identifiable only after they are brought to the surface. NDAS.

PEARL OF GREAT PRICE *a pearl of great price*. Something that is highly valued and highly treasured. Source: OYSTER. This expression derives from the Book of Matthew (13:45,46): " . . . the kingdom of heaven is like unto a merchant man, seeking goodly pearls; Who when he had found one pearl of great price, went and sold all that he had, and bought it." (It is also the title of one of the doctrinal works of the Mormons.) The pearl of *greatest* price is from the Great Pearl Oyster of the Orient. BDPF. *See also* Cast Pearls before Swine.

PEARL ONION *a pearl onion*. A tiny, pickled onion used as garnish or in martinis. WNNCD: ca. 1890. Source: OYSTER. An onion and a pearl are formed in much the same way: layer upon layer. In the case of the pearl, it is one layer of "nacre," or *mother-of-pearl* (q.v.), deposited over a piece of grit, followed by another layer, etc. The Romans used the same word, *unio* "united," for both onion and pearl. EWPO. *See also* Pearl.

PEARLS OF WIT AND WISDOM Gems of humor and knowledge. Source: OYSTER. The oyster is not the only animal that can turn a piece of grit into a priceless pearl: humans can do it too, with the proper preparation and timing. Pearls have been highly valued as gems and jewelry from biblical times, but this metaphor is not from the Bible. *See also* Cast Pearls before Swine; Pearl of Great Price.

PEARLY WHITE *to have pearly white teeth*. To have pure, white, glistening teeth. Source: OYSTER. Teeth that are pearl-colored ought to be bluish gray, not white. The metaphor overlooks the actual color of the pearl and focuses on its iridescence or glistening effect. The term *pearly whites* is sometimes used to refer to a person's complete set of beautiful teeth. *See also* Mother-of-pearl; Oyster White; Pearl.

PEARLY WHITES   *See* Pearly White.

PEBBLE PUP   *See* Hound (n).

PECK   *a peck on the cheek.* A quick, light kiss on the cheek. Source: BIRD. Birds do not usu. transfer food to their mouth with their feet. (Raptors do.) Instead, they strike, or *peck*, at it with their beak, as chickens do to pick up grain or grit from the ground and woodpeckers do to get at insects behind the bark of a tree. Chickens also peck each other, according to their *pecking order* (q.v.), although not in the friendly way that people do. Besides pecking at cheeks, humans also *hunt and peck* (q.v.) at the keys of a typewriter, word processor, or computer. ATWS.

PECKING ORDER   *a pecking order.* The hierarchy within a social structure that indicates rank or status. SPD: 1929. Source: CHICKEN. A flock of chickens has a rigid social structure. Any given bird can peck those lower on the scale without being pecked back, but must submit to pecking by those higher on the scale without retaliating. Rank or status is based on strength and aggressiveness. The same hierarchy can be found in human social organizations, where it is sometimes subtle but is often associated with wealth, politics, and position. (E.g., the boss can criticize the secretary, but the secretary had better not criticize the boss.) The metaphor is based on W. L. Allee's 1928 study of the pecking order of hens. ATWS; CI; DEI; EWPO; IRCD; LCRH. *See also* Henpeck; Henpecked.

PECULIAR   *to be peculiar.* To be distinctive or special; to be unusual or strange. WNNCD: 15th cent. Source: CATTLE. The "distinctive" sense of this word comes from Lat. *peculiaris* "of private property," which is based on Lat. *pecu* "cattle." The idea was that your cattle—the most valuable property that you could own—made you what you were. The meaning of Eng. *peculiar* was broadened to include not only private property but anything about you that was different or special. More recently, the meaning has come to apply to anything that is unusual, odd ("funny peculiar"), strange, or eccentric. ATWS; EWPO; LCRH. *See also* Pecuniary.

PECUNIARY   *to be pecuniary.* To pertain to money. WNNCD: 1502. Source: CATTLE. The Eng. word *pecuniary* is based on the Lat. word *pecunia* "money or property," which derives fr. Lat. *pecu* "cattle." The association of cattle with wealth is still common in many societies and goes back to the time before coinage was invented. *Pecuniary* matters are matters of monetary policy. To be *impecunious* (WNNCD: 1596) is to lack money—to be penniless, "without a cent." ATWS; EWPO; LCRH. *See also* Capital; Chattel; Fee.

PEDIGREE   *a pedigree.* A genealogical record or chart. WNNCD: 15th cent. Source: CRANE. *Pedigree* is from M.Fr. *pie de grue* "crane's foot," probably because of the resemblance of the foot of a crane to the wavering lines of descent on a genealogical chart in the 1400s. The phrase was borrowed into M.E. as *pedegru* and was soon changed to *pedigree*. EWPO. *Compare* Chicken Scratches; Hen Scratching.

PEEP   *a peep.* The slightest sound: "We didn't hear a *peep* out of him." Source: BIRD. *Peep* is echoic for the *cheep* or *chirp* of a baby bird (WNNCD: 15th cent.), which is soft and high-pitched. Baby birds peep only when the parent arrives with food; otherwise, they remain silent. Children are sometimes told by their parents, "I don't want to hear another *peep* out of you," because it is not instinctive for children to keep quiet. A related term is *pipe* (WNNCD: 1889), as in to *pipe up* "to speak up"; and the *pip* of *pipsqueak* (WNNCD: 1910) "a small, insignificant person (usu. male)" may also come from *peep*. ATWS; DEI; ROE; WNWD.

PEN   *a pen.* An instrument for writing or drawing with ink. WNNCD: 14th cent. Source: BIRD. The bird figures in this metaphor because *pen* derives from Lat. *penna* "feather." In the 14th cent., the word came to be applied also to a goose feather, or *quill*, that was sharpened and dipped in ink for writing; and in the 15th cent., *pen* came to function also as a verb, as in "to *pen* a letter." (*Pencil* [q.v.] has a different derivation.) ATWS.

PENCIL   *a pencil.* A writing or drawing instrument that employs graphite as its marking substance. Source: ANIMAL. Literally, a *pencil* is a "little tail" (fr. Lat. *penicillus*, the dim. of Lat. *penis* "tail"). Figuratively, a pencil was orig. a "little brush," of the sort used by painters and illuminators (WNNCD: 14th cent.)— i.e., a brush composed of hairs from the tails of cattle or horses. A modern *pencil* is either a wooden rod filled with solid graphite (i.e., carbon—not lead!) or a metal or plastic case containing an independently retractable rod of graphite. ATWS. *Compare* Pen.

PERCH   *a perch; to perch.* A narrow, elevated seat; to sit on a narrow, elevated seat or on the edge of something. Source: BIRD. Birds perch on wires, fences, or branches while resting or sleeping. The perch of domestic fowl and pet birds is constructed to resemble the height and width of a natural perch. Humans *perch* on the arms of chairs; on the hoods, tops, and trunks of cars; and on the edges of buildings and cliffs—in order to get a better or closer look at something. When a person is told to *come down off your perch*, or is *knocked off his/her perch*, he/she is regarded as being—or having been—haughty or conceited. ATWS; HTB.

PESKY   *See* Pest.

PEST   *a pest.* An annoying person: a nuisance. Source: ANIMAL. Literally, a pest is an animal that carries the pestilence, or plague: e.g., a rat. Figuratively, a *pest* is either an animal that destroys human property or a human that *pesters* (from a different source) other humans. The adj. *pesky* (WNNCD: 1775), meaning "troublesome or annoying," is a modified derivative of *pesty*, which it has replaced; lit., it means "behaving like a pest."

PESTER   *to pester someone.* To annoy or irritate someone. Source: HORSE. Literally, to *pester* someone is to hobble them—i.e., to tie their legs together, as one would an unharnessed or unsaddled horse during a layover. Metaphorically, to *pester* someone is to harass or worry them the way a hobble annoys a horse. ATWS. *See also* Hobbled.

PET   *a pet.* A pampered child; a loving spouse; a favorite student; etc. Source: ANIMAL (*). The animal that is kept for pleasure and companionship—such as a cat or dog—is not the source of this noun. The word derives from the Eng. alteration of Fr. *petit* "small," and it orig. applied to the spoiled child (WNNCD: 1508), not the coddled animal. By 1584, however, the word was being used attributively for both cats and dogs and young farm animals (e.g., a *pet* pig, a *pet* lamb); and by 1629 a verb had developed for the indulging of these beloved animals, such as stroking and pampering them. From this behavior toward animal pets has developed the word *petting* for the amorous kissing, fondling, caressing, and embracing—also called "necking"—that goes on between lovers. Some of the modern uses of *pet*—as in *pet peeve* (WNNCD: ca. 1919) and *pet rock*—also seem to derive from the animal sense of the word, as does *teacher's pet* (WNNCD: ca. 1930). AID; ATWS; CE; DEI; WNWD.

PETCOCK   *See* Cock (n).

PET PEEVE   *See* Pet.

PET ROCK   *See* Pet.

PETTING   *See* Pet.

PHOENIX   *See* Rise like a Phoenix.

PHOENIXLIKE   *See* Rise like a Phoenix.

PHOTO FINISH   *See* Go down to the Wire.

PICK OF THE LITTER   *See* Litter.

PIE   *a pie.* A food dish consisting of a pastry shell filled with fruit, meat, or vegetables. WNNCD: 14th cent. Source: MAGPIE (?). WNNCD: 1605. The names for the pastry dish and the large bird (orig. a *pie*) may both derive from Lat. *pica* "magpie." It is also possible that the magpie's habit of building a large, domed nest (or inverted "pie") in which it stores objects of all kinds may have suggested the metaphor. ATWS. *See also* Magpie.

PIEBALD   *to be piebald.* To consist of at least two colors, esp. black and white: e.g., a *piebald* horse is covered with black and white blotches. WNNCD: 1594. Source: MAGPIE. WNNCD: 1605. The American magpie is mostly black, with white shoulders and wingtips and a green tail. The *pie* in *piebald* is from the black part of the magpie, and the *bald* is from the white. ATWS; HF. *Compare* Bald as a Coot; Bald as an Eagle.

PIG (1)   *a pig.* A rough-cast ingot of iron. IRCD: 1570s. Source: PIG. WNNCD: 13th cent. Molten iron was once poured directly into a channel in a bed of sand, from which smaller channels extended from each side. The main channel was called a *sow*, and the side channels were called *pigs*, based on the resemblance of the formation to a sow nursing her piglets. The result was a number of crude ingots, called *pig iron* (WNNCD: 1665), which were later refined to produce wrought iron and steel. ATWS; BDPF; LCRH. *See also* Sow.

PIG (2)   *a pig.* A greedy, gluttonous, filthy, or obese person. Source: PIG. WNNCD: 13th cent. A domestic pig is a swine that weighs up to approx. 150 pounds. Little pigs are sometimes called *piglets*; and pigs larger than 150 pounds are called *hogs*. Pigs of any size always seem to be sloppy, dirty, and overweight— characteristics that are regarded as undesirable in humans. ATWS; IRCD. *See also* Make a Pig of Yourself.

PIG (3)   A police officer: a "cop." IHAT: 1848. Source: PIG. WNNCD: 13th cent. Student demonstrators against the War in Vietnam in the 1960s may have believed that they were coining a term when they referred to the police as *pigs*. But they were simply reviving a slang term that had been alive in the last half of the 19th cent. but died in the first half of the 20th. *Pig* was selected because it was the worst thing that the demonstrators could think of to call their "oppressors." EWPO; IHAT; SHM. *See also* Pig (2); Screw.

PIG BOAT   *a pig boat.* A submarine. WNNCD: 1921. Source: PIG. WNNCD: 13th cent. The submarine does look a little bit like a pig—long and round, with a "screw" at the end—but it lacks the blunt snout and long ears (and, of course, the legs). Actually, it looks more like a *porpoise* (q.v.), which is also named after the pig. But the steel boat probably gets its name from a *pig* of iron (or *pig iron* [q.v.]), which is oblong and legless. *Compare* Tin Fish.

PIGEON   *a pigeon.* A person who is gullible or easily fooled: a "sucker"; a dupe; a *gull* (q.v.). SOED: 1593. Source: PIGEON. WNNCD: 14th cent. A gullible person is an easy mark for con artists: a *pigeon* ready to be plucked. The analogy is to the vulnerability of the rock pigeon, which was introduced into North America from Europe and exists in great numbers in cities and rural areas. Pigeons are easily taken by net, snare, or shotgun. ATWS; BDPF; IRCD; LTA; NDAS; ST. *See also* Pigeon Drop; Pluck a Pigeon; Stool Pigeon.

PIGEON-BREASTED   *to be pigeon-breasted.* To have a protuding breast bone. IRCD: ca. 1850. Source: PIGEON. WNNCD: 14th cent. *Pigeon breast* (WNNCD: 1842) is a deformity of the human chest, caused by rickets, which is marked by a sharply projecting sternum. For the pigeon itself, the protruding breast bone is normal and is a sign of a healthy bird. *See also* Pigeon-livered; Pigeon-toed.

PIGEON DROP   *a pigeon drop.* An address, different from your own, at which you receive your mail; a con game or scam. Source: PIGEON. WNNCD: 14th cent. In the con game known as a *pigeon drop*, a *pigeon* or "mark" (A) is approached by a stranger (B) who tells A that B has found a wallet, purse, or envelope containing a large amount of money. B calls on a "complete stranger" (C, actually an accomplice of B) to hold the money and proposes that if A will contribute an equal amount of "good faith" money, B will do the same. If the owner is not found, A and B will split the total amount equally. A complies, and A's money and the con artists (B and C) are never seen again. In a variation of the game, after C has put A and B's money in an envelope, C pretends to get cold feet, returns the envelope to A, and departs hurriedly with B. When A opens the envelope, there is nothing in it but strips of paper. *See also* Pigeon; Pluck a Pigeon. *Compare* Badger Game.

PIGEON HAS FLOWN   *The pigeon has flown.* The suspect has escaped. Source: PIGEON. WNNCD: 14th cent. To the hunter, a *pigeon* is a target; to a con artist it is a "mark"; and to the police it is a person under surveillance. The hunter is happy when the pigeon "flies," but the con artist and the police are not. One thing about the pigeon, though: it will always return. *See also* Clay Pigeon; Pigeon; Stool Pigeon. *Compare* Eagle Flies on Friday.

PIGEONHOLE (n)   *a pigeonhole.* A single compartment in a bank of compartments (EWPO: late-19th cent.); a stereotypical category into which people can be conveniently placed. Source: PIGEON. WNNCD: 14th cent. An avian pigeonhole is the small hole in a dovecote through which a pigeon climbs to reach its nest. *Pigeonhole* is a name for a pattern of small compartments that was first extended to the openended boxes in a rolltop desk and now applies also to a bank of open mailboxes in an office. Placing a person in a *pigeonhole* involves oversimplifying that person's accomplishments and capabilities. ATWS; BDPF; CE; IRCD. *See also* Pigeonhole (v).

PIGEONHOLE (v)   *to pigeonhole someone or something.* To stereotype someone; to shelve something. Source: PIGEON. WNNCD: 14th cent. To *pigeonhole* a person is to compartmentalize them—e.g., as a nerd, a hunk, a bitch, etc. Such narrow labeling overlooks the person's broader accomplishments and abilities. To *pigeonhole* a proposal is to file it away so deeply that it can never be found. ATWS; BDPF; DEI; EWPO; IRCD. *See also* Pigeonhole (n).

PIGEON-LIVERED   *to be pigeon-livered.* To be mild-mannered to the point of cowardice. WNNCD: 1602. Source: PIGEON. WNNCD: 14th cent. The pigeon, like its cousin the dove, is a gentle bird that does not prey on other animals but feeds on seeds, grains, and berries. However, it is easily frightened and never stands its ground. (*Chicken-livered* [q.v.] is gradually replacing *pigeon-livered* as a label of cowardice.) *See also* Pigeon-breasted; Pigeon-toed.

PIGEON-TOED   *to be pigeon-toed.* To have feet that turn inward when standing or walking. WNNCD: 1801. Source: PIGEON. WNNCD: 14th cent. The poor pigeon is maligned for a lot of things—for being *pigeon-breasted, pigeon-livered,* and *pigeon-toed.* But the fact is that the pigeon has to walk "*pigeon-toed*" because it has very short legs and a large chest and must turn its entire body with every step. (The dove does the same thing.) ATWS; CI; IRCD. *Compare* Duck Walk.

PIGGY   *a piggy.* A child's toe. Source: PIG. WNNCD: 13th cent. It is not certain why children's toes are called *piggies.* The reason may be that the toes are lined up to the foot like little pigs nursing a sow. There is a nursery rhyme that goes as follows (the adult grabbing each of the toes on one foot, in order, starting with the big toe): "This little piggy went to market. This little piggy stayed home. This little piggy had roast beef. This little piggy had none. And this little piggy"—the adult wiggles the little toe, as if it were a pig's tail—"cried 'oink oink oink' all the way home." ID. *See also* Pig (1). *Compare* Pinky.

PIGGYBACK (adv.)   *to ride piggyback.* For a young child to be carried on the back or shoulders of an adult. WNNCD: 1565. Source: PIG (?). WNNCD: 13th cent. This is probably not an animal metaphor, although the best way to carry a medium-sized pig is to drape it around your neck. The original form of the adverb was *a pick pack,* which evolved into *pick-a-pack, pick-a-back, pig-a-back, pigaback,* and eventually, *piggyback.* The metaphor has been expanded, in the 20th cent., to include semitrailers that *ride piggyback* on railroad flatcars—and, by alteration, to include semitrailers that are carried *birdieback* in the holds of cargo planes. ATWS; BDPF; EWPO; HF; ID; IRCD; MDWPO; NDAS; ST. *See also* Piggyback (n); Piggyback (v).

PIGGYBACK (n)   *a piggyback.* A railroad flatcar carrying loaded semitrailers; an "elbow" on an IV tube for injecting an additional drug into the line. Source: PIG (?). WNNCD: 13th cent. The noun *piggyback* is derived from the adverb *piggyback* (q.v.), which may or may not have been inspired by a farmer carrying a pig on his/her back or shoulders. In the case of both the semitrailer and the elbow, something smaller is carried by, or attached to, something similar but larger. *See also* Piggyback (v).

PIGGYBACK (v) *to piggyback something on(to) something else.* To use something large to carry something similar but smaller. Source: PIG (?). WNNCD: 13th cent. The verb *piggyback* is derived from the adverb *piggyback* (q.v.), which may or may not be an animal metaphor but recalls the pastoral scene of a farmer carrying a pig on his/her back or shoulders. In the 20th cent., a loaded semitrailer can be *piggybacked* on a railroad flatcar, and an additional drug can be piggybacked on an IV that is already carrying another solution, such as saline. *See also* Piggyback (n).

PIGGY BANK *a piggy bank.* A coin bank. WNNCD: 1941. Source: PIG. WNNCD: 13th cent. The *piggy bank* is so called because in the early 1900s (EWPO: 1909) it was made in the shape of a pig; and before that, coins were sometimes collected in an earthenware jar called a *pygg* (IRCD: 15th cent.). Nowadays, a *piggy bank* can be made in any shape and can store both coins and bills. ATWS; BDPF.

PIGHEADED *to be pigheaded.* To be stubborn. WNNCD: 1620. Source: PIG. WNNCD: 13th cent. Pigs are thought to be *as stubborn as mules* (q.v.); but mules are beasts of burden, while pigs are providers of pork. In the animal kingdom, stubbornness is often associated with intelligence: the more intelligent the animal is, the more stubborn it is. Pigs are among the most intelligent of farm animals, so that may account for their refusal to be herded or driven. ATWS; CH; DEI; IRCD. *Compare* Bullheaded; Mulish.

PIG IRON *See* Pig (1).

PIG LATIN Mock Latin: a popular "secret language" of children in which the initial consonants of English words are transferred to the ends of those words, followed by the syllable *ay*: e.g., *igpay atinlay* "pig latin" (or "pig Latin"). WNNCD: 1931. Source: PIG. WNNCD: 13th cent. *Pig latin*, earlier called *hog latin*, is much older than 1931, when it was first recorded. (Both terms were preceded by *dog latin* [q.v.].) *Pig latin* was so named because it sounded—to adults—like the grunting of pigs or hogs. ATWS; EWPO; IRCD.

PIG OUT *to pig out.* To gorge yourself on your favorite food. WNNCD: 1978. Source: PIG. WNNCD: 13th cent. *Pigging out* is usu. done after a period of restraint from overeating. *Bulimics* (q.v.) do it, i.e., "binge," and then follow up with a "purge"; but most people just accept the consequences of *pigging out*: a stomach ache and an eventual weight gain. IRCD. *See also* Eat like a Pig; Make a Pig of Yourself.

PIGPEN   *a pigpen*. A dirty, messy room or building. Source: PIG. WNNCD: 13th cent. Pigs are usu. pictured wallowing in the mud, rooting up the barnyard, or dirtying their own pen. They are regarded as filthy animals. Human "pigs" copy the domestic pig's behavior by failing to clean up or straighten up their room or home until it acquires the reputation of being a slovenly place, fit only for pigs. ATWS; CH; IRCD. *See also* Pig (2); Pigsty; Steward.

PIGS IN THE BLANKET   Frankfurters wrapped in biscuit dough and baked. Source: PIG. WNNCD: 13th cent. In this metaphor the franks are the "pigs" and the dough is the "blanket." The delicacy is probably the forerunner of the *hot dog* (q.v.) in a bun. The "pigs" and the "dogs" suggest that these meals were eaten primarily by children. A variation of this dish is oysters wrapped in bacon and baked—also called *pigs in the blanket* or *angels on horseback*. EWPO.

PIGSKIN   *a pigskin*. A football. IRCD: late 1890s. Source: PIG. WNNCD: 13th cent. From about 1880, the American football was made of pigskin, but now it is made of either cowhide (for college or professional use) or synthetic rubber (for high school or intramural use). The rubber football retains the pebbly surface of pigskin, but big-time players prefer the "tacky" feel of leather. LTA. *Compare* Horsehide.

PIGSTICKER   *a pigsticker*. A bayonet of the type used in WWI and WWII. NDAS: ca. 1918. Source: PIG. WNNCD: 13th cent. The Army bayonet was a thick, double-edged dagger about a foot long that was carried by a soldier and attached to the end of his rifle for close combat. The term *pigsticker* was employed earlier for a blade used to bleed a pig for slaughter. The original *pigsticker* (WNNCD: 1890) was a spear carried by a rider on horseback during a wild boar hunt. *Compare* Frog Sticker.

PIGSTY   *a pigsty*. A dirty, messy room or building. Source: PIG. WNNCD: 13th cent. The term *pigsty*, for a building in which pigs are housed, dates back to 1591. The term *pigpen* (q.v.), for a pen in which pigs are kept, appeared in 1803. Today, both terms are used, metaphorically, for filthy, unkempt places of human habitation—so disgusting they are suitable only for pigs. ATWS; IRCD. *See also* Steward.

PIG SWEAT   *See* Sweat like a Pig.

PIGTAIL   *a pigtail*. A twist of hair. WNNCD: ca. 1750. Source: PIG. WNNCD: 13th cent. A *pigtail* was orig. a twist of tobacco that resembled the curly tail of a pig (WNNCD: 1688). Then the name was applied to the *queue* (q.v.) worn by Chinese peasants and copied by British sailors (IRCD: early-18th cent.). Now, a *pigtail* is a braided or unbraided twist of hair—sometimes one on either side of the head—worn by young women and girls. ATWS; BDPF; EWPO. *See also* Screw. *Compare* Ponytail.

PINION   *See* Pinnacle.

PINK ELEPHANTS   Imaginary objects seen in alcohol- or drug-induced hallucinations. WNNCD: 1940. Source: ELEPHANT. WNNCD: 14th cent. During withdrawal from alcohol or LSD, persons sometimes experience delerium tremens (the DTs), in which imaginary animals and objects dance and float about the room. The image was captured beautifully in Walt Disney's *Fantasia*. DEI; IHAT. *Compare* Cold Turkey; White Elephant.

PINNACLE   *the pinnacle of success*. The acme, or highest point, of an illustrious career. Source: BIRD. *Pinnacle* is from Lat. *pinnaculum* "gable," the dim. of Lat. *pinna* "wing." A medieval *pinnacle* was a spire that anchored a flying buttress on a Gothic cathedral (WNNCD: 14th cent.). A modern *pinnacle* is either the summit of a mountain or the peak of a successful career. Other metaphors from Lat. *pinna* are *pinion* and *panache*. To *pinion* someone is to prevent them from escaping by binding their arms—similar to the way a domestic fowl is prevented from flying by clipping the *pinions*, or ends, of its wings (WNNCD: 1577). A *panache* (fr. It. *pennacchio*) was orig. an ornamental tuft of feathers worn on a helmet (WNNCD: 1553), but the abstract noun *panache* now means flamboyance of style or extreme self-confidence of manner. ATWS; MDWPO; WNWD.

PIN THE TAIL ON THE DONKEY   *to play "pin the tail on the donkey."* To play the children's game in which a blindfolded child attempts to pin a paper "tail" in the proper place on a paper donkey on the wall. Source: DONKEY. WNNCD: ca. 1785. To make the game more difficult, the child is spun around several times before starting off. The results are usu. amusing—and sometimes obscene. The selection of the donkey for the game illustrates the lack of respect that the hardworking animal has received over the centuries. ST. *Compare* Put a Tail on; Talk the Hind Leg off a Donkey.

PIPE UP   *See* Peep.

PIPSQUEAK   *See* Peep.

PIRANHA   *a piranha*. A vicious, bloodthirsty person. EWPO: 1914. Source: PIRANHA. WNNCD: 1869. The *piranha*, or "tooth-fish" (Braz. Port. *pira* "fish" + *ranha* "tooth," fr. an Amazonian Indian word), is a vicious carnivore that attacks humans and other large animals and strips their flesh to the bone in minutes. It was first reported by Theodore Roosevelt after a trip to the Amazon.

PIT AGAINST   *to pit someone against someone else.* To match someone against someone else in a campaign or athletic competition. SOED: 1754. Source: COCK. The verb *pit* derives from the noun *pit*, as in *cockpit* "a cockfighting arena." Two gamecocks, each equipped with sharp metal spurs (or "spars"), are *pitted against* each other in a contest of *sudden death* (q.v.). In politics and sports, the loser, although *crestfallen* (q.v.), survives. ATWS; MDWPO; ST.

PIT BULL   *a pit bull.* A bullterrier. Source: DOG. The *pit bull* is a cross between a bulldog and a terrier, bred for guarding and fighting. The bulldog provides the tenacious nature of the English bullbaiting dog, and the terrier contributes the longer legs of the French burrowing dog. The word *pit* indicates that the *pit bull* was orig. bred for fighting in the *pits*—i.e., in dogfights—but the modern *pit bull* is usu. kept as a guard dog or attack dog. ST. *See also* Bulldog (n).

PITFALL   *a pitfall.* A hidden danger. Source: ANIMAL. An animal *pitfall* (WNNCD: 14th cent.) is a deep pit camouflaged with a covering of light branches and leaves. When the wild animal walks across the covering, it falls into the pit and is unable to escape. A human *pitfall* (SOED: 1586) is a problem that you don't recognize until you encounter it, such as contaminated soil on a building site. A *bottomless pit* (DOC: 1835) is a need that can never be completely satisfied or a debt that can never be fully paid. The reference is to the *pitfall*, from which the animal cannot escape. ST.

PLAY CAT AND MOUSE   *to play cat and mouse with someone.* To toy with someone. HTB: 1913. Source: CAT; MOUSE. WNNCD: O.E. A cat loves to toy with a mouse that it has caught, esp. in view of its kittens. The cat holds the mouse down with one paw, pretends to ignore the mouse by turning aside, then pounces on the mouse as it tries to escape. Then the cycle starts all over again, until the cat decides to kill the mouse. Some sources say that the *cat and mouse game* (WNNCD: 1923) is intended as a demonstration of hunting techniques for the benefit of the kittens. People in authority and power sometimes play this sadistic game of "capture and release" with political prisoners—pretending to *let them off the hook* (q.v.) in return for information, then locking them up again until the next round of *cat and mouse* begins. The game gets its name from the nickname for a 1913 law passed by the British Parliament, the "Cat and Mouse Bill," which discharged fasting suffragettes from prison until they recovered their health—then imprisoned them again. The children's game of *cat and mouse*, in which a "cat" chases a "mouse," is not the source of the term. AID; ATWS; BDPF; CI; DEI; IRCD; LCRH; ST.

PLAY CHICKEN   *to play chicken.* To play a lethal game of "dare." LTA: 1930s. Source: CHICKEN. WNNCD: O.E. The game of *chicken* (q.v.) started with motorcycles and progressed to automobiles and motorboats. The object of the game is to determine which of two drivers, headed toward each other at high speed, will veer from the course at the last minute to avoid a collision. The one who does is said to *chicken out* (q.v.) or be a *chicken* (q.v.). IRCD. *See also* Chicken (adj.).

PLAYFUL AS A KITTEN *to be as playful as a kitten*. Source: CAT. Baby kittens love to play with a ball of yarn—chasing it when it rolls away, catching it and holding on for dear life, and enjoying every minute of it. Young women or girls who are as cute and *playful as a kitten* are said to be *kittenish* (WNNCD: 1754) and are sometimes addressed as "Kitten" by their fathers. The young of some other furbearing animals are also referred to as *kittens* (WNNCD: 14th cent.), and the *kit fox* of the western United States is so called because it is only a third the size of a red or gray fox. (Its young are called "cubs," however.) ATWS; CE; IRCD. *See also* Sex Kitten.

PLAY POSSUM *to play possum*. To feign ignorance, lack of interest, sleep, or death. DAE: 1822. Source: POSSUM. WNNCD: 1613. The possum (or *opossum*, 1610) of the eastern United States is the only American marsupial. The female has a pouch for its very young but carries its older offspring on its back. When cornered or captured, the possum curls up in a ball and feigns death. AID; ATWS; BDPF; CI; DEI; DOC; EWPO; HTB; IRCD; LCRH; MDWPO; SHM; ST. *See also* Roll over and Play Dead.

PLAY THE SEDULOUS APE *to play the (sedulous) ape*. To imitate your superiors unthinkingly and uncritically. MDWPO: late-19th cent. Source: APE. WNNCD: O.E. The best mimics among the apes are the nonanthropoid monkey and the anthropoid chimpanzee, both of which "ape" the actions of their caretakers and spectators in the zoo. ATWS. *See also* Ape (v); Jackanapes.

PLENTY MORE FISH IN THE OCEAN *There are plenty more fish in the ocean (or sea)*. There will be plenty of other opportunities to succeed. IRCD: 16th cent. Source: FISH. WNNCD: O.E. This expression is used when a big fish wiggles off your hook and gets away: There are lots of others where that one came from. In business, it is used when a bid fails or a prospective deal falls through. In courtship, it is used by a suitor when he/she is spurned by a potential lover. Also: X is *not the only fish in the ocean*. AID; ATWS; CH; CI; ST. *See also* Other Fish to Fry.

PLUCK (n) *to have a lot of pluck*. To have a lot of guts. Source: BIRD. The noun *pluck* derives from the verb *pluck* (q.v.); but what is plucked in this case is not the feathers of a bird but the internal organs (or *pluck*) of a dead animal, such as the heart, liver, and lungs. A person who has a lot of *pluck*, or is *plucky* (WNNCD: 1842), has courage, is willing to fight for a cause, and never gives up, regardless of the odds. LCRH.

PLUCK (v)   *to pluck someone or something.* To rob someone; to pick the strings of a musical instrument; to snatch someone from danger. Source: BIRD. All senses of the verb *pluck* derive from the action of pulling feathers from the skin of a bird (WNNCD: O.E.). Robbing someone of their possessions is like separating a bird from its feathers; picking the individual strings of a guitar (etc.) is like removing a bird's feathers one at a time; and snatching someone from danger is like saving a bird's beautiful plumage. ID. *See also* Pluck (n); Pluck a Pigeon.

PLUCK A PIGEON   *to pluck a pigeon.* To "con a sucker"; to "fleece a mark." IRCD: 16th cent. Source: PIGEON. WNNCD: O.E. To *pluck a pigeon* is to relieve a "sucker" of his/her money, as in the con game called a *pigeon drop* (q.v.). The analogy is to relieving a real pigeon of its feathers after shooting, snaring, or netting it and before cooking, baking, or roasting it. The "mark" and the bird are then *plucked pigeons.* BDPF; DEI. *See also* Pigeon.

PLUCKED PIGEON   *See* Pluck a Pigeon.

PLUCKY   *See* Pluck (n).

PLUMBER'S SNAKE   *See* Snake (n) (2).

PLUME   *a plume.* A tall, thin, lacy shaft of water, smoke, or snow. Source: BIRD. *Plume* is from Lat. *pluma* "a small, soft feather," but the 16th cent. ornamental feather, or *plume,* that was worn on a hat or helmet was as large and long as could be found. A sheet or curtain of water, smoke, or snow is also large and long, but it is as diaphonous as a soft, downy feather. The term *nom de plume* (WNNCD: 1873, fr. Fr. "pen name") is based on the early use of a large goose quill, or *plume,* that was sharpened to a point for writing with ink. *Compare* Rooster Tail.

POKE YOUR NOSE INTO SOMEONE ELSE'S BUSINESS   *See* Stick Your Nose into Someone Else's Business.

POLECAT   *a polecat.* A skunk. WNNCD: 14th cent. Source: CAT; CHICKEN. WNNCD: O.E. A polecat is neither a chicken (Fr. *poule,* as in Eng. *poultry*) nor a cat; but it *is* catlike, and it does like to eat chickens. Although the European *polecat* lacks stripes, the early American colonists applied the name to the black and white "chicken thief" that the Native Americans called a *skunk* (q.v.). The names *skunk* and *polecat* have coexisted ever since. CE; EWPO; HF; MDWPO.

POLITICAL ANIMAL   *a political animal.* A person with a passion and talent for politics. SPD: ca. 1933. Source: ANIMAL. Animals are not political, of course, because they lack civilization and formal government. Humans have civilization and government, but few of them are actively involved in the affairs of state, and even fewer regard themselves as professional politicians. George Bernard Shaw used the term *political animal* for the first time in Eng., but the originator of the term was Aristotle, who was reported to have said that "man is by nature a *political animal*." SPD.

POLTROON   *a poltroon*. A coward. WNNCD: ca. 1529. Source: HORSE. *Poltroon* is fr. O.It. *poltrone*, the augmentative of *poltro* "colt"; i.e., a *poltroon* is a "big baby." Young colts are timid and distrustful, and the metaphor *skittish as a young colt* fits them perfectly. A human *poltroon* is not only cowardly but lazy and spiritless as well. CH; EWPO.

POMMEL HORSE   *a pommel horse*. An apparatus on which male gymnasts perform certain individual balancing routines, supported only by their hands. WNNCD: 1908. Source: HORSE. WNNCD: O.E. The pommel horse, or *side horse* (WNNCD: ca. 1934), is probably so called because it is essentially a *vaulting horse* (q.v.) with two handles, parallel to each other but perpendicular to the length of the apparatus. The word *pommel* is appropriate, because it is another name for a saddle horn. ATWS.

PONY   *a pony*. A race horse; a small glass for beer or liquor; a crib sheet. Source: HORSE. All of the senses of *pony* (fr. Fr. *poulenet* "small horse, or colt") describe something smaller than normal. A *race horse* is smaller than a *draft horse*; a "shot glass," or *jigger* (q.v.), is smaller than a drinking glass; and a *crib*, or *trot* (for cheating on tests), is small enough to hide in your pocket. The verb *to pony up* "to hand over, or pay up, a small amount of money" (WNNCD: 1824) may or may not be related to the noun *pony*. ATWS; BDPF; EWPO; IRCD.

PONYTAIL   *a ponytail*. A bundle of hair. WNNCD: 1951. Source: HORSE. Literally, a pony tail is the tail of a small horse, or pony. Figuratively, a *ponytail* is an unbraided bundle of hair, held together with a ribbon or elastic band, at the back of the head of a woman—or at the back or on either side of the head of a girl. A single bundle of hair at the back of the head, held together by a rubber band, has also become popular among some men and boys. Even the horse has been given *ponytails*: a horse's mane is sometimes cut short and tied in a series of little "tails." ATWS; GTP; IRCD. *Compare* Pigtail; Queue.

PONY UP   *See* Pony.

POODLE CLOTH   *See* Poodle Cut.

POODLE CUT   *a poodle cut*. A woman's haircut that features short, tight curls. (Also called a *poodle perm*.) LTA: early 1950s. Source: POODLE. WNNCD: 1820. The poodle (fr. Ger. *pudelhund* "puddle hound") has a coat of heavy, tight curls, somewhat like that of a Persian lamb, which is trimmed to accentuate the head and chest and the extremities: the feet and tail. It has also inspired the word *poodle cloth*, or "terry cloth," which has a nubby surface. *Compare* Beehive Hairdo.

POODLE PERM   *See* Poodle Cut.

POOL SHARK   *a pool shark*. A pool "hustler": a skilled player who suckers others into losing money playing against him/her in pool. Source: SHARK. WNNCD: 1569. Just as the marine shark preys on the weaker and smaller fish in the sea, the *pool shark* preys on the young and innocent, who cannot resist a bet that they have no chance of winning. IRCD. *See also* Card Shark; Loan Shark; Shark.

POOR AS A CHURCH MOUSE   *to be as poor as a church mouse*. To be indigent or destitute. EWPO: 17th cent. Source: MOUSE. WNNCD: O.E. A *church mouse* is not a subspecies of mouse but a house mouse that inhabits a church. Nowadays that shouldn't be such a bad deal, what with the potluck dinners and the inevitable garbage. But 17th cent. churches lacked dining rooms and kitchens, so the mice had to subsist on bread and wine—no cheese. AID; ATWS; BDPF; DEI; DOC; HTB; ID; IRCD. *Compare* Poor as Job's Turkey.

POOR AS JOB'S TURKEY   *to be as poor as Job's turkey*. To be stripped of all your money and possessions. HOI: early-19th cent. Source: TURKEY. WNNCD: 1555. According to the book of Job, the Lord gave Satan permission to test Job's faith, so Satan stripped Job of all his livestock and possessions. The turkey was added by Haliburton's character Sam Slick, who said that Job's turkey survived, but it was so weak that it had to lean against something in order to gobble. BDPF; EWPO; MDWPO. *Compare* Poor as a Church Mouse.

POP FLY   *See* Fly (n) (1).

POPINJAY   *a popinjay*. A vain, supercilious, emptyheaded man. WNNCD: 1528. Source: PARROT; JAY. The bird called a *popinjay* (fr. M.Fr. *papejai*) is not a jay at all but a West African parrot. It was kept as a cage bird for many years because of its beautiful plumage and its ability to "talk." The human *popinjay* is also "beautiful," like the parrot, but he talks about as intelligently as a jay. *Popinjay* was once also the name for a wooden target, on a pole, in the shape of a parrot. ATWS; WNWD.

PORCELAIN   Fine, white, translucent chinaware. WNNCD: ca. 1540. Source: PIG. WNNCD: 13th cent. *Porcelain* derives from Lat. *porcellus* "little pig," the dim. of Lat. *porcus* "pig," by way of Italian and French. The word was first applied, metaphorically, to the cowrie shell, which resembles the part of the sow (the vulva) where little pigs come from. Later, it was transferred to Chinese earthenware, which has the same glossy white finish as the inside of a cowrie shell. BDPF; EWPO.

PORCUPINE   *a porcupine*. A hedgehog. WNNCD: 15th cent. Source: PIG. Both of the popular names for this prickly rodent derive from swine: *porcupine* fr. Lat.

porcus "pig," and *hedgehog* fr. O.E. *hog* "adult pig." *Pig* fits the animal better than *hog*, however, because an adult porcupine or hedgehog weighs between 40 and 50 pounds, the weight of a medium size pig. HF; ROE. *See also* Porpoise (n).

PORCUPINEFISH *a porcupinefish.* A prickly marine fish. Source: PORCUPINE. WNNCD: 15th cent. The *porcupinefish*, also called a "balloon fish," has spikelike spines that are erected, for protection, when the fish inflates itself with water— or, when caught, with air. The American porcupine also erects its prickly spines when threatened, and it may even curl up like a ball of spikes. *See also* Bristle with Anger; Prickly as a Hedgehog.

PORK BARREL *a pork barrel.* A legislative appropriation that benefits only a small congressional district and its representative. WNNCD: 1904. Source: PIG. *Pork barrel politics* has been practiced since Civil War times, but the label was not applied until the early-20th cent. The reference is to the preserving of *pork* (fr. Lat. *porcus* "pig") by curing it with salt and storing it in barrels. Before the abolition of slavery, plantation owners doled out allowances of the salted pork, or "fatback," to the slaves at regular intervals. BDPF; EWPO; GTP; HTB; LCRH; SPD. *See also* Fat Cat.

PORK BARREL POLITICS *See* Pork Barrel.

PORKER *a little porker.* A chubby little child. Source: PIG. On the farm, a *porker* (fr. Lat. *porcus*) is a pig weighing approx. 125 pounds that is being fattened for local consumption. Pigs that weigh more than 150 pounds, called "hogs," are usu. fattened for sale and eventual slaughter. A chubby child, crawling around on all fours, does bear a resemblance to the fat little pig. *Compare* Rug Rat.

PORKPIE HAT *a porkpie hat.* A hat with a flat, indented top and a narrow brim. WNNCD: 1860. Source: PIG. The *porkpie hat* is so called because someone thought it looked like a pork pie. Actually, it looks like any double-crusted pie in which the edge is higher than the center. The brim does not figure in the metaphor. GTP.

PORPOISE (n) *a porpoise.* A dolphin. WNNCD: 14th cent. Source: PIG. A porpoise is lit. a "pig fish" (fr. Lat. *porcus* "pig" + *piscis* "fish"—"the pig of the sea"). The analogy is based on the shape and size of the beak of the porpoise and the snout of the pig—and on the smooth skin of the porpoise and the almost hairless skin of the pig. EWPO; ROE. *See also* Porpoise (v).

PORPOISE (v) *to porpoise.* For a swimmer to propel him-/herself underwater by undulating the body in an up-and-down motion, with the arms at the side of the body and the legs held tightly together. Source: PORPOISE. WNNCD: 14th cent. The *porpoise* (fr. Lat. for "pig fish") is a small, toothed whale which, like the larger dolphin, propels itself through the ocean water in a similar manner. *See also* Porpoise (n). *Compare* Dolphin Kick.

POUNCE *to pounce on someone or something.* To leap on someone; to seize an opportunity. Source: BIRD. The verb *pounce* (WNNCD: 1744) derives from the noun *pounce* "the claw or talon of a bird of prey" (WNNCD: 15th cent.). A raptor, such as an eagle, is said to *pounce* on a prey when it swoops down on it and seizes it in its talons. The meaning was first extended to other animals—e.g., to a cat *pouncing* on a mouse—and then to humans—e.g., to a child *pouncing* on a cat. A more abstract sense of *pounce* is *to leap at the chance*—i.e., to take advantage of an opportunity or to profit from someone else's misfortune. IRCD.

POUND OF FEATHERS *See* Feather (n).

PRAIRIE DOG *a prairie dog.* A burrowing rodent of the Western prairie. WNNCD: 1774. Source: DOG. WNNCD: O.E. The prairie dog, which is related to the woodchuck, or *groundhog* (q.v.), looks more like a cat than a dog; but it does bark like a dog, and that's how it got its name. EWPO.

PRAIRIE OYSTERS The testicles of a bull calf—fried and served as a delicacy, esp. to unsuspecting tourists in the Wild West. IHAT: 1905. Source: OYSTER. WNNCD: 14th cent. Oysters, which are marine bivalve mollusks, aren't found anywhere near the Western Prairie, so pioneers from the East Coast substituted the next best thing—calf testicles, which are routinely removed by cattle raisers to produce tamer and bulkier steers. Some people regard them as aphrodisiacs. The term *prairie oyster* (sing.) is also applied to a "morning after" drink—a remedy for a hangover. It consists of a raw egg (the "oyster") in tomato juice, fruit juice, beer, or whiskey, seasoned with Worchestershire sauce. DEOD; EWPO. *See also* Calf Fries; Mountain Oyster.

PRANCE *to prance around.* To leap about in a lively manner; to strut around in an arrogant manner. Source: HORSE. A horse "prances" when it springs up on its hind legs, moving forward like a kangaroo. This is gen. a sign of spirit and playfulness, although the same action while standing still, called *rearing up*, is a sign of displeasure with the rider and an attempt to unseat him or her. Children *pounce* about in a playful manner also, but adults sometimes *prance* about in a haughty or pretentious manner, as if they were showing off or mocking an adversary. WNWD. *See also* Like a Young Colt; Rampant.

PREDATOR *a predator.* A person who exploits others for his/her own benefit. WNNCD: 1912. Source: ANIMAL (*). *Predator* is not an animal metaphor. The term was orig. employed for a person who plundered, pillaged, or raped. The labeling of animals as "predators" did not occur until later in the 20th cent., when the notion of *food chain* (WNNCD: 1926) was developed. Now it is common to lump cats and dogs with humans as predatory animals, or animals of prey. *See also* Low on the Food Chain. *Compare* Parasite; Scavenger.

PREEN *to preen.* To primp. WNNCD: 14th cent. Source: BIRD. Birds clean, trim, and align their feathers with their beaks. Humans dress themselves up in their best finery, then add finishing touches, with their hands, to an already perfect appearance. With birds, the action of preening is done for cleanliness and preventive maintenance; with humans, it is an act of vanity. ATWS; WNWD.

PREY *See* Prey on.

PREY ON *to prey on your mind.* For something worrisome to preoccupy your thoughts. SOED: 1798. Source: ANIMAL (*). The original meaning of the verb *prey* was "to raid and plunder for the sake of spoils or booty" (WNNCD: 13th cent.), and the booty was known as the *prey.* So the original predators were humans, not animals. However, the verb *prey* is now also associated today with predatory animals, such as big cats and raptorial birds, that hunt down their victims (or *prey*) and kill them for food. A person with a worried mind has *fallen prey* to the troubles that are plaguing him or her; and a person who has been swindled has *fallen prey* to con artists. CI; ST.

PRICES ARE SOARING *See* Soar.

PRICKLY AS A HEDGEHOG *to be as prickly as a hedgehog.* To be as thorny as a rose bush; to be irritable and unapproachable. Source: HEDGEHOG. WNNCD: 15th cent. The *hedgehog* (q.v.) is the larger European counterpart (up to 57 pounds) of the smaller American porcupine (up to 40 pounds). While both animals are covered with spines, those on the hedgehog can be as long as 16 inches. DEI. *See also* Hedgehog Gene. *Compare* Porcupine; Sea Urchin; Urchin.

PRICK UP YOUR EARS *to prick up your ears.* To pay close attention. DOC: 1610. Source: ANIMAL. Many animals, such as dogs and horses, elevate their ears when they hear a sudden or unfamiliar sound; and horses are able to rotate their ears in the direction of the sound. Humans do not have such control over their ears, but they fig. *prick up their ears* when they suddenly raise their head or cock it toward the source of the sound. This occurs when they hear something interesting or surprising, esp. when it concerns themselves. ATWS; BDPF; CI; DEI; GTP. *Compare* Cock Your Head.

PRIDE OF PLACE *one's pride of place.* The apex of one's career. WNNCD: 1623. Source: FALCON. The falcon, or female hawk trained for the hunt, soars up to two miles high searching for its game. The apex of its flight, just before it dives for the kill, is called its *pride of place.* (*See* Shakespeare's *Macbeth*, 1606: Act I, Scene 4.) CI; ST.

PRIZE CATCH   *See* Good Catch.

PROUD AS A PEACOCK   *to be as proud as a peacock.* To be filled with self-pride. EWPO: 14th cent. Source: PEACOCK. WNNCD: 14th cent. The Indian peacock is regarded as the most beautiful bird in the world, and it seems to know that, as it struts about during the mating season with its lacy, five-foot wide, brilliantly colored tail fan backgrounding its blue neck and head. AID; ATWS; BDPF; CI; DEI; EWPO; IRCD. *See also* Strut like a Peacock; Stuck-up.

PROWL   *to prowl (around).* To wander about stealthily. WNNCD: 14th cent. Source: ANIMAL. Predatory animals prowl around in search of prey. Predatory humans *prowl around* on someone else's property looking for trouble (i.e., *prowlers*); they *prowl around* in squad cars (i.e., *prowl cars*) looking for lawbreakers; and they *prowl around* (or go *on the prowl*) looking for sexual partners. CE.

PROWL CAR   *See* Prowl.

PROWLER   *See* Prowl.

PUCE   *the color puce.* Dark red. WNNCD: 1787. Source: FLEA. The flea is a tiny (1 mm) insect that nests in rugs and carpets and feeds on the blood of animals and humans. How the French were able to observe the *color* of the tiny flea (*puce*, fr. Fr. *puce* "flea, or flea color") is uncertain; but it must have been with a microscope, and the flea must have been filled with dark red blood at the time. ATWS. *See also* Flea-bitten; Flea Market. *Compare* Tight as a Tick.

PUFFED WITH PRIDE   *to be puffed with pride.* To be so proud of yourself that you are about to burst. Source: BIRD. The word *pride* in this expression reveals that it is not a fish or reptile metaphor: the puffer fish (or "blowfish") and the puff adder (and the false puff adder, or *hognose snake* [q.v.]) cause their heads to swell up when they are threatened, not when they are showing off. Among the birds, however, the male turkey, grouse, and partridge puff up their chests—and fan their tail feathers—when they are courting. It's as if they are saying to the female: "See how handsome I am!" Humans also *puff up with pride* over the birth and accomplishments of their children.

PUFF UP WITH PRIDE   *See* Puffed with Pride.

PUG NOSE   *a pug nose.* A short, flat nose; a short, turned-up nose. WNNCD: 1778. Source: DOG. The *pug nose* is named for that of the *pug* dog (WNNCD: 1749), which has a flattened face with exposed nostrils. On humans, a *pug nose* is thought to be rather cute, probably because many people have such long noses. The *pug nose* also makes a person look younger than he/she really is, like the "button nose" of a baby. ATWS; EWPO; MDWPO.

PULL A RABBIT OUT OF A HAT   *to pull a rabbit out of a hat.* To save the day: to snatch victory from the jaws of defeat. DOC: 1967. Source: RABBIT. WNNCD: 14th cent. The magician displays an empty top hat, places it top-down on a table, and pulls out a white rabbit. This is the kind of magic that heroes perform when they do the impossible—making something out of nothing. A rabbit is probably used because it is docile; a white one is probably used because it is highly visible. ATWS; DEI; IRCD. *Compare* Make a Silk Purse out of a Sow's Ear.

PULL AWAY FROM THE FIELD   *to pull away from the field.* To take a commanding lead. Source: HORSE. In a horse race, the "field" is the string of horses that leave the starting gate at exactly the same time but soon spread out into a loose pack. As the race continues, one of the horses may *break out of the pack* and take a commanding lead. If the leader then begins to *fade in the stretch* (q.v.), it is said to *come back to the field:* i.e., rather than the field catching up with the leader, the leader falls back into the pack. At the end of the race, the horse that finishes last is said to *trail the field.* All of these racing terms apply equally well, as metaphors, to athletes and political candidates. ST.

PULL CHESTNUTS OUT OF THE FIRE   *See* Cat's Paw.

PULL IN YOUR EYES   *Pull in your eyes!* (Said by one spouse—usu. female—to the other.) Stop ogling that attractive member of the opposite sex! Source: SNAIL. The land snail has eyes at the ends of the middle two of its four tentacles (or "horns"), which extend from the front part of its external "foot." If the snail senses danger, it backs into the shell that it has been dragging along at the rear, and the horns, including the ones with the eyes, are pulled in after it. (There may be a sexual connotation here also.) ATWS. *Compare* Draw in Your Horns.

PULL THE WOOL OVER SOMEONE'S EYES   *to pull the wool over someone's eyes.* To *hoodwink* someone (q.v.). Source: SHEEP. The sheep is the source of this metaphor, whether it derives from pulling a jurist's woolen wig down over his/ her eyes or pulling the unsheared skin of a dead sheep upward over its head. The latter activity is certainly older than the former. ATWS; DEI; DOC; HOI; ID.

PULL YOUR WEIGHT   *See* Put out to Pasture.

PUNCH THIS COW   *Punch this cow!* Step on the gas! Source: COW. WNNCD: O.E. *Punching cows* comes from the work of *cowpunchers* (WNNCD: 1878), or cowboys, who round up a herd of cattle and drive them from corral to range, range to range, back to the corral, and from the corral to market. Cowboys don't actually *hit* the "cows" (more likely steers) the way one would tromp on the accelerator to increase the speed of a vehicle.

PUPPY DOG   *a puppy dog.* A gentle giant. Source: DOG. WNNCD: O.E. Literally, a *puppy dog* (WNNCD: 1595) is a grown dog that is as playful and lovable as a young puppy. Figuratively, a *puppy dog* is a grown man, esp. one of large size, who may appear to be intimidating but is just as friendly and gentle as a puppy. *Compare* Pussycat; Teddy Bear.

PUPPY LOVE   Young love, between a boy and a girl. WNNCD: 1834. Source: DOG. Puppies fall in love with everybody—their siblings, their parents, the other pets in the house, and their human caretakers—and they will *follow them anywhere* (q.v.). That lasts for about a year, until they are no longer puppies. *Puppy love* among children is also temporary: Boy meets girl (or vice versa); boy falls in love with girl (or vice versa); and nobody worries about it, because they know it is only temporary and will end when school starts (or ends). A *lovesick puppy* is a young man who is head-over-heels in love with a young woman who doesn't even know he exists—like a puppy whose affection for its caretakers is not returned. ATWS; DEI; IRCD.

PUP TENT   *a pup tent.* A small tent in the shape of an inverted V. WNNCD: 1863. Source: DOG. The *pup tent* originated during the Civil War as a temporary shelter for two men. Each man contributed a canvas sheet, which they fastened together and supported with poles. The name *pup*—short for *puppy*—was given to the tent because it was not much bigger than a doghouse. IRCD.

PURPLE   *the color purple.* A color somewhere between red and blue: reddish blue; bluish red. WNNCD: 15th cent. Source: MOLLUSK. The mollusk (Gk. *porphyra*) that is the source of the color purple (Lat. *purpura*) is a variety in the eastern Mediterranean that yields a reddish blue dye called "Tyrian purple," a color long identified with royalty. ATWS; THT.

PURR LIKE A KITTEN   *to purr like a kitten.* For an engine to run smoothly and quietly. Source: CAT. A cat's purr is an audible, sustained vibration of its vocal cords when it is happy and contented. A kitten's purr is the same, except softer and barely audible. An internal combustion engine that *purrs like a kitten* is one that is well tuned and well muffled. A motorcycle engine *purrs* more like a cat. ATWS.

PUSSY   *a pussy; some pussy.* The female pudenda; sexual intercourse. WNNCD: 1878. Source: CAT. *Pussy* may be a loan translation of Fr. *minette* "kitten" or *chat* "cat," both of which are slang terms in the language for "vulva." The metaphor was first recorded in Eng. in the late-19th cent. but had been in popular use since the 17th cent. DEOD; IRCD; NDAS. *Compare* Beaver.

PUSSYCAT   *a pussycat.* A softy. Source: CAT. WNNCD: O.E. *Pussycat*—or *pussy* or *puss*—has been a nursery word for "cat" since the early-19th cent. (WNNCD:

1805), and it has also become a popular term of address for a lover or a child. With the metaphorical sense of "softy," a *pussycat* is either a person who is inherently harmless and likable, like a kitten, or one who is not as *bearish* (q.v.) as he/she seems but is more like a cuddly *teddy bear* (q.v.). IRCD; NDAS. *Compare* Puppy Dog.

PUSSYFOOT   *to pussyfoot around.* To move among people and issues quietly, in order to avoid confrontation. WNNCD: 1903. Source: CAT. Before its first recorded appearance as a metaphor, *pussyfoot* meant to tread softly and cautiously, like a cat stalking a mouse. In the early-20th cent. it acquired the additional sense of sidestepping issues, hedging, avoiding commitment, and gen. displaying cowardice. ATWS; DEI; EWPO; IRCD; LTA; SPD. *Compare* Weasel out.

PUSSY WILLOW   *a pussy willow.* A willow tree or shrub whose twigs bear velvety "catkins." WNNCD: 1869. Source: CAT. The *catkins* (WNNCD: 1578) on a pussy willow branch are little balls of silvery gray "velvet" that look and feel remarkably like the fur of a shorthaired cat or kitten. *Pussy* (q.v.) as an independent word for "cat" did not appear until the following decade (WNNCD: 1878). IRCD; WNWD. *See also* Pussycat.

PUT A BUG IN SOMEONE'S EAR   *See* Bug in Your Ear.

PUT ALL YOUR EGGS IN ONE BASKET   *See* Don't Put All Your Eggs in One Basket.

PUT A MUZZLE ON   *See* Muzzle (v).

PUT A TAIL ON   *See* Tail (n).

PUT DOWN   *See* Put Someone Out of Their Misery.

PUT IN MOTHBALLS   *to put something in mothballs.* To put military equipment in protective storage. WNNCD: 1943. Source: MOTH. WNNCD: O.E. Garments made of wool, feathers, or fur can be protected from the hungry larvae of the clothes moth by storing them with mothballs made of camphor or naphthalene. Military equipment made of metal can be protected from the ravages of rust by spraying it with plastic. DOC. *See also* Cocoon; Mothball; Mothball Fleet.

PUT ON THE DOG   *to put on the dog.* To put on airs; to show off. LTA: 1871. Source: DOG. WNNCD: O.E. This metaphor probably alludes to the *lap dog,* which, dressed up in a jeweled collar and fancy jacket, once sat on its owner's lap, rode in the owner's carriage, and was carried in the owner's arms wherever he/she went, even to restaurants and parties. This practice led to the transfer of "showing off the dog" to showing off the dog owner's wealth, jewelry, and style in general. AID; ATWS; BDPF; EWPO; HTB; ID; IRCD; MDWPO.

PUT ON THE FEED BAG   *to put on—or strap on—the (old) feed bag.* To eat. Source: HORSE. A feed bag is a canvas bag containing oats or other grain that fits over the muzzle of a horse. It is used when the horse is fully harnessed and hitched to a load, esp. in town, so that the horse will not have to be unharnessed and allowed to graze. When a person says, "Let's *strap on the old feed bag,*" he/she means "Let's eat!" AID; ATWS.

PUT OUT TO PASTURE   *to be put out to pasture.* To be retired or forced to retire. Source: HORSE. *Workhorses* (q.v.) are put out to pasture with the cows when they can no longer *pull their weight.* Racehorses are put out to pasture by themselves or with other *old war horses* (q.v.) when they can no longer *keep pace with the field* (q.v.). People are *put out to pasture* when they reach a certain age or become expendable. ATWS.

PUT SOMEONE ON A SHORT LEASH   *See* On a Short Leash.

PUT SOMEONE OUT OF THEIR MISERY   *to put someone out of their misery.* To give someone the object or information that they have been "dying for." Source: ANIMAL. A household pet is put out of its misery—from old age or illness—when it is *put to sleep* by the owner or veterinarian, and a racehorse is put out of its misery when it breaks its leg and is *put down* by the track's veterinarian. Soldiers were once *put out of their misery* by a coup de grace from a sword or pistol, but the metaphor in question is based on the termination of the life of a sick or injured animal. DEI.

PUT SOMEONE THROUGH THEIR PACES   *to put someone through their paces.* To force someone to demonstrate their skills and/or capabilities. Source: HORSE. A show horse *goes through its paces* for judges or prospective buyers to demonstrate its discipline and to perform the various gaits that it has been taught. People are *put through their paces* when they are auditioned for a job or a role: They must demonstrate their skills and versatility to the employers or judges. ATWS; CI; ST.

PUT THE CART BEFORE THE HORSE   *to put the cart before the horse.* To get your priorities mixed up. DOC: 1520. Source: HORSE. WNNCD: O.E. Normally, the horse comes first, followed by the cart—although donkeys in mines push the empty cart in and pull the loaded cart out. (The carts are on tracks.) Homer *put the cart before the horse* when he revealed the moral of his story before telling it. A coed puts the *heart* before the *course* when she drops out of school to get married. And the term *backasswards* is a graphic example of a horse/cart reversal (of *ass backwards*). AID; ATWS; BDPF; CI; DEI; EWPO; HOI; ID; IRCD; NDAS. *See also* Lock the Barn Door.

PUT THE FOX IN CHARGE OF THE HENHOUSE *to put the fox in charge of the henhouse.* To put the predator in charge of the prey. Source: FOX. WNNCD: O.E. A fox would like nothing better than to be put in charge of a henhouse, because chickens are its natural prey. A comparable mistake on the human level would be to appoint an embezzler as chief accountant or a child molester as principal of a school. *See also* Fox Guarding the Henhouse.

PUT THE STING ON *See* Sting (n).

PUT TO SLEEP *See* Put Someone Out of Their Misery.

PUT YOUR HEAD IN THE LION'S MOUTH *to put your head in the lion's mouth.* To place yourself in great danger. Source: LION. WNNCD: 12th cent. The *lion's mouth* (q.v.) was a metaphor for danger as far back as biblical times, but no one was foolhardy enough to deliberately stick his head in one until modern times. Now the trick is the highlight of a lion tamer's act in the circus. CI; DEI.

PUT YOUR NECK ON THE LINE *See* Stick Your Neck out.

Q

Q   *the letter "Q."* The "monkey" letter. Source: MONKEY. Q is the 17th letter of the English alphabet and the 19th letter of the Hebrew "alphabet." In the Phoenician "alphabet," which was the source of the Hebrew "alphabet," the letter Q (𝒫) was called *qoph* "monkey." Whether or not the tail of the Q represents the tail of the monkey is uncertain, but it has always been there. ATWS. *See also* Alphabet. *Compare* A; C; G; R.

QUACK   *a quack.* A charlatan; an unlicensed or incompetent physician. WNNCD: 1638. Source: DUCK. *Quack* is short for *quacksalver* (WNNCD: 1579): a "medicine man" who once peddled phony cure-alls in the streets and at fairs, carnivals, and tent shows. The charlatan was so called because he *quacked* (or cried out, like a duck) the merits of his *salves* (or bogus medicines) to anyone who would listen. When *quack* is applied to a physician, it implies not only the prescription of the wrong medicines but the faulty diagnosis and treatment of illnesses or injuries. ATWS; BDPF; CE; EWPO; IRCD. *Compare* Barker.

QUAHOG   *a quahog.* A thick-shelled New England clam. WNNCD: 1753. Source: HOG. WNNCD: O.E. The association of the clam with a hog is due to folk etymology. *Quahog* is a shortening and modification of Narraganset *poquahock*, which has the same meaning. That such confusion is excusable is evidenced in such other metaphors as *groundhog* (q.v.) and *sweathog* (q.v.), both of which are also East Coast terms. HF.

QUAIL (n)   *a quail.* A sexually attractive young woman. EWPO: CA. 1850. Source: QUAIL. WNNCD: 14th cent. The quail, a small game bird related to the partridge, grouse, and bobwhite, employs camouflage, esp. on the female, for protection. It is the male, in some subspecies, not the female, that is attractively colored. *See also* San Quentin Quail.

QUAIL (v)   *to quail.* To cower before something that is frightening or terrible. WNNCD: 1902. Source: QUAIL (*). WNNCD: 14th cent. The quail is indeed a timorous bird, but it is not the source of this metaphor. Instead, the source is M.E. *quailen* "to curdle" (15th cent.), as when one's blood curdles in terror. EWPO; GTP. *See also* Quail (n). *Compare* Chicken out; Cower.

QUARRY   *a quarry.* A prey. SOED: 1615. Source: DEER. In the 13th cent., a *querre* (fr. M.Fr. *cuirée* "skinned") was the entrails of a deer that were placed on the skin of the animal for the hounds to eat. In the 14th cent., a *quarry* was the pile of small game that had been killed in a hunt; and in the 15th or 16th cent., a *quarry* was the game that was being pursued, esp. by a falcon. By the 17th cent., *quarry* had assumed its modern meaning of "prey": the animal or person that is the object of pursuit. In the case of humans, this object is usu. a suspected or escaped criminal. ATWS; BDPF; EWPO; ST; THT.

QUEEN BEE   *a queen bee.* The dominant woman in an organization composed primarily of women. IRCD: early-17th cent. Source: BEE. WNNCD: O.E. In a beehive, females outnumber males approx forty-nine to one. There is only one queen, and the worker bees who attend her make up ninety percent of the rest of the hive. The worker bees are all infertile females, and the few (fertile) male drones die immediately after mating with the queen. So the queen bee has things pretty much to herself—at least for the four years or so of her life. *Compare* Dragon Lady; Mother Hen.

QUEER DUCK   *a queer—or odd—duck.* A strange or eccentric person. Source: DUCK. WNNCD: O.E. *Duck* is used in England to address close friends and relatives, and that may be the basis for this metaphor. However, *queer duck* may also have been inspired by the *ugly duckling* (q.v.), which was not a duck at all but a baby swan. The mother duck that raised it must indeed have thought it looked "queer" and behaved eccentrically for a duck. DOC. *See also* Duck Test. *Compare* Queer Fish.

QUEER FISH   *a queer fish.* A strange, odd, or eccentric person. Source: FISH. WNNCD: O.E. There are a lot of strange fish in the ocean, but their appearance and behavior are innate and cannot be changed. People who are regarded as *queer fish*, however, are not odd by nature but by nurture—either their own or that of society. BDPF; CI; DOC. *Compare* Queer Duck.

QUEUE   *a queue; to queue (up).* A *pigtail* (WNNCD: 1748); to get—or wait—in line (WNNCD: 1777). Source: ANIMAL. *Queue* was borrowed fr. Fr. *Queue* "tail," which derives from Lat. *cauda* "tail of an animal." In Britain, a *queue* is both a *pigtail* (q.v.) and a waiting line, and to *queue* (without *up*) is to form or stand in such a line. An alternative form of Lat. *cauda*, i.e., *coda*, has been borrowed into English from It., where it also means "tail." A *coda* (WNNCD: ca. 1753) is the final section of a literary, dramatic, or musical work that rounds it out, caps it off, and brings it to a conclusion. ATWS; EWPO; WNWD. *See also* Tail (n); Tail (v).

QUEUE UP   *See* Queue.

QUICK AS A CAT   *See* Move like a Cat.

QUICK LIKE A BUNNY   *to move quick like a bunny.* To move fast and without delay. NDAS: 1940s. Source: RABBIT. *Bunny* (or "little tail") is an affectionate name for the rabbit, which, like the white-tailed deer, only shows its fluffy tail when it is "spooked." Rabbits often sit motionless for an extended period; but when they are frightened, they leap straight up in the air, turn on a dime, and are gone. The metaphor is sometimes used in a parent's request to a child: "Would you go get the paper, quick like a bunny?"

QUID   *See* Ruminate.

QUIET AS A MOUSE   *to be as quiet as a mouse.* To be seen but not heard. DOC: 1859. Source: MOUSE. WNNCD: O.E. The common house mouse is usu. neither seen nor heard: it goes about its business of trashing your house in silence—and usu. at night. When you promise to be *as quiet as a mouse*, you are agreeing not to utter a single syllable if you are allowed to attend a movie, concert, etc. Also: "quiet as a *dormouse*" (q.v.). AID; ATWS; ID.

QUILTING BEE   *See* Bee.

R

R   *See* Dog's Letter.

RABBIT (1)   *a rabbit.* A prolific breeder. Source: RABBIT. WNNCD: 14th cent. The rabbit is one of the most prolific mammals. With a gestation period of approx. one month, the female rabbit can produce up to four litters a year, with up to 12 offspring in each, for a total of 48 offspring. Human *rabbits* are couples who produce approx. one child per year. *See also* Multiply like Rabbits.

RABBIT (2)   *a rabbit.* A mechanical figure that speeds along the inside rail of a race track just in front of the pursuing dogs. Source: RABBIT. WNNCD: 14th cent. The mechanical figure is that of a rabbit, and the dogs are greyhounds or whippets. It is unlikely that these intelligent dogs are fooled into thinking that the lure is a real bunny, but it probably does urge them on to greater speed. Dog racing—without the mechanical *rabbit*—goes back to at least medieval times. *See also* Quick like a Bunny; Rabbit (3).

RABBIT (3)   *a rabbit.* A runner who sacrifices his/her own chances of winning a long-distance race by setting an unusually fast pace from the very start. Source: RABBIT. WNNCD: 14th cent. The *rabbit's* purpose is to wear out the opposition and allow a teammate, who has lagged behind, to come to the front and establish a new record—or at least win the race. The term, which derives from the mechanical *rabbit* used in dog racing, also applies in car racing, where prize money is sometimes paid for the number of laps led. ATWS; IRCD. *See also* Quick like a Bunny; Rabbit (2).

RABBIT BALL   *a rabbit ball.* A home run in baseball. LTA: 1920. Source: RAB-BIT. WNNCD: 14th cent. A *rabbit ball* is a fast-pitched ball that leaps off the hitter's bat into the stands. This seldom happened until 1920, when a new, harder ball was introduced. (Babe Ruth promptly hit 54 home runs.) The analogy is to the speed and *jackrabbit start* (q.v.) of the rabbit. IRCD. *See also* Quick like a Bunny. *Compare* Dying Quail.

RABBIT DIED   *The rabbit died.* You're pregnant. Source: RABBIT. WNNCD: 14th cent. Until the 1960s, the *rabbit test* (q.v.) was the standard 20th cent. determiner of pregnancy. The female rabbit did not die from being injected with a woman's urine but was killed so that its ovaries could be examined for hemorrhaging. In other words, the rabbit *always* died, whether the woman was pregnant or not. (On a TV episode of M*A*S*H, Radar's rabbit was anesthesized and survived.)

RABBIT EARS   An indoor television antenna consisting of two movable rods extending from a single base. WNNCD: 1952. Source: RABBIT. WNNCD: 14th cent. The rods of a *rabbit ear antenna*, when in their typical V-shaped position, resemble the ears of a jackrabbit as seen from the front or back. The jackrabbit's ears are a lot shorter, but they are just as good at pulling in VHF signals as an indoor antenna. ATWS; IRCD. *Compare* Elephant Ear.

RABBIT FOOD   Salads and raw vegetables. IRCD: early-20th cent. Source: RAB-BIT. WNNCD: 14th cent. Rabbits are vegetarians. They eat everything, from roots to stalks to leaves to the bark of trees. Most humans are not vegetarians, and they—esp. husbands and children—sometimes complain about being served raw roots (e.g., carrots), stalks (e.g., celery), and "leaves" (e.g., lettuce). Humans do not eat bark, but they do eat rabbits. *See also* Welsh Rabbit.

RABBIT PUNCH   *a rabbit punch.* An illegal blow to the back of a boxer's neck or head. WNNCD: 1915. Source: RABBIT. WNNCD: 14th cent. *Rabbit punches* are outlawed in boxing because of the danger of damage to the opponent's central nervous system. This is exactly why the blow was once—and probably still is—used by trappers, hunters, and breeders to incapacitate rabbits. It is the quickest and most humane way to kill a wounded rabbit. ATWS; IRCD; SHM.

RABBIT'S FOOT   *a rabbit's foot.* A good-luck charm. IRCD: early-19th cent. Source: RABBIT. WNNCD: 14th cent. Rabbits are killed for their meat, their fur (esp. as lining for gloves), and their hind feet. Each dead rabbit can yield two "lucky" *rabbit's feet*, one of which can be carried in your pocket (usu. on a key chain) and rubbed for good luck. This talisman may bring good luck to you, but even two of them were not enough to bring good luck to the rabbit. MDWPO; SHM; WNWD.

RABBIT TEST *a rabbit test.* A pregnancy test. Source: RABBIT. WNNCD: 14th cent. *Rabbit test* has been a receding metaphor since the 1960s, when the use of a rabbit for testing for pregnancy was discontinued. Before then, the test worked as follows: A urine specimen from a woman was concentrated and injected into the ear vein of an adult female rabbit. After 48 hours the rabbit was killed and its ovaries were examined. If the ovaries had hemorrhages, the woman was pregnant. *See also* Rabbit Died. *Compare* Duck Test.

RACCOON EYES *to have raccoon eyes.* To have two black eyes—as from an automobile accident in which your head hit the steering wheel, dashboard, or windshield. Source: RACCOON. WNNCD: 1608. The raccoon (or *coon:* 1742) is a nocturnal animal of North America that is usu. seen raiding garbage cans. This "bandit" looks the part, with a black mask around both eyes. *See also* Coon's Age; Gone Coon.

RAGING BULL *a raging bull.* A violent man who is out of control and unstoppable. Source: BULL. WNNCD: O.E. Down on the farm, bulls become enraged by just about anything. They don't like people, they don't like to be penned up, they don't like to be moved, and they esp. don't like other bulls. In the rodeo, bulls don't like to be ridden; and in the bullring, bulls don't like to be stuck with bandilleros. Among people, a *raging bull* is a boxer, like Rocky Graziano (the subject of the movie *Raging Bull*), who fought his heart out and refused to quit.

RAGTAG AND BOBTAIL *See* Bobtail.

RAIL *to rail at someone.* To scold someone in harsh, abusive language. WNNCD: 15th cent. Source: ASS. The origin of this verb is assumed to be V.Lat. *ragolare* "to bray," by way of Old Provencal and M.Fr. The ass, or donkey, *rails* about its condition by making an unusual *hee haw* sound: *hee* on inspired air and *haw* on expired air. People find it harsh and abusive. *See also* Bray like a Donkey.

RAILBIRD *a railbird.* A spectator or bettor at a racetrack who stands at the rail fence, which separates the track from the grandstand, to get a better view of the finish. WNNCD: 1892. Source: BIRD. WNNCD: O.E. *Railbird* may have been patterned after the earlier *jailbird* (WNNCD: 1618), not only for the rhyme but because both "birds" are behind bars. (There really is a bird called a "rail.") ST.

RAIN CATS AND DOGS *to rain cats and dogs.* To rain extremely hard. IRCD: 1738. Source: CAT; DOG. WNNCD: O.E. No storm has ever been documented in which cats and dogs rained from the sky, although that could conceivably happen in a tornado or hurricane; but it once rained so hard in England that cats and dogs were drowned and swept away by the raging torrent. However, the metaphor probably derives from the fact that in Germanic mythology the cat was associated with storms, which it was thought to be able to predict, and the dog was associated with rain; so when it was *raining cats and dogs*, there was both wind and rain. It didn't hurt that cats and dogs are both familiar animals and natural enemies. AID; ATWS; BDPF; CI; DEI; DOC; EWPO; HOI; HTB; ID; LCRH; MDWPO; SHM.

RAISE SOMEONE'S HACKLES   *to raise someone's hackles*. (Also: *to make someone's hackles rise*.) To anger or infuriate someone. DOC: 1883. Source: COCK. When a rooster or gamecock becomes angry and is about to fight, it raises its long neck-feathers, or "hackles," provoking the same reaction in its opponent. For humans, it is the hair on the back of the neck that rises, and for cats and dogs it is the hair on the back *and* the neck. AID; CI; DEI; ST. *See also* Get Your Hackles Up. *Compare* Get Your Back Up.

RAM (n)   *See* Battering Ram; Ramrod (n).

RAM (v)   *to ram home an idea; to ram something down someone's throat*. To force an issue; to force someone to accept something that they don't want to accept. Source: SHEEP. The female sheep is a passive animal, but the adult male, or "ram," is an aggressive defender of its territory and status, butting heads with other males with tremendous force. This behavior was the basis for the words *battering ram* (q.v.) and *ramrod* (q.v.), the latter of which carries the sense of forcing something down a narrow passage. ATWS; DEI; IRCD.

RAMPAGE   *See* Rampant.

RAMPANT   *to run rampant*. To spread unrestrained. Source: ANIMAL. On a coat of arms, an animal (e.g., a horse) is *rampant* when it is *rearing up* on its hind legs and pawing the air with its forelegs (WNNCD: 14th cent.). A disease *runs rampant* when it spreads like wildfire, and the same applies to poverty, bankruptcy, and violence. The word *rampage* (WNNCD: 1861), meaning "reckless or riotous behavior," as in *to go on a rampage*, derives from the same source as *rampant*, as if the rioters were rising up to take arms against an opponent. ATWS.

RAMROD (n)   *a ramrod*. A metal rod used for loading or cleaning a firearm; a person who is responsible for overseeing discipline and productivity. Source: SHEEP. Muzzle-loading guns were, as the name implies, loaded from the end of the barrel. A charge, a ball, and a wadding were successively forced down the barrel by the use of a metal rod (WNNCD: 1757). Later, a shorter *ramrod*, equipped with a piece of cloth at the end, was used to clean the barrel of a shotgun, rifle, or small firearm. The analogy is to the *battering ram* (q.v.), which gets its name from the head-butting of the adult male sheep, or "ram." A human *ramrod* is one who pushes others to their limits, like a drill sergeant in the Army or a supervisor in a factory. IRCD. *See also* Ramrod (v); Stiff as a Ramrod.

RAMROD (v) *to ramrod something through.* To force the acceptance of an idea or the passage of a bill. WNNCD: 1940. Source: SHEEP. The forcing of a bill through a legislature is seen as analogous to the forcing of a charge, ball, and wadding through the barrel of a muzzle-loading gun. The loading was done with a long metal rod that got its name from the *battering ram* (q.v.), which in turn was named for the powerful charge of the adult male sheep, or "ram." ST. *See also* Ram (v); Ramrod (n).

RAPTURE A feeling of ecstasy, passion, or overwhelming emotion. WNNCD: 1605. Source: BIRD. Experiencing *rapture* is like being seized in the talons of a giant bird and carried to great heights. Birds of prey that catch their game in this fashion—such as eagles, hawks, and owls—are called *raptors* (fr. Lat. *rapere* "to snatch or seize"). *Rapture* can also be experienced by humans who go too far, for too long, into the depths of the ocean—called *rapture of the deep* or "nitrogen narcosis"—although birds can't be blamed for that problem. ST; WNWD.

RARE BIRD *a rare bird.* A special person with an unusual combination of skills and talents. Source: BIRD. WNNCD: O.E. Among animals, a "rare" bird is not one that is "underdone" but a bird that is (1) native but seldom seen, (2) nonnative or exotic, or (3) a member of an endangered species. Among humans, a *rare bird* is someone out of the ordinary, esp. one with contradictory interests, such as brain surgery and boxing. A *rare bird* is not to be confused with an *old bird*, which is simply an eccentric person. CE; DEI; EWPO. *Compare* Queer Duck; Tough Old Bird.

RARING TO GO *See* At the Drop of a Hat.

RASCAL *See* Erase.

RASH *See* Erase.

RAT (n) (1) *a rat.* A despicable person. Source: RAT. WNNCD: O.E. Rats are among the most despised animals because they are poor housekeepers, they damage buildings and their contents, and they threaten people with bites and diseases. Human *rats* betray trusts, desert comrades, and think only of themselves. ATWS; DEI. *See also* Like Rats Leaving a Sinking Ship; Rat (n) (2). *Compare* Rattlesnake; Snake; Weasel; Worm.

RAT (n) (2) *a rat.* An informer; a squealer. SHM: Early 1900s. Source: RAT. WNNCD: O.E. Besides deserting sinking ships, rats refuse to live in harmony with the humans who have fed and housed them for centuries. Human *rats* betray "honor among thieves" by informing on their fellows: i.e., they *rat* on them (WNNCD: 1812). Other names for squealers are *canary*, *fink*, *rat fink*, *stoolie*, and *stool pigeon*—all of which *see*. ATWS; DEI.

RAT (n) (3)   *a rat.* A pad, or roll, over which a woman's hair can be formed to give it greater bulk. Source: RAT. WNNCD: O.E. A *rat* is placed in the hair at the back of the neck to form a "pageboy bob." The pad is so called because it is long and narrow and resembles the shape of a rodent. To "do" hair in this fashion is to *rat* it. There is no evidence that an actual rat was ever used for this purpose. *See also* Ratty.

RAT (v)   *See* Rat (n) (2); Rat (n) (3).

RAT FINK   *a rat fink.* An informer. WNNCD: 1964. Source: RAT. WNNCD: O.E. *Rat fink* is stronger than *fink* (q.v.) but weaker than *rat* (q.v.). It is a term of contempt for a person who betrays his/her associates. The rat is held in even greater contempt by humans than the snake, probably because the rat is a mammal and has lived in human homes and barns for centuries. This unwelcome guest eats the food, trashes the buildings, and passes diseases to the occupants. EWPO; IRCD. *Compare* Canary; Stoolie; Stool Pigeon.

RATHOLE   *a rathole.* A dirty, messy room or building. Source: RAT. WNNCD: O.E. Some rats live in burrows underground, some nest in the underbrush, and some gnaw through the boards of a building and set up housekeeping inside. (Never buy an old wooden house that has tin can covers nailed here and there on the outside.) Solving the Savings and Loan Crisis in the early 1990s was described as "pouring money down a rathole": it goes down, but it never comes back out. ATWS. *See also* Rat's Nest; Rattrap. *Compare* Pigpen; Pigsty.

RAT KANGAROO   *a rat kangaroo.* A small Australian marsupial that has the body and tail of a rat but the hind legs and pouch of a kangaroo. Source: RAT. WNNCD: O.E. The *rat kangaroo*, which is about a yard long, is not to be confused with the much smaller southwestern U.S. *kangaroo rat* (q.v.), whose tail is much longer than its compact body. However, both animals have long hind feet, they both hop instead of walk, and they are both nocturnal.

RAT PACK   *a rat pack.* A band of young movie stars who hang out together, party together, and sometimes act in the same movies together. Source: RAT. WNNCD: O.E. The original Rat Pack, in the early 1960s, consisted of Joey Bishop, Sammy Davis, Jr., Peter Lawford, Dean Martin, and Frank Sinatra—the *Leader of the Pack* (q.v.). (A younger generation of "rat-packers," in the mid 1980s, called themselves the Brat Pack.) A major difference between a human *rat pack* and a pack of rats is that the latter has no leader.

RAT RACE   *a rat race.* The mad scramble for survival in the modern world of business. WNNCD: 1939. Source: RAT. WNNCD: O.E. When threatened, rats scurry away in mass confusion. The appearance is like that of a tide churning up a narrow channel; and, indeed, that is the sense of the I.E. root from which both *rat* and *race* develop. The tidal current of the modern business world is the competition that humans face every single day. It is a relentless struggle, not only to get ahead but just to maintain your position. ATWS; BDPF; CI; DEI; DOC; IRCD; LCRH; ST; WNWD. *Compare* Dog-eat-dog; It's a Jungle out there; Law of the Jungle.

RATS *Rats!* An exclamation of disappointment, annoyance, anger, or disgust: Damn! Source: RAT. WNNCD: O.E. *Disgust* is the key word here. The exclamation may have originated in an actual cry to alert others to the presence of rats, the most disgusting of household pests. Rats do not have to be present for humans to express the same disgust—over getting some bad news, discovering that your repair job doesn't work, or learning that your in-laws are coming. ATWS; BDPF; ID; IRCD.

RAT'S NEST *a rat's nest.* A dirty, messy room or building. Source: RAT. WNNCD: O.E. The rat's nest referred to in this metaphor is probably not the well-organized underground home of burrowing rats, which people seldom see. It is more likely the indoor dwelling of a black or brown rat, which frequents structures from homes to barns to boats and ships and builds its nest of products of human manufacture. *See also* Rathole; Rattrap. *Compare* Pigpen; Pigsty.

RATTAIL COMB *a rattail comb.* A comb with a long, slender, tapering handle. Source: RAT. WNNCD: O.E. The handle of the *rattail comb* resembles the long (up to 19 inches), slender, tapering tail of a rat, although the rat's tail is covered with rough scales and the comb's handle is smooth. The business end of the comb bears no resemblance to a rat. ATWS. *Compare* Rat-tail File.

RAT-TAIL FILE *a rat-tail file.* A long, round, slender, tapered file. WNNCD: 1744. Source: RAT. WNNCD: O.E. Most rats have long (up to 19 inches), slender, hairless (usu. scaled), tapering tails, some of which are prehensile. The *rat-tail file* bears a strong resemblance to a straight rat's tail, even down to the coloring (gray) and the texture (rough). The short handle of the file is also tapered, but square-cut. *Compare* Rattail Comb.

RATTLESNAKE *a rattlesnake.* A dirty, rotten, dangerous scoundrel. Source: SNAKE. A rattlesnake has rattles on the tip of its tail that it activates, when coiled, to warn off intruders. If the warning is not heeded, the snake may then deliver a poisonous strike. Human *rattlesnakes* also issue a warning, but they strike even if the warning is heeded. They are as worthless as the rattlesnake is thought to be (but isn't). *See also* Snake (n) (1).

RATTLE SOMEONE'S CAGE *to rattle someone's cage.* To shake someone up. SPD: ca. 1970. Source: MONKEY. The purpose of *rattling someone's cage* is to stir them into action or merely upset or annoy them. This works with monkeys also, but monkeys sometimes rattle the bars of their own cage to show their annoyance at being locked up. A related expression, *to shake someone's tree*, has approx. the same meaning. NDAS. *See also* Have Your Cage Rattled. *Compare* Get Someone's Goat.

RATTRAP   *a rattrap.* A dirty, dilapidated, deserted structure. Source: RAT. WNNCD: O.E. A run-down building is likened to a *rattrap* because it attracts rats. The lure to the rat is the shelter, the absence of people, and the prospect of colonization. A real *rattrap* (WNNCD: 15th cent.), which is about three times the size of a conventional mousetrap, is neither dirty nor dilapidated. It must be either new or sanitized, and its moving parts must be in good working order. The term *rattletrap* (WNNCD: 1822) "a run-down vehicle" may have been fashioned after *rattrap*. ATWS. *See also* Caught like a Rat in a Trap; Rat Trap Cheese. *Compare* Rathole; Rat's Nest.

RAT TRAP CHEESE   Cheddar cheese. WNNCD: 1927. Source: RAT. WNNCD: O.E. American cheddar was once called *rat trap cheese* because it was the favorite bait to use in a *rattrap* (q.v.). That was before the time of processed cheeses, when cheddar, which has a distinctive smell, was the cheese of choice. Because *people* liked it, it was assumed that *rats* would also. Actually, rats prefer peanut butter.

RATTY   *to be ratty.* To be shabby, ragged, and unkempt. Source: RAT. WNNCD: O.E. *Ratty* can apply to a person's clothing, hair, or domicile. The comparison is with the nest of the indoor rat, such as the brown or black rat, which disgusts the property owner because it is lined with his/her old clothes. *Ratty* can also describe a person's low morals or bad temper. ATWS; IRCD. *See also* Rathole; Rat's Nest.

RAVEN-HAIRED   *to be raven-haired.* To have glossy black hair. (Usu. said of a female.) WNNCD: 1634. Source: RAVEN. WNNCD: O.E. The common raven of the western United States and Canada is entirely black: its feathers, beak, legs, and feet. It is a cousin of the American crow but is about four inches longer and fifty percent heavier. GTP; IRCD. *See also* Ravenous.

RAVENOUS   *to be ravenous.* To have a voracious appetite for something: blood, food, money, power, recognition, sex, etc. WNNCD: 15th cent. Source: RAVEN (*). WNNCD: O.E. Watching a raven tear apart a dead rabbit, one would assume that the metaphor was based on the bird's behavior; but it is not. The source is the M.Fr. verb *raviner* "to take by force," which has the same origin as *rape* and *rapacious*. Ravens prefer carrion over live prey. IRCD.

RAZE   *See* Erase.

REAR ITS UGLY HEAD   *for something monstrous to rear—or raise—its ugly head.* For something unpleasant or frightening to suddenly appear. Source:

ANIMAL (?). The literal reference may be to a *mythical* monster (such as a *behemoth, chimera,* or *leviathan,* all of which *see*), to an *alleged* monster (such as Big Foot or Nessie, the Loch Ness monster), or to a *real* monster (such as a king cobra or a gila monster). At any rate, the figurative reference is to something disastrous, unavoidable, and unstoppable, such as famine, flood, pestilence, or poverty. DEI.

REAR UP   *See* Rampant.

RECOIL   *to recoil from something.* To draw back from something fearful or terrible. Source: SNAKE (*). Many poisonous snakes must strike from a coiled position, after which they must coil again, or *re-coil.* However, *recoil* is not based on the snake's behavior: it lit. means "to move backwards" (fr. Fr. *reculer,* fr. *cul* "bottom"). Since snakes have no "bottoms," they cannot, technically, *recoil* at all.

RED AS A LOBSTER   *to be as red as a lobster.* To have a severe case of sunburn. Source: LOBSTER. WNNCD: O.E. Maine lobsters don't get sunburned, but their shells do turn from dark green to red when they are plunged, alive, into boiling water. Light-colored human skin also turns red (or pink) when it is exposed to hot water or steam, but the expression is usu. associated with sunburn. *See also* In Hot Water; Look like a Boiled Lobster.

RED DOG   *a red dog; to red dog.* A blitz; to blitz. WNNCD: 1953. Source: DOG. WNNCD: O.E. A "blitz" in football is an attempt to break through the offensive line and "sack" the quarterback. In the 1950s, there were three code words to indicate the number of linebackers (only) who would attempt the blitz: (1) *red dog,* (2) *blue dog,* and (3) *green dog.* Since the 1960s, the green and blue signals have disappeared, and *red dog* has come to mean that any number of defensive linebackers *or* linesmen will rush, or *red dog,* the quarterback. *Dog* was probably selected for the code because attack dogs are trained to go after a particular individual. ATWS; EWPO; IRCD; LTA; MDWPO. *Compare* Yellow Dog.

RED FLAG TO A BULL   *to be like a red flag to a bull.* To be a cause of instant anger. Source: BULL. WNNCD: O.E. The bullfighter waves his/her red cape in front of the bull in order to incite its anger and provoke it into charging. However, it is the cape itself, not its color, that angers the animal, since bulls are color-blind. Humans are incited to anger by *red flags,* such as personal or political insinuations. CI; DEI; DOC; LCRH. *See also* See Red; Wave a Red Flag in Front of a Bull.

RED HERRING   *a red herring.* A deliberate diversion or distraction. DOC: 19th cent. Source: HERRING. WNNCD: O.E. Literally, a red herring is a salted herring (or "bloater") that has been smoked to a dark, reddish-brown color and gives off a strong odor. Beginning in the 17th cent., the odiferous herring was dragged along the ground to train dogs to follow a track for fox hunting. Escaping criminals—and opponents of fox hunting—dragged a red herring *across* their own path—or the path of the fox—to divert the hounds, or set them *at fault* (q.v.). In modern times, mystery writers create *red herrings*, or "false clues," to mislead their readers; and politicians use them—sometimes in connection with the "red menace," or communism—to divert attention from the real issue. (Also called a *herring*). ATWS; BDPF; CI; DEI; EWPO; HOI; IRCD; LCRH; MDWPO; SHM; SPD; ST. *See also* Dead as a Herring; Draw a Red Herring; Neither Fish nor Fowl.

REEL IN/OFF   *to reel someone in; to reel something off*. To convince a customer to buy something; to recite a long list of names, events, or jokes (LTA: 1840). Source: FISH. In flycasting, or flyfishing, the line is wound around a spool, or reel, that can shorten it or lengthen it. When the line is tightened, the fish is *reeled in*; and when the line is loosened, the fish swims off with the lure until it tires itself out. Legitimate and illegitimate salespersons *reel in* their customers and "marks" with a line of talk; witnesses and commedians *reel off* names and jokes in rapid order, one right after the other. CI. *See also* Give Someone Some Line.

REIN SOMEONE IN   *See* Bridle.

RELAY   *a relay*. A succession of workers on shifts, or runners in a track race; an automatic electrical switch. Source: DOG; HORSE. The original *relay* (M.Fr. *relais*) was a series of packs of *hounds*, situated in advance along the expected course of the fox hunt, that could be released when the exhausted pack approached. When the word was borrowed into Eng. (WNNCD: 1659), a fresh supply of *horses* was added to the meaning—something like the stagecoach runs or the Pony Express. Today, factory workers work in *relays*, or "shifts," and athletes succeed each other in *relay races* on the track or in the pool. The electromagnetic switch that is called a *relay* responds to conditions in one circuit by activating others. ROE; WNWD.

RETURN TO THE FOLD   *to return to the fold*. To return to the home, family, neighborhood, or group where you were once sheltered but from which you fled. Source: SHEEP. The analogy is to the sheep that has wandered away from the flock or the *sheepfold* (a sheep pen) but has found its way back or been recovered by the shepherd (as in the Parable of the Lost Sheep, Matthew 18:12–13). The expression also applies to a return to the church by lapsed Christians.

RICH BITCH   *See* Bitch (n).

RIDE A HIGH HORSE   *See* Get on Your High Horse.

RIDE A HOBBYHORSE   *See* Hobby.

RIDE A TIGER   *to be riding a tiger.* To be in a no-win situation. Source: TIGER. WNNCD: O.E. ATWS cites a Chinese proverb that states that a person who is *riding a tiger* is "afraid to dismount." That sums up the predicament of the pilot of a passenger plane or the driver of a car or truck whose craft or vehicle is out of control: you can't bail out to avoid harm. The *tiger* will attack you if you get off its back, and it will eventually devour you if you stay on. However, the allusion may be to playing a poker hand that contains no face cards, no pairs, and no potential for a flush or straight: a *tiger hand.* The hand is sure to lose unless you bluff; and if you win by bluffing, you are sure to incur the wrath of the other players. DEI. *See also* Have a Tiger by the Tail.

RIDE ROUGHSHOD   *to ride roughshod over someone.* To treat someone deplorably, despicably, and disdainfully. WNNCD: 1813. Source: HORSE. A horse is *roughshod* (WNNCD: 1688) when the heads of the nails that attach the shoes to its hooves are left protruding—intentionally. The idea is that the protruding nailheads will give the horse better traction in the dirt, as at a racetrack, so that it can *ride roughshod* over the opposition. People *ride roughshod* over other people when they take unfair advantage of them or show no consideration for their human or civil rights. AID; ATWS; CI; DOC; EWPO; SOED; ST.

RIDE SHANK'S MARES   *See* Shank's Mares.

RIGHT-WING   *See* Wing (n).

RINGER   *a ringer.* An illegal substitute. Source: HORSE. In horse racing, a *ringer* is either (1) a fast horse that is entered in a race under the name and colors of an unknown horse or (2) a fast horse that is substituted for a slower horse with that horse's name and colors. The idea is to take advantage of the long odds on the unknown or inferior horse by *bringing in a ringer.* In other forms of competition, a *ringer* is (1) an accomplished athlete who is added to a team under false credentials, (2) a *card shark* (q.v.) or *pool shark* (q.v.) whose talents are misrepresented to the other players, or (3) a voter who registers under the name of another voter. *Ringer* is short for *dead ringer* ("X is a dead ringer for Y")—a person who looks almost exactly like another person, i.e., could be that person's double. CI; LCRH; MDWPO; NDAS; ST. *See also* Dark Horse; Horse of a Different Color.

RISE ABOVE THE HERD   *See* Herd (n).

RISE LIKE A PHOENIX   *to rise like a phoenix from the ashes.* To come to life again after almost total defeat or destruction. Source: BIRD. The phoenix was an immortal bird of Greek mythology that renewed itself every 500 years by consuming itself on a pyre and then rising to live another 500 years. A person who rises, *phoenixlike,* from a personal catastrophe to achieve success in his/her new life is sometimes called a *phoenix*, as are businesses, industries, cities, and nations that have survived ruin to prosper once again. ATWS; BDPF; DEI; EWPO.

RIVER HOG   *a river hog.* A 19th cent. lumberjack who rode logs down the river to the sawmill. Source: HOG. WNNCD: O.E. The *river hog's* job was to prevent the logs from jamming, or, if a logjam occurred, to break it up. Hogs don't ride logs, but they do like water holes, where their wallowing around probably makes them look like logs in a river. *Compare* River Rat.

RIVER RAT   *a river rat.* Someone who fishes from the banks of a river rather than from a boat. Source: RAT. WNNCD: O.E. Fishing from the banks is often not as profitable, but it is cheaper, safer, and just as much fun. People who do it are likened to the large *brown rat*, which lives near water, such as a river or a sewer, and feeds on fish as well as other small animals. It is the infamous transmitter of plague and typhus. *Compare* Desert Rat; Dock Rat.

ROACH   *a roach.* A marijuana joint: the unsmoked butt of a marijuana cigarette. IRCD: late 1930s. Source: COCKROACH. WNNCD: 1623. A marijuana joint is about the size and color of a cockroach and, when discarded, often remains unseen, like the nocturnal insect. *See also* Roach Clip.

ROACH CLIP   *a roach clip.* A tweezerlike metal clip that is used to hold a marijuana joint, or *roach*, when it is smoked down too far to be held in the fingers. WNNCD: 1968. Source: COCKROACH. WNNCD: 1623. *Cockroach* (q.v.) is shortened to *roach* (q.v.); then *roach* is combined with *clip* to form *roach clip.* IRCD; NDAS. *Compare* Alligator Clip.

ROAD HOG   *a road hog.* A driver who takes up more than his/her fair share of the road. WNNCD: 1891. Source: HOG. WNNCD: O.E. The date of this metaphor is just one year later than the date of the word *automobile* (WNNCD: 1890), indicating that it didn't take long for drivers of cars to crowd the slower buggies off the road. The analogy is to the behavior of hogs at a feeding trough, when each of them attempts to take more than its fair share and crowd the others out. ATWS; BDPF; CI; DEI; IRCD.

ROAR LIKE A BULL   *to roar like a bull.* To shout in a loud, deep, powerful voice: to *bellow* (q.v.). Source: BULL. WNNCD: O.E. *Roaring like a bull* is usu. a sign of indignation, anger, or pain. Related metaphors are *bullroar* "nonsense" (a euphemism for *bullshit*) and *bull-roarer* "a flat piece of wood tied to a string that makes a roaring sound when twirled above your head." BDPF; WNWD. *Compare* Roar like a Lion.

ROAR LIKE A LION   *to roar like a lion.* For one or more persons to create a mighty roar. Source: LION. WNNCD: 12th cent. The male lion is famous for its mighty roar, as might be expected from the King of Beasts. The sound is loud, deep, and sustained, and it is probably meant to frighten off other male lions rather than to scare off predators, because there are none. *Compare* Roar like a Bull.

ROBIN'S EGG BLUE Bluish-green, greenish blue, aquamarine, or turquoise. Source: ROBIN. WNNCD: 1549. The American robin is named after the English robin, which is about half its size. Both robins lay greenish-blue eggs in nests not far above the ground. The nests are often dislodged by the wind, so it is not uncommon to find robin's eggs on the lawn. *See also* Who Killed Cock Robin?

ROCK HOUND *See* Hound (n).

ROCKING HORSE *See* Hobby.

ROCK LOBSTER *See* Crayfish.

RODE HARD AND PUT AWAY WET *See* At the Drop of a Hat.

RODENT *See* Erode.

ROGUE COP *See* Rogue Elephant.

ROGUE ELEPHANT *a rogue elephant.* A military, police, or undercover officer who takes the law into his/her own hands. Source: ELEPHANT. WNNCD: 14th cent. Literally, a rogue elephant is one that turns vicious, deserts the herd, and lays waste to the countryside (WNNCD: 1859). A military officer who turns bad is also called a "loose cannon," and a police officer who turns bad is also called a *rogue cop.* DEI; LCRH. *Compare* Maverick.

ROLLING IN CLOVER *to be rolling in clover.* To be enjoying the good life. Source: PIG. Pigs—and hogs—normally do their rolling, or wallowing, in mud, for the purpose of cooling their thick skin, which lacks sweat glands. However, when pigs break out of their pen and invade the neighboring field of clover, they love to roll around in it and root it up. Humans feel this way when they win the lottery. DOC; NDAS. *See also* Hog Heaven; Like a Pig in Clover.

ROLL OVER AND PLAY DEAD *to roll over and play dead.* To concede defeat without a fight. Source: POSSUM. The American possum (or *opossum,* 1610) is the only marsupial native to the United States. The female carries its offspring in its pouch when they are very young and on its back when they are older. If cornered, the possum curls up in a ball and plays dead. *Hedgehogs* (q.v.) do the same thing, and so do *hognose snakes* (q.v.). ST. *See also* Play Possum.

ROOK *to rook someone.* To cheat, defraud, or swindle someone. Source: CROW; RAVEN. The rook is the European cousin of the American crow. They have approx. the same size and appearance, and both are somewhat smaller than the common raven. All three birds steal cloth for their nests and plunder the nests of other birds for their eggs and hatchlings. A person who defrauds or swindles people was once called a *rook*; the victim of the fraud or swindle is currently said to have been *rooked*. The *rook* (or "castle") of chess, and the *rookie* of sports and military life, are from other sources. ATWS; BDPF; EWPO.

ROOKED *See* Rook.

ROOM TO SWING A CAT IN *enough—or not enough—room to swing a cat in.* Enough—or not enough—room to live or work in. IRCD: 1771. Source: CAT. WNNCD: O.E. There are two likely candidates for the origin of this metaphor: (1) the Elizabethan practice of swinging a live cat in a leather sack on a rope around one's head for archers to shoot at (Shakespeare's *Much Ado about Nothing,* 1600, Act I, Scene 1); and (2) the 17th cent. practice of punishing sailors on British ships by whipping them with a *cat-o'-nine-tails* (WNNCD: 1665), an act that was discontinued in the late-19th cent. (HF: 1881). The former practice lends itself to variations such as swinging a live cat by the tail, just for "fun," as Huck and Tom might have done back in Hannibal. The latter practice involves a weapon that is already named for the cat, either because the cat *has nine lives* (q.v.) or because the marks on the backs of the sailors left by the nine knotted lines looked like cat scratches. Both activities required an ample amount of space, either in the woods or on the deck of a ship. AID; ATWS; BDPF; CI; DEI; EWPO; HOI; ID; LCRH; MDWPO; ST.

ROOST *a roost; to roost.* A place to sleep; to spend the night. Source: CHICKEN. Originally, a roost was a wooden structure built to house chickens at night (WNNCD: O.E.). However, the word *roost* has come to mean any resting place for fowl—and even the group of birds themselves. (Technically, a *rooster* ought to be any roosting chicken, male or female; but the word was rushed into use early in the 19th cent. as a euphemism for *cock.*) When humans find themselves temporarily homeless, they ask their friends for a place to *roost*; and "The Roost" is a popular name for a vacation home or cottage. ATWS.

ROOSTER TAIL *a rooster tail.* An almost vertical spray of water that occurs just behind a fast-moving speedboat, motor boat, or power ski. WNNCD: 1946. Source: ROOSTER. WNNCD: 1822. The high-arching spray resembles the fanned tail of a rooster or gamecock. The tail of the latter may be the basis for the word *cocktail* (q.v.); it is also where a cowardly bird *shows its white feather* (q.v.). *Rooster* itself is a euphemism for *cock.*

ROOT OUT   *to root out the cause of something.* To uncover the cause of a problem. Source: PIG. A pig—or hog—uses its snout to turn up the earth in search of roots, grubs, and truffles. If allowed to run free, it can turn a lawn into a plowed field. Humans use their brains to *root out* evil (etc.) wherever it may lurk, including underground. A variation of *root* is *rout*, which is applied to gouging out grooves in wood. ATWS.

ROPE IN   *to rope someone in.* To draw someone into a group or scheme by forceful or deceptive tactics. Source: CATTLE. Cowboys have the unpleasant task of roping calves and drawing them in for such operations as branding, castrating, and doctoring. Ordinary people use words instead of ropes to convince others to join a group, take a job, or buy a product that they don't really want or need. ATWS.

ROSTRUM   *a rostrum.* A speaker's platform. Source: BIRD. In the Roman Forum, a *rostrum* was a raised platform for orators. It was so called because the platform was decorated with the *prows* (Lat. *rostra*) of captured ships, many of which were carved in the shape of a bird's *beak* (Lat. *rostrum*). The modern raised platform on a stage gives no hint of a bird's beak, a ship's prow in the shape of a bird's beak, or a platform decorated with ships' prows in the shapes of birds' beaks. ATWS; BDPF; MDWPO; THT.

ROTTEN EGG   *See* Bad Egg.

ROUND ROBIN   *a round-robin tournament.* A sports tournament in which each contestant—team or individual—plays each other contestant—win or lose—as if completing a circle. Source: ROBIN (*). WNNCD: 1549. The robin circles the lawn looking for worms, but it is not the source of this metaphor. The origin is the signing of a petition in the form of a wheel, with each signature functioning as a spoke of the wheel, so that the name of the first signer cannot be identified (WNNCD: ca. 1730). *Round-robin* may derive from an inversion of 17th cent. Fr. *rubon rond* "round ribbon." BDPF; DEI; EWPO; HOI; IRCD; MDWPO.

ROUND UP   *to round people up.* To recruit volunteers, subpoena witnesses, arrest suspects, etc. WNNCD: 1844. Source: CATTLE. Cowboys in the western United States round up cattle that have been running free on the range by herding them into a group and driving them back to a fenced-in area of the ranch. People are *rounded up* when they have talents or information that are needed or when they are suspected of breaking the law. Both activities are called a *roundup* (WNNCD: 1873), and the noun is also applied to a summary of the news on radio and television: a *news roundup*. ATWS.

ROUNDUP   *See* Round up.

ROUSE   *to rouse someone.* To awaken someone from their sleep or lethargy. Source: HAWK. The hawk, or falcon, shakes its wings in order to cause smaller game—both birds and mammals—to break cover and run or fly into the open, where they can be seized (WNNCD: 1531). ATWS. *See also* Roust.

ROUST   *to roust someone.* To force someone to get out of bed. WNNCD: 1658. Source: HAWK. *Roust* is an alteration of *rouse* (q.v.), which is a gentler form of waking someone up. Both words refer to the behavior of a hawk or falcon, which shakes its feathers noisily to drive small game from their cover. With humans, a glass of cold water usu. does the trick. ATWS.

ROUT   *See* Root out.

RUBBER-CHICKEN CIRCUIT   *the rubber-chicken circuit.* The lecture circuit. Source: CHICKEN. WNNCD: O.E. Candidates for office, authors of new books, and other celebrities have given this name to the lecture circuit because the meals that they are served by their hosts always seem to look and taste like rubber chicken. The *rubber chicken* originated in the circus as a favorite prop of the clowns. SPD; ST. *See also* Chicken in every Pot.

RUB SOMEONE'S NOSE IN IT   *to rub someone's nose in it.* To constantly remind someone of a past mistake or failure. Source: DOG. One method of housebreaking a puppy is to rub its nose in the "mistake" that it has just made on the floor or carpet. That technique may work with dogs, but it doesn't work with people, who resent the implication that they can be conditioned like animals. A person who is not yet *housebroken* doesn't mess on the rug but does lack acceptable social graces. CI; DEI.

RUB SOMEONE THE WRONG WAY   *to rub someone the wrong way.* To irritate or annoy someone. EWPO: 1862. Source: CAT. The *correct* way to pet—or brush—a *cat* is to stroke it *with* the grain of the hair. The *wrong* way is to stroke it *against* the grain, which may provoke a hiss or claw or bite. What is pleasurable to a *person* is not always readily evident, so it is not difficult to upset or offend someone, after only a short acquaintance, by doing or saying the wrong thing. CH; CI; DOC; LCRH.

RUFFLE SOMEONE'S FEATHERS   *to ruffle someone's feathers.* To upset, annoy, or threaten someone. WNNCD: 14th cent. Source: BIRD. Birds' feathers become ruffled, or out of alignment, when they are attacked by a predator or by a member of their own species. Male birds also ruffle their feathers when they are trying to impress female birds during the courting season. Human "feathers," or feelings, become *ruffled* when they are hurt, rejected, or falsely accused. In these cases, it is then necessary to *smooth their ruffled feathers*, or sooth their wounded pride. ATWS; CI; DEI. *Compare* Raise Someone's Hackles.

RUG RAT   *a rug rat.* A young child. Source: RAT. WNNCD: O.E. During the second half of the first year of its life, a child spends much of its time on the living room rug, scurrying about like a rat on the barn floor. *Rug rat* is an affectionate term for a child of this age, and in some families it is applied to preschool children of any age. NDAS. *Compare* Dock Rat; River Rat; Shop Rat.

RULE THE ROOST   *to rule the roost.* To wear the pants in the family. HOI: 15th cent. Source: COCK. The ruler of the chicken coop, or *roost*, is the *cock*, or *rooster*, who is at the top of the *pecking order* (q.v.). The dominant rooster perches wherever he wants to, eats whatever and whenever he wants to, and services whichever hens he wants to. He is the master of the henhouse. ATWS; DEI; DOC; EWPO; ID; LCRH. *See also* Cock of the Walk.

RUMINATE   *to ruminate.* To contemplate, meditate, or mull something over in your mind. WNNCD: 1553. Source: ANIMAL. An animal that ruminates brings up the contents of the first of its four stomachs—its *cud*—and chews it over and over. (The *ruminants* are split-hoofed animals such as the domestic cow, sheep, and goat and the wild buffalo, bison, and deer.) *People* who *ruminate* do not regurgitate their food, but they do turn a thought over and over in their mind—and they do assume the preoccupied look of a contented cow standing still, *chewing its cud* (DOC: 1547). A variant of *cud* is *quid* (WNNCD: 1727) "a wad of tobacco"; both words are from the O.E. words for "cud": *cwudu* and *cwidu*, respectively. ATWS; HTB; IRCD; LCRH; MDWPO; WNWD.

RUMP   *the rump.* The buttocks. Source: ANIMAL. The rump of a four-legged animal is the upper part of its hindquarters (WNNCD: 15th cent.). The *rump* of a two-legged human is the buttocks, or "bottom," which is used for sitting. Dissidents who sit apart from the rest of the group, with whom they disagree, make up a *rump session* (SPD: 1860), a term based on the English "Rump Parliament" of 1648. ATWS; HF.

RUMP SESSION   *See* Rump.

RUN AROUND IN CIRCLES   *See* Chase Your Tail.

RUN AROUND LIKE A CHICKEN WITH ITS HEAD CUT OFF   *See* Like a Chicken with Its Head Cut off.

RUN CIRCLES AROUND   *to run circles around someone.* To surpass someone in performance or intelligence. Source: HARE. In Aesop's fable of the *Tortoise and the Hare* (q.v.), the hare "ran circles around" the tortoise to flaunt his superior speed. However, the tortoise won the race, because its pace, though slow, was steady. DOC.

RUN FOR YOUR MONEY   *See* Off and Running.

RUN LIKE A DEER   *to run like a deer.* To run fast and effortlessly. Source: DEER. WNNCD: O.E. This expression is often used for an athlete, such as a track star or a cross-country runner, who attains great speed while maintaining both poise and control. The deer is the epitome of a graceful, effortless runner, and the John Deere Company has adopted the slogan, "Nothing Runs Like A Deere" (a registered trademark) for its tractor/mower advertisements. *Compare* Run like a Scalded Cat; Run like a Scared Rabbit.

RUN LIKE A SCALDED CAT   *to run like a scalded cat.* To take off as if your life depended on it. Source: CAT. WNNCD: O.E. Cats that hang around the stove are in danger of having scalding water spilled on them. If that should happen, they would jump straight up in the air, let out a screech, and exit by the nearest door. *Compare* Run like a Scared Rabbit.

RUN LIKE A SCARED RABBIT   *to run like a scared rabbit.* To run like a coward from danger. Source: RABBIT. WNNCD: 14th cent. Rabbits are often seen at sunrise or sunset sitting motionless; but when they are frightened, they bound away rapidly, in a zig-zag fashion, to evade capture. (Surprisingly, they usu. don't go very far; and even more surprisingly, they often double back to their original spot.) A human who runs from danger takes the easiest way out. CE. *See also* Jackrabbit Start; Quick like a Bunny. *Compare* Coward; Show the White Feather; Tail between Your Legs.

RUNNING DOG   *a running dog.* An "Ugly American." Source: DOG. WNNCD: O.E. A running dog is a wild dog, running in a pack of wild dogs that terrorize the populace and brutalize the children, showing no mercy. From the 1950s to the 1970s, *running dog* was a term used for Americans by the Communist Chinese. Originally (WNNCD: 1927), the term meant a "lackey," or servile follower. An earlier term, *imperialist dog*, was used for the British (and other Europeans) by Communists in "third world" countries of the former empires.

RUNNING MATE   *a running mate.* A candidate running for vice president or lieutenant governor. Source: HORSE. The job of the subordinate candidate in a political campaign is to be the "point" person for the primary candidate of the same party. The "running" image derives from horse racing, where an expendable horse sometimes *sets the pace* (q.v.) for a faster horse of the same *stable* (q.v.). The subordinate and primary candidates, and the inferior and superior horses, are all called *running mates* or *stablemates* (q.v.). SPD; ST. *See also* Pacemaker; Pacesetter. *Compare* Rabbit (3).

RUN RAMPANT   *See* Rampant.

RUN RIOT *See* At Fault.

RUNT *a runt.* An undersize person. Source: PIG. On the farm, a *runt* is an undersize pig in a large litter of pigs: the *runt of the litter.* The assumption is that there were more pigs than there were nipples, and the runt simply never got its share of milk. Among humans, *runt* is a derogatory term for a person of small stature, regardless of the reason. ATWS. *See also* Pick of the Litter; Suck the Hind Tit.

RUN TO EARTH *to run someone or something to earth.* To track someone or something down; to get to the bottom of a problem. Source: DOG. A foxhound runs its quarry to earth when the fox dives into its hole. The fox hunt is over at this point, and the fate of the fox is up to the huntsman. The police *run* fugitives *to earth* when they *hole them up* (q.v.) or corner them; researchers *run* the truth *to earth* when they discover the facts; and scientists *run* a problem *to earth* when they solve it. An alternative expression, *to run to ground,* may have its ultimate roots in sailing rather than in hunting. AID; BDPF; CI; HOI; LCRH; ST.

RUNT OF THE LITTER *See* Runt.

RUN TO GROUND *See* Run to Earth.

RUNWAY *a runway.* A landing strip at an airport; a narrow platform extending into the center aisle from a stage. Source: ANIMAL. The original *runway* was a path beaten down by the constant passage of animals in the wild (WNNCD: 1833). A human *runway* is a path cleared for the takeoff and landing of airplanes or a path constructed for the parading of performers at a fashion show or a beauty pageant. EWPO.

RUN WITH THE HARE *to run with the hare and run with the hounds.* To support both sides in an argument; to "work both sides of the street." DOC: 1440. Source: HARE; HOUND. WNNCD: O.E. In hunting, the hounds chase the hare; and in the game of *hare and hounds* (q.v.), the pursuing team follows a trail of paper left by the pursued. You can't have it both ways; or, if you could, it would be duplicitous. BDPF; DEI; IRCD.

RUN WITH THE LINE *See* Give Someone Some Line.

S

SACRED COW *a sacred cow.* A person, group of persons, institution, idea, belief, custom, or tradition that is regarded as sacrosanct, untouchable, off limits, and above criticism. WNNCD: 1921. Source: COW. WNNCD: O.E. The allusion is to the sacred cow of India, which, according to the Hindu religion, is a gift from God and cannot be killed or eaten. The metaphorical *sacred cow* is an anachronism that is so well established that no would dare attack it for fear of *ostracism* (q.v.). ATWS; CI; DEI; DOC; EWPO; HTB; IRCD; LCRH. *Compare* Cash Cow.

SACRIFICIAL LAMB *a sacrificial lamb.* An innocent person who is singled out for suffering as an example to others. Source: LAMB. WNNCD: O.E. In ancient times, animals were selected for sacrifice on the basis of their value to the community. The sacrificial animals ranged from the ox to the calf to the sheep to the goat and, finally, to the lamb (or the kid), which was the youngest and therefore the most innocent and least deserving of death. *See also* Like a Lamb to Slaughter. *Compare* Scapegoat.

SADDLED WITH *to be saddled with something unpleasant.* To be burdened with excessive work, debts, responsibilities, etc. SOED: 1693. Source: HORSE. The burden that a racing or riding horse carries is not only the saddle but the rider that occupies the saddle, and most horses would prefer not to have either one. People who are *saddled with responsibilities* feel as though they are being treated like horses: the saddle is bad enough, but to have to carry an additional burden is reprehensible. An even worse condition is to *have a burr under your saddle,* which exacerbates the burden and makes both horses and humans irritable and agitated. ATWS; BDPF; CH; DEI; ST.

SADDLE HORN *See* Horn.

SAID THE SPIDER TO THE FLY *"Come into my parlor," said the spider to the fly.* Com' on in, sucker. IRCD: 1821. Source: SPIDER (WNNCD: 14th cent.); FLY (WNNCD: O.E.). The quotation (actually a paraphrase) is from an early-19th cent. nursery rhyme, in which a spider entices a fly into its delicate but deadly web (the "parlor"). The expression is used in jest by a host to a guest, or by a boss to any employee. DEI. *See also* Cobweb; Spider; Spider's Web.

SALAMANDER *a salamander.* A temporary wood or coal stove: e.g., a fire barrel at a construction site or picket line at which workers can warm their hands in the wintertime. LTA: 1852. Source: SALAMANDER. WNNCD: 14th cent. The salamander is a lizardlike amphibian which was thought in ancient times to be able to survive immersion in fire. ATWS. *See also* Salamander's Wool. *Compare* Rise like a Phoenix.

SALAMANDER'S WOOL An early name for *asbestos* (WNNCD: 1607), a mineral fiber that was orig. defined as "inextinguishable" but is now defined as "noncombustible." BDPF: 16 cent. Source: SALAMANDER. WNNCD: 14th cent. The salamander, a lizardlike but scaleless amphibian, was compared with asbestos because the ancients believed that it could not be consumed in fire. *See also* Salamander. *Compare* Rise like a Phoenix.

SALMON *the color salmon.* A bright yellowish pink. Source: FISH. The North Atlantic and North Pacific salmon are not pink on the outside, but their flesh is. Because the former variety has been known in Eng. since the 14th cent., the name of the color is probably almost as old. The O.E. word for *salmon* was *leax*, which is cognate to Ger. *lahs* and Yiddish *laks*, the basis for Eng. *lox*, as in "lox and bagels." ATWS. *Compare* Purple; Sepia.

SANDHOG *a sandhog.* An underwater tunnel worker. WNNCD: 1903. Source: HOG. WNNCD: O.E. Hogs are not burrowers, but they *are* rooters. The name *sandhog* derives just as much from the working conditions as from the work itself: as wet, sloppy, and muddy as a hog wallow. The channel-tunnel, or "chunnel," under the English Channel was constructed by sandhogs working from opposite ends. The job of a *sewer hog*, or "ditch digger," is not quite so glamorous. MDWPO; NDAS. *Compare* River Hog.

SAND IN YOUR CRAW *to have sand in your craw.* To have guts, or grit. DOC: 1867. Source: BIRD. Birds are unable to fully digest their food without the help of some form of grit: pebbles, gravel, or sand. Pebbles can be a problem, because one that is too large can *stick in the bird's craw* (q.v.) and cause the bird to starve to death. A bird with sand in its craw, or "crop," is in good shape, ready to take on the world. The grit that dinosaurs, the ancestors of birds, ingested for the same purpose consisted of rocks, which, if they were too large, sometimes caused death.

SAN QUENTIN QUAIL *a San Quentin quail.* An underage girl: "jail bait." Source: QUAIL. WNNCD: 14th cent. A sexually attractive young woman has been called a *quail* since the middle of the 19th cent. Sex with one who is *too* young—below the legal age of consent—could get a man sent to San Quentin prison (Calif.). *See also* Quail (n).

SARCASM Biting or cutting remarks that are intended to cause pain. WNNCD: 1579. Source: DOG. The word *sarcasm* comes, by way of Lat., from Gk. *sarkasmos*, which is derived from *sarkazein* "to tear flesh like dogs." Sarcastic remarks are biting or cutting taunts or jibes that are intended to give the recipient as much pain as the victim of an attack dog. HF; THT; WNWD.

SAUCE FOR THE GOOSE *What's sauce for the goose is sauce for the gander.* (Also: What's *good* for the goose is *good* for the gander.) Two can play this game: If you (the female) can get away with this, so can I (the male). DOC: 1670. Source: GOOSE. WNNCD: O.E. Male and female geese look almost exactly alike, whether on land, on water, on the wing, or on the dinner table, where they are served with the same sauce. The insistence on sexual equity could just as well have been expressed with "What's *good/sauce* for the *gander* is *good/sauce* for the *goose*." AID; BDPF; CI; DEI; IRCD. *See also* Take a Gander.

SAVE YOUR BACON *to save your bacon.* To save your life (or *ass*, or *butt*). Source: PIG. As a cut of pork, *bacon* comes from the lower side, above the belly and below the loin. The hindquarter portion is called the "ham," so a more accurate metaphor would be "to save your *ham*." (Bacon and ham cuts retain their names even after they are smoked, which is usu. the case.) BDPF attributes the expression to protecting smoked bacon from the dogs by hanging it out of their reach. DEI. *Compare* Save Your Own Hide.

SAVE YOUR OWN HIDE *See* Hide nor Hair.

SAWBUCK *a sawbuck.* A ten-dollar bill. WNNCD: 1850. Source: DEER. A woodcutter's sawbuck is a pair of connected X-frames in which a log is placed for cutting with a *bucksaw* (q.v.) or a crosscut saw. The X-shape of the frames was the inspiration for the association with a ten-dollar bill (Lat. X = "ten"); and the bucking motion of the saw was analogized to the charging motion of a male deer, or *buck* (q.v.). ATWS; BDPF; EWPO. *Compare* Sawhorse.

SAWHORSE *a sawhorse.* A carpenter's "trestle." WNNCD: 1778. Source: HORSE. WNNCD: O.E. A *sawhorse* is sometimes equated with a *sawbuck* (q.v.); but the former is a narrow bench, on a pair of which a *board* can be laid, while the latter is a pair of X-frames in which a *log* can be placed. Both frameworks are used for sawing, but the *sawhorse* can also be equipped with several boards to form a table, as for a picnic. *Horse* figures in this word as it does in *cheval glass* (q.v.), *clotheshorse* (q.v.), and *vaulting horse* (q.v.)—i.e., as a framework on which something is supported. ATWS; EWPO; THT. *Compare* Easel.

SCALAWAG *a scalawag (or scallywag).* A rascal. WNNCD: 1848. Source: HORSE. *Scalawag* derives from the name given to the ponies on the Shetland Island of Scalaway. In America, *scalawag* (or *scallywag*) was first used by Southern Democrats to refer to white Southern Republicans who supported Northern carpetbaggers during reconstruction. Now, a *scalawag* is an any adult reprobate or young scamp. MDWPO; WNWD.

SCALE *a scale.* A small, thin, rigid plate or flake. Source: FISH. Not all fish have scales, but those that do have provided us with the notion of a multitude of small, thin plates. The term has been applied to the *scales* on a moth's wings, the *scales* on a reptile, the plates on a coat of armor, the flakes that make up a piece of mica, and the flakes of dandruff on a human head. (Graduated scales and balance scales are from a different source: Lat. *scalae* "stairs, or rungs of a ladder.") ATWS.

SCALLOP (n) *a scallop.* One of a series of undulations in the decorative edging of wood or cloth. IRCD: 17th cent. Source: SCALLOP. WNNCD: 15th cent. The scallop is a bivalve mollusk whose two shells have undulations on their edges. (The familiar symbol of the Shell Oil Company is a scallop shell.) ATWS. *See also* Scallop (v); Scalloped Potatoes.

SCALLOP (v) *to scallop something.* To create a series of undulations on the edges of cloth, wood, etc., for the purpose of decoration. Source: SCALLOP. WNNCD: 15th cent. The undulations on the edges of a scallop shell are the basis for this metaphor. *See also* Scallop (n). *Compare* Scalloped Potatoes.

SCALLOPED POTATOES Thin-sliced potatoes that are baked in a milk sauce with bread or crackers. WNNCD: 1737. Source: SCALLOP. WNNCD: 15th cent. The bivalve mollusk does not figure in this metaphor because of its wavy outer edges but because this potato delicacy was originally baked in a dish shaped like a scallop's shell. *See also* Scallop (n); Scallop (v).

SCAPEGOAT *a scapegoat.* An innocent person who is chosen to take the blame for the faults of others: a "fall guy." Source: GOAT. WNNCD: O.E. Biblically, a scapegoat was an "escape goat," i.e., the one of two young goats at an ancient Hebrew "sin offering" (Leviticus 16:5–10) that was *not* selected by lot for sacrifice but was let go into the wilderness as atonement for the sins of the people. The modern *scapegoat* is also randomly selected but is identified more with the goat that was sacrificed than with the goat that was spared. ATWS; BDPF; DEI; IRCD; LCRH; SHM; THT. *See also* Get Someone's Goat; Hero to Goat.

SCARAB *a scarab.* A pendant or amulet, made of polished stone or glazed ceramic, that was used as an ornament or talisman in ancient Egypt. Source: BEETLE. The scarab is a dung beetle that is native to both Egypt and southwestern United States. Dung beetles lay their eggs in a ball of fresh dung, on which the larvae feed until they emerge as adults. This development was a symbol of resurrection to the Egyptians. BDPF. *See also* Rise like a Phoenix.

SCARCE AS HEN'S TEETH *to be as scarce as—or scarcer than—hen's teeth.* To be rare or nonexistent. DOC: 1862. Source: HEN. WNNCD: O.E. Hens don't have teeth, so something that is *as scarce as hen's teeth* is very rare indeed. The expression has the typical exaggeration of a mid-19th cent. rural Americanism. AID; EWPO; HTB; IRCD; LTA.

SCARECROW *a scarecrow.* A tall, skinny, gaunt, and ragged person (usu. male). Source: CROW. WNNCD: O.E. The "ghostly" person is named for the *scarecrow* erected in gardens and cornfields to scare off crows (WNNCD: 1589). It consists of a human effigy made of a wooden cross dressed in human (usu. male) clothing stuffed with straw and topped off with a straw hat. Earlier (EWPO: 1553), it was a real person hired to do the same job. IRCD.

SCAREDY-CAT *a scaredy-cat.* A cowardly child. WNNCD: 1933. Source: CAT. WNNCD: O.E. Cats are careful, cautious, and rather skittish animals. They don't do anything without first investigating it thoroughly (except, perhaps, climbing trees). A child who is reluctant to put him-/herself in possible danger, even on a dare, is likely to be called a *scaredy-cat* by his/her peers. An earlier term with the same meaning was *fraidy-cat* (LTA: 1870). ATWS; IRCD.

SCAVENGER *a scavenger.* A person who gleans usable material from piles of garbage or trash. Source: ANIMAL (*). *Scavenger* is not an animal metaphor. The original scavenger was a collector of sales taxes from out-of-town merchants in England (WNNCD: 1530). Later, the term was applied to collectors of garbage, junk, and trash (WNNCD: 1644) and to salvagers of discarded materials from these sources. Only in recent times has the term *scavenger* been applied to animals—such as the hyena, the vulture, and the rat—that clean the bones of animals that have been killed by others. *Compare* Parasite; Predator.

SCHMALTZ Sticky sentimentality. WNNCD: 1935. Source: CHICKEN. *Schmaltz*—actually, *shmalts*—is a Yiddish word meaning "chicken fat." (*Compare* Ger. *Schmaltz* "grease or lard.") The meaning has been broadened to apply to music (esp.) and art that is corny and sentimental, and is as inspired as chicken fat. EWPO; LCRH.

SCREW (n) (1)   *a screw.* A small tapered metal pin with spiral grooves and a wider slotted head. Source: PIG. The screw is named for the adult female pig (Lat. *scrofa* "sow")—or, more specifically, for the sow's curly tail. The word *screw* was first applied to the water screw, which consisted of a metal tube surrounding a flanged metal corkscrew with a handle at the end. When the handle was turned, water could be raised to the container at the top. Later, it was applied to the *wood screw*, to the propeller of a boat or ship, to the grain elevator, and to the *metal screw*. EWPO.

SCREW (n) (2)   *a screw.* A prison guard. EWPO: mid-19th cent. Source: PIG. *Screw* meaning "prison guard" was derived from *screw* meaning "a tapered, nutless bolt." The association may have been with the outdated practice of guards using thumbscrews on recalcitrant prisoners, or it may have been related to the turnkey locking the prisoners in their cells by "screwing" the key into the lock. Whatever the origin, the source of *screw* is the curly tail of the pig (or sow). *See also* Screw (n) (1).

SCROFULA   Tuberculosis of the lymph glands of the neck. WNNCD: 15th cent. Source: PIG. The swollen lymph glands, or "nodes," resemble little pigs—or, rather, little sows (fr. Lat. *scrofalae*, dim. pl. of *scrofa* "breeding sow"). See also other metaphors that are based on a resemblance to the shape of a pig's body: *pig boat, pig iron,* and *pigs in the blanket.* ATWS.

SEA COW   *a sea cow.* A manatee or dugong. WNNCD: 1613. Source: COW. WNNCD: O.E. A manatee is a large aquatic mammal of the Caribbean; a dugong is a smaller, but similar, aquatic mammal of the tropical Indian and Pacific oceans. What the two animals have in common is that they are large, herbivorous, and practically helpless—like a cow. Although sea cows are not domesticated, they are as dependent on humans for their survival as bovine cows are. *Compare* Sea Horse; Sea Lion; Sea Urchin.

SEA DOG   *a sea dog.* A veteran sailor. WNNCD: 1840. Source: DOG. WNNCD: O.E. A *sea dog* is a sailor who has the age, experience, and wisdom of an old hunting dog. When the hunting dog dies, the hunter loses a highly skilled worker, and it takes years to train a replacement. When an "old salt" retires or dies, the business or sport of sailing loses a wealth of experience and knowledge of the sea. EWPO; ID; IRCD. *Compare* Sea Wolf; Sly Old Dog.

SEA HORSE   *a sea horse.* A "pipefish" that swims upright in the shallow sea. Source: HORSE. WNNCD: O.E. The *sea horse* is so called because it has the head, neck, and "ears" of a horse, although the unusual fish is only five inches long and, of course, has no legs. The male *sea horse* is also unusual because it raises the female's eggs in its pouch. The term *sea horse* orig. meant "walrus" (WNNCD: 15th cent.). EWPO.

SEA LION   *a sea lion*. The largest of the "eared" seals. WNNCD: 1697. Source: LION. WNNCD: 12th cent. Of the two species of large, eared seals, the Steller sea lion of the North Pacific (over one ton) is quite a bit larger than the familiar California sea lion of the mid-Pacific. However, the "lion of the sea" is not named for its size but for the large mane that is present on the males. *Compare* Lion Tamarin; Mountain Lion.

SEA SQUAB   *a sea squab*. A northern puffer, or "blowfish." Source: PIGEON. A *squab* (WNNCD: 1682) is a fledgling pigeon, about four weeks old. It likes to ruffle its feathers above its rapidly growing breast. A *sea squab* is a fish that is able to inflate itself with either water or air in order to make itself appear bigger and more formidable. Both are edible, although some puffers are toxic. DEOD. *See also* Pigeon-breasted.

SEA URCHIN   *a sea urchin*. A ball-shaped marine animal covered with long movable spines. (It resembles the casing of a *horse chestnut* [q.v.].) WNNCD: 1591. Source: HEDGEHOG. When the European hedgehog, orig. called an *urchin*, is frightened, it rolls up into a spiny ball. EWPO. *See also* Prickly as a Hedgehog; Urchin. *Compare* Sea Dog; Sea Wolf.

SEA WOLF   *a sea wolf*. A pirate. Source: WOLF. WNNCD: O.E. A band of pirates was compared to a pack of wolves because both were fierce and fearsome and preyed on innocent beings. Pirates, however, were outlaws; wolves just do what nature expects of them—chase an animal, surround it, kill it, and eat it. The wolf is the nobler of the two. ATWS; ID. *Compare* Sea Dog.

SEE A MAN ABOUT A DOG   *to see a man about a dog*. To pay a visit to the bathroom. IRCD: 1860s. Source: DOG. WNNCD: O.E. There are many euphemisms—such as *water the horse*—for taking leave of others in order to "use the facilities," but this is one of the oldest and most indirect. Are you going to see a man about *buying* a dog? (*Your* dog? *His* dog?) Did the man's dog trespass on your property? (Or vice versa?) Did it bite one of your children? (Or did one of your children bite the dog?) Nobody knows how this metaphor arose. AID; ATWS; LTA.

SEEING-EYE   *a seeing-eye single*. A baseball that is struck exactly between the infielders for a hit. Source: DOG. WNNCD: O.E. *Seeing-eye single* is patterned after a *Seeing Eye* (Registered Trademark) *dog*: a dog trained to guide the blind. The baseball travels through the infield as if it were guided by such a dog. EWPO.

SEE NO EVIL   *See no evil, hear no evil, speak no evil*. When it comes to evil, keep your eyes closed, your ears covered, and your mouth shut. Source: MONKEY. The admonitions are translations of the postures of the "three wise monkeys," a popular statuette of the second half of the 19th cent. The monkey at the left has its paws over its eyes, the one in the middle has its paws over its ears, and the monkey on the right has its paws over its mouth. No doubt the admonitions preceded the statuette. DEI; DOC; IRCD.

SEE RED   *to see red.* To be, or become, extremely angry. DOC: 1901. Source: BULL. A bullfighter waves his/her red cape in front of the bull in order to provoke it to charge. The color is not really significant, since bulls are color-blind; but red has long been associated with violence, and the eyes of a tired or wounded bull are probably bloodshot anyway. AID; DEI; EWPO; MDWPO; ST. *See also* Red Flag to a Bull; Wave a Red Flag in Front of a Bull.

SEE THE ELEPHANT   *to see the elephant.* To experience "baptism under fire." EWPO: early 1860s. Source: ELEPHANT. WNNCD: 14th cent. This expression was used by soldiers in the Civil War to describe their first experience in combat: they had *seen the elephant.* The metaphor probably derives from their actually seeing an elephant for the first time, as children, when it appeared in a traveling circus. The other side of the coin is *not* to see the elephant: i.e., either (1) to ignore *the elephant in the room* (something that is "hidden in plain sight" or ignored because it is too frightening to think about), or (2) to arrive at a *description of an elephant* the way the blind men in the fable did (being "unable to see the woods for the trees" and proclaiming the trunk a snake, the ear a flag, the leg a tree, and the tail a whip). ATWS. *Compare* See the Lions.

SEE THE LIONS   *to see the lions.* To see the sights of the city. IRCD: 1834. Source: LION. WNNCD: 12th cent. When lions were housed in the Tower of London (fr. ca. 1600 to 1830), they were a "must see" for tourists, who could then brag that they had *seen the lions.* After 1830, the expression became a metaphor for having seen everything worth seeing in the city, including the sites and the celebrities. The metaphor is the basis for the term *lionize* (q.v.). ATWS; CI; EWPO. *Compare* See the Elephant.

SEE WHAT I CAN DIG UP   *I'll see what I can dig up.* I'll see what I can find in the kitchen to fix for dinner. Source: DOG. A hunting dog sometimes buries an unfinished bone in the ground for future use. The practice probably derives from the dog's wild cousins, who bury some of the bones of a kill to last them through the winter. Some dogs, such as *terriers* (WNNCD: 15th cent.), are trained to dig up live animals in the ground. A homemaker who says "I'll *see what I can dig up*" actually means "Let's go to a restaurant." The expression is also used by investigators and researchers.

SEE WHICH WAY THE CAT WILL JUMP   *See* Which Way the Cat Will Jump.

SEE YOU LATER, ALLIGATOR *See you—or dig you—later, alligator!* See you later, friend! ATWS: ca. 1930. Source: ALLIGATOR. WNNCD: 1568. *Alligator* (q.v.) was probably added to the older parting, "See you later," because it rhymes with *later. Compare* After a While, Crocodile; What's the Word, Hummingbird.

SEGREGATE *See* Congregate.

SEND A DOG OUT *I wouldn't send a dog out on a night like this.* The weather is so bad tonight that I wouldn't even put my *dog*—the lowest-ranking member of my family—outside, so I certainly wouldn't ask *you* to go. SOURCE: DOG. WNNCD: O.E. The dog is regarded as the lowest of all domesticated animals, probably because it provides no milk, eggs, fiber, nor meat, and works only sporadically as a hunter, herder, or protector. A related expression, *It shouldn't happen to a dog,* illustrates the low status of *man's best friend* (q.v.). NDAS.

SEPARATE THE SHEEP FROM THE GOATS *to separate the sheep from the goats.* To distinguish good from evil. Source: SHEEP; GOAT. WNNCD: O.E. The metaphor is from the New Testament description of Judgment Day (Matthew 25: 31–46), on which the Lord will reward the faithful (the sheep) with Heaven and the faithless (the goats) with Hell. The harmless sheep is often identified with Jesus in the Bible (*agnus dei* "lamb of God"), and the horned goat (or *Judas sheep* [q.v.]) with the Devil. Similar expressions are "to separate the wheat from the chaff" and "to separate the men from the boys." ATWS; BDPF; CI; DEI; DOC; EWPO; IRCD; LCRH; MDWPO; SHM.

SEPIA *the color sepia.* A grayish brown. Source: FISH. *Sepia* is a Greek and Latin word meaning "cuttlefish," or the inky secretion of a cuttlefish, which is not a fish at all but a squidlike mollusk. The ink from this mollusk was used to make a dye that ranged in color from light grayish brown to dark olive brown. Early photographs produced on metal plates, such as the daguerreotype and tintype, developed in this range of colors and were called *sepias*; and when newspapers age, both the paper and the ink turn a grayish brown color that is also called *sepia.* ATWS; EWPO. *Compare* Purple.

SERPENT *a serpent.* A malicious or treacherous person. Source: SNAKE. O.E. *Snaka* meant either "snake" or "worm." Latin *serpent* (the present participle of *serpere* "to creep") was borrowed into Eng. in the 14th cent. to refer to either a real snake or a mythical one, esp. if it was poisonous. Calling a person a *serpent* is pretty much the same as calling them a *rattlesnake* or a *viper* (both of which *see*): vicious and venomous. *See also* Herpes; Serpentine.

SERPENTINE *to be serpentine.* To have a winding form or sinuous motion. WNNCD: 15th cent. Source: SNAKE. Many snakes move in a twisting fashion, rather than a straight line; that is, as seen from above, the snake's body looks like the profile of a spring, a banana curl, or a telephone cord. The track that the snake leaves in the dirt is also wavy or winding. A *serpentine* path or road is one that winds its way through the countryside; a *serpentine* wall is one that features a compound curve; and a *serpentine* movement, as of a modern or exotic dancer, is one that is *slinky* (q.v.) or sinuous, like that of a serpent. ATWS; CE. *See also* Snake (v) (1); Snakelike.

SET A TRAP   *See* Trap.

SET THE HOOK   *to set the hook.* To clinch the deal. Source: FISH. An angler sets the hook firmly in a fish's mouth by jerking on the line or keeping constant pressure on it. A salesperson *sets the hook* in a customer by sweetening the deal at the last minute, esp. if the customer seems to be trying to back out. The baited hook may also have been the inducement that brought the customer there in the first place.

SET THE PACE   *to set the pace.* To take the lead; to set an example. Source: HORSE. In horse racing, a *pacesetter* (WNNCD: 1895) or *pacemaker* (WNNCD: 1884) is a horse that sets the pace for the race by taking an early lead and exhausting all of the other horses except its *running mate* (q.v.) or *stablemate* (q.v.), a fast horse that has been held back during the mad rush but then forges ahead to win the race. The same sort of pacesetting goes on in footracing and car racing. A *pacemaker* is also an electric device that regulates human heartbeats. BDPF; CI; ST.

SEWER HOG   *See* Sandhog.

SEX KITTEN   *a sex kitten.* A sexy young woman: a "nymphette." WNNCD: 1958. Source: CAT. Once kittens open their eyes and find their legs, they are regarded as among the cutest and most affectionate of young animals. They are also playful and get in all sorts of trouble. A *sex kitten* is cute (and she knows it), affectionate, playful, and looking for trouble. The role has been played in the movies by such actresses as Marilyn Monroe, Jane Fonda, and Ann-Margret. IHAT. *See also* Playful as a Kitten.

SHAGGY-DOG STORY   *a shaggy-dog story.* A long, involved story, intended to be humorous or suspenseful, that bores its audience and finally ends with a totally unsatisfactory "punch line." WNNCD: 1946. Source: DOG. WNNCD: O.E. The *shaggy-dog story* is so called because it often involves such characters as a shaggy dog: "Have you heard the one about the shaggy dog that went into a bar and ordered a boilermaker? Well, the bartender . . . ." Scary *shaggy-dog stories* are popular with children around a campfire. ATWS; BDPF; CI; MDWPO.

SHAKE SOMEONE'S TREE   *See* Rattle Someone's Cage.

SHANK'S MARES   *to ride shank's (or shanks') mares (or mare)*. To go on foot: to walk. HOI: ca. 1750. Source: HORSE. A mare is an adult female horse, and a mare's shanks are its legs between the ankle and the knee. When a person *rides*— or *takes* or *goes by*—*shank's mares*, he/she is walking as if on the front legs of a horse (a mare)—or as if each of his/her legs were a horse's (a mare's) leg. AID; ATWS; BDPF; CH; CI; EWPO; ID; IRCD; LCRH; MDWPO; NDAS.

SHARK   *a shark*. A person who takes advantage of others for their money: a con artist, a cheat, a swindler. WNNCD: 1599. Source: SHARK. WNNCD: 1569. A shark in the ocean preys on other fish, including other sharks, for their meat. A human *shark* preys on other humans—esp. the elderly, the young, the weak, and the naive—for their hard-earned money. Both are relentless—the fish because it can't stop swimming or it will sink and die. BDPF; DEI; EWPO; IRCD. *See also* Card Shark; Loan Shark; Pool Shark.

SHARK REPELLENT   A stock maneuver by a corporation to discourage an unfriendly takeover by another corporation. IRCD: 1980s. Source: SHARK. WNNCD: 1569. The predator shark is out to take your life. The predator corporation is out to take your livelihood. Various sprays have been tried to ward off real sharks. The measures used to ward off corporate *sharks* include buying up existing stock and raising the number of votes necessary to approve a merger. *See also* Swim with Sharks.

SHARKSKIN   *a sharkskin suit*. A suit made of worsted wool woven in a tight twill or basket weave. Source: SHARK. WNNCD: 1569. The sharkskin suit eventually becomes hard and shiny, like the skin of a shark, which itself is used for such wearing apparel as cowboy boots and purses (WNNCD: 1851). *Compare* Moleskin.

SHARPER THAN A SERPENT'S TOOTH   Ingratitude—esp. from one's own child. Shakespeare's *King Lear* (1607). Source: SNAKE. In Act I, Scene 4, Lear speaks to "Nature" of his daughter Goneril: "Turn all her mother's pain and benefits/ To laughter and contempt, that she may feel/ How sharper than a serpent's tooth it is/ To have a thankless child!" Earlier in the scene, Lear describes ingratitude as "a marble-hearted fiend." To him, the bite of a poisonous snake is less painful than the ingratitude of his own child. MDWPO.

SHAVETAIL   *a shavetail*. A second lieutenant in the U.S. Army. IHAT: 1898. Source: MULE. A newly broken pack mule in the Army was called a *shavetail* because its tail was shaved to distinguish it from a seasoned one, as a warning to mule packers. A newly commissioned lieutenant—i.e., a *second* lieutenant rather than a *first* lieutenant—is also untested and untried. EWPO. *See also* Mule (1). *Compare* Chicken Colonel.

SHEEP *a sheep.* A timid person. Source: SHEEP. WNNCD: O.E. The sheep is, at the same time, both the most forceful mammal (the ram) and the most defenseless mammal (the ewe), and the lamb is the most defenseless of all sheep. A person who is a *sheep* is vulnerable, gullible, impressionable, and easily influenced by others. The analogy is to the ewe or lamb, not to the ram. ATWS. *See also* Like a Flock of Sheep.

SHEEP-DIP *to taste like sheep-dip.* To taste awful. Source: SHEEP. WNNCD: O.E. On the farm, *sheep-dip* (WNNCD: 1864) is an antiseptic bath through which sheep are run in order to rid them of harmful parasites. It probably tastes about as bad to the sheep as cheap liquor—also called *sheep-dip*—or vermifuge—a dewormer—tastes to humans. LTA.

SHEEP-DIPPING Planting a *mole* (q.v.) in a subversive or otherwise illegal operation. Source: SHEEP. WNNCD: O.E. The undercover operative is the innocent sheep, and the organization is the unpleasant dip. (The bad guys are the parasites that must be eliminated.) *Sheep-dipping* is also a CIA term for loaning military equipment or personnel to a clandestine civilian operation. SPD. *See also* Sheep-dip.

SHEEPISH *to be sheepish.* To be awkward, bashful, embarrassed, shy, or timid. WNNCD: 13th cent. Source: SHEEP. WNNCD: O.E. The (female) sheep is the meekest of all animals: no one's predator and everyone's prey. A *sheepish* person is one who is naive, guileless, defenseless, and lacking in aggression. BDPF; DEI; IRCD. *See also* Sheepish Grin.

SHEEPISH GRIN *a sheepish grin.* A look of guilt and embarrassment. Source: SHEEP. WNNCD: O.E. A *sheepish grin* is not worn by a *sheepish person*, who is innocent and without guile. It is more likely to be found on the face of someone who has been exposed for committing a petty crime or indiscretion: guilt is written all over his/her face. DEI. *See also* Sheepish.

SHEEP'S EYES *to make or cast sheep's eyes at someone.* To glance longingly or lovingly at someone. WNNCD: 1529. Source: SHEEP. WNNCD: O.E. Sheep are passive—almost helpless—animals with fleecy coats and large, dark eyes. When they look up at you they seem to be asking, "Can you help me?" or "Will you hug me?" Children who want favors *make sheep's eyes* at their parents, and lovers amorously *cast sheep's eyes* at their loves. ATWS; BDPF; DEI; HOI; ID; IRCD. *Compare* Sheepish Grin.

SHEEPSHANK *a sheepshank.* A knot used for shortening a rope. WNNCD: ca. 1627. Source: SHEEP. WNNCD: O.E. Why the knot known as a *sheepshank* is named after the shank of a sheep is unknown. It may be because the doubled-over rope looks like the muscles and tendons in the upper front leg of a sheep, or the knot may have been used by farmers for hobbling sheep. *Compare* Cat's Paw.

SHEEPSHEAD   *a sheepshead.* A large, spiny-finned, saltwater food fish of the Atlantic and Pacific coasts. WNNCD: 1643. Source: SHEEP. WNNCD: O.E. The early English settlers in America saw a resemblance between the head of this fish and the head of a sheep. Both have steeply sloping foreheads, pronounced lips, and broad teeth. (Calif. sheepsheads—called *sheepheads*—are all female for the first seven or eight years of their lives.) *Compare* Muttonhead.

SHEEPSKIN   *a sheepskin.* A diploma. Source: SHEEP. WNNCD: O.E. The college or university diploma was orig. written on *parchment* (EWPO: 14th cent.), the skin of a sheep (or a goat). Modern diplomas are written or printed on vegetable parchment, or imitation sheepskin. The term *sheepskin* is also used, more broadly, to describe a garment made from the unsheared skin of a sheep, worn with the wool either on the inside or the outside: e.g., a *sheepskin* coat. ATWS; BDPF; ID; IRCD. *See also* Fleece (v).

SHELL (n)   *a shell.* An outer covering. Source: ANIMAL. The original shell was the outer covering of a mollusk, crustacean, turtle, or bird's egg (WNNCD: O.E. *sciell*). From these animal sources derive all modern senses of *shell*: the outer covering of a fruit, vegetable, or seed (e.g., a *pumpkin shell*, a *nutshell*); the outer covering of a manmade structure (e.g., the *shell of a house*, a *pie shell*); the outer covering of a round of ammunition (e.g., a *shotgun shell*, a *shell casing*); the hull of a boat (e.g., a *racing shell*); a sleeveless blouse (e.g., a ladies' *shell*). A *band shell* (WNNCD: 1926) is a large sounding board, in the shape of a concave mollusk shell, located behind an outdoor stage; a *shell company* is a phony or nonexistent company, one that is hollow and without substance; and a *shell game* is a con game that was orig. played with empty English walnut shells and a dried pea. BDPF; WNWD. *See also* Shell (v).

SHELL (v)   *to shell something.* To remove the outer casing from something (WNNCD: 1562); to destroy something with, or as if with, bombs. Source: ANIMAL. All senses of the verb *shell* derive from the noun *shell* (q.v.). To *shell* orig. meant to separate the outer covering from the inner body of a mollusk: e.g., to shell, or "shuck," oysters or clams. Later, the use was extended to preparing vegetable products: e.g., to *shell*, or "pod," peas; to *shell*, or "shuck," corn. In the case of peas, it is what is inside the shell that is sought, although the pods can also be eaten. In the case of corn, it is the covering itself that is sought for eating; the cob is inedible, except by hogs. More recently, the use of the verb *shell* has been extended to dropping bombs on military targets, as from airplanes, artillery, or mortars: e.g., to *shell a village.* The verb has even found its way into baseball and softball, where *to shell a pitcher* is to bombard him or her with hits.

SHELL A PITCHER *See* Shell (v).

SHELL A VILLAGE *See* Shell (v).

SHELL COMPANY *See* Shell (n).

SHELL GAME *See* Shell (n).

SHEPHERD (n) *a shepherd.* The leader of a congregation. Source: SHEEP. WNNCD: O.E. The analogy is to the caretaker of a flock of sheep: a "sheepherder," or *shepherd.* The shepherd makes sure that the sheep do not stray from the flock (*see* Lost Sheep), are not stolen by rustlers (*see* As Well be Hanged for a Sheep as a Lamb) or attacked by wild animals (*see* Cry Wolf), and have plenty of grass to eat. A religious leader—such as a rabbi, a priest, or a minister—is the spiritual caretaker of his/her "flock" or congregation, making sure that the members are provided with worship services and religious education. The metaphor of the spiritual leader as *shepherd* is found in the Old Testament: e.g., Psalm 23:1, "The Lord is my shepherd." ATWS. *See also* Shepherd (v).

SHEPHERD (v) *to shepherd a group of children.* To guide a group of children safely from one place to another, as on a field trip. WNNCD: 1790. Source: SHEEP. WNNCD: O.E. The verb *shepherd* derives from the noun *shepherd* (q.v.) "the leader of a congregation," but there is no religious sense in the verb. The sheepherder looks after his/her flock, making sure that they are safe and sound and well fed. The teacher sees that his/her *flock* stick together and move along peacefully. DEI.

SHOOFLY PIE *a shoofly pie.* A bottom-crusted pie filled with a mixture of molasses and brown sugar and topped with crumbs made of butter, sugar, and flour. WNNCD: 1926. Source: FLY. WNNCD: O.E. This Pennsylvania Dutch dessert is just as attractive to flies as to humans. "Shoo, fly!" is the command that gave rise to the name *shoofly.* IRCD; LCRH; MDWPO.

SHOO-IN *See* At the Drop of a Hat.

SHOOT A BEAVER *to shoot a beaver.* To sneak a look at, or photograph, the adult female pudenda, or vulva. Source: BEAVER. WNNCD: O.E. The American beaver has long been prized for its thick brown fur, which is used to make capes, coats, and hats, although the semiaquatic animal is usu. trapped rather than shot. A *beaver shot* is a filmed or taped picture of the female genitals. NDAS.

SHOOT THE BULL *to shoot the bull.* To engage in idle, often boastful, conversation. Source: BULL. WNNCD: O.E. *Shooting the bull* is an avocation of younger men (esp.) and women who have nothing better to do. The *bull* in question is a shortened and euphemized form of *bullshit*, so to "shoot the bull" is lit. to sling manure at one another: to *bullshit* each other. AID; DOC; HOI; HTB; IRCD. *See also* Bull (4); Bull Session; Bullshit (n); Bullshit (v). *Compare* Shoot a Beaver; Shoot the Duck.

SHOOT THE DUCK   *to shoot the duck.* To skate crouched down, sitting on one foot, with the other leg extended off the floor or ice. Source: DUCK. WNNCD: O.E. *Shooting the duck* is a roller skating or ice skating version of the *duck walk* (q.v.). The performer resembles a Russian Cossack dancer kicking from the squatting position. Chuck Berry's hunkered-down walk while playing the guitar features this extension of the leg on every step. *Compare* Shoot the Bull.

SHOP RAT   *a shop rat.* A blue-collar worker in a factory, esp. an automobile plant. Source: RAT. WNNCD: O.E. Factory workers often spend their lives in conditions resembling those of the lowly rat: dirty, difficult, and dangerous. *Shop rat* is not a derogatory term, however, but a label in which blue-collar workers take a certain amount of pride. *Compare* Desert Rat; Dock Rat; River Rat; Rug Rat.

SHOULDN'T HAPPEN TO A DOG   *See* Send a Dog out.

SHOW THE WHITE FEATHER   *to show the white feather.* To display cowardice. WNNCD: ca. 1785. Source: COCK. A white feather in the tail of a gamecock was once thought to be an indicator of cowardice and inferior breeding, and gamblers bet against that particular bird. The feather, however, was usu. not displayed until the bird was already losing and had lowered its tail feathers in a sign of defeat. ATWS; BDPF; CI; DEI; EWPO; HOI; LCRH; MDWPO; ST. *Compare* Coward; Tail between Your Legs.

SHOW YOUR TEETH   *to show—or bare—your teeth.* To display extreme hostility toward someone. Source: DOG. A guard dog barks to alert its owner to the presence of intruders and to scare them away. If an intruder persists, the dog moves on to stage two of its defense: a growl, combined with a retraction of the lips and a baring of the "fangs," or *canine teeth* (q.v.). When *people* are in the final stage of anger, they adopt a menacing attitude, make verbal threats, point fingers and wave fists, and otherwise indicate that they are prepared to fight. They may also actually *show their teeth.* ATWS; BDPF; DEI. *See also* Foam at the Mouth.

SHREW   *a shrew.* A nagging, scolding, sharp-tongued, bad-dispositioned, ill-tempered woman. IRCD: 14th cent. Source: SHREW. WNNCD: O.E. The shrew is a small animal that resembles both the mouse (for its long tail and slim legs) and the mole (for its tiny eyes and soft fur), but it is distinguished from them by its pointed snout and its extremely pugnacious behavior. Shrews were once thought to poison livestock—no doubt contributing to the metaphor. ATWS; EWPO; LCRH; THT. *See also* Shrewd; Shrewish. *Compare* Vixen.

SHREWD   *to be shrewd.* To be keen-witted and clever: a "shrewd" operator. Source: SHREW. WNNCD: O.E. The tiny, molelike shrew has lent its name to a sharp-tongued woman (as in Shakespeare's *Taming of the Shrew*) and to a sharp-witted—and not necessarily scrupulous—deal-maker of either sex. This is a large influence for such a small creature. EWPO; IRCD; LCRH; THT. *See also* Shrew; Shrewish.

SHREWISH   *to be shrewish.* To be ill-natured and bad-tempered (said esp. of a woman). WNNCD: 1565. Source: SHREW. WNNCD: O.E. The mouselike shrew may be tiny, but it has a voracious appetite, eating more than its bodyweight every day. It also has a bad attitude, killing and eating other shrews that get in its way. CE. *See also* Shrew; Shrewd.

SHRIMP   *a (little) shrimp.* A small, short, puny, or unimportant person. LTA: 1891. Source: SHRIMP. WNNCD: 14th cent. The shrimp, a small decapod crustacean, serves as food for many marine animals. *Little shrimp* is a redundancy; *jumbo* (q.v.) *shrimp* is an oxymoron. All shrimp are delicious. ATWS; EWPO; IRCD. *See also* Shrimpy.

SHRIMPY   *to be shrimpy.* To be small, short, puny, or unimportant. (Often confused with *skimpy.*) Source: SHRIMP. WNNCD: 14th cent. In the ocean, the shrimp is probably the ultimate prey. *Shrimp* may be an altered borrowing of the O.N. verb *skrympa* "to shrink," which may also be the source of Eng. *skimpy.* *See also* Shrimp.

SHUFFLE OFF THIS MORTAL COIL   *to shuffle off this mortal coil.* To die. Shakespeare's *Hamlet*: 1601. Source: SNAKE. In Hamlet's famous "To be, or not to be" soliloquy (Act III, Scene 1), he notes: "For in that sleep of death what dreams may come/ When we have shuffled off this mortal coil/ Must give us pause." Shakespeare was comparing death, or the soul leaving the body, to the snake's shedding of its skin. Crustaceans do the same thing (their shells), but the presence of *coil* restricts the interpretation to snakes. MDWPO. *See also* Slough off.

SHUTTERBUG   *See* Bug (n) (1).

SHUTTLECOCK   *a shuttlecock.* A badminton "bird." WNNCD: 1522. Source: COCK. WNNCD: O.E. The missile of badminton resembles a *cock* because it has feathers—stuck in one side of a light rubber ball—and it "flies" back and forth over the net. The *shuttle* portion of the word comes from the name of the weaver's instrument that passes to and fro between the vertical threads. HF; IRCD.

SHUT UP LIKE A CLAM   *to shut up like a clam.* ("When John mentioned marriage, she shut up like a clam.") To close your mouth and remain silent. Source:

CLAM. WNNCD: 1520. The *shut up* part of this metaphor (WNNCD: 1857) alludes to the raising of the lower jaw, by a human, to close the mouth. The hard-shell clam clamps both of its halfshells together when threatened. *See also* Clam up.

SHUT YOUR TRAP   *See* Trap.

SIC   *to sic someone on someone else.* To divert someone's attack to someone else. Source: DOG. *Sic 'em* is a command given to a dog by its handler to cause it to attack a human, another dog, or some other animal. The word *sic* is a modification of the word *seek*; it was orig. used (WNNCD: 1845) to set a hunting dog on a quarry, or a guard dog on an intruder. The expression *don't know sic 'em* is used of a dog—or a person—that is not too bright. WNWD. *Compare* Harass.

SICK AS A CAT   *to be as sick as a cat.* To be violently ill. Source: CAT. WNNCD: O.E. When a cat eats a bad mouse, it gets violently ill, vomiting up the mouse and everything else that it ate that day. The same thing happens when a cat gets distemper or becomes allergic to certain food, such as cow's milk. People who are *as sick as a cat* usu. have the same reaction—"losing their lunch" or "tossing their cookies." BDPF. *Compare* Sick as a Dog; Sick as a Horse.

SICK AS A DOG   *to be as sick as a dog.* To be miserably ill. Source: DOG. WNNCD: O.E. A person who is *as sick as a dog* usu. has a high temperature, a bad headache, pains in all the joints, diarrhea, and nausea—probably as a result of influenza or some other virus. Dogs don't get any sicker than humans, but they do it more openly—on the living room carpet, the dining room floor, the bedroom rug, etc. AID; ATWS; BDPF; DEI; DOC; IRCD. *Compare* Sick as a Cat; Sick as a Horse.

SICK AS A HORSE   *to be as sick as a horse.* To be so sick that they may have to shoot you. Source: HORSE. WNNCD: O.E. Cats and dogs usu. recover from their sickness, because they emit the "poison" from their stomachs; but a horse usu. remains listless, wheezes, and heaves its flanks. And if a cat or dog breaks a leg, you put the leg in a cast; but if a horse breaks a leg, you have to shoot it. People who are *as sick as a horse* can't get rid of the problem and wish someone would put them out of their misery. CH. *Compare* Sick as a Cat; Sick as a Dog.

SIDE HORSE   *See* Pommel Horse.

SIGN OF GOOD BREEDING   *See* Thoroughbred.

SILK   The fibers protruding from the top end of an unhusked ear of corn: "corn silk." WNNCD: 1861. Source: SILKWORM. WNNCD: O.E. The silkworm constructs its cocoon of a fine protein fiber, called *silk*, which is the basis not only for *corn silk* but for the name of the shirt and cap of a jockey, the *silks*, and the nickname for a parachute: "to hit the *silk*." ATWS. *See also* Silken; Silky.

SILKEN *to be silken*. To have a smooth, soft, delicate feeling and a lustrous appearance. Source: SILKWORM. WNNCD: O.E. The silkworm, or larva of the Asian moth, produces a filament that it uses to spin its cocoon. Humans then unwind the filament for weaving silk fabric. ATWS. *See also* Silk; Silky.

SILKY *to be silky*. To be smooth, soft, and delicate: e.g., a "silky voice." WNNCD: 1611. Source: SILKWORM. WNNCD: O.E. Of all the moth larvae that spin cocoons, the larva of the Asian moth (*Bombyx mori*) produces the finest and strongest filament. When unwound and respun into cloth, the result is smooth, soft, and delicate. ATWS. *See also* Bombast; Silk; Silken.

SILLY AS A GOOSE *See* Silly Goose.

SILLY ASS *a silly ass*. ("Don't be such a silly ass!") An unreasonable or unrealistic person. Source: ASS. WNNCD: O.E. The ass, or donkey, hasn't gotten any respect for many centuries. It has been characterized as stupid, stubborn, and laughable. A *silly ass* is someone who makes a fool of him-/herself. *See also* Ass; Make an Ass of Yourself; Smart Ass. *Compare* Silly Goose.

SILLY GOOSE *You silly goose!* You silly fool! LTA: 1547. Source: GOOSE. WNNCD: O.E. *Silly goose*, or just plain *goose*, is a polite appellation for someone who has done or said something foolish but is assumed to have known better. The goose has been regarded as a stupid bird for centuries, perhaps because of its tendency to follow the leader in a flock. Also: *silly as a goose*. ATWS; BDPF; CH; IRCD. *Compare* Silly Ass.

SILVERFISH *a silverfish*. A small, wingless insect that invades homes and damages bound books and starched clothing. Source: FISH. WNNCD: O.E. The insect is named after the fish known as a *silversides* (WNNCD: 1703), or "tarpon," which has silver-colored scales. The terrestrial *silverfish* is a silvery gray color but has no scales and, of course, is not a fish at all. It is, in fact, much older than any fish and is thought to be one of the most primitive of all living creatures. WNWD.

SINCE HECTOR WAS A PUP *See* Young Pup.

SING LIKE A BIRD *to sing like a bird*. For a female singer to sing beautifully and naturally; for a criminal to "squeal" on his/her fellow criminals. Source: BIRD. WNNCD: O.E. All birds make vocal sounds, but only the passerine birds are regarded as songbirds. Passerine birds are small perching birds that have a highly developed set of muscles connecting the syrinx (comparable to the human larynx) with the bronchial tubes. Two of the most melodious songbirds are the bold and beautiful cardinal and the shy and plainlooking robin. Female singers are said to *sing like birds* because the bird's song is high-pitched, but the singer among birds is usu. the male. The male bird sings to establish dominance, lay claim to a territory, or court a female. Criminals usu. *sing like a bird* to satisfy a plea bargain or earn a reduced sentence. WNWD. *Compare* Sing like a Canary; Sing like a Lark; Sing like a Nightingale.

SING LIKE A CANARY (1) *to sing like a canary.* For a female singer (esp. a soprano) to sing beautifully. EWPO: late-19th cent. Source: CANARY. (N.D.) The canary has been a popular pet in America for over a century. It is valued mostly for its song and its ability to sing along with a piano, organ, or voice. A woman who *sings like a canary* is also called a *canary* (q.v.). *See also* Sing like a Bird; Sing like a Lark; Sing like a Nightingale. *Compare* Sing like a Canary (2).

SING LIKE A CANARY (2) *to sing like a canary.* For a criminal to *rat* (q.v.) on his/her accomplices in crime. LTA: 1930. Source: CANARY. (N.D.) The caged finch from the Canary Islands loves to sing its own song and to imitate a song played or sung by humans. This is exactly what the caged human, also called a *canary* (q.v.), does. *Compare* Sing like a Canary (1).

SING LIKE A LARK *to sing like a lark.* To sing beautifully. Source: LARK. WNNCD: O.E. A female singer, esp. a soprano, who sings beautifully is said to *sing like a lark*; but it is the male lark (or skylark) that does the singing, and he does it up to 800 feet in the air, during breeding season, as part of the courtship ritual. ATWS. *See also* Bright as a Lark; Happy as a Lark. *Compare* Sing like a Bird; Sing like a Canary (1); Sing like a Nightingale.

SING LIKE A NIGHTINGALE *to sing like a nightingale.* To possess a beautiful soprano voice. Source: NIGHTINGALE. WNNCD: O.E. The *nightingale* (fr. O.E. *nihtegale* "night singer") is an Old World nocturnal bird. The lovely voice is that of the male, however, not the female. *See also* Nightingale. *Compare* Sing like a Bird; Sing like a Canary (1); Sing like a Lark.

SIREN *a siren.* A bewitching female singer; a beautiful, seductive woman; a loud mechanical or electronic warning signal. Source: BIRD. In Greek mythology, a *Siren* (WNNCD: 14th cent.) was a bird with the head of a woman that sang so enchantingly that it could cause unsuspecting sailors to crash their ships on the rocks. In modern times, a *siren* is a woman who sings or acts as seductively as the mythological bird. Oddly enough, it can also be a sound that warns people *against* danger, rather than attracting them *to* it. EWPO.

SITTING DUCK *a sitting duck.* A defenseless person: an "easy mark." WNNCD: 1942. Source: DUCK. WNNCD: O.E. Ducks are hunted *on the wing* (q.v.). Shooting them while they are sitting on the ground or in the water is both unsporting (because it is too easy) and illegal (in most places). A naive, innocent, and overly trusting person is a *sitting duck* for con artists and swindlers. AID; ATWS; CI; DEI; DOC; ST. *See also* Dead Duck; Duck Soup; Lame Duck.

SIT UP AND TAKE NOTICE   *to sit up and take notice.* To suddenly show interest in something. Source: DOG. A watchdog wakes up, sits up, *pricks up its ears* (q.v.), and looks in the direction of a suspicious sound. People *sit up and take notice* when they see or hear something unusual or unexpected, such as a mention of their own name.

SIX-HUNDRED POUND GORILLA   *a six-hundred pound gorilla.* Question: Where does a six-hundred pound gorilla sleep? Answer: Anywhere it wants to. Source: GORILLA. WNNCD: 1853. The allusion is to a gigantic corporation that always seems to get its own way. The male gorilla is large (but usu. not over 500 pounds), and it is intimidating (although its *bark is worse than its bite* [q.v.]). *Also:* Seven-hundred Pound Gorilla; Eight-hundred Pound Gorilla. *See also* Gorilla.

SKIN THE CAT   *See* More than One Way to Skin a Cat.

SKUNK (n)   *You skunk!* You dirty rat! Source: SKUNK. WNNCD: 1634. *Skunk* is derived from an Algonquian word for a distinctly American animal, related to the European *polecat* (q.v.). The skunk is attractively colored (black with white stripes), but it shoots a vile-smelling liquid from beneath its tail when threatened. The human *skunk* is as offensive as the spray. ATWS; EWPO. *See also* Skunk (v).

SKUNK (v)   *to skunk someone.* To defeat someone totally. WNNCD: 1846. Source: SKUNK. WNNCD: 1634. The skunk protects itself by shooting a vile-smelling liquid from beneath its tail at its attacker. No animal wants to deal with that. Humans *skunk* their opponents when they defeat them so badly that they can't score a single point. ATWS; IRCD; ST. *See also* Skunk (n).

SKUNK CABBAGE   *a skunk cabbage.* A large North American plant that in spring sends forth a flower that has a very unpleasant odor. WNNCD: 1751. Source: SKUNK. WNNCD: 1634. The *skunk cabbage,* which is not a real cabbage, was named after the skunk because of its offensive smell. The skunk, like the plant, has a beautiful appearance, but it shoots a vile-smelling liquid from beneath its tail when threatened. EWPO; IRCD. *See also* Skunk (n).

SLEEPER   *a sleeper.* Something that has gone unnoticed but suddenly shows promise. EWPO: 1930s. Source: CATTLE (?). The origin of this sense of *sleeper* is uncertain, but it may derive from an unbranded steer of the same name that goes unnoticed but manages to develop on its own. A metaphorical *sleeper* is a candidate, athlete, or theatrical production that receives little attention from the media but attains prominence anyway. EWPO. *Compare* Dark Horse.

SLEEP WITH THE FISHES   *See* Feed the Fishes.

SLEUTHHOUND   *See* Hound (n).

SLICK AS AN EEL   *See* Slippery as an Eel.

SLICK CHICK   *See* Chick.

SLIMEBALL   *a slimeball.* A lowlife. Source: SNAIL. Literally, a slimeball is the mucous secretion produced by a land snail, or *slug* (q.v.). It is sticky and gooey and totally repulsive. The same adj. also describes a human "greaser," who loads his hair with gobs of gook and thinks he is God's gift to women. At any rate, a human *slimeball*, male or female, is an odious person, as repulsive as snail mucous. *See also* Slug; Snail. *Compare* Lounge Lizard.

SLINK   *to slink around; to slink away.* To move sinuously or provocatively; to steal away stealthily or furtively. WNNCD: 14th cent. Source: SNAKE. The snake is the ultimate "creeper." When encountered uncoiled, most snakes slink away— out of fear and in a sinuous fashion. Humans also *slink* away quietly, out of fear or shame; and females sometimes *slink* sinuously and provocatively, as on the runway of a fashion show. CE. *See also* Snake (v) (1).

SLINKY   *a slinky dress.* A long, flowing dress of silk or satin that clings to the body of the woman who wears it the way a snakeskin clings to a snake: when the woman moves, the dress moves. WNNCD: 1918. Source: SNAKE. The *serpent* is etymologically the "creeper" (fr. Lat. *serpere* "to creep"), and *slinky* derives fr. O.E. *slincan* "to creep." CE. *See also* Serpentine; Snakelike.

SLIPPERY AS AN EEL   *to be as slippery—or as slick—as an eel.* To be hard to pin down (e.g., a politician), hard to catch (e.g., a criminal), or hard to get a handle on (e.g., a football). DOC: 1412. Source: EEL. WNNCD: O.E. The eel, a snakelike "fish," is long, scaleless, and "slippery when wet." AID; DEI; IRCD; SHM. *See also* Like Catching a Greased Pig.

SLIP THE COLLAR   *See* Dog Collar.

SLOUGH OFF   *to slough something off.* To get rid of something that is useless, disadvantageous, or objectionable. Source: SNAKE. Periodically, a snake sheds its old skin, or *slough* (WNNCD: 14th cent.), just as a crustacean sheds its shell, a bird its feathers, and a deer its antlers. Humans *slough off*, or dispose of, a disadvantageous card in the game of bridge by "discarding" it. *Compare* Shuffle off this Mortal Coil.

SLOW AND STEADY WINS THE RACE   Constant effort is more often successful than intermittent spurts of energy. (The moral of the Aesop fable, "The Tortoise and the Hare.") Source: TORTOISE; HARE. In the fable, the tortoise (a large land turtle) maintained a slow and steady pace, while the hare (a European wild rabbit) raced in fits and starts. The tortoise won. ATWS. *See also* Tortoise and the Hare.

SLOW AS A SNAIL   *to be as slow as a snail.* To move at an exceedingly slow rate of speed. Source: SNAIL. WNNCD: O.E. You too would move slowly if you had only one "foot," no legs, and were obliged to carry your house around on your back. The only thing slower than a snail (a univalve mollusk) is probably an oyster (a bivalve mollusk), which attaches itself to a rock and never moves at all. CH. *See also* Snaillike Pace; Snail-paced; Snail's Pace. *Compare* Solitary as an Oyster.

SLUG   *a slug.* A small lump of metal, such as a musket ball. Source: SLUG. WNNCD: 15th cent. The slug is a wormlike, shell-less land snail whose shape is somewhat like that of a bullet but whose speed is considerably slower. ROE. *Compare* Snail.

SLUGABED   *a slugabed.* One who hates to—or refuses to—get up in the morning. Shakespeare's *Romeo and Juliet*: 1592. Source: SLUG. WNNCD: 15th cent. In the play (Act IV, Scene 5), the Nurse chastises the drugged Juliet for being so slow to arise: "Fie, you slug-abed." The slug, a large land snail, is very slow and very vulnerable, since it has no legs to run away on and no shell to hide in. *See also* Slug; Sluggard; Sluggish.

SLUGGARD   *a sluggard.* A lazy or indolent person. Source: SLUG. WNNCD: 15th cent. The slug is an extremely slow-moving land snail. It seems to take forever to get from here to there. A *sluggard* moves about as fast as a slug. CE. *See also* Slug; Slugabed; Sluggish. *Compare* Snail.

SLUGGISH   *to be sluggish.* To be slow or inactive (e.g., your digestion; the economy). WNNCD: 15th cent. Source: SLUG. WNNCD: 15th cent. The slug, a shell-less land snail, is one of the slowest moving animals in the world. *See also* Slugabed; Sluggard. *Compare* Slow as a Snail; Snaillike Pace.

SLY AS A FOX   *to be as sly—or clever, or cunning, or smart—as a fox.* To be crafty and cunning. Source: FOX. WNNCD: O.E. The analogy is probably to the red fox, familiar as the animal chased by horses and hounds in a fox hunt and cursed by chicken ranchers everywhere. When hunted, the fox is often able to escape the dogs by retracing its steps or by running in a stream or in the tracks of another animal. In the henhouse, the fox is often able to kill a number of chickens before the farmer is aware of its presence; then, with its lithe body, it can slip through the tiniest opening, like a *weasel* (q.v.). The fox was the subject of many animal fables in the classical period, when it usually got bested, and in the medieval period, when it usu. came out on top. AID; DOC; SHM. *See also* Sly Old Fox.

SLY OLD DOG   *a sly old dog.* A person who displays previously hidden talents. Source: DOG. WNNCD: O.E. Since you *can't teach old dogs new tricks* (q.v.), an old dog that suddenly demonstrates youthful behavior must have been capable of it all the time. People—usu. males—are called *sly old dogs* when they reveal interests or talents that no one ever knew they had. For example, they may become suddenly romantic, athletic, stylish, or vulgar. *You sly old dog!* is usu. an expression of admiration for having kept the secret for such a long time. BDPF; DEI.

SLY OLD FOX   *a sly old fox.* A clever old man. Source: FOX. WNNCD: O.E. A clever old man with silver hair is compared here to the silver fox, which inhabits subarctic regions of Europe, Asia, and North America. (In more temperate climes it is called a "red fox.") The silver fox has to be clever in order to survive harsh winters, when its usual fare of mice, voles, hares, and birds is seldom seen. ATWS; DEI; ID. *See also* Sly as a Fox. *Compare* Sly Old Dog.

SMALL FRY   Young children (EWPO: 1852); unimportant people (WNNCD: 1897). Source: FISH. *Fry* are the young of fish (fr. O.Fr. *frier* "to spawn") and, metaphorically, of some other animals, such as frogs and bees. The word was first used of children in the late-17th cent. (EWPO: 1697) and was expanded to *small fry* in Harriet Beecher Stowe's *Uncle Tom's Cabin*. In the late-19th cent., *small fry* (or *small-fry*) was applied also to small-time operators, such as "a small-fry politician." A false etymology of *small fry* holds that a catch of small fish, when fried, will amount to a very small meal. ATWS; BDPF; CI; DEI; HOI; LCRH; LTA; NDAS; ST.

SMART AS A FOX   *See* Sly as a Fox.

SMART ASS   *a smart ass.* A pretentious or scarcastic person. Source: ASS. WNNCD: O.E. *Smart ass* is an oxymoron. The ass, or donkey, has always been regarded as a stupid animal: a horse wannabe. A *smart ass* is a person who pretends to be a horse but is only as smart as a donkey. *See also* Ass; Make an Ass of Yourself. *Compare* Silly Ass.

SMART OLD BIRD   *See* Tough Old Bird.

SMELL A RAT   *to smell a rat.* To suspect that things are not as they seem. IRCD: ca. 1550. Source: RAT. WNNCD: O.E. Cats and dogs (esp. rat terriers) can smell live rats without actually seeing them, and these animals are often kept on farms to control the rat population. Humans can only smell rats that are dead, as Hamlet affirmed when asked by King Claudius of the whereabouts of Polonius, whom

Hamlet had recently killed, suspecting him to be a "rat": " . . . if you find him not within this month, you shall nose him as you go up the stairs . . . ." (Hamlet: Act IV, Scene 3). AID; ATWS; BDPF; CI; DEI; DOC; EWPO; LCRH; MDWPO; ST.

SMOKE OUT   *to smoke someone or something out*. To force someone to come out of hiding; to bring something suspicious into public view. WNNCD: 1605. Source: ANIMAL. To smoke an animal out of its den or hole is to build a fire at the entrance, cover it with damp grass or green twigs, and blow the smoke inside until the animal is forced to exit. Result: death. To *smoke* a criminal *out* of a hiding place is to either perform the same operation or to use tear gas or loud noise. Result: capture. To *smoke out* corruption is to publicize it through the mass media. Result: truth. CI; DOC; SOED; ST.

SMOOTH SOMEONE'S RUFFLED FEATHERS   *See* Ruffle Someone's Feathers.

SNAIL   *a snail*. A slow-moving or lethargic person. Source: SNAIL. WNNCD: O.E. The snail is a gastropod mollusk that inhabits a single ("univalve") shell, which it enlarges, from birth, in a spiral shape. Unlike the two-shelled (or "bivalve") mollusks—such as the clam, mussel, and oyster—the snail is not permanently attached to its shell but is free to leave it or carry it around on its back. However, the snail's pace is extremely slow—approx. four miles a year. ATWS; EWPO. *See also* Slow as a Snail; Snail's Pace.

SNAIL DARTER   *a snail darter*. A tiny, nearly extinct, freshwater fish of the eastern United States. Source: SNAIL. WNNCD: O.E. *Snail darter* appears to be a contradiction. Snails don't dart: they are among the slowest-moving animals on earth. The feeding habits of the *snail darter* are unknown (it may feed on baby snails), but its notoriety is great. In the 1970s it held up the building of a TVA dam in Tennessee because of its endangered status. WNNCD: *See also* Snail.

SNAILLIKE PACE   *See* Snail's Pace.

SNAIL-PACED   *See* Snail's Pace.

SNAIL'S PACE   *to move at a snail's pace (or a snaillike pace)*. To move at an excruciatingly slow rate of speed. EWPO: 1592. Source: SNAIL. WNNCD: O.E. Drivers become frustrated when bumper-to-bumper traffic moves only a few miles an hour, as do crowds when the line moves only a few feet a minute—i.e., is *snail-paced* (WNNCD: 1594). Imagine how the poor snail feels, moving only a little over an inch a minute, or four miles a year! The pace is so slow because the snail has no legs (and only one "foot"!) and usu. carries its shell (the original "mobile home") around with it wherever it goes. AID; ATWS; CI; DEI. *See also* Slow as a Snail; Snail.

SNAKE (n) (1) *a snake.* A worthless, no-good person. Source: SNAKE. WNNCD: O.E. Snakes are neither worthless (they help reduce the rat and mouse population) nor bad (they usu. don't go looking for trouble). But they *are* frightening to most humans because of their ability to move rapidly (or "slither") without legs, to lurk unseen under the cover of leaves or grass, and to strike out at intruders with potentially lethal results (although the poisonous ones sometimes hiss or rattle before doing so). Human *snakes* are sneaky persons who abuse others without provocation. They are the "lowest" of the vertebrates. *Compare* Dirty Rat.

SNAKE (n) (2) *a snake.* A long, flexible metal cable used for unplugging sewer pipes—a *plumber's snake* (WNNCD: 1938)—or for cleaning out the tubes of musical instruments. Source: SNAKE. WNNCD: O.E. The body of a snake is long and flexible, and, unlike the worm, it has a spine of connected vertebrae. For this reason, the snake has been compared to a steel cable or a braided whip. *Plumber's snakes* are sometimes motorized so that they twist as they enter the "hole." ATWS; IRCD.

SNAKE (v) (1) *to snake your way.* For a line of animals or people, or a road or river, to wind its way toward its destination. WNNCD: 1653. Source: SNAKE. WNNCD: O.E. Some animals, such as ducks and geese, travel on the ground in a single file, *snaking their way* forward but not necessarily in a straight line. A long waiting line of people may wind its way, slowly, around several corners. A road *snakes its way* through the hills and valleys, and a river of water or lava follows its sinuous path of least resistance. Snakes don't have legs, so they move by twisting and turning. The pattern of movement is referred to as *serpentine* (q.v.). IRCD. *See also* Slink; Snake (v) (2).

SNAKE (v) (2) *to snake a log.* To drag a log out of the woods. Source: SNAKE. WNNCD: O.E. When a log is dragged out of the woods on a chain, as behind a team of horses or a tractor, it moves from side to side, and rolls slightly, as the driver dodges other logs and trees. The scene is very much like the sinuous, or *serpentine* (q.v.), movement of a snake on the ground. *See also* Snake (v) (1).

SNAKEBIT *to be snakebit.* To be plagued with a sudden onset of bad luck: to be *jinxed* (q.v.). Source: SNAKE. WNNCD: O.E. Job must have felt that he was *snakebit* when the Devil began to test his resolve: all of a sudden everything seemed to be going wrong. Victims of snakebite also ask "Why me?" after they are ambushed by a rattlesnake or a copperhead. The answer: They were in the wrong place at the wrong time. ATWS.

SNAKE DANCE *a snake dance.* A procession of people in single file that follows a *serpentine* path (q.v.) and is often accompanied by live or recorded band music. Source: SNAKE. WNNCD: O.E. The modern *snake dance* is usu. performed by high school or college students—sometimes around a huge bonfire—the night before a homecoming football game, although it may also occur *after* the game if the local team wins. It somewhat resembles a "conga line," although there are no "steps," and touching is not required. The original snake dance was a ceremonial dance, performed by certain Native American tribes, in which real or symbolic snakes were handled. ATWS; IRCD.

SNAKE DOCTOR *a snake doctor.* A dragonfly. (Also called a *snake feeder.*) WNNCD: 1862. Source: SNAKE. WNNCD: O.E. This regional expression (from inland Virginia) implies that the *dragonfly* (q.v.) ministers to the snake, caring for and feeding it. The fact is that snakes care very much for, even relish, *snake doctors*, which are among its favorite food. Dragonflies, which are long-tailed four-winged insects, inhabit waterways and wetlands of America, as do many snakes.

SNAKE EYES *to come up (with) snake eyes.* To come up with nothing to show for your efforts. IRCD: ca. 1930. Source: SNAKE. WNNCD: O.E. In the game of craps, to throw *snake eyes* is to throw "craps": two ones, the *lowest* combination of the dice (and a losing count if it is the first throw). The two black dots, against a contrasting background, resemble the eyes of a snake, the *lowest* vertebrate to the ground. ATWS; BDPF; ST.

SNAKE FEEDER *See* Snake Doctor.

SNAKE IN THE GRASS *a snake in the grass.* A person who appears trustworthy but is really a faithless, and perhaps dangerous, friend. WNNCD: 1696. Source: SNAKE. WNNCD: O.E. Vergil referred to a hidden danger in *Eclogue* III as "a snake . . . lurking in the grass," and both Chaucer and Shakespeare described a hidden enemy in such terms. A poisonous viper usu. ambushes its prey, waiting under the cover of brush or tall grass for its innocent victim to appear. AID; ATWS; BDPF; CI; DEI; DOC; EWPO; HTB; ID; IRCD; MDWPO. *See also* Rattlesnake; Serpent; Snake (n) (1); Viper. *Compare* Wolf in Sheep's Clothing.

SNAKELIKE *to be snakelike.* To be narrow and winding. Source: SNAKE. WNNCD: O.E. A *snakelike* path or passageway winds its way through the forest or fortress the way a snake moves through the grass. As seen from above, the snake's body resembles the profile of a coiled spring. In motion, every part of the snake follows the same path, the way all pedestrians must follow the same sidewalk. *See also* Serpentine; Slinky.

SNAKE MEDICINE Moonshine: cheap, illegal whiskey. LTA: 1865. Source: SNAKE. WNNCD: O.E. *Snake medicine* sounds like an antidote for snakebite, but it is just the opposite: liquor as powerful as a snake's venom. Enough venom, or enough alcohol, can kill you. *Snake medicine* may be the basis for the later *snake oil* (q.v.), which was worthless as a medicine but contained enough alcohol to make you forget that you were sick. Neither concoction contained any snake by-products. *See also* Snake Poison. *Compare* Mule; Sheep Dip.

SNAKE OIL   Patent medicine that was once sold at traveling medicine shows as a panacea or cure-all. WNNCD: 1927. Source: SNAKE. WNNCD: O.E. *Snake oil* contained no "oil of snake." It was probably so named because the suckers who bought it eventually came to realize that it was a fraud, like a false puff adder. It couldn't attack anything, although its high alcoholic content kept the buyers from realizing that until the show had left town. *Snake oil* has been extended to cover any deceptive or oversimplified "solution" to a problem. ATWS; IRCD; MDWPO. *Compare* Snake Medicine; Snake Poison.

SNAKE PIT   *a snake pit.* An insane asylum (WNNCD: 1946); any place of chaos or disorder. Source: SNAKE. WNNCD: O.E. It is said that insane persons were once thrown into a real snake pit to shock them back to sanity. Whether or not this is true, a pit full of hundreds of snakes, poisonous or not, would be a horrible place to find yourself in. Since 1946 the meaning has been extended to describe the pit of the stock market and other scenes of bedlam. ATWS; IRCD.

SNAKE POISON   Cheap, potent whiskey. NDAS: late 1800s. Source: SNAKE. WNNCD: O.E. Technically, "snake poison" is snake venom, which is regularly extracted from poisonous snakes to produce antidotes. However, it is not an ingredient in whiskey. The metaphor is based on the fact that cheap, probably illegal, and high-proof whiskey can kill you as fast as snake venom can. *See also* Snake Medicine; Snake Oil. *Compare* Mule; Sheep Dip.

SNARL   *See* Bark like a Dog.

SNATCH FROM THE JAWS   *to snatch victory from the jaws of defeat* (complimentary); *to snatch defeat from the jaws of victory* (sarcastic). To achieve unexpected success—or suffer unexpected failure—at the last moment. Source: ANIMAL. It is uncertain to which animal to attribute the "jaws," but lions and tigers will do, as will alligators and crocodiles. The expressions derive from the jargon of sports reporters. ST. *See also* Pluck (v).

SNIFF OUT   *to sniff something out.* To detect or uncover trouble of any kind. SOED: 1864. Source: DOG. A hunting dog can sniff out a quarry by following its track with its nose, and police dogs can be trained to sniff out drugs or explosives simply by the scent. Investigative reporters *sniff out* crime and corruption by following a paper trail; and a reporter who has a *nose for news* is able to smell trouble a mile away, just as the bloodhound is able to track a criminal a great distance from the scene of the crime. CI; DEI; ST. *See also* Cast about.

SNIPE *to snipe at someone.* To fire bullets or snide remarks at someone from a safe distance. WNNCD: 1832. Source: SNIPE. WNNCD: 14th cent. The snipe— a small, long-billed wetlands bird related to the woodcock—is a difficult prey to hunt. Besides being small, it flies very close to the ground until it is out of range of the shotgun shells. ATWS; IRCD. *See also* Sniper. *Compare* Carp.

SNIPE HUNT *a snipe hunt.* An elaborate practical joke played on an initiate by a group of high school or college students. LCRH: ca. 1900. Source: SNIPE. WNNCD: 14th cent. The snipe is a real gamebird, but the *snipe hunt* is a prank. A new member of the group is taken out into the swamp at night and told to hold a sack or pillowcase open while the rest of the members locate the snipe and drive it in that direction. They disappear, and the initiate is *left holding the bag* (q.v.) all night. HTB; NDAS; SPD; ST.

SNIPER *a sniper.* A person who shoots at exposed individuals from a concealed position. Source: SNIPE. WNNCD: 14th cent. The sniper may be a crazed civilian or a member of the police or military. The crazed civilian picks off people—and the police pick off crazed civilians—as if they were birds, such as the *snipe*. IRCD. *See also* Snipe; Snipe Hunt.

SNOOT *See* Snout.

SNOOTY *See* Snout.

SNORE LIKE A MOOSE *to snore like a moose.* To snore loudly and deeply. Source: MOOSE. WNNCD: 1603. It is not known whether moose snore; but if they do, it must sound like thunder. The metaphor is based either on the huge size of the male moose (over six feet tall at the shoulders and approx. two-thirds of a ton in weight) or on the loud call of the female moose during the mating season.

SNOUT *a snout.* A human nose. Source: ANIMAL. Literally, a *snout* (fr. M.E. *snute*) is the *muzzle*, or projecting jaws and nose of an animal, such as a hog (WNNCD: 13th cent.). Figuratively, a *snout* is the large, or grotesquely large, nose of a human. *Snout* is also the source of Mod. Eng. *snoot* (WNNCD: 1861), which has the same meaning. To be *snooty* (WNNCD: ca. 1920) is to look down your nose at someone, i.e., with snobbery or disdain; and a *snooty* person is a snob. ATWS; WNWD. *Compare* Pug Nose.

SNOWBIRD *a snowbird.* A northerner who travels south for the winter. NDAS: ca. 1900. Source: BIRD. WNNCD: O.E. Nowadays, *snowbirds* are people who can afford to spend the winter in the *South*, but an earlier use of the term applied to migratory workers who couldn't afford to spend the winter in the *North*. The earliest use of the term, in the 1880s, applied to Northern men who enlisted in the Army in the winter and then deserted in the spring. The metaphor is based on the fact that some migratory birds, also called *snowbirds* (WNNCD: 1674), show up in the South only in the winter. *Snowbird* is also slang for "cocaine addict." EWPO. *Compare* Bird of Passage.

SNOW BUNNY   *a snow bunny.* A female groupie who frequents ski resorts but spends less time on the slopes than in the lodge. IHAT: 1960s. Source: RABBIT. The *snow bunny* is like the snowshoe hare, whose coat changes with the seasons. In the winter, the *snow bunny* dresses up in furs and hangs out at the ski lodge, showing off and looking for attention and alliances. IRCD. *See also* Beach Bunny; Bunny.

SNUG AS A BUG IN A RUG   *to be as snug as a bug in a rug.* To be cozy, comfortable, and contented. EWPO: 1772. Source: BUG. WNNCD: 1622. *Bug* and *rug* were probably selected for this metaphor only to rhyme with *snug*, but bugs do inhabit rugs, and they are reluctant to leave them. The clothes moth, for example, feeds not only on woolen clothes but on woolen carpets. Benjamin Franklin is credited with the first written use of this expression. AID; ATWS; CE; DOC; IRCD; LTA.

SOAR   *to soar.* To rise to great heights. Source: BIRD. When *prices soar,* they increase dramatically. When a bird soars, it rises on the solar thermals and updrafts. Pilots also *soar*—in gliders and hot-air balloons—and ballet dancers *soar to great heights* on the stage. *See also* Soar like an Eagle.

SOAR LIKE AN EAGLE   *to soar like an eagle.* To glide through the air with the greatest of ease. Source: EAGLE. WNNCD: 13th cent. The eagle is known for its ability to soar high in the air, silently and effortlessly, without flapping its wings. This behavior has been associated with the glider and the balloon—and with trapeze artists, ballet dancers, platform divers, and gymnasts. To *soar with the eagles* is to be flying high. *See also* Soar.

SOAR TO GREAT HEIGHTS   *See* Soar.

SOAR WITH THE EAGLES   *See* Soar like an Eagle.

S.O.B.   *See* Son of a Bitch.

SOCIAL BUTTERFLY   *a social butterfly.* A person who flits from one social event to another, seeking pleasure and visibility. Source: BUTTERFLY. WNNCD: O.E. The butterfly flutters (by) from one flower to another, gathering nectar and showing off its beautiful wings to a possible mate. It does not stay in one place very long. ATWS; BDPF; EWPO; MDWPO. *Compare* Social Lion.

SOCIAL LION *a social lion.* A person who is prominent in social circles: a celebrity. Source: LION. WNNCD: 12th cent. Lions are social animals, but their society is rather small: a "pride" of ten or so, including a couple of males, a couple of females, and youngsters of various ages. The dominant adult male is the head of the family, but he is seldom invited to "do lunch" with other animals. WNWD. *See also* King of Beasts. *Compare* Social Butterfly.

SOFT SELL *See* Hard-shell/Soft-shell.

SOFT-SHELL *See* Hard-shell/Soft-shell.

SOFT-SHELL TACO *See* Hard-shell/Soft-shell.

SOLITARY AS AN OYSTER *to be as solitary as an oyster.* To be cloistered, like a monk in a monastery. EWPO: 1843 (Dickens' *Christmas Carol*). Source: OYSTER. WNNCD: 14th cent. The oyster has many enemies. Although it "beds" with other oysters, it spends most of its time with its shell closed, fearful of being sucked out by a limpet or a starfish. It simply attaches itself to a object on the sea floor and remains in that place forever. WNWD. *Compare* Cocoon (v).

SON OF A BITCH *a son of a bitch.* A bastard; a despicable person. WNNCD: 1712. Source: DOG. A *bitch* is an adult female dog; therefore, technically, all male dogs are sons of bitches. The association of *bitch* with *bastard* is due to the fact that female dogs are not monogamous but will mate with any dog of the same or different breed. The offspring, then, are likely to be despised by a fastidious breeder. *Son of a bitch!* is an expression of surprise or disappointment, but the abbreviation *S.O.B.* (WNNCD: ca. 1925) is heard in more polite society. DEI; IHAT; IRCD; LTA. *See also* Bitch (n).

SON OF A SEA COOK *You son of a sea cook!* You old stinker! Source: SKUNK. WNNCD: 1634. The Algonquian Indian name for the American polecat is *segonku*. The European colonists pronounced the word *sea-konk*, which later became *sea cook*. So a *son of a sea cook* is lit. a "son of a skunk"—not quite as bad as being the adult skunk itself. EWPO. *Compare* Son of a Bitch.

SOREHEAD *See* Cross as a Bear.

SOUND LIKE A CAT IN HEAT *See* Like a Cat in Heat.

SOUP AND FISH Formal dinner clothes for men. NDAS: early 1900s. Source: FISH. WNNCD: O.E. Soup and fish are the first two courses, in that order, of a formal, six-course dinner. The appropriate dress for men at such a dinner is—or at least *was*—white tie ("soup") and tails ("fish"). Earlier, men's formal evening dress was nicknamed a *monkey suit* (q.v.), and later it came to be known as a *tuxedo*. EWPO; NDAS. *Compare* White Tie and Tails.

SOUR GRAPES   Disparagement of a goal that you have failed to reach. WNNCD: 1760. Source: FOX. In the Aesop fable, the fox's goal was to reach some grapes overhead. Having failed to do so, he consoled himself by saying that they were probably sour anyhow. Human "foxes" sometimes utter *sour grapes* when they are unsuccessful at getting a job or a date or putting together a toy for which "some assembly is required." ATWS; WNWD.

SOUTHPAW   *See* Paw.

SOW   *a sow*. The main channel into which molten iron was once poured. IRCD: 1570s. Source: PIG. Casting iron in the 16th cent. was crude and colorful. Molten iron was poured directly into a channel in the sand (the "sow") that led to numerous but smaller side channels (the "pigs"). To the workers, this formation looked like a mother sow nursing two rows of piglets. The resulting lumps of iron were called *pig iron* (WNNCD: 1665). ATWS; BDPF; LCRH. *See also* Pig (1).

SPANISH FLY   A 17th cent. diuretic, counterirritant, and (supposed) aphrodisiac. Source: FLY. WNNCD: O.E. *Spanish fly* was a powder made of ground-up Spanish "flies" (WNNCD: 1634), i.e., Southern European blister beetles. A beetle is not a fly, and a fly is not an aphrodisiac, so this is a double metaphor. EWPO; IHAT; WNWD. *Compare* Spanish Worm.

SPANISH WORM   *a Spanish worm*. A nail, hidden in a log or a board, that damages the implement of the lumberman or carpenter who tries to cut it. Source: WORM. WNNCD: O.E. This metaphor was probably coined during the time of the Spanish Armada, when England and Spain were enemies. (*Spanish worm* is reminiscent of "German Measles" and "The French Disease.") The larvae of some beetles do infest some trees, but they are neither "true" worms nor Spanish. BDPF. *Compare* Spanish Fly.

SPAR   *to spar with someone*. To engage in a practice boxing match with someone; to engage in a verbal exchange with someone. SOED: 1698. Source: COCK. WNNCD: O.E. A *spar* (a variant of *spur*) is the sharp metal device, attached to the back of the lower leg of a gamecock, which serves as its primary weapon in a cockfight. The cocks attack each other, or *spar*, feet first, like kickboxers. Hand-boxers *spar* with each other for practice, wearing headguards to avoid injury. Debaters engage in *verbal sparring*, which, like practice boxing, is restrained and not intended to draw blood. ATWS; ST. *See also* Sparring Partner.

SPARRING PARTNER   *a sparring partner*. A training companion for practice boxing matches (WNNCD: 1908); a close friend with whom you can argue without any hard feelings. Source: COCK. The physical sparring of boxers is derived from the *sparring* (or "spurring") of gamecocks in a cockfight. The cocks are out for blood, but the boxers wear headgear and try to avoid injury. *Verbal sparring* is even less violent, although it is sometimes hard to tell, given the insults and jibes of the participants. CI; ST. *See also* Spar.

SPARROW-GRASS Asparagus. (A folk etymology.) Source: SPARROW. WNNCD: O.E. The American sparrow—either the house sparrow or the tree sparrow—does not eat grass, and it does not nest in the grass. *Sparrow-grass* is the result of an attempt to make some English sense of a Latin word: *asparagus*. EWPO.

SPARROW HAWK *a sparrow hawk.* A small Eurasian hawk, related to the larger American *goshawk* (q.v.). WNNCD: 15th cent. Source: SPARROW. WNNCD: O.E. Although the *sparrow hawk* does catch birds in flight—including an occasional sparrow—the raptor was probably so named because of its small size, as hawks go. (The *goshawk* is almost twice as long as the *sparrow hawk.*) *Compare* Mosquito Hawk.

SPARROW-LEGGED *to be sparrow-legged.* To have short, skinny legs. Source: SPARROW. WNNCD: O.E. The house sparrow (or English sparrow) is a small bird that seems to have no legs at all—just two huge feet that are longer than its leg bones. Sparrows are such common birds that they have helped to name many other organisms. EWPO. *See also* Sparrow-grass; Sparrow Hawk.

SPAWN *to spawn something.* To produce, generate, or bring forth something. Source: FISH. All fish—both "true" fish and shellfish—are said to *spawn* when they produce or deposit eggs in large numbers. The "many from one" notion has been applied to an invention that *spawns*, or generates, rapid development in a particular field—as the PC did in the computer field. *Spawn* is also used for the birth of a single individual or social concept that would change history: e.g., the country that *spawned* Adoph Hitler; the nation that *spawned* Communism. ATWS.

SPEAK OF THE DEVIL *Speak of the devil!* Here comes the person we were just talking about. Source: BIRD. The "bird" part of the metaphor appears in the second half of the proverb: "Speak of the Devil and he always appears; speak of the Angels and you can hear the *flutter of their wings.*" The Devil, a fallen angel, is usu. portrayed as a male, clad in black, with black wings. The good angels are usu. young men, dressed in white, with white wings. The full proverb means something like this: "If you ask for trouble, you'll always get it; if you ask for help, you never will." Translation: "There's never a cop around when you need one." Good angels were given the wings of birds so that they could fly from Heaven to earth and back. BDPF.

SPEAK WITH FORKED TONGUE *to speak with forked tongue.* To speak doubletalk—saying one thing and meaning another. Source: SNAKE. Many snakes (and small lizards) have tongues that are split at the end, presumably for increasing the tongue's olfactory ability. A human who *speaks with forked tongue* is like the poisonous snake that shows its harmless tongue while hiding its venomous fangs. The opposite is to *talk turkey* (q.v.). CI; WNWD.

SPELLING BEE   *See* Bee.

SPIDER   *a spider.* A large, cast iron frying pay. MDWPO: 17th cent. Source: SPIDER. WNNCD: 14th cent. In the late 1600s, when cooking was done in the huge fireplaces of American farmhouses, most cookware had four short legs so that it could sit above the hot coals. The black, round, four-legged frying pan called to mind the web-spinning spider (which, however, has eight legs). *Spider* is also the name for a trivet. IRCD.

SPIDER CRAB   *a spider crab.* A marine crustacean with ten extremely long legs. WNNCD: ca. 1710. Source: SPIDER. WNNCD: 14th cent. A spider has only eight legs, but in some subspecies of arachnids the legs are extremely long, as with the *daddy longlegs* (WNNCD: 1814). Of the *spider crab's* ten legs, the front pair are small; so it looks as though it only has eight. *Compare* Spider Monkey; Spider Veins.

SPIDER MONKEY   *a spider monkey.* A Central and South American monkey that has extremely long, thin arms and legs. WNNCD: 1764. Source: SPIDER. WNNCD: 14th cent. The spider is well-known for its long, thin legs (esp. the *daddy longlegs*). Although the *spider monkey* has only four "legs," as opposed to the spider's eight, it also has a prehensile tail, longer than its body, that apparently makes up for the other four. *Compare* Spider Crab; Spider Veins.

SPIDER'S WEB   *a spider's web.* A delicate complex network that is affected as a whole by a change in any one of its parts. Source: SPIDER. WNNCD: 14th cent. The computer program called a "spreadsheet" is often compared to a *spider's web* (WNNCD: 1535), because when you change one figure (or "touch it"), all of the other figures change (or "vibrate"). *See also* Cobweb.

SPIDER VEINS   Tiny blood vessels on the surface of the skin that connect or radiate. Source: SPIDER. WNNCD: 14th cent. The analogy is probably to the spider's *web*, in which tiny strands of "silk" radiate from the spider's resting place in the center. However, it could also be to the spider itself, whose long thin legs radiate from its tiny body. *See also* Cobweb; Spider's Web; Spidery. *Compare* Crow's Feet; Pedigree.

SPIDERY   *to be spidery.* To consist of a light, delicate, and intricate arrangement of lines or threads. Source: SPIDER. WNNCD: 14th cent. Spiders are light, but they are neither delicate nor intricate. It is, of course, the spider's *web* that is being referred to in this metaphor. *Spidery* applies to lace produced by crocheting or tatting, such as shawls, tablecloths, and doilies, which often bear a resemblance to a *cobweb* (q.v.). ATWS.

SPINELESS JELLYFISH *See* Jellyfish.

SPINNING BEE *See* Bee.

SPINY LOBSTER *See* Crayfish.

SPOIL *to spoil; the spoils of war.* To ruin, or be ruined; the rewards of victory. Source: ANIMAL. The verb *spoil* derives from the noun *spoil*, which comes fr. Lat. *spolium* "the skin or hide of an animal." When an animal was killed in the wild, its hide was sometimes removed and the carcass left to decay, or "spoil." The hide was the hunter's reward, or "*spoils* of victory." By analogy, the rewards of victory in battle, i.e., the plunder taken from the enemy, came to be known as the *spoils of war* (EWPO: 1697). Today, *spoils* are also the loot taken in a robbery, and the verb *spoil* can be used, transitively, for ruining someone's fun or plans or, intransitively, for *spoiling for a fight*, i.e., being eager to take *spoils*. WNWD.

SPOILING FOR A FIGHT *See* Spoil.

SPOILS OF WAR *See* Spoil.

SPONGE (n) *a sponge.* A manufactured product used to absorb, hold, or dispense liquids. Source: SPONGE. WNNCD: O.E. The original *sponge* is the soft, elastic, and porous skeleton of the marine animal by the same name. However, other products have adopted the name because of their absorbency: the cellulose *sponge* for washing and wiping, and the gauze *sponge* for soaking up blood. A drunk is also called a *sponge* (for absorbing too much alcohol), and a freeloader is called a *sponge* or *sponger* (q.v.). ATWS; HF; ID. *See also* Sponge (v).

SPONGE (v) *to sponge someone or something off; to sponge something up.* To apply water with an absorbent cloth or pad; to soak up water with such a pad. WNNCD: 14th cent. Source: SPONGE. WNNCD: O.E. The *sponge*, or skeleton of the marine animal by this name, is the supreme holder of water. However, because of its expense, it has been replaced with wash cloths, gauze bandages, and cellulose products. *See also* Sponge (n).

SPONGE BATH *a sponge bath.* A tubless, showerless bath given to a patient in bed or taken by a person using water from a sink or bucket. Source: SPONGE. WNNCD: O.E. The *sponge bath* orig. involved the use of a real sponge, i.e., the skeleton of the marine animal by that name. Nowadays, however, it is more common to use a synthetic *sponge* or a wash cloth. WNWD. *See also* Sponge (n).

SPONGE CAKE   *a sponge cake.* A soft, moist cake made without shortening. WNNCD: 1805. Source: SPONGE. WNNCD: O.E. The sponge is a marine animal whose soft, elastic, porous skeleton has been used for centuries for bathing and cleaning, but not for eating. The texture of the *sponge cake* is also light and *spongy* (q.v.)—and it is edible. ATWS.

SPONGE OFF/ON   *to sponge off or on someone.* To live off someone, like a parasite. IRCD: 14th cent. Source: SPONGE. WNNCD: O.E. One who lives at someone else's expense is a *sponge* or *sponger* (q.v.), i.e., a person who soaks up the livelihood of another the way the skeleton of the marine animal known as a *sponge* soaks up water. The human is a *parasite* (q.v.); the animal is not. BDPF; DEI. *See also* Sponge (v).

SPONGER   *a sponger.* A human parasite who lives off others: a "freeloader." IRCD: 16th cent. Source: SPONGE. WNNCD: O.E. The marine animal known as a *sponge* is not a parasite, but it does spend its life attached to a rock. A human *sponge*, or *sponger*, attaches him-/herself to another person, soaking up that person's provisions and money. ATWS. *See also* Sponge (n); Sponge off/on.

SPONGE RUBBER   Foam rubber, filled with air pockets that make it soft and elastic. WNNCD: 1886. Source: SPONGE. WNNCD: O.E. The skeleton of the marine animal known as a *sponge* is the ultimate in softness and elasticity. However, its expense has led to the development of both rubber and synthetic substitutes, used for cushioning and weather stripping. *See also* Sponge (n).

SPONGY   *to be spongy.* To be soft, elastic, and porous: e.g., *spongy* ice; *spongy* ground. WNNCD: 1539. Source: SPONGE. WNNCD: O.E. It took half a century for the adjective *spongy* to develop from the noun *sponge*, but it was a welcome addition. There is no other word in the language for something that is at the same time soft, elastic, and porous—like the skeleton of the marine animal. *See also* Sponge Cake; Sponge Rubber.

SPREAD EAGLE   *a spread eagle.* A leap in figure skating in which both the arms and the legs are extended, straight and to the side, at a 45° angle to the torso. Source: EAGLE. WNNCD: 13th cent. The skating nomenclature is based on the position of the *spread eagle* on the Great Seal of the United States, in which the wings and the legs are extended at 45° angles to the body. The *spread eagle* is also found on the back of a dollar bill. ATWS; IRCD. *See also* American Eagle; Double Eagle; Spread-eagle.

SPREAD-EAGLE   *to spread-eagle someone.* To make someone lean against a wall or a car—or lie face-down on the ground—with arms extended at a 45° angle to the body. Source: EAGLE. WNNCD: 13th cent. The police do this for frisking *spread-eagled* suspects. The eagle does it on the Great Seal of the United States—

and on the back of a dollar bill—with wings and feet extended. ATWS; BDPF. *See also* American Eagle; Double Eagle; Spread Eagle.

SPREAD-EAGLED *See* Spread-eagle.

SPRINKLE SALT ON ITS TAIL *Question:* What's the best way to catch a bird? *Answer:* Sprinkle salt on its tail. IRCD: 16th cent. Source: BIRD. WNNCD: O.E. This advice is sometimes given to children or naive adults who don't realize that if you're close enough to sprinkle salt on a bird's tail, you're close enough to grab it. The expression has been broadened to include other animals, and even humans: "How are we going to catch the criminal?" "Well, we could sprinkle salt on his tail." ATWS; BDPF; IRCD. *Compare* Catchpole.

SPROUT ANTLERS *to sprout antlers.* To become sexually excited. Source: DEER. WNNCD: O.E. All members of the deer family—caribou, deer, elk, and moose—sprout antlers in the summer that grow to full size in the fall, during the mating season, and then are shed before the end of winter. This cycle is reflected in the degree of sexual excitement in the human before and after mating. *See also* Horny.

SPROUT WINGS *to sprout wings.* ("Since when did *you* sprout wings?") To become suddenly and uncharacteristically righteous. NDAS: late-19th cent. Source: BIRD. A person who sprouts wings aligns him-/herself unexpectedly with the angels, who have the wings of birds. To become a *real* angel, you must first *earn your wings*—i.e., prove that you are worthy of the honor—as pilots do when they complete their rigid training and receive a pair of silver wings. Then they are ready to *try their wings*, like a fledgling bird on its first solo flight. AID; ATWS.

SPURRED ON *to be spurred on.* To be urged on or incited by someone or something. Source: HORSE. A *spur* is a pointed wheel that is set vertically in a metal frame on the heel of a medieval knight or a Western cowboy. The purpose of the spur is to incite the horse to action—something that is done by jockeys with a whip and Eastern riders with their boot heels. People are *spurred on* to action by less physical means, such as cheerleaders and inspirational speakers, while the economy is *spurred on* by lower taxes and lower interest rates. ATWS.

SQUEAL *to squeal on someone.* To inform on a partner in crime. Source: PIG. The first thing a pig does when it is picked up is to squeal. This is often the first thing a crook does, too: *squeal* on his/her fellow crooks in exchange for a plea bargain. Other animals that have loaned their names to "informing" are the rat (to *rat* on someone [q.v.]), the canary (to *sing like a canary* [q.v.]), and the pigeon (to be a *stool pigeon* [q.v.]). GTP.

SQUEAL LIKE A PIG *to squeal like a pig.* For children or young women to make a high-pitched cry of fear or delight. Source: PIG. WNNCD: 13th cent. Hogs *grunt*, but pigs *squeal*—esp. when they are hungry or helpless or when they are picked up for treatment or castration. Young women started squealing at Frank Sinatra in the 1940s and haven't stopped since. *See also* Squeal.

SQUIRREL AWAY *to squirrel something away.* To store something away for future use. WNNCD: 1925. Source: SQUIRREL. WNNCD: 14th cent. The squirrel is well known for its activity in the fall: storing acorns and nuts away in its nest for consumption during the winter months. (Squirrels don't hibernate.) The squirrel also buries nuts and acorns in the ground in the summer for digging up again in the fall or spring. AID; ATWS; NDAS. *See also* Pack Rat.

SQUIRRELLY *to be squirrelly.* To be crazy, odd, eccentric. WNNCD: 1932. Source: SQUIRREL. WNNCD: 14th cent. Squirrels are indeed "nutty." They spend most of their time either chasing each other or scolding cats and dogs and other squirrels. They bury acorns and nuts in the summer only to dig them up again in the fall. However, squirrels are really quite sensible: they use their tail as an umbrella, and they know how to come down a tree head first. (Cats don't.) ATWS; ID; NDAS.

STABLE *a stable.* A group of actors, boxers, dancers, models, race cars, or race drivers under a single management. Source: HORSE. A stable was orig. a building in which horses were kept in stalls: a *horse stable* (WNNCD: 14th cent.). Later, the racehorses of a single owner or farm were called a *stable*; and the farm itself, where the horses were bred, raised, and trained, came to be called a *stable* (or *stables*). A *stable* of actors is now a group of actors under contract to a single studio, and a *stable* of boxers is under contract to a single promoter. The members of such groups are called *stablemates* (WNNCD: 1926). ATWS; GTP; ST.

STABLEMATE *See* Stable.

STAG LINE *a stag line.* A line of men or boys, on the sidelines of a dance floor, who came without dates and are waiting patiently to be asked to dance, to ask an unaccompanied female to dance, or to "cut in" on a couple that is on the dance floor. Source: DEER. Real *stags*, the adult males of the European red deer, don't wait patiently to get at the females but engage in violent encounters with other stags over who is to rule the harem. BDPF; IRCD. *See also* Go Stag; Stag Movie; Stag Party.

STAG MOVIE *a stag movie.* A pornographic or "adult" film. LTA: 1940s. Source: DEER. *Stag movie* gets its name from the *stag party* (q.v.) at which it is shown. The presumption is that "dirty" movies are suitable only for the eyes and ears of *stags*, or adult males. Real *stags* are the adult males of European red deer, which are larger by half than the *bucks* (q.v.) of American white-tailed deer. IRCD. *See also* Go Stag; Stag Line.

STAG PARTY *a stag party.* A party for men only: a bachelor party. IRCD: 1854. Source: DEER. While the bride and her female friends are having a *hen party* (q.v.), the groom and his male companions are throwing a *stag party*—for *stags* ("men") only. Sometimes these bachelor parties get pretty wild, with pornographic films (or *stag movies* [q.v.]) and a stripper bursting out of a cake. It is the *stag's* final fling before the mating season starts. ATWS; BDPF; DEI. *See also* Go Stag; Stag Line.

STALKING HORSE *a stalking horse.* A person or thing that is used to disguise one's true purpose. Source: HORSE. WNNCD: O.E. The original *stalking horse* was a real horse that a hunter used to shield himself from his quarry (WNNCD: 1519). Later, the horse was replaced by a figure of a horse, which led to the metaphor of a *stalking horse* as a "front" to conceal one's real intentions (SOED: 1579). Human *stalking horses* are political candidates who are entered in the lists to (1) test the waters for or conceal the identity of the real candidate, or (2) divide or siphon votes from the legitimate candidates (SOED: 1612). ATWS; BDPF; DEI; DOC; HF; HOI; IRCD; LCRH; MDWPO; SPD; ST.

STALLION *See* Stud.

STAMPEDE *a stampede; to stampede.* A headlong rush of a mass of people; for a mass of people to make a headlong rush toward or away from something. Source: ANIMAL. Literally, a stampede is the wild rush of a herd of frightened animals, such as bison, cattle, and caribou (WNNCD: 1834). Figuratively, a *stampede* is a mass movement of people *toward* something attractive, such as a celebrity or a sale, or *away* from something frightening, such as an earthquake or a fire. To stampede a herd of cattle is to "spook" them, or cause them to run away en masse in a panic (WNNCD: 1843). To *stampede* a group of people is to cause them to flee en masse in panic as a result of, for example, a shooting or a terrorist attack. The verb *stampede* derives from the noun *stampede*, which derives from Gmc. *stamp* by way of Sp. *estampida.* IHAT.

STAND THE GAFF *to stand the gaff.* (Usu. neg.: *to be unable to stand the gaff.*) To bear up under pressure. (Neg: to give in under pressure.) DOC: 1900. Source: COCK (?). *Gaff* is another name for the sharp metal spur (or *spar*) worn by gamecocks on the lower back portion of their legs. A cock that succumbs to the slashes of its opponent is said to have been *unable to stand the gaff.* A competing origin for this metaphor is Provencal *gaf*, a boathook that was once used for docking boats and landing fish. ATWS; BDPF; EWPO; HOI; LCRH; MDWPO; ST. *See also* Spar (v); Well-heeled.

STAND THERE WITH YOUR TONGUE HANGING OUT   *See* Lick Your Chops.

STEEL WOOL   A light mass of long, fine steel shavings that is used for cleaning or scouring hard surfaces. WNNCD: ca. 1900. Source: SHEEP. *Steel wool* is so named because it resembles a ball of wool from a sheep. For many of its uses it has been replaced by sandpaper or emory cloth; but its popularity has been restored by saturating it with soap, letting it dry, and using it to scrub barbeque grills, the bottoms of pots and pans, and whitewall tires.

STEWARD   *a steward.* A union member elected to deal with management; an employee who looks after the provisions or passengers on an airplane, ship, or train; a temporary director of a business or other institution. Source: PIG. Literally, a steward is a "sty ward" (fr. O.E. *stī* "pigpen or pigsty" + *weard* "guardian")— i.e., one who looks after the pigs on a farm. Figuratively, a *steward* is (1) a person who represents employees in negotiations with management; (2) an attendant who looks after passengers on a commercial aircraft or provisions on a ship or train; or (3) a temporary manager of a business or estate that is in "stewardship." HF. *See also* Pigpen; Pigsty.

STEWED TO THE GILLS   *See* Loaded to the Gills.

STICK IN YOUR CRAW   *for something to stick in your craw.* For something to be objectionable, repugnant, or hard to accept. Source: BIRD. The upper alimentary canal of a bird consists of its throat, or *gullet*; its craw, or *crop*; and its stomach, or *gizzard*. Birds normally swallow pebbles to assist their crop and gizzard in digesting their food; but if they ingest one that is too large, it can get stuck in their *gullet*, in their *crop* (the first stomach), or in their *gizzard* (the second stomach). Then the bird will die of starvation. People who find something *hard to swallow* don't die from their condition, but the troubling matter *sticks in their throat* for a long time. AID; ATWS; BDPF; DOC; EWPO. *Compare* Sand in Your Craw.

STICK IN YOUR GIZZARD   *See* Stick in Your Craw.

STICK IN YOUR GULLET   *See* Stick in Your Craw.

STICK IN YOUR THROAT   *See* Stick in Your Craw.

STICK TO SOMEONE LIKE A LEECH   *to stick to someone like a leech.* To become financially or psychologically dependent on someone. Source: LEECH. WNNCD: O.E. Anyone who has waded in a shallow lake or stream has likely come in contact with the American leech, or "bloodsucker." This little brownish black worm sticks tightly to your legs and is hard to remove. EWPO. *See also* Bloodsucker; Cling like a Leech; Leech.

STICK TO YOUR RIBS   *See* Hidebound.

STICK YOUR HEAD IN THE SAND   *See* Bury Your Head in the Sand.

STICK YOUR NECK OUT   *to stick your neck out.* To voluntarily expose yourself to criticism or danger: to ask for trouble. LTA: 1940. Source: CHICKEN. The metaphor alludes to the unexplainable action of a chicken when it is held over a chopping block for decapitation: it stretches its neck out on the block to accommodate the chopper. (Some say that the chicken is simply hypnotized by being held tightly by the executioner.) People *put their necks on the line* for more logical reasons: to support an unpopular viewpoint or to represent the views of others who are reluctant to express them themselves. BDPF; CI; DEI; DOC; EWPO; HOI; HTB; LCRH. *See also* Get It in the Neck; Like a Chicken with Its Head Cut off.

STICK YOUR NOSE INTO SOMEONE ELSE'S BUSINESS   *to stick—or poke—your nose into someone else's business.* To intrude into other people's lives; to interfere with other people's affairs. Source: DOG. *Curiosity once killed a cat* (q.v.), but dogs do not hesitate to poke their noses in the "business," or spoor, of other animals. It is their way of determining whose territory they are invading, whether they are friend or foe, whether they are male or female, etc. Dogs also smell *each other*, for the same reason, but get in trouble, as do people, for *sticking their nose where it doesn't belong.* CI. *See also* Cast about.

STICK YOUR NOSE WHERE IT DOESN'T BELONG   *See* Stick Your Nose into Someone Else's Business.

STIFF AS A RAMROD   *to be as stiff—or straight—as a ramrod.* To "stand tall," with your head and shoulders back, your chest out, and your abdomen sucked in, like a military person at attention. Source: SHEEP. A *ramrod* (q.v.) is a long metal rod used for loading and cleaning firearms. It gets its name from the *battering ram* (q.v.), which in turn is named for the adult male sheep. *Also*: "ramrod-straight." ST.

STILL WET BEHIND THE EARS   *to be still wet behind the ears.* To be inexperienced or unsophisticated. HOI: late-19th cent. Source: ANIMAL. When a foal, calf, or fawn is born, its mother begins to clean it up by licking the amniotic fluid from its body. Before the cleanup is finished, however, the newborn often tries to get to its feet and take its first steps, still having a little bit of fluid remaining in the recesses behind its ears. People who are *not yet dry behind the ears* are as naive and innocent as a young animal struggling to find its land legs. AID; ATWS; BDPF; CI; DEI; DOC; EWPO; MDWPO.

STING (n)   *a sting.* A sharp, piercing pain; an elaborate confidence game. Source: BEE. A bee sting is as painful to the bee as it is to the human: the human suffers a sharp, piercing pain, but the honeybee dies shortly after depositing its stinger. The police who *put the sting on* criminals are luckier than the bee: they survive, but the crooks go to jail. *Sting operations* range from setting up a bogus store for buying stolen goods to inviting known criminals to an appearance by a famous ballplayer (who never shows up) and then arresting them on the spot. ATWS; CE; IRCD. *See also* Sting (v).

STING (v)   *for something to sting; for someone to sting someone else.* For something to cause a sharp, piercing pain (WNNCD: O.E.); for someone to swindle or cheat someone else. Source: BEE. Many insects—such as the honeybee, wasp, and scorpion—sting their aggressors, but only the bee loses its stinger and dies following the process. For people, shots *sting*, hail *stings*, remorse *stings*, and death *stings*. Police *put the sting on* crooks by beating them at their own game—swindling other people out of their money or property. ATWS; CE. *See also* Sting (n).

STING OPERATION   *See* Sting (n).

STING TO THE QUICK   *to sting to the quick.* ("That stings me to the quick.") To insult someone's intelligence; to wound someone's pride. DOC: 1722. Source: HORNET. The sting is that of the hornet, a yellow jacket or other large wasp, which can attack again and again. The "quick" is the flesh beneath the skin. DOC. *See also* Mad as a Hornet.

STIR UP A HORNET'S NEST   *to stir up a hornet's nest.* To open Pandora's box: to cause a violent and hostile reaction. DOC: 1739. Source: HORNET. WNNCD: O.E. The hornet, a large wasp such as a yellow jacket, takes offense at having its fragile paper nest, hanging from the limb of a tree, disturbed, and retaliates with multiple stings. AID; CI; IRCD; MDWPO. *See also* Hornet's Nest; Mad as a Hornet; Sting to the Quick.

STONE FOX   *See* Foxy Lady.

STOOLIE   *See* Stool Pigeon.

STOOL PIGEON   *a stool pigeon.* A "decoy" employed by the police to trap criminals (EWPO: ca. 1830); a criminal who "rats" on his/her fellows: a police informer or *stoolie* (EWPO: ca. 1900). Source: PIGEON. WNNCD: 14th cent. As early as the late-18th cent. live pigeons were used as decoys to lure other pigeons into shooting or netting range. They were tied to a stool or perch, where they flapped their wings and attracted the attention of the flock, which descended and was caught or killed. ATWS; BDPF; DAE; DEI; HF; HTB; IRCD; LCRH; MDWPO; ST. *See also* Decoy. *Compare* Fink; Rat; Rat Fink.

STOP BUGGING ME   *See* Bug (v) (2).

STOP DEAD IN YOUR TRACKS   *See* Track down.

STORK BROUGHT ME   *Question*: Where did you come from? *Answer*: The stork brought me. Source: STORK. WNNCD: O.E. Gmc. folklore credits the European white stork with delivering human babies to their families, suspended in a diaper from the stork's bill. Actually, what the stork delivers is fish and crustaceans to its own babies in its large, permanent nest on the top of a roof or chimney. *See also* Look What the Stork Brought; Stork Is Coming. *Compare* Birds and the Bees.

STORK IS COMING   *The stork is coming.* "I'm pregnant." Source: STORK. WNNCD: O.E. *Pregnant* was a forbidden word in the mass media until the 1970s, so many old euphemisms were relied on, such as "The stork is coming." In Gmc. folklore, the stork—a large, heronlike bird—was credited with delivering human babies from the "cabbage patch" to the families' homes. ATWS. *See also* Look What the Stork Brought; Stork Brought Me. *Compare* Rabbit Died.

STRAIGHT AS A DOG'S HIND LEG   *See* Dogleg.

STRAIGHT FROM THE HORSE'S MOUTH   *to come—or get it—straight from the horse's mouth.* To come—or to get it—directly from the highest authority. EWPO: ca. 1900. Source: HORSE. WNNCD: O.E. At the racetrack, bettors who are reluctant to reveal the source of a "hot tip" on a racehorse say that it came— or they got it—*straight from the horse's mouth*, i.e., directly from the horse itself. The expression derives from the practice of estimating a horse's age by examining its teeth: a horse is old if the gums have receded from its worn, permanent teeth. AID; ATWS; BDPF; CI; DEI; DOC; HOI; LCRH; MDWPO; SHM; ST. *See also* Long in the Tooth; Look a Gift Horse in the Mouth.

STRAIN AT THE LEASH   *to strain at the leash.* To be *raring to go* (q.v.). Source: DOG. Leash laws require that dogs—and, in some cases, cats—be walked on a short leash. Most dogs don't like the restraint and try to stretch the leash as far as it will go. Dogs that enjoy going for a walk strain at the leash in order to get the outing underway. Children who are kept *on a short leash* (q.v.) by their parents, or husbands who are kept *on a short leash* by their wives, try to stretch the rules as far as they will go, usu. to no avail. *Unleashing* a barrage of insults, invectives, propaganda, or missiles (WNNCD: 1671) is like unleashing a pack of vicious dogs. ATWS; BDPF. *Compare* Chomp at the Bit.

STRAIN OUT GNATS AND SWALLOW CAMELS   *to strain out gnats and swallow camels.* To focus on minor issues and overlook major ones. Source: GNAT; CAMEL. WNNCD: O.E. Jesus accused the scribes and Pharisees of doing this:

"Ye blind guides, which strain at a gnat, and swallow a camel" (Matthew 23:24). The gnat is a tiny biting fly that could scarcely be removed from water by straining it; but there would be no way to miss the large camel. ATWS; BDPF; DEI; DOC; HTB.

STRAP ON THE OLD FEED BAG   See Put on the Feed Bag.

STRAW THAT BROKE THE CAMEL'S BACK   *the straw that broke the camel's back.* The limit to one's patience or endurance. WNNCD: 1848. Source: CAMEL. WNNCD: O.E. Dickens is credited with this metaphor, but it reads more like an ancient proverb. The North African/Middle Eastern camel, or "dromedary," is a domesticated beast of burden and transportation. If the camel is loaded with straw, there is a limit to the amount of straw that it can carry. That one last straw will break its back. ATWS; CI; EWPO; ID; IRCD. *See also* Last Straw.

STRING ALONG   *to string along with someone.* To accompany someone; to go along with someone's plans. WNNCD: 1944. Source: HORSE. A string of horses is a line of horses in single file that are attached to each other with a rope and are led by the rider of the lead horse. People *string along* with other people when they accompany them on a trip or to an event ("Is it okay if I string along?") or when they agree to abide by their decisions. EWPO.

STRONG AS A BULL   *to be as strong as a bull.* To have enormous strength. Source: BULL. WNNCD: O.E. The bull is probably the strongest of all farm animals, although, as with the stallion, its strength is seldom tested as a draft animal (for pulling wagons, plows, etc.). Its strength lies in its ability to protect its herd— or itself—against all enemies, including humans. *See also* Strong as a Bull Moose; Strong as a Horse; Strong as an Ox.

STRONG AS A BULL MOOSE   *to be as strong as a bull moose.* To have great size and physical strength. Source: MOOSE. WNNCD: 1203. The moose, the largest member of the deer family, is of great size (over six feet tall at the shoulders, up to two-thirds of a ton in weight) and great strength. "Bull Moose" was selected by Theodore Roosevelt as the name for his (losing) independent party in the presidential campaign of 1912. IRCD. *See also* Strong as a Bull; Strong as a Horse; Strong as an Ox.

STRONG AS A HORSE   *to be as strong as a horse.* To combine great strength with elegance. Source: HORSE. WNNCD: O.E. Of the two major draft animals in American history—the ox and the horse—the ox is probably the stronger, because it is built closer to the ground, works better as a member of a team, and is more durable. But the horse is much faster than the ox, and it is more spirited and more beautiful. The strongest of all horses is the stallion. When a team of two horses is having trouble pulling a heavy load a short distance, seesawing back and forth, the stallion is sometimes hitched up alone to do the job. ATWS; BDPF. *See also* Strong as a Bull; Strong as a Bull Moose; Strong as an Ox.

STRONG AS AN OX *to be strong as an ox.* To be extremely strong and durable. (Usu. said of a male.) Source: OX. WNNCD: O.E. An ox is a castrated bull that is employed as a draft animal. It can weigh well over a ton. The ox was the largest beast of burden in Europe before the horse appeared. Horses are faster, but oxen have greater endurance. AID; ID. *See also* Big as an Ox; Strong as a Bull; Strong as a Bull Moose; Strong as a Horse.

STRUT LIKE A PEACOCK *to strut like a peacock.* To parade around with a swelled chest, a deliberate gait, a pompous air, and an overabundance of pride. Source: PEACOCK. WNNCD: 14th cent. During the mating season, the Indian peacock struts among his potential conquests with his brilliant five-foot wide tail fan extended, as if in recognition of his handsome appearance. BDPF; EWPO. *See also* Proud as a Peacock; Stuck-up.

STUBBORN AS A MULE *to be as stubborn as a mule.* To be obstinate, unreasonable, inflexible, and unyielding. DOC: 1809. Source: MULE. WNNCD: 13th cent. The mule is a sterile offspring of a male donkey (a *jackass*) and a female horse (a *mare*). From its mother it gets its size (as large as a horse), and from its father it gets its temperament (as stubborn as a jackass). Its stubbornness has also given it an undeserved reputation for stupidity. AID; ATWS; CI; DEI. *See also* Mule (1); Mulish.

STUCK-UP *to be stuck-up.* To be pretentious, conceited, and snobbish. WNNCD: 1829. Source: PEACOCK. WNNCD: 14th cent. The Indian peacock attempts to impress its potential conquests during the mating season by raising it five-foot wide tail into a five-foot wide fan: i.e., it "sticks up" its tail fan. People can be *stuck-up* without carrying a fan. BDPF. *See also* Proud as a Peacock; Strut like a Peacock.

STUD *a stud.* A virile or promiscuous young man. IHAT: 1803. Source: HORSE. Literally, a stud is an uncastrated adult male horse, esp. one kept for breeding (WNNCD: O.E.). Earlier, it was called a *studhorse* (WNNCD: O.E.) or a *stallion* (WNNCD: 14th cent.). When a stallion has completed a successful career on the racetrack, it is *kept at stud*, or *retired to stud*, on a *stud farm*, where it services willing mares for a fee. Human *studs* are so called because of their natural virility or their *track record* (q.v.) as sexually active males. *Stud poker* (WNNCD: 1864) is so called because, unlike draw poker, it permits some of the cards to be dealt face up, with a round of betting after each deal. The assumption is that only a macho male can handle such exposure. ATWS; CE. *Compare* Put out to Pasture.

STUD POKER *See* Stud.

STUFFED TO THE GILLS   *to be stuffed to the gills*. To have eaten so much that you can't eat any more. Source: FISH. The gills of a fish are located on either side of its "neck." If humans had gills, they would also be located on the neck, just below the lower jaw. People who are *stuffed to the gills* are full of food from their stomach to their throat: there isn't room for another bite. ATWS; BDPF; DOC. *See also* Green around the Gills; Loaded to the Gills.

SUBJUGATE   *to subjugate someone*. To bring someone under your control. WNNCD: 15th cent. Source: OX. In Latin, *subjugare* meant, lit., "to bring under the yoke" (fr. *sub* "under" + *jugum* "yoke"), i.e., to defeat or conquer. In fact, victorious Roman generals sometimes made defeated armies march under a yoke, like oxen, to symbolize their submission. The practice has also been used in modern times. LCRH. *See also* Oxbow; Syzygy; Yoke.

SUCK THE HIND TIT   *to suck the hind tit*. To get the worst of the deal. Source: ANIMAL. Mammals usu. have more teats (or tits or nipples) than the number of young that they typically bear at a given time: e.g., the horse has two nipples and usu. delivers a single foal; the cow has four nipples and usu. delivers one or two calves; etc. Mammals that produce large numbers of young (i.e., "litters") at one time—such as the dog, cat, and pig—have a large number of nipples running down both sides of the belly. It has long been presumed that the supply of milk into the nipples decreases progressively from front to back, and that the kitten, puppy, or piglet that *sucks the hind tit* will get less than its fair share of nourishment. The matter is complicated by the fact that some litters are larger than the number of available nipples, in which case some of the excess young will probably die. The expression *suck the hind tit* is applied to humans who feel that they have been shortchanged or have gotten the "short end of the stick." HTB; NDAS. *See also* Runt.

SUDDEN DEATH   The elimination of one of two competitors who are tied at the end of an election (by the toss of a coin, the drawing of straws or cards, or the roll of a die) or at the end of a regulation game of professional football or hockey (the first to score wins the game) or at the end of a regulation golf match (the first to win a hole wins the match). Source: COCK. The sudden death of a gamecock in a cockfight results in an instant win by its opponent. The same is true in other illegal "sports," such as dog fights, in which killing the opponent is the ultimate goal. MDWPO; ST. *See also* Stand the Gaff.

SUN DOG   *a sun dog*. A parhelion. WNNCD: 1635. Source: DOG. WNNCD: O.E. A parhelion is a chromatic ring around the sun caused by light shining through the ice crystals of cirrus clouds on a very cold day. Essentially, the parhelion is a complete halo that contains all of the colors of the rainbow plus a multicolored spot that appears on either side of the sun. (A *sun dog* is sometimes called a "sunbow.") A *moon dog* is a halo of ice crystals around a full moon, but without the spots on either side. The question, of course, is what the dog has to do with all this, unless the metaphor refers to a dog's collar. WNWD.

SWALLOW SOMETHING HOOK, LINE, AND SINKER   *See* Hook, Line, and Sinker.

SWALLOWTAIL COAT   *a swallowtail coat.* A men's formal coat, the back of which is long, V-shaped, and split in the middle. Source: SWALLOW. WNNCD: O.E. *Swallowtail* (WNNCD: 1703) was first used to describe the long, forked tail of the barn swallow. It has since been extended to other birds (e.g., the South American swallow-tailed manakin), to butterflies (e.g., the North American giant swallowtail), and to the full-dress coat, also called a *tailcoat* (WNNCD: 1847). *See also* Soup and Fish; White Tie and Tails.

SWALLOW THE BAIT   *See* Hook, Line, and Sinker.

SWAN DIVE   *a swan dive.* A competitive forward dive in which the legs are kept straight and together, the back is arched, the head is back, and the arms are extended straight out, at right angles to the body. WNNCD: 1898. Source: SWAN. WNNCD: O.E. Swans are not diving birds, but they do soar this way, creating a beautiful sight with their seven-and-one-half-foot wingspread and long necks. (The legs, however, are not prominent.) ATWS: ID. *See also* Graceful as a Swan.

SWAN SONG   *a swan song.* The final work of a famous artist or performer, just before his/her death or retirement. Source: SWAN. WNNCD: O.E. The pure-white European "mute" swan, now introduced into North America, makes no sound during its lifetime except for a warning hiss. However, the ancient Greeks believed that when the swan was dying, it became capable of producing a song of great sweetness and beauty. ATWS; BDPF; CI; DEI; EWPO; HOI; ID; IRCD; LCRH; SHM.

SWAP HORSES WHILE CROSSING THE RIVER   *See* Change Horses in Midstream.

SWARM (n)   *a swarm of people.* A throng of people, esp. in motion. Source: BEE. *Swarm* is applied to a crowd of sightseers, onlookers, reporters, etc., who are either milling about or moving forward in order to get a better view of or access to the object of attention. The effect is that of a colony of honeybees, led by the queen, migrating in search of a new home. The murmur among both the human and insect *swarms* is appropriate, since the word derives from an I.E. root meaning "to hum or buzz." ATWS. *See also* Swarm (v).

SWARM (v)   *to swarm.* To move as a crowd. Source: BEE. Honeybees swarm when the entire colony, led by the queen, flies from an old hive in search of a new one (WNNCD: 14th cent.). Termites also swarm in this fashion, and for the same reason; but flies swarm only when they find a common source of food. People *swarm* toward an object of attraction, murmuring as they go. The verb *swarm* is derived from the noun *swarm* (q.v.). ATWS. *Compare* Swarm like Locusts.

SWARM LIKE LOCUSTS   *to swarm like locusts.* For a large crowd of people to move en masse toward an attraction, e.g., into a stadium, theater, store, etc. Source: LOCUST. WNNCD: 14th cent. *Locust* is another name for a migratory grasshopper that swarms to another field after it has cleared the first one of vegetation. DEI. *See also* Swarm (v).

SWEAT HOG   *a sweat hog.* A slow-learner; an underachiever. Source: HOG. WNNCD: O.E. *Sweat hogs* are students (esp. high school students) who sweat like hogs to do more or better work but fail to achieve a minimum level of proficiency. (The term may have originated with the TV series, *Welcome Back, Kotter*, in which Mr. Kotter was the unlucky teacher of a remedial class of "sweat hogs.") The problem is that hogs don't sweat: they have no sweat glands. At the college level, *sweat hog* is a slang term for an unattractive or promiscuous female. NDAS. *See also* Sweat like a Pig.

SWEAT LIKE A PIG   *to sweat like a pig.* To sweat profusely. Source: PIG. WNNCD: 13th cent. This is a misguided metaphor: pigs don't sweat. Like all pachyderms, they don't have sweat glands. That's why they wallow in the mud— to cool their skin. The expression may be an alteration of to *bleed like a stuck pig* (q.v.); but whatever the origin, the myth of perspiration persists in the slang term *pig sweat*, meaning "beer." GTP; NDAS. *See also* Sweat Hog.

SWEET AS HONEY   *to be as sweet as honey.* To be as nice and kind as could be. Source: BEE. Nothing is quite as sweet as the honey produced by honeybees, who make it for no altruistic reason but simply because that's what honeybees do. People who are *as sweet as honey*, however, are often suspected of some ulterior motive—of being overly sweet for their own benefit: "One minute she was as sweet as honey, and then . . . ." DEI. *See also* Mealy-mouthed.

SWEETEN THE KITTY   *to sweeten the kitty.* To increase the size of the "pot" (in poker); to make a bid or offer more attractive. Source: CAT. *Kitty* is an affectionate name for a cat, and it is used in the standard cat call: "Here Kitty, Kitty, Kitty!" A poker *kitty* (q.v.) is probably named for the game from which poker derived: faro, or "Tiger." To *feed the kitty* is to ante into the pot before the next hand, and to *sweeten the kitty* is to increase it even more by raising the ante. In finance, to *sweeten the kitty* is to raise the stakes until the potential buyer—or lender—gives in. AID; HTB; NDAS.

SWEETNESS AND LIGHT Beauty and intelligence combined. EWPO: 1697 (Johnathan Swift's "Preface" to *The Battle of the Books*). Source: BEE. For Swift, *sweetness and light* represented honey and wax, respectively: the ancient products of the beehive. In more recent times, the phrase has come to be used in a negative construction, *not all sweetness and light*, meaning "not all harmony and reason,"— i.e., "Things are not as they seem."

SWEET-TALKER *See* Mealy-mouthed.

SWELLED HEAD *to get—or have—a swelled head.* To get or have an exaggerated opinion of yourself. WNNCD: 1891. Source: ANIMAL. Various animals— birds, mammals, reptiles—cause their heads or throats to swell when they are excited. The sage grouse inflates its brilliant air sacs during mating season; the howler monkey inflates its huge throat sac when howling to establish its territory; and the false puff adder (or blowhead snake) inflates not only its head but its entire body when threatened. The purpose of the swelled head for animals (esp. males) is to impress a member of the opposite sex (the grouse), to impress a member of the same sex (the monkey), or to impress a predator of any sex or species (the snake). Humans affect a *swelled head* when they become conceited or believe that they are more important than they really are. AID.

SWIM LIKE A FISH *to swim like a fish.* To swim skillfully and effortlessly. Source: FISH. WNNCD: O.E. The only animal that actually swims like a fish is the "true"—or vertebrate—fish itself, which propels itself by wiggling its vertical tail from side to side, aided to some extent by its pectoral fins. Humans may swim like *porpoises* (q.v.), and they may *crawfish* (q.v.) on certain issues, but they don't swim at all like a fish, and neither do penguins and seals, which use their wings or flippers to propel themselves. But penguins and seals take naturally to water, while a human who does so is regarded as unusual. *See also* Fishtail.

SWIM WITH SHARKS *to swim with sharks.* To associate or do business with hustlers, swindlers, usurers, extortionists, or just plain crooks. Source: SHARK. WNNCD: 1569. "If you swim with sharks, you're going to be eaten by them." The shark has a double row of very sharp teeth in a very large mouth. It is not advisable to swim with them. *See also* Shark Repellent.

SWINE *a swine.* A disgusting person. IRCD: before 1600. Source: PIG. Of the three Eng. words for "porkers"—*pigs, hogs,* and *swine—swine* is probably the oldest and broadest. Like *cattle,* it is a collective noun for the entire family. When applied to humans, *swine* is much more severe than *pig* or *hog,* because it captures the entire character and personality of the individual: hateful and loathsome. The implication is that the person is as uncultured, uncouth, and uncivilized as a dirty pig. ATWS. *See also* Male Chauvinist Pig; Pig (2).

SYZYGY *a syzygy.* The occurrence of the sun, the earth, and the moon in a straight line, resulting either in an eclipse of the sun (the moon between the sun and the earth) or an eclipse of the moon (the earth between the sun and the moon). WNNCD: ca. 1847. Source: OX. WNNCD: O.E. Gk. *syzygos* lit. meant "yoked together," like a team of oxen (fr. *syn* "together" + *zygon* "yoke"). Oxen were usu. yoked in pairs, however, not in threes. *See also* Oxbow; Subjugate; Yoke.

T

TACKY   *to be tacky.* To be shabby or seedy (WNNCD: 1883); to be showy or gaudy. Source: HORSE. *Tacky* was once a Southern term for a low-class horse; later, it was applied to a low-class person and that person's possessions. Now, *tacky* usu. refers to something that is lacking in style and good taste. ATWS.

TADPOLE   *a tadpole.* The larval stage of a frog or toad: a "polliwog." WNNCD: 15th cent. Source: TOAD. WNNCD: O.E. Both frogs and toads are *tadpoles* in their aquatic larval stage; but the word itself is derived from M.E. *taddepol* "toad head." *Tadpoles* appear to be all head and tail, with no body or legs. EWPO; HF.

TAIL (n)   *a tail.* The back or bottom of something; an extension from the back or bottom of something. Source: ANIMAL. All senses of *tail* derive from O.E. *tægel* "tail of an animal." Most animals—whether mammals, birds, fish, or reptiles— have a tail of some sort or at some stage of their development. The major exceptions are the anthropoidal primates (or "apes"): orangutans, chimpanzees, and gorillas. Humans also lack tails, but they have applied the term *tail* to everything from kites and coats (which actually do have tails) to lights and gates (which are attached to the *tail end* of vehicles). Coins have heads and *tails* and nothing much in between, and winds come from either the front ("headwinds") or the rear (*tailwinds*). You can *put a tail on* someone ("have someone followed"), and you can *work your tail off* ("bust your buns"). The last example may allude to the banded gecko, which sacrifices its tail to a predator rather than submit to capture. (The tail grows back.) ATWS; CH; ST. *See also* Queue; Tail (v).

TAIL (v)   *to tail someone; to tail off.* To follow someone surreptitiously; to become smaller or fainter. Source: ANIMAL. The verb *tail* derives from the noun *tail* (WNNCD: O.E.) but appears more than half a century later (WNNCD: 1523). In its transitive function it orig. meant "to tie or splice the ends of two ropes together"; then the meaning was broadened to include both *removing* ("docking" or "bobbing") the tail of an animal and *adding* a tail to something, such as a *kite* (q.v.). The modern sense of "follow" suggests attaching yourself to the subject as if you were their *tail*. In its intransitive function, *tail* orig. meant to follow in single file (i.e., head to *tail*); then, with *off*, it came to mean "to become progressively less audible or visible," like a diminishing sound, or a person riding off into the sunset. The verb *curtail* "to shorten or reduce" (WNNCD: 1580) would seem to suggest cutting off the tail of a dog, or *cur*, but the word is derived fr. M.Fr. *courtault* "a docked animal," and the Eng. words *cur* (q.v.) and *tail* have been read into the word only because of folk etymology. ATWS; ST. *See also* Tail (n).

TAIL BETWEEN YOUR LEGS   *to leave with your tail between your legs.* To leave in humiliation or disgrace. DOC: ca. 1400. Source: DOG. A dog that is beaten in a fight with another dog, or is caught red-handed violating the rules of the household, sneaks away with its head lowered and its tail between its legs. A *coward* (fr. Lat. *cauda* "tail" by way of O.Fr. *coart*) is a person who fig. retreats with *his/her tail between his/her legs* as a result of an ignominious defeat or a public disgrace. AID; ATWS; BDPF; CI; EWPO; HTB; ID; LCRH. *Compare* Turn Tail.

TAIL END   *See* Tail (n).

TAIL IS WAGGING THE DOG   *The tail is wagging the dog.* The minority is in control of the majority. Source: DOG. WNNCD: O.E. The dog is the only animal that wags its tail, from side to side, to express happiness or pleasurable anticipation: the faster the wag, the greater the pleasure. The opposite does not occur, however. *The tail wags the dog* only in human metaphor, as when a minority stockholder forces a corporation to take a certain action, or a vocal minority pressures a government to move in a certain direction. The *tail that wags the dog* at a college or university is often the alumni, esp. those who value athletics over education. AID; ATWS; DEI.

TAIL OFF   *See* Tail (v).

TAIL THAT WAGS THE DOG   *See* Tail Is Wagging the Dog.

TAKE A GANDER   *to take a gander at something.* To take a look at something. WNNCD: 1914. Source: GOOSE. A *gander* (WNNCD: O.E.), or adult male goose, looks almost exactly like a *goose* (WNNCD: O.E.), or adult female goose. Both have long necks that they can straighten in order to see over the rest of the flock on the ground. Human *ganders* are glances achieved by stretching the neck as far up or around as it will go, as at a parade. AID; ATWS; CE; IRCD. *See also* Gooseneck. *Compare* Crane Your Neck.

TAKE COVER *See* Break Cover.

TAKE SOMEONE TO THE WIRE *See* Go down to the Wire.

TAKE SOMEONE UNDER YOUR WING *to take someone under your wing.* To provide someone with care, guidance, support, or protection. Source: HEN. Matthew 23:37 contains the following passage: "O Jerusalem, Jerusalem . . . how often would I have gathered thy children together, even as a hen gathereth her chickens under her wings, and ye would not." Many birds shield their young with their wings in times of danger, but the metaphor is usu. associated with the familiar hen and her chicks. ATWS; CI; DEI; EWPO; HTB; ID. *See also* Mother Hen. *Compare* Aegis.

TAKE SOMETHING IN STRIDE *to take something in stride.* To maintain your equilibrium in the face of obstacles. Source: HORSE. A horse takes a fence in stride when it jumps it without altering its pace or rhythm. People who *take* adversity *in stride* are able to "keep their cool," maintain their sense of balance, cope with the problem, and "stay the course" (to mix a few metaphors). To *make great strides* is to achieve remarkable progress, as a race horse does when it lengthens its stride and covers more ground. To *catch someone off stride* is to take someone by surprise or catch someone off balance. ATWS; CI; ST.

TAKE THE BAIT *See* Bait (1).

TAKE THE BIT *to take the bit in—or between—your teeth.* To take charge; to take control. DOC: ca. 1589. Source: HORSE. The bit is that part of a bridle that fits crosswise in a horse's mouth and is controlled by the reins that are attached at either end. When the rider or driver pulls on the left rein, the left end of the bit pulls back the left side of the horse's mouth, as a signal for the horse to turn left. If a horse becomes fed up with being *jerked around* (q.v.) this way, it may bite down on the bit, preventing it from moving. In this case the horse has taken control of its own destiny and can go wherever it wants. A horse that makes a habit of taking the bit between its teeth is said to be *hard-bitten* (WNNCD: 1784); and a *hard-bitten* person is one who is tough and stubborn. People who *take the bit in their teeth* are taking charge of their own lives and forging ahead in their own direction. AID; ATWS; BDPF; DEI; LCRH. *See also* Chomp at the Bit.

TAKE THE BULL BY THE HORNS *to take the bull by the horns.* To face a difficult problem head on. EWPO: 1873. Source: BULL. WNNCD: O.E. There are three possible origins for this metaphor: bull vaulting, bullfighting, and bulldogging. Minoan bull vaulters ran straight at the bull, grasped its horns, and somersaulted over its back. Spanish bullfighters face the defeated bull, grasp its horns, and force its head to the ground. Bulldoggers in an American rodeo leap from a horse onto the neck of a running bull calf (or steer), grab its horns from the rear, and twist its head until the animal falls over. In all of these activities there is a considerable amount of danger involved, and evading it would make one a coward. AID; ATWS; BDPF; CI; DEI; DOC; HOI; ID; IRCD; LCRH; MDWPO; ST.

TAKE THE COLLAR   *See* Draw the Collar.

TAKE TO SOMETHING LIKE A DUCK TO WATER   *See* Like a Duck to Water.

TAKE WING   *See* Wing (n).

TALK THE HIND LEG OFF A DONKEY   *to talk the hind leg off a donkey.* To talk endlessly or coercively. Source: DONKEY. WNNCD: ca. 1785. A person who can *talk the hind leg off a donkey* may not only be an endless speaker but may also be trying to "con" someone out of their prized possession. The metaphor may have developed from a story about a donkey who kicked one of its hind legs off trying to ward off an abusive rider or driver. CI; DEI; *Compare* Pin the Tail on the Donkey.

TALK TURKEY   *to talk turkey.* To speak frankly, bluntly, and truthfully. LTA: 1830. Source: TURKEY. WNNCD: 1555. This expression comes from a probably apocryphal story about an American colonist and his Indian hunting companion. After killing a number of crows and turkeys, the colonist divided them up un- equally, considering the amount of edible meat: "a crow for you, a turkey for me; a crow for you . . . " etc. The Indian pointed out that the colonist was always "talking turkey" for himself but never for him; and he redistributed the game. AID; ATWS; BDPF; CE; CI; DEI; DOC; EWPO; IRCD; LCRH; NDAS.

TAME (adj.)   *to be tame.* To be subdued. Source: ANIMAL. A *tame* animal is one that was once wild, either as an individual or a species, but has been do- mesticated for the benefit of humans (WNNCD: O.E.). A *tame* joke, novel, play, or movie is one that is inhibited and not offensive or risqué. The verb *tame* developed in the 14th cent. to express the process of domesticating animals, but it soon came to apply to clearing the land (i.e., *taming the wilderness*), *harnessing* natural energy, and toning down language.

TAME (v)   *See* Tame (adj.).

TAME THE WILDERNESS   *See* Tame (adj.).

TAN SOMEONE'S HIDE   *See* Hide nor Hair.

TAR AND FEATHER *to tar and feather someone.* To expose someone to public disgrace. Source: CHICKEN; GOOSE. People have been *tarred and feathered,* for various reasons, since at least 1189, when an English statute ordered the punishment for certain thieves. In America, the operation was first carried out on a traitor in 1768. The procedure involved stripping the individual, covering him with hot tar, rolling him in chicken or goose feathers, and riding him out of town on a rail. The practice continued well into the 19th cent. In more recent times, people who "ought to be *tarred and feathered*" are submitted to public disgrace of a less physical and more vocal nature. AID; BDPF; EWPO; HTB; IHAT.

TARRED AND FEATHERED *See* Tar and Feather.

TARRED WITH THE SAME BRUSH *to be tarred with the same brush.* For the innocent to be treated the same as the guilty. HOI: late-18th cent. Source: SHEEP. Tar was used for several centuries to treat the sores on sheep that resulted from shearing and tail-docking. (It was later replaced by turpentine.) Tar was also used for "branding" unsheared sheep with the farmer's special mark. (It was later replaced by paint, and then by ear tags.) So all of the sheep were *tarred with the same brush.* BDPF; CI; DEI; DOC; EWPO. *See also* Knock the Tar out of Someone.

TEACH AN OLD DOG NEW TRICKS *You can't teach an old dog new tricks.* When people reach a certain age, they become set in their ways and can no longer learn new tasks nor adapt to new circumstances. DOC: 1670. Source: DOG. WNNCD: O.E. The proverb is true neither of old dogs nor elderly humans, although they may both take a little longer to master the "tricks." The expression is used, after the fact, by particular individuals under specific circumstances— usu. as an admission of failure on the part of the veteran. AID; ATWS; BDPF; DEI; IRCD.

TEACHER'S PET *See* Pet.

TEACH YOUR GRANDMOTHER TO SUCK EGGS *to teach your grandmother (how) to suck eggs.* To give advice to an expert. HOI: early-18th cent. Source: CHICKEN. The presumption is that all women old enough to be grandmothers already know how to suck eggs out of their shells with a straw: they need no instruction. Sucking raw eggs may be a lost art, but the expression *Go suck an egg!* (meaning "Get lost!") remains with us. ATWS; DEI; EWPO; LCRH.

TEAM *a team.* Two or more persons working or playing together as a unit. Source: ANIMAL. The first *team* was either a pair of oxen yoked together to pull a cart or a pair of horses harnessed together to pull a chariot (WNNCD: O.E.). When draft animals are *linked* together, they must *work* together: if one animal refuses to move, or moves too slowly or too fast, the purpose of the team is defeated, and the vehicle will make little or no progress. When people band together as a *team*, or *team up*, they understand that they must *work as a team*, i.e., display *teamwork* (WNNCD: 1886), or they will accomplish nothing. From sports come the terms *team spirit* and *team player*, both of which refer to the subordination of one's personal interests to those of the *team*; and from education comes the term *team teaching*, which involves two or more persons working together to teach a class.

TEAM PLAYER   *See* Team.

TEAM SPIRIT   *See* Team.

TEAM TEACHING   *See* Team.

TEAM UP   *See* Team.

TEAMWORK   *See* Team.

TEDDY BEAR   *a teddy bear.* A stuffed toy in the likeness of a bear (WNNCD: 1907); a bearlike man who is actually as harmless as a teddy bear. Source: BEAR. WNNCD: O.E. The *teddy bear* is named after President Theodore ("Teddy") Roosevelt, who, although rough and tough, once refused to shoot a bear cub that had been captured on a bear hunt. The sportsmanship was depicted in a cartoon in 1902, and the bear cub, rendered in brown plush, was soon put on sale under the name "Teddy" (later *teddy*). A *bear of a man* (q.v.), who has a rough exterior but a soft heart (like TR), is sometimes called a *teddy bear*. BDPF; EWPO; IRCD. *See also* Bear (3). *Compare* Puppy Dog; Pussycat.

TELL IT TO THE MARINES   *See* Horse Marines.

TENACIOUS AS A BULLDOG   *See* Bulldog (n).

TEXAS TURKEY   *a Texas turkey.* An armadillo. EWPO: 1930s. Source: TURKEY. WNNCD: 1555. During the Great Depression of the 1930s, poor people in the southwestern United States came to rely on the armadillo for food, presumably even for their Thanksgiving dinner, at which turkey was the traditional fare. Previously, it had been regarded only as a pest. EWPO. *See also* Cape Cod Turkey. *Compare* Hoover Hog.

THAT AIN'T HAY   That's no small amount of money. Source: HORSE. Horses are sometimes called *hayburners*, because, unlike *iron horses* (q.v.) that produce energy by burning wood, horses produce energy by eating hay (and grain). A pile of dollar bills may look like a haystack, but it is capable of producing much more energy for humans, and it is not the sort of thing you would feed to a horse. AID.

THAT BIRD HAS FLOWN *See* Bird Has Flown.

THICK AS FLEAS *to be as thick as fleas.* For two people, or two groups of people, to be in close association (i.e., "in cahoots") with each other. SOURCE: FLEA. WNNCD: O.E. Two people who are *as thick as fleas* are as close as two fingers (the usual sign). The analogy is to the density of fleas on a dog's (or cat's) back. *See also* Flea-bitten.

THICK-SKINNED *to be thick-skinned.* To be callous or insensitive. Source: ELEPHANT. To be *thick-skinned* is to be as resistant to "barbs" as an elephant or other *pachyderm* (fr. Gk. *pachys* "thick" + *derma* "skin"—WNNCD: ca. 1847). The other pachyderms are the rhinocerous, the hippopotamus, and the pig. All are nonruminant hoofed animals with little hair. MDWPO.

THIS LITTLE PIGGY *See* Piggy.

THOROUGHBRED *a thoroughbred.* A person of impeccable background. Source: HORSE. Technically, a thoroughbred is a horse whose lineage goes back to an English mare and an Arabian stallion (WNNCD: 1842); but in America a thoroughbred is determined not so much by foreign ancestry as by descendance from at least one racehorse with a great *track record* (q.v.). People who are *thoroughbreds* are well-bred, well mannered, and cultured. A *sign of good breeding* is an indication of "class" in either a thoroughbred horse or a thoroughbred person. BDPF; ST; WNWD.

THREE BLIND MICE A disparaging name for the umpires in a baseball game. Source: MOUSE. WNNCD: O.E. In the nursery rhyme—"Three blind mice, three blind mice; see how they run, see how they run . . . "—the farmer's wife cut off the tails of the three blind mice with a carving knife. This is what some of the fans at a baseball game would like to do to the three "umps" (now four in regular games, six in playoff games). After a bad "call" in a baseball (or hockey) game, the organist sometimes plays this little ditty.

THREE-DOG NIGHT *See* Man's Best Friend.

THREE-LEGGED MARE *See* Two-legged Mare.

THROW A SHOE *to throw a shoe.* For an athlete's shoe to come off during the course of play. Source: HORSE. Horses (and mules) are the only animals that wear shoes. When one of a horse's shoes comes off—i.e., when the horse "throws a shoe"—the shoe must be replaced before the horse can go back to work. The same is true of an athlete, who can't compete without the proper equipment. Cars can also *throw a shoe*; however, the missing equipment is not a brake shoe but a wheel with a tire on it. *See also* Horseshoes.

THROW A WRENCH IN THE WORKS   *to throw a (monkey) wrench in the works.* To sabotage someone's plans, project, or operation. IRCD: 1920. Source: MONKEY. WNNCD: ca. 1530. The expression, which orig. included the word *monkey*, is a free translation of the Fr. word *sabotage* "the throwing of wooden shoes (*sabots*) into machinery in order to still the wheels of industry." *Sabotage* was borrowed into Eng. and first used as a verb in 1913. AID; DOC; HTB. *See also* Monkey Wrench.

THROW IN THE SPONGE   *to throw in the sponge.* To admit defeat; to give up; to surrender. LTA: 1860. Source: SPONGE. WNNCD: O.E. The soft, elastic, porous skeleton of the marine porifera, or *sponge*, was formerly used to wash off a prizefighter between rounds. However, if the boxer was losing or was about to suffer serious injury, the cornerperson could stop the fight by throwing the sponge in the ring. (When the sponge was replaced by a towel, the expression was changed accordingly.) ATWS; BDPF; CI; DEI; DEOD; HTB; IRCD; LCRH; MDWPO; ST.

THROW IT TO THE DOGS   *See* Go to the Dogs.

THROW SOMEONE A BONE   *See* Bone to Pick.

THROW SOMEONE OFF THE SCENT   *to throw someone off the scent.* To misinform someone about the whereabouts of another person or thing. Source: DOG. Hunting dogs are thrown off the scent of a particular quarry when they encounter the fresher scent of another animal or when someone *draws a red herring across their path* (q.v.) in order to deliberately distract them. The police are *thrown off the scent* of an escaped criminal when they are deliberately misled about his/her location; and investigators are *thrown off the scent* when they are faced with a deliberate coverup. CI; ST. *See also* Throw Someone off the Track.

THROW SOMEONE OFF THE TRACK   *to throw someone off the track.* To mislead or distract someone. Source: FOX. WNNCD: O.E. In a fox hunt, the wily fox attempts to throw the hounds off its track by doubling back on its own tracks, running in the tracks of another animal, or running in or across a stream or on top of a stone wall. Humans *throw* other humans *off the track* by creating diversions, deceptions, and alibis. AID; ST. *See also* Cover Your Tracks; Throw Someone off the Scent.

THROW SOMEONE TO THE LIONS   *to throw someone to the lions.* To put someone in an extremely vulnerable position. Source: LION. WNNCD: 12th cent. The allusion is to the Roman "sport" of putting Christians and other "undesirables" in the arena and allowing lions and other wild animals to attack and kill them. The modern version might feature a rookie teacher/lawyer/pitcher being thrown into his/her first major assignment. CI; ST. *Compare* Throw Someone to the Wolves.

THROW SOMEONE TO THE WOLVES   *to throw someone to the wolves.* To sacrifice someone else to protect yourself. Source: WOLF. WNNCD: O.E. In its mildest form, this metaphor may derive from the practice of throwing *something*, such as raw meat, from the back of a sleigh in hopes of slowing up a pack of pursuing wolves and allowing the passengers to escape. In its grossest form, the metaphor may derive from an Aesop fable about the nursemaid of some naughty children who *threatened* to throw them to the pursuing wolves unless they behaved—or to a Russian folktale about a family that actually *did* throw their children to the wolves, one at a time, until they reached their destination. At any rate, it is obvious that wolves have been regarded as a major threat to humans for a very long time. Modern "wolves" demand that *someone* be sacrificed—fired, demoted, reassigned, charged, convicted, etc.—for the common good. AID; ATWS; BDPF; DEI; EWPO; IRCD; LCRH. *Compare* Sacrificial Lamb; Scapegoat.

TICKLE THE IVORIES   *to tickle the ivories.* To play the piano. Source: ELEPHANT. The keys of a piano are called *ivories* because, before 1955, they were made of the creamy-white dentine from the tusks of elephants. The word *ivory* itself derives from the ancient Egyptian word for "elephant," although it has also been applied to the tusks of other mammals, such as walruses and narwhals. Piano keys are now made of plastic. ATWS. *See also* Ivory Tower.

TIED UP   *See* Hog-tie.

TIE FLIES   *to tie flies.* To manufacture artificial lures for fly fishing. WNNCD: ca. 1880. Source: FLY. WNNCD: O.E. Artificial lures for fly fishing do not consist of live—or dead—flies tied to a bare hook. Instead, they are hooks adorned with feathers to give the appearance of a large flying insect, such as a caddis fly. One who *ties flies* is called a *flytier* (WNNCD: 1881). *See also* Fly (n) (2); Fly Fishing.

TIGER   *a tiger.* A fierce competitor; a bloodthirsty person; a sexually aggressive male. Source: TIGER. WNNCD: O.E. The tiger is the largest of the "big cats"— larger than the lion, which coexists with it only in India. The tiger is also a formidable hunter—not only ambushing its prey, like the lion, but also pursuing it. The two sexes look alike, and both hunt. The tiger is regarded as courageous because it attacks animals much larger than itself, such as water buffalo, and doesn't give up until it has made a kill. The transfer of the name to humans may derive from the game of poker, where a *tiger* is the worst possible hand that you can be dealt: no face cards, no pairs, no potential flush or straight. It takes a lot of nerve (or "courage") to bluff with a hand like that. ATWS; BDPF; DEI; ID; IRCD. *See also* Arouse the Tiger; Have a Tiger by the Tail; Kitty; Ride a Tiger.

TIGER HAND   *See* Ride a Tiger.

TIGER LILY   *a tiger lily.* An Asian garden lily whose orange-colored flowers are covered with black spots. WNNCD: 1824. Source: TIGER. WNNCD: O.E. This is one of the few tiger metaphors that is based on the animal's color and markings, rather than its size and ferocity. In fact, the metaphor is based entirely on contrasting colors—orange and black—because the tiger is renowned for having stripes, not spots. *Compare* Tiger Shark.

TIGER SHARK   *a tiger shark.* A man-eating shark of the warm waters of the Atlantic and Pacific. WNNCD: 1784. Source: TIGER. WNNCD: O.E. The *tiger shark* is so called because of its stripes. The vertical brown stripes, contrasting with a gray background, occur on the upper sides of the body and extend from the pectoral fins to the second dorsal fins; from there to the end of the tail they are spots rather than stripes. The vertical stripes of the tiger begin on the face and extend to the hind legs and tail, where they become rings. The tiger's stripes are black against an orangish brown background.

TIGHT AS A TICK   *to be as tight as a tick.* To be either stingy with your money or totally inebriated. IRCD: ca. 1875. Source: TICK. WNNCD: 14th cent. The bloodsucking tick attaches itself tightly to the skin of a warm-blooded animal and is hard to remove; it also gorges itself on blood until its body is "tight as a drum." DOC. *See also* Full as a Tick. *Compare* Drunk as a Skunk.

TILL THE COWS COME HOME   *to stay out till the cows come home.* To stay out all night. DOC: 1620. Source: COW. WNNCD: O.E. Cows are milked twice a day. They are usu. driven out to pasture after the morning milking and driven back to the barn for the evening milking. However, if the cows wander off, or if the farmer or his/her dog is not available to retrieve them, they may stay out all night, eventually coming home in the morning complaining about their painfully full udders. AID; ATWS; BDPF; CH; CI; DEI; EWPO; HOI; LCRH.

TIN FISH   *See* Torpedo (n).

TITMOUSE   *a titmouse.* A small bird resembling the nuthatch but possessing a longer tail. WNNCD: 14th cent. Source: MOUSE. WNNCD: O.E. *Titmouse* is a folk etymology for *titmose* (fr. *tit* "little," as in "a jot or a *tittle*," + *mose*, the original name of the bird). M.E. *mose* must have been too similar to M.E. *mous* "mouse" to prevent the association of the small common bird with the small common rodent. MDWPO. *Compare* Dormouse.

TOAD   *a toad.* An ugly or contemptible person. Source: TOAD. WNNCD: O.E. The toad has always had a bad reputation, esp. when compared with its relative, the frog. (Princes turn into frogs, not toads.) Toads are not as pretty as frogs, they are less active and nimble, they are fatter and squattier, and they have warts. ATWS. *See also* Toadfish; Ugly as a Toad.

TOADEATER *a toadeater*. One who will perform the most distasteful task in order to stay in favor: a sycophant; a brownnoser. WNNCD: 1572. Source: TOAD. WNNCD: O.E. A *toadeater*, or *geek*, was a charlatan's assistant who would eat a toad, believed to be poisonous in the 16th cent., and then be cured by downing the charlatan's magic elixir. ATWS; BDPF; EWPO; IRCD; MDWPO. *See also* Toady (n).

TOADFISH *a toadfish*. A scaleless brown bottomfeeding marine fish that has a huge wide head and a huge wide mouth with puffy lips. WNNCD: 1612. Source: TOAD. WNNCD: O.E. The toadfish resembles a toad in color, compactness, large-headedness, lethargy, ugliness, and status. Ugliness was probably the key feature in its naming. *See also* Toad; Ugly as a Toad.

TOAD STICKER *a toad sticker*. A short dagger. Source: TOAD. WNNCD: O.E. The *toad sticker* was probably never used to kill *toads*, since they are inedible and sometimes poisonous. Its purpose is to kill *people*. It was named for the toad because it is a very small weapon, used only at close quarters. *Compare* Frog Sticker; Pig Sticker.

TOADSTOOL *a toadstool*. An inedible poisonous mushroom with a domed cap. WNNCD: 14th cent. Source: TOAD. WNNCD: O.E. Unlike frogs, which are aquatic and like to sit on lily pads, toads are terrestrial, although they don't sit on toadstools. The metaphor is based partly on the appearance of the fungus—like a toad sitting on a stick—but mostly on the poisonous nature of some toads and most toadstools. ATWS; EWPO; HF. *See also* Padlock; Tadpole; Toad.

TOAD STRANGLER *a toad strangler*. An extremely heavy rainstorm that causes flash flooding. Source: TOAD. WNNCD: O.E. *Toad strangler* is an American regional expression that comes close to the mark. Unlike frogs, which are primarily aquatic, toads are primarily terrestrial. If caught in a torrential rainstorm, they could very easily drown. CH. *Compare* Rain Cats and Dogs.

TOADY (n) *a toady*. A fawning flatterer: a sycophant; a brownnoser. WNNCD: 1826. Source: TOAD. WNNCD: O.E. *Toady* is short for *toadeater* (q.v.). Just as the 16th cent. conjurer's assistant was willing to eat a "poisonous" toad and then be miraculously cured, the 19th cent. *toady* was willing to do anything, however distasteful, to please his employer. ATWS; CE; EWPO; IRCD; LCRH; THT. *See also* Toady (v).

TOADY (v) *to toady*. To behave obsequiously toward a superior in order to stay or rise in favor: to "brownnose"; to "suck up." WNNCD: 1861. Source: TOAD.

WNNCD: O.E. The verb *toady* is derived from the noun *toady* (q.v.), which is a shortening of the word *toadeater* (q.v.). Dickens' character Uriah Heep, in *David Copperfield*, was probably the classic literary example of a *toady*. CE; MDWPO.

TOMBOY *See* Tomcat.

TOMCAT *a tomcat.* A sexually active male. Source: CAT. WNNCD: O.E. Literally, a tomcat, or *tom*, is simply a male cat, esp. a sexually active one that *cats around* the neighborhood at night looking for available females (WNNCD: 1789). Figuratively, a *tomcat* is a sexually active man who *tomcats* around like the feline, seeking sexual encounters wherever he can find them. *Tom* has also been applied to the male of other species, such as the turkey (a *tom turkey*) and to a girl who behaves like a boy (a *tomboy*). ATWS; IRCD; WNWD. *Compare* Alley Cat.

TOOTHLESS LION *a toothless lion.* A once-powerful entity that has grown old and feeble and is no longer feared or respected. Source: LION. WNNCD: 12th cent. A lion *does* lose its teeth when it grows old, but a lion's teeth are not its primary weapon: its limbs are. The lioness waits in ambush while the adult males drive a quarry her way. Then she kills it by striking it on the back and breaking its spine. So even a toothless lion should be feared. DEI. *Compare* Toothless Tiger.

TOOTHLESS TIGER *a toothless tiger.* A fierce-looking opponent who poses no real threat because of old age, illness, injury, etc. Source: TIGER. WNNCD: O.E. Even a toothless tiger would pose a serious threat, not only because of its huge size—up to 12 feet long, from tip of nose to tip of tail, and 650 pounds in weight—but also because of its strong legs and menacing claws. However, *toothless* usu. implies age and infirmity, so such tigers—and humans—would only be as threatening as *pussycats* (q.v.). *See also* Paper Tiger. *Compare* Toothless Lion.

TOP DOG *the top dog.* The boss; the leader; the champion. WNNCD: 1900. Source: DOG. WNNCD: O.E. In a pack of dogs, the top dog is the male that can beat, or has beaten, all of the other male dogs—i.e., the one that is both at the top of the domination hierarchy and on top of the other dog at the end of a dogfight. Among humans, a *top dog* is someone who is at the top of his/her competitive field. An *underdog* (WNNCD: 1887) is a person, team, or organization that is a predicted loser in an upcoming competition on the basis of their past record. Among dogs, an underdog is the male dog on the bottom at the end of a dogfight: a loser. ATWS; BDPF; CI; DEI; EWPO; IRCD; MDWPO; ST.

TORPEDO (n) *a torpedo.* An underwater missile; a hired gun. Source: FISH. Literally, a torpedo is a fish: a disc-shaped ray that stuns its victim with a charge of up to 220 volts of electricity (fr. Lat. *torpedo* "stiffness or numbness"). The stunning behavior of the electric ray was first associated with naval explosives in

1786, when a floating mine was named for the fish (and referred to by Admiral Farragut: "Damn the torpedoes! Full speed ahead!"). In WWI, the cigar-shaped, self-propelled, underwater missile that was fired at ships from a submarine was likewise called a *torpedo*, and a decade later it was nicknamed a *tin fish* (WNNCD: ca. 1925). In WWII, *torpedoes* were also fired from airplanes, and the term *torpedo juice* "homemade whiskey made from the alcohol in a torpedo" first appeared. More recently, *torpedo* has been applied to a professional hit person; and a verb, *to torpedo something*, has developed with the meaning "to wreck someone's plans." BDPF; EWPO; HF; IHAT; ROE.

TORPEDO (v)   *See* Torpedo (n).

TORPEDO JUICE   *See* Torpedo (n).

TORTOISE AND THE HARE   *the tortoise and the hare.* A situation which supports the moral of the Aesop fable, "The Tortoise and the Hare": *Slow and steady wins the race* (q.v.). Source: TORTOISE (WNNCD: 14th cent.); HARE (WNNCD: O.E.). The tortoise, or large land turtle, is a very slow-moving animal, while the hare, or long-eared rabbit, is a very fast-moving one. When they raced, in the fable, the tortoise won, because it maintained a steady pace, while the hare moved in fits and starts. A silhouette of the *tortoise* is now a symbol for "slow speed" on the throttle of some lawn mowers, and an outline of the *hare* is a symbol for "fast speed." BDPF; IRCD.

TOUGH OLD BIRD   *a tough old bird.* An elderly person who refuses to give in to adversity or infirmity. Source: BIRD. WNNCD: O.E. A person who refuses to grow old, become incapacitated, or die is like an old rooster or tom turkey that is allowed to live because it is too tough to eat. The metaphor may also allude to a fighting cock that is beyond its prime but is still eager to return to the pits. A *smart old bird* is a senior citizen who is too shrewd to be *gulled* (q.v.). *Compare* Tough Turkey.

TOUGH TURKEY   *Tough turkey!* That's your problem! Source: TURKEY. WNNCD: 1555. *Tough turkey* is a WWII euphemism for *Tough shit!* (or *T.S.*), which was further euphemized as *tough*, as in *That's tough!* The inspiration for *tough turkey* was probably an old tom turkey that was worthless as food because it was too tough to eat. CE. *See also* Tough Old Bird.

TRACK DOWN   *to track someone or something down.* To search for someone or something until you find them/it. Source: ANIMAL. Animal predators, such as the cat and the dog, track down their prey by sight, sound, and scent. Human predators, such as hunters, rely primarily on sight and sound: i.e., they look for animal tracks and listen for animal calls. Police investigators *track down* perpetrators of crime and corruption by following both a physical trail and a paper trail.

Once they are *on the track of* the criminals, their goal is to *keep track of* them until they are apprehended. If the objects of pursuit *backtrack*, or *double back* on their tracks, the pursuers may *lose track of* them temporarily. When the criminals are surrounded, however, with no way out, they usu. *stop dead in their tracks*. Private investigators, insurance investigators, scientific investigators, and investigative reporters employ the same techniques, although their goal is more likely evidence, knowledge, or the solution to a problem. Ordinary people try to *track down* the cause of a leaky roof; they sometimes *backtrack* to an earlier issue when speaking; they try to *keep track of* their friends; they sometimes *lose track of* their friends; and they *stop dead in their tracks* when they finally spot them again. AID; CI; DA; DAE; DEI; ST. *See also* Cover Your Tracks; On the Right/Wrong Track.

TRACK RECORD *a track record.* A history of one's successes and failures. WNNCD: 1952. Source: HORSE. The track record of a horse is the history of its successes and failures on the racetrack: the number of races it has participated in; the number of times it has finished in the money; the number of times it has won; the amount of money it has paid; etc. For people, a *track record* is a written (as in a *résumé*) or unwritten history of their successes (esp.) and failures in the world of work. Both types of records—horse and human—are used by people for betting on the chances of success of the individual in the future. CI; DEI; DOC; NDAS; ST.

TRAGEDY *a tragedy.* A drama in which the noble but flawed protagonist fights the good fight but comes to a disastrous and pitiable end; any loss of life, livelihood, property, etc. Source: GOAT. The founders of Greek tragedy, the dramatists of classical Greece, called their art form a "goat song" (Gk. *tragōidia*, fr. *tragos* "goat" + *ōidē* "song"), although no one is certain why. It may have been that the actors or chorus orig. wore goatskins in honor of the satyrs (half man, half goat), or that a goat was sacrificed before or after the performance, or that a goat was awarded to the winning dramatist. At any rate, the metaphor has been broadened and weakened so much in modern times that *any* misfortune is now a *tragedy*. ATWS; BDPF; EWPO; THT.

TRAIL THE FIELD *See* Pull away from the Field.

TRAP *a trap.* An ambush; a deception. Source: ANIMAL. All senses of *trap*—both noun and verb, and both concrete and abstract—derive from the mechanical device for capturing game or pests (WNNCD: O.E.). Trappers hunt game by setting out spring-operated devices with steel jaws that snap together when the animal accidentally steps on them, or tries to get to the bait that they sometimes contain. Householders capture mice and rats by setting out boards with a spring-operated bail that snaps down on the rodent's neck when it touches the cheese that is used as bait. The spring-operated nature of the trap leads to the name of another mechanical device, a *trap* that throws clay pigeons into the air in *trap* *shooting*; and the sense of "capture" carries over to the U-shaped device, a *plumber's trap*, that catches solids and gas but allows liquids to flow through the pipe. A *trap play* in football is a play in which an offensive lineman pulls back and lures the opposing defensive lineman into following him, thereby allowing the ballcarrier to plunge through the hole in the line. A mouth is sometimes called a *trap* because of its hinged lower jaw ("Shut your *trap*!"); and a set of drums in a jazz band is called a *trap* because of its pedal-operated cymbals. A person who has a *mind like a steel trap* seizes upon everything and retains it forever; but a person who lacks such a mind is likely to *fall into a trap* or be *caught in a trap*. A *death trap* (WNNCD: 1835) is a building that is unsafe to be in; and to be *trapped* (WNNCD: 14th cent.) in such a building or other enclosure is to be unable to escape. The police sometimes *set a trap* for a suspected criminal, but they are careful to avoid charges of *entrapment*. AID; ATWS; CI; ST.

TRAPPED   *See* Trap.

TRAP PLAY   *See* Trap.

TRAP SHOOTING   *See* Trap.

TRAVEL BUG   *See* Bug (n) (1).

TRAVEL IN DOUBLE HARNESS   *See* Get Hitched.

TREACLE   Molasses. Source: ANIMAL. In ancient Greece, the etymon of *treacle*, Gk. *thēriakē*, meant an antidote against the poisonous bite of an animal (fr. *thēr* "wild animal," a cognate of Eng. *deer*). Over the centuries, the antidote passed from a salve, applied to the wound itself, to a liquid, taken internally and sweetened with molasses. Eventually, the word *treacle* came to be identified with the sweetener itself (esp. in Britain) and became synonymous with *molasses*. In America, *treacle* became a metaphor for anything excessively sentimental or cloying. THT; WNWD. *See also* Schmaltz. *Compare* Hair of the Dog.

TREAT SOMEONE LIKE A DOG   *to treat someone like a dog.* To deal with someone shabbily or abusively. Source: DOG. WNNCD: O.E. Many dogs *lead a dog's life* (q.v.): caged in a pen or chained to a stake; left outside in the heat, cold, rain, and snow; fed food unsuitable for human consumption or tossed an occasional bone; yelled at, kicked, and sometimes beaten. A person who is *treated like a dog* is either being denied his/her human and civil rights or is being dealt with unfairly or vindictively. DEI.

TREAT WITH KID GLOVES   *See* Handle with Kid Gloves.

TRIPE   Trash. Source: ANIMAL. Literally, *tripe* is the lining of the stomach, esp. the second stomach, of a ruminant animal, such as an ox, that is eaten as a delicacy (WNNCD: 14th cent.). Figuratively, *tripe* is anything that is regarded as worthless or offensive, ranging from the arts to arguments. The metaphorical meaning was probably created by someone who found the eating of animal stomachs to be disgusting and uncivilized. ATWS. *Compare* Pluck (n).

TROJAN HORSE   *a Trojan horse*. A hidden danger; a deceptive scheme. WNNCD: ca. 1574. Source: HORSE. WNNCD: O.E. After ten years of frustration fighting the Trojans, the Greeks set sail for home, leaving behind a huge *wooden horse*—the Trojan horse—on the sand outside the city of Troy. The Trojans, taking the horse to be a gift from the departing Greeks, drew it inside the city walls. That night the Greek soldiers who had been hidden inside the horse let themselves out, opened the gates of the city, and let in the rest of the Greeks, who had turned around and sailed back to Troy. The fall of the city ensued, as described in Virgil's *Aeneid*. From this experience comes the expression, "Never trust Greeks bearing gifts." ATWS; BDPF; DEI; EWPO. *See also* Look a Gift Horse in the Mouth.

TROT (n)   *a trot; the trots*. A jog; diarrhea. Source: HORSE. Literally, a *trot* (WNNCD: 14th cent.) is the diagonal gait of a riding, fox hunting, or harness racing horse. Figuratively, a *trot* is a brisk walk or a slow run by humans— although when humans get *the trots*, or "the runs," they sometimes *gallop* (q.v.) to the nearest bathroom. A *trot* is also a *pony* (q.v.), or "crib": a translation that is smuggled into a foreign language or literature class for cheating on a test (WNNCD: 1860s). IRCD; ST. *See also* Trot (v).

TROT (v)   *to trot*. To move briskly; to jog. Source: HORSE. A horse *trots* (WNNCD: 14th cent.) by advancing its legs in diagonal pairs: e.g., left front leg and right hind leg; right front leg and left hind leg; etc. The trotting gait is some-where between a fast walk and a run, although the animal never completely leaves the ground, as it does in a *gallop* (q.v.). People *trot* by walking fast or running slowly. A horse that is "hot to trot" is eager or impatient for the race or the hunt to start; a person who is *hot to trot* is eager to engage in sex. To "trot out" a horse (WNNCD: 1838) is to *put it through its paces* (q.v.); to *trot out* a person or a product is to put them on display. ATWS; CE; CI; DEI; ST. *See also* Trot (n).

TROT OUT   *See* Trot (v).

TROTS   *See* Trot (n).

TRY IT ON THE DOG   *to try it on the dog*. To try out a play in a smaller city before taking it to Broadway. HTB: late-19th cent. Source: DOG. WNNCD: O.E. This metaphor derives from the ancient practice of using a dog as a food taster:

If the food looks tainted, feed some of it to the dog. If the dog gets sick or refuses to eat it, you were probably right; if not, it is probably safe for humans. (After all, there are plenty more dogs where that one came from.) In the late 1800s, the show business "dog," called a *dogtown*, was usu. a city in the northeastern United States, such as Philadelphia, Hartford, or Boston. If the play proved to be a *dog* (q.v.) there, it would probably never make it to the Great White Way. ATWS.

TRY YOUR WINGS   *See* Sprout Wings.

TURKEY (1)   *a turkey.* A stupid fool. EWPO: ca. 1930. Source: TURKEY. WNNCD: 1555. The domesticated turkey is regarded as a stupid, awkward bird, in spite of its beautiful plumage. It can't fly; it walks funny; it makes a gurgling sound; it doesn't recognize its own food; it doesn't know enough to come in out of the rain (and can drown); it panics at the sound of a loud noise (and can suffocate in the resulting pile-up); and it is cannibalistic. A human *turkey* (or *jive turkey*, in black slang) is presumably capable of the same behavior. ATWS; LTA. *See also* Turkey (2); Turkey (3).

TURKEY (2)   *a turkey.* A theatrical (or other) production that is a flop or a failure. EWPO: 1940s. Source: TURKEY. WNNCD: 1555. On Broadway, a *turkey* is a flop show that opens and closes on the same night. The connection here is not to the opening and closing of the beautiful tail fan of the tom turkey but to the nature of turkeys in general: they are regarded as losers, esp. around Thanksgiving time. ATWS; EWPO; LCRH; LTA; MDWPO. *See also* Turkey (1); Turkey (3).

TURKEY (3)   *a turkey.* Three strikes in succession in a single game of bowling. Source: TURKEY (?). WNNCD: 1555. The turkey is a large American bird (up to four feet tall and 40 pounds in weight), and the male has a magnificent tail fan three feet across. It is possible that the three side-by-side "X's" on a scoring sheet once reminded a bowler of the tom's fantail; or there may be some connection to the *turkey shoot* (q.v.). *See also* Turkey (1); Turkey (2).

TURKEY BUZZARD   *a turkey buzzard.* An American vulture. WNNCD: 1846. Source: TURKEY. WNNCD: 1555. The turkey buzzard of the eastern United States is not so called because it preys on turkeys—vultures don't prey on anything that large—but because its orangish red and purplish blue neck resembles that of a male turkey. (The turkey buzzards return to Hinckley, Ohio, from their southern migration on March 15.) *See also* Buzzards Are Circling.

TURKEY SHOOT   *a turkey shoot.* A cinch; a piece of cake; a no-lose situation. Source: TURKEY. WNNCD: The turkey shoot was a contest of marksmanship in the 19th cent. in which a turkey was either the prize (WNNCD: 1845) or the target (tied behind a log with only its head visible to the shooter). The expression has since come to mean "an easy task," such as *shooting fish in a barrel* (q.v.). EWPO; NDAS. *Compare* Duck Soup; Sitting Duck.

TURKEY TROT   *a turkey trot.* A ragtime dance popular in the United States in the early 1900s. WNNCD: 1908. Source: TURKEY. WNNCD: 1555. The metaphor is based on the similarity between the dance step—raising the shoulders, rising on the balls of the feet—and the unusual stiff-legged gait of the turkey. A Thanksgiving middle-distance run is also called a *turkey trot.* IRCD; LTA.

TURKEY WATTLES   Bags of loose skin hanging below the chin of an elderly person. Source: TURKEY. WNNCD: 1555. Both chickens and turkeys have wattles of red skin hanging below their beak, but the wattles of the turkey are much larger—and lower—and they contrast strongly with the blue skin on the turkey's head. Human *wattles* are not red, but they do increase from chicken-size to turkey-size as a person ages. *Compare* Dewlap.

TURN A HAIR   *See* Didn't Turn a Hair.

TURN ON YOU   *See* Bite the Hand that Feeds You.

TURN TAIL   *to turn tail (and run).* To beat a hasty retreat. Source: FALCON. This is what an untrained falcon does when it encounters an uncooperative prey: turns its tail to the prey and flies off. Birds have been the source of other "cowardice" metaphors, such as *chicken out* and *show the white feather,* both of which *see.* ATWS; CE; SOED; ST. *See also* Coward; Tail between Your Legs.

TURN TURTLE   *to turn turtle.* To be rendered helpless; to *go belly up* (q.v.). DOC: 1830s. Source: TURTLE. WNNCD: 1657. When a boat or ship capsizes—i.e., turns over so that its keel is above water and its decks below—it is said to have *turned turtle.* Male tortoises render each other helpless in this way during the mating season, and sailors once stored sea turtles on board ship in this position during long voyages. However, the fact has been ignored that a *capsized* boat or ship looks very much like the *upright* shell of a large turtle in the water. So *turn turtle* could just as well mean "turn into a turtle." ATWS; BDPF; CI; DEI; EWPO; HOI; IRCD; LCRH.

TURTLEDOVE   *a turtledove.* A small gray pigeon of Europe, Africa, and the Middle East—essentially equivalent to the American mourning dove. WNNCD: 14th cent. Source: TURTLE (*). WNNCD: 1657. This is a false metaphor. The *turtle* in *turtledove* derives fr. Lat. *turtur,* an echoic word for the mournful sound made by the bird, not fr. V.Lat. *tartaruca* "turtle." Because of its affection for its mate, the turtledove is sometimes confused with the *lovebird* (q.v.), which is a parrot. *Turtledoves* were first mentioned in The Song of Solomon. ATWS; EWPO; HF; IRCD; MDWPO; WNWD. *See also* Voice of the Turtle.

TURTLENECK   *a turtleneck*. A knit sweater, or shirt-sweater, with a long, tight-fitting neck that can be pulled up to the face and then turned down, over the other material, to provide extra warmth for the neck. WNNCD: ca. 1908. Source: TURTLE. WNNCD: 1657. When the head of some of the smaller American turtles, such as the pond turtle and the box turtle, is only partially extended from the shell, the excess skin that will cover the neck when the head is fully extended is doubled over and looks exactly like the neck of a turtleneck sweater. ATWS; IRCD. *See also* Mock Turtleneck.

TWO-LEGGED MARE   *a two-legged mare*. An empty gallows. Source: HORSE. A mare has four legs; but seen from the side, while standing, it does resemble a two-legged gallows. *Two-legged mare* was an early American term; an even earlier British term for the gallows was *three-legged mare*. The assumption is that, when seen from a distance, a gallows with a victim hanging from it looked like a *mare with three legs*. BDPF; CH; DOC.

U

UGLY AS A TOAD *to be as ugly as a toad.* To be extremely unattractive. Source: TOAD. WNNCD: O.E. Some animals, such as the platypus, are bizarre; but the toad has always been regarded as just downright ugly. The reason is probably that it has a close relative, the frog, that is not only pretty, nimble, and smooth-skinned but is also edible (the legs). (Some toads are also poisonous.) ATWS. *See also* Toad; Toadfish. *Compare* Ugly Duckling.

UGLY DUCKLING *an ugly duckling.* An unattractive, awkward, or otherwise unpromising child who turns into a beautiful, graceful, and talented adult. WNNCD: 1883. Source: DUCK. WNNCD: O.E. The metaphor is based on "The Ugly Duckling," a children's story by Hans Christian Andersen about a cygnet that is raised by a mother duck. To the ducks and ducklings, the cygnet is ugly, awkward, and untalented; but, as you may have guessed, it grows up to be a beautiful swan. ATWS; BDPF; CI; DEI; DOC; EWPO; IRCD. *Compare* Black Sheep.

UKULELE *a ukulele (or ukelele).* A small, four-stringed guitar. WNNCD: 1913. Source: FLEA. When this musical instrument was introduced into Hawaii by the Portuguese (ca. 1880), it was named *ukulele* by the Hawaiians—lit., "flea" (*uku*) "jumping" (*lele*): a "jumping flea"—perhaps because of the way the player's fingers leap across the strings. ATWS; EWPO; LTA. *See also* Flea-flicker; My Dog Has Fleas.

UNABLE TO STAND THE GAFF *See* Stand the Gaff.

UNBRIDLED *See* Bridle.

UNDERDOG   *See* Top Dog.

UNDER THE WIRE   *See* Go down to the Wire.

UNFLAPPABLE   *to be unflappable.* To be imperturbable. WNNCD: 1954. Source: BIRD. When birds are cornered, they raise themselves to their full height and flap their wings rapidly and noisily. A person who is *unflappable* is self-assured, not easily excited, and calm in a crisis. SPD; WNWD.

UNTIL THE LAST DOG IS HUNG   *See* Hangdog Look.

UNTRAMMELED   *to be untrammeled.* To be unimpeded or unrestrained. Source: FISH. Literally, a fish that is untrammeled is one that is not caught in a *trammel*, or three-layered net (fr. Lat. *tres* "three" + *macula* "mesh"). Catching fish in a net is more ancient than catching them on a baited hook—and trapping them in a wicker basket is the most ancient method of all. People are *untrammeled* when they are free to do and go as they please. ATWS.

UP A TREE   *to be up a tree.* To be trapped in a difficult situation. DOC: 1825. Source: ANIMAL. When an animal such as a bear, possum, raccoon, or squirrel is pursued by dogs and hunters, it often tries to escape by climbing a tree. Unless the tree is surrounded closely by other trees, however, this is a mistake, because the prey then becomes an easier target for the hunter. People who have gotten themselves into a predicament from which they can't escape are like the treed animal: trapped by their own doing. A worse situation for the animal is to go out on a limb, because the limb will break and the prey will either fall to its death or land at the hunter's feet. Animals go out on a limb to save themselves, but humans usu. *go out on a limb* to help someone else or support an unpopular cause (HOI: 1897). Nevertheless, both the animal and the human that are *out on a limb* are taking a risk and putting themselves in a precarious position. AID; ATWS; BDPF; CI; DEI; LCRH; ST. *Compare* Stick Your Neck Out.

URCHIN   *an urchin.* A little rascal (usu. male). Source: HEDGEHOG. The European hedgehog was orig. called an *urchin* (fr. M.Fr. *herichon* "the bristly one") because of its sharp spines (WNNCD: 14th cent.). Figuratively, an *urchin* is a mischievous child, like the children in Dickens' *Oliver Twist* or the "Our Gang" comedies. These children lack the spines, but they are just as irritating. ATWS; EWPO; THT. *See also* Prickly as a Hedgehog; Sea Urchin.

V

VAMPIRE   *a vampire.* A dead person who rises from the coffin at night and sucks the blood of sleeping people. WNNCD: 1734. Source: BAT (*). *Vampire* is not an animal metaphor. There *is* such a thing as a vampire bat (of Mexico, Central America, and South America) that sucks the blood of cattle and horses and sometimes attacks humans; but the vampire *bat* is named after the folkloric *human* vampire, as described in Bram Stoker's *Dracula. Compare* Bloodsucker.

VARMINT   *a varmint.* A thieving rascal. Source: WORM. WNNCD: O.E. *Varmint* is an alteration of *vermin* (q.v.), which derives from Lat. *vermis* "worm." In British regional Eng. a *varmint* was an animal pest that was always in season (WNNCD: 1539). In the American West, *varmint* was applied to a thieving human (usu. male) who rustled cattle, or stole horses or other men's women. All of this unpleasantness began with the worm, esp. one that robs animals or crops of their life. EWPO.

VAULTING HORSE   *a vaulting horse.* An apparatus in gymnastics on which the running gymnast places his/her hands in order to elevate him-/herself into the air for a tumbling routine. WNNCD: ca. 1875. Source: HORSE. WNNCD: O.E. The vaulting horse, also known as a *long horse* (WNNCD: ca. 1934), is probably named for the horse because it is about the length of a horse's body, it is cylindrical, it is covered with brown leather, and it stands on (two) legs. At one time there may have been a sport of vaulting from or onto the back of a real horse, as in bull vaulting. ATWS. *See also* Pommel Horse. *Compare* Take the Bull by the Horns.

VENISON   Deer meat. Source: ANIMAL. Originally, *venison* was the meat of animals killed in the hunt (fr. Lat. *venatio* "hunting"). When the word came into

Eng. (via Fr. *veneison* "hunting or game"), it was applied to the meat of "small wild mammals"—i.e., *deer* (WNNCD: 13th cent.). When the word *deer* was narrowed in meaning to a member of the family *Cervidae* (e.g., the white-tailed deer), the word *venison* went along with it, taking on the meaning of "deer meat." EWPO.

VENOM   Poison. Source: ANIMAL. Animal venom is the poison delivered to a victim by a reptile, fish, or insect. Human *venom* is the poisonous language directed at one person by another, who is said to "spew venom." The language takes the form of bitterness, malice, and abuse and is intended to bite or sting.

VERBAL SPARRING   *See* Spar.

VERMICELLI   Very thin spaghetti. WNNCD: 1669. Source: WORM. In It., *vermicelli* lit. means "little worms" (fr. Lat. *vermis* "worm" + It. *-ell-* "dim." + *-i* "pl."). That's something not to think about the next time you're eating these small-diameter strings of pasta. It could be worse: you could be eating the "little worms" in a room painted *vermilion* (q.v.) "the color of earthworms." Bon appetit! ATWS; EWPO.

VERMILION   *the color vermilion.* A bright red or reddish orange. WNNCD: 14th cent. Source: WORM. *Vermilion* derives ultimately fr. Lat. *vermiculus* "little worm." In L.Lat., *vermiculus* took on the meaning "crimson"; but in O.Fr., which is the immediate source of the Eng. word, the color was lightened, brightened, and moved closer to orange than to purple. Thus, *vermilion* means "the color or earthworms," although, like *crimson* (q.v.), it is actually produced from crushed *kermes* insects. ATWS.

VERMIN   Small animal pests, such as bugs and rats; larger animal predators, such as coyotes and wolves. WNNCD: 14th cent. Source: WORM. The meaning of the Lat. word *vermin*, "worm," has been extended in Eng. to include many objectionable animals, such as despicable humans. The reference is probably to the worms that destroy agricultural crops. ATWS; EWPO. *See also* Varmint; Vermicelli; Vermilion.

VERMOUTH   A sweet or dry aromatic wine used in mixed drinks, such as the martini. WNNCD: 1806. Source: WORM (*). *Vermouth* is the Eng. version of a Fr. alteration (*vermout*) of a Ger. word (*Wermut*) meaning "wormwood." *Wormwood* is a false metaphor, because it has nothing to do with either worms or wood, and neither does *vermouth*. But *vermouth*, like wormwood, is a potent liqueur that is an essential ingredient in certain drinks. (In the case of wormwood, that is absinthe.) *See also* Bitter as Wormwood.

VIPER   *a viper.* A disloyal, spiteful, vicious, treacherous, or evil person. Source: SNAKE. Vipers, or "pit vipers," are members of the family of snakes known as

Viperidae. The name of the family has been thought to mean "live-bearing" (Lat. *vivus parere*), but that is highly unlikely, since some of the members lays eggs, including the Malayan pit viper. *Pit vipers,* such as the *rattlesnake* (q.v.), are so called because they have heat-sensing pits, or cavities, in their skull, resembling the sinus area in humans, which allow them to locate warm-blooded prey without moving from ambush. Suffice it to say that a viperous snake is a venomous, thick-bodied, nonconstricting one, while a *viperous* human is one with a poisonous attitude or intention. ATWS; IRCD. *See also* Serpent; Snake.

VIXEN *a vixen.* An ill-tempered or shrewish woman: a *shrew* (q.v.). EWPO: ca. 1595 (Shakespeare's *A Midsummer Night's Dream*). Source: FOX. *Vixen* is a Southern English modification of M.E. *fixen,* fr. O.E. *fyxe* "a female fox." In Act III, Scene 2, of the play, Helena describes Hermia as being angry, keen, shrewd, and fierce: "She was a vixen when she went to school." The female fox, unlike the shrew, is not pugnacious, but it is a fierce defender of its cubs. IRCD. *See also* Fox.

VOICE OF THE TURTLE *The voice of the turtle is heard in the land.* Spring is here. (The Song of Solomon 2:12: "The flowers appear on the earth; the time of the singing of birds is come, and the voice of the turtle is heard in our land...") Source: TURTLE (*). WNNCD: 1657. This is a false metaphor: turtles make no sound. The "voice" is actually that of the *turtledove* (q.v.), equivalent to the American mourning dove, which is named for its distinctive sound (*turtur* in Lat.). The sound was perceived as a happy one in the Old World, a sad one in the new.

VULTURE *a vulture.* A human predator: a ravenous, rapacious, voracious individual. IRCD: ca. 1600. Source: VULTURE. WNNCD: 14th cent. Interestingly, the vulture, although a huge and ominous-looking bird, does not usu. prey on living creatures. Its main source of food is carrion and—because of its weak jaws—dead animals that have already been opened up by other animals. It does, however, prey on weak or dying animals, just as the human *vulture* does. ATWS; CE. *See also* Vulture for Culture; Vultures Are Circling.

VULTURE FOR CULTURE *a vulture for culture.* A dilettante: one who immerses him-/herself in the arts, usu. as a spectator or benefactor. Source: VULTURE. WNNCD: 14th cent. The human hunger for culture is compared here to the vulture's hunger for food. Unfortunately, the food that the vulture prefers is not alive and well but dead or dying: i.e., carrion and *roadkill* (q.v.). Once the kill is opened up by some other animal, however, the vulture is ravenous and voracious. CI. *See also* Vulture; Vultures Are Circling.

VULTURES ARE CIRCLING *The vultures are circling.* The relatives are assembling in anticipation of the death of a wealthy family member. Source: VULTURE.

WNNCD: 14th cent. Vultures circle in the air above a dying animal, waiting for (1) the animal to die, (2) another animal to come along and open up the body, and (3) everybody else to go away. When the dead animal is unattended, the vultures descend and eat their fill. *See also* Vulture. *Compare* Buzzards Are Circling.

W

WADDLE LIKE A DUCK   *to waddle like a duck*. To swing the lower part of the body from side to side, in unison with short steps and outturned feet. WNNCD: 1592. Source: DUCK. WNNCD: O.E. Ducks are round-figured birds with short legs and large webbed feet. When they walk, they swing their entire body along with their feet, which are turned outward in order to avoid stepping on each other. Humans who *waddle like ducks* usu. do so because they are obese, are not athletic, or are not concerned about their appearance. WNWD. *See also* Duck Walk.

WAIT IN THE WINGS   *See* Wing (n).

WALK LIKE A DUCK   *See* Duck Walk; Waddle like a Duck.

WALK ON EGGS   *to walk on eggs*. To be very careful what you say and do in order not to upset a delicate situation or offend a sensitive individual. DOC: 1591. Source: CHICKEN; WEASEL. Parents *walk on eggs* (i.e., "tread lightly") in order not to waken a sleeping infant. Weasels sneak into chicken coops at night, walking gingerly on the eggs to get to the birds themselves; they may also suck the eggs, in which case they may have to exit by walking on the empty eggshells. AID; ATWS; BDPF; CE; EWPO. *See also* Weasel out.

WALK THE DOG   *to walk the dog*. To perform the trick of letting a yo-yo spin at the end of the string and propel itself along the floor. Source: DOG. WNNCD: O.E. The spinning yo-yo resembles a dog being walked on a leash, pulling the human along behind. Walking the dogs was once a method of showing them—

and their owner—off. Now, it is a necessity for people who live in the city, where laws require all dogs to be on a leash when they are off their own property.

WALLOP *See* Gallop.

WALLOW IN SELF-PITY *to wallow in self-pity* (etc.). To devote yourself to, or delight in, feeling sorry for yourself (etc.). Source: HOG. Hogs make it a practice to roll around in the mud (a *hogwallow*), but the action is more for prevention than pleasure. Hogs have no sweat glands, and in order to protect their thick skin from the heat of the sun, esp. when there is no available shade, they must coat it with mud or dirt. Human *wallowing* serves more of a masochistic purpose than a therapeutic one. Humans punish themselves by *wallowing in self-pity*, ignorance, guilt, etc. IRCD. *See also* Sweat Hog; Sweat like a Pig.

WALRUS *a walrus.* A large marine mammal of the northern regions that is prized by native hunters for its long ivory tusks, its oil-yielding blubber, and its thick, tough hide. WNNCD: 1728. Source: WHALE; HORSE. The Anglo-Saxons were acquainted with the walrus, but they had no separate name for it. (They called it a *hwæl* "whale," and in M.E. it was called a *seahorse*.) The Norse word *hvalros* "whale-horse" was borrowed, by way of Dutch, almost a century later to fill the void. ATWS; EWPO; IRCD. *See also* Walrus Mustache.

WALRUS MUSTACHE *a walrus mustache.* A long, large, bushy mustache. IRCD: early-20th cent. Source: WALRUS. WNNCD: 1728. The walrus (or "whale-horse") is a large (up to 12 feet long and 2,600 pounds in weight) mammal of the northern regions that has stiff brown whiskers on its upper lip just above its foot-long tusks. The professional golfer Craig Stadler was nicknamed "The Walrus" by his colleagues in the 1980s because of his bushy mustache. ATWS; IRCD. *See also* Walrus.

WARD HEELER *a ward heeler.* A worker for the boss of a political ward. WNNCD: 1888. Source: DOG. On the command "Heel!" an obedient dog stations itself at the back or side of its trainer—i.e., at the trainer's heels. An obedient *ward heeler* follows his/her political boss around wherever he/she goes and does whatever he/she wants—like an obedient dog. SPD.

WAR HORSE *See* Old War Horse.

WARM THE COCKLES OF YOUR HEART *to warm the cockles of your heart.* For something to give you a feeling of immense satisfaction or pleasure. WNNCD: 1671. Source: COCKLE. WNNCD: 14th cent. The heart-shaped shell of the cockle (or scallop) gave its name to the ventricles (Lat. *cochlea*) of the heart, which has long been regarded as the seat of affection and pleasure. ATWS; BDPF; EWPO.

WASP   *a wasp.* A member of the American majority: White, Anglo-Saxon, and Protestant. (Also: *Wasp* and *WASP.*) WNNCD: 1960. Source: WASP. WNNCD: O.E. Parasitic wasps are some of the most numerous and abusive of insects. Besides their painful sting, they either lay their eggs in the larvae of other insects or provision their nests with paralyzed insects for their own larvae to feed on. (During WWII, American women who transported military aircraft were called WASPs, an acronym for Women's Auxiliary Service Pilots.) EWPO; IRCD; NDAS; SPD. *See also* Waspish.

WASPISH   *to be waspish.* To be rude, irritable, or insolent. WNNCD: 1566. Source: WASP. WNNCD: O.E. The wasp has one of the most painful stings of any insect, and, unlike the bee, can sting again and again, esp. when anyone disturbs its dirt, mud, or paper nest. The wasp also uses its stinger to paralyze other insects, or their larvae, so that it can drag them to its nest as food for its own larvae. ATWS; IRCD; SPD. *See also* Wasp.

WASP WAIST   *a wasp waist.* A very slender waist—either of a woman or her dress. WNNCD: 1870. Source: WASP. WNNCD: O.E. The waist of the wasp is extremely slender—merely a slim stalk connecting the thorax and the abdomen. No woman has a waist that small, but the use of corsets in the 19th cent. helped to achieve that effect. CE; DEI. *See also* Wasp-waisted.

WASP-WAISTED   *to be wasp-waisted.* For a woman—or her dress—to have a very slender waist. IRCD: 19th cent. Source: WASP. WNNCD: O.E. Unlike its cousin the bee, the wasp has an abdomen that is connected to its thorax by a (sometimes long) slender stalk. The corsetmakers of the late-19th cent. held this up as an ideal for all fashionable women. (It was never achieved.) *See also* Wasp Waist.

WATCHDOG   *a watchdog.* A person or group that monitors the practice of business or government and "blows the whistle" on them whenever they find crime, waste, or corruption. SPD: 1827. Source: DOG. WNNCD: O.E. The canine *watchdog* (WNNCD: 1610) is a guard dog or alarm dog for homes, farms, businesses, and industries. A *guard dog* is one that is physically capable of preventing intruders from entering the establishment; an *alarm dog* is one that is vocally capable of alerting the residents so that they can react themselves or call the police. The earliest human *watchdogs* were government committees that probed waste in the U.S. Treasury. A *watchdog organization* is one like that of consumer advocate Ralph Nader that investigates and exposes waste and corruption in government and industry. ATWS.

WATCHDOG ORGANIZATION   *See* Watchdog.

WATCH SOMEONE LIKE A HAWK   *to watch someone like a hawk.* To keep a sharp eye on someone you don't trust. Source: HAWK. WNNCD: O.E. The hawk is noted for its keen vision: it can see a mouse from a quarter of a mile away. It can also see small animals under the brush—and fish underwater. The hawk does not distrust its prey, but they are the objects of its remarkable eyesight. ATWS; CI. *See also* Eye like a Hawk; Hawk-eyed.

WATCH WITH AN EAGLE EYE   *See* Eagle Eye.

WATER FLEA   *a water flea.* A tiny, active crustacean. WNNCD: 1585. Source: FLEA. WNNCD: O.E. This metaphor is based on the size of the crustacean (as tiny as a flea—approx. 1 mm. in length) and its activity (as good a leaper and jumper as the flea). The flea, of course, is an insect, not a shellfish. *See also* Ukulele.

WATER WINGS   *See* Wing (n).

WAVE A RED FLAG IN FRONT OF A BULL   *to wave a red flag in front of a ball.* To ask for trouble. Source: BULL. WNNCD: O.E. The matador is asking for trouble when he/she waves a red cape in front of the bull; but trouble—i.e., for the bull to charge—is what makes a bullfight, and the cape could just as well be yellow, because bulls are color-blind. Humans use insinuations to provoke other humans into anger or action. EWPO; LCRH. *See also* Red Flag to a Bull; See Red.

WEAK AS A KITTEN   *to be as weak as a kitten.* To be feeble, exhausted, or sick. Source: CAT. A newborn kitten is blind and helpless, and even a week-old kitten is wobbly and fragile. People who feel *as weak as a kitten* are usu. exhausted from too much work or exercise or are recovering from a dangerously high fever. AID; ATWS; CI; DEI. *See also* Sick as a Cat.

WEAR THE HORNS   *See* Make Horns.

WEASEL (1)   *a weasel.* (You little weasel!) A sneaky, untrustworthy person. SHM: 1920s. Source: WEASEL. WNNCD: O.E. The weasel is a small, long-bodied carnivore that sneaks into henhouses at night, kills as many chickens as it can, sucks the eggs, and sneaks back out with *egg on its face* (q.v.). The human *weasel* can also be an informer, or squealer. ATWS. *See also* Walk on Eggs; Weasel (2); Weasel out.

WEASEL (2)   *a weasel.* A small, light-tracked vehicle that can negotiate just about any kind of terrain: snow, sand, mud, water. Source: WEASEL. WNNCD: O.E. The weasel is a small, light, short-legged animal that is famous for its ability to *weasel out of* (q.v.)—or into—just about any kind of chicken coop. It is so light that it can even *walk on eggs* (q.v.). *See also* Weasel (1); Egg on Your Face.

WEASEL OUT   *to weasel out of something.* To back out of a commitment or obligation for reasons that are less than honorable. LTA: 1925. Source: WEASEL. WNNCD: O.E. The human *weasels out* of a sticky situation by making up lame excuses, although the recipient may be well aware of their inadequacy. The weasel sneaks into chicken coops at night, has its fill of chickens and eggs, then sneaks out with *egg on its face* (q.v.). ATWS; IRCD; SHM. *See also* Walk on Eggs.

WEASEL WORDS   Words that inadvertently cancel each other out or deliberately evade or mislead. (Usu. associated with politics.) WNNCD: 1900. Source: WEASEL. WNNCD: O.E. Weasels are noted for their ability to get themselves out of tight spots, such as locked henhouses. Politicians can avoid commitment to one or another side of an issue by employing words with the same effect. ATWS; BDPF; DEI; DOC; EWPO; HTB; IRCD; LCRH; LTA; SHM; WNWD.

WEATHERCOCK   *a weathercock.* A fickle person; a changeable thing. Source: COCK. WNNCD: O.E. Literally, a weathercock is a weather vane in the shape of a rooster (WNNCD: 14th cent.). It is designed to point into the wind and change directions as the wind does. Figuratively, a *weathercock* is a person who lacks direction and blows with the wind—or a fashion or style that changes frequently and unpredictably. ATWS; DEI; MDWPO; WNWD.

WEB OF DECEIT   *a web of deceit.* An intricate form of deception: a snare. Source: SPIDER (?). The spider spins an intricate web to ensnare passing insects, which see the spider, in the center of the web, as an easy catch. They are *caught in the web* before they can reach their goal. Intricate forms of extortion are designed for the same purpose. The question about the source is due to the fact that *web* derives from the fabric on a loom (O.E. *web*), not from the spider's *cobweb* (meaning "spider's web"). IRCD. *See also* Said the Spider to the Fly.

WELL-GROOMED   *See* Groom.

WELL-HEELED   *to be well-heeled.* To be well-off; to be well-to-do. WNNCD: 1897. Source: COCK. A well-heeled fighting cock is one that is equipped with a sharp metal spur (or "spar") on the back of each lower leg. The cockfight is no contest if the opponent lacks such spurs or has dull ones. The connection with money came when the cockfighting term was first applied to the carrying of a handgun in the back pocket—and then to the carrying of a wallet in that same pocket instead. AID; ATWS; DEI; EWPO; HTB; LCRH; ST. *See also* Spar; Stand the Gaff.

WELSH RABBIT   Melted cheese on toast. WNNCD: 1725. Source: RABBIT. WNNCD: 14th cent. *Welsh rabbit* contains no rabbit. The term was an invention of the English to ridicule the meager fare of the poor people of Wales. However, when the name was changed again, to *Welsh rarebit* (WNNCD: ca. 1785), melted cheese on toast came to be regarded as a delicacy, as it is today. BDPF; DEOD; EWPO; IRCD; LCRH. *Compare* Cape Cod Turkey; City Chicken; Mock Turtle Soup; Texas Turkey.

WEREWOLF   *a werewolf.* A person (esp. a "man": O.E. *wer*) who can transform himself—or be transformed—wholly or partially into a wolf. WNNCD: O.E. Source: WOLF. WNNCD: O.E. Modern *werewolves* grow long hair on their body, fangs on their teeth, and claws on their hands, but they walk upright; ancient *werewolves* simply became four-legged wolves. Both ancient and modern *werewolves* are impervious to knives or bullets, and both have a taste for human flesh. (A *werewolf* is also known as a *wolfman*.) BDPF; MDWPO. *Compare* Wolf Boy.

WET BEHIND THE EARS   *See* Still Wet behind the Ears.

WHALE (n)   *a whale of a time; a whale of a job; a whale of a difference.* A great time; a great job; a big difference. IRCD: ca. 1890. Source: WHALE. WNNCD: O.E. The *whale* is a symbol of great size. It is the largest animal that ever lived: almost 200 tons in weight, almost 100 feet in length—bigger than the dinosaurs. It is "the greatest." ATWS; BDPF; CE; CI; DEI. *See also* Whale (v) (1); Whale (v) (2).

WHALE (v) (1)   *to whale the daylights out of someone.* To punish someone physically; to defeat someone soundly. Source: WHALE. WNNCD: O.E. The metaphor probably derives from the old-fashioned thrashing of a naughty child or miscreant adult with a *whalebone whip* (ca. 1790). *Whalebone* is itself a metaphor: it comes from the upper jaw of certain whales, but it is keratin (the material of horns and fingernails), not bone. AID; ATWS. *Compare* Whale (v) (2).

WHALE (v) (2)   *to whale (away) with someone.* To hit tennis balls back and forth with an opponent as hard as you can, esp. from the baseline, either in practice or competition. Source: WHALE (?). WNNCD: O.E. Whale (v) (2) probably derives from Whale (v) (1), although it lacks the sense of physical punishment. *See also* Whale (v) (1).

WHALE AWAY   *See* Whale (v) (2).

WHALEBACK   *a whaleback.* A loaded iron ore barge or freighter on the Great Lakes. WNNCD: 1886. Source: WHALE. WNNCD: O.E. There are no whales in the Great Lakes, but the seamen who worked there saw a resemblance between the long convex load of iron ore on a barge or boat and the back of a mammoth whale. (The boats were over 400 feet long!) *See also* Whale (n).

WHALEBONE   *See* Whale (v) (1).

WHALE SHARK   *a whale shark.* The largest *fish* in the oceans (the Atlantic and Pacific), measuring up to 60 feet long. Source: WHALE. WNNCD: O.E. The whale is the largest *animal* in the oceans (or anywhere else, for that matter—past or present), measuring up to 98 feet long (the blue whale). Its name has become synonymous with enormous size. *See also* Whale (n).

WHALING   *a whaling.* A severe beating. Source: WHALE. WNNCD: O.E. *Whaling* is an old-fashioned term now, but it was quite familiar to people (and horses) in the late-19th cent. It referred to a severe beating with a *whalebone* whip of the type still used by riders to whip their horses on to greater speed. (Spurs once served the same purpose.) EWPO. *See also* Whale (v) (1).

WHAT HAS FOUR WHEELS AND FLIES   *See* Fly (n) (1).

WHAT'S EATING YOU   *See* Fret.

WHAT'S THE WORD, HUMMINGBIRD   *What's the word, hummingbird?* What's new, friend? Source: BIRD. This animal-based greeting is comparable to such partings as *After awhile, crocodile* and *See you later, alligator* (both of which *see*). All are based solely on rhyme: e.g., *word* and *bird*. The hummingbird metaphor probably developed about twenty years after the other two: ca. 1950.

WHAT TIME IS THE NEXT SWAN   *What time is the next swan?* When does the next bus/train/plane leave? EWPO: 19th cent. Source: SWAN. WNNCD: O.E. This question was an ad-lib by an anonymous tenor who sang the part of Lohengrin in a performance of Wagner's opera by the same name in the second half of the 19th cent. His ride, in a boat pulled by a swan, inadvertently left without him: hence the quip. BDPF.

WHEELHORSE   *a wheelhorse.* One who bears the brunt of the hard work; one who is a dependable and effective worker (esp. for a political party). SPD: 1848. Source: HORSE. WNNCD: O.E. Before the advent of automotive vehicles, a wheelhorse was the horse, in a team of horses, closest to the wheels of a carriage, wagon, or piece of farm equipment (WNNCD: 1708). The assumption was that the wheelhorse, because of its proximity to the vehicle, had to do more work than the other horses in the team, although that is questionable, at least when the team was moving steadily forward; when the team was backing up, or trying to prevent the vehicle from sliding down a hill, however, the wheelhorse was definitely the one most likely to get its tail singed by the front wheels. A political *wheelhorse* is a worker for a political party who is steady and dependable. BDPF. *Compare* Workhorse.

WHEN PIGS FLY   Never. Source: PIG. WNNCD: 13th cent. If someone makes an unreasonable demand of you, you might say, "When pigs fly!", meaning that you will never do it, because pigs can't fly. The expression—and its variant: *when pigs have wings*—is based on a line from the poem "The Walrus and the Carpenter," from *Through the Looking Glass* (1871), the sequel to Lewis Carroll's *Alice's Adventures in Wonderland* (1865): "The time has come, the Walrus said,/ To talk of many things:/ Of shoes and ships and sealing wax/ Of cabbages and kings/ And why the sea is boiling hot/ And *whether pigs have wings!*" (italics added). BDPF; ID.

WHEN PIGS HAVE WINGS   *See* When Pigs Fly.

WHEN THE CAT'S AWAY, THE MICE WILL PLAY   When the boss is absent, the employees will do as they please. IRCD: ca. 1600. Source: CAT; MOUSE. WNNCD: O.E. In the 17th cent. cats were more valued as mousers than as pets. Their job was to patrol the house, barns, stables, and granaries looking for and killing destructive mice (and rats). When the cats were raiding another building, the mice were free to eat all the grain and gather all the nesting materials they wanted. Children are like mice in this regard: when their parents (the "cats") are gone, they feel no pressure to behave. AID; ATWS; BDPF; CI; ID; ST.

WHEN THE EAGLE FLIES   On payday. Source: EAGLE. WNNCD: 13th cent. This expression, attributed to Black slang, is thought to allude to the payment of workers in ten-dollar gold coins, nicknamed "eagles," in the late 1800s. However, many pieces of American currency, both coins and bills, have borne the image of the *spread eagle* (q.v.) on the reverse side. NDAS. *See also* Eagle Flies on Friday.

WHICH CAME FIRST, THE CHICKEN OR THE EGG   *Which came first, the chicken or the egg?* An unanswerable question: a conundrum. Source: CHICKEN. WNNCD: O.E. The fact that *chicken* appears before *egg* in the question suggests that that is the proper order: the chicken came first, then produced the egg. But the chicken must have developed from an egg, so the egg must have come first. The thing about a cycle is there *is* no clear starting point. CI; DEI.

WHICH WAY THE CAT WILL JUMP   *to guess—or see—which way the cat will jump.* To hazard a guess about something totally unpredictable; to delay making a decision until further events have transpired. Source: CAT. WNNCD: O.E. Cats are very predictable animals: they hunt at pretty much the same time and place every day; they bring their kill back to the house to show it off; they keep regular hours; and they always use the litter box while in the house—and even teach their kittens how to use it. Just about the only thing that is unpredictable about a cat is which way it will jump when the wash water is thrown on it—or, if the cat is stalking the canary, when it will finally pounce. ATWS.

WHIPPED   *See* Work Yourself into a Lather.

WHIP YOUR WEIGHT IN WILDCATS   *to be able to whip your weight in wild-cats.* To be able to beat up on any man in the saloon. Source: WILDCAT. WNNCD: 14th cent. The *wildcat* (q.v.), a medium-size "cat" such as the bobcat or ocelot, weighs approx. 35 pounds; so a two-hundred pound mountain man should be able to defeat approx. six wildcats in a fight, provided that he takes them on one at a time. If he took all of them on at once, the wildcats would win. WNWD.

WHIRLYBIRD   *a whirlybird.* A helicopter. WNNCD: 1951. Source: BIRD. WNNCD: O.E. Airplanes are sometimes called *birds,* but a helicopter is a different breed of bird: its lift is created not by fixed wings but by rotating blades. When the blades rotate at a very high speed they create a powerful downdraft and make a deafening whirling sound. The "copter" was nicknamed *whirlybird* during the Korean War, but that was changed to *chopper* during the War in Vietnam. *Helicopter* (WNNCD: 1887) is itself a metaphor, consisting of *helikos* "spiral" + *pteron* "wing." IRCD; MDWPO.

WHISTLING GIRLS AND CROWING HENS   *Whistling girls and crowing hens/ Always come to some bad ends.* Girls who act like boys are asking for trouble. Source: HEN. WNNCD: O.E. In the barnyard, the roosters do the crowing, while the hens do the egg laying and chick raising. Their roles are clear. Animal behavior is being held up, in this Victorian jingle, as a model for girls: "Don't act like boys!" MDWPO. *See also* Tomboy.

WHITE BUCKS   White suede shoes. IRCD: 1940s. Source: DEER. *White bucks* were popular in the decades of the 1940s and 1950s. They were not manufactured from the skin of albino male deer but from the bleached or dyed skins of normally colored deer (i.e., *buckskins* [q.v.]) or cattle. The leather was either split or given a napped or suede-like surface. The singer Pat Boone was famous for his *white bucks.* (Elvis's were blue.)

WHITE ELEPHANT   *a white elephant.* Something that is too valuable to throw away but too expensive to keep. MDWPO: 1850s. Source: ELEPHANT. WNNCD: 14th cent. The Asian or small-eared elephant of South and Southeast Asia is sometimes venerated in its albino form. The story goes that whenever an ancient King of Siam (now Thailand) became dissatisfied with one of his courtiers, he would present him with one of his sacred white elephants. The courtier would experience his punishment when the elephant, which could not be sold, would eat him out of house and home. A modern version of the story concerns P. T. Barnum, owner of the Greatest Show on Earth: when a competitor imported a real white elephant for his show, Barnum reportedly whitewashed a gray elephant, thereby leaving the competitor with a metaphorical *white elephant* on his hands. ATWS; BDPF; CI; DEI; DOC; EWPO; HOI; IRCD; LCRH; SHM; ST. *Compare* Pink Elephants.

WHITE TIE AND TAILS   *a white-tie and tails affair*. An affair requiring men to wear formal evening dress, including a white tie and a tailcoat. (A "black-tie" affair is semiformal.) Source: SWALLOW. *Tails* is a shortening of *tailcoat*, which in turn is a shortening of *swallow-tail coat* (q.v.). All of the terms are based on the long, inverted V-shaped tail of the barn swallow. *Compare* Soup and Fish.

WHOA, NELLIE   *Whoa, Nellie!* Slow down! Stop! Source: HORSE. When horses replaced oxen as the draft animals of choice in America, some of the old commands were retained for the newcomers: *Whoa* "stop" (WNNCD: 15th cent.); *Gee* "turn right" (1628); and *Haw* "turn left" (1777). (*Giddyup*—earlier *giddayap* or *giddap*—is a late-19th cent. term.) On the farm, there were occasions when a team of horses pulling a wagon in a field had to be controlled by voice rather than by rein, because all of the hands were busy pitching hay or straw or tossing bundles of corn or grain. *Nellie* was probably the name of the "old gray mare" that was pulling the wagon at the time this term was invented. *Compare* Home, James.

WHO KILLED COCK ROBIN   *Who killed cock robin?* Who is responsible for the death of this public figure? Source: ROBIN. WNNCD: 1549. *Cock Robin* was the unfortunate victim of murder in the 19th cent. nursery rhyme "Who Killed Cock Robin?" The murderer was the sparrow, who admitted, in the first verse of the poem, that he did it with his bow and arrow. In each of the thirteen verses that followed, a different animal volunteered to assist at the funeral. *Robin* is short for *robin red-breast* (WNNCD: 15th cent.), and a *cock robin* is an adult male robin. Robins are colorful, melodious, and numerous; so why would anyone want to kill them? That is, who would want to murder such a solid citizen?

WHOSE BULL IS BEING GORED   *See* Whose Ox Is Being Gored.

WHOSE OX IS BEING GORED   *That depends on whose ox is being gored.* That depends on who is suffering the damage. DOC: 1802. Source: OX. WNNCD: O.E. If *my* ox is goring *your* ox with its horns, that's one thing; but if *your* ox is goring *my* ox, that's an entirely different matter. An ox is a large adult steer that is used as a draft animal. It may or may not have horns. *See also* Bugle; Greenhorn.

WIGGLE OFF THE HOOK   *See* Off the Hook.

WILD AND WOOLY   *to be wild and wooly.* For a tale or an experience to be scary or harrowing. DOC: 1891. Source: SHEEP. In the American West of the 19th cent., the sheepskin coat, with the fleece intact, was a popular sight. It was worn—with the fleece either inside or outside—by homesteaders, cowboys, hunters, trappers, and mountain men and was associated, in literature, with the danger and adventure of the Wild West. ATWS; EWPO.

WILDCAT (n)   *a wildcat.* A person (esp. a female) with a fierce, savage, and uncontrollable temper. Source: WILDCAT. WNNCD: 14th cent. In Europe, a *wildcat* is a wild, thick-coated, gray cat of medium size (up to 30 pounds) that is the probable ancestor of all domestic cats. In America, *wildcat* can refer to the bobcat (which most closely resembles the European wildcat except for its bobbed tail), the ocelot, the lynx, and even the mountain lion—all of which are fierce predators. ATWS; BDPF.

WILDCAT (v)   *to wildcat.* To prospect for oil or natural gas on the basis of a hunch rather than scientific information. WNNCD: ca. 1903. Source: WILDCAT. WNNCD: 14th cent. The verb *wildcat* is a back-formation from the noun *wildcatter* (WNNCD: 1883), "an independent prospector who drills for oil or gas where nobody else wants to." To *wildcat* is, lit., to "hunt in the dark," the way the nocturnal *wildcat* (q.v.) does. It never knows if it will get lucky and make a killing on any particular night. A human participant in a *wildcat strike* (q.v.) is also known as a *wildcatter.* IRCD.

WILDCAT BANK   *a wildcat bank.* A financially unsound and irresponsible banking establishment. WNNCD: 1838. (An Americanism.) Source: WILDCAT. WNNCD: 14th cent. The first establishment to receive the label was a bank in Michigan that went bankrupt because it issued more bank notes, or *wildcat currency,* than it had assets to cover. On the notes was a picture of a wildcat. BDPF; EWPO; IRCD. *See also* Wildcat (n); Wildcat Strike; Wildcat Venture; Wildcat Well.

WILDCAT CURRENCY   *See* Wildcat Bank.

WILDCAT STRIKE   *a wildcat strike.* A localized work stoppage that is not authorized by the union and is perhaps in violation of the contract with the company. Source: WILDCAT. WNNCD: 14th cent. The maverick behavior of a group of striking workers is compared to the undomesticated nature of the wildcat, which is a solitary hunter. DEI; IRCD. *See also* Wildcat (n); Wildcat (v); Wildcat Bank; Wildcat Venture; Wildcat Well.

WILDCATTER   *See* Wildcat (v); Wildcat Well.

WILDCAT VENTURE   *a wildcat venture.* A business undertaking that is speculative, risky, reckless, precarious, unsound, uncontrolled, financially irresponsible, or illegitimate. Source: WILDCAT. WNNCD: 14th cent. *Wildcat* was first applied to an unsound banking venture in Michigan in 1838, probably because there was a picture of a wildcat on the unredeemable bank notes. ATWS; BDPF; EWPO; IRCD. *See also* Wildcat (n); Wildcat Bank; Wildcat Strike; Wildcat Well.

WILDCAT WELL *a wildcat well.* A speculative oil or natural gas well that is drilled in untested territory or at a greater depth in a depleted area. IRCD: ca. 1910. Source: WILDCAT. WNNCD: 14th cent. The driller of a *wildcat well,* a *wildcatter,* is an independent operator who relies on "hunch" rather than research. The American wildcat is also a solitary hunter. ATWS; EWPO. *See also* Wildcat (n); Wildcat Bank; Wildcat Strike; Wildcat Venture.

WILDERNESS *a wilderness.* A wasteland. WNNCD: 13th cent. Source: ANIMAL. *Wilderness* derives fr. O.E. *wildēoren* "of wild animals" (fr. *wilde* "wild" + *dēor* "animal"). Literally, a wilderness is a place that is inhabited by wild animals but has never been inhabited, or disturbed, by humans. Figuratively, a *wilderness* is a human creation that is a *bewildering* and frightening tangle of complexity and confusion: e.g., a code of laws; a government budget; a tax guide; a college catalogue. Dangers lurk everywhere. *See also* It's a Jungle out there.

WILD-GOOSE CHASE *a wild-goose chase.* A futile pursuit; a hopeless quest. WNNCD: 1592. Source: GOOSE. WNNCD: O.E. Trying to catch a barnyard goose is hard enough, but catching a wild goose with your bare hands is practically impossible. The difficulty of this pursuit was reflected in the 16th cent. game of "follow the leader," called a *wild-goose chase,* as described in Act II, Scene 4 of Shakespeare's *Romeo and Juliet* (1595). It was a kind of crosscountry horseback race in which the riders had to go wherever the lead rider went and do exactly what he did—like a flock of geese. Nowadays, a *wild-goose chase* is an impossible dream, like the one pursued by Don Quixote. AID; ATWS; BDPF; CI; DEI; DOC; EWPO; HOI; ID; IRCD; LTA; ST. *Compare* Like Catching a Greased Pig.

WILD HORSES *Wild horses couldn't drag it out of me (or drag me there).* Nothing could persuade me to reveal my secret or attend that event. Source: HORSE. WNNCD: O.E. Wild horses still roam the West, where they are much admired for their free spirit and ability to evade capture. Once broken, however, they become as obedient and workable as any domesticated horse. The allusion may be to a team of partially broken horses that don't respond well to commands and tend to get out of control. Nothing is quite as frightening as being on a hay wagon behind a team of runaway horses—unless it is being forced to attend a party, reunion, or wedding that you wouldn't be caught dead at, or being tricked into giving away a secret that you have promised to keep. AID; CI; DEI.

WIN BY A NOSE *to win by a nose (or a whisker).* To win by the slightest margin. Source: HORSE. The nose of a horse is the most forward part of its body when it is standing still, although a front foot could conceivably extend beyond the nose when running. In a horse race, the winner is the horse that gets its nose across the finish line first, regardless of where the feet are. The leading horse in a close race is said to *lead by a nose,* and the winning horse in a close finish is said to *nose the others out.* A bet placed *on the nose* is one that gambles that that horse will win. All of these horse racing expressions can be applied metaphorically to candidates in any sort of contest, and *on the nose* can be applied more generally to any figure or statement that is exactly right. AID; ATWS; CI; ST.

WIN BY A WHISKER   *See* Win by a Nose.

WING (n)   *a wing.* An extension to either side of a center. Source: BIRD. The wings of a bird come in pairs, and so do most metaphorical wings. The arms of a human are sometimes called *wings,* and a *broken wing* is a broken arm. The *wingspan* of a boxer is the distance from the tips of the fingers of one hand to the tips of the fingers of the other hand when they are outstretched to either side. *Water wings* (WNNCD: ca. 1908) are flotation devices for novice swimmers that are worn under the arms. The wings of a *wingback chair* (WNNCD: 1904) are the forward projections of the sides near the top of the high back, and a *wingback* (WNNCD: 1938) in American football is a player who lines up outside one of the tight ends. The *wings* of a stage are the left or right portions that are out of sight of the audience, and someone who is *waiting in the wings* is ready to perform when needed. The *wings* of a legislative body are the seats to the left or right side of the center aisle that are occupied by *right-wing* conservatives (WNNCD: 1905) and *left-wing* liberals (WNNCD: 1919). The *wings* of a building are the extensions to the right or left, or both, of the main edifice: e.g., the *east wing,* the *west wing.* Finally, of course, there are the *wings* of an airplane, which are the closest things to the wings of a bird: when they both take off, they *take wing.* ATWS; BDPF.

WING (v)   *to wing someone; to wing it.* To shoot someone in the arm; to improvise (DOC: 1920). Source: BIRD. The surest way to shoot a bird in flight is to hit it on the wing or shoulder. Shooting a human in the *wing* (q.v.), or arm, does not bring them down to earth, but it does disable them, especially if the arm is holding a gun. To *wing it* is to *fly blind:* to make it up as you go along. Pilots do this when they "fly by the seat of their pants"—i.e., without a map or flight plan. Actors in the theater *wing it* when they forget their lines and have to be prompted from the *wings,* or when something unforeseen occurs on the stage. ATWS; ST.

WINGBACK   *See* Wing (n).

WINGBACK CHAIR   *See* Wing (n).

WIN GOING AWAY   *See* Off and Running.

WINGSPAN   *See* Wing (n).

WING TIPS   Men's oxford shoes with a serrated leather overpiece that curves from the tip of the toe along each side. WNNCD: ca. 1908. Source: BIRD. The serrated leather piece resembles the wings of a bird. (Hermes, or Mercury, wore his on the back of each sandal.) Spelled solid, *wingtips* are the tips of the wings of an airplane. ATWS.

WINGTIPS *See* Wing Tips.

WISE AS AN OWL *to be as wise as an owl.* To be as smart as Athena, the Greek goddess of wisdom. Source: OWL. WNNCD: O.E. Athena's mascot was the owl, which backed her on Greek coins. The owl's supposed wisdom may have been due to its solemn stare and unusual tameness (for a bird of prey), which suggests superior knowledge and power. However, in Asia Minor the owl was, and still is, a symbol of evil and death. AID; ATWS; DEI. *See also* Wise Old Owl.

WISE OLD OWL *a wise old owl.* A person who is thought to be wise because he/she listens and watches attentively but says very little. Source: OWL. WNNCD: O.E. The owl was a symbol of wisdom in ancient Greece, associated with the Goddess Athena. That may have been because the owl has a humanlike face (flat, with large eyes and "ears") and a solemn stare; and it spend its days sitting motionless on a perch, seldom uttering a sound. *See also* Wise as an Owl.

WISHBONE *a wishbone.* An offensive alignment in American football. LTA: 1960s. Source: CHICKEN; TURKEY. Literally, a wishbone is the forked breastbone of a fowl that is prepared for holiday dinner. When the wishbone has been allowed to dry, two people each grasp a prong and pull upward until the bone breaks. The person who is left holding the longer piece is supposed to be granted the wish that he/she made before the exercise. The metaphorical *wishbone* is a formation in which the halfbacks are placed farther back from the line than the fullback, who is located directly behind the quarterback, giving the appearance of a breastbone as seen from above. The alignment was invented by Darrel Royal of the University of Texas. HF.

WISH I COULD BE A LITTLE MOUSE *I wish I could be a little mouse.* I wish I could hear what's going on behind those closed doors (without being noticed). Source: MOUSE. WNNCD: O.E. The little mouse, although seldom seen or heard, is privy to all our conversations. If it had the intelligence and linguistic ability of a human, oh what stories the mouse could tell! *Also:* "I wish I could be a *fly on the wall*" (q.v.). CI.

WITHDRAW INTO YOUR SHELL *to withdraw into your shell.* To become defensive, uncompromising, uncommunicative, or unsocial. Source: TORTOISE; TURTLE. Most *tortoises*, or "land turtles," and some *turtles*, or "aquatic turtles," are able to draw their head, legs, and tail inside their shell when threatened. (Sea turtles cannot, nor can snapping turtles.) When they withdraw into their shell this way they are almost totally impregnable. ATWS; BDPF. *See also* Crawl into Your Shell. *Compare* Come out of Your Shell.

WOLF (n)   *a wolf.* A man who makes sexual advances to women. IHAT: 1940s. Source: WOLF. WNNCD: O.E. The animal called the *wolf* has a ravenous appetite for the meat of other animals. The human *wolf* has a ravenous appetite for members of the opposite sex. In the 1940s, the human *wolf* was regarded as pretty much of a joke. More recently, he is taken more seriously as a potential sexual abuser. *Canis lupus* comes off better in a comparison. ATWS; HOI; IRCD. *See also* Wolf Call; Wolf Whistle.

WOLF (v)   *to wolf down your food.* To devour your food quickly and greedily, with a minimum of chewing, as if there were no tomorrow. WNNCD: 1862. Source: WOLF. WNNCD: O.E. Wolves are carnivores, and when they have pursued, surrounded, and killed a wild (or domestic) animal, they devour it ravenously, probably because they could be scared off by a larger carnivore, such as a mountain lion, at any time. ATWS; DEI; IRCD. *See also* Wolf (n).

WOLF BAIT   A sexually attractive female. IHAT: 1940s. Source: WOLF. WNNCD: O.E. A pretty young woman was called *wolf bait* during WWII because she attracted the *wolf calls* (q.v.) and *wolf whistles* (q.v.) of male *wolves* (q.v.). The term was complimentary in those days, but nowadays it implies that the bait is deliberately leading the wolves on. *Compare* San Quentin Quail.

WOLF BOY   *a wolf boy.* A feral child believed to have been raised in the wilderness with—and possibly by—animals. Source: WOLF. WNNCD: O.E. The most famous *wolf boy* was Romulus, son of Mars, who killed his twin brother Remus and founded Rome. (They were suckled by a wolf.) A more recent example was Victor (*L'enfant Sauvage*; *The Wild Boy of Aveyron*), who was discovered at the age of twelve, in the late-18th cent., in a forest near Paris, living like a wild animal. He may have lived *among* wolves, but he was not raised *by* them.

WOLF CALL   *a wolf call.* A howling sound made by a man to a passing woman whom he regards as sexually attractive. Source: WOLF. WNNCD: O.E. Wolves, which are *canids* (like the coyote, fox, and dog), howl at the moon for no apparent reason except to let other wolves know that they exist. Human *wolves* (q.v.) used to howl—or *hoot* (q.v.)—at attractive females to express their admiration, but the action is now regarded as sexual abuse. ATWS; IRCD; WNWD. *See also* Wolf Whistle.

WOLFFISH   *a wolffish.* An eellike Atlantic blenny with a large head, large jaws, and long, sharp teeth. WNNCD: 1569. Source: WOLF. WNNCD: O.E. Fish must have been the last animals to be named, because so many of them are named after birds, reptiles, and mammals. The *wolffish* probably got its name because of its fierce appearance and its ferocious behavior: it will attack just about anything, including humans. It is regarded as one of the most dangerous species of fish. ATWS.

WOLF IN SHEEP'S CLOTHING   *a wolf in sheep's clothing.* A person who pretends to be good but is really evil: a "smiling villain." (Matthew 7:15, "Beware of false prophets, which come to you in sheep's clothing, but inwardly they are ravening wolves.") Source: WOLF. WNNCD: O.E. There is also an Aesop fable about a wolf who wrapped himself in a sheepskin, stole into a sheepfold, and devoured all of the lambs. Modern rustlers have succeeded in stealing sheep from a flock by using the same disguise. Moral: Don't trust anyone. AID; ATWS; CI; DEI; DOC; EWPO; HOI; IRCD.

WOLFMAN   *See* Werewolf.

WOLF PACK   *a wolf pack.* A squadron of submarines or fighter planes in pursuit of their natural prey. WNNCD: 1942. Source: WOLF. WNNCD: O.E. The natural prey of a pack of wolves is an herbivorous animal of just about any size, wild or domestic. The pack pursues the animal until it tires, then surrounds it until it falls. Now the wolves, which are carnivorous, can devour it at their leisure. The term *wolf pack* was applied to German submarines that made coordinated attacks on Allied vessels in WWII, and it was also applied to a group of enemy planes in the same war. BDPF; IRCD. *See also* Pack of Wolves; Leader of the Pack.

WOLFSBANE   A yellow-flowered poisonous herb of the buttercup family, approx. equivalent to *monkshood* (also poisonous), which has a bluish flower. Source: WOLF (?). WNNCD: O.E. It is uncertain why *wolf* (apparently possessive) appears in the name of this plant. The reason may be that it was the killer (or *bane*) of the wolves that came in contact with it; or perhaps its poison (also *bane*) was being compared with the danger, to people, of the dreaded wolf. Both are the *bane* (or death) of an existence. LCRH.

WOLF WHISTLE   *a wolf whistle.* A two-part whistle, consisting of a high note followed by the same high note sliding to a low note, that is uttered by a male to a sexually attractive female. WNNCD: 1946. Source: WOLF. WNNCD: O.E. Wolves don't whistle (they howl), but *human* wolves do. Often it is an expression of admiration toward a female family member who is wearing a new dress or has a new hairdo, but sometimes it is directed at a stranger, from a safe distance, who cannot identify the whistler and file charges. ATWS; DEI; IHAT; IRCD; WNWD. *See also* Wolf Call.

WOODEN HORSE   *See* Trojan Horse.

WOOD PUSSY   *a wood pussy.* A skunk. WNNCD: ca. 1899. Source: CAT. A skunk does not live in the woods but in a burrow in the ground, and it is not a member of the cat family but a relative of the weasel. However, to a child a skunk probably looks like a pretty striped cat that is completely harmless. English has come up with many other nicknames for dangerous animals, such as *bee-wolf* for "bear" and *whale-horse* for "walrus." EWPO.

WOOF   *See* Bark like a Dog.

WOOLGATHERING   Daydreaming. WNNCD: 1553. Source: SHEEP. Sheep are the source of wool that catches on bushes and fences and was once collected by women and children. The job was so monotonous and unchallenging—moving aimlessly from bush to bush, sometimes finding wool and sometimes not—that the name of the activity came to be associated with mind-wandering or idle daydreaming, in which the gatherers probably participated. ATWS; CI; DEI; EWPO; HOI; ID; LCRH. *See also* Count Sheep.

WORK AS A TEAM   *See* Team.

WORK FOR CHICKEN FEED   *See* Chicken Feed.

WORK FOR PEANUTS   *to work for peanuts*. To have a job that pays practically nothing. Source: ELEPHANT; MONKEY. In the zoo, both the elephant and the monkey work for peanuts that are thrown to them by the spectators: the former picking them up with its nimble trunk and swallowing them whole, and the latter picking them up with its nimble fingers, shelling them, and popping them in its mouth. The organ grinder's monkey works for coins, but those go to the grinder, who then feeds the monkey peanuts for its labors. Peanut growers, such as former President Jimmy Carter, lit. *work for peanuts*. AID; DEI; SPD.

WORKHORSE   *a workhorse*. A person who works longer and harder than anyone else on a team; a machine that is more useful or durable than any other in an industry. Source: HORSE. WNNCD: O.E. Literally, a workhorse is a draft horse, i.e., one that is used for drawing heavy loads rather than for racing, riding, or pulling a buggy (WNNCD: 1543). Figuratively, a *workhorse* is either (1) someone on whom a team relies for the long, hard, dirty jobs, or (2) a vehicle that has proved to be the most dependable for long, hard, dirty hauls. (In WWII, that was the 2.5 ton truck.) Someone who *works like a horse* (IRCD: 16th cent.) works longer and harder than anyone should be expected to. AID; ATWS; DEI; EWPO. *Compare* Wheelhorse.

WORK LIKE A BEAVER   *to work like a beaver*. To work fast, hard, and long. DOC: 1775. Source: BEAVER. WNNCD: O.E. The beaver is renowned for its industriousness: cutting down large trees, floating them into the stream to form a pond, building an underwater lodge, etc.—all before winter comes. (So many trees; so little time!) ATWS; CI; DOC; HOI; IRCD. *See also* Busy as a Beaver; Eager Beaver. *Compare* Work like a Dog.

WORK LIKE A DOG *to work like a dog.* To work extremely hard, for long hours, under the most difficult conditions. Source: DOG. WNNCD: O.E. Dogs that are kept as either pets or watchdogs have a pretty easy life, but "working dogs," such as herding dogs and hunting dogs, work harder than their owners do, at least during certain times of the year. The metaphor probably refers to these hardworking dogs, not to the house dogs or yard dogs. ID. *Compare* Work like a Beaver.

WORK LIKE A HORSE *See* Workhorse.

WORK YOURSELF INTO A LATHER *to work yourself into a lather.* To become agitated, angry, excited, flustered, overwrought, upset, or worried. EWPO: mid-19th cent. Source: HORSE. A horse gets *in a lather* (NDAS: 17th cent.) when it is worked too hard or run too hard and develops a white foam of perspiration along each piece of harness or saddle that it is carrying. When people begin to get angry, other people advise them, "Don't *work yourself into a lather,*" i.e., don't get *hot and bothered,* like a horse. A similar expression is "to be *whipped,*" i.e., to be worn out or exhausted, like a horse at the end of a hard race. AID; CI. *See also* Rode Hard and Put away Wet. *Compare* Foam at the Mouth.

WORK YOUR TAIL OFF *See* Tail (n).

WORLD IS YOUR OYSTER *The world is your oyster.* You're sitting on top of the world, and it's all there for your taking. BDPF: 1602 (Shakespeare's *The Merry Wives of Windsor,* Act II, Scene 2). Source: OYSTER. WNNCD: 14th cent. In *Merry Wives,* after Falstaff refuses to lend Pistol a penny, Pistol replies: "Why, then the world's mine oyster,/ Which I with sword will open." The implication is that if you have power (the sword), your wealth (the pearl in the oyster) is unlimited. ATWS; CI; DEI; DOC; EWPO.

WORM (1) *a worm.* Any small, soft-bodied, legless animal. Source: WORM. WNNCD: O.E. The animal that *worm* orig. referred to was an earthworm, i.e., an annelid worm with multiple rings around its body. However, the meaning of the word has been broadened to include most insect larvae (such as caterpillars, grubs, and maggots), certain burrowing lizards (known as *blindworms* and *slow worms*), and even some marine clams (called *shipworms*), none of which are "true" worms. *See also* Worm (2); Worm (3).

WORM (2) *You worm!* You lowlife! Source: WORM. WNNCD: O.E. The earthworm may not be the lowest form of life, but it is certainly one of the lowest to the ground—as low as a *serpent* (also known as a *wyrm* in O.E.). Worms are maligned because of their small size, slow movement, slimy appearance, and association with rotten food and rotting flesh. A human *worm* is a person of low moral character and despicable social behavior: a loathsome, contemptuous individual. ATWS; DEI. *See also* Varmint; Vermin; Worm (1); Worm (3). *Compare* Snake.

WORM (3)   *a worm*. A tapered metal screw; a nontapered metal screw whose threads mesh with the teeth of a *worm wheel* to form a *worm gear* (WNNCD: 1876). Source: SNAKE; WORM. WNNCD: O.E. The threads of a screw are analogous to the coils of a snake or the rings of an earthworm. (O.E. *wyrm*, the source of Mod. Eng. *worm*, meant both "worm" and "serpent," although there was also a separate word for "snake": *snaca*.) The snake's spiraling coils and the earthworm's rings are also the basis for the name of the condensing tube used in distilling: the *worm*. The term *worm* is also applied to the nontapered sheathed "screw" that is used to lift grain and water. *See also* Screw (n) (1); Worm (1); Worm (2).

WORM-BURNER   *a worm-burner*. A hard, low golf shot from the tee that sails only a few feet above the ground. (Also used in baseball and softball.) Source: WORM. WNNCD: O.E. The *worm-burner* travels so fast, and so close to the ground, that it could "burn" any worm that raised its "head" into the ball's path. This is one of the many colorful animal metaphors that relate to sports. *Compare* Dying Quail; Wounded Duck.

WORM-EATEN   *to be worm-eaten*. To be worn-out or antiquated. Source: WORM. WNNCD: O.E. Worm-eaten wood has actually been eaten by worms— or, more likely, by the larvae of certain beetles. Metaphorically, a *worm-eaten* piece of wooden furniture may look as if it has been eaten by worms but is simply old and decrepit. Even inorganic objects and abstract ideas can be *worm-eaten*. ATWS. *See also* Food for Worms. *Compare* Moth-eaten.

WORM'S-EYE VIEW   *a worm's-eye view*. A view from ground level or below. Source: WORM. WNNCD: O.E. The "true" worm, or annelid worm, such as an earthworm or night-crawler, spends its entire lifetime at ground level—either in a hole in the ground or, when the ground is wet (esp. at night), on top of it; but when it emerges from its hole it "sees" everything from ground level. DEI. *Compare* Bird's-eye View.

WORM SOMETHING OUT   *to worm something out of someone*. To extract information from someone who doesn't want to give it up and may not realize that he/she is doing so. IRCD: early-18th cent. Source: WORM. WNNCD: O.E. This metaphor is based on the use of a vermifuge, or dewormer, to "worm" animals or humans, usu. in the springtime (WNNCD: 1564). The dewormer is an indirect means of relieving the body of worms, just as *worming out* is an indirect means of relieving another person of a secret—through cunning and insidious questioning. AID; ATWS; BDPF; DEI. *See also* Worm Your Way.

WORM WILL TURN *Even a worm will turn.* Even a 97-pound weakling will fight back if you kick enough sand in his face. IRCD: ca. 1592 (Shakespeare's *Henry VI, Part III*, Act II, Scene 2). Source: SNAKE; WORM. WNNCD: O.E. In O.E., *wyrm* meant both "serpent" and "worm," and both senses are captured in this metaphor. The worm is pretty low in the animal hierarchy, yet even the lowly worm will turn on you if you step on it. Shakespeare wrote: "Who scapes the lurking serpent's mortal sting?/ Not he that sets his foot upon her back./ The smallest worm will turn, being trodden on,/ And doves will peck in safeguard of their brood." Also: *The worm turns.* ("The shoe is on the other foot.") ATWS; BDPF; CE; CI; DEI; DOC; ID.

WORMWOOD *See* Vermouth.

WORM YOUR WAY *to worm your way into or out of something.* To insinuate yourself into the good graces of someone; to wiggle out of a sticky problem or unwanted responsibility. Source: WORM. WNNCD: O.E. The worm eats its way into a perfectly good apple, causing its decay and unsuitability for eating. The process is slow and almost imperceptible—until you bite into the apple! When a robin plucks an earthworm from its hole in the ground, the worm tries to wiggle (or *wriggle*) out of the bird's beak and return to its hole. Human *worms* crawl into and wiggle out of social situations in much the same way. AID; BDPF; DEI. *See also* Worm Something Out.

WORSHIP THE GOLDEN CALF *to worship the golden calf.* To value money over all else. Source: CALF. WNNCD: O.E. The source of this metaphor is the golden calf constructed by Aaron and worshipped by the Isrealites while Moses was on Mount Sinai (Exodus 32:4). This account may also have been the inspiration for the expression, "The love of money is the root of all evil" (I Timothy 6:10). BDPF; DEI; EWPO; IRCD; WNWD. *Compare* Kill the Fatted Calf.

WORTH THE WHISTLE *to be worth the whistle.* To be worth the trouble. BDPF: 1606 (Shakespeare's *King Lear*, Act IV, Scene 2). Source: DOG. In *Lear*, Goneril, one of Lear's daughters, says to the Duke of Albany, "I have been worth the whistle," but Albany disagrees. The reference is to the calling of a dog by whistling.

WOULDN'T HURT A FLEA *X wouldn't hurt a flea.* X is a kind and gentle person, not capable of even the smallest degree of violence. Source: FLEA. WNNCD: O.E. The flea, a bloodsucking insect, is one of the smallest animals (only 1 mm in length), yet it is also one of the deadliest, transmitting diseases such as bubonic plague from rats to humans. ATWS. *Compare* Wouldn't Hurt a Fly.

WOULDN'T HURT A FLY *X wouldn't hurt a fly.* X wouldn't think of injuring another person or animal. Source: FLY. WNNCD: O.E. Flies are so widespread, so abundant, and so annoying that only a devout pacificist would object to swatting, stomping, squishing, or squashing one of them. (The jury is still out on the use of flypaper: Is it a deadly weapon or an attractive nuisance?) CI; DEI; IRCD. *Compare* Wouldn't Hurt a Flea.

WOUNDED BIRD   *See* Bird.

WOUNDED BIRD TRICK   *the wounded bird trick.* A pretense of injury in order to decoy an attacker away from his/her primary object. Source: BIRD. The wounded bird trick is practiced by the *killdeer* (and certain ducks), which walks away from its nest on the ground while dragging one of its wings as if it were broken. The attacker, usu. a bird of prey, then focuses its attention on the "wounded" bird, which seems to be an easy target—that is, until the killdeer suddenly *flies in the face* (q.v.) of the attacker or darts away. Humans sometimes employ this tactic to protect their children when attacked by dogs, bears, etc. *See also* Killdeer; Wounded Bird.

WOUNDED DUCK   *a wounded duck.* A wobbly pass in football. Source: DUCK. WNNCD: O.E. When a duck is shot, but not killed, it may continue to fly, in a wobbly fashion, for a short distance. A forward pass from the quarterback that tumbles end over end, or at least fails to spiral properly, has a similar appearance. *See also* Duck Hook; Lame Duck. *Compare* Dying Quail.

WRIGGLE OFF THE HOOK   *See* Off the Hook.

Y

YAP   *See* Bark like a Dog.

YARDBIRD   *See* Jailbird.

YELLOW-BELLIED   *See* Yellow Dog.

YELLOW BELLY   *See* Yellow Dog.

YELLOW DOG   *a yellow dog*. A mean, contemptible, coward. LTA: 1880. Source: DOG. WNNCD: O.E. For some reason, a yellow dog has been regarded as worthless or cowardly: i.e., a mongrel, a cur. It may be because lazy, good-for-nothing dogs lie in their own urine and develop a *yellow belly*—also a metaphor for "coward," along with the adj. *yellow-bellied* (LTA: 1847). CH; IRCD; MDWPO. *See also* Yellow-dog Contract. *Compare* Red Dog; Show the White Feather.

YELLOW-DOG CONTRACT   *a yellow-dog contract*. A bargaining agreement between employer and employees in which the employees agree not to form or join a union during the life of the contract. WNNCD: 1920. (*Yellow-dog contracts* were outlawed by Congress in 1935.) Source: DOG. WNNCD: O.E. The *yellow dog* in such an agreement was the employee who signed the contract, not the employer who concocted it. A related metaphor, *yellow-dog Democrat* (SPD: 1928), refers to a party member who supports the party ticket regardless of who is running—even if it's a yellow dog. BDPF; EWPO; IRCD; LCRH; LTA; SHM.

YELLOW-DOG DEMOCRAT   *See* Yellow-dog Contract.

YELP   *See* Bark like a Dog.

YIP   *See* Bark like a Dog.

YOKE   *to bear a yoke.* To be in a state of oppression, servitude, bondage, or marriage. Source: OX. The original *yoke* was borne by a pair of oxen, which were hitched together under a double-bowed beam resembling a pair of modern eyeglasses. This is the source of the marriage metaphor. Later, prisoners and defeated soldiers were placed, individually, under a single beam, with arms raised and tied above it. Single-beamed yokes have also been used for centuries for carrying equal loads suspended at either end of the beam. ATWS. *See also* Subjugate; Syzygy. *Compare* Get Hitched; In Double Harness.

YOKEL   *a yokel.* A country bumpkin. WNNCD: ca. 1812. Source: BIRD. Literally, *yokel* is an imitative word for the cry of the green woodpecker, which is found in Europe, North Africa, and Asia Minor. Figuratively, *yokel* came to be associated with the people of rural England who lived in the countryside with the *yokel* bird. The word—but not the bird—came to America to refer to naive or gullible people from farms or small towns. EWPO.

YOU CAN LEAD A HORSE TO WATER   *See* Lead a Horse to Water.

YOU CAN'T MAKE AN OMELET WITHOUT BREAKING EGGS   *See* Can't Make an Omelet without Breaking Eggs.

YOUNG BUCK   *a young buck.* An energetic, brash, or impetuous young man. Source: DEER. A *buck* is an adult male deer, or *stag* (q.v.). A *young* buck is a buck "wannabe"—a cocky and ambitious young male that thinks it can challenge the stags for dominance over the harem. The same phenomenon occurs in the ranks of most animals, but among humans the prize is more often money or glory. ATWS; CE. *See also* Buck Private. *Compare* Young Lion.

YOUNG CHICK   *See* Chick.

YOUNG LION   *a young lion.* One of a group of enthusiastic young members of an organization—such as a corporation or a political party—who is fearless and lacks respect for tradition. Source: LION. WNNCD: 12th cent. The young male lion is a problem in the wild, where he thinks he can do whatever he wants to— until the senior member of the pride puts him in his place. Eventually, however, he will succeed him as *King of Beasts* (q.v.). CE. *Compare* Young Buck.

YOUNG PUP   *a young pup.* An insolent or arrogant young man. Source: DOG. *Pup* (WNNCD: 1773) is short for *puppy* (WNNCD: 1591) "a young dog less than a year old." A human *young pup* is a know-it-all who talks back to his parents and is too big for his britches. However, like the cute little innocent puppy, the youngster is somewhat admired for his arrogance. A related expression is "He's been around *since Hector was a pup*." Hector, son of Priam, was a young man around the end of the second millenium B.C. DEI; IRCD; MDWPO. *See also* Puppy Dog. *Compare* Young Buck; Young Lion.

Z

ZEBRA *a zebra*. A referee who wears a shirt with alternating black and white vertical stripes, called *zebra stripes*, as in basketball, football, and ice hockey. Source: ZEBRA. WNNCD: 1600. The African zebra, although related to the equines of other continents, has a distinctive coat of black and white stripes: mostly vertical on the neck and shoulders, horizontal on the rump and legs. It has never been domesticated. NDAS. *See also* Zebra Mussel.

ZEBRA FINCH *a zebra finch*. A small Australian cage bird that has black bars on its grayish white tail feathers. WNNCD: 1889. Source: ZEBRA. WNNCD: 1600. The zebra, a medium-sized African "horse," has alternating black and white stripes on its entire body. The pattern has inspired the naming of several other animals. *See also* Zebra Fish; Zebra Mussel.

ZEBRA FISH *a zebra fish*. A "barred" fish—i.e., one with vertical and/or horizontal contrasting bars or stripes. WNNCD: 1771. Source: ZEBRA. WNNCD: 1600. The African zebra, which is of the same genus (*Equus*) as the horse, has a coat of black and white alternating stripes. It has competed with the Bengal tiger, which has alternating black and orange stripes, as the model for naming newly discovered striped animals. *See also* Zebra Finch; Zebra Mussel.

ZEBRA MUSSEL *a zebra mussel*. A small (one-inch long) trianglar shellfish with alternating ribs of black and white. Source: ZEBRA. WNNCD: 1600. Originally from the Baltic Sea, the *zebra mussel* has now reached the Great Lakes, to which it has brought both good news (it cleans the water) and bad news (it clogs intake pipes along the shores). The African zebra is famous for its coat of alternating black and white stripes. *See also* Zebra Finch; Zebra Fish.

ZEBRA STRIPES *See* Zebra.

ZODIAC *See* Zoo.

ZOO *a zoo.* A crowded, confused, and boisterous assemblage of people. Source: ANIMAL. An animal *zoo* (short for London's *Zoological Garden*) is a collection of (usu.) wild animals for public viewing (WNNCD: ca. 1847). The animals are noisy, unrestrained, and uninhibited, as they are in the wild. A human *zoo* is a home or workplace in which the people behave like animals in the zoo: pushing, shoving, yelling, and fighting. A *zoo plane* is an airplane crowded full of reporters that trails a Presidential candidate's plane wherever it goes (SPD: ca. 1970). A *zodiac* (fr. Gk. *zoidiakos* "pertaining to animals") is a symbolic representation of the major constellations, many of which are named after animals (WNNCD: 14th cent.). ATWS; BDPF; EWPO. *Compare* It's a Jungle Out There.

ZOO PLANE *See* Zoo.

CLASSIFICATION OF METAPHORS ACCORDING TO ANIMAL

ALBATROSS
Albatross around Your Neck
ALLIGATOR
Alligator (n)
Alligator (v)
Alligator Clip
Alligator Gar
Alligator Pear
Alligator Snapper
See You Later, Alligator
ANIMAL (general)
Aggregate
Animal
Animal Cracker
Animal Instincts
Animal Magnetism
Animal Passions
Asphalt Jungle
At Loggerheads
At the End of Your Tether
Backbite
Backtrack

Bag
Bait (1)
Bait (2)
Bait and Switch
Bait the Hook
Bait the Trap
Band Shell
Barnyard Epithet
Barnyard Humor
Barnyard Language
Beast
Beastly
Beast of Burden
Beast with Two Backs
Beauty and the Beast
Behave like an Animal
Bestial
Bestiality
Bête Noire
Bewilder
Bloodthirsty
Bonfire

Bottomless Pit

Brand

Brand Name

Break Cover

Breed (n)

Breed (v)

Browse

Brutal

Brute

Brute Force

Brute Strength

Brutish

Burrow

By Leaps and Bounds

By the Nape of the Neck

Caught in a Trap

Caught Napping

Chew Someone out

Chew Your Cud

Claw (v)

Claw Your Way out

Claw Your Way to the Top

Clutch (n) (1)

Clutch (v)

Clutch Bag

Clutch Hit

Clutch Hitter

Coda

Cold-blooded

Come through in the Clutch

Come to the End of Your Tether

Congregate

Congregation

Cornet

Corral

Crawl under a Rock

Creature Comforts

Creature of Habit

Cub Reporter

Cud

Curtail

Death Trap

Den

Den Mother

Den of Thieves

Different Animal

Double Back

Drink from the Same Trough

Earmark (v)

Eat out of Your Hand

Egregious

End of Your Tether

Entrapment

Fair Game

Fall into a Trap

Fall Prey to

Fenced in

Feral

Ferocious

Fierce

Fit for neither Man nor Beast

Flock

Fret

Fur Will Fly

Get on the Horn

Get Wind of Something

Go around in Circles

Go for the Jugular

Go into Hibernation

Good in the Clutch

Go on a Rampage

Go out on a Limb

Go to Pot

Graze

Great Horned Owl

Gregarious

Grow by Leaps and Bounds

Hard Sell

Hard-shell Conservative

Hard-shell/Soft-shell

Hard-shell Taco

Have a Ring through Your Nose

Have Someone in Your Clutches

Herd (n)

Herd (v)

Herd Mentality

Hide

Hide nor Hair

Hightail It

Hole up

Hoofer

Hoof It

Horn

Horned Question

Horned Toad

Hornet

Horn in on

Horns of a Dilemma

Horny

In Season

Instinct for the Jugular

In the Bag

It's a Jungle out there

Jump through Hoops

Jungle Gym

Keep Track of

Lap

Lap Something up

Law of the Jungle

Lead Someone around by the Nose

Leap at the Chance

Leave No Stone Unturned

Led around by the Nose

Lick Your Wounds

Lie Low

Like a Caged Animal

Like a Cornered Animal

Like a Hunted Animal

Like an Animal

Litter

Lock Horns

Look like Roadkill

Look like Something that just Crawled out from under a Rock

Lose Track of

Lower than the Animals

Low on the Food Chain

Make Heads or Tails

Make Horns

Make the Fur Fly

Mind like a Steel Trap

Mixed Bag

Nature of the Beast

Neither Hide nor Hair

Not Fit for Man nor Beast

Not yet Dry behind the Ears

Old Stomping Ground

On the Prowl

On the Track of

Open Season

Out for Blood

Out of Season

Out on a Limb

Parasite

Party Animal

Pastor

Pastoral

Paw

Pencil

Pesky

Pest

Pet

Pet Peeve

Pet Rock

Petting

Pick of the Litter

Pitfall

Political Animal

Predator

Prey

Prey on

Prick up Your Ears

Prowl

Prowl Car

Prowler

Put a Tail on

Put down

Put Someone out of Their Misery

Put to Sleep

Queue

Queue up

Quid

Rampage

Rampant

Rear Its Ugly Head

Rise above the Herd

Ruminate

Rump

Rump Session

Run Rampant

Runway

Saddle Horn

Save Your own Hide

Scavenger

Segregate

Set a Trap

Shell (n)

Shell (v)

Shell a Pitcher

Shell a Village

Shell Company

Shell Game

Shut Your Trap

Smoke out

Snatch from the Jaws

Snoot

Snooty

Snout

Soft Sell

Soft-shell

Soft-shell Taco

Southpaw

Spoil

Spoiling for a Fight

Spoils of War

Stampede

Still Wet behind the Ears

Stop Dead in Your Tracks

Suck the Hind Tit

Swelled Head

Tail (n)

Tail (v)

Tail End

Tail off

Take Cover

Take the Bait

Tame (adj.)

Tame (v)

Tame the Wilderness

Tan Someone's Hide

Teacher's Pet

Team

Team Player

Team Spirit	Big Ape
Team Teaching	Go Ape
Team up	Go Ape over
Teamwork	Jackanapes
Track down	Play the Sedulous Ape
Trap	**ARTHROPOD**
Trapped	Antenna
Trap Play	**ASS**
Trap Shooting	Asinine
Treacle	Ass
Tripe	Easel
Up a Tree	Feel like an Ass
Venison	Jackass
Venom	Jackrabbit
Wear the Horns	Make an Ass of Yourself
Wet behind the Ears	Rail
What's Eating You	Silly Ass
Wilderness	Smart Ass
Work as a Team	**BABOON**
Work Your Tail off	Big Baboon
Zodiac	**BADGER**
Zoo	Badger
Zoo Plane	Badger Game
ANT	**BAT**
Ant Lion	Bat House
Ants in Your Pants	Batman
Antsy	Bats
Doodlebug	Bats in Your Belfry
Have Ants in Your Pants	Batty
Myrmidons of the Law	Blind as a Bat
ANTELOPE	Drive Someone Bats
Chamois	Like a Bat out of Hell
APE	Old Bat
Above the Apes	Vampire
Ape (adj.)	**BEAR**
Ape (n)	Angry as a Bear
Ape (v)	Arctic

Bear (1)

Bear (2)

Bear (3)

Bear (4)

Bear for Punishment

Bear for Work

Bear Hug

Bear in the Air

Bearish

Bear Market

Bear of a Man

Bear of a Task

Bears in the Woods

Berserk

Bugbear

Cross as a Bear

Cuddly as a Bear

Growl like a Bear

Have a Bear by the Tail

Hungry as a Bear

Koala Bear

Lick into shape

Like a Bear with a Sore Head

Loaded for Bear

Panda Bear

Sorehead

Teddy Bear

BEAVER

Beaver

Beaverboard

Beaver Shot

Busy as a Beaver

Eager Beaver

Shoot a Beaver

Work like a Beaver

BEDBUG

Bedbug Letter

Crazy as a Bedbug

Don't Let the Bedbugs Bite

BEE

Abuzz

Bee

Beehive Hairdo

Beehive of Activity

Bee in Your Bonnet

Beeline

Bee's Knees

Beeswax

Birds and the Bees

Busy as a Bee

Busy Bee

Buzz (n)

Buzz (v)

Buzz Bomb

Buzzer

Buzz off

Buzz Session

Buzzword

Drone (n) (1)

Drone (n) (2)

Drone (v)

Float like a Butterfly

Honey

Honeycomb

Honeycombed

Honeymoon

Honeymoon Is over

Hum

Humdrum

Husking Bee

Make a Beeline

Makes Things Hum

Mealy-mouthed

Mellifluous

Mind Your Own Beeswax

None of Your Beeswax

Put the Sting on

Queen Bee

Quilting Bee

Spelling Bee

Spinning Bee

Sting (n)

Sting (v)

Sting Operation

Swarm (n)

Swarm (v)

Sweet as Honey

Sweetness and Light

Sweet-talker

BEETLE

Beetle (n)

Beetle (v)

Beetlebrain

Beetlebrained

Beetle-browed

Scarab

BIRD (general)

All Aflutter

Augur

Augury

Auspices

Auspicious

Aviation

Beak

Bill

Bird

Birdbrain

Birdbrained

Birdcage

Bird Didn't Fly

Birdfarm

Bird Has Flown

Birdie

Birdieback

Bird in the Hand

Bird Legs

Bird of Ill Omen

Bird of Paradise

Bird of Passage

Birds and the Bees

Bird's-eye View

Birds of a Feather

Boobird

Break out of Your Shell

Broken Wing

Brood

Chat

Chatter

Chatterbox

Claw (n)

Clawhammer

Clip Someone's Wings

Come off Your Perch

Covey

Decoy

Down

Down-to-earth

Early Bird

Early Bird Catches the Worm

Earn Your Wings

Eat like a Bird

Empty Nest

Empty Nester

Empty-nest Syndrome

Feather (n)

Feather (v)

Featherbed

Featherbrain

Featherbrained

Feather in Your Cap

Featherweight

Feathery

Feather Your Nest

Fink

Fledgling

Flies

Flip the Bird

Flush out

Flutter

Fly (n) (1)

Fly (v)

Fly Ball

Fly Blind

Fly-by-night

Fly by the Seat of Your Pants

Fly in the Face of

Fly in the Teeth of

Flyleaf

For the Birds

Foul Your Own Nest

Free as a Bird

Full-fledged

Get up with the Birds

Give Someone the Bird

Go Fly a Kite

Hard to Swallow

Hatch

Have Your Wings Clipped

Helicopter

High as a Kite

Hover

How Do You Get Down off an Elephant

Hungry Mouths to Feed

Hunt-and-peck

Hunt-'n-pecker

Inaugurate

In Fine Feather

In Full Feather

Jailbird

Jinx

Kibitz

Kibitzer

Kill Two Birds with one Stone

Kite (n)

Kiwi

Kiwi Fruit

Knock Me over with a Feather

Knock Someone off Their Perch

Left-wing

Light as a feather

Little Bird Told Me

Love

Lovebird

Love Nest

Make the Feathers Fly

Make Your Hair Stand on End

Mechanical Claw

Mugwump

Nasty

Neither Fish nor Fowl

Nest (n)

Nest (v)

Nested Embeddings

Nesting Instinct

Nestle

Nom de Plume

Old Bird

On the Fly

Panache

Peck

Peep

Pen

Perch

Phoenix

Phoenixlike

Pinion

Pinnacle

Pipe up

Pipsqueak

Pluck (n)

Pluck (v)

Plucky

Plume

Pop Fly

Pounce

Pound of Feathers

Preen

Prices Are Soaring

Puffed with Pride

Puff up with Pride

Railbird

Rapture

Rare Bird

Rat Fink

Right-wing

Rise like a Phoenix

Rostrum

Ruffle Someone's Feathers

Sand in Your Craw

Sing like a Bird

Siren

Smart Old Bird

Smooth Someone's Ruffled Feathers

Snowbird

Soar

Soar to Great Heights

Speak of the Devil

Sprinkle Salt on Its Tail

Sprout Wings

Stick in Your Craw

Stick in Your Gizzard

Stick in Your Gullet

Stick in Your Throat

Take Wing

That Bird Has Flown

Tough Old Bird

Try Your Wings

Unflappable

Wait in the Wings

Water Wings

What's the Word, Hummingbird

Whirlybird

Wing (n)

Wing (v)

Wingback

Wingback Chair

Wingpan

Wing Tips

Wingtips

Wounded Bird

Wounded Bird Trick

Yardbird

Yokel

BOOBY

Booby Hatch

BUFFALO

Buff (adj.)

Buff (n) (1)

Buff (n) (2)

Buff (v)

Buffalo

Buffaloed

Buffalofish

Buffalo Wings

In the Buff

BUG

Bitten by the Bug

Bug (n) (1)

Bug (n) (2)

Bug (n) (3)

Bug (n) (4)

Bug (v) (1)

Bug (v) (2)

Bugaboo

Bugbear

Bug Boy

Bug-eyed

Buggy (adj.)

Buggy (n)

Buggy (v)

Bughouse

Bug in Your Ear

Bug off

Bug out

Come Down with the Bug

Cute as a Bug's Ear

Debug

Doodlebug

Firebug

Jitterbug

Litterbug

Lovebug

Put a Bug in Someone's Ear

Shutterbug

Snug as a Bug in a Rug

Stop Bugging Me

Travel Bug

BULL

Bellow

B.S.

Bull (1)

Bull (2)

Bull (3)

Bull (4)

Bulldog (n)

Bulldoze

Bulldozer

Bullfinch

Bullfrog

Bullhead

Bullheaded

Bullhorn

Bull in a China Shop

Bullish

Bull Market

Bullnecked

Bullpen

Bullroar

Bull-roarer

Bull Session

Bull's-eye

Bull's-eye Glass

Bull's-eye Lantern

Bull's-eye Lens

Bull's-eye Window

Bullshit (n)

Bullshit (v)

Bullshot

Bull Snake

Bullwhip

Bully

Bully Beef

Bull Your Way

Bulrush

Cock-and-bull Story

Croon

Crooner

Have a Ring through Your Nose

Have Someone in the Bullpen

Hit the Bull's-eye

Like a Bull out of a Chute

Moment of Truth

No Bull

Raging Bull

Red Flag to a Bull

Roar like a Bull

See Red

Shoot the Bull

Strong as a Bull

Take the Bull by the Horns

Wave a Red Flag in front of a Bull

Whose Bull Is Being Gored

BULLDOG

Bulldog (v)

Bulldog Edition

BURRO

Burrito

BUTTERFLY

Butterflies in Your Stomach

Butterfly Fish

Butterfly Shrimp

Butterfly Stroke

Butterfly Table

Butterfly Valve

Feel the Butterflies

Float like a Butterfly

Pavilion

Social Butterfly

BUZZARD

Buzzards Are Circling

Old Buzzard

CALF

Calf

Calf Eyes

Calf Fries

Kill the Fatted Calf

Worship the Golden Calf

CAMEL

C

Camel

Camelopard

Camel's Hair

Camel that Poked Its Head in the Tent

G

Go through the Eye of a Needle

Last Straw

Strain out Gnats and Swallow Camels

Straw that Broke the Camel's Back

CANARY

Canary (1)

Canary (2)

Canary Yellow

Cat that Ate the Canary

Sing like a Canary (1)

Sing like a Canary (2)

CAT

Alley Cat

Bell the Cat

Cat

Catamaran

Cat and Mouse Game

Cat around

Cat Burglar

Catcall

Caterpillar

Caterwaul

Catfight

Catfish

Cat Got Your Tongue

Catgut

Cathouse

Cat Is out of the Bag

Catkin

Catlike

Catnap

Cat on a Hot Tin Roof

Cat-o'-nine-tails

CAT Scan

Cat's Cradle

Cat's-eye

Cat's Meow

Cat's Pajamas

Cat's Paw

Catsup

Cat's Whiskers

Cattail

Cat that Ate the Canary

Catty

Catty-corner

Catwalk

Copycat

Copycat Crime

Copycat Killer

Curiosity Killed the Cat

Different Breed of Cat

Don't Give a Lick

Dust Pussy

Eyes like a Cat

Fat Cat

Feed the Kitty

Feline

Fight like Cats and Dogs

Fight like Cats in a Bag

Fight Tooth and Nail

Fraidy-cat

Get Burned

Get Your Back up

Green-eyed Monster

Grin like a Cheshire Cat

Guess Which Way the Cat Will Jump

Hair-raising Experience

Hairy

Have as Many Lives as a Cat

Have Eyes like a Cat

Have Kittens

Have Nine Lives

Hellcat

Hepcat

Holy Cats

Kitten

Kittenish

Kitty

Kitty-corner

Land on Your Feet

Let the Cat out of the Bag

Lick and a Promise

Like a Cat in Heat

Look like Something the Cat Dragged in

Look like the Cat that Ate the Canary

Look what the Cat Dragged in

Make the Fur Fly

More than One Way to Skin a Cat

Move like a Cat

Nine Lives

Old Cat

Play Cat and Mouse

Playful as a Kitten

Polecat

Pull Chestnuts out of the Fire

Purr like a Kitten

Pussy

Pussycat

Pussyfoot

Pussy Willow

Quick as a Cat

Rain Cats and Dogs

Chicken Scratches

Chickenshit

Chicken Switch

Chicken Tracks

Chickweed

City Chicken

Clip Someone's Wings

Clutch (n) (2)

Come Home to Roost

Coop

Cooped up

Count Your Chickens

Curses, like Chickens, always Come Home to Roost

Darning Egg

Don't Count Your Chickens before They Hatch

Don't Put All Your Eggs in One Basket

Dumb Cluck

Egghead

Egg on

Eggplant

Fly the Coop

Get It in the Neck

Get the Ax

Get up with the Chickens

Good Egg

Go Suck an Egg

Go to Bed with the Chickens

Hard-boiled

Have Your Wings Clipped

Hip Chick

Last One in Is a Rotten Egg

Like a Chicken with Its Head Cut off

Lose Your Head

Love

Mother Carey's Chickens

Nest Egg

Nobody here but Us Chickens

No Chicken

No Spring Chicken

Oval

Pecking Order

Play Chicken

Polecat

Put all Your Eggs in One Basket

Put Your Neck on the Line

Roost

Rotten Egg

Rubber-chicken Circuit

Run around like a Chicken with Its Head Cut off

Schmaltz

Slick Chick

Stick Your Neck out

Tar and Feather

Tarred and Feathered

Teach Your Grandmother to Suck Eggs

Walk on Eggs

Which Came First, the Chicken or the Egg

Wishbone

Work for Chicken Feed

You Can't Make an Omelet without Breaking Eggs

Young Chick

CHIPMUNK

Chipmunk Cheeks

CLAM

Clam

Clambake

Clammy

Clamshell

Clam up

Happy as a Clam

Hard-shell/Soft-shell

Shut up like a Clam

COCK

Battle Royal

Cock (n)

Cock (v)

Cockade

Cock-and-bull Story

Cockboat

Cockeyed

Cockfight

Cockhorse

Cock of the Walk

Cockpit

Cockroach

Cocksure

Cocktail

Cocky

Cock Your Arm

Cock Your Ears

Cock Your Eye

Cock Your Hat

Cock Your Head

Cock Your Wrist

Coquet

Coquetry

Coquette

Coxcomb

Coxswain

Crest (n)

Crest (v)

Crestfallen

Crow

Game

Get Your Hackles up

Grit

Live like Fighting Cocks

Make Someone's Hackles Rise

Make the Feathers Fly

Petcock

Pit against

Raise Someone's Hackles

Rule the Roost

Show the White Feather

Shuttlecock

Spar

Sparring Partner

Stand the Gaff

Sudden Death

Unable to Stand the Gaff

Verbal Sparring

Weathercock

Well-heeled

COCKROACH

Cockroach

Come out of the Woodwork

Roach

Roach Clip

COCKLE

Cockle Finish

Warm the Cockles of Your Heart

COCOON

See Insect

COD

Codfish Aristocracy

Codpiece

COOT

Bald as a Coot

Crazy as a Coot

Old Coot

COW

Andirons

Bawl

Black Cow

Brown Cow

Bucolic

Cash Cow

Cow (n)

Cow (v)

Cowcatcher

Cow College

Cower

Cow-eyed

Cow Eyes

Cowlick

Cowslip

Cow Town

Cry over Spilled Milk

Dewlap

Have a Cow

Holy Cow

Make Cow Eyes

Milk

Milk a Cash Cow

Punch this Cow

Sacred Cow

Sea Cow

Till the Cows Come Home

COYOTE

Coyote

CRAB

Boston Crab

Cancer

Canker

Catch a Crab

Crab (n)

Crab (v)

Crab Apple

Crabbed

Crabby

Crabgrass

Crab Louse

Crabs

CRANE

Cranberry

Crane

Cranesbill

Crane Your Neck

Geranium

Pedigree

CRAYFISH

Crawfish

Crayfish

CRICKET

Cricket (1)

Cricket (2)

Jimminy Crickets

Not Cricket

CROCODILE

After awhile, Crocodile

Crocodile Tears

Leviathon

CROW

As the Crow Flies

Black as a Crow

Crow

Crowbar

Crowberry

Crowfoot

Crow's-feet

Crow's Nest

Eat Crow

Old Crow

Rook

Scarecrow

CUCKOO

Cloud-cuckoo-land

Coccyx

Cuckold

Cuckoo (adj.)

Cuckoo (n)

Cuckoo Clock

Cuckoo's Nest

Cuckoo Spit

DEER

Big Bucks

Buck (n)

Buckeye

Buck Fever

Buck Naked

Buck Passer

Buck Private

Buckskin

Buck Slip

Buck Stops here

Buck Tooth

Eat Humble Pie

Fast Buck

Fawn

Go Stag

Hightail It

Killdeer

Pass the Buck

Quarry

Run like a Deer

Sawbuck

Sprout Antlers

Stag Line

Stag Movie

Stag Party

White Bucks

Young Buck

DINOSAUR

Dinosaur

Last Dinosaur

DODO

Dead as a Dodo

Dodo

Dumb Dodo

DOG

Abet

At Bay

At each Other's Throats

At Fault

Atta Boy

Autograph Hound

Bark

Bark at the Moon

Barker

Barking Dogs

Barking Dogs seldom Bite

Bark Is Worse than Your Bite

Bark like a Dog

Bark up the Wrong Tree

Bawl

Baying

Bird Dog

Bird-dog

Bitch (n)

Bitch (v)

Bitching

Bitchy

Bite the Hand that Feeds You

Bloodhound

Bone of Contention

Bone to Pick

Bring to Bay

Bring to Heel

Brought to Bay

Brought to Heel

Call off Your Dogs

Canine Appetite

Canine Tooth

Cannibal

Cast

Cast about

Chase Your Tail

Chili Dog

Chowhound

Clean as a Hound's Tooth

Close on Someone's Heels

Corn Dog

Coward

Crooked as a Dog's Hind Leg

Cur

Cynic

Cynosure

Dead Set on

Die like a Dog

Dirty Dog

Dog (n)

Dog (v)

Dog and Pony Show

Dog-cheap

Dog Collar

Dog Days

Dog-ear

Dog-eared

Dog Eat Dog

Dog-eat-dog World

Dogface

Dogfight

Dogged

Doggedly

Doggedness

Doggerel

Doggie Bag

Doggone

Doghouse

Dog in the Manger

Dog It

Dog Latin

Dogleg

Dog Paddle

Dog Rhyme

Dog's Age

Dogs Are Barking

Dogs Are in the Manger

Dogs Are Tired

Dog's Letter

Dog's Life

Dogs of War

Dog Someone's Heels

Dog Tags

Dog-tired

Dogtown

Dog Watch

Dog Years

Don't Know Sic 'em

Down, Boy

Every Dog Has His Day

Fawn on

Feed the Bulldog

Feisty

Fight like Cats and Dogs

Fight Tooth and Nail

Firedogs

Foam at the Mouth

Follow Someone around like a Puppy Dog

Follow You anywhere

Gabriel's Hounds

Go around in Circles

Go to the Dogs

Green Dog

Growl

Gun-shy

Gun Them down like Dogs

Hair of the Dog

Hangdog Look

Harass

Hard on Someone's Heels

Hare and Hounds

Hark back

Hold at Bay

Horehound

Hot Diggity Dog

Hotdog

Hot Dog

Hot Dog!

Hotdogger

Hot on the Trail

Hound (n)

Hound (v)

Hound Dog

Hounds of Hell

Houndstooth Check

Housebroken

Howl

Hush Puppy

Imperialist Dog

In Abeyance

In at the Death

In at the Kill

In Full Cry

In Hot Pursuit

In the Doghouse

Jerk Someone around

Jerk Someone's Chain

Keep at Bay

Lap Dog

Lead a Dog's Life

Let Sleeping Dogs Lie

Let Slip the Dogs of War

Lick Someone's Boots

Lick Your Chops

Lie like a Dog

Lost-puppy Look

Love Me, Love My Dog

Lovesick Puppy

Lucky Dog

Mad Dog

Make Your Mouth Water

Man Bites Dog

Mangy

Man's Best Friend

Moon Dog

More Money than a Dog Has Fleas

Mud Puppy

Muzzle (n)

Muzzle (v)

My Dog Has Fleas

Nip at the Heels

Nippy

Nose for News

On a Cold Trail

On a Short Leash

Once Bitten, Twice Shy

One-ring Circus

On Someone's Tail

On the Right/Wrong Track

Pavlovian Response

Pebble Pup

Pit Bull

Poke Your Nose into Someone else's
Business

Prairie Dog

Prick up Your Ears

Pug Nose

Puppy Dog

Puppy Love

Pup Tent

Put a Muzzle on

Put on the Dog

Put Someone on a Short Leash

R

Rain Cats and Dogs

Red Dog

Relay

Rich Bitch

Rock Hound

Rub Someone's Nose in It

Run around in Circles

Running Dog

Run Riot

Run to Earth

Run to Ground

Run with the Hare

Sarcasm

Sea Dog

See a Man about a Dog

Seeing-eye

See What I Can Dig up

Send a Dog out

Shaggy-dog Story

Shouldn't Happen to a Dog

Show Your Teeth

Sic

Sick as a Dog

Since Hector Was a Pup

Sit up and Take Notice

Sleuthhound

Slip the Collar

Sly Old Dog

Snarl

Sniff out

S.O.B.

Son of a Bitch

Stand there with Your Tongue Hanging out

Stick Your Nose into Someone else's Business

Stick Your Nose where It Doesn't Belong

Straight as a Dog's Hind Leg

Strain at the Leash

Sun Dog

Tail between Your Legs

Tail Is Wagging the Dog

Tail that Wags the Dog

Teach an Old Dog New Tricks

Tenacious as a Bulldog

Three-dog Night

Throw It to the Dogs

Throw Someone a Bone

Throw Someone off the Scent

Top Dog

Treat Someone like a Dog

Try It on the Dog

Turn on You

Underdog

Until the Last Dog Is Hung

Walk the Dog

Ward Heeler

Watchdog

Watchdog Organization

Woof

Work like a Dog

Worth the Whistle

Yap

Yellow-bellied

Yellow Belly

Yellow Dog

Yellow-dog Contract

Yellow-dog Democrat

Yelp

Yip

Young Pup

DOLPHIN

Delphinium

Dolphin Kick

DONKEY

Bray like a Donkey

Carrot-and-stick

Donkey Engine

Donkey's Years

Donkey Work

Hee Haw

Like a Carrot to a Donkey

Pin the Tail on the Donkey

Talk the Hind Leg off a Donkey

DOVE

Bill and Coo

Columbine

Coo

Dove

Dove of Peace

Dovetail (n)

Dovetail (v)

Dovish

Gentle as a Dove

Hold out the Olive Branch

Lovey-dovey

Palomino

DRAGON

Draconian

Dragonfly

Dragonhead

Dragon Lady

Dragon's Blood

Dragon's Teeth

Komodo Dragon

DUCK

Canard

Cold Duck

Dead Duck

Duck (n)

Duck (v)

Duckbilled Platypus

Duck Hook

Ducks and Drakes

Duck's Egg

Duck Soup

Ducktail

Duck Test

Duck Walk

Ducky

Easy as Duck Soup

Fine Day for Ducks

Get All Your Ducks in a Row

How Do You Get Down off an Elephant

Lame Duck

Lay an Egg

Like a Duck to Water

Like Water off a Duck's Back

Mock Duck

Nice Day for Ducks

Nice Weather for Ducks

Nice Weather if You're a Duck

Odd Duck

Quack

Queer Duck

Shoot the Duck

Sitting Duck

Take to Something like a Duck to Water

Ugly Duckling

Waddle like a Duck

Wounded Duck

EAGLE

American Eagle

Aquiline

Bald as an Eagle

Double Eagle (1)

Double Eagle (2)

Fish Eggs

Fisheye

Fish-eye Lens

Fish for Compliments

Fish for Information

Fishing Expedition

Fish in Troubled Waters

Fish or Cut Bait

Fish out

Fish out of Water

Fish Story

Fishtail

Fishwife

Fishy

Flat as a Flounder

Flounder

Get a Bite

Get a Nibble

Get a Rise out of Someone

Get Hooked

Ghoti

Give Someone Some Line

Go Belly up

Good Catch

Go on a Fishing Expedition

Green around the Gills

Hooked

Hook, Line, and Sinker

ICHTHUS

In Cold Blood

In the Swim

Isinglass

Jellyfish

Keeper

Kettle of Fish

Kingfish

Land

Let Someone off the Hook

Like a Fish out of Water

Like Shooting Fish in a Barrel

Loaded to the Gills

N

Neither Fish nor Fowl

Not the only Fish in the Ocean

Off the Hook

One that Got away

On Your own Hook

Other Fish to Fry

Plenty more Fish in the Ocean

Prize Catch

Queer Fish

Reel in/off

Run with the Line

Salmon

Scale

Sepia

Set the Hook

Silverfish

Sleep with the Fishes

Small Fry

Soup and Fish

Spawn

Spineless Jellyfish

Stewed to the Gills

Stuffed to the Gills

Swallow Something Hook, Line, and Sinker

Swallow the Bait

Swim like a Fish

Take the Bait

Tin Fish

Torpedo (n)

Torpedo (v)

Torpedo Juice

Untrammeled

Wiggle off the Hook

Wriggle off the Hook

FLEA

Fleabag

Flea-bitten

Flea-flicker

Flea in Your Ear

Flea Market

Have More Money than Fleas

More Money than a Dog Has Fleas

My Dog Has Fleas

Puce

Thick as Fleas

Ukulele

Water Flea

Wouldn't Hurt a Flea

FLY

Barfly

Catch More Flies

Draw People like Flies

Drop like Flies

Firefly

Fly (n) (2)

Fly Fishing

Fly in the Ointment

Fly on the Wall

Flyspeck

Flyweight

Gadfly

Musket

No Flies on Me

Said the Spider to the Fly

Shoofly Pie

Spanish Fly

Tie Flies

What Has Four Wheels and Flies

Wouldn't Hurt a Fly

FOX

Bright-eyed and Bushy-tailed

Clever as a Fox

Cover Your Tracks

Crazy like a Fox

Cunning as a Fox

Flying Fox

Fox

Fox and Geese

Foxfire

Fox Guarding the Henhouse

Foxhole

Fox Squirrel

Fox-trot

Foxy Lady

No Atheists in the Foxholes

Old Fox

Outfox

Put the Fox in Charge of the Henhouse

Sly as a Fox

Sly Old Fox

Smart as a Fox

Sour Grapes

Stone Fox

Throw Someone off the Track

Vixen

FROG

Croak

Frog (1)

Frog (2)

Frog (3)

Frog (4)

Frog (5)

Frog Hair

Frog in Your Throat

Frog Kick

Frogman

Frog Spit
Frog Sticker
Leapfrog (n)
Leapfrog (v)
Padlock
GNAT
Strain out Gnats and Swallow Camels
GOAT
Aegis
Buck (v)
Buck a Trend
Buck for a Raise
Buckram
Bucksaw
Buck the Odds
Buck up
Butcher
Butt
Butt in
Cab
Cabriole (1)
Cabriole (2)
Cabriolet
Caper
Caprice
Capricious
Capriole
Chevron
Chimera
Cut a Caper
Fleecy
Get Someone's Goat
Goat
Goatee
Goatsucker
Handle with Kid Gloves
Hero to Goat

Kid (n)
Kid (v)
Kidding
Kid-glove Treatment
Kidnap
Old Goat
Scapegoat
Separate the Sheep from the Goats
Tragedy
GOOSE
Barnacle
Cook Someone's Goose
Fox and Geese
Gandy Dancer
Give Someone the Bird
Gone Goose
Goose (n)
Goose (v)
Gooseberry
Goose Bumps
Goose Egg
Gooseflesh
Goose Hangs High
Goose Is Cooked
Gooseneck
Gooseneck Lamp
Goose Pimples
Goose Step
Goose that Laid the Golden Eggs
Goshawk
Gossamer
Honk (n)
Honk (v)
Honker
Kill the Goose that Laid the Golden Eggs
Lay an Egg
Loose as a Goose

Loosey-goosey

Sauce for the Goose

Silly as a Goose

Silly Goose

Take a Gander

Tar and Feather

Wild-goose Chase

GOPHER

Do Goobers Eat Gophers or Do Gophers
   Eat Goobers

Gopher

Gopher Ball

Gopher Pitch

GORILLA

Gorilla

Six-hundred Pound Gorilla

GRASSHOPPER

Grasshopper (1)

Grasshopper (2)

Grasshopper Pie

Knee-high to a Grasshopper

GREYHOUND

Greyhound

GROUSE

Grouse

GULL

Gull (n)

Gull (v)

Gullible

Gull-wing

HARE

Hare and Hounds

Harebrained

Harelip

Harrier

Mad as a March Hare

Paper Chase

Paper Trail

Run Circles around

Run with the Hare

Slow and Steady Wins the Race

Tortoise and the Hare

HAWK

Ballhawk

Bat an Eye

Eye like a Hawk

Hawk (n) (1)

Hawk (n) (2)

Hawk (v) (1)

Hawk (v) (2)

Hawk-eyed

Hawkish

Hawk-nosed

Know a Hawk from a Handsaw

Mosquito Hawk

Nighthawk

Rouse

Roust

Watch Someone like a Hawk

HEDGEHOG

Caprice

Capricious

Hedgehog Gene

Prickly as a Hedgehog

Sea Urchin

Urchin

HEN

Fox Guarding the Henhouse

Hen Party

Henpeck

Henpecked

Henpecked Husband

Mad as a Wet Hen

Mother Hen

Old Biddy

Old Hen

Scarce as Hen's Teeth

Take Someone under Your Wing

Whistling Girls and Crowing Hens

HERRING

Dead as a Herring

Draw a Red Herring

Herringbone

Herringbone Pattern

Herringbone Suit

Herringbone Twill

Red Herring

HIPPOPOTAMUS

Behemoth

HOG

Brush-hog

Bush-hog

Disgruntled

Eat High off the Hog

Gas Hog

Go Hog-wild

Go Whole Hog

Groundhog

Grunt (n)

Grunt (v)

Ham (1)

Ham (2)

Ham Actor

Ham-handed

Ham It up

Ham Radio

Ham Radio Operator

Hedgehog

Hog (n) (1)

Hog (n) (2)

Hog (v)

Hogback

Hog Heaven

Hog Latin

Hognose Snake

Hogshead

Hog the Limelight

Hog the Road

Hog-tie

Hogwash

Hoover Hog

Hyena

Independent as a Hog on Ice

Kick the Bucket

Live High on the Hog

Pork Barrel

Pork Barrel Politics

Porkpie Hat

Quahog

River Hog

Road Hog

Sandhog

Sewer Hog

Sweat Hog

Tied up

Wallow in Self-pity

HORNET

Hornet

Hornet's Nest

Like an Angry Hornet

Mad as a Hornet

Sting to the Quick

Stir up a Hornet's Nest

HORSE

Also-ran

Amble

Angels on Horseback

At the Drop of a Hat

Back in Harness

Back the Wrong Horse

Beat a Dead Horse

Beggar on Horseback

Be there with Bells on

Big Enough to Choke a Horse

Blaze

Blaze a Trail

Bobtail

Break out of the Pack

Bridal Path

Bridle

Bring in a Ringer

Catch Someone off Stride

Cavalcade

Change Horses in Midstream

Change of Pace

Charley Horse

Cheval Glass

Chivalry Is not Dead

Chomp at the Bit

Clotheshorse

Cockhorse

Coltish

Come a Cropper

Come Back to the Field

Come off It

Come Straight from the Horse's Mouth

Constable

Cool Your Heels

Count Noses

Curry Favor

Dark Horse

Dead Horse

Dead Ringer

Didn't Turn a Hair

Die in Harness

Dog and Pony Show

Don't Look a Gift Horse in the Mouth

Down the Stretch

Draw the Collar

Eat a Horse

Eat like a Horse

Fade in the Stretch

Fall Neck and Crop

Fall off a Horse

Fall off the Pace

Feel Your Oats

Filly

Finish out of the Money

Fire Horse

Flog a Dead Horse

Fox-trot

Frisky as a Young Colt

Full of Beans

Gallop

Gambit

Gambol

Gams

Get Hitched

Get It Straight from the Horse's Mouth

Get off Your High Horse

Get on the Stick

Get on Your High Horse

Get on Your Horse

Get out of Hand

Gift Horse

Give Someone Free Rein

Give Someone Their Head

Go Down to the Wire

Go Full Tilt

Good Judge of Horse Flesh

Go through the Paces

Groom

Hack

Hackney

Hackneyed

Hack Writer

Halter

Hard-bitten

Harness

Harridan

Have a Burr under Your Saddle

Hell Bent for Leather

Hightail It

Hippopotamus

Hobbled

Hobble Skirt

Hobby

Hobbyhorse

Hobson's Choice

Hold Your Horses

Home, James

Horse

Horse-and-buggy

Horse-and-buggy Days

Horse around

Horse Chestnut

Horse-collar

Horsefeathers

Horsehide

Horse Latitudes

Horselaugh

Horseless Carriage

Horse Marines

Horse of a Different Color

Horse of Another Color

Horse Opera

Horseplay

Horsepower

Horse Race

Horseradish

Horse's Ass

Horse Sense

Horses for Courses

Horseshit

Horseshoe Bat

Horseshoe Bend

Horseshoe Crab

Horseshoes

Horse Thief

Horse Trade

Horse Trader

Horse Trading

Horsey Set

Hot and Bothered

Hot to Trot

If Wishes Were Horses

In a Lather

Inside Track

In the Homestretch

In the Running

Iron Horse

Jade

Jaded

Jockey for Position

Keep a Tight Rein

Keep Pace with

Kick over the Traces

Kick up Your Heels

Know Your Oats

Lead a Horse to Water

Lead by a Nose

Lead from Wire to Wire

Left at the Post

Like a Young Colt

Lock the Barn Door after the Horse Is
Stolen

Long Horse

Long in the Tooth

Look a Gift Horse in the Mouth
Make Great Strides
Man on a White Horse
Man on Horseback
Mare's Nest
Mare with Three Legs
Marshal (n)
Marshal (v)
Neck and Neck
Never Look a Gift Horse in the Mouth
Nightmare
Nose Someone out
Off and Running
Off Your Feed
Old Fire Horse
Old War Horse
One-hearse Town
One-horse Race
One-horse Town
One-ring Circus
One-trick Pony
On the Nose
Out of the Running
Pacemaker
Pacesetter
Pack a Wallop
Pay for a Dead Horse
Pester
Photo Finish
Poltroon
Pommel Horse
Pony
Ponytail
Pony up
Prance
Prick up Your Ears
Pull away from the Field

Pull Your Weight
Put on the Feed Bag
Put out to Pasture
Put Someone through Their Paces
Put the Cart before the Horse
Ragtag and Bobtail
Raring to Go
Rear up
Rein Someone in
Relay
Ride a High Horse
Ride a Hobbyhorse
Ride Roughshod
Ride Shank's Mares
Ringer
Rocking Horse
Rode Hard and Put away Wet
Run for Your Money
Running Mate
Saddled with
Sawhorse
Scalawag
Sea Horse
Set the Pace
Shank's Mares
Shoo-in
Sick as a Horse
Side Horse
Sign of Good Breeding
Spurred on
Stable
Stablemate
Stalking Horse
Stallion
Straight from the Horse's Mouth
Strap on the Old Feed Bag
String along

Strong as a Horse

Stud

Stud Poker

Swap Horses while Crossing the River

Tacky

Take Someone to the Wire

Take Something in Stride

Take the Bit

Take the Collar

Tell It to the Marines

That Ain't Hay

Thoroughbred

Three-legged Mare

Throw a Shoe

Track Record

Trail the Field

Travel in Double Harness

Trojan Horse

Trot (n)

Trot (v)

Trot out

Trots

Turn a Hair

Two-legged Mare

Unbridled

Under the Wire

Vaulting Horse

Wallop

Walrus

War Horse

Well-groomed

Wheelhorse

Whipped

Whoa, Nellie

Wild Horses

Win by a Nose

Win by a Whisker

Win Going away

Wooden Horse

Workhorse

Work like a Horse

Work Yourself into a Lather

You Can Lead a Horse to Water

HYENA

Laugh like a Hyena

INSECT

Cocoon (n)

Cocoon (v)

Cocooning

Cocoon Stage

Creep

Creeps

Creep Show

Creepy

Crimson

Get under Your Skin

Grub

Grubby

Hover

Insect

Jigger

Paparazzi

JACKAL

Jackal

JAY

Cajole

Jay

Jaywalk

Jaywalker

Naked as a Jaybird

Popinjay

KANGAROO

Kangaroo Court

Kangaroo Rat

Kangaroo Ticket

KINGFISHER

Halcyon Days

KITE

At one Fell Swoop

Kite (n)

Kite (v)

LAMB

As well Be Hanged for a Sheep as a Lamb

Come in like a Lamb

Gentle as a Lamb

Innocent as a Lamb

In two Shakes of a Lamb's Tail

Lamb

Like a Lamb to Slaughter

Lion Shall Lie down with the Lamb

Meek as a Lamb

Sacrificial Lamb

LARK

Bright as a Lark

Happy as a Lark

Lark

Larkspur

Sing like a Lark

LEECH

Bloodsucker

Cling like a Leech

Leech

Stick to Someone like a Leech

LEMMING

March like Lemmings

LEOPARD

Camelopard

Leopard

Leopard Frog

Leopard never Changes Its Spots

Leopard Seal

LIMPET

Limpet

LION

Ant Lion

Beard the Lion

Bold as a Lion

Brave as a Lion

Brave the Lion's Den

Caged Lion

Come in like a Lion

Dandelion

King of Beasts

Leonine

Leonine Contract

Leonine Verse

Leopard

Like a Female Lion Protecting Her Cubs

Lion

Lionhearted

Lionize

Lion's Den

Lion Shall Lie down with the Lamb

Lion's Mouth

Lion's Share

Lion-tailed Macaque

Lion Tamarin

Lord of the Jungle

Mane

Mountain Lion

Put Your Head in the Lion's Mouth

Roar like a Lion

Sea Lion

See the Lions

Social Lion

Throw Someone to the Lions

Toothless Lion

Young Lion

LIZARD

Alligator (n)

Leaping Lizards

Lounge Lizard

LOBSTER

In Hot Water

Lobster (1)

Lobster (2)

Lobster Shift

Look like a Boiled Lobster

Red as a Lobster

Rock Lobster

Spiny Lobster

LOCUST

Swarm like Locusts

LOON

Crazy as a Loon

Loony

Loony Bin

LOUSE

Get in Your Hair

Louse

Louse up

Lousy

Lousy with

MACKEREL

Cold as a Mackerel

Dead as a Mackerel

Holy Mackerel

Mackerel Sky

MAGGOT

Mawkish

MAGPIE

Chatter like a Magpie

Magpie

Pie

Piebald

MITE

Mighty Mite

MOLE

Holy Moley

Make a Mountain out of a Molehill

Mole (1)

Mole (2)

Moleskin

MOLLUSK

Purple

MONKEY

Climb like a Monkey

Drive Someone Bananas

Get the Monkey off Your Back

Go Bananas

Grease Monkey

Have a Monkey on Your Back

Have Your Cage Rattled

Jungle Gym

Little Monkey

Make a Monkey out of Someone

Monkey

Monkey around

Monkey Bars

Monkey Business

Monkey See, Monkey Do

Monkeyshines

Monkey Suit

Monkey's Uncle

Monkey with

Monkey Wrench

More Fun than a Barrel of Monkeys

Q

Rattle Someone's Cage

See No Evil

Shake Someone's Tree

Throw a Wrench in the Works

Work for Peanuts

MOOSE

Moose

Snore like a Moose

Strong as a Bull Moose

MOSQUITO

Canapé

Canopy

Mosquito Boat

Mosquito Hawk

MOTH

Gypsy Moth

Like a Moth to Flame

Mothball

Mothball Fleet

Moth-eaten

Put in Mothballs

MOUSE

Are You a Man or a Mouse

Build a Better Mousetrap

Cat and Mouse Game

Dormouse

Mickey Mouse

Mickey-mouse

Mouse (1)

Mouse (2)

Mousetrap

Mouse Type

Mousy

Muscle

Mussel

Play Cat and Mouse

Poor as a Church Mouse

Quiet as a Mouse

Three Blind Mice

Titmouse

When the Cat's away, the Mice Will Play

Wish I Could Be a Little Mouse

MULE

Build a Fire under

Kick like a Mule

Mule (1)

Mule (2)

Mule (3)

Mule Deer

Mule Ear

Mule Rabbit

Mulish

Shavetail

Stubborn as a Mule

NIGHTINGALE

Nightingale

Sing like a Nightingale

NIT

Nitpick

Nitpicker

Nit-picking

Nitty-gritty

Nitwit

OCTOPUS

Like an Octopus

Octopus

OSTRICH

Bury Your Head in the Sand

Head-in-the-sand

Hide Your Head in the Sand

Ostrichlike

Stick Your Head in the Sand

OWL

Ain't that a Hoot

Hoot (n)

Hoot (v)

Night Owl

Not Give a Hoot

Not Worth a Hoot
Owlish
Owl Show
Wise as an Owl
Wise Old Owl
OX
A
Adam's Off Ox
Alphabet
Big as an Ox
Big Ox
Boo
Bugle
Bulimia
Clumsy as an Ox
Dumb as an Ox
Dumb Ox
Dummox
Greenhorn
Jugular
Kick against the Pricks
L
Lummox
Oxbow
Strong as an Ox
Subjugate
Syzygy
Whose Ox Is Being Gored
Yoke
OYSTER
Cast Pearls before Swine
Eat Your First Oyster
Mother-of-pearl
Mountain Oysters
On the Half Shell
Ostracism
Ostracize

Oyster White
Pearl
Pearl Diver
Pearl of Great Price
Pearl Onion
Pearls of Wit and Wisdom
Pearly White
Pearly Whites
Prairie Oysters
Solitary as an Oyster
World Is Your Oyster
PARASITE
Parasite
PARROT
Lovebirds
Parrot (n)
Parrot (v)
Parrot-fashion
Parrot Fish
Popinjay
PEACOCK
Proud as a Peacock
Strut like a Peacock
Stuck-up
PIG
Aardvark
Bleed like a Stuck Pig
Blind Pig
Bring Home the Bacon
Buy a Pig in a Poke
Cast Pearls before Swine
Chauvinist Pig
Eat like a Pig
Fat as a Pig
Guinea Pig
In a Pig's Eye
Like a Pig in Clover

Like Catching a Greased Pig

Make a Pig of Yourself

Make a Silk Purse out of a Sow's Ear

Male Chauvinist Pig

Pig (1)

Pig (2)

Pig (3)

Pig Boat

Piggy

Piggyback (adv.)

Piggyback (n)

Piggyback (v)

Piggy Bank

Pigheaded

Pig Iron

Pig Latin

Pig out

Pigpen

Pigs in the Blanket

Pigskin

Pigsticker

Pigsty

Pig Sweat

Pigtail

Porcelain

Porcupine

Pork Barrel

Pork Barrel Politics

Porker

Porkpie Hat

Porpoise

Rolling in Clover

Root out

Rout

Runt

Runt of the Litter

Save Your Bacon

Screw (n) (1)

Screw (n) (2)

Scrofula

Sow

Squeal

Squeal like a Pig

Steward

Sweat like a Pig

Swine

This Little Piggy

When Pigs Fly

When Pigs Have Wings

PIGEON

Bill and Coo

Clay Pigeon

Coo

Pigeon

Pigeon-breasted

Pigeon Drop

Pigeon Has Flown

Pigeonhole (n)

Pigeonhole (v)

Pigeon-livered

Pigeon-toed

Pluck a Pigeon

Plucked Pigeon

Sea Squab

Stoolie

Stool Pigeon

PIRANHA

Piranha

POODLE

Poodle Cloth

Poodle Cut

Poodle Perm

PORCUPINE

Bristle with Anger

Porcupine Fish

PORPOISE

Flipper

Porpoise (v)

POSSUM

Play Possum

Roll over and Play Dead

QUAIL

Dying Quail

Quail (n)

Quail (v)

San Quentin Quail

RABBIT

Beach Bunny

Breed like Rabbits

Bunny

Bunny Hop

Buns

Dumb Bunny

Dust Bunny

Hightail It

Jackrabbit Start

Multiply like Rabbits

Pull a Rabbit out of a Hat

Quick like a Bunny

Rabbit (1)

Rabbit (2)

Rabbit (3)

Rabbit Ball

Rabbit Died

Rabbit Ears

Rabbit Food

Rabbit Punch

Rabbit's Foot

Rabbit Test

Run like a Scared Rabbit

Snow Bunny

Welsh Rabbit

RACCOON

Coon's Age

Gone Coon

Raccoon Eyes

RAT

Caught like a Rat in a Trap

Corrode

Desert Rat

Dirty Rat

Dock Rat

Drowned Rat

Erase

Erode

Like Rats Leaving a Sinking Ship

Pack Rat

Rascal

Rash

Rat (n) (1)

Rat (n) (2)

Rat (n) (3)

Rat (v)

Rat Fink

Rathole

Rat Kangaroo

Rat Pack

Rat Race

Rats

Rat's Nest

Rattail Comb

Rat-tail File

Rattrap

Rat Trap Cheese

Ratty

Raze

River Rat

Rodent

Rug Rat	Pool Shark
Shop Rat	Shark
Smell a Rat	Shark Repellent
RAVEN	Sharkskin
Cormorant	Swim with Sharks
Raven-haired	**SHEEP**
Ravenous	As well Be Hanged for a Sheep as a Lamb
Rook	Battering Ram
ROBIN	Bellwether
Robin's Egg Blue	Black Sheep
Round Robin	Buckram
Who Killed Cock Robin	Butt Heads
ROOK	Cape Hope Sheep
Rook	Cold Shoulder
Rooked	Count Sheep
ROOSTER	Dyed-in-the-wool
Bantam	Fleece
Bantam Rooster	Fleecy
Bantamweight	Judas Sheep
Rooster Tail	Knock Heads
SALAMANDER	Knock the Tar out of Someone
Gerrymander	Like a Flock of Sheep
Salamander	Like a Sheep Being Led to Slaughter
Salamander's Wool	Lost Sheep
SARDINE	Mutt
Packed like Sardines	Mutton Chops
SCALLOP	Muttonhead
Scallop (n)	Pull the Wool over Someone's Eyes
Scallop (v)	Ram (n)
Scalloped Potatoes	Ram (v)
SEAL	Ramrod (n)
Flipper	Ramrod (v)
Like a Trained Seal	Return to the Fold
Mukluks	Separate the Sheep from the Goats
SHARK	Sheep
Card Shark	Sheep-dip
Loan Shark	Sheep-dipping

Sheepish

Sheepish Grin

Sheep's Eyes

Sheepshank

Sheepshead

Sheepskin

Shepherd (n)

Shepherd (v)

Steel Wool

Stiff as a Ramrod

Tarred with the Same Brush

Wild and Wooly

Wolf in Sheep's Clothing

Woolgathering

SHREW

Shrew

Shrewd

Shrewish

SHRIMP

Shrimp

Shrimpy

SILKWORM

Bombast

Silk

Silken

Silky

SKUNK

Drunk as a Skunk

Make a Stink

Skunk (n)

Skunk (v)

Skunk Cabbage

Son of a Sea Cook

SLUG

Slug

Slugabed

Sluggard

Sluggish

SNAIL

Come out of Your Shell

Crawl into Your Shell

Draw in Your Horns

Pull in Your Eyes

Shell (n)

Slimeball

Slow as a Snail

Snail

Snail Darter

Snaillike Pace

Snail-paced

Snail's Pace

SNAKE

Aspic

Boa

Copperhead

Deaf as an Adder

Herpes

If It Had Been a Snake

Lower than a Snake's Belly

Nourish a Snake in Your Bosom

Rattlesnake

Recoil

Serpent

Serpentine

Sharper than a Serpent's Tooth

Shuffle off this Mortal Coil

Slink

Slinky

Slough off

Snake (n) (1)

Snake (n) (2)

Snake (v) (1)

Snake (v) (2)

Snakebit

Snake Dance

Snake Doctor

Snake Eyes

Snake Feeder

Snake in the Grass

Snakelike

Snake Medicine

Snake Oil

Snake Pit

Snake Poison

Speak with Forked Tongue

Viper

Worm (3)

Worm Will Turn

SNIPE

Guttersnipe

Left Holding the Bag

Snipe

Snipe Hunt

Sniper

SPARROW

Fall of a Sparrow

Sparrow-grass

Sparrow Hawk

Sparrow-legged

SPIDER

Caught in the Web

Clear away the Cobwebs

Cobwebs in Your Head

Lobster (1)

Said the Spider to the Fly

Spider

Spider Crab

Spider Monkey

Spider's Web

Spider Veins

Spidery

Web of Deceit

SPONGE

Fungus

Sponge (n)

Sponge (v)

Sponge Bath

Sponge Cake

Sponge off/on

Sponger

Sponge Rubber

Spongy

Throw in the Sponge

SQUIRREL

Bright-eyed and Bushy-tailed

Squirrel away

Squirrelly

STORK

Look what the Stork Brought

Stork Brought Me

Stork Is Coming

SWALLOW

One Swallow Does not Make a Summer

Swallowtail Coat

White Tie and Tails

SWAN

Graceful as a Swan

Swan Dive

Swan Song

What Time Is the Next Swan

TICK

Full as a Tick

Tight as a Tick

TIGER

Arouse the Tiger

Blind Tiger

Fight like a Tiger

Go Get 'em, Tiger

Have a Tiger by the Tail

Kitty

Lady-or-tiger

WHALE
Beached Whale
Blubber
Walrus
Whale (n)
Whale (v) (1)
Whale (v) (2)
Whale Away
Whaleback
Whalebone
Whale Shark
Whaling
WILDCAT
Whip Your Weight in Wildcats
Wildcat (n)
Wildcat (v)
Wildcat Bank
Wildcat Currency
Wildcat Strike
Wildcatter
Wildcat Venture
Wildcat Well
WOLF
Cry Wolf
Keep the Wolf from the Door
Leader of the Pack
Lone Wolf
Lupus
Pack of Wolves
Sea Wolf
Throw Someone to the Wolves
Werewolf
Wolf (n)
Wolf (v)
Wolf Bait
Wolf Boy
Wolf Call

Wolffish
Wolf in Sheep's Clothing
Wolfman
Wolf Pack
Wolfsbane
Wolf Whistle
WORM
Bitter as Wormwood
Bookworm
Can of Worms
Crimson
Crocodile
Early Bird Catches the Worm
Food for Worms
Open a Can of Worms
Spanish Worm
Varmint
Vermicelli
Vermilion
Vermin
Vermouth
Worm (1)
Worm (2)
Worm (3)
Worm-burner
Worm-eaten
Worm's-eye View
Worm Something out
Worm Will Turn
Wormwood
Worm Your Way
ZEBRA
Zebra
Zebra Finch
Zebra Fish
Zebra Mussel
Zebra Stripes

About the Author

ROBERT A. PALMATIER is Professor Emeritus of Linguistics, Department of Foreign Languages and Literatures, Western Michigan University. His earlier works dealt with Middle English syntax, technical terms in transformational grammar, sports metaphors (*Sports Talk*, Greenwood, 1989), and sports idioms. He is currently conducting research on popular metaphors derived from the arts, the entertainment industry, and the mass media.